IBM® PC ASSEMBLY LANGUAGE AND PROGRAMMING

Second Edition

PETER ABEL

*British Columbia
Institute of Technology*

PRENTICE HALL
Englewood Cliffs, New Jersey 07632

Library of Congress Cataloging-in-Publication Data

Abel, Peter
    IBM PC assembly language and programming / Peter Abel. -- 2nd ed.
        p.   cm.
    Rev. ed. of: IBM PC assembler language and programming. c1987.
    Includes index.
    ISBN 0-13-448945-4
    1. IBM Personal Computer--Programming. 2. Assembler language
(Computer program lanmguage) 3. IBM Personal System/2 (Computer
system) I. Abel, Peter   IBM PC assembler language and
programming. II. Title.
QA76.8.I2594A236 1991
005.265--dc20   90-39012
                                                         CIP

Editorial/production supervision and interior design: JENNIFER WENZEL
Manufacturing buyers: LORI BULWIN/LINDA BEHRENS/PATRICE FRACCIO

© 1991, 1987 by Prentice-Hall, Inc.
A Division of Simon & Schuster
Englewood Cliffs, New Jersey 07632

The author and publisher of this book have used their best efforts in preparing this book. These efforts include the development, research, and testing of the theories and programs to determine their effectiveness. The author and publisher make no warranty of any kind, expressed or implied, with regard to these programs or the documentation contained in this book. The author and publisher shall not be liable in any event for incidental or consequential damages in connection with, or arising out of, the furnishing, performance, or use of these programs.

UNIX is a registered trademark of AT&T (Bell Laboratories).
Apple and MacIntosh are registered trademarks of Apple Computer, Inc.
Intel is a registered trademark of Compuview Products, Inc.
Microsoft Window is a trademark and Microsoft is a registered trademark of the Microsoft
    Corporation.
IBM and IBM PC/XT/AT are registered trademarks of International Business Machines
    Corporation.

Printed in the United States of America

10 9 8 7 6 5 4 3 2

ISBN   0-13-448945-4

PRENTICE-HALL INTERNATIONAL (UK) LIMITED, *London*
PRENTICE-HALL OF AUSTRALIA PTY. LIMITED, *Sydney*
PRENTICE-HALL CANADA INC., *Toronto*
PRENTICE-HALL HISPANOAMERICANA, S.A., *Mexico*
PRENTICE-HALL OF INDIA PRIVATE LIMITED, *New Delhi*
PRENTICE-HALL OF JAPAN, INC., *Tokyo*
SIMON & SCHUSTER ASIA PTE. LTD., *Singapore*
EDITORA PRENTICE-HALL DO BRASIL, LTDA., *Rio de Janeiro*

CONTENTS

2 MACHINE EXECUTION

3 ASSEMBLY LANGUAGE REQUIREMENTS

15 DISK STORAGE ORGANIZATION   248

16 DISK PROCESSING I: FILE CONTROL BLOCKS   258

17 DISK PROCESSING II: FILE HANDLES AND EXTENDED DOS FUNCTIONS   289

18 DISK PROCESSING III: BIOS DISK OPERATIONS   314

19 PRINTING   324

20 MACRO WRITING   337

PREFACE

The microprocessor had its origin in the 1960s when research designers devised the integrated circuit (IC). They combined various electronic components into a single component on a silicon "chip." The manufacturers set this tiny chip into a device resembling a centipede, and connected it into a functioning system. In the early 1970s, the Intel 8008 chip in a computer terminal ushered in the first generation of microprocessors.

By 1974, the 8008 evolved into the 8080, a second-generation microprocessor with general-purpose use. Its success prompted other companies to manufacture 8080 or similar processors.

In 1978, Intel produced the third-generation 8086 processor, which provided some compatibility with the 8080 and significantly advanced the design. Intel developed a variation of the 8086 to provide a slightly simpler design and compatibility with current input/output devices—the 8088 processor, which IBM selected for its announced personal computer in 1981. An enhanced version of the 8088 is the 80188, and enhanced versions of the 8086 are the 80186, 80286, 80386, and 80486, which provide additional operations and processing power.

The spread of microcomputers has also caused a renewed interest in assembly language. First, a program written in assembly language requires considerably less memory space and execution time. Second, a knowledge of assembly language and its resulting machine code provides an understanding of machine architecture that no high-level language such as Pascal and C can possibly provide. Although most software specialists develop new applications in high-level languages, which are easier to write and maintain, a common practice is to recode bottleneck routines in assembly language. Programs such as terminate-and-stay-resident (TSRs) and interrupt service routines are almost always developed in assembly language.

High-level languages were designed to eliminate the technicalities of a particular computer. An assembly language, however, is designed for a specific computer or, more accurately, for a specific processor. Consequently, to write a program in assembly language for your PC, you have to be familiar with its architecture, and this book supplies all the necessary basic material. Among the material and knowledge required for this topic are the following:

- Access to an IBM personal computer (XT, AT, or PS/2) or equivalent compatible.
- A copy of PC-DOS or MS-DOS operating system, preferably a recent version, and familiarity with its use.
- A diskette containing an assembler translator program, preferably a recent version. The IBM version is MASM, Microsoft versions are MASM and Quick-Assembler, Borland's is TASM, and SLR System's is OPTASM.

The following are not required for this topic:

- Knowledge of a programming language, although such knowledge may help you grasp some programming concepts more readily.
- Prior knowledge of electronics or circuitry. This book provides the necessary information about PC architecture that you require for assembly language programming.

OPERATING SYSTEMS

The purpose of an operating system is to allow a user to instruct a computer as to what action to take (such as execute a particular program) and to provide means to store (catalog) information on disk and to access it.

The most common operating system for the PC and its compatibles is MS-DOS from Microsoft, known as PC-DOS on the IBM PC. Among the enhancements, version 2.0 provided support for hard disk, version 3.0 provided support for the AT, and version 4.0 provided a user shell. A discussion of the advanced operating systems, OS/2 and UNIX, is outside the scope of this book.

THE APPROACH TO TAKE

This book can act as both a tutorial and a permanent reference. To make the most effective use of your investment in a microcomputer and software, work through each chapter carefully, and reread any material that is not immediately clear. Key in the example programs, convert them to executable "modules," and execute them. Work through the exercises at the end of each chapter.

The first eight chapters furnish the foundation material for the book and for the assembly language. After these chapters, you can begin with Chapter 11, 12, 14, 15, 19, 20, or 21. Chapters 23, 24, and 25 are intended as reference. Related chapters are

- 8 through 10 (screen and keyboard operations)
- 12 and 13 (arithmetic operations)
- 15 through 18 (disk processing)
- 21 and 22 (subprograms and memory management)

When you have completed this book, you will be able to:

- Understand the hardware of the personal computer.
- Understand machine language code and hexadecimal format.
- Understand the steps involved in assembly, link, and execute.
- Write programs in assembly language to handle the keyboard and screen, perform arithmetic, convert between ASCII and binary formats, perform table searches and sorts, and perform disk input and output.
- Trace machine execution as an aid in debugging.
- Write your own macro instructions.
- Link separate programs into one executable program.

Learning assembly language and getting your programs to work is an exciting and challenging experience. For the time and effort invested, the rewards are sure to be great.

NOTES ON THE SECOND EDITION

This second edition reflects a considerable number of changes since the first edition of this book:

- Inclusion of DOS features through version 4.01.
- Information unique to the IBM PS/2 series.
- Features of Borland's Turbo Assembler.
- Features of the Intel 80386 and 80486 processors.
- Use of simplified segment directives.
- Additional interrupts.

Other material new to this edition includes memory management, program overlays, and keyboard buffer details, as well as many more questions at the end of each chapter.

NOTE TO INSTRUCTORS

An Instructors' Manual is available containing additional questions and answers and transparency masters. Included is a diskette containing the additional questions and answers as well as all the source programs in the book.

Acknowledgments

The author is grateful for the assistance and cooperation of all those who contributed suggestions, reviews, and corrections to earlier editions. Special thanks goes to Michael Cafferty, Michael Cafferty and Associates, Inc.; Keith B. Olson, Montana Tech.; Ernie F. Philipp, Northern Virginia Community College; and James F. Peters III, Kansas State University for reviewing the second edition of this manuscript.

1

INTRODUCTION TO PC ARCHITECTURE

OBJECTIVE

To explain features of microcomputer hardware and program organization.

INTRODUCTION

Writing a program in assembly language requires knowledge of the computer's instruction set, the rules of its use, and the hardware on which it runs. The instruction set and its use are developed throughout this book. An explanation of the basic hardware (or architecture)—bits, bytes, registers, memory, processor, and data bus—is provided in this chapter.

The fundamental building blocks of a computer are the bit and the byte. These supply the means by which a computer can represent data and instructions in memory.

The main hardware features are internal memory, a microprocessor, and registers. A computer stores a program temporarily in its internal memory for execution. (This is the memory that people mean when they claim that their computer has, for example, 640K of memory.) The microprocessor executes the program instructions, and the registers handle arithmetic, data movement, and addressing.

An assembly language program consists of one or more segments for defining data and for machine instructions and a segment named the stack that contains stored addresses.

This chapter covers all this material so that you can get going right away in Chapter 2 on your first machine language program.

BITS AND BYTES

The smallest unit of data in a computer is a *bit*. A bit may be magnetized as *off* so that its value is zero, or as *on* so that its value is one. A single bit doesn't provide much information, but it is surprising what a bunch of them can do.

A group of nine bits represents a *byte,* eight bits for *data* and one bit for *parity:*

$$\left|\begin{array}{c} 0\mid 0\mid 0\mid 0\mid 0\mid 0\mid 0\mid 0 \\ \underline{\hspace{1cm}} \text{ data bits } \underline{\hspace{1cm}} \end{array}\right|\begin{array}{c} 1 \\ \text{parity} \end{array}\left|\right.$$

The eight data bits provide the basis for binary arithmetic and for representing characters such as the letter A and the symbol *. Eight bits provide for 256 different combinations of on/off conditions, from all off (00000000) through all on (11111111). For example, a representation of the on- and off-bits for the letter A is 01000001 and for the asterisk is 00101010, although you don't have to memorize such facts. Each byte in memory has a unique address beginning with zero for the first byte.

Parity requires that the on-bits for a byte are always an odd number. Since the letter A contains two on-bits, the processor automatically sets its parity bit on (01000001-1), and since the asterisk contains three on bits, the processor sets its parity bit off (00101010-0). When an instruction references a byte in storage, the computer checks its parity. If parity is even, the system assumes that a bit is "lost" and displays an error message. A parity error may be a result of a hardware fault or an electrical disturbance; either way, it is a rare event.

You may have wondered how a computer "knows" that the bit value 01000001 represents the letter A. When you key in A on the keyboard, the system delivers a signal from that particular key into memory and sets a byte (in an input location) to the bit value 01000001. You can move this byte about in memory as you will, and may even print it or display it on the screen as the letter A.

For reference purposes, the bits in a byte are numbered 0 to 7 from right to left as shown here for the letter A:

Bit number:	7	6	5	4	3	2	1	0
Bit contents for A:	0	1	0	0	0	0	0	1

The number 2^{10} equals 1024, which happens to be the value K, for kilobytes. Thus a computer with a 640K memory has 640×1024, or 655,360 bytes.

A 16-bit (two-byte) field is known as a *word* and a 32-bit field is a *doubleword.* The bits in a word are numbered 0 through 15 from right to left as shown here for the letters PC:

Bit number:	15	14	13	12	11	10	9	8	|	7	6	5	4	3	2	1	0
Bit contents:	0	1	0	1	0	0	0	0	|	0	1	0	0	0	0	1	1

BINARY NUMBERS

Because a computer can distinguish only between 0 and 1 bits, it works in a base-2 numbering system known as binary. In fact, the word bit derives its name from "binary digit."

A collection of bits can represent any value. The value of a binary number is based on the relative position of each bit and the presence of 1-bits. The following eight-bit number contains all 1-bits:

Position value:	128	64	32	16	8	4	2	1
On-bit:	1	1	1	1	1	1	1	1

The rightmost bit assumes the value 1, the next digit to the left assumes 2, the next assumes 4, and so forth. The total of the 1-bits in this case is $1 + 2 + 4 + \cdots + 128$, or 255 (or $2^8 - 1$).

For the binary number 01000001, the 1-bits represent the values 1 plus 64, or 65:

Position value:	128	64	32	16	8	4	2	1
On-bit:	0	1	0	0	0	0	0	1

But wait . . . isn't 01000001 the letter A? Indeed it is. Here's the part that you have to get clear. Bits 01000001 can represent either the number 65 or the letter A:

- If a program defines a data item for arithmetic purposes, then 01000001 represents a binary number equivalent to the decimal number 65.
- If a program defines a data item (one or more adjacent bytes) meant to be descriptive such as a heading, then 01000001 represents a letter, also known as "string" data.

When you start programming, you will see this distinction more clearly, because you define and use each data item for a specific purpose; in practice, this is rarely a source of confusion.

A binary number is not limited to 8 bits. A processor that uses 16-bit (or 32-bit) architecture handles 16-bit (or 32-bit) numbers automatically. For 16 bits, $2^{16} - 1$ provides values up to 65,535, and for 32 bits, $2^{32} - 1$ provides values up to 4,294,967,295.

Binary Arithmetic

A microcomputer performs arithmetic only in binary format. Consequently, an assembly language programmer has to be familiar with binary format and binary addition. The following examples illustrate binary addition:

$$
\begin{array}{cccc}
0 & 0 & 1 & 1 \\
+\underline{0} & +\underline{1} & +\underline{1} & +1 \\
0 & 1 & 10 & +\underline{1} \\
 & & & 11
\end{array}
$$

Note the carry of a 1-bit in the last two examples. Now, let's add 01000001 and 00101010. The letter A and an asterisk? No, the decimal values 65 and 42:

Decimal	Binary
65	01000001
+42	+00101010
107	01101011

Check that the binary sum 01101011 is actually 107. Let's try another example that adds the decimal values 60 and 53:

Decimal	Binary
60	00111100
+53	+00110101
113	01110001

Negative Numbers

The preceding binary numbers are all positive values because the leftmost bit contains zero. A negative binary number contains a 1-bit in its leftmost position. However, it's not as simple as changing the leftmost bit to 1, such as 01000001 (+65) to 11000001. A negative value is expressed in *two's complement notation;* that is, to represent a binary number as negative, reverse the bits and add 1. Let's use 01000001 as an example:

Number 65:	01000001
Reverse bits:	10111110
Add 1:	10111111 (equals −65)

A binary number is known to be negative if its leftmost bit is 1, but if you add the 1-bit values for 10111111, you won't get 65. To determine the absolute value of a negative binary number, simply repeat the previous operation: reverse the bits and add 1:

Binary value: 10111111
Reverse bits: 01000000
Add 1:   01000001   (equals +65)

The sum of +65 and −65 should be zero. Let's try it:

$$\begin{array}{rl} +65 & 01000001 \\ -65 & +\underline{10111111} \\ \hline \overline{00} & (1)00000000 \end{array}$$

The 8-bit value is all zeros. The carry of the 1-bit on the left is lost. However, if there is a carry *into* the sign bit and a carry *out* as in this example, the result is correct.

Binary subtraction is a simple matter: Convert the number being subtracted to two's-complement format and add the numbers. Let's subtract 42 from 65. The binary representation for 42 is 00101010 and its two's complement is 11010110:

$$\begin{array}{rl} 65 & 01000001 \\ +(-42) & +\underline{11010110} \\ \hline 23 & (1)00010111 \end{array}$$

The result, 23, is correct. Once again, there was a valid carry into the sign bit and a carry out.

If the justification for two's-complement notation isn't immediately clear, consider the following proposition: What value would you have to add to binary 00000001 to make it equal to 00000000? In terms of decimal numbers, the answer would be −1. The two's complement of 1 is 11111111. Add +1 and −1 as follows:

$$\begin{array}{rl} 1 & 00000001 \\ +(-1) & \underline{11111111} \\ \text{Result:} & (1)00000000 \end{array}$$

Ignoring the carry of 1, you can see that the binary number 11111111 is equivalent to decimal −1. You can also see a pattern form as the binary numbers decrease in value:

+3	00000011
+2	00000010
+1	00000001
0	00000000
−1	11111111
−2	11111110
−3	11111101

In fact, the 0-bits in a negative binary number indicate its value: Treat the positional value of each 0-bit as if it were a 1-bit, sum the values, and add 1.

You'll find this material on binary arithmetic and negative numbers particularly relevant when you get to Chapters 12 and 13 on arithmetic.

HEXADECIMAL REPRESENTATION

Imagine that you want to view the contents of four adjacent bytes (a doubleword) that contain a binary value. Although a byte may contain any of the 256 bit combinations, there is no way to display or print many of them as standard ASCII characters. (Examples include the bit configurations for tab, enter, form feed, and escape.) Consequently, the computer designers have developed a shorthand method of representing binary data. The method divides each byte in half and expresses the value of each half-byte. Consider the following four bytes:

```
Binary:    0101  1001    0011  0101    1011  1001    1100  1110
Decimal:    5     9       3     5       11    9        12    14
```

Since some of these numbers still require two digits, let's extend the numbering system so that $10 = A$, $11 = B$, $12 = C$, $13 = D$, $14 = E$, and $15 = F$. Here's the shorthand number that represents the contents of the bytes just given:

59   35   B9   CE

The numbering system involves the "digits" 0 through F, and since there are 16 such digits, it is known as *hexadecimal representation*. Figure 1-1 provides the binary, decimal, and hexadecimal values of the numbers 0 through 15.

Assembly language makes considerable use of hexadecimal (or hex) format. Listings of an assembled program show in hexadecimal all addresses, machine code instructions, and the contents of constants. Also, for debugging you can use the DOS DEBUG program, which also displays addresses and contents of bytes in hexadecimal format.

You soon get used to working with hexadecimal format. Keep in mind that the number following hex F is hex 10, which is decimal value 16. Following are some simple examples of hex arithmetic.

```
  6        5        F        F       10        FF
 +4       +8       +1       +F      +10       + 1
 ---      ---      ---      ---      ---      -----
  A        D       10       1E       20       100
```

Binary	Decimal	Hexadecimal	Binary	Decimal	Hexadecimal
0000	0	0	1000	8	8
0001	1	1	1001	9	9
0010	2	2	1010	10	A
0011	3	3	1011	11	B
0100	4	4	1100	12	C
0101	5	5	1101	13	D
0110	6	6	1110	14	E
0111	7	7	1111	15	F

Figure 1-1   Binary, Decimal, and Hexadecimal Representation

Note also that hex 20 equals decimal 32, hex 100 is decimal 256, and hex 1000 is decimal 4096.

To indicate a hex number in a program, code an "H" immediately after the number, as 25H (decimal value 37). A hex number always begins with a decimal digit 0–9; thus you code B8H as 0B8H. In this book we indicate a hexadecimal number as, for example, hex 4C or 4CH, a binary number as binary 01001100 or 01001100B, and a decimal number as 76—the absence of a description assumes a decimal number. An occasional exception occurs where the base is obvious from its context.

In Appendix B we explain how to convert hex numbers to decimal, and vice versa.

ASCII CODE

To standardize the representation of characters, microcomputer manufacturers have adopted the ASCII (American National Standard Code for Information Interchange) code. A standard code facilitates transfer of data between different computer devices. The 8-bit extended ASCII code that the PC uses provides 256 characters, including symbols for foreign alphabets. For example, the combination of bits 01000001 (hex 41) indicates the letter A. In Appendix A we supply a list of the ASCII characters, and in Chapter 8 we show how to display most of the 256 characters on a screen.

PC HARDWARE

An important hardware element of the PC is the system unit, which contains a system board, power supply, and expansion slots for optional boards. Features of the system board are an Intel microprocessor, read-only memory (ROM), and random access memory (RAM).

Processor

The brain of the PC and compatibles is an Intel microprocessor based on the 8086 family, which performs all processing of instructions and data. The processors vary in speed and capacity of memory, registers, and data bus. A *data bus* transfers data between the processor, memory, and external devices, and in effect manages the traffic.

8088/80188. These processors have 16-bit registers and an 8-bit data bus and can address up to 1 million bytes of memory. The registers can process two bytes at a time, whereas the data bus can transfer only one byte at a time. The 80188 is a souped-up 8088 with additional instructions. These processors run in what is known as *real mode,* that is, one program at a time.

8086/80186. These processors are similar to the 8088/80188, but have a 16-bit data bus and can run faster. The 80186 is a souped-up 8086 with additional instructions.

80286. This processor can run faster than the preceding processors and can address up to 16 million bytes. It can run in real mode or in *protected mode* for multitasking.

80386. This processor has 32-bit registers and a 32-bit data bus and can address up to 4 billion bytes of memory. It can run in real mode or in protected mode for multitasking.

80486. This processor also has 32-bit registers and a 32-bit data bus and is designed for enhanced performance. It can run in real mode or in protected mode for multitasking.

Execution Unit and Bus Interface Unit

The processor is partitioned into two logical units: an execution unit (EU) and a bus interface unit (BIU), as illustrated in Figure 1-2. The role of the EU is to execute instructions, whereas the BIU delivers instructions and data to the EU. The EU contains an arithmetic and logic unit (ALU), a control unit (CU), and a number of registers. These features provide instruction execution, arithmetic, and logic (comparison for high, low, and equal).

Important functions of the BIU are the bus control unit, segment registers, and instruction queue. First, the BIU controls the buses that transfer data to the EU, to memory, and to external input/output devices. Second, the segment registers control memory addressing.

The third function of the BIU is instruction access. Since all program instructions are in memory, the BIU must access instructions from memory into an *instruction queue*. Because the queue is four or more bytes in size, depending on the processor, the BIU is able to look ahead and prefetch instructions so that there is always a queue of instructions ready to execute.

The EU and BIU work in parallel, with the BIU keeping one step ahead. The EU notifies the BIU when it needs access to data in memory or an I/O device. Also, the EU requests machine instructions from the BIU instruction queue. The top instruction is the currently executable one, and while the EU is occupied executing an instruction, the BIU fetches another instruction from memory. This fetching overlaps with execution and speeds up processing.

Internal Memory

A microcomputer contains two types of internal memory, RAM (random access memory) and ROM (read-only memory). Memory locations are numbered consecutively beginning with 00 so that each location has a unique address.

RAM comprises the first part of memory, and ROM comprises the last part.

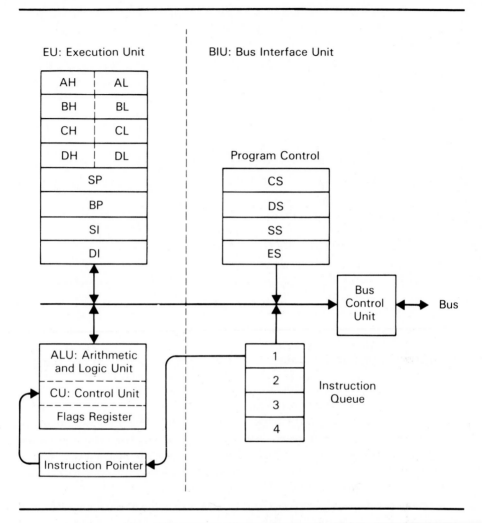

Figure 1-2 Execution Unit and Bus Interface Unit

According to the physical memory map of an 8086-type PC in Figure 1-3, the first 640K is RAM on the system board, most of which is available for your own use.

Read-only memory.   ROM (read-only memory) is a special memory chip that (as the name suggests) can only be read. Since instructions and data are permanently "burned into" the memory chip, they cannot be altered. ROM BIOS begins at address 768K and handles input/output devices, such as a hard disk controller. ROM beginning at 960K controls the computer's basic functions, such as power-on self-test, dot patterns for graphics, and the disk self-loader.

One function of ROM is to handle start-up procedures. When you switch on

Start Address		Purpose
Dec	Hex	
zero	0	640K of RAM memory on system board
640K	A0000	128K monochrome and graphics/display video buffer (RAM)
768K	C0000	192K memory expansion area (ROM)
960K	F0000	64K base system ROM

Figure 1-3   Physical Memory Map

the power, ROM performs various checkouts and loads into RAM special data from a system disk. For programming purposes, an important feature of ROM is the Basic Input/Output System (BIOS), covered in later chapters. (*Basic* here means the conventional word, not the programming language.)

Random access memory.   A programmer is concerned mainly with RAM (random access memory), which would be better named read-write memory. RAM is available as a "worksheet" for temporary storage and execution of programs.

Since the contents of RAM are lost when you turn off the power, you need separate external storage for keeping programs and data. If you have a DOS diskette inserted or hard disk installed, when you turn on the power, the ROM boot-up procedure causes, among other operations, the DOS COMMAND.COM program to load into RAM. You then request COMMAND.COM to perform actions, such as load a program from a disk into RAM. Since COMMAND.COM occupies only a small part of RAM, there is also space for other programs. Your program executes in RAM and normally produces output on the screen, printer, or disk. When finished, you may ask COMMAND.COM to load another program into RAM, an action that overwrites the previous program. All further discussions of RAM use the general term *memory*.

Addressing Memory Locations

The processor, depending on model, can access one or more bytes of memory at a time. Consider the decimal number 1025. The hex representation of this value, 0401, requires two bytes, or one word, of memory. It consists of a high-order (most significant) byte, 04, and a low-order (least significant) byte, 01. The system stores them in memory in *reverse byte sequence:* the low-order byte in the low memory address and the high-order byte in the high memory address. The processor would transfer hex 0401 from a register into memory locations 5612 and 5613 like this:

| 01 | 04 |
          | |
location 5612,   location 5613,
least significant byte   most significant byte

The processor expects numeric data in memory to be in reverse byte sequence and processes it accordingly. When the processor retrieves the word from memory, it again reverses the bytes, restoring them correctly in the register as hex 01 04. Although this feature is entirely automatic, you have to be alert to this fact when programming and debugging assembly language programs.

An assembly language programmer has to distinguish clearly between the address of a memory location and its contents. In the preceding example, the contents of location 5612 is 01 and the contents of location 5613 is 04.

SEGMENTS AND ADDRESSING

A *segment* is an area in memory that begins on a paragraph boundary, that is, at any location evenly divisible by 16, or hex 10. Although a segment may be located almost anywhere in memory and in real mode may be up to 64K bytes in size, it requires only as much space as the program requires for execution.

The fact that a segment in real mode can be up to 64K in size and there are four kinds of segments suggests that the amount of available RAM memory is $4 \times 64K$, or 256K. But there may be any number of segments; to address another segment, it is only necessary to change the address in a segment register. The three main segments are code, data, and stack.

Code Segment

The code segment contains the machine instructions that are to execute. Typically, the first executable instruction is at the start of this segment, and the operating system links to this location for program execution. The CS (code segment) register addresses this segment.

Data Segment

The data segment contains a program's defined data, constants, and work areas. The DS (data segment) register addresses this segment.

Stack Segment

In simple terms, the stack contains any data and addresses that you need to save temporarily for your own "called" subroutines to return to your main program. The SS (stack segment) register addresses this segment.

Segment Boundaries

The segment registers contain the starting address of each segment. Figure 1-4 provides a graphic view of the CS, DS, and SS registers, although the registers and segments are not necessarily in this sequence. Extra segment registers are the ES and, on the 80386/486, the FS and GS registers, which have specialized uses.

As discussed earlier, a segment begins on a paragraph boundary, which is an address evenly divisible by decimal 16 or hex 10. Assume that a data segment begins at memory location hex 045F0. Since in this and all other cases the rightmost hex digit is zero, the computer designers decided that it would be unnecessary to store the zero digit in the segment register. Thus hex 045F0 is stored as 045F, with the rightmost zero understood. In this book, where appropriate, we refer to the rightmost zero in square brackets as 045F[0].

Segment Offsets

Within a program, all memory locations are relative to the start of a segment. The distance in bytes is expressed as an *offset* (or displacement) from the start of a segment. A two-byte (16-bit) offset can range from hex 0000 through hex FFFF, or

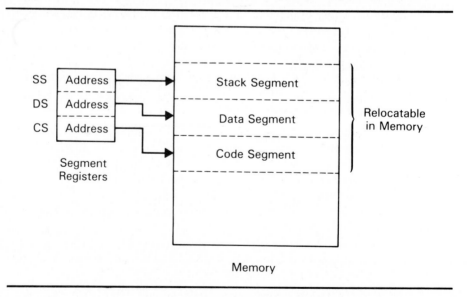

Figure 1-4 Segments and Registers

zero through 65,535. Thus the first byte of the code segment is at offset 00, the second byte is at offset 01, and so forth, through to offset 65,535. To reference any memory address in a segment, the computer combines the address in a segment register with an offset.

In the following example, the DS register contains the starting address of the data segment at hex 045F[0] and an instruction references a location with an offset of 0032 within the data segment. The actual memory location of the byte referenced by the instruction is therefore hex 04622:

DS address:	045F0
Offset:	+ 0032
Actual address:	04622

Note that a program contains one or more segments and that they may begin almost anywhere in memory, may be almost any size, and may be in any sequence.

Memory Capacity

The PC series has used a number of Intel processors that provide different addressing capability.

8086/8088 addressing.   The registers of the 8086/8088 processors provide 16 bits. Since a segment address is on a paragraph boundary, the rightmost four bits of its address are zero. As discussed earlier, an address is stored in a segment register and the computer assumes four rightmost zero bits (one hex digit), as hex nnnn[0]. Now, hex FFFF[0] allows addressing up to 1,048,560 bytes. If you are uncertain, decode each hex F as binary 1111, allow for the 0-bits, and add the values for the 1-bits.

80286 addressing.   In real mode, the 80286 processor works the same as an 8086, except that it is faster. In protected mode, the processor uses 24 bits for addressing, so that FFFFF[0] allows addressing up to 16 million bytes. The segment registers act as selectors for accessing a 24-bit base address from memory and adds this value to a 16-bit offset address:

Segment register:	16 bits [0000]
Base address:	24 bits

80386/486 addressing.   In real mode, the 80386/486 processors work the same as an 8086, except that they are faster. In protected mode, the processors use 48 bits for addressing, which allows addressing segments up to 4 billion bytes. The 16-bit segment registers act as selectors for accessing a 32-bit base address from memory and adds this value to a 32-bit offset address:

| Segment register: | 16 bits [0000] |
| Base address: | 32 bits |

REGISTERS

The processor's registers are used to control instructions being executed, to handle addressing of memory, and to provide arithmetic capability. The registers are addressable by name. Bits are conventionally numbered from right to left, as

$$\dots 15\ 14\ 13\ 12\ 11\ 10\ 9\ 8\ 7\ 6\ 5\ 4\ 3\ 2\ 1\ 0$$

Segment Registers

A segment register is 16 bits long and provides for addressing an area of memory, known as the current segment. As discussed earlier, a segment aligns on a paragraph boundary and its address in a segment register assumes four 0-bits to the right.

CS register.   The code segment register contains the initial address of a program's code segment. This address plus an offset value in the instruction pointer (IP) register indicates the address of an instruction to be fetched for execution. For normal programming purposes, you need not reference the CS.

DS register.   The data segment register contains the initial address of a program's data segment. In simple terms, this address plus an offset value in an instruction causes a reference to a specific byte location in the data segment.

SS register.   The stack segment register permits implementation of a stack in memory, used for temporary storage of addresses and data. The SS register contains the starting address of the program's stack segment. This address plus an offset value in the stack pointer (SP) register indicates the current word in the stack being addressed. For normal programming purposes, you need not reference the SS register.

ES register.   Some string (character data) operations use the extra segment register to handle memory addressing. In this context, the ES register is associated with the DI register. If the ES is required, the program must initialize it.

FS and GS registers.   These are additional extra segment registers on the 80386/486.

Instruction Pointer Register

The 16-bit IP register contains the offset address of the instruction that is to execute next. The IP is associated with the CS register such that the IP indicates the current instruction within the currently executing code segment. You would not normally reference this register in a program, but you can change its value when using the DOS DEBUG program to test a program. The 80386/486 have an extended 32-bit instruction pointer, the EIP.

In the following example, the CS register contains hex 25A4[0] and the IP contains hex 412. To find the next instruction to be executed, the processor combines the addresses in the CS and IP:

Contents of CS register:	25A40
Contents of IP register:	+ 412
Address of next instruction:	25E52

Pointer Registers

The pointer registers, SP and BP, are associated with the SS register and permit the system to access data in the stack segment.

SP register. The 16-bit stack pointer is associated with the SS register and provides an offset value that refers to the current word being processed in the stack. The 80386/486 have an extended 32-bit stack pointer, the ESP register. The system automatically handles these registers.

In the following example, the SS register contains hex 27B3[0] and the SP contains 312. To find the current word being processed in the stack, the computer combines the addresses in the SS and SP:

Contents of SS register:	27B30
Contents of SP register:	+ 312
Address in stack:	27E42

Stack segment:

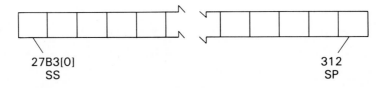

    27B3[0]   312
      SS   SP

BP register. The 16-bit base pointer facilitates referencing parameters, which are data and addresses passed via the stack. The 80386/486 have an extended 32-bit base pointer, the EBP register.

General-Purpose Registers

The AX, BX, CX, and DX general-purpose registers are the workhorses. They are unique in that you can address them as one word or as a one-byte portion. The leftmost byte is the "high" portion and the rightmost byte is the "low" portion. For example, the CX register consists of a CH and a CL portion, and you can reference any of the three names. The following instructions move zeros to the CX, CH, and CL registers, respectively:

```
MOV  CX,00
MOV  CH,00
MOV  CL,00
```

The 80386/486 support all the general-purpose registers plus 32-bit extended versions of them: the EAX, EBX, ECX, and EDX. These processors can reference the 8-bit, 16-bit, and 32-bit registers.

AX register. The AX register, the primary accumulator, is used for operations involving input/output and most arithmetic. For example, multiply, divide, and translate instructions assume use of the AX. Some instructions generate more efficient code if they reference the AX rather than another register.

BX register. The BX is known as the base register since it is the only general-purpose register that can be used as an "index" to extend addressing. Another common purpose is for computations.

CX register. The CX is known as the count register. It may contain a value to control the number of times a loop is repeated or a value to shift bits left or right. The CX is also used for computations.

DX register. The DX is known as the data register. Some input/output operations require its use, and multiply and divide operations that involve large values assume the DX and AX pair.

```
                      DX:  | DH | DL |
         EDX:  |_____|____|
```

You may use any of these general-purpose registers for addition and subtraction of 8-bit, 16-bit, or 32-bit values.

Index Registers

The index registers are available for extended addressing and for use in addition and subtraction.

SI register. The 16-bit source index register is required for some string (character) operations. In this context, the SI is associated with the DS register. The 80386/486 support a 32-bit extended register, the ESI.

DI register. The 16-bit destination index register is also required for some string operations. In this context, the DI is associated with the ES register. The 80386/486 support a 32-bit extended register, the EDI.

Flags Register

Nine of the 16 bits of the flags register are common to all 8086-family processors to indicate the current status of the machine and the results of execution. Many instructions involving comparisons and arithmetic change the status of the flags, which some instructions may test to determine subsequent action. Briefly, the common flag bits are the following:

OF (overflow). Indicates overflow of a high-order bit following arithmetic.

DF (direction). Designates left or right direction for moving or comparing string (character) data.

IF (interrupt). Indicates that an external interrupt such as keyboard entry is processed (1) or ignored (0).

TF (trap). Permits operation of the processor in single-step mode. Debugger programs such as DEBUG set the trap flag; you can step through execution one instruction at a time to examine the effect on registers and memory.

SF (sign). Contains resulting sign of arithmetic operation (0 = plus and 1 = minus).

ZF (zero). Indicates result of arithmetic or compare operation (0 = nonzero and 1 = zero result).

AF (auxiliary carry). Contains a carry out of bit 3 on 8-bit data, for specialized arithmetic.

PF (parity). Indicates parity of low-order 8-bit data operation (1 = even and 0 = odd number).

CF (carry). Contains carries from high-order (leftmost) bit following an arithmetic operation, and contents of last bit of a shift or rotate.

These flags are in the register in these locations:

Bit number:	15	14	13	12	11	10	9	8	7	6	5	4	3	2	1	0
Flag:					O	D	I	T	S	Z		A		P		C

The flags that are most relevant to assembly language programming are O, S, Z, and C for comparisons and arithmetic, and D for direction of string operations. The 80286/386/486 have some flags used for internal purposes, concerned primarily with protected mode. The 80386/486 have a 32-bit extended flags register known as Eflags. Subsequent chapters contain more detail about the flags register.

KEY POINTS

- The computer distinguishes only between bits that are 0 (off) and 1 (on) and performs arithmetic only in binary format.
- The value of a binary number is determined by the placement of 1-bits. Thus binary 1111 equals $2^3 + 2^2 + 2^1 + 2^0$, or 15.
- A negative binary number is represented by two's complement notation: Reverse the bits of its positive representation and add 1.
- The value K equals 1024 bytes.
- A single character of memory is a byte, comprised of eight data bits and one parity bit. Two adjacent bytes comprise a word, and four adjacent bytes comprise a doubleword.
- Hexadecimal format is an important shorthand notation for representing groups of 4 bits. The hex digits 0–9 and A–F represent binary 0000 through 1111.
- The representation of character data is done in ASCII format.
- The heart of the PC is a microprocessor that can access bytes or words.
- The two types of internal memory are ROM (read-only memory) and RAM (random access memory).
- The processor stores numeric data in words in memory in reverse byte sequence.

- An assembly language program consists of one or more segments: a stack segment for maintaining return addresses, a data segment for defined data and work areas, and a code segment for executable instructions. Locations in a segment are expressed as an offset relative to its start.
- The CS, DS, and SS registers provide for addressing the code, data, and stack segments, respectively.
- The IP register contains the offset address of the instruction that is to execute next.
- The SP and BP pointer registers are associated with the SS register and permit the system to access data in the stack segment.
- The AX, BX, CX, and DX general purpose registers are the workhorses. The leftmost byte is the "high" portion and the rightmost byte is the "low" portion. The AX (primary accumulator) is used for input/output and most arithmetic. The BX (base register) can be used as an "index" to extend addressing. The CX is known as the count register and the DX is known as the data register.
- The index registers are available for extended addressing and for use in addition and subtraction. The SI and DI registers are required for some string (character) operations.
- The flags register indicates the current status of the machine and the results of execution.

QUESTIONS

1-1. Provide the binary bit configuration for the following numbers: **(a)** 5; **(b)** 13; **(c)** 21; **(d)** 27; **(e)** 31.

1-2. Add the following binary numbers:

    (a) 00010101   **(b)** 00111110   **(c)** 00011111   **(d)** 01010101
         00001101   00101001   00000001   00111111

1-3. Determine the two's complement for the following binary numbers: **(a)** 00010011; **(b)** 00111100; **(c)** 00111001.

1-4. Determine the positive (absolute) value of the following negative binary numbers: **(a)** 11001000; **(b)** 10111101; **(c)** 11111110; **(d)** 11111111.

1-5. Determine the hex representation for the following: **(a)** ASCII letter Q; **(b)** ASCII number 7; **(c)** binary 01011101; **(d)** binary 01110111.

1-6. Add the following hex numbers:

    (a) 23A6   **(b)** 51FD   **(c)** 7779   **(d)** EABE   **(e)** FBAC
        0022   0003   0887   2 6 C4   0CBE

1-7. Determine the hex representation for the following decimal numbers. Refer to Appendix B for the conversion method. You could also check your result by converting the hex to binary and adding the 1-bits. **(a)** 19; **(b)** 33; **(c)** 89; **(d)** 255; **(e)** 4095; **(f)** 63,398.

1-8. Provide the ASCII bit configuration for the following one-byte characters. Use Appendix A as a guide: **(a)** P; **(b)** p; **(c)** #; **(d)** 5.

1-9. What is the purpose of the processor?

1-10. What are the two main kinds of memory on the PC and what are their main purposes?

1-11. Show how the processor stores hex 012345 in memory.

1-12. Explain the following: **(a)** segments; **(b)** offsets; **(c)** boundaries.

1-13. What are **(a)** the three kinds of segments, **(b)** their maximum size, and **(c)** the address boundary on which they begin?

1-14. Explain which registers are used for the following purposes: **(a)** addition and subtraction; **(b)** counting for looping; **(c)** multiplication and division; **(d)** addressing segments; **(e)** indication of a zero result; **(f)** address of an instruction that is to execute.

1-15. Show the EAX register and the size and position of the AH, AL, and AX within it.

2

MACHINE EXECUTION

OBJECTIVE

To introduce machine language and the entering and execution of a program in memory.

INTRODUCTION

This chapter begins with a general description of the boot process (how the system loads itself when you power up) and how an executing instruction addresses memory. The main part of this chapter uses a DOS program named DEBUG that allows you to view memory, to enter programs, and to trace their execution. In the text we describe how you can enter these programs directly into memory in a code segment and provide an explanation of each execution step. Some readers may have access to sophisticated debuggers such as CODEVIEW or TurboDebugger; however, we'll use DEBUG since it is simple and universally available.

The initial exercises have you inspect the contents of particular locations in memory. The first program example uses "immediate" data defined within the instructions for loading into registers and performing arithmetic. The second program example uses data defined separately in the data segment. Tracing these instructions through machine execution provides insight into the operation of a computer and the role of the registers.

You can start right in with no prior knowledge of assembly language or even of programming. All you need is an IBM PC or equivalent micro and a disk containing the DOS operating system. This book does assume, however, that you are familiar with booting up a computer, handling diskettes, and selecting disk drives and files.

THE BOOT PROCESS

Turning on the power causes a "cold boot." The processor enters a reset state, clears all memory locations to 0, performs a parity check of memory, and sets the CS register to FFFF[0]H and the IP register to zero. The first instruction to execute therefore is at FFFF0H, the entry point to BIOS in ROM.

BIOS checks the various ports to identify and initialize devices that are attached. BIOS then establishes an interrupt service table that contains addresses for interrupts that occur. Except for advanced processors, this table begins at location 0 in memory. BIOS also establishes its own data area beginning at location 40[0].

BIOS next determines whether a disk containing DOS is present, and if so, it accesses the bootstrap loader from the disk. This program loads DOS files IBMBIO.COM, IBMDOS.COM, and COMMAND.COM from disk into memory. (Under MS-DOS, IBMBIO.COM and IBMDOS.COM are known as IO.SYS and MSDOS.SYS, respectively.) At this point, memory appears as follows:

Interrupt services table
BIOS data area
IBMBIO.COM and IBMDOS.COM (or IO.SYS and MSDOS.SYS)
COMMAND.COM resident portion (resides permanently)
Available for program's use
COMMAND.COM transient portion (executing programs may erase it)
ROM BIOS

MACHINE ADDRESSING

As discussed in Chapter 1, the CS register contains the address of the beginning of a program's code segment and the DS register contains the address of the beginning of its data segment. The code segment contains instructions that are to execute, whereas the data segment contains data that the instructions reference. The IP register indicates the address of the current instruction in the code segment to be executed. An instruction operand indicates an offset address in the data segment to reference.

Consider an example in which the CS register contains hex 04AF[0], the DS contains 04B1[0], and the IP contains 0013. The CS:IP determine the address of the next instruction to execute as

$$
\begin{array}{ll}
\text{CS:} & \text{04AF0} \\
\text{IP:} & +\ \ 0013 \\
\hline
\text{Instruction address:} & +\,04B03
\end{array}
$$

Let's say that the instruction beginning at 04B03 copies the contents of a byte in memory into the AL register; the byte is at offset 0012 in the data segment. Here is the machine code and symbolic code for this operation:

A01200   MOV AL,[0012]
     |
Location 04B03

Memory location 04B03 contains the first byte of the instruction to be accessed. The second and third bytes contain the offset value, in reversed byte sequence. To access the data item, the processor determines its location from the contents of the DS register plus the offset (0012) in the instruction operand. Since the DS contains hex 04B1[0], the actual location of the referenced data item is

$$
\begin{array}{ll}
\text{DS:} & \text{04B10} \\
\text{Offset:} & +\ \ 0012 \\
\hline
\text{Address of data item:} & +\,04B22
\end{array}
$$

Let's say that location 04B22 contains hex 1B. The processor extracts the 1B at location 04B22 and copies it in the AL register, as shown in Figure 2-1.

As the processor fetches each byte of the instruction, it increments the IP register so that it contains the offset (0016) for the next instruction. The processor is now ready to execute the next instruction, which it derives once again from the contents of the CS (04AF0) plus the current offset in the IP (0026), in effect 04B06.

An instruction may also access more than one byte at a time. For example, an

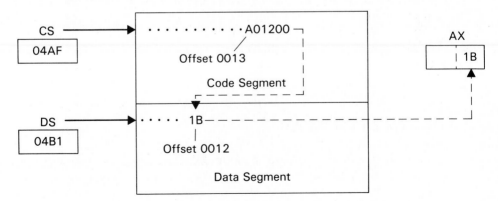

Figure 2-1 Segments and Offsets

instruction is to store the contents of the AX register (hex 0123) in two adjacent bytes in the data segment beginning at offset 0012: MOV [0012],AX. The processor stores them in reversed byte sequence as

Contents of bytes: 23   01
| |
Offset in data segment: 0012   0013

The instruction MOV AX,[0012] subsequently would retrieve these bytes by copying them from memory back into the AX. The operation reverses (and corrects) the bytes in the AX as 01 23.

Even-Numbered Addresses

The 8086, 80286, 80386, and 80486 processors execute more efficiently if an accessed word begins on an even-numbered address. In the previous MOV example, the processor can access the full word at offset 0012 directly into a register. But the word could begin on an odd-numbered address such as 0013:

Memory contents: | xx | 23 | 01 | xx |
| | | |
Offset: 0012   0013   0014   0015

In this case, the processor has to perform two accesses. The processor first accesses the bytes at 0012 and 0013 and delivers the byte from 0013 to the AL register. It then accesses the bytes at 0014 and 0015 and delivers the byte from 0014 to the AH register. The AX now contains 0123.

You don't have to perform any special programming for even or odd locations, nor do you have to know whether an address is even or odd. The accessing operation reverses a word from memory into a register so that it resumes its correct sequence.

Assembly language has an EVEN directive that you can use to align data on even memory locations for efficiency. Also, since the beginning of the data segment is always an even address, the first data field begins on an even number, and as long as successive data fields are defined as even-numbered words, they all begin on even addresses. For most purposes, however, these processors execute at such rapid speed that you'll never notice the effects of this alignment.

VIEWING MEMORY LOCATIONS

In the first exercise, you use the DOS DEBUG program to view the contents of selected memory locations. Insert the DOS diskette containing DEBUG in the default drive or set the system to the directory on hard disk containing DEBUG. To initiate the program, key in DEBUG and press Enter. DEBUG should load from disk into memory. When DEBUG's prompt, a hyphen (-), appears on the screen,

DEBUG is ready to accept your commands. The only command with which this exercise is concerned is D (dump).

Checking Memory Size

The first step is to examine the amount of memory that DOS thinks you have installed. Depending on computer model, the value may be based on switches set internally, and may indicate less memory than is actually installed. The value is in the ROM BIOS data area at locations hex 413 and 414, which you can view from DEBUG by means of a two-part address: 400 is the segment address, which you type as 40 (the last zero is assumed), and 13 is the offset from the segment address. Key in the following exactly as you see it:

D 40:13 [and press Enter]

The first two bytes displayed should be kilobytes of memory size in hexadecimal, with the bytes in reverse sequence. Some examples showing reversed hex, corrected hex, and the decimal equivalent follow:

Reversed Hex	Corrected Hex	Decimal (K)
00 01	01 00	256
80 01	01 80	384
00 02	02 00	512
80 02	02 80	640

Checking Serial Number

The computer's serial number is embedded in ROM at location hex FE000. To see it, type in

D FE00:0 [and press Enter]

The screen should display a seven-digit number followed by a copyright date in hex format.

Checking ROM BIOS Date

The date of your ROM BIOS begins at hex location FFFF5, recorded as mm/dd/yy. Type

D FFFF:05 [and press Enter]

Knowing this date could be useful to determine a computer's age and model.

Checking Copyright Notice

The copyright notice on conventional machines is at hex location F000:E005. Use the DEBUG D command to view it.

Checking Model ID

The model ID is at hex location F000:FFFE:

Code	Model
FF	IBM PC ('81, '82)
FE	PC-XT ('82), portable ('82)
FD	PCjr
FC	PC-AT ('84), PC-XT model 286, PS/2 models 50 and 60
FB	PC-XT ('86)
FA	PS/2 model 30
F9	PC convertible
F8	PS/2 models 70 and 80

Now that you know how to use the dump command, you can set an address to view the contents of any valid location. You can also step through memory simply by pressing D repeatedly—DEBUG displays locations continuing from the last operation.

When you've completed your inspection, press Q (for "quit") and the Enter key to exit from DEBUG.

MACHINE LANGUAGE EXAMPLE: IMMEDIATE DATA

Let's now use DEBUG to enter programs directly into memory and trace their execution. The next example illustrates a simple machine language program as it appears in main storage and the effect of its execution. The following program steps are in hexadecimal format:

Instruction	Explanation
B82301	Move the hex value 0123 to the AX.
052500	Add the hex value 0025 to the AX.
8BD8	Move the contents of the AX to the BX.
03D8	Add the contents of the AX to BX.
8BCB	Move the contents of the BX to CX.
2BC8	Subtract the contents of the AX from CX.
2BC0	Subtract the contents of the AX from AX (clear AX).
90	No operation (do nothing).
C3	Return to DOS.

You may have noticed that machine instructions may be one, two, or three bytes in length. The first (or only) byte is the actual operation, and other bytes are *operands*—references to an immediate value, a register, or a memory location. Also, machine instructions appear in memory one immediately following the other. Program execution begins with the first instruction and steps through each instruction one after another. Do not, at this point, expect to make much sense of the machine code. For example, in one case move is hex B8 and in another case move is hex 8B.

You can enter this program directly into memory and execute it one instruction at a time. At the same time, you can view the contents of the registers after each instruction. Begin this exercise just as you did for the preceding one—key in the command DEBUG and press Enter. When DEBUG has fully loaded, it displays its prompt (-). To print this exercise, turn on your printer and press Ctrl and PrtSc together.

To enter the machine language program directly, key in the following E (enter) command, including the blanks where indicated:

```
E CS:100 B8 23 01 05 25 00 [press Enter]
```

CS:100 indicates the starting memory address where the data is to be stored—hex 100 (256) bytes following the start of the code segment (the normal starting address for machine code under DEBUG). The E command causes DEBUG to store each pair of hexadecimal digits into a byte in memory, from CS:100 through CS:105.

The next E command stores six bytes starting at CS:106 through 107, 108, 109, 10A, and 10B:

```
E CS:106 8B D8 03 D8 8B CB [followed by Enter]
```

The last E command stores six bytes starting at CS:10C through 10D, 10E, 10F, 110, and 111:

```
E CS:10C 2B C8 2B C0 90 C3 [followed by Enter]
```

If you have keyed in an incorrect command, you can simply repeat it.

Now it's a simple matter of executing these instructions. Figure 2-2 shows all the steps, including the E commands. Your screen should display similar results as you enter each DEBUG command.

Key in the command R (register), followed by the Enter key to view the contents of the registers and flags. DEBUG now shows the contents of the registers in hexadecimal format, for example as

$$AX = 0000 \qquad BX = 0000 \ldots$$

Because of differences in DOS versions, the register contents on your screen may not be identical to those shown in Figure 2-2, which was run under DOS 4.01. The IP (instruction pointer) register displays IP = 0100, indicating that instruction

```
-E CS:100 B8 23 01 05 25 00
-E CS:106 8B D8 03 D8 8B CB
-E CS:10C 2B C8 2B C0 90 C3
-R
AX=0000  BX=0000  CX=0000  DX=0000  SP=FFEE  BP=0000  SI=0000  DI=0000
DS=21C1  ES=21C1  SS=21C1  CS=21C1  IP=0100  NV UP EI PL NZ NA PO NC
21C1:0100 B82301        MOV    AX,0123
-T

AX=0123  BX=0000  CX=0000  DX=0000  SP=FFEE  BP=0000  SI=0000  DI=0000
DS=21C1  ES=21C1  SS=21C1  CS=21C1  IP=0103  NV UP EI PL NZ NA PO NC
21C1:0103 052500        ADD    AX,0025
-T

AX=0148  BX=0000  CX=0000  DX=0000  SP=FFEE  BP=0000  SI=0000  DI=0000
DS=21C1  ES=21C1  SS=21C1  CS=21C1  IP=0106  NV UP EI PL NZ NA PE NC
21C1:0106 8BD8          MOV    BX,AX
-T

AX=0148  BX=0148  CX=0000  DX=0000  SP=FFEE  BP=0000  SI=0000  DI=0000
DS=21C1  ES=21C1  SS=21C1  CS=21C1  IP=0108  NV UP EI PL NZ NA PE NC
21C1:0108 03D8          ADD    BX,AX
-T

AX=0148  BX=0290  CX=0000  DX=0000  SP=FFEE  BP=0000  SI=0000  DI=0000
DS=21C1  ES=21C1  SS=21C1  CS=21C1  IP=010A  NV UP EI PL NZ AC PE NC
21C1:010A 8BCB          MOV    CX,BX
-T

AX=0148  BX=0290  CX=0290  DX=0000  SP=FFEE  BP=0000  SI=0000  DI=0000
DS=21C1  ES=21C1  SS=21C1  CS=21C1  IP=010C  NV UP EI PL NZ AC PE NC
21C1:010C 2BC8          SUB    CX,AX
-T

AX=0148  BX=0290  CX=0148  DX=0000  SP=FFEE  BP=0000  SI=0000  DI=0000
DS=21C1  ES=21C1  SS=21C1  CS=21C1  IP=010E  NV UP EI PL NZ AC PE NC
21C1:010E 2BC0          SUB    AX,AX
-T

AX=0000  BX=0290  CX=0148  DX=0000  SP=FFEE  BP=0000  SI=0000  DI=0000
DS=21C1  ES=21C1  SS=21C1  CS=21C1  IP=0110  NV UP EI PL ZR NA PE NC
21C1:0110 90            NOP
-T

AX=0000  BX=0290  CX=0148  DX=0000  SP=FFEE  BP=0000  SI=0000  DI=0000
DS=21C1  ES=21C1  SS=21C1  CS=21C1  IP=0111  NV UP EI PL ZR NA PE NC
21C1:0111 C3            RET
-
```

Figure 2-2 Trace of Machine Instructions

execution is to begin 100 bytes past the start of the code segment. (That is why you used E CS:100 to enter the start of the program.)

The flags register in Figure 2-2 shows the following flags setting:

NV   UP   EI   PL   NZ   NA   PO   NC

These settings mean no overflow, up (right) direction, enable interrupt, plus sign, nonzero, no auxiliary carry, parity odd, and no carry, respectively. At this time, none of these flags is important to us.

The R command also displays at offset 0100 the first instruction to be executed. Note that in Figure 2-2 the CS register contains 21C1. Since your CS value may differ, we'll show it as xxxx in this example. The instruction is the following:

`XXXX:0100 B82301 MOV AX,0123`

- xxxx indicates the start of the code segment as xxxx[0]. The value xxxx:0100 means 100 (hex) bytes following the CS address xxxx[0].
- B82301 is the machine code that you entered at CS:100.
- MOV AX,0123 is the symbolic assembly instruction for the machine code. This instruction means, in effect, "Move the immediate value 0123 into the AX register." DEBUG has "unassembled" the machine instruction so that you may more easily interpret it. In later chapters, you code assembly instructions exclusively.

At this point, the MOV instruction has not executed. For this purpose, key in T (trace) and press the Enter key. The machine code is B8 (move to AX register) followed by 2301. The operation moves the 23 to the low half (AL) of the AX register and the 01 to the high half (AH) of the AX register:

AX: |01|23|

DEBUG displays the results in the registers. The contents of the IP register is 0103 to indicate the offset location in the code segment of the next instruction to be executed:

xxxx:0103 052500 ADD AX,0025

To execute this instruction, enter another T. The ADD instruction adds 25 to the low half (AL) of the AX register and 00 to the high half (AH) of the AX, in effect adding 0025 to the AX. AX now contains 0148, and IP contains 0106 for the next instruction to be executed:

xxxx:0106 8BD8 MOV BX,AX

Key in another T command. The MOV instruction moves the contents of the AX register to the BX register-note that BX now contains 0148. AX still contains 0148 because MOV actually copies the data from one location to another.

Now key in T commands to step through the remaining instructions. The ADD instruction adds the contents of AX to BX, giving 0290 in BX. Then the program moves (copies) the contents of BX into CX, subtracts AX from CX, and subtracts AX from itself. After this last operation, the zero flag is changed from NZ (nonzero) to ZR (zero) to indicate that the result of the last operation was zero (subtracting AX from itself cleared it to zero).

If you want to reexecute these instructions, reset the IP register and trace through again. Enter R IP, enter 100, then R, and the required number of T commands, all followed by the Enter key.

Although you can also press T for the last instructions, NOP (no-operation) and RET (return), it is not recommended exiting DEBUG this way. To view the machine language program in the code segment, key in D (dump) as follows:

D CS:100

DEBUG now displays 16 bytes (32 hex digits) to the left of each line. To the right is the ASCII representation (if printable) of each byte (pair of hex digits). In the case of machine code, the ASCII representation is meaningless and may be ignored. In later sections we discuss the right side of the dump in more detail.

The first line of the dump begins at 00 and represents the contents of locations CS:100 through CS:10F. The second line represents the contents of CS:110 through CS:11F. Although your program ends at CS:111, the Dump command automatically displays eight lines from CS:100 through CS:170.

Figure 2-3 shows the results of the D CS:100 command. Expect only the machine code from CS:100 through 111 to be identical to your own dump; the bytes that follow could contain anything.

One more point: Figure 2-3 shows that the DS, ES, SS, and CS registers all contain the same address. DEBUG treats the program area as one segment, with code and data (if any) in the same segment, although you must keep them separate.

To terminate the DEBUG session, enter Q (quit). This operation returns you to DOS. If you printed the session, press Ctrl/PrtSc again to terminate printing.

```
-D CS:100
21C1:0100  B8 23 01 05 25 00 8B D8-03 D8 8B CB 2B C8 2B C0   .#..%.......+.+.
21C1:0110  90 C3 8D 46 14 50 51 52-FF 76 28 E8 74 00 8B E5   ...F.PQR.v(.t...
21C1:0120  B8 01 00 50 FF 76 32 FF-76 30 FF 76 2E FF 76 28   ...P.v2.v0.v..v(
21C1:0130  E8 88 15 8B E5 FF 36 18-12 FF 36 16 12 8B 76 28   ......6...6...v(
21C1:0140  FF 74 3A 89 46 06 E8 22-CE 8B E5 30 E4 3D 0A 00   .t:.F.."...0.=..
21C1:0150  75 32 A1 16 12 2D 01 00-8B 1E 18 12 83 DB 00 53   u2...-.........S
21C1:0160  50 8B 76 28 FF 74 3A A3-16 12 89 1E 18 12 E8 FA   P.v(.t:.........
21C1:0170  CD 8B E5 30 E4 3D 0D 00-74 0A 83 06 16 12 01 83   ...0.=..t.......
```

Figure 2-3   Dump of the Code Segment

MACHINE LANGUAGE EXAMPLE: DEFINED DATA

The preceding example used immediate values defined directly within MOV and ADD instructions. We next illustrate a similar example that defines data values 0123 and 0025 within the program. The program is to access the memory locations that contain these data values.

Working through this example should provide insight into how a computer accesses data by means of the DS register and offset addresses. The example defines the following data items and contents:

DS Offset	Hex Value	Bytes Occupied
0200	2301	0 and 1
0202	2500	2 and 3
0204	0000	4 and 5
0206	2A2A2A	6, 7, and 8

Remember that a hex character occupies a half-byte, so that, for example, 23 is stored in byte 0 (the first byte) of the data area, and 01 is stored in byte 1 (the second byte).

Here are the machine language instructions that process these items:

Instruction	Explanation
A10002	Move the word (two bytes) beginning at DS location 0200 into the AX register.
03060202	Add the contents of the word (two bytes) beginning at DS location 0202 to the AX register.
A30402	Move the contents of the AX register to the word beginning at DS location 0204.
C3	Return to DOS.

You may have noticed that two MOV instructions have different machine codes: A1 and A3. The actual machine code is dependent on the registers that are referenced, the number of bytes (byte or word), the direction of data transfer (from or to a register), and the reference to immediate data or memory.

Again, you can use DEBUG to enter this program and to watch its execution. When DEBUG signals its hyphen prompt, it is ready for your commands. First key in the E (enter) commands for the data segment:

```
E DS:0200 23 01 25 00 00 00 [press Enter]
E DS:0206 2A 2A 2A [press Enter]
```

The first E command stores the three words (six bytes) at the start of the data area, DS:0200. Note that you have to enter words with the bytes reversed so that 0123 is 2301 and 0025 is 2500. When a MOV instruction accesses these words into a register, it "unreverses" the bytes so that 2301 becomes 0123 and 2500 becomes 0025.

The second E command stores three asterisks (***) so that you can view them later using the D (dump) command—the asterisks serve no particular purpose in the data segment. Now key in the instructions, once again beginning at CS:100, as follows:

```
E CS:100 A1 00 02 03 06 02 02 [press Enter]
E CS:107 A3 04 02 C3 [press Enter]
```

Figure 2-4 shows all the steps including the E commands. Your screen should display similar results, although the CS and DS addresses probably differ. To examine the stored data (at DS:200 through 208) and the instructions (at CS:100 through 10A), key in the following D commands:

```
-E DS:200 23 01 25 00 00 00
-E DS:206 2A 2A 2A
-E CS:100 A1 00 02 03 06 02 02
-E CS:107 A3 04 02 C3
-D DS:200,208
21C1:0200   23 01 25 00 00 00 2A 2A-2A                          #.%...***
-R
AX=0000  BX=0000  CX=0000  DX=0000  SP=FFEE  BP=0000  SI=0000  DI=0000
DS=21C1  ES=21C1  SS=21C1  CS=21C1  IP=0100   NV UP EI PL NZ NA PO NC
21C1:0100 A10002        MOV     AX,[0200]                     DS:0200=0123
-T

AX=0123  BX=0000  CX=0000  DX=0000  SP=FFEE  BP=0000  SI=0000  DI=0000
DS=21C1  ES=21C1  SS=21C1  CS=21C1  IP=0103   NV UP EI PL NZ NA PO NC
21C1:0103 03060202      ADD     AX,[0202]                     DS:0202=0025
-T

AX=0148  BX=0000  CX=0000  DX=0000  SP=FFEE  BP=0000  SI=0000  DI=0000
DS=21C1  ES=21C1  SS=21C1  CS=21C1  IP=0107   NV UP EI PL NZ NA PE NC
21C1:0107 A30402        MOV     [0204],AX                     DS:0204=0000
-T

AX=0148  BX=0000  CX=0000  DX=0000  SP=FFEE  BP=0000  SI=0000  DI=0000
DS=21C1  ES=21C1  SS=21C1  CS=21C1  IP=010A   NV UP EI PL NZ NA PE NC
21C1:010A C3           RET
-D DS:0200,0208
21C1:0000   23 01 25 00 48 01 2A 2A-2A                          #.%.H.***
-Q
```

Figure 2-4   Trace of Machine Instructions

To view the data: D DS:200,208 [press Enter]
To view the code: D CS:100,10A [press Enter]

Check that the contents of both areas are identical to that of Figure 2-4.

You can execute these instructions just as you did earlier. Press R to view the contents of the registers and flags and to display the first instruction. The registers contain the same values as at the start of the first example. The first displayed instruction is

xxxx:0100 A10002 MOV AX,[0200]

CS:0100 references your first instruction, A10002. DEBUG interprets this instruction as a MOV and has determined that the reference is to the first location [0200] in the data area. The square brackets are to tell you that this reference is to a memory address and not an immediate value. (An immediate value for moving 0200 to the AX register would appear as MOV AX,0200.)

Now key in the DEBUG T (trace) command. The instruction MOV AX,[0200] moves the contents of the word at offset 0200 to the AX register. The contents are 2301, which the operation reverses in the AX as 0123.

Enter another T command to cause execution of the next instruction, ADD. The operation adds the contents of the word in memory at DS offset 0202 to the AX register. The result in the AX is now the sum of 0123 and 0025, or 0148.

The next instruction is MOV [0204],AX. Key in a T command for it to execute. The instruction moves the contents of the AX register to the word in memory at DS offset 0204. To view the changed contents of the data from 200 through 208, key in

D DS:200,208 [Enter]

The displayed values should be

Value in data area:	23	01	25	00	48	01	2A	2A	2A
	|	|	|	|	|	|	|	|	|
Offset:	200	201	202	203	204	205	206	207	208

The value 0148 is moved from the AX register to the data area at offsets 204 and 205 and is reversed as 4801. The left side of the dump shows the actual machine code as it appears in memory. The right side of a dump simply helps you locate alphabetic (string) data more easily. Note that these hex values are represented on the right of the screen by their ASCII equivalents. Thus hex 23 generates a number (#) symbol and hex 25 generates a percent (%) symbol, while the three hex 2A bytes generate asterisks (*).

Enter Q (quit) to terminate the DEBUG session.

MACHINE LANGUAGE EXAMPLE: MEMORY SIZE DETERMINATION

In the first exercise in this chapter, you checked locations 413 and 414 for the amount of memory (RAM) that your computer contains. ROM BIOS has a routine that delivers memory size. You can access BIOS through INT (interrupt) instructions, in this case INT 12H. BIOS returns the value to the AX register in terms of 1K bytes. Load DEBUG into memory and enter the following machine code for INT 12H and RET:

E CS:100 CD 12 C3 [and press Enter]

Press R (and Enter) to display the registers and the first instruction. The AX contains 0000 and the IP contains 0100. The instruction, INT 12H, passes control to a routine in BIOS that delivers the size of memory to the AX. Press T (and Enter) repeatedly to see the following BIOS instructions execute. (DEBUG shows the symbolic instructions, although it is the machine code that actually executes.) Comments to the right are the author's:

```
STI                      ; Set interrupt
PUSH   DS                ; Save DS address in stack
MOV    AX,0040           ; Segment 40[0]
MOV    DS,AX             ;   plus
MOV    AX,[0013]         ;   offset 0013
POP    DS                ; Restore address in DS
IRET                     ; Return from interrupt
```

At this point, the AX contains the size of memory in hex format. Now enter another T command to exit from BIOS and to return to your program. The displayed instruction is RET for the machine code C3 that you entered. Don't press T to continue the trace; instead, press Q to quit.

SPECIAL DEBUG FEATURES

You can use DEBUG to enter either assembly language statements or machine language instructions. You may find occasions to use both methods.

The A Command

The A (assemble) command tells DEBUG to begin accepting symbolic assembly instructions and to convert them into machine language. Initialize the starting address as

```
                           A 100 [Enter]
```

DEBUG displays the value of the code segment and the offset, as xxxx:0100. Type in each instruction followed by the Enter key. When you've entered the program, press Enter again to exit the A command. Try entering the following program:

```
                 MOV  AL,25     [Enter]
                 MOV  BL,32     [Enter]
                 ADD  AL,BL     [Enter]
                 RET            [Enter]
```

On completion, the screen should display the following:

```
                 xxxx:0100      MOV  AL,25
                 xxxx:0102      MOV  BL,32
                 xxxx:0104      ADD  AL,BL
                 xxxx:0106      RET
```

At this point, DEBUG is ready to accept another instruction. Just press Enter again to terminate the operation.

You can see that DEBUG has determined the starting location of each instruction. But before executing the program, let's examine the machine language generated.

The U Command

DEBUG's U (unassemble) command displays the machine code for your assembly instructions. You have to tell DEBUG the locations of the first and last instructions that you want to see, in this case, 100 and 106. Key in

U 100,106 [Enter]

The screen should display

```
xxxx:0100    B025    MOV    AL,25
xxxx:0102    B332    MOV    BL,32
xxxx:0104    00D8    ADD    AL,BL
xxxx:0106    C3      RET
```

Now trace execution of the program. Begin with R to display the registers and the first instruction, and T to trace subsequent instructions.

 You can now see how to enter a program in either machine or assembly language. A common use for entering assembly language is for very small programs. However, DEBUG is really intended for what its name implies—debugging programs—and most of your efforts will involve use of assembly language.

Saving a Program from within DEBUG

You may use DEBUG to save a program on disk under two circumstances.

  1. You have read a program, modified it, and now want to save it. Follow these steps:
  • Read the program under its name: DEBUG n:filename.
  • Use the D command to view the program and E to enter changes.
  • Use the W (write) command to write the revised program.
  2. You have used DEBUG to write a very small program that you now want to save.
  • Request the DEBUG program.
  • Use A (assemble) and E (enter) to create the program.
  • Name the program: N filename.COM. The program extension must be COM. (See Chapter 6 for details of COM files.)
  • Since only you know where the program really ends, tell DEBUG the length of the program in bytes. In the preceding example, the last instruction was

xxxx:0106 C3 RET

The last instruction is one byte, and therefore the program size is 100 through 106 inclusive, or 7.
  • First request the CX register as R CX [Enter].
  • DEBUG replies with CX 0000 (zero value).
  • You reply with the program length, 7.
  • Write the revised program: W [Enter].

 For both methods, DEBUG displays a message "Writing nnnn bytes." If the number is zero, you have failed to enter the program length; try again.

 Appendix E contains a complete description of DEBUG commands and is a useful reference for debugging your programs. The relevant parts at this time are the commands D (dump), E (enter), H (hexadecimal), N (name), Q (quit), R (register), T (trace), and W (write).

THE STACK

The two types of executable programs are name.COM and name.EXE. Both types require an area in the program reserved as a stack. The purpose of the stack is to provide a space for temporary storage of addresses and data items.

You must explicitly define a stack for an EXE program, whereas DOS defines the stack for a COM program. Each data item in the stack is one word (two bytes). The SS register, as initialized by DOS, contains the address of the beginning of the stack, and initially an offset in the SP register points to the end (or "top") of the stack:

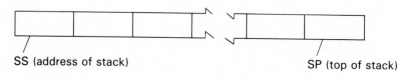

SS (address of stack)   SP (top of stack)

The PUSH, CALL, and INT instructions decrement the SP by 2 to the next lower storage word in the stack and store (or push) values there. The POP, RET, and IRET instructions return values from the stack and increment the SP.

The following example pushes the AX and BX registers onto the stack and then pops them. Assume that the AX contains hex 015A, the BX contains 03D2, and the SP contains 28.

1. *Pushing the AX.* The instruction PUSH AX decrements the SP by 2 and stores the contents of the AX, 015A, in the stack. Note that the stored bytes are reversed:

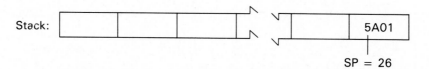

SP = 26

2. *Pushing the BX.* The instruction PUSH BX decrements the SP by 2 and stores the contents of the BX, 03D2, in the stack:

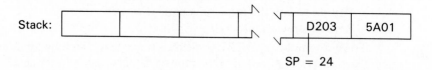

SP = 24

3. *Popping the BX.* The instruction POP BX restores the word from where the SP points in the stack to the BX register and increments the SP. The BX now contains 03D2, with the bytes correctly reversed:

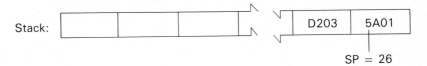

SP = 26

4. *Popping the AX.* The instruction POP AX restores the word from where the SP points in the stack to the AX register and increments the SP. The AX now contains 015A, with the bytes correctly reversed:

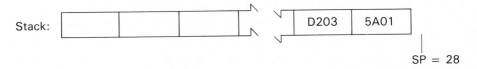

SP = 28

Note that POP instructions are coded in a reverse sequence from PUSH instructions. Thus the example pushed the AX and BX but popped the BX and AX. Also, the values pushed on the stack are still there, although the SP no longer points to them.

You have to ensure that your program coordinates pushing onto the stack and popping off it. Although this is a fairly straightforward requirement, an error can result in a program crash. Also, an EXE program has to define a stack that is large enough to contain all values that could possibly be pushed onto it.

THE INTERRUPT INSTRUCTION: INT

The INT instruction interrupts processing and accesses the interrupt services table in low memory to determine the address of a required routine. The operation transfers to DOS or to BIOS for specified action, and returns to the program to continue processing. Most often, an interrupt is to perform an input or output operation. Interrupts require a trail that facilitates exiting a program and returning to it. For this purpose, INT performs the following:

- Decrements the stack pointer by 2 and pushes the flags register onto the stack
- Clears the interrupt and trap flags
- Decrements the stack pointer by 2 and pushes the CS register onto the stack
- Decrements the stack pointer by 2 and pushes the instruction pointer onto the stack
- Causes the required operation to be performed

To return from the interrupt, the routine issues an IRET (interrupt return), which pops the registers off the stack and returns to the instruction following the INT.

Since this process is entirely automatic, your only concern is to define a stack segment large enough for the necessary pushing and popping.

KEY POINTS

- Turning on the power causes a "cold boot." The processor enters a reset state, clears all memory locations to 0, performs a parity check of memory, and sets the CS register and the IP register to the entry point to BIOS in ROM.

- As the processor fetches each byte of an instruction, it increments the IP register so that it contains the offset for the next instruction.

- The DOS DEBUG program is useful for debugging assembly language programs, but be careful in its use, especially the E (enter) command. Entering data at a wrong location or entering incorrect data may cause unpredictable results. You may find your screen filled with strange characters or have your keyboard lock. You are not likely to cause any damage, but you may get a bit of a surprise and may lose data that you entered during the DEBUG session.

- If you enter an incorrect value in the data segment or code segment, reenter the E command to correct it. To resume execution at the first instruction, set the instruction pointer (IP) register to 0100. Key in the R (register) command followed by the designated register as R IP [Enter]. DEBUG displays the contents of the IP and waits for an entry. Key in the value 0100 (followed by Enter). To check the result, key in an R command (without the IP). DEBUG displays the registers, flags, and the first instruction to be executed. You can now use T to retrace the instruction steps. If your program accumulates totals, you may have to clear some memory locations and registers. But be sure not to change the contents of the CS, DS, SP, and SS registers, all of which have specific purposes.

- The purpose of the stack is to provide a space for temporary storage of addresses and data items. Each data item in the stack is one word (two bytes).

- You must explicitly define a stack for an EXE program, whereas DOS defines the stack for a COM program.

- The INT instruction interrupts processing, transfers to DOS or to BIOS for specified action, and returns to the program to continue processing.

QUESTIONS

2-1. During execution of a program, the CS contains 5A2B[0], the SS contains 5B53[0], the IP contains 52, and the SP contains 48. Calculate the addresses for **(a)** the instruction to execute and **(b)** the current location in the stack.

2-2. The DS contains 5B24[0] and an instruction that moves data from memory to the AL is A03A01. Calculate the referenced memory address.

2-3. Provide the machine code instructions for the following operations: **(a)** move the hex value 4629 to the AX register; **(b)** add the hex value 036A to the AX register.

2-4. Assume that you have used DEBUG to enter the following E command:

E CS:100 B8 45 01 05 25 00

The hex value 45 was supposed to be 54. Code another E command to correct only the one byte that is incorrect; that is, directly change 45 to 54.

2-5. Assume that you have used DEBUG to enter the following E command:

E CS:100 B8 04 30 05 00 30 C3

(a) What are the three instructions here? (The first program in this chapter gives a clue.)

(b) On executing this program, you discover that the AX register ends up with 6004 instead of the expected 0460. What is the error, and how would you correct it?

(c) Having corrected the instructions, you now want to reexecute the program from the first instruction. What two DEBUG commands are required?

2-6. The following is a machine language program:

B0 25 D0 E0 B3 15 F6 E3 C3

The program performs the following:
- Moves the hex value 25 to the AL register
- Shifts the contents of the AL one bit left (the result is 4A)
- Moves the hex value 15 to the BL register
- Multiplies AL by BL

Use DEBUG's E command to enter this program beginning at CS:100. Remember that these are hexadecimal values. After entering the program, key in D CS:100 to view it. Then key in R and enough successive T commands to step through the program until reaching RET. What is the final product in the AX register?

2-7. Use DEBUG's E command to enter the following machine language program:

Data:	25	15	00	00							
Machine code:	A0	00	02	D0	E0	F6	26	01	02	A3	02	02	C3

The program performs the following:
- Moves the contents of the one-byte at DS:0200 (25) to the AL register
- Shifts the AL contents one bit left (the result is 4A)
- Multiplies the AL by the one byte contents at DS:0201 (15)
- Moves the product from the AX to the word beginning at DS:0202

After entering the program, key in D commands to view the data and the code. Then key in R and enough successive T commands to step through the program until reaching RET. At this point, the AX should contain the product 0612. Key in another D DS:0200 and note that the product at DS:0202 is stored as 1206.

2-8. For Question 2-7, code the commands that write the program on disk under the name TRIAL.COM.

2-9. Use DEBUG's A command to enter the following instructions:

```
MOV     BX,25
ADD     BX,30
SHL     BX,01
SUB     BX,22
NOP
RET
```

Unassemble and trace execution through to the NOP.

2-10. What is the purpose of the stack?

2-11. In what way is the stack defined for **(a)** a COM program and **(b)** an EXE program? (That is, who or what defines it?)

2-12. **(a)** What is the size of each entry in the stack?
(b) Where initially is the "top" of the stack and how is it addressed?

2-13. **(a)** How do the instuctions PUSH, CALL, and INT affect the stack?
(b) How do the instructions POP, RET, and IRET affect the stack?

2-14. What in general terms is the purpose of the INT instruction?

3

ASSEMBLY LANGUAGE REQUIREMENTS

OBJECTIVE

To cover the basic requirements for coding an assembly language program.

INTRODUCTION

In Chapter 2 we showed how to key in and execute a machine language program. No doubt you were also very aware of the difficulty in deciphering the machine code even for a small program. Probably no one seriously codes in machine language other than for the smallest programs. A higher level of coding is at the assembly level in which a programmer uses symbolic instructions in place of machine instructions and descriptive names for data items and memory locations.

In this chapter we explain the basic requirements for an assembly language program, including the use of comments, the general coding format, the directives for printing a program listing, and the directives for defining segments and procedures. The chapter also covers the general organization of a program, including initialization and terminating execution.

ASSEMBLY LANGUAGE COMMENTS

The use of comments throughout a program can improve clarity, especially in assembly language where the purpose of a set of instructions is often unclear. A comment always begins with a semicolon (;), and wherever you code it, the assembler assumes that all characters to its right are comments. A comment may contain any printable character, including a blank.

A comment may appear on a line by itself or following an instruction on the same line, as the following two examples illustrate:

1. ;This entire line is a comment
2. ADD AX,BX ;Comment on same line as instruction

Since a comment appears only on a listing of an assembled source program and generates no machine code, you may include any number of comments without affecting program execution. In this book, assembly instructions are in uppercase letters and comments are in lowercase, only as a convention and to make programs more readable.

CODING FORMAT

In general, a *name* refers to the address of a data item, whereas a *label* refers to the address of an instruction. Since the same rules apply to both names and labels, this section uses the term *name* to mean either name or label. Here is the general format for an instruction:

| [name] | operation | [operand(s)] |

A name (if any), operation, and operand (if any) are separated by at least one blank or tab character. There are a maximum of 132 characters on a line, although most people prefer to stay within 80 characters because of the screen width. Two examples follow:

Name	Operation	Operand	Comment
COUNT	DB	1	;Name, operation, one operand
	MOV	AX,0	;Operation, two operands

Name, operation, and operand may begin at any column. However, consistently starting at the same column for these entries makes a more readable program. Also, most program editors provide useful tab stops every eight positions.

Name

A name or label can use the following characters:

     Alphabetic letters: A through Z and a through z
     Digits: 0 through 9

Special characters: question mark (?)
                        period (.) (only first character)
                        at (@)
                        underline (_)
                        dollar ($)

The first character of a name must be an alphabetic letter or a special character. The assembler treats uppercase and lowercase letters the same. The maximum length is 31 characters. Examples of valid names are COUNT, PAGE25, and $E10. Descriptive, meaningful names are recommended. The names of registers, such as AX, DI, and AL, are reserved for referencing registers. Consequently, in an instruction such as

```
ADD AX,BX
```

the assembler automatically knows that AX and BX refer to registers. However, in an instruction such as

```
MOV REGSAVE,AX
```

the assembler can recognize the name REGSAVE only if you define it in the program. Appendix C provides a list of reserved words.

Operation

For a data item, an operation such as DB or DW defines a field, work area, or constant. For an instruction, an operation such as MOV or ADD indicates an action.

Operand

For a data item, an operand defines its initial value. In the following definition of a data item named COUNTER, the operand initializes its contents with 0:

Name	Operation	Operand	Comment
COUNTR	DB	0	;Define byte (DB) with 0 value

For an instruction, an operand indicates where to perform the action. An operand may contain one, two, or even no entries. Here are three examples:

	Operation	Operand	Comment
No operand	RET		;Return
One operand	INC	CX	;Increment CX register
Two operands	ADD	AX,12	;Add 12 to AX register

DIRECTIVES

Assembly language supports a number of instructions that enable you to control the way in which a program assembles and lists. These instructions, named *directives* (or pseudo-operations), act only during the assembly of a program and generate no machine-executable code. The most common directives, are explained in the next sections. Chapter 24 covers all of the directives in detail; there is too much information to cover at this point, but you can use that chapter as a reference.

Listing Directives: PAGE and TITLE

The PAGE and TITLE directives help to control the format of an assembled listing.

Page.   The PAGE directive at the start of a program designates the maximum number of lines to list on a page and the maximum number of characters on a line. Its general format is

```
PAGE [[length],[width]
```

The following example sets 60 lines per page and 132 characters per line:

```
PAGE 60,132
```

Lines per page may range from 10 to 255, and characters per line may range from 60 to 132. Omission of a PAGE statement causes the assembler to assume PAGE 50,80.

Assume that the line count is set to 60. When the assembled program has listed 60 lines, it ejects the forms to the top of the next page and increments a page count. You may also want to force a page to eject at a specific line, such as at the end of a segment. At the required line, simply code PAGE with no operand. The assembled listing automatically ejects the page on encountering PAGE.

Title.   You can use the TITLE directive to cause a title for a program to print on line 2 of each page. You may code TITLE once, at the start. Its general format is

```
TITLE text
```

For text, a recommended technique is to use the name of the program as cataloged on disk. For example, if the program is named ASMSORT, code that name plus a descriptive comment, all up to 60 characters in length, as follows:

```
TITLE ASMSORT Assembly program to sort customer names
```

SEGMENT Directive

An assembly language program consists of one or more segments. A code segment provides for executable code, a data segment defines data items, and a stack segment defines stack storage. The directive for defining a segment, SEGMENT, has the following format:

Name	*Operation*	*Operand*	
name	SEGMENT	[options]	;Begin segment
⋮			
name	ENDS		;End segment

The segment name must be present, must be unique, and must follow the naming conventions of the language. The ENDS statement indicates the end of a segment and contains the same name as the SEGMENT statement. The maximum size of a segment is 64K. A SEGMENT statement may contain three types of options: alignment, combine, and class, coded in this format:

name	SEGMENT	align combine 'class'

Alignment type.   This entry indicates the boundary on which the segment is to begin. For the typical requirement, PARA, the segment aligns on a paragraph boundary, so that the starting address is evenly divisible by 16 or hex 10. Omission of an operand causes the assembler to assume (default to) PARA.

Combine type.   This entry indicates whether to combine with other segments when "linked" after assembly (explained later under "Linking the Program"). Types are STACK, COMMON, PUBLIC, and AT expression. For example, the stack segment is defined as

```
name SEGMENT   PARA STACK
```

You may use PUBLIC and COMMON when separately assembled programs are to be combined when linked. Otherwise, a program that is not to be combined with other programs may omit this option or code NONE.

Class type.   This entry, enclosed in apostrophes, is used to group related segments when linking. This book uses the classes 'code' for the code segment (recommended by MicroSoft), 'data' for the data segment, and 'stack' for the stack segment.

The following example defines a stack segment with alignment, combine, and class types:

```
name SEGMENT  PARA STACK 'Stack'
```

The partial program in Figure 3-1 in a later section illustrates SEGMENT statements with various options.

PROC Directive

The code segment contains the executable code for a program. This segment also contains one or more procedures, defined with the PROC directive. A segment that contains only one procedure would appear as follows:

```
segnam      SEGMENT   PARA   Comment
procname    PROC      FAR    ;One
               .              ;procedure
               .              ;within
               .              ;the code
procname    ENDP             ;segment
segname     ENDS
```

The procedure name must be present, must be unique, and must follow naming conventions for the language. The operand FAR indicates to the DOS program loader that this PROC is the entry point for program execution. The ENDP directive indicates the end of a procedure and contains the same name as the PROC statement.

The code segment may contain any number of procedures used as subroutines, which you usually code as NEAR; we cover this condition in Chapter 7.

ASSUME Directive

The processor uses the SS register to address the stack, the DS register to address the data segment, and the CS register to address the code segment. You have to tell the assembler the purpose of each segment. The directive for this purpose is ASSUME, coded in the code segment as follows:

Operation	*Operand*
ASSUME	SS:stackname,DS:datasegname,CS:codesegname

For example, SS:stackname means that the assembler is to associate the name of the stack segment with the SS register. The operands may appear in any sequence. ASSUME may also contain an entry for the ES, as ES:datasegname; if your program does not use the ES register, you may omit its reference or code ES:NOTHING.

Like other directives, ASSUME is just a message to the assembler; you may still have to code an instruction that at execute time physically loads an address in a segment register.

END Directive

As already seen, the ENDS directive terminates a segment, and the ENDP directive terminates a procedure. An END directive terminates the entire program. Its general format is

Operation	Operand
END	[procname]

The operand may be blank if the program is not to execute; for example, you may want to assemble only data definitions, or the program is to be linked with another (main) module. For typical programs, the operand contains the name of the first or only PROC designated as FAR where program execution is to begin.

MEMORY AND REGISTER REFERENCES

One feature to get clear is the use in instruction operands of names, of names in square brackets, and of numbers. In the following examples, assume that WORDA is defined as a word (two bytes) in memory:

```
MOV   AX,BX        ;Move contents of BX to AX
MOV   AX,WORDA     ;Move contents of WORDA to AX
MOV   AX,25        ;Move value 25 to AX
MOV   AX,[BX]      ;Move contents of memory location specified by BX
```

The only new item is the use of square brackets, which you'll use in later chapters.

PROGRAM ORGANIZATION

The two basic types of executable programs are EXE and COM. We'll develop the requirements for EXE first and leave COM for Chapter 6. Figure 3-1 provides a skeleton of an EXE program showing stack, data, and code segments.

The sequence in which you define segments is usually unimportant. The example defines the segments as follows:

```
STACKSG   SEGMENT   PARA   STACK 'Stack'
DATASG    SEGMENT   PARA   'Data'
CODESG    SEGMENT   PARA   'Code'
```

INITIALIZING A PROGRAM

Figure 3-1 illustrates common initialization and exit requirements for an EXE program. The two requirements for initializing are: (1) notify the assembler the segments to associate with segment registers, and (2) load the DS with the address of the data segment.

ASSUME in the code segment is a directive that notifies the assembler to

```
          page 60,132
          TITLE    EXASM1 Skeleton of an Assembly Program
; ---------------------------------------------------------------
STACKSG   SEGMENT   PARA STACK 'Stack'
          ...
STACKSG   ENDS
; ---------------------------------------------------------------
DATASG    SEGMENT   PARA 'Data'
          ...
DATASG    ENDS
; ---------------------------------------------------------------
CODESG    SEGMENT   PARA 'Code'
BEGIN     PROC      FAR
          ASSUME    CS:CODESG,DS:DATASG,SS:STACKSG
          MOV       AX,DATASG      ;Get address of data segment

          MOV       DS,AX          ;Store it in DS
          ...
          MOV       AH,4CH         ;Request terminate
          INT       21H            ;Exit to DOS
BEGIN     ENDP
CODESG    ENDS
          END       BEGIN
```

Figure 3-1   Skeleton of an EXE Program

associate certain segments with certain segment registers, in this case, CODESG with the CS, DATASG with the DS, and STACKSG with the SS:

```
ASSUME   CS:CODESG,DS:DATASG,SS:STACKSG
```

By associating segments with segment registers, the assembler can determine offset addresses of items within each segment. For example, each instruction in the code segment is a specific length. The first instruction is at offset 0, and if it is two bytes long, the second instruction is at offset 2, and so forth.

Two instructions initialize the address of the data segment in the DS register:

```
MOV     AX,DATASG     ;Get address of data segment
MOV     DS,AX         ;Store address in DS
```

The first MOV loads the address of the data segment in the AX register and the second MOV copies the address from the AX into the DS. Two MOVs are required because no instruction can move data directly from memory to a segment register. Thus MOV DS,DATASG is illegal. In Chapter 4 we discuss initializing segment registers in more detail.

When DOS loads an EXE program from disk into memory for execution, it performs the following operations:

1. Constructs a 256-byte (hex 100) program segment prefix (PSP) on a paragraph boundary in available memory.
2. Loads the EXE program immediately following the PSP.
3. Stores the address of the PSP in the DS and ES registers.
4. Stores the address of the code segment in the CS and sets the IP to the offset of the first instruction, usually at zero.
5. Stores the address of the stack in the SS and sets the SP to the size (the "top") of the stack.
6. Transfers control to the EXE program for execution.

Thus the DOS loader initializes the CS:IP and SS:SP registers correctly. Since the loader program sets the address of the PSP in the DS and ES registers, you have to initialize the DS, as shown by the two MOV instructions in Figure 3-1.

Now, even if this initialization is not clear at this point, take heart. Every EXE program has virtually identical initialization steps that you can duplicate each time you code a program.

TERMINATING PROGRAM EXECUTION

In this section we cover the various ways that DOS provides for normal termination of program execution. You'll find all these methods used in assembly language programs.

DOS Service Call 4CH

This operation requires running the program under DOS 2.0 or later and is the currently recommended practice, as shown in Figure 3-1. INT 21H recognizes 4CH in the AH is a service call for terminating. You can also pass a return code in the AL for subsequent testing in a batch file (via the IF ERRORLEVEL statement).

```
MOV AH,4CH          ;DOS service call
MOV AL,retcode      ;Return code (optional)
INT 21H             ;Terminate and return to DOS
```

The return code for normal termination is usually 0. You may also code the two MOVs as one statement:

```
MOV AX,4C00H     ;DOS service call and return code
```

DOS Interrupt 20H

This operation has been available in all versions of DOS. Since it may be made obsolete, its use is no longer recommended.

```
INT 20H     ;Terminate and return to DOS
```

DOS Service Call 0

This operation has been available in all versions of DOS.

```
MOV AH,0    ;DOS service call
INT 21H     ; for program termination
```

The RET Instruction

The use of RET requires that you set up the program to facilitate return to DOS when execution is complete. Immediately following the ASSUME statement, push on the stack first, the current address in the DS register, and second, a zero address. RET returns to the beginning of the program segment prefix (PSP) where an INT 20H instruction is stored.

```
ASSUME     CS;CSEG,DS:DSEG,SS:SSEG,ES:DSEG
PUSH       DS                    ;Push DS onto stack
SUB        AX,AX                 ;Set AX to zero
PUSH       AX                    ;Push zero onto stack
MOV        AX,DSEG               ;Initialize
MOV        DS,AX                 ; DS register
. . .
RET                              ;Terminate and return to DOS
```

The DS initially contains the starting address of the PSP, which the first PUSH stores in the stack. The SUB instruction clears the AX to zero by subtracting it from itself, and the second PUSH stores this value on the stack. The stack now contains two values:

$$| \, \ldots \, | \, \texttt{0000} \, | \, \texttt{addr of PSP} |$$

RET exits from your program and returns to DOS by means of the address that was pushed onto the stack at the start (PUSH DS). In effect, RET (a far return since the procedure is labeled FAR) pops the word at the top of the stack (the zeros) onto the IP and increments the SP by 2. It then pops the next word at the top of the stack (the address of the PSP) onto the CS and increments the SP by 2. The new CS:IP values—segment and offset—now point to the beginning of the PSP, where an INT 20H instruction resides. Control transfers to this location and the INT instruction returns to DOS.

EXAMPLE OF A SOURCE PROGRAM

Figure 3-2 combines the preceding information into a simple assembly language source program based on Figure 2-3 that added two data items in the AX register.

STACKSG contains one entry, DW (Define Word), that defines 32 words initialized to zero, an ample size for most programs.

DATASG defines three data words named FLDA, FLDB, and FLDC.

CODESG contains the executable instructions for the program, although the

```
            page 60,132
    TITLE   EXASM1 (EXE)  Move and add operations
    ; -------------------------------------------------
    STACKSG SEGMENT PARA STACK 'Stack'
            DW        32 DUP(0)
    STACKSG ENDS
    ; -------------------------------------------------
    DATASG  SEGMENT PARA 'Data'
    FLDA    DW        250
    FLDB    DW        125
    FLDC    DW        ?
    DATASG  ENDS
    ; -------------------------------------------------
    CODESG  SEGMENT PARA 'Code'
    BEGIN   PROC      FAR
            ASSUME    CS:CODESG,DS:DATASG,SS:STACKSG
            MOV       AX,DATASG   ;Set address of DATASG
            MOV       DS,AX       ;  in DS register

            MOV       AX,FLDA     ;Move 0250 to AX
            ADD       AX,FLDB     ;Add  0125 to AX
            MOV       FLDC,AX     ;Store sum in FLDC
            MOV       AH,4CH      ;Return to DOS
            INT       21H
    BEGIN   ENDP
    CODESG  ENDS
            END       BEGIN
```

Figure 3-2   EXE Source Program with Conventional Segments

first statement, ASSUME, generates no executable code. The ASSUME directive assigns CODESG to the CS register, DATASG to the DS register, and STACKSG to the SS register. In effect, the statement tells the assembler to use the address in the CS register for addressing CODESG, the address in the DS register for addressing DATASG, and the address in the SS register for addressing STACKSG. When loading a program from disk into memory for execution, the system loader sets the actual addresses in the SS and CS registers, but you have to initialize the DS (and ES) register, as shown by the first two MOV instructions.

We'll trace the assembly, linkage, and execution of this program in Chapter 4.

INITIALIZING FOR 80386 PROTECTED MODE

For protected mode under an 80386/486 processor, use DWORD to align segments on a doubleword address. This alignment speeds up accessing memory for 32-bit data buses. In the following, the .386 directive tells the assembler to accept instructions that are unique to the 80386 (and 80486). The USE32 use type tells the assembler to generate code appropriate to 32-bit protected mode.

```
.386
segname   SEGMENT     DWORD   USE32
```

Initialization of the data segment register could look like this, since the 80386 DS register is still 16 bits in size:

```
MOV     EAX,DATASEG     ;Get address of data segment
MOV     DS,AX           ;Load 16-bit portion
```

SIMPLIFIED SEGMENT DIRECTIVES

MicroSoft Assembler version 5.0 and Borland Turbo Assembler introduced some shortcuts in defining segments. To use this feature, you initialize the *memory model* before defining any segment. The general format (including the leading period) is

```
.MODEL   memory-model
```

The memory model may be SMALL, MEDIUM, COMPACT, or LARGE. (Another model, HUGE, need not concern us here.) The requirements are:

Model	Number of Code Segments	Number of Data Segments
SMALL	1	1
MEDIUM	More than 1	1
COMPACT	1	More than 1
LARGE	More than 1	More than 1

You may use any of these models for a stand-alone program (that is, one not linked to another program). The SMALL model requires that code fits within a 64K segment and data fits within another 64K segment, and is suitable for most of the examples in this book. The .MODEL directive automatically generates the required ASSUME statement.

The general formats (including the leading period) for the directives that define the code, data, and stack segments are

```
.CODE [name]
.DATA
.STACK [size]
```

For each directive, the address generates a SEGMENT statement and its matching ENDS. The default segment names are _TEXT (for the code segment), _DATA, and STACK. The underline (or break) character preceding _TEXT and _DATA is intended. As the format indicates, you may override the default name for the code segment. The default stack size is 1024 bytes, which you may also override. You identify where the three segments are to begin and the assembler generates them. Note, however, that the instructions that initialize the data segment are

```
MOV   AX,@data
MOV   DS,AX
```

Earlier, Figure 3-2 gave an example of a program using conventionally defined segments. Figure 3-3 now provides the same example, but this time using the simplified segment directives .STACK, and .DATA, .CODE. The stack is defined as 96 bytes (48 words). Note the missing SEGMENT, ENDS, and ASSUME statements.

```
          page   60,132
    TITLE   EXASM1A (EXE)  Move and add operations
;-----------------------------------------------------
          .MODEL SMALL
          .STACK 64            ;Define stack
          .DATA                ;Define data
    FLDA    DW      250
    FLDB    DW      125
    FLDC    DW      ?

          .CODE                ;Define code segment
    BEGIN   PROC    FAR
          MOV     AX,@data     ;Set address of DATASG
          MOV     DS,AX        ;   in DS register

          MOV     AX,FLDA      ;Move 0250 to AX
          ADD     AX,FLDB      ;Add  0125 to AX
          MOV     FLDC,AX      ;Store sum in FLDC

          MOV     AX,4C00H     ;Return to DOS
          INT     21H
    BEGIN   ENDP                 ;End of procedure

          END     BEGIN        ;End of program
```

Figure 3-3   EXE Source Program with Simplified Segment Directives

KEY POINTS

- A semicolon precedes comments on a line.
- A program consists of one or more segments, each of which begins on a paragraph boundary.
- ENDS terminates each segment, ENDP terminates each procedure, and END terminates the program.
- The ASSUME directive associates segment registers CS, DS, and SS with their appropriate segment names.
- EXE programs (but not COM programs) should provide at least 32 words for stack addressing.
- You normally initialize the DS register in EXE programs with the address of the data segment.
- For the simplified segment directives, you initialize the memory model before defining any segment. Options are SMALL (one code segment and one data segment), MEDIUM (any number of code segments and one data segment), COMPACT (one code segment and any number of data segments), and LARGE (any number of code segments and data segments).

QUESTIONS

3-1. What commands cause the assembler **(a)** to print a heading at the top of a page of the listing and **(b)** to eject to a new page?

3-2. Determine which of the following names are valid: **(a)** PC–AT; **(b)** $50; **(c)** @$_Z; **(d)** 34B7; **(e)** AX.

3-3. What is the purpose of each of the three segments described in this chapter?

3-4. Distinguish between a directive and an instruction.

3-5. The format for the SEGMENT directive is

```
name SEGMENT align combine 'class'
```

What is the purpose of **(a)** align, **(b)** combine, and **(c)** 'class'?

3-6. **(a)** What is the purpose of a procedure?
(b) How do you define the beginning and the end of a procedure?
(c) When would you define a procedure as FAR and as NEAR?

3-7. What particular END statements are concerned with terminating **(a)** a program, **(b)** a procedure, and **(c)** a segment?

3-8. Distinguish between statements that terminate an assembly and statements that terminate execution.

3-9. **(a)** What does DOS construct and store in front of an executable module when the module is loaded for execution?
(b) What is its size?

3-10. DOS performs certain operations when it loads an EXE program for execution. What values does DOS initialize **(a)** in the CS and IP registers, **(b)** in the SS and SP registers, and **(c)** in the DS and ES registers?

3-11. Given the names CDSEG, DATSEG, and STKSEG for the code segment, data segment, and stack, respectively, code the ASSUME.

3-12. (a) What are the four ways to provide normal termination of an assembly language program?
(b) Which is the recommended way?

3-13. For the simplified segment directives, the .MODEL directive provides for SMALL, MEDIUM, COMPACT, and LARGE models. Under what circumstances would you use each model?

4

ASSEMBLING, LINKING, AND EXECUTING A PROGRAM

OBJECTIVE

To cover the steps in assembling, linking, and executing an assembly language program.

INTRODUCTION

In this chapter we explain the procedure for keying in an assembly source program and for assembling, linking, and executing it. The symbolic instructions that you code in assembly language are known as the source program. You use the assembler program to translate the source program into machine code, known as the object program. Finally, you use the linker program to complete the machine addressing for the object program, generating an executable module.

In the sections on assembling we explain how to request execution of the assembler program, which provides diagnostics (including any error messages) and generates the object program. Also explained are details of the assembler listing and in general terms how the assembler processes a source program.

In the sections on linking we explain how to request execution of the linker program so that you can generate an executable module. Also explained are details of the generated link map as well as the diagnostics. Finally, we explain how to request execution of the executable module.

PREPARING A PROGRAM FOR EXECUTION

Figure 3-2 illustrated only source code for a program that is not yet in executable format. At this point, you could use DOS EDLIN or preferably a full-screen editor to key in this program. Insert the editor diskette in disk drive A and a formatted diskette in drive B. Users of hard disk or RAM disk should substitute the appropriate drive in the following examples. Call up the editor program and key in the statements for the source program, EXASM1.

Although spacing is not important to the assembler, a program is more readable if you keep the name, operation, operand, and comments consistently aligned. Most editors have tab stops at every eight positions to facilitate aligning columns.

Once you have entered the program, check the code for accuracy. You can verify that the program is cataloged on disk by keying in

```
       DIR B:                (for all files)
    or DIR B:EXASM1.ASM      (for one file)
```

For a printout of the program, turn on your printer and adjust the paper. You can request the DOS program PRINT:

```
    PRINT B:EXASM1.ASM [Enter]
```

As it stands, EXASM1.ASM is just a text file that cannot execute—you must first assemble and link it. (Users of BASIC are used to keying in a source program and executing it directly; however, assembler and compiler languages require steps to assemble and link.) The *assembly step* involves translating the source code to machine object code and generating an OBJ (object) file, or module. (You have already seen examples of machine code in Chapter 2 and examples of source code in Chapter 3.) The OBJ module is not quite in executable form. The *link step* involves converting the OBJ module to an EXE (executable) machine code module. Figure 4-1 provides a chart of steps involved in assembling, linking, and executing a program.

ASSEMBLING A PROGRAM

The diskette included in the assembler package contains the translator program. The IBM and MicroSoft program is MASM.EXE, whereas the Borland Turbo program is TASM.EXE. (Some assembler packages may also contain a smaller version named ASM.EXE with some minor features omitted.)

Insert the assembler diskette in drive A and your program diskette containing EXASM1.ASM in drive B. Users of hard disks can substitute their own drive numbers in the examples. You can also gain a lot of productivity by loading all the programs and files into RAM disk. You can key in MASM or TASM with or without a command line.

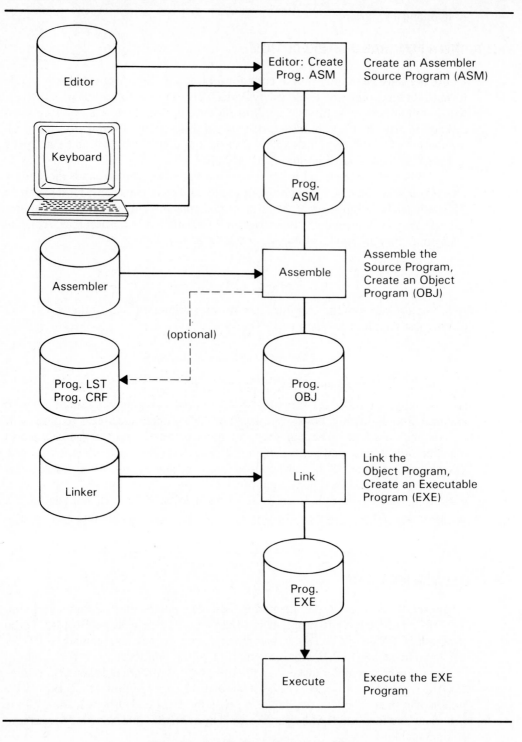

Figure 4-1   Steps in Assembly, Link, and Execute

Assembling with a Command Line

The general format for using a command line to assemble is

```
MASM/TASM [options] source[,object][,listing][,crossref]
```

- Options provide for such features as setting levels of warning messages, and are explained in Appendix D. Since the assembler's defaults are usually adequate, you'll seldom need to use options.
- Source identifies the source program, such as EXASM1.ASM. The assembler assumes the extension .ASM, so you need not enter it. You can also enter a disk drive number if you don't want to accept the current default drive.
- Object provides for a generated OBJ file. The filename and drive may be the same as or different from the source.
- Listing provides for a generated LST file that contains the source and object code. The filename and the drive may be the same or different.
- Crossref provides for a generated cross-reference file containing symbols for cross-reference listing. The extension is .CRF for MASM and .XRF for TASM. The filename and the drive may be the same or different.

You always enter the name of the source file and you usually request an OBJ file, which is required for linking a program into executable form. You'll probably often request LST files, especially when you want to examine the machine code generated. A CRF file is useful for very large programs where you want to see which instructions reference which data items. Also, the entry causes the assembler to generate line numbers on the LST file to which the CRF file refers. Later sections cover LST and CRF files.

Example 1.   Reference filename EXASM1.ASM on drive B and generate object, listing, and cross-reference files. If a filename is to be the same as that of the source, you need not repeat it. The reference to drive number is sufficient to indicate requesting the file.

```
MASM/TASM B:EXASM1,B:,B:,B:
```

Example 2.   Generate only an object file. In this case, you can omit the reference to the listing and cross-reference files.

```
MASM/TASM B:EXASM1,B:
```

The assembler converts your source statements into machine code and displays on the screen any errors. Typical errors include a name that violates naming conventions, an operation that is spelled incorrectly (such as MOVE instead of MOV), and an operand containing a name that is not defined. There are about 100 error messages, explained in the assembler manual. The assembler attempts to correct some errors, but in any event you should reload your editor, correct the source program (EXASM1.ASM), and reassemble.

Assembling without a Command Line

You can also enter just the name of the program with no command line, although TASM and MASM respond differently. TASM displays the general format for the command line and an explanation of the options, whereas MASM displays a list of prompts. Here are the MASM prompts to which you reply:

```
Source filename      [.ASM]:
Object filename      [source.OBJ]:
Source listing       [NUL.LST]:
Cross-reference      [NUL.CRF]:
```

- Source filename identifies the name of the source file. Type the drive (if it's not the default) and the name of the source file, as B:EXASM1 without the extension ASM.
- Object filename provides for the object file. The prompt assumes the same file name, although you could change it. If necessary, enter drive number, B:.
- Source listing provides for an assembler listing, although the prompt assumes that you do not want one. To get one on drive B, type B: and press Enter.
- Cross-reference provides for a cross-reference listing, although the prompt assumes that you do not want one. To get one on drive B, type B: and press Enter.

For the last three prompts, just press Enter if you want to accept the default.

Assembler Listing of Conventional
Segment Definitions

Figure 4-2 provides the listing that the assembler produced under the name EXASM1.LST. The line width is 132 positions because of the PAGE entry. You can also print this listing if your printer can compress the print line. For 132 characters per inch and six lines per inch, turn on the printer and key in the DOS command

MODE LPT1:132,6

Note at the top of the listing how the assembler has acted on the PAGE and TITLE directives. None of the directives, including SEGMENT, PROC, ASSUME, and END, generates machine code, since they are just messages to the assembler.

At the extreme left is the number for each line. The second column shows the

```
Microsoft (R) Macro Assembler Version 5.10
EXASM1 (EXE)  Move and add operations                      Page  1-1

  1                                page 60,132
  2                        TITLE   EXASM1 (EXE)  Move and add operations
  3                        ; --------------------------------------------
  4 0000                   STACKSG SEGMENT PARA STACK 'Stack'
  5 0000  0020[            DW      32 DUP(0)
  6         0000
  7              ]
  8
  9 0040                   STACKSG ENDS
 10                        ; --------------------------------------------
 11 0000                   DATASG  SEGMENT PARA 'Data'
 12 0000  00FA             FLDA    DW      250
 13 0002  007D             FLDB    DW      125
 14 0004  0000             FLDC    DW      ?
 15 0006                   DATASG  ENDS
 16                        ; --------------------------------------------
 17 0000                   CODESG  SEGMENT PARA 'Code'
 18 0000                   BEGIN   PROC    FAR
 19                                ASSUME  CS:CODESG,DS:DATASG,SS:STACKSG
 20 0000  B8 ---- R        MOV     AX,DATASG    ;Address of DATASG
 21 0003  8E D8            MOV     DS,AX        ;   in DS register
 22
 23 0005  A1 0000 R        MOV     AX,FLDA      ;Move 0250 to AX
 24 0008  03 06 0002 R     ADD     AX,FLDB      ;Add  0125 to AX
 25 000C  A3 0004 R        MOV     FLDC,AX      ;Store sum in FLDC
 26 000F  B4 4C            MOV     AH,4CH       ;Return to DOS
 27 0011  CD 21            INT     21H
 28 0013            BEGIN  ENDP
 29 0013            CODESG ENDS
 30                        END     BEGIN
```

```
Segments and Groups:
                  N a m e         Length  Align  Combine Class
CODESG . . . . . . . . . . . . 0013    PARA   NONE    'CODE'
DATASG . . . . . . . . . . . . 0006    PARA   NONE    'DATA'
STACKSG  . . . . . . . . . . . 0040    PARA   STACK   'STACK'

Symbols:
                  N a m e         Type    Value   Attr
BEGIN  . . . . . . . . . . . . F PROC  0000    CODESG  Length = 0013

FLDA . . . . . . . . . . . . . L WORD  0000    DATASG
FLDB . . . . . . . . . . . . . L WORD  0002    DATASG
FLDC . . . . . . . . . . . . . L WORD  0004    DATASG

@CPU . . . . . . . . . . . . . TEXT    0101h
@FILENAME  . . . . . . . . . . TEXT    exasm1
@VERSION . . . . . . . . . . . TEXT    510
```

Figure 4-2   Assembled Program with Conventional Segments

hex addresses of data fields and instructions. The third group of columns shows the translated machine code in hexadecimal format. To the right is the original source code.

Stack segment.   The stack segment "begins" at offset location 0000. Actually, it loads in memory according to an address that will be in the SS register and is offset zero bytes from that address. The SEGMENT directive causes alignment of an address divisible by hex 10 and notifies the assembler that this is a stack—the statement itself generates no machine code.

The stack segment contains a DW (Define Word) directive that defines 32 words, each generating a zero value designated by (0). This definition of 32 words is a realistic size for a stack because a large program may require many "interrupts" for input/output and "calls" to subprograms, all involving use of the stack. The stack segment ends at address hex 0040, which is the equivalent of decimal value 64 (32 × 2).

Define a size of at least 32 words for the stack. If the size is too small to contain all the items pushed on it, neither the assembler nor the linker warn you, and the program may crash in an unpredictable way.

Data segment.   The program defines a data segment, DATASG, containing three defined values all in DW (Define Word) format. FLDA defines a word (two bytes) with the decimal value 250, which the assembler has translated to hex 00FA (shown on the left). FLDB defines a word with the decimal value 125, assembled as hex 007D. The actual storage values of these two constants are, respectively, FA00 and 7D00, which you can check with DEBUG.

FLDC is coded as a DW with ? in the operand to define a word with an unknown constant.

Code segment.   The code segment also begins at offset location 0000. It loads in memory according to an address that will be in the CS register and is offset zero bytes from that address. The ASSUME directive relates DATASG to the DS register. This program does not require the ES register, but some programmers define its use as a standard practice.

Two instructions establish addressability for the data segment:

```
0000   B8 - - - - R          MOV    AX,DATASG
0003   8E D8                 MOV    DS,AX
```

The first MOV instruction "stores" DATASG in the AX register. Now, an instruction cannot actually store a segment in a register—the assembler recognizes an attempt to load the address of DATASG. Note the machine code to the left: B8 - - - - R. The four hyphens mean that the assembler cannot determine the address of DATASG; the system determines this only when the object program is linked and loaded for execution. Since the system loader may locate a program anywhere in memory, the assembler leaves the address open and indicates the fact with an R; the linker is to replace (or relocate) the incomplete address with the actual one.

The second MOV instruction moves the contents of the AX register to the DS register. Since there is no valid instruction for a direct move from memory to the DS register, you have to code two instructions to initialize the DS.

The DOS loader automatically initializes the SS and CS when it loads a program for execution, but it is your responsibility to initialize the DS, and the ES if required.

For the simplified segment directives, initialize the DS like this:

```
MOV     AX,@data
MOV     DS,AX
```

While all this business may seem unduly involved, at this point you really don't have to understand it. Subsequent programs in this book use a standard definition and initialization. You simply have to reproduce this code for each of your programs. To this end, store a skeleton program on disk, and for each new program, COPY it into a file with its correct name, and use your editor to complete the additional instructions.

The first instruction after initialing the DS register is MOV AX,FLDA, which begins at offset location 0000 and generates machine code A1 0000. The space between A1 (the operation) and 0000 (the operand) is only for readability. The next instruction is ADD AX,FLDB, which begins at offset location 0003 and generates four bytes of machine code. In this example, machine instructions are two, three, or four bytes in length.

The last statement in the program, END, contains the operand BEGIN, which relates to the name of the PROC at offset 0000. This is the location in the code segment where the program loader is to transfer control for execution.

Following the program listing are a segment and group table and a symbol table.

Segments and group table. The first table shows any segments and groups defined in the program. Note that the segments are not in the same sequence as coded; the assembler has listed them in alphabetic sequence by name. (This program contains no groups, which is a later topic.) The table provides the length in bytes of each segment, the alignment (both are paragraphs), the combine type, and the class. The assembler converted the class names to uppercase.

Symbols table. The second table provides the names of data fields in the data segment (none in this example) and the labels applied to instructions in the code segment. For BEGIN (the only entry in this example), the type F PROC means far procedure. The value is the offset for the beginning of the segment for names, labels, and procedures. Length gives the size in bytes.

Appendix D explains all the options for these tables. To cause the assembler to omit these tables, code a /N option following the MASM command, as MASM /N.

For the last three entries, @CPU identifies the processor, @FILENAME gives the name of the program, and @VERSION shows the MASM version.

Assembler Listing of Simplified Segment Directives

Figure 3-3 showed how to code a program using the simplified segment directives. Figure 4-3 now provides the assembled listing of this program. The first part of the symbol table under segments and groups shows the three segments as:

```
 1                                    page    60,132
 2                          TITLE     EXASM1A (EXE)  Move and add operations
 3                          ;------------------------------------------------
 4                                    .MODEL SMALL
 5                                    .STACK 64                  ;Define stack
 6                                    .DATA                      ;Define data
 7 0000   00FA     FLDA     DW        250
 8 0002   007D     FLDB     DW        125
 9 0004   0000     FLDC     DW        ?
10
11                                    .CODE                      ;Define code segment
12 0000            BEGIN    PROC      FAR
13 0000   B8 ---- R         MOV       AX,@data                   ;Address of DATASG
14 0003   8E D8             MOV       DS,AX                      ;   in DS register
15
16 0005   A1 0000 R         MOV       AX,FLDA                    ;Move 0250 to AX
17 0008   03 06 0002 R      ADD       AX,FLDB                    ;Add  0125 to AX
18 000C   A3 0004 R         MOV       FLDC,AX                    ;Store sum in FLDC
19
20 000F   B8 4C00           MOV       AX,4C00H                   ;Return to DOS
21 0012   CD 21             INT       21H
22 0014            BEGIN    ENDP                                 ;End of procedure
23
24                          END       BEGIN                      ;End of program
```

```
Segments and Groups:
                  N a m e           Length  Align   Combine Class
DGROUP . . . . . . . . . . . GROUP
  _DATA  . . . . . . . . . .   0006   WORD    PUBLIC  'DATA'
  STACK  . . . . . . . . . .   0040   PARA    STACK   'STACK'
_TEXT  . . . . . . . . . . .   0014   WORD    PUBLIC  'CODE'

Symbols:
                  N a m e           Type    Value   Attr
BEGIN  . . . . . . . . . . . F PROC  0000    _TEXT   Length = 0014

FLDA . . . . . . . . . . . . L WORD  0000    _DATA
FLDB . . . . . . . . . . . . L WORD  0002    _DATA
FLDC . . . . . . . . . . . . L WORD  0004    _DATA

@CODE  . . . . . . . . . . . TEXT    _TEXT
@CODESIZE  . . . . . . . . . TEXT    0
@CPU . . . . . . . . . . . . TEXT    0101h
@DATASIZE  . . . . . . . . . TEXT    0
@FILENAME  . . . . . . . . . TEXT    _exasm1a
@VERSION . . . . . . . . . . TEXT    510
```

Figure 4-3   Assembled Program with Simplified Segment Directives

_DATA, with a length of six bytes

STACK, with a length of 40H (64 bytes)

_TEXT for the code segment, with a length of 14H

Under the heading "Symbols" are names defined in the program or defaulted. The simplified segment directives provide a number of predefined equates, which begin with an @ symbol and which you are free to reference in a program:

@CODE	Equated to the name of the code segment, _TEXT
@CODESIZE	Set to 0 by the small and medium models
@CPU	Model of processor
@DATASIZE	Set to 0 by the small and medium models

@FILENAME   Name of the program
@VERSION   Version of assembler (n.nn)

You may use @code and @data in ASSUME and executable statements, such as MOV AX,@data.

Two-Pass Assembler

The assembler makes two passes through the symbolic program. One of the main reasons is because of forward references—an instruction may reference a label but the assembler has not yet encountered its definition.

During pass 1, the assembler reads the entire source program and constructs a symbol table of names and labels used in the program, that is, names of data fields and program labels and their relative location in the program. Pass 1 determines the amount of code to be generated. MASM starts generating object code in pass 1, whereas TASM does it in pass 2.

During pass 2, the assembler uses the symbol table that it constructed in pass 1. Now that it knows the length and relative positions of each data field and instruction, it can complete the object code for each instruction. It then produces, if requested, the various object, listing, and cross-reference files.

LINKING A PROGRAM

Once your program is free of error messages, your next step is to link the object module, EXASM1.OBJ, which contains only machine code. The linker performs the following functions:

- Completes any addresses that the assembler has left empty in the OBJ module. Because a program can load almost anywhere in memory for execution, the assembler may not have completed all the machine addresses. Many programs contain such addresses, which the assembler lists in object code as ---- R.
- Combines, if requested, more than one separately assembled module into one executable program, such as two or more assembly language programs or an assembly program with a program written in a high-level language such as C or Pascal.
- Generates an EXE module and initializes it with instructions for loading it for execution.

Once you have linked one or more OBJ modules into an EXE module, you may execute the EXE module any number of times. But whenever you need to make a change in the EXE module, you must correct the source program, assemble it into another OBJ module, and link the OBJ module into an EXE module. Even if initially these steps are not entirely clear, you will find that with only a little experience, they become automatic.

Note: You may convert certain types of EXE programs to efficient COM programs, although the preceding examples are not suitable for this purpose. See Chapter 6 for details.

To link an assembled program from diskette, insert the linker diskette in drive A and the program diskette in drive B. Hard disk or RAM disk users can substitute their own drives. The IBM and MicroSoft version is LINK, whereas the Borland version is TLINK—be sure to use the correct version. You can key in LINK or TLINK with or without a command line.

Linking with a Command Line

The general format for using a command line to link is

```
LINK/TLINK objfile,exefile[,mapfile][,libraryfile]
```

- Objfile identifies the object file generated by the assembler. The linker assumes the extension .OBJ, so you need not enter it. You can also enter disk drive number.
- Exefile provides for generating an EXE file. The filename and drive may be the same as or different from the source.
- Mapfile provides for generating a file with an extension .MAP that indicates the relative location and size of each segment and any errors that LINK has found. A typical error is failure to define a stack segment. Entering CON tells the linker to display the map on the screen (instead of writing it on disk) so that you can view the map immediately for errors.
- Libraryfile provides for the libraries option, which you don't need at this early stage.

This example links the object file EXASM1.OBJ that was generated by the earlier assembly. The linker is to write the EXE file on drive B, display the map, and ignore the library option:

```
LINK B:EXASM1,B:,CON
```

If a filename is to be the same as that of the source, you need not repeat it. The reference to drive number is sufficient to indicate requesting the file.

Linking without a Command Line

You can also enter just the name of the linker with no command line, although TLINK and LINK respond differently. TLINK displays the general format for the command and an explanation of options, whereas LINK displays a list of prompts. Here are the LINK prompts to which you reply:

Link prompt	Reply	Action
Object Modules [.OBJ]:	B:EXASM1	Links EXASM1.OBJ
Run File [EXASM1.EXE]:	B:	Creates EXASM1.EXE
List File [NUL.MAP]:	CON	Sends map to screen
Libraries [.LIB]:	[Enter]	Defaults (ignores)

- Object Modules asks for the name of the object module that is to be linked; it defaults to OBJ if you omit the extension.
- Run File requests the name of the file that is to execute and allows a default to the filename EXASM1.EXE. The reply asks the linker to write the file on drive B.
- List File provides for the map file, although the default is NUL.MAP (that is, no map). The reply CON tells the linker to display the map on the screen.
- Libraries asks for the library option, which this reply says to ignore.

The Link Map

For the program EXASM1, LINK produced this map:

```
Start       Stop        Length    Name        Class
00000H      0003FH      0040H     STACKSG     STACK
00040H      00045H     0006H     DATASG      DATA
00050H      00062H      0013H     CODESG      CODE
Program entry point at 0005:0000
```

The stack is the first segment at offset zero bytes from the start of the program. Since it is defined as 32 words, it is 64 bytes long, as its length (hex 40) indicates. The data segment begins at the next paragraph boundary, 40H, and the code segment at the next boundary, 50H. Program entry point 0005:0000 refers to the address of the first executable instruction, segment 0005[0], offset 0000.

Some assemblers may rearrange the segments into alphabetical order. At this stage the only error that you are likely to encounter is entering wrong filenames. The solution is to restart with the link command. Appendix D supplies other options.

Generated Files

Use the DOS DIR command to check the files on your program disk. DIR B:EXASM1.* displays the following filenames and sizes, although their sequence may vary depending on what your disk already contains:

```
EXASM1.ASM    687   date time
EXASM1.OBJ    135   date time
EXASM1.LST   2199   date time
EXASM1.CRF    377   date time
EXASM1.EXE    629   date time
```

No doubt you realize that writing a number of programs causes a shortage of disk space. It's a good idea to use the DOS CHKDSK program regularly to check the remaining space. You can use the DOS ERASE (or DEL) command to erase OBJ, CRF, and LST files. You need the ASM file in case of further changes and the EXE file to execute the program.

EXECUTING A PROGRAM

Having assembled and linked the program, you can now (at last!) execute it. If the EXE file is in drive B, you could cause execution by entering:

```
B:EXASM1.EXE  or  B:EXASM1
```

DOS assumes that the file extension is EXE (or COM) and loads the file for execution. However, since this program produces no visible output, run it under DEBUG and step through with trace commands. Key in the following, including the extension EXE:

```
DEBUG B:EXASM1.EXE
```

DOS loads DEBUG, which in turn loads the EXE program module. Once ready, DEBUG displays its hyphen prompt. To view the stack segment, key in

```
D SS:0
```

The stack contains all zeros because it was initialized that way. To view the data segment, key in

```
D DS:0
```

The operation displays the three data items as FA007D000000, with the bytes for each word in reverse sequence. To view the code segment, key in

```
D CS:0
```

Compare the displayed machine code to the assembled listing:

```
B8 ---- 8ED8A10000 . . .
```

In this case, the assembled listing does not accurately show the machine code, since the assembler did not know the address for the operand of the first instruction. You can determine this address by examining the displayed code.

Key in R to view the registers, and step through program execution with successive T (trace) commands. As you step through the program, note the contents of the registers. When you reach the last instruction, you can use Q (quit) to terminate DEBUG.

CROSS-REFERENCE LISTING

The assembler generates an optional CRF or XRF file that you can use to produce a cross-reference listing of a program's labels, symbols, and variables. However, you still have to convert this file to a proper sorted cross-reference. A program on the assembler disk performs this function: CREF for IBM and MicroSoft or TCREF for Borland. You can key in CREF or TCREF with or without a command line.

Using a Command Line

The general format for using a command line is

```
            CREF/TCREF xreffile,reffile
```

- xreffile identifies the cross-reference file generated by the assembler. The program assumes the extension, so you need not enter it. You can also enter a disk drive number.
- reffile provides for generating a REF file. The filename and drive may be the same as or different from the source.

Appendix D provides a number of options for this command.

Omitting the Command Line

You can also enter just the name of the program with no command line, although TCREF and CREF respond differently. TCREF displays the general format for the command and an explanation of options, whereas CREF displays prompts. Here are the CREF prompts to which you reply:

```
                Cross-reference[.CRF]:
                Listing[filename.REF]:
```

For the first prompt, enter the name of the CRF file, such as B:EXASM1. For the second prompt, you can enter the drive number only and accept the default file name. This choice causes CREF to write a cross-reference file named EXASM1.REF on drive B.

The Listing

Figure 4-4 contains the cross-reference produced by CREF for the program in Figure 4-2. The entries are in sequence followed by the line number in the source program where they are defined and referenced. The first number, shown as n#, indicates the line where the symbol is defined in the LST program. Numbers to its right show where the symbol is referenced. For example, CODESG is defined in line 17 and is referenced in lines 19 and 29.

ERROR DIAGNOSTICS

The assembler provides diagnostics for any programming error that violates its rules. The program in Figure 4-5 is the same as the one in Figure 4-2, except this one has a number of errors. This example was run under MASM; TASM generates a similar error listing.

Line	Explanation
14	FLDC requires an operand.
19	ASSUME does not relate the SS to STACKSG, although the assembler has not noted this.
20	DATSEG should be spelled DATASG.
21	DX should be coded DS, although the assembler does not know that this is an error.
23	AS should be coded AX.

```
        EXASM1 (EXE)  Move and add operations

    Symbol Cross-Reference  (# definition, + modification) Cref-1

    @CPU . . . . . . . . . . . . . .  1#
    @VERSION . . . . . . . . . . . .  1#

    BEGIN. . . . . . . . . . . . . .  18#    28      30

    CODE . . . . . . . . . . . . . .  17
    CODESG . . . . . . . . . . . . .  17#    19      29

    DATA . . . . . . . . . . . . . .  11
    DATASG . . . . . . . . . . . . .  11#    15      19      20

    FLDA . . . . . . . . . . . . . .  12#    23
    FLDB . . . . . . . . . . . . . .  13#    24
    FLDC . . . . . . . . . . . . . .  14#    25+

    STACK. . . . . . . . . . . . . .  4
    STACKSG. . . . . . . . . . . . .  4#     9       19

        12 Symbols
```

Figure 4-4 Cross-Reference Table

```
  1                                  page 60,132
  2                        TITLE     EXASM3 (EXE)  Illustrate assembly errors
  3                        ; ---------------------------------------------------
  4 0000                   STACKSG SEGMENT PARA STACK 'Stack'
  5 0000     0020[                 DW        32 DUP(0)
  6             0000
  7                ]
  8
  9 0040                   STACKSG ENDS
 10                        ; ---------------------------------------------------
 11 0000                   DATASG  SEGMENT PARA 'Data'
 12 0000     00FA          FLDA    DW        250
 13 0002     007D          FLDB    DW        125
 14 0004                   FLDC    DW
exasm3.ASM(11): error A2027: Operand expected
 15 0004                   DATASG  ENDS
 16                        ; ---------------------------------------------------
 17 0000                   CODESG  SEGMENT PARA 'Code'
 18 0000                   BEGIN   PROC      FAR
 19                                ASSUME    CS:CODESG,DS:DATASG
 20 0000  A1 0000 U                MOV       AX,DATSEG    ;Address of DATASG
exasm3.ASM(17): error A2009: Symbol not defined: DATSEG
 21 0003  8B D0                    MOV       DX,AX        ;   in DS register
 22
 23                                MOV       AS,FLDA      ;Move 0250 to AX
exasm3.ASM(20): error A2009: Symbol not defined: AS
 24 0005  03 06 0002 R             ADD       AX,FLDB      ;Add  0125 to AX
 25 0009  A3 0000 U                MOV       FLDD,AX      ;Store sum in FLDC
exasm3.ASM(22): error A2009: Symbol not defined: FLDD
 26 000C  B4 4C                    MOV       AH,4CH       ;Return to DOS
 27 000E  CD 21                    INT       21H
 28 0010                   BEGIN   ENDP
exasm3.ASM(25): error A2006: Phase error between passes
 29 0010                   CODESG  ENDS
```

Figure 4-5   Assembly Diagnostics

25   FLDD should be coded FLDC.

28   Correcting the other errors will cause this message to disappear.

KEY POINTS

- Both MASM and TASM provide a command line for assembling, including (at least) the name of the source program. MASM also provides prompts for entering options.
- The assembler converts a source program to an OBJ file and generates optional listing and cross-reference files.
- The Segments and Group Table following an assembler listing shows any segments and groups defined in the program. The Symbols Table shows all symbols (data names and instruction labels).
- The linker (LINK or TLINK) converts an OBJ file to an executable EXE file. You may link using a command line or by means of prompts (LINK only).
- The simplified segment directives generate the names _DATA for the data segment, STACK for the stack segment, and _TEXT for the code segment. They also generate a number of predefined equates.
- The CREF (or TCREF) program produces a useful cross-reference listing.

QUESTIONS

4-1. Code the MASM or TASM command line to assemble a program named TEMPY.ASM with files LST, OBJ, and CRF. Assume that the program diskette is in drive B.

4-2. Code the MASM command with no command line and replies to prompts to assemble a program named TEMPY.ASM with files LST, OBJ, and CRF. Assume that the program diskette is in drive B.

4-3. Code the commands for TEMPY from Question 4-1 for the following: **(a)** Execution through DEBUG; **(b)** direct execution from DOS.

4-4. Give the purpose of each of the following files: **(a)** file.ASM; **(b)** file.CRF; **(c)** file.LST; **(d)** file.EXE; **(e)** file.OBJ; **(f)** file.MAP.

4-5. Code the two instructions to initialize the DS register. Assume that the name of the data segment is DATSEG.

4-6. Write an assembly language program using conventional segment definitions for the following:
- Move hex 30 (immediate value) to the AL register
- Shift the AL contents one bit left (SHL AL,1)
- Move hex 18 (immediate value) to the BL register
- Multiply AL by BL (code MUL BL)

Remember the instructions required to terminate execution. The program does not need to define or initialize a data segment. Be sure to COPY a skeleton program and use your editor to develop the program. Assemble and link. Use DEBUG to trace and to check the code segment and registers.

4-7. Revise the program in Question 4-6 for simplified segment directives. Assemble and link it, and compare the object code and symbol tables to the original program.

4-8. Revise the program in Question 4-6 as follows:
- Define a one-byte item (DB) named FLDA containing hex 28 and another named FLDB containing hex 14.
- Define a two-byte item (DW) named FLDC with no constant.
- Move the contents of FLDA to the AL register and shift left one bit.
- Multiply the AL by FLDB (MUL FLDB).
- Move the product in the AX to FLDC.

This program requires a data segment. Assemble, link, and use DEBUG to test.

4-9. Revise the program in Question 4-8 for simplified segment directives. Assemble and link it, and compare the object code and symbol tables to the original program.

5

DEFINING AND MOVING DATA

OBJECTIVE

To provide the methods in an assembly language program for defining constants and work areas and for transferring data.

INTRODUCTION

This chapter features the defining of data items and the simple transfer of data. You may define data items with or without initial constant values, and may define them with various lengths, such as byte, word, or doubleword.

The chapter also covers the EQU directive, which you may use to give names to commonly used constant values. Also explained in detail is the MOV instruction, which is frequently used to transfer data between registers and between registers and memory. You can also define a constant value in an instruction operand as an immediate value. Finally, we introduce the basic addressing formats that you will use throughout the rest of the book.

DATA DEFINITION DIRECTIVES

The purpose of the data segment in an EXE program is for defining constants, work areas, and input/output areas. The assembler permits definition of items in various lengths according to the directive that defines data. For example, DB defines a byte and DW defines a word. A data item may contain an undefined value or it may contain a constant defined either as a character string or as a numeric value. Here is the general format for data definition:

```
[name] Dn  expression
```

Name.   If the program references a data item, it does so by means of a name. The name of an item is otherwise optional, as indicated by the square brackets. The section "Coding Format" in Chapter 3 provides the rules of names.

Directive.   The directives that define data items are DB (byte), DW (word), DD (doubleword), DF (farword), DQ (quadword), and DT (tenbytes), each of which indicates the length of the defined item.

Expression.   The expression in an operand may contain a question mark to indicate an uninitialized item, such as

```
FLD1  DB  ?
```

or a constant, such as

```
FLD2  DB  25
```

An expression may contain multiple constants separated by commas and limited only by the length of a line, as follows:

```
FLD3  DB  11, 12, 13, 14, 15, 16, ...
```

The assembler defines these constants in adjacent bytes. A reference to FLD3 is to the first one-byte constant, 11 (you could think of the first byte as FLD3 + 0), and a reference to FLD3 + 1 is to the second constant, 12. For example, the instruction

```
MOV  AL, FLD3 + 3
```

loads the value 14 (hex 0E) into the AL register. The expression also permits duplication of constants of the general form

```
[name] | Dn | repeat-count  DUP(expression) ...
```

The following examples illustrate duplication:

```
DW    10 DUP(?)             ;Ten words, uninitialized
DB    5 DUP(14)             ;Five bytes containing hex 0E0E0E0E0E
DB    3 DUP(4 DUP(8))       ;Twelve 8s
```

The third example generates four copies of the digit 8 (8888) and duplicates that value three times, giving twelve 8s in all.

An expression may contain a character string or a numeric constant.

Character Strings

A character string is used for descriptive data such as people's names and page titles. The string is contained within single quotes as 'PC' or within double quotes as "PC". The assembler stores character strings in object code in normal ASCII format.

DB is the only format that defines a character string exceeding two characters and stores them in normal left-to-right sequence. Consequently, DB is the only sensible format for defining character data. An example is

```
DB  'Character string'
```

Numeric Constants

Numeric constants are used for arithmetic values and for memory addresses. The constant is not stored within quotes. The assembler converts numeric constants to hexadecimal and stores the bytes in object code in reverse sequence—right to left. Following are the various numeric formats.

Decimal.   Decimal format permits the decimal digits 0 through 9 optionally followed by the letter D, as 125 or 125D. Although the assembler allows decimal format as a coding convenience, it converts decimal to binary object code and represents it in hex. For example, decimal 125 becomes hex 7D.

Hexadecimal.   Hex format permits the hex digits 0 through F followed by the letter H, which you can use to define binary values. Since the assembler expects that a reference beginning with a letter is a symbolic name, the first digit of a hex constant must be 0 to 9. Examples are 2EH and 0FFFH, which the assembler stores as 2E and FF0F, respectively. The bytes in the second example are stored in reverse sequence.

Binary.   Binary format permits the binary digits 0 and 1 followed by the letter B. The normal use for binary format is to clearly distinguish bit values for the Boolean instructions AND, OR, XOR, and TEST. Decimal 12, hex C, and binary 1100B all generate the same value: hex 0C or binary 00001100, depending on how you view the contents of the byte.

Octal.   This format permits the octal digits 0 through 7 followed by the letter Q or O, such as 253Q. Octal has specialized uses.

Real. The assembler converts the given real value, a decimal or hex constant followed by the letter R, into floating-point format.

Be sure to distinguish between the use of character and numeric constants. A character constant defined as DB '12' generates ASCII characters, represented as hex 3132. A numeric constant defined as DB 12 generates a binary number, represented as hex 0C.

The program in Figure 5-1 provides examples of directives that define character strings and numeric constants. It has been assembled and shows the generated object code on the left. Since the program consists of only a data segment, it is not suitable for execution.

```
                            page 60,132
                    TITLE   EXDEF (EXE)   Define data directives
                            .MODEL SMALL
                            .DATA
                    ;       Define Byte - DB:
                    ;       ----------------
0000  00            FLD1DB  DB   ?              ;Uninitialized
0001  20            FLD2DB  DB   32             ;Decimal constant
0002  20            FLD3DB  DB   20H            ;Hex constant
0003  59            FLD4DB  DB   01011001B      ;Binary constant
0004  000A[ 00 ]    FLD5DB  DB   10 DUP(0)      ;Ten zeros
000E  50 65 72 73 6F 6E FLD6DB DB 'Personal Computer'
      61 6C 20 43 6F 6D
                                               ;Character string
      70 75 74 65 72
001F  33 32 36 35 34 FLD7DB DB  '32654'        ;Numbers as chars
0024  01 4A 61 6E 02 46 FLD8DB DB 01,'Jan',02,'Feb',03,'Mar'
      65 62 03 4D 61 72                        ;Table

                    ;       Define Word - DW:
                    ;       ----------------
0030  FFF0          FLD1DW  DW   0FFF0H         ;Hex constant
0032  0059          FLD2DW  DW   01011001B      ;Binary constant
0034  001F R        FLD3DW  DW   FLD7DB         ;Address constant
0036  0003 0004 0007 FLD4DW DW   3,4,7,8,9      ;Table of 5 constants
      0008 0009
0040  0005[ 0000]   FLD5DW  DW   5 DUP(0)       ;Five zeros

                    ;       Define Doubleword - DD:
                    ;       -----------------------
004A  00000000      FLD1DD  DD   ?              ;Uninitialized
004E  00007F3C      FLD2DD  DD   32572          ;Decimal value
0052  0000000E 00000031 FLD3DD DD 14,49         ;Two constants
005A  00000001      FLD4DD  DD   FLD3DB - FLD2DB
                                               ;Diff betw addresses
005E  00005043      FLD5DD  DD   'PC'           ;Character string

                    ;       Define Quadword - DQ:
                    ;       ---------------------
0062  0000000000000000 FLD1DQ DQ ?              ;Uninitialized
006A  474D0000000000000 FLD2DQ DQ 04D47H        ;Hex constant
0072  3C7F000000000000 FLD3DQ DQ 32572          ;Decimal constant

                    ;       Define Tenbytes - DT:
                    ;       ---------------------
007A  0000000000000000 FLD1DT DT ?              ;Uninitialized
      0000
0084  5634120000000000 FLD2DT DT 123456         ;Decimal constant
      0000
008E  4350000000000000 FLD3DT DT 'PC'           ;Character string
      0000
                            END
```

Figure 5-1 Definitions of Character Strings and Numeric Values

```
Segments and Groups:
                N a m e          Length  Align  Combine Class
DGROUP . . . . . . . . . . . GROUP
   _DATA . . . . . . . . . . 0098    WORD   PUBLIC  'DATA'
_TEXT  . . . . . . . . . . . 0000    WORD   PUBLIC  'CODE'

Symbols:
                N a m e          Type    Value   Attr
FLD1DB . . . . . . . . . . . L BYTE   0000    _DATA
FLD1DD . . . . . . . . . . . L DWORD  004A    _DATA
FLD1DQ . . . . . . . . . . . L QWORD  0062    _DATA
FLD1DT . . . . . . . . . . . L TBYTE  007A    _DATA
FLD1DW . . . . . . . . . . . L WORD   0030    _DATA
FLD2DB . . . . . . . . . . . L BYTE   0001    _DATA
FLD2DD . . . . . . . . . . . L DWORD  004E    _DATA
FLD2DQ . . . . . . . . . . . L QWORD  006A    _DATA
FLD2DT . . . . . . . . . . . L TBYTE  0084    _DATA
FLD2DW . . . . . . . . . . . L WORD   0032    _DATA
FLD3DB . . . . . . . . . . . L BYTE   0002    _DATA
FLD3DD . . . . . . . . . . . L DWORD  0052    _DATA
FLD3DQ . . . . . . . . . . . L QWORD  0072    _DATA
FLD3DT . . . . . . . . . . . L TBYTE  008E    _DATA
FLD3DW . . . . . . . . . . . L WORD   0034    _DATA
FLD4DB . . . . . . . . . . . L BYTE   0003    _DATA
FLD4DD . . . . . . . . . . . L DWORD  005A    _DATA
FLD4DW . . . . . . . . . . . L WORD   0036    _DATA
FLD5DB . . . . . . . . . . . L BYTE   0004    _DATA   Length = 000A
FLD5DD . . . . . . . . . . . L DWORD  005E    _DATA
FLD5DW . . . . . . . . . . . L WORD   0040    _DATA   Length = 0005
FLD6DB . . . . . . . . . . . L BYTE   000E    _DATA
FLD7DB . . . . . . . . . . . L BYTE   001F    _DATA
FLD8DB . . . . . . . . . . . L BYTE   0024    _DATA
```

Figure 5-1   Cont.

Define Byte: DB

Of the directives that define data items, one of the most useful is DB (Define Byte).

A DB numeric expression may contain one or more one-byte constants. This maximum of one byte means two hex digits. The largest positive hex number is 7F; all "higher" numbers 80 through FF represent negative values. In terms of decimal numbers, the limits are +127 and −128. The assembler converts numeric constants to binary object code (represented in hex). In Figure 5-1, numeric constants are FLD2DB, FLD3DB, FLD4DB, and FLD5DB.

A DB character expression may contain a string of any length up to the end of a line. For examples, see FLD6DB and FLD7DB in Figure 5-1. The object code shows the ASCII character for each byte in normal left-to-right sequence; hex 20 represents a blank character.

FLD8DB shows a mixture of numeric and string constants suitable for a table.

Define Word: DW

The DW directive defines items that are one word (two bytes) in length. A DW numeric expression may contain one or more one-word constants. The largest positive hex number is 7FFF; all "higher" numbers 8000 through FFFF represent negative values. In terms of decimal numbers, the limits are +32,767 and −32,768.

The assembler converts DW numeric constants to binary object code (represented in hex), but stores the bytes in reverse sequence. Consequently, the decimal value 12345 converts to hex 3039 but is stored as 3930.

In Figure 5-1, FLD1DW and FLD2DW define numeric constants. FLD3DW defines the operand as an address—in this case as the offset address of FLD7DB. The object code generated is 001F (the R to the right means "relocatable"), and a check above in the figure shows that the offset address of FLD7DB is indeed 001F.

A DW character expression is limited to two characters, which the assembler reverses in object code such that 'PC' becomes 'CP.' For defining character strings, DW is of limited use.

FLD4DW defines a table of five numeric constants. Note that the length of each constant is one word (two bytes).

Define Doubleword: DD

The DD directive defines items that are a doubleword (four bytes) in length. A numeric expression may contain one or more constants, each with a maximum of four bytes (eight hex digits). The largest positive hex number is 7FFFFFFF; all "higher" numbers 80000000 through FFFFFFFF represent negative values. In terms of decimal numbers, these maximums are +2,147,483,647 and −2,147,483,648.

The assembler converts DD numeric constants to binary object code (represented in hex) but stores the bytes in reverse sequence. Consequently, the decimal value 12345 converts to 00003039 but is stored as 39300000.

In Figure 5-1, FLD2DD defines a numeric constant and FLD3DD defines two numeric constants. FLD4DD generates the numeric difference between two defined addresses; in this case, the result is the length of FLD2DB.

A DD character expression is limited to two characters. The assembler reverses the characters and left-adjusts them in the four-byte doubleword, as shown by FLD5DD in object code.

Define Farword: DF   ╳ *NO*

The DF directive defines a farword as six bytes. Its normal use is for the 80386/486 processors.

Define Quadword: DQ

The DQ directive defines items that are four words (eight bytes) in length. A numeric expression may contain one or more constants, each with a maximum of eight bytes or 16 hex digits. The largest positive hex number is 7 followed by 15 Fs. As an indication of the magnitude of this number, hex 1 followed by 15 0s equals the decimal number 1,152,921,504,606,846,976.

The assembler handles DQ numeric values and character strings just like DD and DW. In Figure 5-1, FLD2DQ and FLD3DQ illustrate numeric values.

Define Tenbytes: DT

The DT directive defines data items that are ten bytes long. Its purpose is related to packed BCD (binary-coded decimal) numeric values, which are more useful for 80×87 numeric processors than for standard arithmetic operations. A BCD number is packed with two decimal digits per byte, with the leftmost bit as the sign (0 or 1). For the constant 123456, the assembler stores the bytes in reverse sequence as 56 34 12 00 00 00 00 00 00 00.

Figure 5-1 illustrates DT for an uninitialized item, a numeric value, and a two-character constant.

DUMP OF THE DATA SEGMENT

The program in Figure 5-1 contains only a data segment. Although the assembler generated no error messages, the link map displayed "Warning: No STACK Segment" and the linker displayed "There were 1 errors detected." Despite the warning, you can still use DEBUG to view the object code, which is shown in Figure 5-2. Assemble and link the program, load the EXE file under DEBUG, and press D for display. The right side of the dump in the figure clearly shows the alphabetic data, such as "Personal Computer."

EQU DIRECTIVE

The EQU directive does not define a data item. Instead, it defines a value that the assembler can use to substitute in other instructions. Consider the following EQU statement coded in the data segment:

```
                         TIMES  EQU  10
```

```
-d
2C40:0000   00 20 20 59 00 00 00 00-00 00 00 00 00 00 50 65   .  Y..........Pe
2C40:0010   72 73 6F 6E 61 6C 20 43-6F 6D 70 75 74 65 72 33   rsonal Computer3
2C40:0020   32 36 35 34 01 4A 61 6E-02 46 65 62 03 4D 61 72   2654.Jan.Feb.Mar
2C40:0030   F0 FF 59 00 1F 00 03 00-04 00 07 00 08 00 09 00   ..Y.............
2C40:0040   00 00 00 00 00 00 00 00-00 00 00 00 00 00 3C 7F   ..............<.
2C40:0050   00 00 0E 00 00 00 31 00-00 00 01 00 00 00 43 50   ......1.......CP
2C40:0060   00 00 00 00 00 00 00 00-00 00 47 4D 00 00 00 00   ..........GM....
2C40:0070   00 00 3C 7F 00 00 00 00-00 00 00 00 00 00 00 00   ..<.............
-d
2C40:0080   00 00 00 00 56 34 12 00-00 00 00 00 00 00 43 50   ....V4........CP
2C40:0090   00 00 00 00 00 00 00 00-00 72 03 E9 6B 01 2B C0 50   .........r..k.+.P
2C40:00A0   50 FF 76 04 E8 F5 5D 83-C4 06 0B D0 74 03 E9 57   P.v...].....t..W
2C40:00B0   01 B8 FF FF 50 2B C0 50-FF 76 04 E8 DE 5D 83 C4   ....P+.P.v...]..
2C40:00C0   06 8B 1E A4 43 FF 06 A4-43 D1 E3 D1 E3 A1 0E 3C   ....C...C......<
2C40:00D0   8B 16 10 3C 89 87 8A 32-89 97 8C 32 5E 8B E5 5D   ...<...2...2^..]
2C40:00E0   C3 90 B8 05 00 50 B8 CC-07 50 8D 46 80 50 E8 23   .....P...P.F.P.#
2C40:00F0   6C 83 C4 06 FF 76 04 8D-46 80 50 E8 98 0D 83 C4   l....v..F.P.....

            <-------- hexadecimal representation --------->    <--- ASCII ---->
```

Figure 5-2 Dump of the Data Segment

The name, in this case TIMES, may be any name acceptable to the assembler. Now whenever the word TIMES appears in an instruction or another directive, the assembler substitutes the value 10. For example, the assembler converts the directive

```
FIELDA DB  TIMES DUP(?)
```

to

```
FIELDA DB  10 DUP(?)
```

An instruction may also contain an equated operand, as in the following:

```
COUNTR EQU  05
        . . .
MOV CX,COUNTR
```

The assembler replaces COUNTR in the MOV operand with the value 05, making the operand an immediate value, as if it were coded

```
MOV CX,05  ;Assembler substitutes 05
```

The advantage of EQU is that many statements may use the value defined by COUNTR. If the value has to be changed, you need change only the EQU statement. Needless to say, you can use an equated value only where a substitution makes sense to the assembler. You can also equate symbolic names:

```
TP   EQU  TOTALPAY
MPY  EQU  MUL
```

The first example assumes that the program has defined TOTALPAY in the data segment. For any instruction that contains the operand TP, the assembler replaces it with the address of TOTALPAY. The second example enables a program to use the word MPY in place of the regular symbolic instruction MUL.

MOV INSTRUCTION

The MOV instruction transfers (or copies) data referenced by operand 2 to the operand 1 address. The sending field is unchanged. The operands that reference memory or registers must agree in size, such as both bytes, words, or doublewords. The general format is

```
MOV   {register/memory},{register/memory/immediate}
```

Here are examples of valid MOV operations.

Immediate to register: MOV   AX,25
Immediate to memory: MOV   BYTEVAL,25
Register to register: MOV   EAX,ECX
Register to memory: MOV   BYTEVAL,BH
Memory to register: MOV   BH,BYTEVAL

You can move a byte to a register (MOV AH,BYTEVAL), a word (MOV AX,WORDVAL), or a doubleword (MOV EAX,DWORDVAL). The operand affects only the portion of the register referenced; for example, moving a byte to the AH does not affect the AL.

MOV operations that are not allowed are memory to memory, immediate to segment register, and segment register to segment register. You can code more than one instruction to handle these requirements.

IMMEDIATE OPERANDS

Figure 2-2 illustrated the use of immediate operands. For example, the instruction

MOV AX,0123H

moves the immediate constant hex 0123 to the AX register. The three-byte object code for this instruction is B82301, where B8 means "move an immediate value to the AX register," and the following two bytes (in reverse sequence) contain the value itself. Many instructions provide for two operands; the first operand may be a register or memory location, and the second operand may be an immediate constant.

The use of an immediate operand is more efficient than defining a numeric constant in the data segment and referencing it in the operand of the MOV, for example, as

Data segment: AMT1   DW   0123H
Code segment: MOV   AX,AMT1

Length of Immediate Operands

The length of an immediate constant cannot exceed the length of the first operand. For example, an immediate operand is two bytes, but the AL register is only one byte:

MOV AL,0123H   ;Invalid length

However, if an immediate operand is shorter than a receiving operand, as

```
ADD AX,25H   ;Valid length
```

the assembler expands the immediate operand to two bytes, 0025, and stores the object code as 2500.

The 80386/486 processors permit 4-byte (doubleword) immediate operands, such as

```
MOV EAX,12345678H   ;80386/486
```

Immediate Formats

An immediate constant may be any valid defined format. Here are some examples:

Hexadecimal: 0123H
Decimal: 291 (which the assembler converts to hex 0123)
Binary: 100100011B (which converts to hex 0123)

MOV, ADD, and SUB are three of many instructions that provide for immediate operands. Figure 5-3 provides examples of these instructions with valid immediate operands. The .386 directive allows the assembler to recognize the reference to the EBX register. You don't need an 80386 to assemble this statement but you do need one to execute it. Since the example is not intended for execution, it omits defining a stack and initializing the DS register.

To process items longer than the capacity of a register involves additional coding, covered in later chapters.

```
                    .386      page 60,132
                    TITLE     EXIMM (EXE)   Example immediate operands
                    ;         (Coded for assembly, NOT for execution)
                              .MODEL SMALL
                              .STACK 64          ;Defined stack
                              .DATA              ;Defined data
0000  00            FLDA      DB        ?
0001  0000          FLDB      DW        ?

                              .CODE
0000                BEGIN     PROC      FAR
0000  66| B8 0113             MOV       AX,275   ;Move immediate

0004  66| 05 007D             ADD       AX,125   ;Add immediate

0008  66| 2D 00C8             SUB       AX,200   ;Subtract immediate

000C  BB 00000000            MOV       EBX,0    ;Move immediate (80386)

0011  66| 83 C3 20            ADD       BX,20H   ;Add immediate (hex)
0015                BEGIN     ENDP
                              END
```

Figure 5-3 Immediate Operands

ADDRESSING FORMATS

Up to this point, we have used a number of addressing formats without defining them. Where there are two operands, the operation processes from operand 2 to operand 1. Three instruction types—register, immediate, and direct memory have been used. A fourth type—indexed addressing—is new.

Register Addressing

Processing data between registers is the fastest type of processing, since there is no reference to memory. Here are some examples:

```
MOV  CL,AH    ;Move contents of AH to CL
ADD  AX,BX    ;Add contents of BX to AX
```

Immediate Addressing

In immediate format, operand 2 contains a constant value. The receiving field in operand 1 may be a register or a memory location. Here are some examples:

```
SAVE  DB   ?
      . . .
      ADD  CX,12           ;Add 12 to CX
      MOV  SAVE,25         ;Move 25 to SAVE
      MOV  BX,OFFSET SAVE  ;Load offset of SAVE in BX
```

The last instruction initializes the BX with the offset address of the data item SAVE. This is a feature that you'll use in later programs.

Direct Memory Addressing

In this format, one operand references a memory location and the other references a register. Here are some examples:

```
WORD1   DW   0
BYTE1   DB   0
        . . .
        MOV  AX,WORD1    ;Load WORD1 in AX
        ADD  BYTE1,CL    ;Add CL to BYTE1
```

Indexed Addressing

Indexed addressing is a more sophisticated technique that makes use of the computer's segment:offset addressing capability. The only registers used for this purpose on the 8086 and 80286 are BX, DI, SI, and BP, contained in square brackets as an index operator. The BX, DI, and SI are associated with the DS register. The BP, which is associated with the SS register, is discussed in a subsequent chapter. Either instruction operand may contain the indexed address; the other operand references a register or immediate value. An indexed address such as [BX] tells the assembler to use the memory address currently in the BX register.

In the following example, the first MOV initializes the BX with the address of DATAFLD. In the second MOV, the computer is to use the address in the BX to store 0 in the memory location where it points, in this case, DATAFLD.

```
DATAFLD  DB   ?
         . . .
         MOV  BX,OFFSET DATAFLD  ;Load BX with offset
         MOV  [BX],0             ;Move 0 to DATAFLD
```

The effect is the same as coding MOV DATAFLD,0, although the uses for indexed addressing are usually not so trivial. For example, you may combine registers in an indexed address as

```
[BX + SI]      Address in BX plus address in SI
[BX + 2]       Address in BX plus 2
```

80386/486 indexing.   The 80386/486 processors allow generation of an address from any combination of one or more general registers, a offset, and a scaling factor (1, 2, 4, or 8), associated with the contents of one of the registers. For example, the instruction

```
         MOV  EBX,[ECX*2 + ESP + 4]
```

moves an address into the EBX that consists of the contents of the ECX times 2 plus the contents of the ESP plus 4.

KEY POINTS

- Names of data items should be unique and descriptive. For example, an item for an employee's wage could be named EMPWAGE.

- DB is the preferred format for defining character strings since it permits strings longer than two bytes and converts them to normal left-to-right sequence.

- Decimal and a binary (hex) constants generate different values. Consider the effect of adding decimal 25 and adding hex 25:

```
         ADD  AX,25   ;Add 25
         ADD  AX,25H  ;Add 37
```

- DW, DD, and DQ store numeric values in object code with the bytes in reverse sequence.
- DB items are used for processing half registers (AL, BL, etc.), DW for full registers (AX, BX, etc.), and DD for extended registers (EAX, EBX, etc.). Longer numeric items require special handling.
- Immediate operands should match the size of a register: a one-byte constant with a one-byte register (AL, BH) and a one-word constant with a one-word register (AX, BX).
- Four instruction types are register, immediate, direct memory, and indexed addressing.

QUESTIONS

5-1. What are the lengths in bytes generated by the following data directives: **(a)** DW; **(b)** DD; **(c)** DT; **(d)** DB; **(e)** DQ?

5-2. Define a character string named TITLE1 containing the constant RGB Electronics.

5-3. Define the following numeric values in data items named FLDA through FLDE, respectively:
   (a) A four-byte item containing the hex equivalent to decimal 115.
   (b) A one-byte item containing the hex equivalent to decimal 25.
   (c) A two-byte item containing an undefined value.
   (d) A one-byte item containing the binary equivalent to decimal 25.
   (e) A DW containing the consecutive values 16, 19, 20, 27, 30.

5-4. Show the generated hex object code for **(a)** DB '26' and **(b)** DB 26.

5-5. Determine the assembled hex object code for **(a)** DB 26H; **(b)** DW 2645H; **(c)** DD 25733AH, and **(d)** DQ 25733AH.

5-6. Code the following as instructions with immediate operands: **(a)** store 320 in the AX; **(b)** compare FLDB to zero; **(c)** add hex 40 to BX; **(d)** subtract hex 40 from CX; **(e)** shift FLDB one bit left; **(f)** shift the CH one bit right.

5-7. Key in and assemble the data items and instructions for Questions 5-2, 5-3, and 5-6 using either conventional segment names or simplified segment directives. Also, define a stack. Assemble and link the program and run it under DEBUG to check the assembled code. Print the LST listing when it is free of error messages.

6

COM PROGRAMS

OBJECTIVE

*To explain the purpose and uses of COM files and how to prepare an
assembly language program for that format.*

INTRODUCTION

Up to now, you have written, assembled, and executed programs in EXE format.
The linker automatically generates a particular format for an EXE program, and
when storing it on disk precedes it with a special header block that is at least 512
bytes long. (Chapter 22 provides details of header blocks.)

You can also generate a COM program for execution. One example of a
commonly used COM program is COMMAND.COM. The advantages of COM
programs are that they are smaller than comparable EXE programs and are more
easily adapted to resident programs.

DIFFERENCES BETWEEN EXE AND COM PROGRAMS

There are some significant differences between a program that is to execute as EXE
and one that is to execute as COM.

Program Size

An EXE program may be virtually any size, whereas a COM program is restricted to one segment and a maximum of 64K, including the program segment prefix (PSP). The PSP is a 256-byte (hex 100) block that DOS inserts immediately preceding a COM and EXE program when it loads them in memory. A COM program is always smaller than its original EXE program; one reason is that the 512-byte header block that precedes an EXE program on disk does not precede a COM program. A COM program is an absolute image of the executable program, with no relocatable information.

Segments

Stack segment.   You define an EXE program with a stack segment, whereas a COM program automatically generates a stack. Thus, when you write an assembly language program that is to be converted to COM format, you omit the stack.

Data segment.   An EXE program usually defines a data segment and initializes the DS register with its address. A COM program defines its data within the code segment. As you'll see, there are simple ways to handle this situation.

Code segment.   An entire COM program consists of one code segment, with a maximum of 64K, including the PSP, stack, and data.

Initialization

When DOS loads a COM program for execution, it initializes all segment registers with the address of the program segment prefix. Since the CS and DS registers contain the correct initial address, your program does not have to load them.

Because addressing begins at an offset of hex 100 bytes from the beginning of the PSP, code an ORG directive as ORG 100H immediately following the code SEGMENT or .CODE statement. This statement tells the assembler to begin the object code hex 100 bytes past the start of the PSP. Otherwise, the assembler calculates offsets from the start of the PSP.

CONVERSION

If your source program is already written in EXE format, you can use an editor to convert the instructions into COM format. MASM and TASM coding formats for COM programs are identical; however, their methods for conversion differ. When conversion is complete, you can delete the OBJ and EXE files.

MicroSoft Conversion

For both EXE and COM programs under MicroSoft MASM, you assemble and
produce an OBJ file, and link the OBJ file to produce an EXE program. If you
wrote the program to run as an EXE program, you can now execute it. If you wrote
the program to run as a COM program, the linker produces a message:

```
Warning: No STACK Segment
```

You may ignore this message, since there is supposed to be no defined stack. A
program named EXE2BIN converts MicroSoft EXE programs to COM programs.
Actually, it converts to a BIN (binary) file; the program name means "convert
EXE-to-BIN," but you should name your output file extension COM. Assuming
that EXE2BIN is in drive A and a linked file named CALC.EXE is in drive B, type

```
EXE2BIN B:CALC B:CALC.COM[Enter]
```

Since the first operand of the command always references an EXE file, do not code
the EXE extension. The second operand could be a name other than CALC.COM.
If you omit the extension, EXE2BIN assumes BIN, which you would have to
rename subsequently as COM.

Borland Conversion

As long as your source program is coded according to COM requirements, you can
convert your object program directly into a COM program. Use the /T option for
TLINK:

```
TLINK /T B:CALC
```

EXAMPLE OF A COM PROGRAM

The program in Figure 6-1, named EXCOM1, is the same as the one in Figure 4-2
revised to conform to COM requirements. Note the following changes in this COM
program:

- There is no defined stack or data segment.
- An ASSUME statement tells the assembler to begin offsets from the start of
  the code segment. The CS register also contains this address, which is that of
  the PSP. The ORG directive, however, causes the program to begin hex 100
  bytes from this point, past the PSP.

```
                  page 60,132
        TITLE     EXCOM1  COM program to move and add
        CODESG    SEGMENT PARA 'Code'
                  ASSUME  CS:CODESG,DS:CODESG,SS:CODESG,ES:CODESG
                  ORG     100H          ;Start at end of PSP

        BEGIN:    JMP     MAIN          ;Jump past data
        ; -----------------------------------------------------
        FLDA      DW      250           ;Data definitions
        FLDB      DW      125
        FLDC      DW      ?
        ; -----------------------------------------------------
        MAIN      PROC    NEAR
                  MOV     AX,FLDA       ;Move 0250 to AX
                  ADD     AX,FLDB       ;Add  0125 to AX
                  MOV     FLDC,AX       ;Store sum in FLDC
                  MOV     AH,4CH        ;Return to DOS
                  INT     21H
        MAIN      ENDP
        CODESG    ENDS
                  END     BEGIN
```

Figure 6-1   COM Source Program with Conventional Segments

- ORG 100H sets an offset address for the start of execution. The program loader stores this in the instruction pointer.
- A JMP instruction transfers control of execution around the defined data. Some programmers code data items following the instructions, so that no initial JMP instruction is required. Coding data items first speeds up the assembly process slightly but provides no other advantage.
- INT 21H service 4CH terminates processing and exits to DOS. You may also use the RET instruction for this purpose.

The steps to convert this program for MASM are

```
        MASM B:EXCOM1,B:
        LINK B:EXCOM1,B:
        EXE2BIN B:EXCOM1 B:EXCOM1.COM
```

The steps to convert this program for TASM are

```
        TASM B:EXCOM1,B:
        TLINK/T B:EXCOM1,B:
```

The EXE and COM programs are 788 bytes and 20 bytes in size, respectively, partly because the linker stores a 512-byte header block at the beginning of an EXE module. Type DEBUG B:EXCOM1.COM to trace execution up to (but not including) the last instruction.

You may also code simplified segment directives when coding a COM program, as shown in Figure 6-2. You define only a code segment, not a stack or data segment.

```
            page 60,132
TITLE       EXCOM2   COM program to move and add data
            .MODEL   SMALL
            .CODE

            ORG      100H            ;Start at end of PSP
BEGIN:      JMP      MAIN            ;Jump past data
; --------------------------------------------------------
FLDA        DW       250             ;Data definitions
FLDB        DW       125
FLDC        DW       ?
; --------------------------------------------------------
MAIN        PROC     NEAR
            MOV      AX,FLDA         ;Move 0250 to AX
            ADD      AX,FLDB         ;Add  0125 to AX
            MOV      FLDC,AX         ;Store sum in FLDC
            MOV      AH,4CH          ;Return to DOS
            INT      21H
MAIN        ENDP
            END      BEGIN
```

Figure 6-2 COM Source
Program with Simplified
Segment Directives

THE COM STACK

For a COM program, DOS automatically defines a stack and sets the same segment address in all four segment registers. If the 64K segment for the program is large enough, DOS sets the stack at the end of the segment and loads the SP register with hex FFFE, the top of the stack. If the 64K segment does not contain enough space for a stack, DOS sets the stack at the end of memory. For both cases, DOS then pushes a zero word onto the stack, which acts as an offset for the IP if you use RET to terminate execution.

Where your program is large or memory is restricted, you may have to take care in pushing words onto the stack. The DIR command indicates the size of a file and will give you an idea as to the space available for a stack. In general, the smaller programs in this book are COM and should be clear from their format.

DEBUGGING TIPS

Omission of only one COM requirement may cause a program to fail. If EXE2BIN finds an error, it simply notifies you that it cannot convert the file but does not provide a reason. Check the SEGMENT, ASSUME, and END statements. If you omit ORG 100H, the program incorrectly references data in the program segment prefix, with unpredictable results.

If you run a COM program under DEBUG, use D CS:100 to view the data and instructions. Do not follow the program through termination; instead, use DEBUG's Q command.

An attempt to execute the EXE module of a program written as COM will fail.

KEY POINTS

- A COM program is restricted to one 64K segment, although you may code additional SEGMENT AT statements.
- A COM program is smaller than its original EXE program.
- A program written to run as COM does not define a stack or data segment, nor does it initialize the DS register.
- A program written to run as COM uses ORG 100H immediately following the code SEGMENT statement. The statement sets the offset address to the beginning of execution following the program segment prefix.
- For MicroSoft MASM, the EXE2BIN program converts an EXE file to COM format. Borland's TLINK can convert an object program directly into COM format.
- DOS defines a stack for a COM program either at the end of the program or, if insufficient space, at the end of memory.

QUESTIONS

6-1. What is the maximum size of a COM program?

6-2. For a source program to be converted to COM format, what segments can you define?

6-3. Why do you define ORG 100H at the beginning of a program to be converted to COM format?

6-4. How does the system handle the fact that you do not define a stack for a COM program?

6-5. A source program is named SAMPLE.ASM. Provide the commands to convert it to COM format under **(a)** MASM and **(b)** TASM.

6-6. Revise the program in Question 4-6 for COM format. Assemble, link, and execute it under DEBUG. Use EXE2BIN for MASM programs.

7

PROGRAM LOGIC AND CONTROL

OBJECTIVES

To cover the requirements for program control (looping and jumping), for logical comparisons, and for program organization.

INTRODUCTION

Up to this chapter, program examples have executed in a straight line, with one instruction sequentially following another. Seldom, however, is a programmable problem that simple. Most programs consist of a number of loops in which a series of steps repeats until reaching a specific requirement and various tests to determine which of several actions to take. A common requirement is to test whether a program is to terminate execution.

These requirements involve a transfer of control to the address of an instruction that does not immediately follow the one currently executing. A transfer of control may be *forward* to execute a new series of steps or *backward* to reexecute the same steps.

Certain instructions can transfer control outside the normal sequential steps by causing an offset value to be added to the instruction pointer (IP). Following are four classes of transfer operations, all covered in this chapter:

- Unconditional Jump: JMP
- Looping: LOOP

- Conditional Jump: Jnnn (such as JE, JNH, and JL)
- Call a procedure: CALL

SHORT, NEAR, AND FAR ADDRESSES

The three types of addresses are short, near, and far. A *short* address is reached by an offset and is limited to a distance of −128 to 127 bytes. A *near* address is reached by an offset and is limited to a distance of −32,768 to 32,767 bytes within the same segment. A *far* address is in another segment and is reached by a segment address and offset.

Distance	Short	Near	Far
Instructions	−128 to 127 same segment	−32,768 to 32,767 same segment	Another segment
JMP	yes	yes	yes
Jnnn	yes	80386/486	no
LOOP	yes	no	no
CALL	N/A	yes	yes

INSTRUCTION LABELS

The JMP, Jnnn, and LOOP instructions require an operand that refers to the label of an instruction. The following example jumps to A90, which is the label given to a MOV instruction:

```
             JMP    A90
             . . .
    A90:     MOV    AH,00
             . . .
```

The label of an instruction such as A90: is followed by a colon to give it the near attribute—that is, the label is inside a procedure in the same code segment. *Watch out:* Omission of the colon is a common error. Note that an address label in an instruction operand (such as JMP A90) does not have a colon.

You can also code the label on a separate line as

```
    A90:
             MOV    AH,00
```

In both cases, the address of A90 references the first byte of the MOV instruction.

THE JMP INSTRUCTION

A commonly used instruction for transferring control is the jump (JMP) instruction. A jump is unconditional since the operation transfers control under all circumstances. JMP also flushes the processor's prefetch instruction queue. The general format is

[label]	JMP	short, near, or far address

A JMP operation within the same segment may be short or near. On its first pass through a source program, the assembler generates the length of each instruction. However, a JMP instruction may be either two or three bytes long. A JMP operation to a label within −128 to +127 bytes is a short jump. The assembler generates one byte for the operation (EB) and one byte for the operand. The operand acts as an offset value that the computer adds to the IP register when executing the program. The limits are hex 00 to FF, or −128 to +127. The assembler may have already encountered the designated operand (a backward jump) within −128 bytes:

```
                    A50:
                          . . .
                    JMP  A50
```

In this case, the assembler generates a two-byte machine instruction. A JMP that exceeds −128 to +127 bytes becomes a near jump, for which the assembler generates different machine code (E9) and a two-byte operand (8086/80286) or four-byte (80386/80486). In a forward jump, the assembler has not yet encountered the designated operand:

```
                    JMP  A90
                          . . .
                    A90:
```

Since the assembler doesn't know at this point whether the jump is short or near, it automatically generates a three-byte instruction. However, provided that the jump really is short, you can use the SHORT operator to force a short jump and a two-byte instruction, as

```
                    JMP  SHORT A90
                          . . .
               A90:
```

Example of a Program Using JMP

The COM program in Figure 7-1 illustrates the use of the JMP instruction. The program initializes the AX, BX, and CX registers to the value of 1 and a loop performs the following:

> Add 1 to AX
> Add AX to BX
> Double the value in CX

At the end of each loop, the instruction JMP A20 transfers control to the instruction labeled A20. The effect of repeating the loop causes AX to increase as 1, 2, 3, 4, . . . ; BX to increase according to the sum of the digits 1, 3, 6, 10, . . . ; and CX to double as 1, 2, 4, 8, ... Since this loop has no exit, processing is endless—usually not a good idea.

In this program, A20 is -9 bytes from the JMP. You can confirm this distance by examining the object code for the JMP: EBF7. EB is the machine code for a near JMP and F7 is a negative value for -9 in two's-complement notation. The JMP operation adds the F7 to the instruction pointer (IP), which contains the offset 0112 of the instruction following the JMP:

	Decimal	*Hex*	
Instruction pointer:	274	0112	
JMP operand:	−9	FFF7	(two's complement)
Transfer address:	265	(1)0109	

The jump address calculates as hex 0109, where the carry out of 1 is ignored, just as a check of the program listing for the offset address of A20 shows. Conversely, the operand for a forward JMP is a positive value.

As a useful experience, key in the program, assemble it, link it, and convert it to COM format. No data definitions are required, since immediate operands gener-

```
                          page 60,132
                  TITLE   EXJUMP (COM)  Illustrate JMP for looping
                          .MODEL SMALL
                          .CODE
0000              MAIN    PROC    NEAR
0000  B8 0001             MOV     AX,01          ;Initialize AX,
0003  BB 0001             MOV     BX,01          ;   BX, and
0006  B9 0001             MOV     CX,01          ;   CX to 01
0009              A20:
0009  05 0001             ADD     AX,01          ;Add 01 to AX
000C  03 D8               ADD     BX,AX          ;Add AX to BX
000E  D1 E1               SHL     CX,1           ;Double CX
0010  EB F7               JMP     A20            ;Jump to A20 instr'n
0012              MAIN    ENDP
                          END     MAIN
```

Figure 7-1   Use of the JMP Instruction

ate all the data. Use DEBUG to trace the COM module for a number of iterations. Once AX contains 08, BX and CX will be incremented to hex 24 (decimal 36) and hex 80 (decimal 128), respectively. Use DEBUG's Q command to exit.

THE LOOP INSTRUCTION

The JMP instruction as used in Figure 7-1 causes an endless loop. But a routine is more likely to loop a specified number of times or until it reaches a particular condition. The LOOP instruction, which serves this purpose, requires an initial value in the CX register. For each iteration, LOOP automatically deducts 1 from the CX; if CX is zero, control drops through to the following instruction, and if nonzero, control jumps to the operand address. The distance must be a short jump, within −128 to +127 bytes. For an operation that exceeds this limit, the assembler issues a message "relative jump out of range." The general format is

[label]	LOOP	short—address

The program in Figure 7-2 illustrates use of LOOP and performs the same operation as Figure 7-1 except that it terminates after ten loops. A MOV instruction initializes CX with the value 10. Since LOOP uses the CX, this program now uses DX in place of CX for doubling the initial value 1. The LOOP instruction replaces JMP A20, and for efficiency INC AX (increment the AX by 1) replaces ADD AX,01.

Just as for JMP, the machine code operand contains the distance from the end of the LOOP instruction to the address of A20, which is added to the IP.

As a useful exercise, modify your copy of Figure 7-1 for these changes and assemble, link, and convert it to COM. Use DEBUG to trace the entire ten loops.

```
                              page 60,132
                      TITLE   EXLOOP (COM)   Illustration of LOOP
                              .MODEL  SMALL
                              .CODE
      0100                    ORG     100H
      0100            BEGIN   PROC    NEAR
      0100  B8 0001           MOV     AX,01      ;Initialize AX,
      0103  BB 0001           MOV     BX,01      ;   BX, &
      0106  BA 0001           MOV     DX,01      ;   DX to 01
      0109  B9 000A           MOV     CX,10      ;Initialize no. of loops
      010C            A20:
      010C  40                INC     AX         ;Add 01 to AX
      010D  03 D8             ADD     BX,AX      ;Add AX to BX
      010F  D1 E2             SHL     DX,1       ;Double DX
      0111  E2 F9             LOOP    A20        ;Decr CX, loop if nonzero
      0113  B4 4C             MOV     AH,4CH     ;Terminate
      0115  CD 21             INT     21H
      0117            BEGIN   ENDP
                              END     BEGIN
```

Figure 7-2 Use of the LOOP Instruction

Once CX is reduced to zero, the contents of AX, BX, and DX are, respectively, hex 000B, 0042, and 0400. Use DEBUG's Q command to exit.

Two variations on the LOOP instruction are LOOPE/LOOPZ (loop while equal/zero) and LOOPNE/LOOPNZ (loop while not equal/zero). Both operations decrement the CX by 1. LOOPE continues looping as long as the CX is not zero or the zero condition is set. LOOPNE continues looping as long as the CX is not zero or the nonzero condition is set.

FLAGS REGISTER

The remaining material in this chapter requires a more detailed knowledge of the flags register. This register contains 16 bits, which various instructions set to indicate the status of an operation. In all cases, a flag remains set until another instruction changes it. The flags register contains the following commonly used bits:

Bit no.:	15	14	13	12	11	10	9	8	7	6	5	4	3	2	1	0
Flag:					O	D	I	T	S	Z		A		P		C

CF (Carry flag).   Contains a carry (0 or 1) from the high-order bit following arithmetic operations and some shift and rotate operations.

PF (Parity flag).   Contains a check of the low-order 8 bits of data operations. An odd number of data bits sets the flag to 0 and an even number to 1—not to be confused with the parity bit and seldom of concern for conventional programming.

AF (Auxiliary carry flag).   Set to 1 if arithmetic causes a carry out of bit 3 (fourth from the right) of a register one-byte operation. This flag is concerned with arithmetic on ASCII and BCD packed fields.

ZF (Zero flag).   Set as a result of arithmetic or compare operations. Unexpectedly, a nonzero result sets it to 0 and a zero result sets it to 1. However, the setting, if not apparently correct, is logically correct: 0 means no (the result is not equal to zero) and 1 means yes (the result equals zero). JE and JZ test this flag.

SF (Sign flag).   Set according to the sign (high-order or leftmost bit) after an arithmetic operation: positive sets to 0 and negative sets to 1. JG and JL test this flag.

TF (Trap flag).   When set, causes the processor to execute in single-step mode, that is, one instruction at a time under user control. You have already set this flag when you entered the T command in DEBUG, and that's about the only place where you'd expect to find its use.

IF (Interrupt flag). Disables interrupts when 0 and enables interrupts when 1.

DF (Direction flag). Used by string operations to determine the direction of data transfer. When 0, the operation increments the SI and DI registers, causing left-to-right data transfer; when 1, the operation decrements the SI and DI, causing right-to-left data transfer.

OF (Overflow flag). Indicates a carry into and out of the high-order (leftmost) sign bit following a signed arithmetic operation.

As an example, the CMP instruction compares two operands and affects the AF, CF, OF, PF, SF, and ZF flags. However, you do not have to test these flags individually. The following tests the BX register for a zero value:

```
        CMP   BX,00              ;Compare BX to zero
        JZ    B50                ;Jump if zero to B50
        .     (action if nonzero)
        .
B50:    ...                      ;Jump point if BX zero
```

If the BX contains zero, CMP sets the ZF to 1 and may or may not change other flags. The JZ (Jump if Zero) instruction tests only the ZF flag. Since ZF contains 1 (meaning a zero condition), JZ transfers control (jumps) to the address indicated by operand B50.

CONDITIONAL JUMP INSTRUCTIONS

The assembler supports a variety of conditional jump instructions that transfer control depending on settings in the flags register. For example, you can compare two fields and then jump according to flag values that the compare sets. The general format is

```
[label]| Jnnn | short-address
```

As explained earlier, the LOOP instruction decrements and tests the CX register; if nonzero, the instruction transfers control to the operand address. You could replace the LOOP A20 statement in Figure 7-2 with two statements—one that decrements CX and another that performs a conditional jump:

```
        DEC   CX     ;Equivalent to LOOP
        JNZ   A20
```

DEC and JNZ perform exactly what LOOP does: Decrement the CX by 1 and jump to A20 if CX is nonzero. DEC also sets the zero flag in the flags register either to zero or nonzero. JNZ then tests the setting of the zero flag. In this example, LOOP, although it has limited uses, is more efficient than the two instructions DEC and JNZ.

Just as for JMP and LOOP, the machine code operand contains the distance from the end of the JNZ instruction to the address of A20, which is added to the instruction pointer. For the 8086/286, the distance must be a short jump, within −128 to +127 bytes. For an operation that exceeds this limit, the assembler issues a message "relative jump out of range." The 80386/486 provide for 8-bit (short) or 32-bit (near) offsets that allow reaching any address in a segment.

Signed and Unsigned Data

Distinguishing the purpose of conditional jumps should clarify their use. The type of data (unsigned or signed) on which you are performing comparisons or arithmetic can determine which instruction to use. An *unsigned* data item treats all bits as data bits; typical examples are character strings such as names and addresses and numeric values such as customer numbers. A *signed* data item treats the leftmost bit as a sign, where 0 is positive and 1 is negative. Many numeric values may be either positive or negative.

In the next example, the AX contains 11000110 and the BX contains 00010110. The instruction

```
CMP  AX,BX
```

compares the contents of the AX to the BX. As unsigned data, the AX value is larger; as signed data, the AX value is smaller.

Jumps Based on Unsigned Data

The following conditional jump instructions apply to unsigned data:

Symbol	Description	Flags Tested
JE/JZ	Jump Equal or Jump Zero	ZF
JNE/JNZ	Jump Not Equal or Jump Not Zero	ZF
JA/JNBE	Jump Above or Jump Not Below/Equal	CF, ZF
JAE/JNB	Jump Above/Equal or Jump Not Below	CF
JB/JNAE	Jump Below or Jump Not Above/Equal	CF
JBE/JNA	Jump Below/Equal or Jump Not Above	CF, AF

You can express each test in one of two symbolic codes. For example, JB and JNAE generate the same object code, but, for example, the positive test JB is easier to understand than the negative test JNAE.

Jumps Based on Signed Data

The following conditional jump instructions apply to signed data:

Symbol	Description	Flags Tested
JE/JZ	Jump Equal or Jump Zero	ZF
JNE/JNZ	Jump Not Equal or Jump Not Zero	ZF
JG/JNLE	Jump Greater or Jump Not Less/Equal	ZF, SF, OF
JGE/JNL	Jump Greater/Equal or Jump Not Less	SF, OF
JL/JNGE	Jump Less or Jump Not Greater/Equal	SF, OF
JLE/JNG	Jump Less/Equal or Jump Not Greater	ZF, SF, OF

The jumps for testing equal/zero (JE/JZ) and for not equal/zero (JNE/JNZ) are included in both lists for unsigned and signed data. An equal/zero condition occurs regardless of the presence of a sign.

Special Arithmetic Tests

The following conditional jump instructions have special uses:

Symbol	Description	Flags Tested
JS	Jump Sign (negative)	SF
JNS	Jump No Sign (positive)	SF
JC	Jump Carry (same as JB)	CF
JNC	Jump No Carry	CF
JO	Jump Overflow	OF
JNO	Jump No Overflow	OF
JP/JPE	Jump Parity Even	PF
JNP/JPO	Jump Parity Odd	PF

JC and JNC are often used to test the success of disk operations. Another conditional jump, JCXZ, tests the contents of the CX register for zero. This instruction need not be placed immediately following an arithmetic or compare operation. One use for JCXZ could be at the start of a loop to ensure that the CX actually contains a nonzero value.

Now, don't expect to memorize these instructions. For unsigned data, remember that a jump is equal, above, or below. For signed data, remember that a jump is equal, greater, or less. The jumps for testing the carry, overflow, and parity flags have unique purposes. The assembler translates symbolic to object code regardless of which instruction you use, but, for example, JAE and JGE, although apparently similar, do not test the same flags.

The 80386/486 processors permit far conditional jumps. You can indicate a short or far jump as

```
JNE    SHORT address    ;80386/486
JAE    FAR address      ;80386/486
```

CALLING PROCEDURES

Up to now, code segments have consisted of only one procedure, coded as

```
BEGIN    PROC    FAR
           .
           .
           .
BEGIN    ENDP
```

The FAR operand in this case informs the system that this address is the entry point for program execution, whereas the ENDP directive defines the end of the procedure. A code segment, however, may contain any number of procedures all distinguished by PROC and ENDP. The CALL instruction transfers control to a called procedure and the RET instruction returns from the called procedure to the original calling procedure. RET should be the last instruction in a called procedure. The use of procedures can better enable you to organize a program into logical routines that contain related logic.

Details of CALL and RET Operations

CALL and RET generate particular object code depending on whether the operation involves a NEAR or FAR procedure.

Near call and return.   A CALL to a procedure within the same segment is near and performs the following:

- Decrements the SP by 2 (one word)
- Pushes the IP (containing the offset of the instruction following the CALL) onto the stack
- Inserts the offset address of the called procedure in the IP

A RET that returns from a near procedure performs the following:

- Pops the old IP value from the stack into the IP
- Increments the SP by 2

The CS:IP now point to the instruction following the original CALL in the calling procedure, where execution resumes.

Far call and return.   A far CALL permits you to call a procedure labeled FAR in a separate code segment. A far CALL pushes both the CS and IP onto the stack, and RET pops them from the stack. Far calls and returns are the subject of Chapter 21.

Example of a Near Call and Return

A typical organization of near calls and returns appears in Figure 7-3. Note the following features:

- The program is divided into a far procedure, BEGIN, and two near procedures, B10 and C10. Each procedure has a unique name and contains its own ENDP for ending its definition.
- The PROC directives for B10 and C10 contain the attribute NEAR to indicate that these procedures are within the current code segment. Since omission of the attribute causes the assembler to default to NEAR, many subsequent examples omit it.
- In procedure BEGIN, the CALL instruction transfers program control to the procedure B10 and begins its execution.

```
                         TITLE    CALLPROC (EXE) Call procedures
                                  .MODEL   SMALL
                                  .STACK   64
                                  .DATA
                                  .CODE

0000                     BEGIN    PROC     FAR
0000   E8 0007 R                  CALL     B10            ;Call B10
                           ;               ...
0003   B4 4C                      MOV      AH,4CH         ;Terminate
0005   CD 21                      INT      21H
0007                     BEGIN    ENDP
               ;----------------------------------------------------
0007                     B10      PROC     NEAR
0007   E8 000B R                  CALL     C10            ;Call C10
                           ;               ...
000A   C3                         RET                     ;Return to
000B                     B10      ENDP                    ;  caller
               ;----------------------------------------------------
000B                     C10      PROC     NEAR
                           ;               ...
000B   C3                         RET                     ;Return to
000C                     C10      ENDP                    ;  caller
               ;----------------------------------------------------
                                  END      BEGIN
```

Figure 7-3   Effect of Execution on the Stack

- In procedure B10, the CALL instruction transfers control to the procedure C10 and begins its execution.
- In procedure C10, the RET instruction causes control to return to the instruction immediately following CALL C10.
- In procedure B10, the RET instruction causes control to return to the instruction immediately following CALL B10.
- Procedure BEGIN then resumes processing from that point.
- RET always returns to the calling routine. If B10 did not end with a RET instruction, instructions would execute through B10 and drop directly into C10. In fact, if C10 did not contain a RET, the program would execute past the end of C10 into whatever instructions happen to be there (if any), with unpredictable results.

Technically, you can transfer control to a near procedure by means of a jump instruction or even by normal in-line code. But for clarity and consistency, use CALL to transfer control to a procedure, and use RET to terminate its execution.

STACK SEGMENT

Up to this point, our programs have had little need to push data onto the stack. Consequently, these programs needed to define only a very small stack. However, CALL automatically pushes onto the stack the IP containing the offset of the instruction that immediately follows the CALL. In the called procedure, the RET instruction uses this address for returning to the calling procedure and automatically pops the current word in the stack into the IP.

In simple terms, an instruction that pushes onto the stack moves a one-word address or value onto the stack. An instruction that pops the stack accesses the previously pushed word. Both operations change the offset address in the SP (stack pointer) register for the next word. Because of this feature, RET must match its original CALL. Also, a called procedure can CALL another procedure, which in turn can CALL yet another procedure. The stack must be large enough to contain the pushed addresses. All this turns out to be easier than it first appears, and a stack definition of 32 words is ample for most of our purposes.

The instructions PUSH, PUSHF, CALL, INT, and INTO decrement the SP by 2 and save the contents of a register by pushing it onto the stack. The instructions POP, POPF, RET, and IRET return the contents by popping them off the stack and increment the SP by 2.

On loading an EXE program for execution, the system sets the following register values:

DS and ES: Address of the program segment prefix (PSP), a 256-byte (100H) area that precedes an executable program module in memory.

CS: Address of the entry point to your program, the first executable instruction.

IP: Zero, if the first executable instruction is at the beginning of the code segment.

SS: Address of the stack segment.

SP: Offset to the top of the stack. For example, if you define the stack with 32 words (64 bytes) as .STACK 64 (32 words), the SP contains 64, or 40H.

Effect of Program Execution on the Stack

Let's trace the simple EXE program in Figure 7-3 through execution. In practice, called procedures would contain any number of instructions.

The current available location for pushing or popping is the "top" of the stack. In this example, the system loader would have set the SP to the size of the stack, hex 40. The program performs the following operations.

- CALL B10 decrements the SP by 2, to 3EH. It then pushes the IP (containing 0003) onto the stack at offset 3E. This is the address of the instruction following the CALL. The processor uses the CS:IP addresses to transfer control to B10.

- In procedure B10, CALL C10 decrements the SP by 2, to 3CH. It then pushes the IP (containing 000A) onto the stack at offset 3C. The processor uses the CS:IP addresses to transfer control to C10.

- To return from C10, the RET instruction pops the address (000A) from the stack at 3C, inserts it in the IP, and increments the SP by 2 to 3EH. There is an automatic return to offset 000A in procedure B10.

- The RET at the end of procedure B10 pops the address (0003) from the stack at 3E into the IP and increments the SP by 2 to 40H. There is an automatic return to offset 0003 in the code segment, where the program terminates execution.

The following shows the effect on the stack as each instruction executes. Words in memory contain bytes in reverse sequence, such that 0003 becomes 0300. The example shows only offset locations 0036 through 003F and the contents of the SP:

Operation		*Stack*				*SP*
On entry, initially:	xxxx	xxxx	xxxx	xxxx	xxxx	0040
CALL B10 (push 0003)	xxxx	xxxx	xxxx	xxxx	0300	003E
CALL C10 (push 000A)	xxxx	xxxx	xxxx	0A00	0300	003C
RET (pop 000A)	xxxx	xxxx	xxxx	0A00	0300	003E
RET (pop 0003)	xxxx	xxxx	xxxx	0A00	0300	0040
Stack offset:	0036	0038	003A	003C	003E	

If you use DEBUG to view the stack, you may find harmless data from a previously executed program.

EXTENDED MOVE OPERATIONS

Previous programs moved immediate data into a register, moved data from defined memory to a register, moved register contents to memory, and moved the contents of one register to another. In all cases, data length was limited to one or two bytes, and no operation moved data from one memory area directly to another memory area. In this section we explain how to move data that exceeds two bytes. Another method, the use of string instructions, is covered in Chapter 11.

In the EXE program in Figure 7-4, the data segment contains three nine-byte fields defined as NAME1, NAME2, and NAME3. The object of the program is to move the contents of NAME1 to NAME2 and the contents of NAME2 to NAME3. Since these fields are each nine bytes long, more than a simple MOV instruction is required. The program contains a number of new features.

The procedure BEGIN initializes the segment registers and then calls B10MOVE and C10MOVE. B10MOVE moves the contents of NAME1 to NAME2. Since the operation moves one byte at a time, the routine begins with the leftmost byte of NAME1 and loops to move the second byte, the third byte, and so on, as follows:

```
NAME1:   A  B  C  D  E  F  G  H  I
         |  |  |  |  |  |  |  |  |
NAME2:   J  K  L  M  N  O  P  Q  R
```

In order to step through NAME1 and NAME2, the routine initializes the CX register to 9 and uses the index registers, SI and DI. Two LEA instructions load the offset addresses of NAME1 and NAME2 into the SI and DI registers as follows:

```
LEA  SI,NAME1    ;Load offset addresses
LEA  DI,NAME2    ;   of NAME1 and NAME2
```

A looping routine uses the addresses in the SI and DI registers to move the first byte of NAME1 to the first byte of NAME2. The square brackets around SI and DI in the MOV operands mean that the instruction is to use the address in that register for accessing the memory location. Thus

```
MOV  AL,[SI]
```

means: Use the address in SI (NAME1 + 0) to move the referenced byte to the AL register. And the instruction

```
MOV  [DI],AL
```

```
            page    65,132
TITLE   EXMOVE (EXE) Extended move operations
;------------------------------------------------
            .MODEL  SMALL
            .STACK  64
;------------------------------------------------
            .DATA
NAME1   DB      'ABCDEFGHI'
NAME2   DB      'JKLMNOPQR'
NAME3   DB      'STUVWXYZ*'
;------------------------------------------------
            .CODE
BEGIN   PROC    FAR
            MOV     AX,@data        ;Initialize segment
            MOV     DS,AX           ;  registers
            MOV     ES,AX
            CALL    B10MOVE         ;Call jump routine
            CALL    C10MOVE         ;Call loop routine
            MOV     AH,4CH          ;Terminate processing
            INT     21H
BEGIN   ENDP

;           Extended Move using Jump-on-Condition:
;           ------------------------------------
B10MOVE PROC
            LEA     SI,NAME1        ;Initialize address of NAME1
            LEA     DI,NAME2        ;   & NAME2
            MOV     CX,09           ;Initialize to move 9 chars
B20:
            MOV     AL,[SI]         ;Move from NAME1
            MOV     [DI],AL         ;Move to NAME2
            INC     SI              ;Increment next char in NAME1
            INC     DI              ;Increment next pos'n in NAME2
            DEC     CX              ;Decrement loop count
            JNZ     B20             ;Count not zero? Yes, loop
            RET                     ;If count = 0, return to
B10MOVE ENDP                        ;  caller

;           Extended Move using LOOP:
;           -----------------------
C10MOVE PROC
            LEA     SI,NAME2        ;Initialize address of NAME2
            LEA     DI,NAME3        ;   and NAME3
            MOV     CX,09           ;Initialize to move 9 chars
C20:
            MOV     AL,[SI]         ;Move from NAME2
            MOV     [DI],AL         ;Move to NAME3
            INC     DI              ;Increment next char of NAME2
            INC     SI              ;Increment next pos'n of NAME3
            LOOP    C20             ;Decrement count, loop nonzero
            RET                     ;If count = 0, return to
C10MOVE ENDP                        ;  caller
            END     BEGIN
```

Figure 7-4   Extended Move Operations

means: Move the contents of the AL to the address referenced by DI (NAME2 + 0).

The INC instructions increment the SI and DI registers and DEC decrements the CX. If CX is nonzero, the routine loops back to B20. And since SI and DI have been incremented by 1, the next MOV references NAME1 + 1 and NAME2 + 1. The loop continues in this fashion until it has moved NAME1 + 8 to NAME2 + 8.

The procedure C10MOVE is similar to B10MOVE with two exceptions: it moves NAME2 to NAME3 and uses LOOP instead of DEC/JNZ.

Suggestion: Key in the program, assemble and link it, and use DEBUG to trace it. Note the effect on the registers, the instruction pointer, and the stack. Use D DS:0 to view the changes to NAME2 and NAME3.

BOOLEAN OPERATIONS: AND, OR, XOR, TEST, NOT

Boolean logic is important in circuitry design and has a parallel in programming logic. The instructions for Boolean logic are AND, OR, XOR, and TEST, which can be used to clear and set bits and to handle ASCII data for arithmetic purposes (Chapter 13). The general format is

[label]	operation	{register/memory}, {register/memory/immediate}

The first operand references one byte or word in a register or memory and is the only value that is changed. The second operand references a register or immediate value. The operation matches the bits of the two referenced operands and sets the CF, OF, PF, SF, and ZF flags accordingly (AF is undefined).

AND.   If matched bits are both 1, sets the result to 1. All other conditions result in 0.

OR.   If either (or both) of the matched bits is 1, sets the result to 1. If both are 0, the result is 0.

XOR.   If one matched bit is 0 and the other 1, sets the result to 1. If matched bits are the same (both 0 or both 1), the result is 0.

TEST.   Sets the flags like AND but does not change the bits.
The following AND, OR, and XOR operations use the same bit values:

```
              AND      OR     XOR
             0101    0101    0101
             0011    0011    0011
  Result:    0001    0111    0110
```

Examples of Boolean Operations

For the following unrelated examples, assume that the AL contains 1100 0101 and the BH contains 0101 1100.

```
  1. AND    AL,BH     ; Sets AL to 0100 0100
  2. OR     BH,AL     ; Sets BH to 1101 1101
```

```
3. XOR   AL,AL       ;Sets AL to 0000 0000
4. AND   AL,00       ;Sets AL to 0000 0000
5. AND   AL,0FH      ;Sets AL to 0000 0101
6. OR    CL,CL       ;Sets SF and ZF
```

Examples 3 and 4 provide ways of clearing a register to zero. Example 5 zeros the left four bits of the AL. Although the use of CMP may be clearer, you can use OR for the following purposes:

```
1. OR    CX,CX       ;Test CX for zero
   JZ    . . .       ;Jump if zero
2. OR    CX,CX       ;Test CX for sign
   JS    . . .       ;Jump if negative
```

TEST acts like AND but only sets flags. Here are some examples:

```
1. TEST  BL,11110000B ;Any of leftmost bits
   JNZ   . . .        ;   in BL nonzero?
2. TEST  AL,00000001B ;Does the AL contain
   JNZ   . . .        ;   an odd number?
3. TEST  DX,0FFH      ;Does the DX contain
   JZ    . . .        ;   a zero value?
```

Another related instruction, NOT, simply reverses the bits in a byte or word in a register or memory—0s become 1s and 1s become 0s. For example, if the AL contains 1100 0101, the instruction NOT AL changes the AL to 0011 1010. Flags are unaffected. NOT is not the same as NEG, which changes a value from positive to negative, and vice versa, by reversing the bits and adding 1 (see the section "Negative Numbers" in Chapter 1).

CHANGING LOWERCASE TO UPPERCASE

There are various reasons for converting between uppercase and lowercase letters. For example, you may have received a data file from a system that processes only uppercase letters. Or a program has to allow users to enter commands either as uppercase or lowercase (such as YES or yes) and converts to uppercase for testing it. Uppercase letters A through Z are hex 41 through 5A, and lowercase letters a through z are hex 61 through 7A. The only difference is that bit 5 is 0 for uppercase and 1 for lowercase, as the following shows:

	Uppercase		*Lowercase*
Letter A:	01000001	Letter a:	01100001
Letter Z:	01011010	Letter z:	01111010
Bit:	76543210	Bit:	76543210

The COM program in Figure 7-5 converts the contents of a data item, TITLEX, from lowercase to uppercase, beginning at TITLEX + 1. The program initializes the BX with the address of TITLEX + 1 and uses the address to move each character starting at TITLEX + 1 to the AH. If the value is between hex 61 and 7A, an AND instruction sets bit 5 to 0:

```
AND  AH,11011111B
```

All characters other than a through z remain unchanged. The routine then moves the changed character back to TITLEX, increments the BX for the next character, and loops.

Used this way, the BX register acts as an index register for addressing memory locations. You may also use the SI and DI for this purpose.

```
TITLE   CASE   (COM)  Change lowercase to uppercase
        .MODEL SMALL
        .CODE
        ORG    100H
BEGIN:  JMP    MAIN
; -----------------------------------------------
TITLEX  DB     'Change to uppercase letters'
; -----------------------------------------------
MAIN    PROC   NEAR
        LEA    BX,TITLEX+1     ;1st char to change
        MOV    CX,26           ;No. of chars to change
B20:
        MOV    AH,[BX]         ;Character from TITLEX
        CMP    AH,61H          ;Is it
        JB     B30             ;  lower
        CMP    AH,7AH          ;  case
        JA     B30             ;  letter?
        AND    AH,11011111B    ;Yes - convert
        MOV    [BX],AH         ;Restore in TITLEX
B30:
        INC    BX              ;Set for next char
        LOOP   B20             ;Loop 26 times
        MOV    AH,4CH          ;Done -- exit
        INT    21H
MAIN    ENDP
        END    BEGIN
```

Figure 7-5   Changing Lowercase to Uppercase

SHIFTING

The shift instructions, which are part of the computer's logical capability, can perform the following actions:

- Reference a register or memory address
- Shift bits left or right
- Shift up to 8 bits if byte, 16 bits if word, and 32 bits if doubleword (80386/486)
- Shift logically (unsigned) or arithmetically (signed)

The second operand contains the shift value, which is a constant (an immediate value) or a reference to the CL register. For the 8088/8086 processors, the immediate constant may be only 1; a shift value greater than 1 must be contained in the CL register. The 80186-80486 processors allow immediate shift constants up to 31. The general format is

[label]	shift	{register/memory},{CL/immediate}

Shifting Right

A right shift moves the bits in the designated register to the right. A bit that is shifted off enters the carry flag. The right shift instructions provide for unsigned and signed data:

```
SHR    ; Shift (unsigned) right
SAR    ; Shift arithmetic (signed) right
```

The following related instructions illustrate SHR and unsigned data:

```
MOV  CL,03            ;    AL:
MOV  AL,10110111B     ;10110111
SHR  AL,01            ;01011011 Shift right 1
SHR  AL,CL            ;00001011 Shift right 3
SHR  AX,12            ;80186-80486 only
```

The first SHR shifts the contents of the AL one bit to the right. The shifted 1-bit now resides in the carry flag and a 0-bit is filled to the left in the AL. The second SHR shifts the AL three more bits. The carry flag contains successively 1, 1, then 0, and three 0-bits are filled to the left in the AL.

SAR differs from SHR in one important way: SAR uses the sign bit to fill leftmost vacated bits. In this way, positive and negative values retain their sign. The following related instructions illustrate SAR and unsigned data in which the sign is a 1 bit:

```
MOV  CL,03            ;    AL:
MOV  AL,10110111B     ; 10110111
SAR  AL,01            ; 11011011 Shift right 1
SAR  AL,CL            ; 11111011 Shift right 3
SAR  AX,12            ; 80186-80486 only
```

Shifting Left

A left shift moves the bits in the designated register to the left. A bit that is shifted off enters the carry flag. The left shift instructions provide for unsigned and signed data:

```
SHL    ;Shift (unsigned) left
SAL    ;Shift arithmetic (signed) left
```

The following related instructions illustrate SHL and unsigned data:

```
MOV  CL,03          ;     AL:
MOV  AL,10110111B   ; 10110111
SHL  AL,01          ; 01101110 Shift left 1
SHL  AL,CL          ; 01110000 Shift left 3
SHL  AX,12          ; 80186-80486 only
```

The first SHL shifts the contents of the AL one bit to the left. The shifted 1-bit now resides in the carry flag and a 0-bit is filled to the right in the AL. The second SHL shifts the AL three more bits. The carry flag contains successively 0, 1, then 1, and three 0-bits are filled to the right in the AL.

Left shifts always fill 0-bits to the right. As a result, SHL and SAL are identical.

Left shift is especially useful for doubling values and right shift for halving values, and both are significantly faster than multiply and divide. Halving odd numbers such as 5 and 7 generates a smaller value (2 and 3, respectively) and sets the carry flag to 1. Also, if you have to shift two bits, coding two shift instructions is more efficient than storing 2 in the CL and coding one shift.

You can use the JC (Jump if Carry) instruction to test the bit shifted into the carry flag at the end of a shift operation.

ROTATING

The rotate instructions, which are part of the computer's logical capability, can perform the following actions:

- Reference a byte or a word
- Reference a register or memory
- Rotate left or right. The bit that is shifted off rotates to fill the vacated bit position
- Rotate up to 8 bits if byte, 16 bits if word, and 32 bits if doubleword (80386/486)
- Rotate logically (unsigned) or arithmetically (signed)

The second operand contains the rotate value, which is a constant (an immediate value) or a reference to the CL register. For the 8088/8086 processors, the immediate constant may be only 1; a rotate value greater than 1 must be contained in the CL register. The 80186-80486 processors allow immediate constants up to 31. The general format is

[label]	rotate	{register/memory},{CL/immediate}

Rotating Right

A right rotate rotates the bits in the designated register to the right. The right rotate instructions provide for unsigned and signed data:

```
ROR     ;Rotate right
RCR     ;Rotate with carry right
```

The following related instructions illustrate ROR:

```
MOV     CL,03           ;     BH:
MOV     BH,10110111B    ; 10110111
ROR     BH,01           ; 11011011    Rotate right 1
ROR     BH,CL           ; 01111011    Rotate right 3
ROR     BX,12           ; 80186-80486 only
```

The first ROR rotates the rightmost 1-bit of the BH to the leftmost vacated position. The second ROR rotates the three rightmost bits.

RCR causes the carry flag to participate. The shifted off bit on the right moves into the CF, and the CF bit moves into the vacated bit position on the left. You can use the JC (Jump if Carry) instruction to test the bit rotated into the CF at the end of the rotate operation.

Rotating Left

A left rotate rotates the bits in the designated register to the left. The left rotate instructions provide for unsigned and signed data:

```
ROL     ;Rotate left
RCL     ;Rotate with carry left
```

The following related instructions illustrate ROL:

```
MOV     CL,03           ;     BL:
MOV     BL,10110111B    ; 10110111
ROL     BL,01           ; 01101111    Rotate left 1
ROL     BL,CL           ; 01111011    Rotate left 3
ROL     BX,12           ; 80186-80486 only
```

The first ROL rotates the leftmost 1-bit of the BL to the rightmost vacated position. The second ROL rotates the three leftmost bits.

RCL also causes the carry flag to participate. The shifted off bit on the left moves into the CF, and the CF bit moves into the vacated bit position on the right.

Example Shift and Rotate

Consider a 32-bit value of which the leftmost 16 bits are in the DX and the rightmost 16 bits are in the AX, as DX:AX. Instructions to "multiply" the value by two could be

```
SHL   AX,1   ;Multiply DX:AX pair
RCL   DX,1   ; by 2
```

The SHL shifts all bits in the AX to the left, and the leftmost bit shifts into the carry flag. The RCL shifts the DX left and inserts the bit from the CF into the rightmost vacated bit.

PROGRAM ORGANIZATION

The following are typical steps in writing an assembly language program:

1. Have a clear idea of the problem that the program is to solve.
2. Sketch your ideas in general terms and plan the overall logic. For example, if a problem is to test multibyte move operations such as in Figure 7-4, start by defining the fields to be moved. Then plan the strategy for the instructions: routines for initialization, for using a conditional jump, and for using a LOOP. The following, which shows the main logic, is pseudocode that many programmers use to plan a program:

> Initialize segment registers
> Call Jump routine
> Call Loop routine
> Return to DOS

Jump routine could be planned as

> Initialize registers for count, addresses of names
> Jump1:
> Move one character of name
> Increment for next characters of names
> Decrement count: If nonzero, Jump1
> If zero, Return

Loop routine could be sketched in a similar way.

3. Organize the program into logical units such that related routines follow one another. A procedure that is about 25 lines (the size of the screen) is easier to debug.

4. Use other programs as a guide. Attempts to memorize all the technical material and code "off the top of the head" often result in even more program bugs.

5. Use comments to clarify what a procedure is supposed to accomplish, what arithmetic and comparison operations are performing, and what a seldom-used instruction is doing. (An example of the latter is LOOPNE—does it loop while not equal or until not equal?)

6. For keying in the program, use a saved skeleton program that you can copy into a newly named file.

The remaining programs in this text make considerable use of JMP, LOOP, conditional jumps, CALL, and called procedures. Having covered the basics of assembly language, you are now in a position for more advanced and realistic programming.

KEY POINTS

- A short address is reached by an offset and is limited to a distance of -128 to 127 bytes. A near address is reached by an offset and is limited to a distance of $-32,768$ to 32,767 bytes within the same segment. A far address in another segment is reached by a segment address and offset.

- Labels such as B20: within procedures require colons to indicate a near label.

- Labels for conditional jump and LOOP instructions must be short. The operand generates one byte of object code. Hex 01 to 7F covers the range from decimal $+1$ to $+127$, and hex FF to 80 covers the range from -1 to -128. Since machine instructions vary in length from one to four bytes, the limit is not obvious, but about two screens full of source code is a practical guide.

- For using LOOP, initialize the CX with a positive number. Since LOOP checks for a zero value, the program will continue looping if CX is negative.

- When an instruction sets a flag, it remains set until another instruction changes it. For example, you could perform an arithmetic operation that sets flags and if the operation is followed immediately by MOV instructions, the flags remain unchanged. However, to minimize bugs, code a conditional jump instruction immediately following the instruction that set the flag.

- Select an appropriate conditional jump instruction depending on whether the operation processes signed or unsigned data.

- Always CALL a procedure, and include RET at its end for returning. A called procedure may call other procedures, and if you follow the conventions, RET causes the correct address in the stack to pop. The only examples in this book that jump to a procedure are at the beginning of COM programs.

- Be careful when using indexed operands. Consider the following move operations:

```
MOV    AX,SI
MOV    AX,[SI]
```

The first MOV moves the contents of the SI register. The second MOV uses the offset address in the SI to access a word in memory.

- Use shift instructions to double or halve values, but be sure to select the appropriate instruction for unsigned and signed data.

QUESTIONS

7-1. **(a)** What is the maximum number of bytes that a near JMP, a LOOP, and a conditional jump instruction may jump? **(b)** What characteristic of the machine code operand causes this limit?

7-2. A JMP instruction begins at hex location 0624. Determine the transfer address based on the following hex object code for the JMP operand: **(a)** 27; **(b)** 6B; **(c)** C6.

7-3. Code a routine using LOOP that calculates the Fibonacci series: 1, 1, 2, 3, 5, 8, 13, . . . (except for the first two numbers in the sequence, each number is sum of the preceding two numbers). Set the limit for 12 loops. Assemble, link, and use DEBUG to trace.

7-4. Assume that AX and BX contain signed data and that CX and DX contain unsigned data. Determine the CMP (where necessary) and conditional jump instructions for the following:
- **(a)** Does the DX value exceed the CX?
- **(b)** Does the BX value exceed the AX?
- **(c)** Does the CX contain zero?
- **(d)** Is there an overflow?
- **(e)** Is the BX equal to or smaller than the AX?
- **(f)** Is the DX equal to or smaller than the CX?

7-5. In the following, what flags are affected, and what would they contain?
- **(a)** An overflow occurred.
- **(b)** A result is negative.
- **(c)** A result is zero.
- **(d)** Processing is in single-step mode.
- **(e)** A string data transfer is to be right to left.

7-6. Refer to Figure 7-3. What would be the effect on program execution if the procedure B10 did not contain a RET?

7-7. What is the difference between coding a PROC operand with FAR and with NEAR?

7-8. What are the ways in which a program can begin executing a procedure?

7-9. In an EXE program, A10 calls B10, B10 calls C10, and C10 calls D10. As a result of these calls, how many addresses does the stack contain?

7-10. Assume that the BL contains 1110 0011 and that a location named BOONO contains 0111 1001. Determine the effect on the BL for the following: **(a)** XOR BL,BOONO; **(b)** AND BL,BOONO; **(c)** OR BL,BOONO; **(d)** XOR BL,11111111B; **(e)** AND BL,00000000B.

7-11. Revise the program in Figure 7-5 as follows: Define the contents of TITLEX as uppercase letters and code the instructions that convert uppercase to lowercase.

7-12. Assume that the DX contains binary 10111001 10111001 and the CL contains 03. Determine the contents of the DX after the following unrelated instructions: **(a)** SHR DX,1; **(b)** SHR DX,CL; **(c)** SHL DX,CL; **(d)** SHL DL,1; **(e)** ROR DX,CL; **(f)** ROR DL,CL; **(g)** SAL DH,1.

7-13. Use shift, move, and add instructions to multiply the contents of the AX by 10.

7-14. An example routine at the end of the section "Rotating" multiplies the DX:AX by 2. Revise the routine to **(a)** multiply by 4, **(b)** divide by 4, and **(c)** multiply the 48 bits in the DX:AX:BX by 2.

8

INTRODUCTION TO SCREEN AND KEYBOARD PROCESSING

OBJECTIVE

To introduce the requirements for displaying information on a screen and accepting input from a keyboard.

INTRODUCTION

Up to this point, programs have defined data items in the data area or within an instruction operand as immediate data. The number of practical applications for programs that process only defined data is few indeed. Most programs require input data from a keyboard, disk, or modem, and provide answers in a useful format on a screen, printer, or disk. This chapter covers basic requirements for displaying information on a screen and for accepting input from a keyboard.

There are various requirements for telling the system whether processing is to be input or output, and on what device. The INT (Interrupt) instruction handles input and output. The two types of interrupts covered in this chapter are BIOS operation INT 10H for screen handling and DOS operation INT 21H for displaying output and accepting input. These operations use what are known as *service* (or *function*) calls to request an action; you insert an initial value in the AH register to identify the type of operation to be performed.

You can also use INT 10H to handle screen output and INT 16H to handle keyboard input, both of which transfer control directly to BIOS. However, to facilitate some of the more complex operations, INT 21H provides a higher level of interrupt that first transfers control to DOS. For example, input from a keyboard may require a count of characters entered, a check against a maximum number of characters, and a check for the Enter character. The DOS INT 21H operation handles much of this additional processing and transfers automatically to BIOS for the low-level operation.

As a convention, in this book we refer to hex 0DH as Enter for the keyboard and as Carriage Return for the screen and printer.

Chapters 9 and 10 cover advanced screen and keyboard handling features.

THE SCREEN

The screen is a grid of addressable locations at any one of which the cursor can be set. A typical video monitor, for example, has 25 rows (numbered 0 to 24) and 80 columns (numbered 0 to 79). Here are some examples of cursor locations:

Location	Decimal Format		Hex Format	
	Row	Column	Row	Column
Upper left corner	00	00	00	00
Upper right corner	00	79	00	4F
Center of screen	12	39/40	0C	27/28
Lower left corner	24	00	18	00
Lower right corner	24	79	18	4F

The system provides space in memory for a screen buffer. Monochrome memory begins at BIOS location B0000 and supports 4K bytes of memory, 2K of which are available for characters and 2K for an attribute for each character that specifies reverse video, blinking, high intensity, and underlining.

The original color/graphics display supports 16K bytes of memory (display buffer) starting at address hex B8000. You can process either in text mode for normal character display or in graphics mode. For text mode, the display buffer provides for screen "pages" numbered 0 through 3 for an 80-column screen (and 0 through 7 for a 40-column screen):

B8000 : | page 0 | page 1 | page 2 | page 3 |

The default page number is 0, but you may format and display any of the pages in memory. Each page is 4K in size: 2K bytes of 25 rows and 80 columns of characters and 2K bytes for each screen character for its attribute.

The interrupts that handle screen displays transfer your data directly to the memory area, depending on the type of video adapter installed, such as CGA, EGA, or VGA. Although technically your programs may transfer data directly to the screen memory area, there is no assurance that the memory locations will be the same on all models. The recommended practice is to use the appropriate interrupt instructions, such as INT 10H or INT 21H. You can use INT 10H to display, to set the cursor at any location, and to clear the screen, and INT 21H to display.

SETTING THE CURSOR

Setting the cursor is a common requirement for text mode, since its position determines where to display the next character. INT 10H is the BIOS operation for screen handling, and service 02 in the AH tells the operation to set the cursor. Page (or screen) number for color, normally 0, is in the BH register, and row and column must be in the DX. The contents of the other registers is not important. The following instructions set the cursor to row 05, column 12:

```
MOV    AH,02       ;Request set cursor
MOV    BH,00       ;Page number 0
MOV    DH,05       ;Row 05
MOV    DL,12       ;Column 12
INT    10H         ;Interrupt—exit to BIOS
```

To set row and column, you could also use one MOV instruction with an immediate hex value as

```
MOV    DX,050CH    ;Row 5, column 12
```

CLEARING THE SCREEN

Prompts and commands stay on the screen until overwritten or scrolled off. When your program starts executing, you may want the screen cleared. You can clear beginning at any location and ending at any higher-numbered location. BIOS INT 10H also handles screen clearing or scrolling. Insert service 06H in the AH, 00H for full screen in the AL, attribute value in the BH, starting row:column in the CX, and ending row:column in the DX.

The attribute in the following example sets the entire screen to white (foreground) on black (background). If you have a color monitor, you could try, for example, 71H for blue (1) on white (7).

```
MOV    AX,0600H    ;AH 06 (scroll), AL 00 (full screen)
MOV    BH,07       ;Attribute: white (7) on black (0)
MOV    CX,0000     ;Upper left row:column
MOV    DX,184FH    ;Lower right row:column
INT    10H         ;Interrupt—transfer to BIOS
```

If you mistakenly set the lower right location higher than hex 184F, the operation wraps around the screen and clears some locations twice. Although the action causes no harm on monochrome screens, it may cause a serious error on some color monitors. In Chapter 9 we describe scrolling in more detail.

SCREEN AND KEYBOARD OPERATIONS: ORIGINAL DOS

A program often has to display messages indicating completion or errors detected and prompts to a user requesting data or action to take. We'll first examine the methods for original DOS versions, and later examine the extended methods introduced by DOS 2.0. The original DOS operations work under all versions, although the DOS manual recommends use of the extended operations for new development. The display operation for original DOS is a little more involved, but keyboard input is particularly useful because of its built-in checks.

ORIGINAL DOS FOR SCREEN DISPLAY

The original DOS service for displaying requires defining a display string in the data area. The string is immediately followed by a dollar sign ($) delimiter, which the operation recognizes:

```
NAMPRMP    DB    'Customer name?','$'   :Display string
```

You can code the dollar sign immediately following the display string as just shown, inside the string as 'Customer name?$', or on the next line as DB '$'. The effect, however, is that you can't use this service to display a $ character on the screen.

Set service 09 in the AH register, load the address of the string in the DX, and issue an INT 21H instruction. The operation recognizes the end of the message by the dollar sign ($) delimiter.

```
MOV    AH,09        ;Request display
LEA    DX,NAMPRMP   ;Load address of prompt
INT    21H          ;DOS interrupt
```

The LEA (load effective address) instruction loads the address of NAMPRMP in the DX to enable the operation to locate the display string. For the actual memory address, LEA loads the offset address of NAMPRMP, and DOS uses the address in the DS register plus the DX (DS:DX).

If you omit the dollar sign at the end of the string, the operation displays characters from memory until it finds one—if any.

USING DOS TO DISPLAY THE ASCII CHARACTER SET

Most of the 256 ASCII characters are represented by symbols that can display on a video screen. Hex 00 and FF have no symbol and display as blank, although the true ASCII blank character is hex 20.

The COM program in Figure 8-1 displays the entire range of ASCII characters. The program calls three procedures: B10CLR, C10SET, and D10DISP. B10CLR clears the screen and C10SET initializes the cursor to 00,00. D10DISP displays the contents of CHAR, which is initialized to hex 00 and is successively incremented to display each character until reaching hex FF.

```
                page 60,132
        TITLE   DOSASC (COM)  Use DOS to display ASCII characters 00-FF
                .MODEL  SMALL
                .CODE

                ORG     100H
        BEGIN:  JMP     SHORT MAIN
        CHAR    DB      00,'$'

        ;               Main procedure:
        ;               --------------
        MAIN    PROC    NEAR
                CALL    B10CLR          ;Clear screen
                CALL    C10SET          ;Set cursor
                CALL    D10DISP         ;Display characters
                MOV     AH,4CH          ;Exit
                INT     21H
        MAIN    ENDP
        ;               Clear screen:
        ;               ------------
        B10CLR  PROC    NEAR
                MOV     AX,0600H        ;Scroll full screen
                MOV     BH,07           ;Attribute: white on black
                MOV     CX,0000         ;Upper left location
                MOV     DX,184FH        ;Lower right location
                INT     10H
                RET
        B10CLR  ENDP
        ;               Set cursor to 00,00:
        ;               -------------------
        C10SET  PROC    NEAR
                MOV     AH,02           ;Request set cursor
                MOV     BH,00           ;Page number 0
                MOV     DX,0000         ;Row 0, column 0
                INT     10H
                RET
        C10SET  ENDP
        ;               Display ASCII characters:
        ;               ------------------------
        D10DISP PROC
                MOV     CX,256          ;Initialize 256 iterations
                LEA     DX,CHAR         ;Initialize address of char
        D20:
                MOV     AH,09           ;Display ASCII char
                INT     21H
                INC     CHAR            ;Increment for next character
                LOOP    D20             ;Decrement CX, loop nonzero
                RET                     ;Terminate
        D10DISP ENDP
                END     BEGIN
```

Figure 8-1   DOS Service to Display the ASCII Character Set

A problem with DOS service 09 is that it does not display the dollar symbol. Also, special control characters cause the cursor to move: Hex 07 causes a beep, hex 08 causes a backspace (erasing the previous character), hex 0A causes a line feed, and hex 0D causes a carriage return. (As you'll see in Chapter 9, BIOS services can display proper symbols for these special characters.)

Suggestion: Reproduce the program as it stands, assemble it, link it, and convert it to a COM file. For execution, enter its name, such as B:ASCII.COM.

The first displayed line begins with a blank character (hex 00), two "happy faces" (hex 01 and 02), and then a heart, a diamond, and a club (hex 03, 04, and 05). Hex 07 causes the speaker to sound. Hex 06 would have been a spade but the control characters hex 08 through 0D erase it. In fact, hex 0D causes a "carriage return" (Enter) to the start of the next line. The musical note is hex 0E, and the characters above hex 7F include extended ASCII characters.

You can change the program to bypass the control characters. The following instructions bypass all characters between hex 08 and 0D; you may want to experiment with bypassing only, say, hex 08 (Backspace) and 0D (Enter).

```
          CMP   CHAR,08H    ;Lower than 08?
          JB    D30         ;Yes—accept
          CMP   CHAR,0DH    ;Lower/equal 0D?
          JBE   D40         ;Yes—bypass
    D30:
          MOV   AH,40H      ;Display < 08
          . . .             ;      and > 0D
          INT   21H
    D40:
          INC   CHAR
```

ORIGINAL DOS FOR KEYBOARD INPUT

The original DOS service to accept data from a keyboard is particularly powerful. The input area requires a *parameter list* containing specified fields that the INT operation is to process. First, the interrupt needs to know the maximum length of the input data. The purpose is to warn users who key in too many characters; the operation sounds the speaker and does not accept additional characters. Second, the operation delivers to the parameter list the number of bytes actually entered.

The following defines a parameter list for an input area. (If you've worked in a high-level language, you may be used to the term record or structure.) LABEL is a directive with the type attribute of BYTE, which simply causes alignment on a byte boundary. The first byte contains your limit for the maximum number of input characters. The minimum is 0 and, since this is a one-byte field, the maximum is hex FF, or 255. You decide, based on the kind of data you expect the user to enter. The second byte is for the operation to store the actual number of characters entered. The third byte begins a field that is to contain the typed characters.

```
NAMEPAR  LABEL  BYTE          ;Start of parameter list
MAXLEN   DB     20            ;Maximum number of input characters
ACTLEN   DB     ?             ;Actual number of input characters
NAMEFLD  DB     20 DUP(' ')   ;Characters entered from keyboard
```

In the parameter list, the LABEL directive tells the assembler to align on a byte boundary and gives the location the name NAMEPAR. Since LABEL takes no space, NAMEPAR and MAXLEN refer to the same memory location.

To request input, use DOS service 0AH in the AH, load the address of the parameter list (NAMEPAR in the example) into the DX, and issue INT 21H:

```
MOV    AH,0AH         ;Request input service
LEA    DX,NAMEPAR     ;Load address of parameter list
INT    21H            ;DOS interrupt
```

The INT operation waits for a user to enter characters and checks that they do not exceed the maximum in the parameter list (20 in the example). The operation echoes the entered character on the screen and advances the cursor. The user presses the Enter key to signal the end of an entry. The operation also transfers this character (hex 0D) to the input field (NAMEFLD in the example) but does not include it in the actual length. If you key in a name such as BROWN (Enter), the parameter list appears like this:

```
ACSII: | 20 |  5 | B  | R  | O  | W  | N  | #  |    |    |    |    | . . .
  Hex: | 14 | 05 | 42 | 52 | 4F | 57 | 4E | 0D | 20 | 20 | 20 | 20 | . . .
```

The operation delivers the length of the input name, 05, into the second byte of the parameter list, named ACTLEN in the example. The Enter character is at NAMEFLD + 5. The # symbol here is to indicate this character because hex 0D has no printable symbol. Since the maximum length of 20 includes the hex 0D, the actual name may be only 19 characters long.

The operation does not accept more than the maximum number of characters. If the user keys in 20 characters in the preceding example without pressing Enter, the operation causes the speaker to beep; it accepts only the Enter character at this point.

This service is not suitable for entering extended functions such as F1, Home, PgUp, and Arrows. For these, use INT 16H or INT 21H service 01, both covered in Chapter 10.

ACCEPTING AND DISPLAYING NAMES

The EXE program in Figure 8-2 requests that a user enter a name, then displays the name on the center of the screen and sounds the speaker. The program continues accepting and displaying names until the user presses Enter as a reply to a prompt. If a user enters the name Ted Smith, the program performs the following:

1. Divides the length 09 by 2: 9 / 2 = 4, with the fraction ignored

2. Subtracts this value from 40: 40 − 4 = 36

In E10CENT, the SHR instruction shifts the length 09 one bit to the right: Bits 00001001 become 00000100, effectively dividing the length by 2. The NEG instruction reverses the sign, changing +4 to −4. ADD adds the value 40, giving the starting position for the column, 36, in the DL register. With the cursor set at row 12, column 36, the name appears on the screen as follows:

```
            page     60,132
TITLE     CTRNAME (EXE)  Accept names & center on screen
;---------------------------------------------------------
          .MODEL SMALL
          .STACK 64
;---------------------------------------------------------
          .DATA
NAMEPAR LABEL    BYTE              ;Name parameter list:
MAXNLEN DB       20                ;   maximum length of name
NAMELEN DB       ?                 ;   no. of characters entered
NAMEFLD DB       20 DUP(' '),'$'   ;   name and delimiter
                                   ;   for displaying
PROMPT  DB       'Name? ', '$'
;---------------------------------------------------------
          .CODE
BEGIN   PROC     FAR
        MOV      AX,@data          ;Initialize segment
        MOV      DS,AX             ;   registers
        MOV      ES,AX
        CALL     Q10CLR            ;Clear screen
A20LOOP:
        MOV      DX,0000           ;Set cursor to 00,00
        CALL     Q20CURS
        CALL     B10PRMP           ;Display prompt
        CALL     D10INPT           ;Provide for input of name
        CALL     Q10CLR            ;Clear screen
        CMP      NAMELEN,00        ;Name entered?
        JE       A30               ;   no -- exit
        CALL     E10CODE           ;Set bell & '$'
        CALL     F10CENT           ;Center & display name
        JMP      A20LOOP
A30:
        MOV      AH,4CH            ;Return to DOS
        INT      21H
BEGIN   ENDP
;                Display prompt:
;                --------------
B10PRMP PROC     NEAR
        MOV      AH,09             ;Request display
        LEA      DX,PROMPT
        INT      21H
        RET
B10PRMP ENDP
;                Accept input of name:
;                --------------------
D10INPT PROC     NEAR
        MOV      AH,0AH            ;Request input
        LEA      DX,NAMEPAR
        INT      21H
        RET
D10INPT ENDP
```

Figure 8-2 Accepting and Displaying Names

```
;                       Set bell and '$' delimiter:
;                       ---------------------------
E10CODE PROC    NEAR
        MOV     BH,00                   ;Replace Enter char (0D)
        MOV     BL,NAMELEN              ; with bell (07)
        MOV     NAMEFLD[BX],07
        MOV     NAMEFLD[BX+1],'$'  ;Set display delimiter
        RET
E10CODE ENDP
;                       Center and display name:
;                       -----------------------
F10CENT PROC    NEAR
        MOV     DL,NAMELEN              ;Locate center column:
        SHR     DL,1                    ;  divide length by 2,
        NEG     DL                      ;  reverse sign,
        ADD     DL,40                   ;  add 40
        MOV     DH,12                   ;Center row
        CALL    Q20CURS                 ;Set cursor
        MOV     AH,09
        LEA     DX,NAMEFLD              ;Display name
        INT     21H
        RET
F10CENT ENDP
;                       Clear screen:
;                       ------------
Q10CLR  PROC    NEAR
        MOV     AX,0600H                ;Request scroll screen
        MOV     BH,30                   ;Color (07 for BW)
        MOV     CX,0000                 ;From 00,00
        MOV     DX,184FH                ;To 24,79
        INT     10H                     ;Call BIOS
        RET
Q10CLR  ENDP
;                       Set cursor row/column:
;                       ----------------------
Q20CURS PROC    NEAR                    ;DX set on entry
        MOV     AH,02                   ;Request set cursor
        MOV     BH,00                   ;Page #0
        INT     10H                     ;Call BIOS
        RET
Q20CURS ENDP

        END BEGIN
```

Figure 8-2 Cont.


```
Row 12:    Ted Smith
            |   |
Column:    36  40
```

Note the instructions in E10CODE that insert the Bell (07) character in the input area immediately following the name:

```
MOV     BH,00              ;Replace Enter character (0D)
MOV     BL,NAMELEN         ; with Bell (07)
MOV     NAMEFLD[BX],07
```

The first two MOVs set the BX with the length. The third MOV references an index operator in square brackets, which means that the BX is to act as a special index register to provide extended addressing. The MOV combines the length in the BX with the address of NAMEFLD and moves the 07 to this address. Thus for a length of 05, the instruction inserts 07 at NAMEFLD + 05 (replacing the Enter character) following the name. The last instruction in E10CODE inserts a '$' delimiter following the 07 so that when F10CENT displays the name, the speaker also sounds.

Replying with Only the Enter Character

If you key in only the Enter character, the operation accepts it and inserts a length of 0 in the parameter list, as follows:

        Parameter list(hex):|14|00|0D| . . .

To signify end of input data on a prompt for name, a user can simply press Enter. If the length is 0, the program determines that input is ended.

Clearing the Enter Character

You can use input characters for various purposes, such as printing on reports, storing in a table, or writing on disk. For these purposes, you may have to replace the Enter character (hex 0D) somewhere in NAMEFLD with a blank (hex 20). The field containing the actual length, NAMELEN, provides its relative position. If NAMELEN contains 05, this position is NAMEFLD + 5. You can move this length into the BX register for indexing the address of NAMEFLD as follows:

```
MOV   BH,00              ;Set BX
MOV   BL,NAMELEN         ; to 00 05
MOV   NAMEFLD[BX],20H    ;Clear Enter character
```

The first two MOV instructions set the BX with the length 05. The third MOV moves a blank (hex 20) to the address specified in the first operand: the address of NAMEFLD plus the contents of BX, in effect, NAMEFLD + 5.

Clearing the Input Area

Entered characters replace the previous contents in an input area and remain there until other characters replace them. Consider the following successive input:

```
        Input                    NAMEPAR (hex)
   1. BROWN      |14|05|42|52|4F|57|4E|0D|20|20|20| . . .|20|
   2. HAMILTON   |14|08|48|41|4D|49|4C|54|4F|4E|0D| . . .|20|
   3. ADAMS      |14|05|41|44|41|4D|53|0D|45|5A|0D| . . .|20|
```

The name HAMILTON replaces the shorter name BROWN. But because the name ADAMS is shorter than HAMILTON, it replaces HAMIL and the Enter character replaces the T. The remaining letters, ON, still follow ADAMS. You may want to clear NAMEFLD prior to prompting for a name, as follows:

```
          MOV   CX,20            ;Initialize for 20 loops
          MOV   SI,0000          ;Start position for name
B30:
          MOV   NAMEFLD[SI],20H  ;One blank to name
          INC   SI               ;Increment for next character
          LOOP  B30              ;20 times
```

Instead of the SI register, you could use DI or BX. A more efficient method that moves a word of two blanks requires only ten loops. However, because NAMEFLD is defined as DB (byte), you would have to override its length with a WORD and PTR (pointer) operand, as the following indicates:

```
          MOV   CX,10            ;Initialize for ten loops
          LEA   SI,NAMEFLD       ;Initialize start of name
B30:
          MOV   WORD PTR[SI],2020H ;Two blanks to name
          INC   SI               ;Increment two positions
          INC   SI               ;  in name
          LOOP  B30              ;Loop ten times
```

Interpret the MOV at B30 as: Move a blank word to where the address in the SI register points. This example uses LEA to initialize and uses a slightly different method for the MOV at B30 because you cannot code an instruction such as

```
MOV WORD PTR[NAMEFLD],2020H  ;Invalid
```

Clearing the input area solves the problem of short names being followed by previous data. A more efficient practice is to clear only positions to the right of an entered name.

SCREEN AND KEYBOARD OPERATIONS: EXTENDED DOS

We'll now examine the extended method for screen and keyboard operations introduced by DOS 2.0, which is more in the UNIX and OS-2 style. The extended method involves a *file handle,* which you load in the BX register when requesting an I/O operation. Since the following standard file handles are always available, you do not have to define them:

00   Input, normally keyboard (CON), may be redirected
01   Output, normally display (CON), may be redirected

02   Error output, display (CON), may not be redirected
03   Auxiliary device (AUX)
04   Printer (LPT1 or PRN)

Use DOS interrupt INT 21H and load the required service in the AH register: hex 3F for input and hex 40 for output. Set the CX with the number of bytes to read or display, and load the DX with the address of the input or output area.

A successful operation clears the carry flag and inserts in the AX the number of characters actually entered or displayed. An unsuccessful operation sets the carry flag and inserts an error code (6 in this case) in the AX. Since the AX could contain a length or an error code, the only way to determine an error condition is to test the carry flag, although keyboard and display errors presumably would be rare. You also use file handles in a similar way to process disk files, where error conditions are more common.

You can use these services to redirect input and output to other devices, although we won't concern ourselves with this feature here.

EXTENDED DOS FOR SCREEN DISPLAY

DOS service 40H requests display. Load file handle 01 in the BX, the number of characters to display in the CX, and the address of the area to display in the DX. The operation responds like service 09 to 07H (beep), 08H (backspace), 0AH (line feed), and 0DH (carriage return). The following instructions illustrate this service:

```
DISAREA  DB    16 DUP('PC Users Society')    ;Display area
         . . .
         MOV   AH,40H                         ;Request display
         MOV   BX,01                          ;File handle for output
         MOV   CX,16                          ;Maximum 16 characters
         LEA   DX,DISAREA                     ;Display area
         INT   21H                            ;Call DOS
```

LEA loads the address of DISAREA in the DX to enable DOS to locate the information that is to display. A successful operation clears the carry flag (which you may test) and sets the AX with the number of characters displayed. An unsuccessful operation could occur because of an invalid handle. The operation sets the carry flag and inserts an error code (6 in this case) in the AX. Since the AX could contain a length or an error code, the only way to determine an error condition is to test the carry flag, although few programs do so:

```
         JC error-routine    ;Test for display error
```

Exercise: Displaying on the Screen

Let's use DEBUG to examine the internal effects of an interrupt. Load DEBUG, and when its prompt appears, type A 100 to begin entering the following instructions (but not the numbers) at location 100. Remember that DEBUG assumes that all numbers entered are hexadecimal.

```
100    MOV  AH,40
102    MOV  BX,01
105    MOV  CX,xx   (Insert length of your name)
108    MOV  DX,10E
10B    INT  21
10D    RET
10E    DB   'Your name'
```

The program sets the AH to request display and sets the hex value 10E in the DX—the location of the DB containing your name, at the end of the program.

When you have keyed in the instructions, press Enter again. Try the U command (U 100,10D) to unassemble the program and R and then repeat T commands to trace execution. When DEBUG executes INT 21H, it traces through BIOS, so on reaching INT, use the P (proceed) command to execute directly through BIOS to the next instruction. (Don't follow it through BIOS.) Your name should display on the screen. Use the Q command to return to DOS.

EXTENDED DOS FOR KEYBOARD INPUT

DOS service 3FH requests keyboard input, although it's a clumsy operation. The BX contains the file handle 00, the CX the maximum number of characters to accept, and the DX the address of the area to enter characters. The following instructions illustrate the use of DOS service 3FH:

```
INAREA    DB     20 DUP(' ')   ;Input area
          . . .
          MOV    AH,3FH         ;Request input
          MOV    BX,00          ;File handle for keyboard
          MOV    CX,20          ;Maximum 20 characters
          LEA    DX,INAREA      ;Input area
          INT    21H            ;Call DOS
```

LEA loads the offset address of INAREA in the DX. The INT operation waits for the user to enter characters, but does not check whether the number of characters exceeds the maximum in the CX register (20 in the example). Pressing the Enter key (hex 0D) signals the end of an entry. For example, entering the characters "PC Users Group" causes the following in INAREA:

```
PC Users Group|hex 0D|hex 0A
```

The typed characters are immediately followed by Enter (hex 0D), which you typed, and Line Feed (hex 0A), which you did not type. Because of this feature, the maximum number and the length of the input area should provide for an additional two characters. If you type fewer characters than the maximum, the locations in memory following the entered characters still contain the previous contents.

A successful operation clears the carry flag (which you may test) and sets the AX with the number of characters delivered. In the preceding example, this length is 14, plus 2 for the Enter and Line Feed, or 16. Accordingly, a program can determine the actual number of characters entered. Although this feature is trivial for YES and NO type of replies, it is useful for replies with variable length such as names.

An unsuccessful operation could occur because of an invalid handle. The operation sets the carry flag and inserts an error code (6 in this case) in the AX. Since the AX could contain a length or an error code, the only way to determine an error condition is to test the carry flag.

If you key in a name that exceeds the maximum in the CX register, the operation accepts all characters. Consider a situation in which the CX contains 08 and a user enters the characters "PC Exchange." The operation sets the first eight characters in the input area as "PC Excha" with no Enter and Line Feed following, and sets the AX with a length of 08. The next INT operation does not accept a name directly from the keyboard, because it still has the rest of the previous string in its buffer. It delivers "nge" followed by the Enter and Line Feed to the input area and sets the AX to 05. Both operations are "normal" and clear the carry flag.

```
First INT:    PC Excha      AX = 08
Second INT:   nge, 0D, 0A   AX = 05
```

A program can tell whether a user has keyed in a valid number of characters if (a) the number returned in the AX is less than the number in the CX or (b) the number returned is equal and the last two characters in the input area are 0D and 0A.

The built-in checks of original DOS service 0AH for keyboard input offer a far more powerful operation and, at least at the time of this writing, that operation is the preferred choice.

Exercise: Entering Data

Here's an exercise in which you can view the effect of entering data while in DEBUG. The program allows you to key in up to 12 characters, including Enter and

Line Feed. Load DEBUG, and when the prompt appears, type A 100 to begin entering the following instructions at location 100. Remember that DEBUG treats numbers as hexadecimal.

```
100     MOV AH,3F
102     MOV BX,00
105     MOV CX,0C
108     MOV DX,10F
10B     INT 21
10D     JMP 100
10F     DB '  '
```

The program sets the AH and BX to request keyboard input, inserts the maximum length in the CX, and sets hex 10F in the DX—the location of the DB at the end of the program. The entered characters appear beginning at location hex 10F.

When you key in the instructions, press Enter again. Try the U command (U 100,108) to unassemble the program. Use R and repeated T commands to trace execution of the four MOV instructions. When at location 10B, use P (proceed) to execute through the interrupt. (Don't follow it through BIOS.) The interrupt stops to let you key in characters followed by Enter. Check the contents of the AX register, the carry flag, and use D 10F to display the entered characters in memory. You can continue looping indefinitely. Key in Q to quit.

USE OF CARRIAGE RETURN, LINE FEED, AND TAB FOR DISPLAY

One way to make displays execute faster is to use the Carriage Return, Line Feed, and Tab characters. You can code them in ASCII or hex, as

	ASCII	*Hex*
Carriage Return:	13	0DH
Line Feed:	10	0AH
Tab:	09	09H

Use these characters where you display or accept input for advancing the cursor automatically to the start of the next row, either for original or extended DOS. Here's an example:

```
MESSAGE    DB    09,'PC Users Group Annual Report',13,10
           . . .
           MOV   AH,40H        ;Request display
           MOV   BX,01         ;Handle
           MOV   CX,31         ;Length
```

```
LEA   DX,MESSAG1      ;Message
INT   21H             ;Call DOS
```

The use of EQU to define the operations makes a program more readable:

```
CR        EQU   13    (or EQU 0DH)
LF        EQU   10    (or EQU 0AH)
TAB       EQU   09    (or EQU 09H)
MESSAGE   DB    TAB, 'PC Users Group Annual Report', CR, LF
```

KEY POINTS

- Monochrome display supports 4K bytes of memory, 2K of which are available for characters and 2K for an attribute for each character.
- The original color display supports 16K bytes and can operate in color or monochrome. You can process either in text mode for normal character display or in graphics mode.
- Be consistent in using hex notation. For example, INT 21 is not the same as INT 21H.
- INT 10H is the instruction that links to BIOS for display operations. Two common operations are service 02 (set cursor) and 06 (scroll screen).
- INT 21H is a special DOS operation that handles some of the complexity of input/output.
- When using INT 21H service 09 for displaying, define a delimiter ($) immediately following the display area. Be careful when clearing the field not to clear the delimiter as well. A missing delimiter can cause spectacular effects on a screen.
- When using INT 21H service 0AH for keyboard input, define a parameter list carefully. The INT 21H operation expects the first byte to contain a maximum value and automatically inserts an actual value in the second byte.
- For extended DOS service 40H to display, use handle 01 in the BX.
- For extended DOS service 3FH for input, use handle 00 in the BX. The operation returns Enter and Line Feed characters following the typed characters in the input area. The operation does not check for entries that exceed a maximum.

QUESTIONS

8-1. What is the hex value for the bottom rightmost location on an 80-column screen?

8-2. Code the instructions to set the cursor to row 12, column 8.

8-3. Code the instructions to clear the screen beginning at row 12, column 0, through row 22, column 79.

8-4. Code data items and instructions to display a message "What is the date (mm/dd/yy)?." Follow the message with a beep sound. Use **(a)** original DOS services and **(b)** extended DOS services with file handles.

8-5. Code data items and instructions to accept data from the keyboard according to the format in Question 8-4. Use **(a)** original DOS services and **(b)** extended DOS services with file handles.

8-6. What are the standard file handles for **(a)** keyboard input, **(b)** normal screen display, and **(c)** printer?

8-7. Key in the program in Figure 8-2 with the following changes:
- Instead of row 12, center at row 15.
- Instead of clearing the entire screen, clear only rows 0 through 15.
- Assemble, link, and test it.

8-8. Revise Figure 8-2 for use with extended DOS services for input and display. Assemble, link, and test it.

9

ADVANCED SCREEN PROCESSING

OBJECTIVE

To cover advanced features of screen handling, including scrolling, reverse video, blinking, and the use of color/graphics.

INTRODUCTION

In Chapter 8 we introduced the basic features concerned with screen handling and keyboard input. This chapter provides advanced features related to video adapters, setting modes (text or graphics), and screen handling. In the first section we describe the common video adapters and their associated memory storage areas. Next we explain how you can set text or graphics mode.

Text mode allows you to display in monochrome or color, depending on the type of adapter and screen installed. We explain the use of the attribute byte for color, blinking, and high intensity, as well as the instructions to set the cursor size and location, to scroll up or down the screen, and to display characters. Also presented is the use of graphics mode, together with the various instructions used to display colors.

VIDEO ADAPTERS

The common video adapters are:

MDA   Monochrome display adapter
HGC   Hercules graphics card
CGA   Color graphics adapter
EGA   Enhanced graphics adapter
MCGA   Multicolor graphics array (PS/2 models 25 and 30)
VGA   Video graphics array

A video adapter consists of three basic units.

1. A *video controller,* the workhorse unit, generates the monitor's scan signals for the selected text or graphics mode. The computer's processor sends instructions to the controller's registers and reads status information from them.

2. A *video RAM area* in memory contains the information that the monitor is to display. The interrupts that handle screen displays transfer your data directly to the memory area. Following are the beginning segment memory addresses for major video adapters:
   B000:[0] Monochrome text mode for MDA, EGA, and VGA
   B100:[0] For HGC
   B800:[0] Text modes (color or black and white) for CGA, MCGA, EGA, and VGA and graphics modes (color or black and white) for CGA, EGA, MCGA, and VGA
   A000:[0] Used for font descriptors when in text mode and for newer video buffer high-resolution graphics for EGA, MCGA, and VGA
   The actual memory area depends on the video mode in use. The modes are listed later in Figure 9-1.

3. *Video BIOS,* which acts as an interface to the video adapter, contains such routines as setting the cursor and displaying characters.

INT 10H SERVICE 00: SETTING THE MODE

The system provides a special interrupt operation to set the mode to text or graphics. This operation can set the mode for the currently executing program or can switch between text and graphics on a color monitor. Setting the mode also clears the screen. Figure 9-1 provides common modes, with the number to the left. For example, mode 03 requests text mode, color, and a screen resolution value depending on the type of monitor. To set mode, request INT 10H, with service 00 in the AH register and a new mode in the AL. The following example sets the video mode for standard color text on any type of color monitor:

```
MOV   AH,00    ;Request set mode
MOV   AL,03    ;80×25 standard color text
INT   10H      ;Call BIOS
```

Mode	Text/ Graphics	Mono/ Color	Adapter	Resolution	Colors
00	Text (25 rows, 40 cols.)	Mono	CGA	320×200	
			EGA	320×350	
			MCGA	320×400	
			VGA	360×400	
01	Text (25 rows, 40 cols.)	Color	CGA	320×200	16 colors
			EGA	320×350	16 of 64
			MCGA	320×400	16 of 262,144
			VGA	360×400	16 of 262,144
02	Text (25 rows, 80 cols.)	Mono	CGA	640×200	
			EGA	640×350	
			MCGA	640×400	
			VGA	720×400	
03	Text (25 rows, 80 cols.)	Color	CGA	640×200	16 colors
			EGA	640×350	16 of 64
			MCGA	640×400	16 of 262,144
			VGA	720×400	16 of 262,144
04	Graphics	Color	CGA, EGA, MCGA, VGA	320×200	4 colors
05	Graphics	Mono	CGA, EGA, MCGA, VGA	320×200	
06	Graphics	Mono	CGA, EGA, MCGA, VGA	640×200	
07	Text (25 rows, 80 cols)	Mono	MDA	720×350	
			EGA	720×350	
			VGA	720×400	
0D	Graphics	Color	EGA, VGA	320×200	16 colors
0E	Graphics	Color	EGA, VGA	640×200	16 colors
0F	Graphics	Mono	EGA, VGA	640×350	
10	Graphics	Color	EGA, VGA	640×350	16 colors
11	Graphics	Color	MCGA, VGA	640×480	2 of 262,144
12	Graphics	Color	VGA	640×480	16 of 262,144
13	Graphics	Color	MCGA, VGA	320×200	256 of 262,144

Note 1: Modes 08–0A are for the PCjr
Note 2:   MDA: monochrome display adapter
          CGA: color graphics adapter
          MCGA: multicolor graphics array
          VGA: video graphics array

Figure 9-1   Modes for Video Displays

If you write software for unknown video monitors, you can use BIOS INT 11H to determine the device attached to the system, although the information is rather primitive. The operation returns a value to the AX, with bits 5 and 4 indicating video mode:

01:	40 × 25 monochrome using a color adapter
10:	80 × 25 monochrome using a color adapter
11:	80 × 25 monochrome using a monochrome adapter

You can test the AX for the type of monitor, and then set the mode accordingly.

TEXT (ALPHANUMERIC) MODE

Text mode is for normal processing of letters and numbers on the screen. Processing is similar for both monochrome and color, except that color does not support the underline attribute. Text mode provides access to the full extended ASCII 256-character set.

Attribute Byte

An *attribute byte* for both monochrome and color in text (not graphics) mode determines the characteristics of each character displayed. The attribute byte has the following format, according to bit positions:

		Background				Foreground		
Attribute:	BL	R	G	B	I	R	G	B
Bit number:	7	6	5	4	3	2	1	0

Bits 0–2 control the screen foreground (the character being displayed), and bits 4–6 control the background. The letters R, G, and B indicate a bit position for red, green, and blue, respectively, for a color monitor. Bit 3 (I) sets high intensity, and bit 7 (BL) sets blinking. For monochrome, bit 0 sets the underline attribute. On both color and monochrome, 000 is black and 111 is white. For example, 1000 0111 means white on black blinking and 0100 0001 means blue on red.

These attributes are valid for text display in both monochrome and color. When a program sets an attribute, it remains set until another operation changes it. You can use INT 10H operations to generate a screen attribute and perform such actions as scroll up, scroll down, read attribute/character, or display attribute/character. If you use DEBUG to view the video display area, you'll see each one-byte character immediately followed by its one-byte attribute.

Monochrome Display

On most monochrome monitors, the foreground is green, grey, or amber and the background black, although in this book we refer to the display as black and white (BW). To modify attributes, you may combine them as follows:

Attribute	Background				Foreground				Hex
	BL	R	G	B	I	R	G	B	
Black on black (nondisplay)	0	0	0	0	0	0	0	0	00
Underline	0	0	0	0	0	0	0	1	01
White on black, normal video	0	0	0	0	0	1	1	1	07
White on black, blinking	1	0	0	0	0	1	1	1	87
White on black, intense	0	0	0	0	1	1	1	1	0F
Black on white, reverse video	0	1	1	1	0	0	0	0	70
Black on white, reverse blinking	1	1	1	1	0	0	0	0	F0

Color Display

For many color displays, the foreground characters can be one of 16 colors and the background can be one of eight colors. Blinking and intensity apply to foreground. You can also select one of 16 colors for the border. Color monitors do not provide underlining; instead, setting the underline bit selects the blue color as foreground, thereby displaying blue on black.

The attribute byte is used the same way as was shown for a BW monitor. The three basic colors are red, green, and blue. You can combine these in the attribute byte to form a total of eight colors (including black and white), and can set high intensity for a total of 16 colors:

Color	I	R	G	B	Color	I	R	G	B
Black	0	0	0	0	Gray	1	0	0	0
Blue	0	0	0	1	Light blue	1	0	0	1
Green	0	0	1	0	Light green	1	0	1	0
Cyan	0	0	1	1	Light cyan	1	0	1	1
Red	0	1	0	0	Light red	1	1	0	0
Magenta	0	1	0	1	Light magenta	1	1	0	1
Brown	0	1	1	0	Yellow	1	1	1	0
White	0	1	1	1	High-intensity white	1	1	1	1

If foreground and background colors are the same, the displayed character is invisible. You can also use the attribute byte to cause a foreground character to blink. Here are some typical attributes:

Attribute	Background				Foreground				
	7	*6*	*5*	*4*	*3*	*2*	*1*	*0*	
	BL	*R*	*G*	*B*	*I*	*R*	*G*	*B*	*Hex*
Black on black	0	0	0	0	0	0	0	0	00
Blue on black	0	0	0	0	0	0	0	1	01
Red on blue	0	0	0	1	0	1	0	0	14
Cyan on green	0	0	1	0	0	0	1	1	23
Light magenta on white	0	1	1	1	1	1	0	1	7D
Gray on green, blinking	1	0	1	0	1	0	0	0	A8

You may want to use INT 11H to determine the type of monitor. For monochrome, use 07 to set normal attribute and, for color, use any of the color combinations just given. The color stays set until another operation changes it. Color systems for text mode also support screen pages 0–3, where 0 is the normal screen.

As an example, the following INT 10H operation uses service 09 to display five asterisks as light green on magenta, blinking:

```
MOV   AH,09        ;Request display
MOV   AL,'*'       ;Asterisk
MOV   BH,00        ;Page number 0
MOV   BL,0DAH      ;Color attribute
MOV   CX,05        ;Five times
INT   10H          ;Call BIOS
```

BIOS INTERRUPT 10H FOR TEXT MODE

INT 10H, which we used earlier to set the mode, also facilitates full-screen handling. The operation requires a service code in the AH register that determines the function of the interrupt. The interrupt preserves the contents of the BX, CX, DX, DI, SI, and BP registers, but not the AX—a point to remember if you use INT 10H in a loop. Each service is described in the following sections.

INT 10H Service 01: Set Cursor Size

The cursor is not part of the ASCII character set and exists only in text mode. The computer maintains its own hardware for its control, and there are special INT operations for its use. The normal cursor symbol is similar to an underline or break character. You can use INT 10H to adjust the cursor size vertically: Set the CH (bits 4–0) for the top ("start scan line") and the CL (bits 4–0) for the bottom ("end scan line"). You can adjust the size between the top and bottom, 0:13 for monochrome and enhanced graphics, and 0:7 for the color graphics adapter. This example enlarges the cursor from top to bottom positions for monochrome or EGA:

```
MOV  AH,01    ;Request set cursor size
MOV  CH,00    ;Start scan line
MOV  CL,13    ;End scan line
INT  10H      ;Call BIOS
```

The cursor now blinks as a solid rectangle. You can adjust its size anywhere between these bounds, such as 04:08, 03:10, and so forth. The cursor remains at this type until another operation changes it. Using 12:13 (monochrome or EGA) or 6:7 (CGA) resets the cursor to normal. If you are unsure of your monitor's bounds, type and execute service 03 under DEBUG.

INT 10H Service 02: Set Cursor Position

This useful operation sets the cursor anywhere on a screen according to row:column coordinates. Page number is normally 0, but can be 0 through 3 for 80-column text mode. The cursor location on each page is independent of the others. Load 02 in the AH, page number in the BH, and row:column in the DX:

```
MOV  AH,02    ;Request set cursor
MOV  BH,00    ;Page number 0
MOV  DH,row   ;Row
MOV  DL,col   ;Column
INT  10H      ;Call BIOS
```

INT 10H Service 03: Read Cursor Position

A program can use this service to determine the present row, column, and size of the cursor, particularly in situations where a program has to use the screen temporarily and resets the original screen. Set the page number in the BH, just as for service 02.

```
MOV  AH,03    ;Request cursor location
MOV  BH,00    ;Set page number 0 (normal)
INT  10H      ;Call BIOS
```

On return, the CH contains the starting scan line of the cursor, the CL contains the ending scan line, the DH contains the row, and the DL contains the column.

INT 10H Service 05: Select Active Page

For text modes 0–3 and 13–16, this service lets you set the page that is to display. Pages may be 0–3 in 80-column mode or 0–7 in 40-column mode.

```
MOV  AH,05    ;Request active page
MOV  AL,page# ;Page number
INT  10H      ;Call BIOS
```

INT 10H Service 06: Scroll Up Screen

You used this service in Chapter 8 to clear the screen. For text mode, setting the AL to 00 causes a scroll up of the entire screen, effectively clearing it to blank. Top lines scroll off and blank lines appear at the bottom.

Inserting a nonzero value in the AL causes that number of lines to scroll up. When a program displays down the screen past the bottom, the next line wraps around to start at the top. But even if the interrupt operation specifies column 0, the new lines are indented and succeeding lines may be badly skewed. The solution is to scroll the screen. Load the number of lines in the AL, attribute in the BH, starting row:column in the CX, and ending row:column in the DX.

```
MOV   AX,0601H    ;Scroll up one line
MOV   BH,30H      ;Black on cyan
MOV   CX,0000     ;From 00,00
MOV   DX,184FH    ;  to 24,79 (full screen)
INT   10H         ;Call BIOS
```

Here's a standard approach to scrolling one line:

1. Define an item named ROW, initialized to 0, for setting the row location of the cursor.
2. Display a line and advance the cursor to the next line.
3. Test if ROW is near the bottom of the screen (CMP ROW,22).
4. If no, increment ROW (INC ROW) and exit.
5. If yes, scroll one line, use ROW to set the cursor, and clear ROW to 00.

The CX and DX registers permit scrolling any portion of the screen. But watch for matching the AL value with the distance in the CX:DX, especially where you reference a partial screen. The following instructions scroll five lines, in effect creating a *window* at the center of the screen with its own attributes:

```
MOV AX,0605H   ;Scroll five lines
MOV BH,61H     ;Blue on brown
MOV CX,0A1CH   ;From row 10, column 28
MOV DX,0E34H   ;  to row 14, column 52 (part screen)
INT 10H        ;Call BIOS
```

Note that the attribute set for a window remains until another operation changes it. Thus you may set various windows to different attributes at the same time.

INT 10H Service 07: Scroll Down Screen

For text mode, scrolling down the screen causes the bottom lines to scroll off and blank lines to appear at the top. Set the AH to 07 and set the AL, BH, CX, and DX registers just as for service 06, scroll up.

INT 10H Service 08: Read Attribute/Character at Cursor Position

This service can read both character and attribute from the display area in either text or graphics mode. Page number is normally 0, but can be 0 through 3 for 80-column text mode. Load the page number in the BH, as this example shows:

```
MOV  AH,08    ;Request read attribute/character
MOV  BH,00    ;Page number 0 (normal)
INT  10H      ;Call BIOS
```

The operation returns the character in the AL and its attribute in the AH. In graphics mode, the operation returns hex 00 for a non-ASCII character. Since this operation reads one character at a time, you have to code a loop to read successive characters.

INT 10H Service 09: Display Attribute/Character at Cursor Position

Here's a fun operation to display characters in text or graphics mode with blinking, reverse video, and all that. The AL contains a single ASCII character that is to display any number of times. The BH contains the page number, the BL contains the attribute, and the value in the CX determines the number of times to repetitively display the character in the AL, as follows:

```
MOV  AH,09          ;Request display
MOV  AL,character   ;Character to display
MOV  BH,page#       ;Page number
MOV  BL,attribute   ;Attribute (text) or color (graphics)
MOV  CX,repetition  ;Number of repeated characters
INT  10H            ;Call BIOS
```

The operation does not advance the cursor or respond to Bell, Carriage Return, Line Feed, or Tab characters (it attempts to display them as ASCII characters). Displaying different characters requires a loop. The following example displays five blinking hearts with reverse video:

```
MOV  AH,09    ;Request display
MOV  AL,03H   ;Heart
```

```
MOV  BH,00        ;Page number 0 (normal)
MOV  BL,0F0H      ;Blink reverse video
MOV  CX,05        ;Five times
INT  10H          ;Call BIOS
```

In text but not graphics mode, displayed characters automatically carry over from one line to the next. To display a prompt or message, code a routine that sets the CX to 01 and loops to move one character at a time from memory into the AL. (Since the CX is occupied, you can't use the LOOP instruction.) Also, when displaying each character, you have to use service 02 to advance the cursor to the next column.

For graphics mode, use the BL for defining the foreground color. If bit 7 is 0, the defined color replaces present pixel colors; if bit 7 is 1, the defined color is combined (XORed) with them.

You can use this service to change any valid video page and then use service 05 to display the page.

INT 10H Service 0AH: Display Character at Cursor Position

This operation displays characters in text or graphics mode. The only difference between service 0AH and 09H in text mode is that service 0AH uses the current attribute.

```
MOV  AH,0AH       ;Request display
MOV  AL,char      ;Character to display
MOV  BH,page#     ;Page number
MOV  CX,repetition ;Number of repeated characters
INT  10H          ;Call BIOS
```

DOS interrupt 21H services that can print a string of characters and respond to screen control characters are often more convenient.

INT 10H Service 0EH: Write Teletype

This operation lets you use a monitor as a terminal for simple displays. Set the AH to 0EH, the character to display in the AL, page number (normal) in the BH, and foreground color (graphics mode) in the BL.

```
MOV  AH,0EH       ;Request display
MOV  AL,char      ;Character to display
MOV  BH,page#     ;Page number
MOV  BL,color     ;Foreground color (graphics mode)
INT  10H          ;Call BIOS
```

Backspace (08H), Bell (07H), Carriage Return (0DH), and Line Feed (0AH) act as commands for screen formatting. The operation automatically advances the cursor, wraps characters onto the next line, scrolls the screen, and maintains the present screen attributes.

INT 10H Service 0FH: Get Current Video Mode

This operation returns mode (see service 00) in the AL, characters per line in the AH (20, 40, or 80), and page number in the BH.

INT 10H Service 11H: Character Generator

For EGA, MCGA, and VGA systems, this complex service initiates a mode set and resets the video environment. A discussion is outside the scope of this book.

INT 10H Service 12H: Select Alternate Screen Routine

This service supports EGAs and VGAs. To get EGA information, load 10H in the BL; the operation returns:

BH	00H for color and 01H for monochrome
BL	00H for 64K, 01H for 128K, 02H for 192K, and 03H for 256K
CH	Adapter bits
CL	Switch setting

The service supports a number of elaborate functions for PS/2 computers such as 30H (select scan lines), 31H (default palette loading), and 34H (cursor emulation).

INT 10H Service 13H: Display Character String

For EGAs and VGAs, the operation displays strings with options of setting attributes and moving the cursor, and acts on Backspace, Bell, Carriage Return, and Line Feed.

```
MOV  AH,13H          ;Request display
MOV  AL,function     ;0, 1, 2, or 3
MOV  BH,page#        ;Page number
MOV  BL,attribute    ;Screen attribute
LEA  BP,address      ;Address of string in ES:BP
MOV  CX,length       ;Length of string
MOV  DX,screen       ;Relative starting location on screen
INT  10H             ;Call BIOS
```

The four functions in the AL are:

0   Display attribute and string; do not advance cursor.
1   Display attribute and string; advance cursor.
2   Display character then attribute; do not advance cursor.
3   Display character then attribute; advance cursor.

USING BIOS TO DISPLAY THE ASCII CHARACTER SET

Figure 8-1 used DOS to display the ASCII character set, but the operation acted on Backspace, Bell, Carriage Return, and Line Feed control characters. The revised program in Figure 9-2 illustrates the use of BIOS INT 10H for the following services:

08H   Read the attribute at the current cursor position, for use by service 06H.

06H   Scroll up the screen to clear the entire screen using the attribute just read. Also, create a 16-line window with brown foreground and blue background for the displayed characters.

02H   Set the cursor initially and to advance for each displayed character.

0AH   Display each character at the current cursor position, including control characters.

```
        TITLE   BIOASC (COM)  Use BIOS to display ASCII character set
                .MODEL  SMALL
                .CODE
                ORG     100H
        BEGIN:  JMP     SHORT MAIN
        CTR     DB      00              ;Counter for ASCII characters
        COL     DB      24              ;Column of screen
        ROW     DB      04              ;Row of screen
        ;               Main procedure:
        ;               --------------
        MAIN    PROC    NEAR
                CALL    B10CLR          ;Clear screen
        A20:    CALL    C10SET          ;Set cursor
                CALL    D10DISP         ;Display characters
                CMP     CTR,0FFH        ;Last character displayed?
                JE      A30             ;  yes -- exit
                INC     CTR             ;Increment ASCII counter
                ADD     COL,02          ;Increment column
                CMP     COL,56          ;At end of column?
                JNE     A20             ;  no -- bypass
                INC     ROW             ;  yes - increment row
                MOV     COL,24          ;  and reset column
                JMP     A20
        A30:    MOV     AH,4CH          ;Exit to DOS
                INT     21H
        MAIN    ENDP
```

Figure 9-2 BIOS to Display the ASCII Character Set

```
;               Clear screen and create window:
;               ------------------------------
B10CLR  PROC    NEAR
        MOV     AH,08           ;Request get current
        INT     10H             ;  attribute in AH
        MOV     BH,AH           ;Move it to BH
        MOV     AX,0600H        ;Scroll whole screen
        MOV     CX,0000         ;Upper left location
        MOV     DX,184FH        ;Lower right location
        INT     10H
        MOV     AX,0610H        ;Create 16-line window
        MOV     BH,16H          ;Brown on blue
        MOV     CX,0418H        ;Upper left corner 04:24
        MOV     DX,1336H        ;Lower right corner 19:54
        INT     10H
        RET
B10CLR  ENDP
;               Set cursor to row and column:
;               -----------------------------
C10SET  PROC    NEAR
        MOV     AH,02           ;Request set cursor
        MOV     BH,00           ;Page 0 (normal)
        MOV     DH,ROW          ;New row
        MOV     DL,COL          ;New column
        INT     10H
        RET
C10SET  ENDP

                Display ASCII characters:
;               -------------------------
D10DISP PROC    NEAR
        MOV     AH,0AH          ;Display
        MOV     AL,CTR          ;ASCII char
        MOV     BH,00           ;Page 0
        MOV     CX,01           ;One character
        INT     10H
        RET
D10DISP ENDP
        END     BEGIN
```

Figure 9-2 Cont.

Characters display in 16 columns and 16 rows. This program, like others in this book, are written for clarity rather than efficiency. You could revise the program to make it more efficient, such as using registers for the row, column, and ASCII character generator. Also, INT 10H destroys only the AX register, and values in other registers don't have to be reloaded. However, the program won't run noticeably faster and it would lose clarity.

BLINKING, REVERSE VIDEO, AND SCROLLING

The program in Figure 9-3 accepts names from the keyboard and displays them on the screen. This program, however, displays the prompt with reverse video (blue on white), accepts the name normally (white on blue), and displays the name at column 40 on the same row with blinking and reverse video. Here is the format:

```
        Name? Francis Bacon     Francis Bacon [blinking]
         |                        |
   Column 0                 Column 40
```

```
            page     60,132
    TITLE   NMSCROLL (EXE) Reverse video, blinking, scrolling
            .MODEL   SMALL
            .STACK   64
;   ------------------------------------------------------
            .DATA
    NAMEPAR LABEL    BYTE               ;Name parameter list:
    MAXNLEN DB       20                 ;  maximum length of name
    ACTNLEN DB       ?                  ;  no. of chars entered
    NAMEFLD DB       20 DUP(' ')        ;  name

    COL     DB       00
    COUNT   DB       ?
    PROMPT  DB       'Name? '
    ROW     DB       00
;   ------------------------------------------------------
            .CODE
    BEGIN   PROC     FAR
            MOV      AX,@data
            MOV      DS,AX
            MOV      ES,AX
            MOV      AX,0600H
            CALL     Q10SCR             ;Clear screen
    A20LOOP:
            MOV      COL,00             ;Set column to 0
            CALL     Q20CURS
            CALL     B10PRMP            ;Display prompt
            CALL     D10INPT            ;Provide for input of name
            CMP      ACTNLEN,00         ;No name? (indicates end)
            JNE      A30
            MOV      AX,0600H
            CALL     Q10SCR             ;If so, clear screen,
            MOV      AH,4CH             ;  and terminate
            INT      21H
    A30:
            CALL     E10NAME            ;Display name
            JMP      A20LOOP
    BEGIN   ENDP
;                    Display prompt:
;                    --------------
    B10PRMP PROC     NEAR
            LEA      SI,PROMPT          ;Set address of prompt
            MOV      COUNT,05
    B20:
            MOV      BL,71H             ;Reverse video
            CALL     F10DISP            ;Display routine
            INC      SI                 ;Next character in name
            INC      COL                ;Next column
            CALL     Q20CURS
            DEC      COUNT              ;Countdown
            JNZ      B20                ;Loop n times
            RET
    B10PRMP ENDP
;                    Accept input of name:
;                    --------------------
    D10INPT PROC     NEAR
            MOV      AH,0AH             ;Request input
            LEA      DX,NAMEPAR
            INT      21H
            RET
    D10INPT ENDP
;                    Display name with blinking reverse video:
;                    ---------------------------------------
    E10NAME PROC     NEAR
            LEA      SI,NAMEFLD         ;Initialize name
            MOV      COL,40             ;Set screen column
    E20:
            CALL     Q20CURS            ;Set cursor
            MOV      BL,0F1H            ;Blink reverse video
```

Figure 9-3 Blinking, Reverse Video, and Scrolling

```
            CALL    F10DISP          ;Display routine
            INC     SI               ;Next character in name
            INC     COL              ;Next screen column
            DEC     ACTNLEN          ;Countdown name length
            JNZ     E20              ;Loop n times

            CMP     ROW,20           ;Near bottom screen?
            JAE     E30
            INC     ROW              ;  no - increment row
            RET
E30:
            MOV     AX,0601H         ;  yes -
            CALL    Q10SCR           ;  scroll screen
            RET
E10NAME ENDP
;                   Display character:
;                   ------------------
F10DISP PROC        NEAR             ;BL (attribute) set on entry
            MOV     AH,09            ;Request display
            MOV     AL,[SI]          ;Get name character
            MOV     BH,00            ;Page number
            MOV     CX,01            ;One character
            INT     10H              ;Call BIOS
            RET
F10DISP ENDP
;                   Scroll screen:
;                   -------------
Q10SCR  PROC        NEAR             ;AX set on entry
            MOV     BH,17H           ;White on blue
            MOV     CX,0000
            MOV     DX,184FH
            INT     10H              ;Call BIOS
            RET
Q10SCR  ENDP
;                   Set cursor row/col:
;                   -------------------
Q20CURS PROC        NEAR
            MOV     AH,02
            MOV     BH,00
            MOV     DH,ROW           ;Row
            MOV     DL,COL           ;Column
            INT     10H
            RET
Q20CURS ENDP

            END     BEGIN
```

Figure 9-3   Cont.

To control cursor placement, the program defines ROW for incrementing the row and COL for moving the cursor horizontally when displaying the prompt and name. (INT 10H service 09 does not automatically advance the cursor.) The program displays down the screen until it reaches row 20 and then begins scrolling up one line for each additional prompt.

For input, the procedure D10INPT uses DOS operation INT 21H, service 0AH.

EXTENDED ASCII CHARACTERS

ASCII characters 128–255 (hex 80–FF) provide a number of special characters that are useful for displaying prompts, menus, and logos. For example, use these characters to draw a rectangle with solid lines:

Hex	Character
DA	Top left corner angle
BF	Top right corner angle
C0	Bottom left corner angle
D9	Bottom right corner angle
C4	Solid horizontal line
B3	Solid vertical line

The following example uses INT 10H service 09 to draw a solid horizontal line 25 positions long:

```
MOV  AH,09      ;Request display
MOV  AL,0C4H    ;Solid line
MOV  BH,00      ;Page number 0
MOV  BL,0FH     ;White on black, intense
MOV  CX,25      ;25 repetitions
INT  10H        ;Call BIOS
```

Remember that this service does not advance the cursor. The simplest way to display a box is to define it in the data segment and display the whole area. The "dots on" characters for shaded areas can also be useful:

Hex	Character
B0	One-quarter dots on (light)
B1	One-half dots on (medium)
B2	Three-quarter dots on (dark)

You can derive many good ideas from examining the displays of professionally designed software, or let your imagination dream up some original ideas.

DOS SERVICE 02 TO DISPLAY

You may find DOS service 02 useful for displaying single characters. Load in the DL the character that is to display at the current cursor position, and request INT 21H. Tab, Carriage Return, and Line Feed act normally.

```
MOV  AH,02      ;Request display character
MOV  DL,char    ;Character to display
INT  21H
```

GRAPHICS MODE

This section covers the use of graphics mode. The common RGB video monitor used to display color graphics accepts input signals that are sent to three separate electron guns—red, green, and blue, for each of the primary additive colors.

The EGA (enhanced graphics adapter) and the VGA (video graphics array) provide for significantly better resolution than the original color graphics adapter (CGA) and in many ways are compatible. Resolutions are shown in Figure 9-1.

The graphics adapters have two basic modes of operation: text (or alphanumeric) and graphics, with additional modes possible between these basic modes. The default mode is text. Use BIOS interrupt INT 10H service 00 to set graphics mode or to return to text mode, as the following two examples show:

1. Set medium graphics mode:

```
        MOV  AH,00    ;Set mode
        MOV  AL,04    ;Medium graphics
        INT  10H
```

2. Set text mode:

```
        MOV  AH,00    ;Set mode
        MOV  AL,03    ;Color text
        INT  10H
```

Graphics mode uses pixels (picture elements, or pels) to generate color patterns. The color/graphics adapter (CGA) has three resolutions:

1. *Low resolution,* not supported by ROM, provides a display of 100 rows of 160 pixels (that is, four bits per pixel). Each pixel can consist of the standard 16 colors as described earlier. Producing this mode involves direct addressing of the Motorola 6845 CRT Controller.
2. *Medium resolution* for standard color graphics provides 200 rows of 320 pixels. Each byte represents four pixels (that is, two bits per pixel).
3. *High resolution* provides 200 rows of 640 pixels. Since it requires the full 16K bytes of color/graphics storage, high-resolution graphics can support only BW. Each byte represents eight pixels (that is, one bit per pixel) providing for 0 (black) and 1 (white).

Note that for graphics mode, ROM contains dot patterns for only the first (bottom) 128 characters. INT 1FH provides access to a 1K area in memory that defines the top 128 characters, eight bytes per character. The mapping of graphics bytes to video scan lines is the same for both medium- and high-resolution graphics.

Medium-Resolution Mode

Under medium-resolution mode, each byte represents four pixels, numbered 0 through 3, as follows:

byte:

C1 C0	C1 C0	C1 C0	C1 C0

pixel: 0   1   2   3

At any given time there are four available colors numbered 0 through 3. The limitation of four colors is because a 2-bit pixel provides four bit combinations: 00, 01, 10, and 11. You can choose pixel 00 for any one of the 16 available colors for background, and choose pixel 01, 10, and 11 for any one of two three-color palettes:

C1	C0	Palette 0	Palette 1
0	0	background	background
0	1	green	cyan
1	0	red	magenta
1	1	brown	white

Use INT 10H service 0BH to select a color palette and the background. Thus, if you choose background color yellow and palette 0, available colors are yellow, green, red, and brown. A byte consisting of the pixel value 10101010 would display as all red. If you choose background color blue and palette 1, available colors are blue, cyan, magenta, and white. A byte consisting of pixel value 00011011 displays blue, cyan, magenta, and white.

BIOS INTERRUPT 10H FOR GRAPHICS

INT 10H facilitates full screen handling for both graphics and text mode, as described earlier. The operation preserves the contents of the BX, CX, DX, DI, SI, and BP registers, but not the AX. We describe each function in the following sections.

INT 10H Service 00: Set Mode

An earlier section, "BIOS Interrupt 10H for Text Mode," covered this service in detail for setting mode for color or monochrome text and for graphics. Service 00 in the AH and 04 in the AL set standard color graphics mode:

```
MOV  AH,00   ;Set mode for
MOV  AL,04   ;  320 × 200 resolution
INT  10H
```

Setting graphics mode causes the cursor to disappear.

INT 10H Service 04: Read Light Pen Position

Use this service with graphics to determine the status of a light pen. The operation returns the following information:

AH   0 if status is not triggered and 1 if triggered.
DX   Row in the DH and column in the DL.
CH/BX   Pixel location, with raster (horizontal) line in the BH and column/dot in the BX.

INT 10H Service 08: Read Attribute/Character at Cursor Position

This service can read both character and attribute from the display area in either text or graphics mode. See the earlier section "BIOS Interrupt 10H for Text Mode."

INT 10H Service 09: Display Attribute/Character at Current Cursor Position

See the earlier section "BIOS Interrupt 10H for Text Mode."

INT 10H Service 0AH: Display a Character at Cursor Position

See the earlier section "BIOS Interrupt 10H for Text Mode."

INT 10H Service 0BH: Set Color Palette

Use this service to set the color palette and display a graphics character. The value in the BH (00 or 01) determines the purpose of the BL register:

BH = 00   (1) Select the background color for 320×200 graphics, (2) select the border color, or (3) select the foreground color. The BL contains the color value (0–31).
BH = 01   Select the palette for 320×200 graphics. The BL contains the palette (0 or 1).

The following example selects palette 0:

```
MOV  AH,0BH   ;Request color
MOV  BH,01    ;Select palette
MOV  BL,00    ;  number 0 (green, red, brown)
INT  10H      ;Call BIOS
```

To keep the same palette, you need set it only once. But once you change palette, the entire screen changes to that color combination. If you use service 0BH while in text mode, the value set for color 0 for the palette determines the border color.

INT 10H Service 0CH: Write Pixel Dot

Use service 0CH to display a selected color (background and palette). Set the CX for column and DX for row. The minimum value for column or row is 0, and the maximum value depends on the video mode. The AL contains the color of the pixel: 0–3 for medium-resolution graphics and 0–1 for high-resolution graphics.

```
MOV  AH,0CH       ;Request write dot
MOV  AL,color     ;Color of pixel
MOV  CX,column    ;Horizontal position
MOV  DX,row       ;Vertical position
INT  10H          ;Call BIOS
```

INT 10H Service 0DH: Read Pixel Dot

This operation, the opposite of service 0CH, reads a dot to determine its color value. Set the CX for column and DX for row. The minimum value for column or row is 0, and the maximum value depends on the video mode. The operation returns the pixel color in the AL.

INT 10H Service 0EH: Write Teletype

See the earlier section "BIOS Interrupt 10H for Text Mode."

INT 10H Service 10H: Set Palette Registers

This service handles EGA and VGA systems. A function code in the AL determines the operation:

00   Set a palette register, where the BH contains the value to set and the BL contains the register to set.
01   Set the overscan register, where the BH contains the value to set.
02   Set all palette registers and overscan. ES:DX points to a 17-byte table, where bytes 0–15 are palette values and byte 16 is an overscan value.
03   Toggle intensify/blinking bit, where 00 in the BL enables intensify and 01 enables blinking.

Other AL function codes for the VGA are 07 (read individual palette register), 08 (read overscan register), 09 (read all palette registers and overscan), 10H (set individual color register), 12H (set block of color registers), 13H (select color page),

15H (read individual color register), 17H (read block of color registers), and 1AH (read color page state).

INT 10H Service 1AH: Read/Write Display Combination Code

For PS/2 systems, the service returns codes that identify the type of display.

INT 10H Service 1BH: Return Functionality/State Information

For PS/2 systems, the service returns information to a 64-byte buffer identifying video mode, cursor size, page supported, and so forth.

INT 10H Service 1CH: Save/Restore Video State

For PS/2 systems, the service provides for saving and restoring the video state.

SETTING GRAPHICS MODE AND DISPLAYING COLOR

The program in Figure 9-4 uses INT 10H service 10H for setting graphics mode, service 0BH for selecting background color green, and service 0CH for writing pixel dots for 640 rows and 350 columns. The program increments the color for each row, and since only the rightmost three bits are used, the colors repeat after every seven rows. Note that rows and columns are in terms of dots, not characters. The display begins 64 columns from the left and ends 64 columns from the right.

The program resets the display to text mode. You can also change mode by means of the DOS MODE command (MODE CO80 for color or MODE MONO for monochrome) or by your own program that simply uses INT 10H service 00.

DETERMINING TYPE OF VIDEO ADAPTER

Since the video graphics adapters support various services, there may be times when you want to know what type of adapter is installed in a system. The recommended way is to check first for a VGA, then for an EGA, and last for CGA or MDA. Here are the steps:

1. Determine whether a VGA is installed:

```
MOV   AH,1AH      ;Request VGA service
MOV   AL,0        ; and function 0
INT   10H         ;
CMP   AL,1AH      ;If AL contains 1AH on return,
JE    VGAFOUND    ; system contains a VGA
```

```
TITLE     GRAPHIX (COM)  Display color/graphics
          .MODEL SMALL
          .CODE
          ORG    100H
BEGIN     PROC   NEAR
          CALL   B10MODE        ;Set mode and palette
          CALL   C10DISP        ;Display color/graphics
          CALL   D10RSET        ;Reset mode to text
          MOV    AH,4CH         ;Exit
          INT    21H

B10MODE   PROC   NEAR
          MOV    AH,00          ;Set EGA graphics mode
          MOV    AL,10H         ;640 X 350 (04H for CGA)
          INT    10H
          MOV    AH,0BH         ;Set color palette
          MOV    BH,00          ;Background
          MOV    BL,02          ;Green
          INT    10H
          RET
B10MODE   ENDP

C10DISP   PROC   NEAR
          MOV    BX,00          ;Set initial color,
          MOV    CX,64          ;  column,
          MOV    DX,70          ;  and row
C20:
          MOV    AH,0CH         ;Write pixel dot
          MOV    AL,BL          ;Set color
          INT    10H            ;BX, CX, & DX are preserved
          INC    CX             ;Increment column
          CMP    CX,576         ;Column at 576?
          JNE    C20            ;  no -- loop
          MOV    CX,64          ;  yes - reset column
          INC    BL             ;Change color
          INC    DX             ;Increment row
          CMP    DX,140         ;Row at 140?
          JNE    C20            ;  no  - loop
          RET                   ;  yes - terminate
C10DISP   ENDP

D10RSET   PROC   NEAR
          MOV    AH,00          ;Reset text mode
          MOV    AL,03
          INT    10H
          RET
D10RSET   ENDP
BEGIN     ENDP
          END    BEGIN
```

Figure 9-4   Color/Graphics Display

2. Determine whether an EGA is installed:

```
MOV  AH,12H      ;Request EGA service
MOV  BL,10H      ;Amount of EGA memory
INT  10H
CMP  BL,10H      ;If BL no longer contains 10H,
JNE  EGAFOUND    ;  system contains an EGA
```

However, since an EGA may be installed along with an MDA or CGA, you may want to determine whether it is active. The BIOS data area at 40:0087 contains an EGA instruction byte. Check bit 3: 0 means that the EGA is active and 1 means that it is inactive.

3. Determine whether a CGA or MDA is installed. Examine the word at location 40:0063, which contains the base address of the memory controller: 3BxH means MDA and 3DxH means CGA.

KEY POINTS

- The attribute byte is available in text mode for both monochrome and color display and provides for blinking, reverse video, and high intensity. For color text, the RGB bits enable you to select colors but not underlining.
- BIOS INT 10H provides services for full screen processing such as setting mode, setting cursor location, scrolling the screen, reading from the keyboard, and writing characters.
- If your program displays lines down the screen, use BIOS INT 10H service 06 to scroll up before the display reaches the bottom.
- For INT 10H services that display, you have to advance the cursor and possibly echo the character to the screen.
- The 16K memory for color display permits storing additional "pages" or "screens." There are four pages for 80-column screens and eight pages for 40-column screens.
- Graphics mode provides for low resolution (not supported by ROM), medium resolution (for normal color graphics), and high resolution (for BW graphics).
- A pixel (picture element) consists of a specified number of bits depending on the graphics adapter and the resolution (low, medium, or high).
- Under medium-resolution graphics on the color/graphics adapter (CGA), you can select four colors of which one is any of the 16 available colors and the other three are from a color palette.

QUESTIONS

9-1. Provide the attributes in binary for monochrome screens for the following: **(a)** underline only; **(b)** white on black, normal intensity; **(c)** reverse video, intense.

9-2. Provide the attribute bytes in binary for the following: **(a)** magenta on light cyan; **(b)** brown on yellow; **(c)** red on gray; blinking.

9-3. Code the following routines: **(a)** Set the mode for 80-column monochrome; **(b)** set the cursor type for start line 5 and end line 12; **(c)** scroll up the screen 10 lines; **(d)** display ten blinking "dots" with one-half dots on (hex B1).

9-4. Under text mode, how many colors are available for background and for foreground on the color graphics adapter (CGA)?

9-5. Code the instructions for displaying five diamond characters in text mode with light green on magenta.

9-6. What hardware and mode permit the use of screen pages?

9-7. Write a program that uses DOS INT 21H service 0AH to accept data from the keyboard and service 09 to display the data. The program clears the screen, sets screen colors (you decide), and accepts a set of data from the keyboard from the current position of the cursor. The set of data could be four or five lines (say, any length up to 25 characters) entered from the keyboard, each line followed by Enter. You could use a variety of colors, reverse video, or beeping as an experiment. Then set the cursor to a different row and column (you decide), and display the entered data at that location. The program is to accept any number of sets of data. It could terminate when the user presses ⟨Enter⟩ with no data. Write the program with a short main logic routine and a series of called subroutines. Include some concise comments.

9-8. Revise the program in Question 9-7 so that it uses INT 16H for keyboard input and INT 10H service 09 for display.

9-9. Explain the reason for the number of colors available under low-, medium-, and high-resolution graphics.

9-10. Code the instructions to set graphics mode for **(a)** 320 × 200 resolution on the CGA and **(b)** 640 × 200 on the EGA.

9-11. Code the instructions for selecting background color blue in graphics mode.

9-12. Code the instructions to read a dot from row 12, column 13 in graphics mode.

9-13. Revise Figure 9-2 for the following: **(a)** graphics mode for your own monitor; **(b)** background color red; **(c)** row beginning at 10 and ending at 30; **(d)** column beginning at 20 and ending at 300.

10

ADVANCED KEYBOARD PROCESSING

OBJECTIVES

To cover all the keyboard operations and advanced features of keyboard input, including shift status, keyboard buffer, and scan codes.

INTRODUCTION

Chapter 8 used services 0AH and 3FH for INT 21H to handle keyboard input. These are only two of many ways to request keyboard actions. Of these ways, service 0AH and INT 16H should provide almost all the keyboard input you'll require.

Other topics include the keyboard shift state, scan codes, and keyboard buffer area. The shift state in the BIOS area enables you to determine, for example, whether Ctrl, Shift, or Alt have been pressed. The scan code is a unique number assigned to each key on the keyboard that enables the system to identify the source of a pressed key and enables a program to check for non-ASCII keys such as Home, PgUp, and Arrows. Appendix F contains the scan codes for each key on the keyboard. The keyboard buffer area provides space in memory for you to type ahead before a program actually requests input.

SHIFT STATUS

The BIOS data area at segment hex 40[0] contains a number of useful data items. These include the first byte of the current *shift status* at 40:17H, where a 1-bit indicates the following:

Bit	Action	Bit	Action
7	Insert toggled	3	Alt pressed
6	CapsLock state toggled	2	Ctrl pressed
5	NumLock state toggled	1	Left Shift pressed
4	Scroll Lock state toggled	0	Right Shift pressed

You may use INT 16H service 02 (covered later) to check these values. The second byte of the keyboard status is at 40:18H, where a 1-bit indicates the following:

Bit	Action	Bit	Action
7	Insert pressed	3	Ctrl/NumLock (pause) pressed
6	CapsLock pressed	2	SysReq pressed
5	NumLock pressed	1	Left Alt pressed
4	Scroll Lock pressed	0	Left Ctrl pressed

Bits 0, 1, and 2 are associated with the IBM extended (101-key) keyboard. Two other keyboard bytes are described in Chapter 23.

Shift Status Exercise

To see the effect of the Ctrl, Alt, and Shift keys on the shift status bytes, load DEBUG for execution. Enter D 40:17 to view the contents of the status bytes. Press the CapsLock, NumLock, and ScrollLock keys and enter D 40:17 again to see the result on both status bytes. The byte at 40:17 should show 70, and 40:18 is probably 00. You could try various combinations, although it's difficult to type a valid DEBUG command while holding down the Ctrl and Alt keys. Enter Q to quit.

KEYBOARD BUFFER

An item of interest in the BIOS data area at 40:1EH is the *keyboard buffer*. This area allows you to type up to 15 characters ahead before a program requests input. When you press a key, the keyboard's processor generates the key's scan code (its unique assigned number) and requests INT 09.

In simple terms, the BIOS interrupt routine gets the scan code from the keyboard, converts it to an ASCII character, and delivers it to the keyboard buffer area. Subsequently, BIOS INT 16H (the lowest-level keyboard operation) reads the character from the buffer and delivers it to your program. However, your program need never request INT 09, because it occurs automatically when you press a key. A later section covers INT 09 and the keyboard buffer in detail.

DOS INTERRUPT 21H FOR KEYBOARD INPUT

This section covers the DOS services for keyboard input. All of these operations except service 0AH accept only one character. [To handle a string of characters, you would have to code a loop that accepts a character, checks for the Backspace and Enter keys, displays (echoes) the character to the screen (if necessary), and advances the cursor.] For DOS keyboard input, insert a service call in the AH and request INT 21H.

INT 21H Service 01: Keyboard Input with Echo

The operation accepts a character from the keyboard buffer or, if none is available, waits for a keyboard entry. The operation returns one of two actions. If the AL is nonzero, it contains a standard ASCII character, such as a letter or number, which the operation echoes on the screen. Zero in the AL means that the user has pressed an extended function key such as Home, F1, or PgUp. To get its scan code in the AL, immediately repeat the service. The operation also responds to a Ctrl/Break request. The following illustrates:

```
        MOV   AH,01     ;Request keyboard input
        INT   21H
        CMP   AL,00     ;Extended function key pressed?
        JNZ   ...       ;  no--ASCII character
        INT   21H       ;  yes--repeat operation
```

INT 21H Service 06: Direct Console I/O

This rather obscure operation can transfer any possible character and control code with no interference from DOS. There are two versions, for input and for output. For input, load 0FFH in the DL. If no character is in the buffer, the operation sets the zero flag and does not wait for input. If a character is waiting in the buffer, the operation stores the character in the AL and clears the zero flag. The operation does not echo the character on the screen and does not check for Ctrl/Break or Ctrl/PrtSc. If the AL is nonzero, it represents a standard ASCII character, such as a letter or number. Zero in the AL means that the user has pressed a special function key such as Home, F1, or PgUp. To get its scan code in the AL, immediately repeat the service.

```
K10:    MOV   AH,06
        MOV   DL,0FFH   ;Request keyboard input
        INT   21H
        JZ    K10       ;Buffer empty--repeat
        CMP   AL,00     ;Extended function key pressed?
        JNZ   K30       ;  no--ASCII character
        INT   21H       ;  yes--repeat operation
```

You can force the operation to wait for keyboard input by coding the first INT in a loop:

```
K20:    INT   21H
        JZ    K20    ;Buffer empty, try again
```

For output on the screen, store the ASCII character (not 0FFH) in the DL.

INT 21H Service 07: Direct Keyboard Input without Echo

This operation works like service 01 except that the character entered does not echo on the screen and the operation does not respond to a Ctrl/Break request. You could use this operation for password input or where you don't want to disturb the screen.

INT 21H Service 08: Keyboard Input without Echo

This operation works like service 01 except that the character entered does not echo on the screen.

INT 21H Service 0AH: Buffered Keyboard Input

This is the most powerful and useful of the DOS keyboard operations and is covered in detail in Chapter 8.

INT 21H Service 0BH: Check Keyboard Status

The operation returns hex FF in the AL if an input character is available or 00 if no character is available. This service is related to services that do not wait for keyboard input.

INT 21H Service 0CH: Clear Keyboard Buffer and Invoke Service

You may use this operation in association with services 01, 06, 07, 08, or 0AH. Load the required service in the AL:

```
MOV  AH,0CH      ;Request keyboard input
MOV  AL,service  ;Service call
MOV  DX,KBAREA   ;Keyboard area for service 0AH
INT  21H
```

The operation first clears the keyboard buffer, executes the service in the AL, and accepts (or waits for) a character. You could use this operation for a program that does not allow typing ahead, such as some DOS programs.

BIOS INTERRUPT 16H FOR KEYBOARD INPUT

BIOS INT 16H, the basic BIOS keyboard operation used extensively by software developers, provides the following input commands according to a service code in the AH. The operation is fairly dependent on IBM ROM BIOS compatibility.

INT 16H Service 00: Read a Character

The operation checks the keyboard buffer for a character. If none is available, the operation waits for one. If a character is available, the operation returns it in the AL and its scan code in the AH. (A later section covers scan codes.) If the pressed key is an extended function such as Home or F1, the character is 00H. Here are the two possibilities:

Key pressed:	AH	AL
Regular ASCII character:	scan code	ASCII character
Extended function key:	scan code	zero

In this way you can test the AL for zero to determine whether the user pressed a function key:

```
MOV  AH,00    ;Request BIOS input
INT  16H
CMP  AL,00    ;Extended function key?
```

Since the operation does not echo the character to the screen, you have to issue a screen display interrupt for this purpose.

INT 16H Service 01: Determine If a Character Is Available

The operation is similar to service 00. If a character is available in the keyboard buffer, the operation clears the zero flag (ZF = 0) and delivers the character to the AL and its scan code to the AH; the entry remains in the buffer. If no character is available, the operation sets the zero flag and does not wait. Note that the operation provides a look-ahead feature, since the character remains in the keyboard buffer until service 00 reads it.

INT 16H Service 02: Return the Current Shift Status

The operation returns to the AL the status of keyboard shift from the BIOS data area at location hex 417 (40:17). The status byte was described in an earlier section. The following tests whether the Left or Right Shift keys are pressed:

```
MOV  AH,02           ;Request shift status
INT  16H
OR   AL,00000011B    ;Left or right shift?
JE   xxxx
```

INT 16H Service 05H: Keyboard Write

This operation allows you to store characters in the keyboard buffer as if a user had pressed a key. Load the ASCII character in the CH and its scan code in the CL. The operation allows you to enter characters into the buffer until it is full.

INT 16H Service 10H: Read a Character

This operation is the same as service 00 except that it also accepts the additional extended functions (such as F11 and F12) from the IBM extended keyboard. The service works for AT (after 11/15/85), XT-286, and PS/2 computers.

INT 16H Service 11H: Determine If a Character Is Available

This operation is the same as service 01 except that it accepts the additional extended functions from the IBM extended keyboard. The service works for AT (after 11/15/85), XT-286, and PS/2 computers.

INT 16H Service 12H: Return the Current Shift Status

This operation is the same as service 02 except that it also delivers to the AH the extended shift status. The service works for AT (after 11/15/85), XT-286, and PS/2 computers.

Bit	Key	Bit	Key
7	Sys Req pressed	3	Right Alt pressed
6	Caps Lock pressed	2	Right Ctrl pressed
5	Num Lock pressed	1	Left Alt pressed
4	Scroll Lock pressed	0	Left Ctrl pressed

EXTENDED FUNCTION KEYS

The keyboard provides three basic types of keys:

1. *Characters* such as letters A through Z, numbers 0 through 9, and %, $, and #.
2. *Extended function keys* such as Home, End, Backspace, Arrows, Enter, Del, Ins, PgUp, PgDn, and the program function keys.
3. *Control keys* for Alt, Ctrl, and Shift that work in association with other keys.

An extended function key requests an action rather than delivering a character. There is nothing in the design of the keys that compels them to perform a specific action. As programmer, you determine, for example, that pressing the Home key is to set the cursor at the top left corner of the screen, or that pressing the End key sets the cursor at the end of text on the screen. You could as easily program them to perform wholly unrelated operations.

Each key has a designated scan code numbered beginning with 01 for Esc. Refer to Appendix F for a complete list of these codes. By means of these scan codes, a program may determine the source of any keystroke. For example, a request for input of one character could involve INT 16H, service 00. The operation replies in one of two ways, depending on whether you press a character key or an extended function key. For a character such as the letter A, the operation delivers these two items:

1. The ASCII character A (hex 41) in the AL.
2. The scan code for the letter A, hex 1E, in the AH.

```
| 1E | 41 |
| AH | AL |
```

If you press an extended function key such as Ins, the operation delivers these two items:

1. Zero in the AL register.
2. The scan code for Ins, hex 52, in the AH.

```
| 52 | 00 |
| AH | AL |
```

Thus after an INT 16H operation (and some INT 21H operations), you can test the AL. If zero, the request is for an extended function code; if nonzero, the operation has delivered a character. The following tests for an extended function:

```
MOV  AH,00    ;Request input
INT  16H      ;Call BIOS
CMP  AL,00    ;Extended function?
JZ   exit     ;Yes--exit
```

The keyboard contains two keys for such characters as −, + , and *. Pressing the asterisk key, for example, sets the character code hex 2A in the AL and one of two scan codes in the AH, depending on which key was pressed: hex 09 if the asterisk above the number 8, or hex 29 if the asterisk on the PrtSc key.

The following logic tests the scan code for an asterisk:

```
CMP  AL,2AH   ;Asterisk?
JNE  EXIT1    ;No--exit
CMP  AH,09H   ;Which scan code?
JE   EXIT2
```

Let's set the cursor to row 0, column 0 if a user presses the Home key (scan code 47H):

```
MOV  AH,00    ;Request input
INT  16H
CMP  AL,00    ;Extended function?
JNE  EXIT1    ;No--exit
CMP  AH,47H   ;Scan code for Home?
JNE  EXIT2    ;No--exit
MOV  AH,02
MOV  BH,00    ;Set cursor
MOV  DX,00    ;  to 0,0
INT  10H      ;Call BIOS
```

Function keys F1–F10 generate scan codes 3BH–44H, respectively. The following tests for function key F10:

```
CMP  AH,44H   ;Function key F10?
JE   EXIT1    ;Yes--exit
```

At EXIT1, the program could perform any required action.

SELECTING FROM A MENU

The partial program in Figure 10-1 illustrates displaying a menu and letting a user press the Up and Down Arrow keys to select an item. The procedures perform the following:

BEGIN   Calls Q10CLR to clear the screen, calls B10MENU to display the menu items and to set the first item to reverse video, and calls D10INPT to accept keyboard input.

B10MENU   Calls H10DISP to display each line in the menu.

D10INPT   Uses INT 16H for input: Down Arrow to move down the menu, Up Arrow to move up the menu, Enter to accept a menu item, and Esc to quit. All other keyboard entries are ignored. The routine wraps around, so that traveling above the first menu line loops around to the last line, and vice versa. The routine also sets the previous line to normal video and the new (selected) line to reverse video.

```
            page      60,132
TITLE       SELMENU (EXE) Select line from menu
; -------------------------------------------------------------
            .MODEL SMALL
            .STACK 64
; -------------------------------------------------------------
            .DATA
TOPROW   EQU    00                    ;Top row of menu
BOTROW   EQU    07                    ;Bottom row of menu
LEFCOL   EQU    16                    ;Left column of menu
COL      DB     00                    ;Screen column
ROW      DB     00                    ;Screen row
COUNT    DB     ?                     ;Characters per line
LINES    DB     ?                     ;Lines displayed
ATTRIB   DB     ?                     ;Screen attribute
NINTEEN  DB     19                    ;Width of menu
MENU     DB     '                   '
         DB     '  Add records      '
         DB     '  Delete records   '
         DB     '  Enter orders     '
         DB     '  Print report     '
         DB     '  Update accounts  '
         DB     '  View records     '
         DB     '                   '
PROMPT   DB     09, 'To select an item, use up/down arrow'
         DB     ' and press Enter.'
         DB     13, 10, 09, 'Press Esc to exit.'
; -------------------------------------------------------------
            .CODE
BEGIN    PROC   FAR
         MOV    AX,@data              ;Initialize data segment
         MOV    DS,AX
         MOV    ES,AX
         CALL   Q10CLR                ;Clear screen
         MOV    ROW,BOTROW+2
         MOV    COL,00
         CALL   Q20CURS               ;Set cursor
         MOV    AH,40H                ;Request display for prompt
         MOV    BX,01                 ;Handle for screen
         MOV    CX,75                 ;Number of characters
         LEA    DX,PROMPT
         INT    21H
A10LOOP:
         CALL   B10MENU               ;Display menu
         MOV    COL,LEFCOL+1
         CALL   Q20CURS               ;Set cursor
         MOV    ROW,TOPROW+1          ;Set row to top item
         MOV    ATTRIB,16H            ;Set reverse video
         CALL   H10DISP               ;Highlight current menu line
         CALL   D10INPT               ;Provide for menu selection
         CMP    AL,0DH                ;Enter pressed?
         JE     A10LOOP               ;  yes -- continue
         MOV    AX,0600H              ;Esc pressed (indicates end)
         CALL   Q10CLR                ;Clear screen
         MOV    AH,4CH                ;  and terminate
         INT    21H
BEGIN    ENDP
;               Display full menu:
;               ------------------
B10MENU  PROC   NEAR
         MOV    ROW,TOPROW            ;Set top row
         MOV    LINES,08              ;Number of lines
         LEA    SI,MENU
         MOV    ATTRIB,71H            ;Blue on white
B20:
         MOV    COL,LEFCOL            ;Set left column of menu
         MOV    COUNT,19
```

Figure 10-1 Select Item from Menu

```
          B30:
                    CALL      Q20CURS          ;Set cursor next column
                    MOV       AH,09            ;Request display
                    MOV       AL,[SI]          ;Get character from menu
                    MOV       BH,00            ;Page 0
                    MOV       BL,71H           ;New attribute
                    MOV       CX,01            ;One character
                    INT       10H
                    INC       COL              ;Next column
                    INC       SI               ;Set for next character
                    DEC       COUNT            ;Last character?
                    JNZ       B30              ;No -- repeat
                    INC       ROW              ;Next row
                    DEC       LINES
                    JNZ       B20              ;All lines printed?
                    RET                        ;If so, return
          B10MENU ENDP
          ;         Accept input for request:
          ;         -------------------------
          D10INPT PROC        NEAR
                    MOV       AH,0             ;Request input character
                    INT       16H
                    CMP       AH,50H           ;Down arrow?
                    JE        D20
                    CMP       AH,48H           ;Up arrow?
                    JE        D30
                    CMP       AL,0DH           ;Enter key?
                    JE        D90
                    CMP       AL,1BH           ;Escape key?
                    JE        D90
                    JMP       D10INPT          ;None -- retry
          D20:      MOV       ATTRIB,71H       ;Blue on white
                    CALL      H10DISP          ;Set old line to normal video
                    INC       ROW
                    CMP       ROW,BOTROW-1     ;Past bottom row?
                    JBE       D40              ;No -- ok
                    MOV       ROW,TOPROW+1     ;Yes -- reset
                    JMP       D40
          D30:      MOV       ATTRIB,71H       ;Normal video
                    CALL      H10DISP          ;Set old line to normal video
                    DEC       ROW
                    CMP       ROW,TOPROW+1     ;Below top row?
                    JAE       D40              ;No -- ok
                    MOV       ROW,BOTROW-1     ;Yes -- reset
          D40:      CALL      Q20CURS          ;Set cursor
                    MOV       ATTRIB,16H       ;Reverse video
                    CALL      H10DISP          ;Set new line to reverse video
                    JMP       D10INPT
          D90:      RET
          D10INPT ENDP
          ;         Set menu line to normal/highlight:
          ;         ----------------------------------
          H10DISP PROC        NEAR
                    MOV       AH,00
                    MOV       AL,ROW           ;Row tells which line to set
                    MUL       NINTEEN          ;Multiply by length of line
                    LEA       SI,MENU+1        ;  for selected menu line
                    ADD       SI,AX
                    MOV       COUNT,17         ;Characters to display
          H20:
                    CALL      Q20CURS          ;Set cursor next column
                    MOV       AH,09            ;Request display
                    MOV       AL,[SI]          ;Get character from menu
                    MOV       BH,00            ;Page 0
                    MOV       BL,ATTRIB        ;New attribute
                    MOV       CX,01            ;One character
                    INT       10H
```

Figure 10-1 Cont.

```
              INC     COL                   ;Next column
              INC     SI                    ;Set for next character
              DEC     COUNT                 ;Last character?
              JNZ     H20                   ;No -- repeat
              MOV     COL,LEFCOL+1          ;Reset column to left
              CALL    Q20CURS               ;Set cursor
              RET
H10DISP  ENDP
;                     Clear screen:
;                     ------------
Q10CLR   PROC    NEAR
              MOV     AX,0600H
              MOV     BH,61H                ;Blue on brown
              MOV     CX,0000
              MOV     DX,184FH
              INT     10H                   ;Call BIOS
              RET
Q10CLR   ENDP

;                     Set cursor row:column:
;                     ---------------------
Q20CURS  PROC    NEAR
              MOV     AH,02
              MOV     BH,00                 ;Page 0
              MOV     DH,ROW                ;Row
              MOV     DL,COL                ;Column
              INT     10H
              RET
Q20CURS  ENDP
              END     BEGIN
```

Figure 10-1   Cont.

H10DISP   Displays the current selected line according to a provided
             attribute.

Q10CLR   Clears the entire screen to blue foreground and brown back-
             ground.

The program simply illustrates menu selection; a full program would execute a
routine for a selected item. You'll get a better understanding of this program if you
type it in and test it.

INTERRUPT 09 AND THE KEYBOARD BUFFER

When you press a key, the keyboard's processor generates the key's scan code and
requests INT 09. This interrupt (at location 36) points to an interrupt handling
routine in ROM BIOS. The routine issues a request for input from port 96 (hex 60):

```
              IN    AL,60H
```

The routine reads the scan code and compares it to a scan code table for the
associated ASCII character (if any). The routine combines the scan code and the
ASCII character and delivers the two bytes to the keyboard buffer. Figure 10-2
illustrates this procedure.

Exceptions: INT 09 handles the keyboard status bytes at 40:17 and 40:18 for Shift, Alt, and Ctrl. Although they generate INT 09, the interrupt routine doesn't deliver them to the buffer. Also, INT 09 ignores undefined keystroke combinations.

When you *press* a key, the keyboard processor generates a scan code and INT 09. When you *release* the key within ½ second, it generates a second scan code (the first code plus 128—the leftmost bit is set) and issues another INT 09. The second scan code tells the interrupt routine that you have released the key. If you hold the key for more than ½ second, the keyboard process becomes typematic and repeats the key operation.

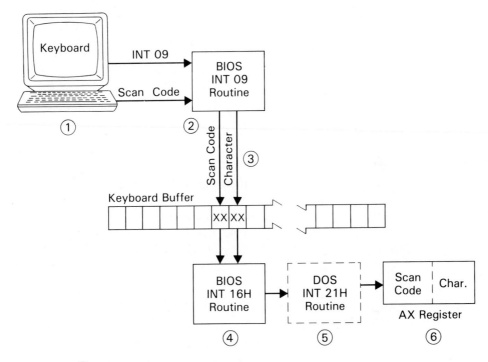

① Keyboard generates INT 09.

② INT 09 routing accepts scan code from keyboard, finds its associated character (if any).

③ INT 09 delivers both to the keyboard buffer.

④ & ⑤ Program requests INT 16H either directly or via INT 21H.

⑥ INT 16H accesses the buffer and delivers the character to the AL and the scan code to the AH.

Figure 10-2 Keyboard Buffer

The Keyboard Buffer

The keyboard buffer requires two addresses: one to tell INT 09 where to insert the next character and another to tell INT 16H where to extract the next character. The addresses are offsets within segment 40[0].

> Hex 41A   Address of current head of the buffer, the next position to be read.
>
> Hex 41C   Address of current tail of the buffer, the next position to store a character.
>
> Hex 41E   The keyboard buffer: 16 words (32 bytes), although it can be longer. The buffer holds keyboard characters and scan codes as entered for later reading via INT 16H. Two bytes are required for each character and its associated scan code.

address of head	address of tail	buffer
41A	41C	41E

When you type a character, INT 09 advances the tail. When INT 16H reads a character, it advances the head. In this way, the process is circular, with the head continually chasing the tail.

When the buffer is *empty,* the head and tail are at the same address. In the following example, a user has keyed 'abcd⟨Enter⟩'. INT 09 has stored the characters in the buffer and has advanced the tail to 428. (For simplicity, the example does not show the scan codes.) The program issued INT 16H five times to read all the characters and has advanced the tail to 428, so that the buffer is now empty:

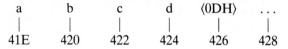

When the buffer is *full,* the tail is immediately behind the head. The user now types 'fghijklmnopqrs'. INT 09 stores the characters beginning with the tail at 428 and circles around to store the 's' at 424, immediately before the head at 426.

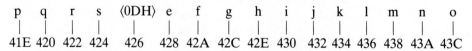

INT 09 does not accept any more characters typed ahead, and indeed accepts only 15 at most, although the buffer holds 16. (Can you tell why?) In this example, if INT 09 accepts another character, it would advance the tail to the same address as the head, and INT 16H would suppose that the buffer is empty.

The Ctrl, Shift, and Alt Keys

INT 09 also handles the status byte at 40:17 in the BIOS data area: right shift (bit 0) left shift (bit 1), Ctrl (bit 2), and Alt (bit 3). When you press one of these keys, the routine sets the appropriate bit to 1, and when you release the key, it clears the bit to 0.

Your program may test for these keys pressed either by means of INT 16H (service 02) or by direct reference to the status byte. The following partial COM program illustrates the use of direct reference.

```
BIODATA     SEGMENT AT 40H          ;Locate BIOS data area
            ORG     17H             ;  and
KBSTATE     DB      ?               ;  status byte
BIODATA     ENDS
CODESG      SEGMENT PARA
            ASSUME  CS:CODESG,DS:BIODATA
            ORG     100H
BEGIN:
            MOV     AX,BIODATA      ;Initialize address of
            MOV     DS,AX           ;  BIODATA in DS
            MOV     AL,KBSTATE      ;Get keyboard status byte
            OR      AL,00000011B    ;Test either shift pressed
            JE      XXX
            . . .
```

The program uses the SEGMENT AT feature to define the BIOS data area, in effect as a dummy segment. (This is not a violation of the rule that a COM program may have only one segment.) KBSTATE identifies the location of the keyboard status byte at 40:17H. The code segment initializes the address of BIODATA in the DS and stores the keyboard status byte in the AL. An OR operation tests the byte for either Shift key pressed.

KEY POINTS

- The shift status bytes in the BIOS data area indicate the current status of Ctrl, Alt, Shift, CapsLock, and NumLock.
- DOS keyboard operations provide a variety of services to echo or not echo on the screen, to recognize or ignore Ctrl/Break, and to accept scan codes.
- BIOS INT 16H provides the basic BIOS keyboard operation for accepting characters from the keyboard buffer. For a character key, the operation delivers the character to the AL and the key's scan code to the AH. For an extended function key, the operation delivers zero to the AL and the key's scan code to the AH.

- The scan code is a unique number assigned to each key that enables the system to identify the source of a pressed key and enables a program to check for non-ASCII keys such as Home, PgUp, and Arrow.
- The BIOS data area at 40:1EH contains the keyboard buffer. This area allows you to type up to 15 characters ahead, before a program requests input.
- When you press a key, the keyboard's processor generates the key's scan code (its unique assigned number) and requests INT 09. When you release the key, it generates a second scan code (the first code plus 128—the leftmost bit is set) and to tell INT 09 that the key is released.
- INT 09 gets the scan code from the keyboard, generates an associated ASCII character, and delivers them to the keyboard buffer area or sets the Ctrl, Alt, Shift status.

QUESTIONS

10-1. **(a)** What is the location of the first byte of the keyboard shift status in the BIOS data area?

(b) What would the contents 00001100B mean?

(c) What would the contents 00000010B mean?

10-2. Explain the features of the following services for INT 21H keyboard input: **(a)** Service 01; **(b)** service 07; **(c)** service 08; **(d)** service 0AH.

10-3. Explain the differences for INT 16H services 00H, 01H, and 10H.

10-4. Provide the scan codes for the following extended functions: **(a)** Up Arrow; **(b)** function key F3; **(c)** Home; **(d)** PgUp.

10-5. Use DEBUG to examine the effects on the AX register for entered keystrokes. To request entry of assembly language statements, type A 100 (assemble), and enter the following instructions:

```
MOV     AH,00
INT     16H
JMP     100
```

Use U 100,104 to unassemble the program and use G 104 to get DEBUG to execute through the INT. Execution stops, waiting for your input. Press any key and examine the AH register. Continue entering G 104 and press a variety of keys. Press Q to quit.

10-6. Code the instructions to enter a keystroke; if the key is PgDn, set the cursor to row 24, column 0.

10-7. Revise Figure 10-1 for the following features.

(a) After the initial clearing of the screen, display a prompt that asks users to press F1 for a menu screen.

(b) On F1 pressed, display the menu.

(c) Allow users to select menu items also by pressing the first character (upper or lower case) of each item.

(d) On request of an item, display a message for that particular selection, such as "Delete Records System."

(e) Allow users to press Esc to return to the main menu for the selected routine.

10-8. Under what circumstances does an INT 09 occur?

10-9. Explain in simple terms how INT 09 handles Ctrl and Shift keys differently from standard keyboard keys.

10-10. (a) What is the BIOS memory location of the keyboard buffer?

(b) What is its size in bytes?

(c) How many keyboard characters can it contain?

10-11. (a) What does it mean when the address of the head and tail in the keyboard buffer are the same?

(b) What does it mean when the address of the tail immediately follows the head?

11

STRING OPERATIONS

OBJECTIVE

To explain the special instructions used to process string data.

INTRODUCTION

Instructions to this point have handled only one byte, word, or doubleword at a time. It is often necessary, however, to move or compare data fields that exceed these lengths. For example, you may want to compare descriptions or names in order to sort them into ascending sequence. Items in this format are known as string data and may be either character or numeric. For processing *string data,* assembly language provides five string instructions:

MOVS Moves one byte, word, or doubleword from one location to another in memory.

LODS Loads from memory a byte into the AL, a word into the AX, or a doubleword into the EAX.

STOS Stores the contents of the AL, AX, or EAX registers into memory.

CMPS Compares byte, word, or doubleword memory locations.

SCAS Compares the contents of the AL, AX, or EAX to a memory location.

An associated instruction, the REP prefix, causes the string instructions to perform repetitively a specified number of times.

FEATURES OF STRING OPERATIONS

A string instruction can specify repetitive processing for one byte, word, or double-word (80386/486) at a time. Thus you could select a byte operation for a string with an odd number of bytes and a word operation for an even number of bytes. The following indicates the registers implied for each string instruction and the byte, word, and doubleword versions. The DI and SI should contain valid addresses.

Instruction	Implied Operands	Byte	Word	Doubleword
MOVS	DI,SI	MOVSB	MOVSW	MOVSD
LODS	AL,SI or AX,SI	LODSB	LODSW	LODSD
STOS	DI,AL or DI,AX	STOSB	STOSW	STOSD
CMPS	SI,DI	CMPSB	CMPSW	CMPSD
SCAS	DI,AL or DI,AX	SCASB	SCASW	SCASD

If you code an instruction simply as MOVS, you include the operands, for example as MOVS BYTE1,BYTE2, where the definition of the operands indicates the length of the move. The standard practice, however, is to load the address of the operands in the DI and SI registers and to code MOVSB, MOVSW, and MOVSD without operands.

The string instructions assume that the DI and SI contain offset addresses that reference memory. The SI register is normally associated with the DS (data segment) register, as DS:SI. The DI register is always associated with the ES (extra segment) register, as ES:DI. Consequently, MOVS, STOS, CMPS, and SCAS require that an EXE program initialize the ES register, usually with the address in the DS register. (Use LEA for this purpose.)

REP: REPEAT STRING PREFIX

The REP prefix immediately before a string instruction, such as REP MOVSB, provides for repeated execution based on an initial count in the CX register. REP executes the string instruction, decrements the CX, and repeats this operation until CX is zero. In this way, you can handle strings of virtually any length.

The direction flag (DF) determines the direction of a repeated operation:

- For left to right (normal), use CLD to clear the DF to 0.
- For right to left, use STD to set the DF to 1.

The following example moves (or copies) the 20 bytes of STRING1 to STRING2. Assume that the DS and ES are both initialized with the address of the data segment.

```
STRING1  DB     20 DUP('*')
STRING2  DB     20 DUP(' ')
         ...
         CLD                    ;Clear direction flag
         MOV    CX,20           ;Initialize for 20 bytes
         LEA    DI,STRING2      ;Initialize receiving name
         LEA    SI,STRING1      ;Initialize sending address
         REP    MOVSB           ;Move STRING1 to STRING2
```

During execution, CMPS and SCAS also set status flags so that the operation can terminate immediately on finding a specified condition. The variations of REP for this purpose are the following:

REP	Repeat the operation until CX decremented to zero.
REPZ or REPE	Repeat the operation while the zero flag (ZF) indicates equal/zero. Terminate when the ZF indicates not equal/zero or CX decremented to zero.
REPNE or REPNZ	Repeat the operation while the ZF indicates not equal/zero. Terminate when the ZF indicates equal/zero or CX decremented to zero.

Since the 8088 processor can handle only one byte at a time, the use of word operations is not necessarily more efficient. For the other processors, word and doubleword operations are often more efficient.

MOVS: MOVE STRING

Earlier, Figure 7-4 illustrated moving a nine-byte field. The operation involved three instructions for initialization and five for looping. MOVS combined with a REP prefix and a length in the CX can move any number of characters. Although you don't code the operands, the instruction looks like this:

```
REP MOVSn [ES:DI,DS:SI]
```

For the receiving string, the segment register is the ES and the offset register is the DI. For the sending string, the segment register is the DS and the offset register is the SI. As a result, at the start of an EXE program, initialize the ES register along with the DS register, and prior to executing the MOVS, use LEA to initialize the DI and SI registers. Depending on the direction flag, MOVS increments or decrements the DI and SI registers by 1 for byte, 2 for word, and 4 for doubleword.

The instructions equivalent to REP MOVSB are

```
          JCXZ      LABEL2        ;Jump if CX zero
LABEL1:   MOV       AL,[SI]       ;Get character
          MOV       [DI],AL       ;Store character
          INC/DEC   DI            ;Increment or decrement
          INC/DEC   SI            ;Increment or decrement
          LOOP      LABEL1
LABEL2:   ...
```

In Figure 11-1, the procedure C10MVSB uses MOVSB to move a ten-byte field, NAME1, one byte at a time to NAME2. The first instruction, CLD, clears the direction flag to 0 so that the MOVSB processes left to right. The direction flag is normally 0 at the start of execution, but CLD is coded here as a wise precaution.

The two LEA instructions load the SI and DI registers with the offset addresses of NAME1 and NAME2, respectively. Since the DOS loader automatically initializes the DS and ES registers for a COM program, the segment/offset addresses are correct for ES:DI and DS:SI. A MOV instruction initializes CX with 10

```
TITLE     STRING1 (COM)  Use of MOVS string operations
          .MODEL   SMALL
          .CODE
          ORG      100H
BEGIN:    JMP      SHORT MAIN
; ------------------------------------------------
NAME1     DB       'Assemblers'    ;Data items
NAME2     DB       10 DUP(' ')
NAME3     DB       10 DUP(' ')
; ------------------------------------------------
MAIN      PROC     NEAR            ;Main procedure
          CALL     C10MVSB         ;MVSB subroutine
          CALL     D10MVSW         ;MVSW subroutine
          MOV      AH,4CH          ;Exit
          INT      21H
MAIN      ENDP
;              Use of MOVSB:
;              ------------
C10MVSB   PROC     NEAR
          CLD                      ;Left to right
          MOV      CX,10           ;Move 10 bytes,
          LEA      DI,NAME2        ;  NAME1 to NAME2
          LEA      SI,NAME1
          REP MOVSB
          RET
C10MVSB   ENDP
;              Use of MOVSW:
;              ------------
D10MVSW   PROC     NEAR
          CLD                      ;Left to right
          MOV      CX,05           ;Move 5 words,
          LEA      DI,NAME3        ;  NAME2 to NAME3
          LEA      SI,NAME2
          REP MOVSW
          RET
D10MVSW   ENDP
          END      BEGIN
```

Figure 11-1 Use of MOVS String Operations

(the length of NAME1 and NAME2). The instruction REP MOVSB now performs the following:

- Moves the leftmost byte of NAME1 (addressed by DS:SI) to the leftmost byte of NAME2 (addressed by ES:DI).
- Increments DI and SI by 1 for the next bytes to the right.
- Decrements CX by 1.
- Repeats this operation, ten loops in all, until CX becomes zero.

Because the direction flag is 0 and MOVSB increments DI and SI, each iteration processes one byte farther to the right, as NAME1+1 to NAME2+1, and so on. At the end of execution, the CX contains 00, the DI contains the address of NAME2+10, and the SI contains the address of NAME1+10—both one byte past the end of the name.

If the direction flag is 1, MOVSB would decrement DI and SI, causing processing from right to left. But in that case, you would have to initialize the SI with NAME1+9 and the DI with NAME2+9.

The next procedure in Figure 11-1, D10MVSW, uses MOVSW to move five words from NAME2 to NAME3. At the end of execution, the CX contains 00, the DI contains the address of NAME3+10, and the SI contains the address of NAME2+10.

Since MOVSW increments the DI and SI registers by 2, the operation requires only five loops. For processing right to left, initialize the SI with NAME1+8 and the DI with NAME2+8.

LODS: LOAD STRING

LODS loads the AL with a byte, the AX with a word, or the EAX with a double-word from memory. The memory address is subject to the DS:SI registers, although you can override the SI. Depending on the direction flag, the operation also increments or decrements the SI by 1 for byte, 2 for word, and 4 for doubleword.

Since one LODS operation fills the register, there is no practical use for the REP prefix. For most purposes, a simple MOV instruction is adequate. But MOV generates three bytes of machine code, whereas LODS generates only one, although it requires that you initialize the SI register. You could use LODS to step through a string one byte, word, or doubleword at a time, examining successively for a particular value.

The instructions equivalent to LODSB are

```
MOV  AL,[SI]   ;Load character in AL
INC  SI        ;Increment SI for next
```

The LODSW instruction in Figure 11-2 processes only one word and inserts the first byte of NAME1 (containing As) in the AL register and the second byte in

```
TITLE    STRING2 (COM)  Use of LODS string operation
         .MODEL   SMALL
         .CODE
         ORG      100H
BEGIN:   JMP      SHORT MAIN
; ----------------------------------------------------
NAME1    DB       'Assemblers'    ;Data item
; ----------------------------------------------------
MAIN     PROC     NEAR            ;Main procedure
         CLD                      ;Left to right
         LEA      SI,NAME1        ;Load 1st word of NAME1
         LODSW                    ;  into AX reg.
         MOV      AH,4CH          ;Exit
         INT      21H
MAIN     ENDP
         END      BEGIN
```

Figure 11-2 Use of LODSW String Operation

the AH (that is, reversed), so that the AX contains sA. Since the operation processes a word, it increments the SI by 2.

STOS: STORE STRING

STOS stores the contents of the AL, AX, or EAX register into a byte, word, or doubleword in memory. The memory address is always subject to the ES:DI registers. Depending on the direction flag, STOS also increments or decrements the DI register by 1 for byte, 2 for word, and 4 for doubleword.

A practical use of STOS with a REP prefix is to initialize a data area to any specified value, such as clearing a display area to blank. The number of bytes, words, or doublewords is in the CX. The instructions equivalent to REP STOSB are

```
         JCXZ     LABEL2      ;Jump if CX zero
LABEL1:  MOV      [DI],AL     ;Store AL in memory
         INC/DEC  DI          ;Increment or decrement
         LOOP     LABEL1
LABEL2:  ...
```

The STOSW instruction in Figure 11-3 repeatedly stores hex 2020 (blanks) five times through NAME1. The operation stores the AL in the first byte and the AH in the next byte (that is, reversed). On termination, the CX contains 00 and the DI contains the address of NAME1+10.

CMPS: COMPARE STRING

CMPS compares the contents of one memory location (addressed by DS:SI) to another memory location (addressed by ES:DI). Depending on the direction flag, CMPS also increments or decrements the SI and DI registers, by 1 for byte, 2 for word, and 4 for doubleword. The operation sets the AF, CF, OF, PF, SF, and ZF

```
TITLE    STRING3 (COM)  Use of STOSW string operation
         .MODEL  SMALL
         .CODE
         ORG     100H
BEGIN:   JMP     SHORT MAIN
; ------------------------------------------
NAME1    DB      'Assemblers' ;Data item
; ------------------------------------------
MAIN     PROC    NEAR               ;Main procedure
         CLD                        ;Left to right
         MOV     AX,2020H           ;Move
         MOV     CX,05              ;  5 blanks
         LEA     DI,NAME1           ;  to NAME1
         REP STOSW
         MOV     AH,4CH             ;Exit
         INT     21H
MAIN     ENDP
         END     BEGIN
```

Figure 11-3 Use of STOSW
String Operation

flags. When combined with a REP prefix and a length in the CX, CMPS can successively compare any string length.

Consider the comparison of two strings containing JEAN and JOAN. A comparison from left to right one byte at a time causes the following:

```
J  :  J    Equal
E  :  O    Unequal (E is low)
A  :  A    Equal
N  :  N    Equal
```

A comparison of the entire four bytes ends with a comparison of N to N: equal/zero. Now since the two names are not "equal," the operation should terminate as soon as it finds an unequal condition. For this purpose, REP has a variation, REPE, which repeats the operation as long as the comparison is equal, or until the CX register equals zero. The coding for repeated one-byte comparisons is REPE CMPSB.

Figure 11-4 consists of two examples that use CMPSB. The first example compares NAME1 to NAME2, which contain the same values. The CMPSB operation continues for the entire ten bytes. At the end of execution, DEBUG shows that the CX contains 00, the DI contains the address of NAME2+10, the SI contains the address of NAME1+10, the sign flag is positive, and the zero flag indicates equal/zero.

The second example compares NAME2 to NAME3, which contain different values. The CMPSB operation terminates after comparing the first byte and results in a high/unequal condition: the CX contains 09, the DI contains the address of NAME3+1, the SI contains the address of NAME2+1, the sign flag is positive and the zero flag indicates unequal.

The first example results in equal/zero and moves 01 to the BH register. The second example results in unequal and moves 02 to the BL register. If you use DEBUG to trace the instructions, the BX register should contain 0102 at the end of execution.

```
TITLE      STRING4 (COM)   Use of CMPS string operations
           .MODEL   SMALL
           .CODE
           ORG      100H
BEGIN:     JMP      SHORT MAIN
; ----------------------------------------------------------
NAME1      DB       'Assemblers'        ;Data items
NAME2      DB       'Assemblers'
NAME3      DB       10 DUP(' ')
; ----------------------------------------------------------
MAIN       PROC     NEAR                ;Main procedure
           CLD                          ;Left to right
           MOV      CX,10               ;Initialize for 10 bytes
           LEA      DI,NAME2
           LEA      SI,NAME1
           REPE CMPSB                   ;Compare NAME1:NAME2
           JNE      G20                 ;Not equal -- bypass
           MOV      BH,01               ;Equal -- set BH
G20:
           MOV      CX,10               ;Initialize for 10 bytes
           LEA      DI,NAME3
           LEA      SI,NAME2
           REPE CMPSB                   ;Compare NAME2:NAME3
           JE       G30                 ;Equal -- exit
           MOV      BL,02               ;Not equal -- set BL
G30:
           MOV      AH,4CH              ;Exit
           INT      21H
MAIN       ENDP
           END      BEGIN
```

Figure 11-4   Use of CMPS String Operations

Warning! These examples use CMPSB to compare one byte at a time. If you use CMPSW to compare a word at a time, initialize CX to 5. But that's not the problem. When comparing words, CMPSW reverses the bytes. For example, let's compare the name SAMUEL to ARNOLD. For the initial comparison of words, instead of comparing SA to AR, the operation compares AS to RA. So, instead of higher, the result is lower—and incorrect. CMPSW works correctly only if the compared strings contain numeric data defined as DW, DD, or DQ.

SCAS: SCAN STRING

SCAS differs slightly from CMPS because it scans a string for a specified byte, word, or doubleword value. SCAS compares the contents of a memory location (addressed by ES:DI) to the AL, AX, or EAX register. Depending on the direction flag, SCAS also increments or decrements the DI register by 1 for byte, 2 for word, and 4 for doubleword. At the end of execution, SCAS sets the AF, CF, OF, PF, SF, and ZF flags. When combined with the REP prefix and a length in the CX, SCAS can scan any string length.

SCAS would be particularly useful for a text-editing application where the program has to scan for punctuation, such as periods, commas, and blanks.

The example in Figure 11-5 scans NAME1 for the lowercase letter 'm'. Since the SCASB operation is to continue scanning while the comparison is not equal or until the CX is zero, the operation is REPNE SCASB.

```
TITLE     STRING5 (COM)  Use of SCAS string operation
          .MODEL   SMALL
          .CODE
          ORG      100H
BEGIN:    JMP      SHORT MAIN
; ----------------------------------------------------------
NAME1     DB       'Assemblers'      ;Data item
; ----------------------------------------------------------
MAIN      PROC     NEAR              ;Main procedure
          CLD                        ;Left to right
          MOV      AL,'m'
          MOV      CX,10             ;Scan NAME1
          LEA      DI,NAME1          ;  for 'm'
          REPNE SCASB
          JNE      H20               ;If found,
          MOV      AH,03             ;  store 03 in AH
H20:
          MOV      AH,4CH
          INT      21H               ;Exit
MAIN      ENDP
          END      BEGIN
```

Figure 11-5 Use of SCASB String Operation

Since NAME1 contains "Assemblers," SCASB finds an equal on the fifth comparison. If you use DEBUG to trace the instructions, at the end of execution of the REP SCASB operation you will see that the zero flag shows zero, the CX is decremented to 05, and the DI is incremented by 05. (The DI is incremented one byte past the actual location of the 'm'.)

The program stores 03 in the AH register to indicate that an "m" was found. If no equal is found, the operation would set the zero flag to nonzero.

SCASW scans for a word in memory that matches the word in the AX register. If you used LODSW or MOV to transfer a word into the AX register, the first byte will be in the AL and the second byte in the AH. Since SCASW compares the bytes in reversed sequence, the operation works correctly.

SCAN AND REPLACE

You may also want to replace a specific character with another character, for example, to clear editing characters such as paragraph and end-of-page symbols from a document. The following partial program scans STRING for an ampersand (&) and replaces it with a blank. If SCASB locates an ampersand, it terminates the operation. In this example there is an ampersand at STRING+8, where the blank is to be inserted. The SCASB operation will have incremented the DI register to STRING+9. Decrementing DI by 1 provides the correct address for the blank replacement character.

```
STRLEN   EQU   15                  ;Length of STRING
STRING   DB    'The time&is now'
         ...
         CLD                       ;Left to right
         MOV   AL,'&'              ;Search character
```

```
              MOV   CX,STRLEN        ;Length of STRING
              LEA   DI,STRING        ;Address of STRING
              REPNE SCASB            ;Scan
              JNZ   K20              ;Found?
              DEC   DI               ;Yes--adjust address
              MOV   BYTE PTR[DI],20H ;Replace with blank
       K20:   ...
```

ALTERNATE CODING FOR STRING INSTRUCTIONS

If you code explicitly with a byte, word, or doubleword instruction such as MOVSB, MOVSW, or MOVSD, the assembler assumes the correct length and does not require operands. For instructions such as MOVS, which have no suffix to indicate byte, word, or doubleword, you must indicate the length in the operands. For example, if FLDA and FLDB are defined as byte (DB), the instruction

```
         REP MOVS FLDA,FLDB
```

implies a repeated move of the byte beginning at FLDB to the byte beginning at FLDA. If you load the DI and SI registers with the addresses of FLDA and FLDB, you could also code the instruction as

```
         REP MOVS ES:BYTE PTR[DI],DS:[SI]
```

Few programs are coded this way, and it is covered here just for the record.

DUPLICATING A PATTERN

The STOS instruction is useful for setting an area according to a specific byte, word, or doubleword value. For repeating a pattern that exceeds these lengths, you can use MOVS with a minor modification. Let's say that you want to set a display line to the following pattern:

```
     ***___**___***___***___***___...
```

Rather than define the entire pattern repetitively, you need only define the first six bytes immediately before the display line. Here is the required coding:

```
         PATTERN   DB    '***___'
         DISAREA   DB    42 DUP(?)
                   ...
                   CLD
                   MOV  CX,21
```

```
LEA  DI,DISAREA
LEA  SI,PATTERN
REP  MOVSW
```

On execution, MOVSW moves the first word of PATTERN (**) to the first word of DISAREA, and then moves the second (* -) and third (- -) words:

```
                   *** _ _ _ *** _ _ _

                    |           |
                 PATTERN     DISAREA
```

At this point the DI contains the address of DISAREA+6, and the SI contains the address of PATTERN+6, which is also the address of DISAREA. The operation now automatically duplicates the pattern by moving the first word of DISAREA to DISAREA+6, DISAREA+2 to DISAREA+8, DISAREA+4 to DISAREA+10, and so forth. Eventually, the pattern is duplicated through to the end of DISAREA:

```
    *** _ _ _ *** _ _ _ *** _ _ _ *** _ _ _ *** _ _ _      . . .     *** _ _ _
     |               |               |                                |
  PATTERN        DISAREA+6       DISAREA+12                       DISAREA+42
```

You can use this technique to duplicate a pattern any number of times. The pattern may be any length, but must be located immediately before the receiving field.

RIGHT-ADJUSTING ON THE SCREEN

The program in Figure 11-6 illustrates most of the material described in this chapter. The procedures perform the following:

B10INPT   Accepts names up to 30 characters in length at the top of the screen.

D10SCAS   Uses SCASB to scan the name and bypasses any input containing an asterisk.

E10RGHT   Uses MOVSB to right-adjust the entered names to the right of the screen, one under the other. The length in ACTNLEN in the input parameter list is used to calculate the rightmost character of a name, as follows:

```
              Jerome Kern
            Richard Rodgers
             Irving Berlin
```

F10CLNM   Uses STOSW to clear the name in memory.

```
        TITLE     EXRIGHT (EXE)  Right-adjust displayed names
                  .MODEL  SMALL
                  .STACK  96
; ---------------------------------------------------------
                  .DATA
NAMEPAR LABEL     BYTE                 ;Name parameter list
MAXNLEN DB        31                   ;Maximum length
ACTNLEN DB        ?                    ;No. of chars entered
NAMEFLD DB        31 DUP(' ')          ;Name

PROMPT  DB        'Name?', '$'
NAMEDSP DB        31 DUP(' '), 13, 10, '$'
ROW     DB        00
; ---------------------------------------------------------
                  .CODE
BEGIN   PROC      FAR                  ;Main procedure
        MOV       AX,@data             ;Initialize
        MOV       DS,AX                ;  data segment
        MOV       ES,AX
        MOV       AX,0600H
        CALL          Q10SCR           ;Clear screen
        SUB       DX,DX                ;Set cursor 00,00
        CALL      Q20CURS
A10LOOP:
        CALL      B10INPT              ;Request input of name
        TEST      ACTNLEN,0FFH         ;No name? (indicates end)
        JZ        A90                  ;  yes - exit
        CALL      D10SCAS              ;Scan for asterisk
        CMP       AL,'*'               ;Found?
        JE        A10LOOP              ;  yes - bypass
        CALL      E10RGHT              ;Right-adjust name
        CALL      F10CLNM              ;Clear name
        JMP       A10LOOP
A90:    MOV       AH,4CH               ;Return to DOS
        INT       21H
BEGIN   ENDP
;                 Prompt for input:
;                 ----------------
B10INPT PROC
        MOV       AH,09
        LEA       DX,PROMPT            ;Display prompt
        INT       21H
        MOV       AH,0AH
        LEA       DX,NAMEPAR           ;Accept input
        INT       21H
        RET
B10INPT ENDP
;                 Scan name for asterisk:
;                 ----------------------
D10SCAS PROC
        CLD                            ;Left to right
        MOV       AL,'*'
        MOV       CX,30                ;Set 30-byte scan
        LEA       DI,NAMEFLD
        REPNE SCASB                    ;Asterisk found?
        JE        D20                  ;  no - exit
        MOV       AL,20H               ;  yes - clear * in AL
D20:    RET
D10SCAS ENDP

;                 Right-adjust & display name:
;                 ---------------------------
E10RGHT PROC
        STD                            ;Right to left
        MOV       CH,00
        MOV       CL,ACTNLEN           ;Length in CX for REP
        LEA       SI,NAMEFLD           ;Calculate rightmost
        ADD       SI,CX                ;  position
        DEC       SI                   ;  of input name
```

Figure 11-6   Right-Adjusting on the Screen

```
            LEA     DI,NAMEDSP+30       ;Right pos'n of display name
            REP MOVSB                   ;Move string right to left
            MOV     DH,ROW
            MOV     DL,48
            CALL    Q20CURS             ;Set cursor
            MOV     AH,09
            LEA     DX,NAMEDSP          ;Display name
            INT     21H

            CMP     ROW,20              ;Bottom of screen?
            JAE     E20                 ;  no --
            INC     ROW                 ;  increment row
            JMP     E90
E20:
            MOV     AX,0601H            ;  yes --
            CALL    Q10SCR              ;  scroll and
            MOV     DH,ROW              ;  set cursor
            MOV     DL,00
            CALL    Q20CURS
E90:        RET
E10RGHT ENDP
;               Clear name:
;               ----------
F10CLNM PROC
            CLD                         ;Left to right
            MOV     AX,2020H
            MOV     CX,15               ;Clear 15 words
            LEA     DI,NAMEDSP
            REP STOSW
            RET
F10CLNM ENDP
;               Scroll screen:
;               -------------
Q10SCR  PROC                            ;AX set on entry
            MOV     BH,30               ;Color (07 for BW)
            MOV     CX,00
            MOV     DX,184FH
            INT     10H
            RET
Q10SCR  ENDP
;               Set cursor row/col:
;               ------------------
Q20CURS PROC                            ;DX set on entry
            MOV     AH,02
            SUB     BH,BH
            INT     10H
            RET
Q20CURS ENDP

            END     BEGIN
```

Figure 11-6   Cont.

KEY POINTS

- For the string instructions MOVS, STOS, CMPS, and SCAS, be sure that your EXE programs initialize the ES register.

- For string instructions, use the suffixes B, W, or D (80386/486) for handling byte, word, or doubleword strings.

- Clear (CLD) or set (STD) the direction flag for the required direction of processing.

- Double-check initialization of the DI and SI registers. For example, MOVS implies operands DI,SI, whereas CMPS implies operands SI,DI.
- Initialize the CX register for REP to process the required number of bytes, words, or doublewords.
- For normal processing, use REP with MOVS and STOS, and use a modified REP (REPE or REPNE) with CMPS and SCAS.
- CMPSW and SCASW reverse the bytes in compared words.
- Where you want to process right to left, watch out for addressing beginning at the rightmost byte of a field. If the field is NAME1 and is ten bytes long, then for processing bytes, the load address for LEA is NAME+9. For processing words, however, the load address for LEA is NAME+8 because the string operation initially accesses NAME+8 and NAME+9.

QUESTIONS

11-1. The string operations assume that the operands relate to the DI or SI registers. Identify these registers for the following: **(a)** MOVS (operands 1 and 2); **(b)** CMPS (operands 1 and 2); **(c)** SCAS (operand 1).

11-2. For string operations using REP, how do you define the number of repetitions that are to occur?

11-3. For string operations using REP, how do you set processing right to left?

11-4. The chapter gives the instructions equivalent to **(a)** MOVSB, **(b)** LODSB, and **(c)** STOSB, each with a REP prefix. For each case, provide equivalent code for processing words.

11-5. Key in, assemble, and link the program in Figure 11-1. Be sure to initialize the ES register. Change the MOVSB and MOVSW operations to move from right to left. Use DEBUG to trace through the procedures and note the contents of the data segment and registers.

11-6. Use the following data definitions and code string operations for the related questions (a)–(f):

```
DATASG    SEGMENT PARA
          CONAME  DB    'SPACE EXPLORERS INC.'
          PRLINE  DB    20 DUP(' ')
```

- **(a)** Move CONAME to PRLINE left to right.
- **(b)** Move CONAME to PRLINE right to left.
- **(c)** Load the third and fourth bytes of CONAME into the AX.
- **(d)** Store the AX beginning at PRLINE+5.
- **(e)** Compare CONAME to PRLINE (they will be unequal).
- **(f)** Scan CONAME for a blank character and if found move it to the BH.

11-7. Revise H10SCAS in Figure 11-5 so that the operation scans NAME1 for "er." A check of NAME1 discloses that the characters "er" do not appear as a word, as shown by the following: /As/se/mb/le/rs/. Two possible solutions are:

   (a) Use SCASW twice. The first SCASW begins at NAME1 and the second SCASW begins at NAME1+1.

   (b) Use SCASB and on finding an "e" compare the following byte for an "r."

11-8. Define a field containing hex 03, hex 04, hex 05, and hex B4. Use MOVSW to duplicate this field 20 times, and display the result.

12

ARITHMETIC I
Processing Binary Data

OBJECTIVE

To cover the requirements for addition, subtraction, multiplication, and division of binary data.

INTRODUCTION

Although we are accustomed to decimal (base 10) arithmetic, a microcomputer performs only binary (base 2) arithmetic. Further, pre-80386 processors are limited to 16-bit registers and large values require special treatment.

This chapter covers addition, subtraction, multiplication, and division and the use of unsigned and signed data. We also provide many examples and warnings of various pitfalls for the unwary traveler in the realm of the microprocessor. Chapter 13 covers special requirements involved with converting between binary and ASCII data formats.

ADDITION AND SUBTRACTION

The ADD and SUB instructions process binary data. A computer performs subtraction by means of two's-complement methodology: Reverse the bits of operand 2, add 1, and add the result to operand 1. Other than the latter step, processing for ADD and SUB is identical. The general formats are

```
ADD/SUB   register,register
ADD/SUB   memory,register
ADD/SUB   register,memory
ADD/SUB   register,immediate
ADD/SUB   memory,immediate
```

Since there is no direct memory-to-memory operation, use a register to handle this situation. The following example adds WORDA to WORDB:

```
WORDA   DW    123         ;Define WORDA
WORDB   DW    25          ;Define WORDB
        ...
        MOV   AX,WORDA     ;Move WORDA to AX
        ADD   AX,WORDB     ;Add WORDB to AX
        MOV   WORDB,AX     ;Move AX to WORDB
```

Figure 12-1 provides examples of ADD and SUB for processing a byte, word, or doubleword (80386/486). The procedure B10ADD uses ADD to process bytes and the procedure C10SUB uses SUB to process words.

Overflows

Be alert for overflows in arithmetic operations. Since a byte provides for only a sign bit plus seven data bits, an arithmetic operation can easily exceed the capacity of a one-byte register, from -128 to $+127$. Thus a sum in the AL register that exceeds its capacity does not automatically overflow into the AH. Suppose that the AL contains hex 60. The instruction

```
ADD  AL,20H
```

generates a sum of hex 80 in the AL. But the operation also sets the overflow flag to overflow and the sign flag to negative. The reason? Hex 80, or binary 10000000, is a negative number. Instead of $+128$, the sum is -128. Since the problem is that the AL register is too small, the sum should be in the AX register.

Extending the Sum

In the next example, the CBW (Convert Byte to Word) instruction extends the hex 60 in the AL by propagating the sign bit of the AL (0) through the AH: hex 0060 in the AX. ADD generates the correct result in the AX: hex 0080, or $+128$:

```
CBW                 ;Extend AL sign into AH
ADD    AX,20H       ;Add to AX
```

```
                  page 60,132
      TITLE       EXADD (COM)  ADD and SUB operations
                  .MODEL  SMALL
                  .CODE
                  ORG    100H
      BEGIN:  JMP    SHORT MAIN
      ; ----------------------------------------------------
      BYTEA   DB   64H                     ;Data items
      BYTEB   DB   40H
      BYTEC   DB   16H
      WORDA   DW   4000H
      WORDB   DW   2000H
      WORDC   DW   1000H
      ; ----------------------------------------------------
      MAIN    PROC   NEAR                  ;Main procedure:
              CALL   B10ADD                ;Call ADD routine
              CALL   C10SUB                ;Call SUB routine
              MOV    AH,4CH
              INT    21H                   ;Exit
      MAIN    ENDP
      ;       Examples of ADD bytes:
      ;       --------------------
      B10ADD  PROC
              MOV    AL,BYTEA
              MOV    BL,BYTEB
              ADD    AL,BL                 ;Register-to-register
              ADD    AL,BYTEC              ;Memory-to-register
              ADD    BYTEA,BL              ;Register-to-memory
              ADD    BL,10H                ;Immediate-to-register
              ADD    BYTEA,25H             ;Immediate-to-memory
              RET
      B10ADD  ENDP
      ;       Examples of SUB words:
      ;       --------------------
      C10SUB  PROC
              MOV    AX,WORDA
              MOV    BX,WORDB
              SUB    AX,BX                 ;Register-from-register
              SUB    AX,WORDC              ;Memory-from-register
              SUB    WORDA,BX              ;Register-from-memory
              SUB    BX,1000H              ;Immediate-from-register
              SUB    WORDA,256H            ;Immediate-from-memory
              RET
      C10SUB  ENDP

              END    BEGIN
```

Figure 12-1 Examples of ADD and SUB

But even a full word allows only for a sign bit plus 15 data bits, from $-32,768$ to $+32,767$. Our next step examines how to handle numbers that exceed this maximum.

Multiword Addition

Let's examine two ways to perform multiword arithmetic. The first is simple and specific, whereas the second is more sophisticated and general.

In Figure 12-2, the procedure D10DWD illustrates a simple way of adding one pair of words (WORD1A and WORD1B) to a second pair (WORD2A and WORD2B) and storing the sum in a third pair (WORD3A and WORD3B). The operation is to add these values:

```
WORD1A and WORD2A:   0123 BC62
WORD2A and WORD2B:   0012 553A
WORD3A and WORD3B:   0136 119C
```

Because of reverse byte sequence in memory, the values are defined with the words reversed: BC62 0123 and 553A 0012, respectively. The assembler stores these values in memory in proper reverse byte sequence:

```
WORD1A and WORD1B:   62BC 2301
WORD2A and WORD2B:   3A55 1200
```

```
TITLE     EXDBADD (COM)  Adding doublewords
          .MODEL   SMALL
          .CODE
          ORG      100H
BEGIN:    JMP      SHORT MAIN
;  -----------------------------------------------
WORD1A    DW       0BC62H            ;Data items
WORD1B    DW       0123H
WORD2A    DW       553AH
WORD2B    DW       0012H
WORD3A    DW       ?
WORD3B    DW       ?
;  -----------------------------------------------
MAIN      PROC     NEAR              ;Main procedure
          CALL     D10DWD            ;Call 1st ADD
          CALL     E10DWD            ;Call 2nd ADD
          MOV      AH,4CH
          INT      21H               ;Exit
MAIN      ENDP
;                  Example of ADD doublewords:
;                  ------------------------
D10DWD    PROC
          MOV      AX,WORD1A         ;Add leftmost word
          ADD      AX,WORD2A
          MOV      WORD3A,AX
          MOV      AX,WORD1B         ;Add rightmost word
          ADC      AX,WORD2B         ;  with carry
          MOV      WORD3B,AX
          RET
D10DWD    ENDP
;                  Generalized add operation:
;                  ------------------------
E10DWD    PROC
          CLC                        ;Clear carry flag
          MOV      CX,02             ;Set loop count
          LEA      SI,WORD1A         ;Leftmost word
          LEA      DI,WORD2A         ;Leftmost word
          LEA      BX,WORD3A         ;Leftmost word of sum
E20:
          MOV      AX,[SI]           ;Move word to AX
          ADC      AX,[DI]           ;Add with carry to AX
          MOV      [BX],AX           ;Store word
          INC      SI                ;Adjust addresses for
          INC      SI                ;  next word to right
          INC      DI
          INC      DI
          INC      BX
          INC      BX
          LOOP     E20               ;Repeat for next word
          RET
E10DWD    ENDP

          END      BEGIN
```

Figure 12-2 Multiword Addition

The first MOV and ADD operations reverse the bytes in the AX and add the leftmost words:

```
WORD1A:   BC62
WORD2A:  +553A
Total:    1119C   (9C11 is stored in WORD3A)
```

Since the sum of WORD1A plus WORD2A exceeds the capacity of the AX, a carry occurs, and the carry flag is set to 1. Next, the example adds the words at the right, but this time using ADC (Add With Carry) instead of ADD. ADC adds the two values, and since the carry flag is set, adds 1 to the sum:

```
WORD1B        0123
WORD2B       +0012
Plus carry  +    1
Total         0136   (3601 is stored in WORD3B)
```

By using DEBUG to trace the arithmetic, you can see the sum 0136 in the AX, and the reversed values 9C11 stored in WORD3A and 3601 in WORD3B.

Again in Figure 12-2, the procedure E10DWD provides an approach to adding values of any length, although this example adds the same pairs of words, WORD1A:WORD1B and WORD2A:WORD2B. The example loops once through the instructions for each pair of words to be added—in this case, two times. The first loop adds the leftmost words and the second loop adds the rightmost words. Since the second loop is to process the words to the right, the addresses in the SI, DI, and BX registers are incremented by 2. Two INC instructions perform this operation for each register.

Note that the instruction ADD reg,02 would clear the carry flag and would cause an incorrect answer, whereas INC does not affect the carry flag.

Because of the loop, there is only one add instruction, ADC. At the start, a CLC (Clear Carry) instruction ensures that the carry flag is initially clear. To make this method work, ensure that (1) the words are defined adjacent to each other, (2) processing is from left to right, and (3) the CX is initialized to the number of words to be added.

For multiword subtraction, the instruction equivalent to ADC is SBB (Subtract With Borrow). Simply replace ADC with SBB in the procedure E10DWD.

80386/486 Arithmetic

The 80386/486 processors provide 32-bit registers for arithmetic. To add the EBX to the EAX, for example, simply code

```
ADD  EAX,EBX     ;80386/486
```

You could add quadwords on the 80386 using the technique covered earlier for adding multiwords.

UNSIGNED AND SIGNED DATA

Some numeric fields are *unsigned;* examples include a customer number and a memory address. Some *signed* numeric fields may contain positive or negative values; examples include customer balance owing (which could be negative if over-paid) and an algebraic number. Other signed numeric fields are supposed to be always positive; examples include rate of pay, day of the month, and the value of pi.

For unsigned data, all bits are intended to be data bits. Instead of a maximum of 32,767, a 16-bit register can contain 65,535. For signed data, the leftmost bit is a sign bit. The ADD and SUB instructions do not distinguish between unsigned and signed data, and indeed simply add and subtract the bits. In the following addition of two binary numbers, the top number contains a 1-bit to the left. For unsigned data, the bits represent 249, but for signed data the bits represent −7. The addition does not set the overflow or carry flags:

```
                      Unsigned      Signed
        Binary        Decimal       Decimal        OF        CF
        11111001        249          -7
      + 00000010      +   2          +2
        11111011        251          -5             0         0
```

The result of binary addition is the same for both unsigned and signed data. However, the bits in the unsigned field represent 251, whereas the bits in the signed field represent −5. In effect, the contents of a field mean whatever you intend.

Arithmetic Carry

The carry flag is set when there is a carry out of the sign bit. Where a carry occurs on unsigned data, the result is invalid. The following example of addition causes a carry. The unsigned operation is invalid, whereas the signed operation is valid:

```
                      Unsigned      Signed
        Binary        Decimal       Decimal        OF        CF
        11111100        252          -4
      + 00000101      +   5          +5
     (1)00000001         1            1             0         1
                      (invalid)     (valid)
```

Arithmetic Overflow

The overflow flag is set when a carry into the sign bit does not carry out, or a carry out occurs with no carry in. Where an overflow occurs on signed data, the result is invalid, as this example shows:

Binary	Unsigned Decimal	Signed Decimal	OF	CF
01111001	121	+121		
+00001011	+ 11	+ 11		
10000100	132	-124	1	0
	(valid)	(invalid)		

An add operation may set *both* a carry and overflow flags. In the next example, the carry makes the unsigned operation invalid, whereas the overflow makes the signed operation invalid:

Binary	Unsigned Decimal	Signed Decimal	OF	CF
11110110	246	- 10		
+10001001	+137	-119		
(1)01111111	127	+127	1	1
	(invalid)	(invalid)		

MULTIPLICATION

For multiplication, the MUL instruction handles unsigned data and the IMUL (Integer Multiplication) instruction handles signed data. Both instructions affect the carry and overflow flags. As programmer, you have control over the format of data that you process and the responsibility of selecting the appropriate instruction. The general format is

MUL/IMUL	register/memory

The basic multiplication operations are byte times byte, word times word, and doubleword times doubleword (80386/80486).

Byte times byte.   The multiplicand is in the AL register and the multiplier is a byte in memory or a register. After multiplication, the product is in the AX register. The operation ignores and erases any data that is already in the AH.

Before:	AH	AL Multiplicand
After:		AX Product

Word times word.   The multiplicand is in the AX register and the multiplier is a word in memory or a register. After multiplication, the product is a doubleword that requires two registers: The high-order (leftmost) portion is in the DX and the low-order (rightmost) portion is in the AX. The operation ignores and erases any data that is already in the DX.

	DX	AX
Before:	DX Ignored	AX Multiplicand
After:	DX High product	AX Low product

Doubleword times doubleword.   The multiplicand is in the EAX register and the multiplier is a doubleword in memory or a register. The product is generated in the EDX:EAX pair. The operation ignores and erases any data that is already in the EDX.

Field Sizes

The operand of MUL or IMUL references only the multiplier. Consider the instruction MUL MULTR:

Definition of MULTR	Operation Assumed
DB	AL times byte
DW	AX times word
DD	EAX times doubleword

When the multiplier is in a register, the size of the register determines the type of operation:

Instruction	Multiplier	Multiplicand	Product
MUL CL	byte	AL	AX
MUL BX	word	AX	DX:AX
MUL EBX	doubleword	EAX	EDX:EAX

Unsigned Multiplication: MUL

The MUL (Multiplication) instruction multiplies unsigned data. In Figure 12-3, C10MUL gives three examples of multiplication: byte times byte, word times word, and word times byte. The first MUL example multiplies hex 80 (128) and hex 40 (64). The product in the AX is hex 2000 (8,192). The second MUL example generates hex 1000 0000 in the DX:AX registers.

The third MUL example involves word times byte and requires extending BYTE1 to a word. Since the values are supposed to be unsigned, the example

```
TITLE    EXMULT (COM)  MUL & IMUL operations
         .MODEL   SMALL
         .CODE
         ORG      100H
BEGIN:   JMP      SHORT MAIN
; --------------------------------------------------
BYTE1    DB       80H
BYTE2    DB       40H
WORD1    DW       8000H
WORD2    DW       2000H
; --------------------------------------------------
MAIN     PROC     NEAR            ;Main procedure
         CALL     C10MUL          ;Call MUL  routine
         CALL     D10IMUL         ;Call IMUL routine
         MOV      AH,4CH
         INT      21H             ;Exit
MAIN     ENDP
;                 Examples of MUL:
;                 ----------------
C10MUL   PROC
         MOV      AL,BYTE1        ;Byte x byte
         MUL      BYTE2           ;  product in AX

         MOV      AX,WORD1        ;Word x word
         MUL      WORD2           ;  product in DX:AX

         MOV      AL,BYTE1        ;Byte x word
         SUB      AH,AH           ;  extend multiplicand in AH
         MUL      WORD1           ;  product in DX:AX
         RET
C10MUL   ENDP
;                 Examples of IMUL:
;                 -----------------
D10IMUL  PROC
         MOV      AL,BYTE1        ;Byte x byte
         IMUL     BYTE2           ;  product in AX

         MOV      AX,WORD1        ;Word x word
         IMUL     WORD2           ;  product in DX:AX

         MOV      AL,BYTE1        ;Byte x word
         CBW                      ;  extend multiplicand in AH
         IMUL     WORD1           ;  product in DX:AX
         RET
D10IMUL  ENDP

         END      BEGIN
```

Figure 12-3 Unsigned and Signed Multiplication

assumes that leftmost bits in the AH register are to be zero. (The problem with using CBW is that the leftmost bit of the AL could be 0 or 1.) The product in the DX:AX is hex 0040 0000.

Signed Multiplication: IMUL

The IMUL (Integer Multiplication) instruction multiplies signed data. In Figure 12-3, D10IMUL uses the same three examples as C10MUL, replacing MUL with IMUL.

The first IMUL example multiplies hex 80 (a negative number) by hex 40 (a positive number). The product in the AX register is hex E000. Using the same data, MUL generated a product of hex 2000, so you can see the difference in using MUL and IMUL. MUL treats hex 80 as +128, whereas IMUL treats hex 80 as −128. The product of −128 times +64 is −8192, which equals hex E000. (Try converting hex E000 to bits, reverse the bits, add 1, and add up the bit values.)

The second IMUL example multiplies hex 8000 (a negative value) times hex 2000 (a positive value). The product in the DX:AX is hex F000 0000 and is the negative of the product that MUL generated.

The third IMUL example extends BYTE1 to a word in the AX. Since the values are supposed to be signed, the example uses CBW to extend the leftmost sign bit into the AH register: hex 80 in the AL becomes hex FF80 in the AX. Since the multiplier, WORD1, is also negative, the product should be positive. And indeed it is: hex 0040 0000 in the DX:AX—the same result as MUL, which assumed multiplication of two positive numbers.

In effect, if the multiplicand and multiplier have the same sign bit, MUL and IMUL generate the same result. But if the multiplicand and multiplier have different sign bits, MUL produces a positive product and IMUL produces a negative product.

You may find it worthwhile to use DEBUG to trace these examples.

EXTENDED MULTIPLICATION OPERATIONS

The 80186-80486 processors have two additional IMUL formats for immediate operands. You can use them for either signed or unsigned multiplication, since the results are the same. The values must be all the same length: 16 bits or (on the 80386/486) 32 bits. The general format for 16 bits is

IMUL	register,immediate

The register contains the multiplicand and the immediate value is the multiplier. The product is generated in the specified register. A product that exceeds the register causes the carry and overflow flags to be set.

The general format for 32 bits has three operands:

IMUL	register,memory,immediate

Operand 2 contains the multiplicand, operand 3 contains the multiplier, and operand 1 contains the generated product.

The 80386/486 processors provide yet another IMUL format for 16 or 32 bits:

IMUL	register,register/memory

Operand 1 contains the multiplicand and operand 2 contains the multiplier. The product is generated in the operand 1 register.

Shifting

If you multiply by a power of 2 (2, 4, 8, etc.), it is more efficient to shift left the required number of bits. For the 8088/8086, a shift greater than 1 requires the shift value in the CL register. In the following examples, the multiplicand is in the AX:

```
Multiply by 2 (shift left 1):    SHL  AX,01
Multiply by 8 (shift left 3):    MOV  CL,03    ;8088/8086
                                 SHL  AX,CL
Multiply by 8 (shift left 3):    SHL  AX,03    ;80186-80486
```

Multiword Multiplication

Conventional multiplication involves multiplying byte by byte, word by word, or doubleword by doubleword. As already seen, the maximum signed value in a word is +32,767. Multiplying larger values on pre-80386 processors involves additional steps. The approach is to multiply each word separately and to add each product to a sum. Consider the following decimal multiplication:

$$
\begin{array}{r}
1365 \\
\times \quad 12 \\
\hline
16{,}380
\end{array}
$$

What if you could multiply only two-digit numbers? You could multiply the 13 and the 65 by 12 separately, like this:

$$
\begin{array}{rr}
13 & 65 \\
\times 12 & \times 12 \\
\hline
156 & 780
\end{array}
$$

Next, add the two products; but remember, since the 13 is at the 100s position, its product is actually 15,600:

$$
\begin{array}{r}
15{,}600 \\
+ \quad 780 \\
\hline
16{,}380
\end{array}
$$

An assembly language program can use the same technique, except that the data consists of words (four digits) in hexadecimal format.

Doubleword by word.   E10XMUL in Figure 12-4 multiplies a doubleword by a word. The multiplicand, MULTCND, consists of two words containing hex 3206 and 2521, respectively. The reason for defining two DWs instead of a DD is to facilitate addressing for MOV instructions that move words to the AX register. The values are defined in reverse byte sequence and the assembler stores each word in reverse byte sequence. Thus MULTCND, which has a true value of hex 3206 2521 is stored as 2125 0632.

```
TITLE    EXDWMUL (COM) Multiplication of doublewords
         .MODEL  SMALL
         .CODE
         ORG     100H
BEGIN:   JMP     SHORT MAIN
; ------------------------------------------------
MULTCND DW      2521H                ;Data items
        DW      3206H
MULTPLR DW      0A26H
        DW      6400H
PRODUCT DW      0
        DW      0
        DW      0
        DW      0
; ------------------------------------------------
MAIN     PROC    NEAR                 ;Main procedure
         CALL    E10XMUL              ;Call 1st multiply
         CALL    Z10ZERO              ;Clear product
         CALL    F10XMUL              ;Call 2nd multiply
         MOV     AH,4CH
         INT     21H                  ;Exit
MAIN     ENDP
;                Doubleword x word:
;                ------------------
E10XMUL PROC
         MOV     AX,MULTCND           ;Multiply left word
         MUL     MULTPLR+2            ;  of multiplicand
         MOV     PRODUCT,AX           ;Store product
         MOV     PRODUCT+2,DX

         MOV     AX,MULTCND+2         ;Multiply right word
         MUL     MULTPLR+2            ;  of multiplicand
         ADD     PRODUCT+2,AX         ;Add to stored product
         ADC     PRODUCT+4,DX
         RET
E10XMUL ENDP
;                Doubleword x doubleword:
;                -----------------------
F10XMUL PROC
         MOV     AX,MULTCND           ;Multiplicand word 1
         MUL     MULTPLR              ;  x multiplier word 1
         MOV     PRODUCT+0,AX         ;Store product
         MOV     PRODUCT+2,DX

         MOV     AX,MULTCND           ;Multiplicand word 1
         MUL     MULTPLR+2            ;  x multiplier word 2
         ADD     PRODUCT+2,AX         ;Add to stored product
         ADC     PRODUCT+4,DX
         ADC     PRODUCT+6,00         ;Add any carry

         MOV     AX,MULTCND+2         ;Multiplicand word 2
         MUL     MULTPLR              ;  x multiplier word 1
         ADD     PRODUCT+2,AX         ;Add to stored product
         ADC     PRODUCT+4,DX
         ADC     PRODUCT+6,00         ;Add any carry

         MOV     AX,MULTCND+2         ;Multiplicand word 2
         MUL     MULTPLR+2            ;  x multiplier word 2
         ADD     PRODUCT+4,AX         ;Add to product
         ADC     PRODUCT+6,DX
         RET
F10XMUL ENDP

;                Clear product area:
;                ------------------
Z10ZERO PROC
         MOV     PRODUCT,0000         ;Clear words
         MOV     PRODUCT+2,0000       ;  left to right
         MOV     PRODUCT+4,0000
         MOV     PRODUCT+6,0000
         RET
Z10ZERO ENDP
         END     BEGIN
```

Figure 12-4 Multiword Multiplication

The multiplier, MULTPLR + 2, contains hex 6400. The field for the generated product, PRODUCT, provides for three words. The first MUL operation multiplies MULTPLR + 2 and the left word of MULTCND; the product is hex 0E80 E400, stored in PRODUCT + 2 and PRODUCT + 4. The second MUL multiplies MULTPLR + 2 and the right word of MULTCND; the product is hex 138A 5800. The routine adds the two products, like this:

```
Product 1:    0000 0E80  E400
Product 2:  + 138A 5800
Total:        138A 6680  E400
```

Since the first ADD may cause a carry, the second add is ADC (Add with Carry). Because numeric data is stored in reversed byte format, PRODUCT will actually contain 00E4 8066 8A13. The routine requires that the first word of PRODUCT initially contain zero.

Doubleword by doubleword. Multiplying two doublewords on pre-80386 processors involves four multiplications:

Multiplicand		Multiplier
word 2	×	word 2
word 2	×	word 1
word 1	×	word 2
word 1	×	word 1

You add each product in the DX and AX to the appropriate word in the final product. In Figure 12-4, F10XMUL gives an example. MULTCND contains hex 3206 2521, MULTPLR contains hex 6400 0A26, and PRODUCT provides for four words.

Although the logic is similar to multiplying doubleword by word, this problem requires an additional feature. Following the ADD/ADC pair is another ADC that adds 0 to PRODUCT. The first ADC itself could cause a carry, which subsequent instructions would clear. The second ADC, therefore, adds 0 if there is no carry and adds 1 if there is a carry. The final ADD/ADC pair does not require an additional ADC; since PRODUCT is large enough for the final generated answer, there is no carry.

The final product is 138A 687C 8E5C CCE6, stored in PRODUCT with the bytes reversed. Try using DEBUG to trace this example.

SHIFTING THE DX:AX REGISTERS

The following routines could be useful for shifting a product in the DX:AX registers to the left or right. You could contrive a more efficient method, but these examples are generalized for any number of loops (and shifts) in the CX. Note that shifting off a 1-bit sets the carry flag.

```
;           Shift Left 4 Bits
            MOV   CX,04            ;Initialize four loops
C20:        SHL   DX,1             ;Shift DX
            SHL   AX,1             ;Shift AX
            ADC   DX,00            ;Add AX carry, if any
            LOOP  C20              ;Repeat
;           Shift Right 4 Bits
            MOV   CX,04            ;Initialize four loops
D20:        SHR   AX,1             ;Shift AX
            SHR   DX,1             ;Shift DX
            JNC   D30              ;If DX carry,
            OR    AH,10000000B     ; insert 1-bit in AH
D30:        LOOP  D20              ;Repeat
```

Here's a more efficient method for left shifting that does not require looping. This example stores a shift factor in the CL register. Although specific to a 4-bit shift, it could be adapted to other shifts.

```
MOV CL,04    ;Set shift
SHL DX,CL    ;Shift DX left 4 bits
MOV BL,AH    ;Store AH in BL
SHL AX,CL    ;Shift AX left 4 bits
SHR BL,CL    ;Shift BL right 4 bits
OR  DL,BL    ;Insert BL 4 bits in DL
```

DIVISION

For division, the DIV (divide) instruction handles unsigned data and IDIV (integer divide) handles signed data. You are responsible for selecting the appropriate instruction. The general format is

DIV/IDIV	register/memory

The basic divide operations are byte into word, word into doubleword, and double-word into quadword (80386/80486).

Byte into word.   The dividend is in the AX and the divisor is a byte in a register or in memory. After division, the remainder is in the AH and the quotient is in the AL. Since a one-byte quotient is very small—a maximum of 255 (hex FF) if unsigned and +127 (hex 7F) if signed—this operation has limited use.

	AX Dividend	
Before:		
After:	AH Remainder	AL Quotient

Word into doubleword.   The dividend is in the DX:AX pair and the divisor is a word in a register or memory. After division, the remainder is in the DX and the quotient is in the AX. The quotient of one word allows a maximum of +32,767 (hex FFFF) if unsigned and +16,383 (hex 7FFF) if signed.

Before:	DX High dividend	AX Low dividend
After:	DX Remainder	AX Quotient

Doubleword into quadword.   The dividend is in the EDX:EAX pair and the divisor is a doubleword in a register or memory. After division, the remainder is in the EDX and the quotient is in the EAX.

Field Sizes

The operand of DIV or IDIV references the divisor. Consider the instruction DIV DIVISOR.

Definition of DIVISOR	*Operation Assumed*
DB	Byte into word
DW	Word into doubleword
DD	Doubleword into quadword

When the divisor is in a register, the size of the register determines the type of operation:

Operation	*Divisor*	*Dividend*	*Quotient*	*Remainder*
DIV CL	byte	AX	AL	AH
DIV CX	word	DX:AX	AX	DX
DIV EBX	doubleword	EDX:EAX	EAX	EDX

Remainder.   If you divide 13 by 3, the result is $4\frac{1}{3}$. The quotient is 4 and the true remainder is 1. Note that a calculator (and a BASIC program) would deliver a quotient of 4.333. . . . The value consists of an integer portion (4) and a fraction portion (.333). The values ⅓ and .333 are fractions, whereas the 1 is a remainder.

Unsigned Division: DIV

The DIV instruction divides unsigned data. In Figure 12-5, D10DIV gives four examples: byte into word, byte into byte, word into doubleword, and word into word. The first DIV example divides hex 2000 (8092) by hex 80 (128). The remainder in the AH is 00 and the quotient in the AL is hex 40 (64).

```
TITLE     EXDIV (COM)  DIV and IDIV operations
          .MODEL   SMALL
          .CODE
          ORG      100H
BEGIN:    JMP      SHORT MAIN
; ------------------------------------------------
BYTE1     DB       80H                ;Data items
BYTE3     DB       16H
WORD1     DW       2000H
WORD2     DW       0010H
WORD3     DW       1000H
; ------------------------------------------------
MAIN      PROC     NEAR               ;Main procedure
          CALL     D10DIV             ;Call DIV  routine
          CALL     E10IDIV            ;Call IDIV routine
          MOV      AH,4CH
          INT      21H                ;Exit
MAIN      ENDP
;                  Examples of DIV:
;                  ---------------
D10DIV    PROC
          MOV      AX,WORD1           ;Word / byte
          DIV      BYTE1              ;  rmdr:quot in AH:AL
          MOV      AL,BYTE1           ;Byte / byte
          SUB      AH,AH              ;  extend dividend in AH
          DIV      BYTE3              ;  rmdr:quot in AH:AL

          MOV      DX,WORD2           ;Doubleword / word
          MOV      AX,WORD3           ;  dividend in DX:AX
          DIV      WORD1              ;  rmdr:quot in DX:AX
          MOV      AX,WORD1           ;Word / word
          SUB      DX,DX              ;  extend dividend in DX
          DIV      WORD3              ;  rmdr:quot in DX:AX
          RET
D10DIV    ENDP
;         Examples of IDIV:
;         ----------------
E10IDIV   PROC
          MOV      AX,WORD1           ;Word / byte
          IDIV     BYTE1              ;  rmdr:quot in AH:AL
          MOV      AL,BYTE1           ;Byte / byte
          CBW                         ;  extend dividend in AH
          IDIV     BYTE3              ;  rmdr:quot in AH:AL

          MOV      DX,WORD2           ;Doubleword / word
          MOV      AX,WORD3           ;  dividend in DX:AX
          IDIV     WORD1              ;  rmdr:quot in DX:AX
          MOV      AX,WORD1           ;Word / word
          CWD                         ;  extend dividend in DX
          IDIV     WORD3              ;  rmdr:quot in DX:AX
          RET
E10IDIV   ENDP

          END      BEGIN
```

Figure 12-5   Unsigned and Signed Division

The second DIV example requires extending BYTE1 to a word. Since the value is supposed to be unsigned, the example assumes that leftmost bits in the AH register are to be zero. The remainder in the AH is hex 12 and the quotient in the AL is hex 05.

For the third DIV, the remainder in the DX is hex 1000 and the quotient in the AX is hex 0080.

The fourth DIV requires extending WORD1 to a doubleword in the DX register. After the division, the remainder in the DX is hex 0000 and the quotient in the AX is hex 0002.

Signed Division: IDIV

The IDIV (integer divide) instruction divides signed data. In Figure 12-5, E10IDIV uses the same four examples as D10DIV, replacing DIV with IDIV. The first IDIV example divides hex 2000 (positive) by hex 80 (negative). The remainder in the AH is hex 00 and the quotient in the AL is hex C0 (−64). (DIV using the same data caused a quotient of +64.)

The results in hex of the remaining three IDIV examples are

IDIV Example	Remainder	Quotient
2	EE (−18)	FB (−5)
3	1000 (4096)	0080 (128)
4	0000	0002

Only Example 4 produces the same answer as DIV. In effect, if the dividend and divisor have the same sign bit, DIV and IDIV generate the same result. But if the dividend and divisor have different sign bits, DIV generates a positive quotient and IDIV generates a negative quotient.

You may find it worthwhile to use DEBUG to trace these examples.

Shifting

If you divide by a power of 2 (2, 4, 8, and so on), it is more efficient simply to shift right the required number of bits. For the 8088/8086, a shift greater than 1 requires a shift value in the CL register. The following examples assume that the dividend is in the AX:

Divide by 2 (shift right 1):	SHR AX,01	
Divide by 8 (shift right 3):	MOV CL,03	;8088/8086
	SHR AX,CL	
Divide by 8 (shift right 3):	SHR CL,03	;80186-80486

Overflows and Interrupts

DIV and IDIV operations can easily cause an overflow. An interrupt occurs, with unpredictable results. The operation assumes that the quotient is significantly smaller than the original dividend. Dividing by zero always causes an interrupt. But dividing by 1 generates a quotient that is the same as the dividend and could easily cause an interrupt.

Here's a useful rule: If the divisor is a byte, its contents must be greater than the left byte (AH) of the dividend; if the divisor is a word, its contents must be greater than the left word (DX) of the dividend. Here's an illustration using a divisor of 1, although other values could serve:

Divide Operation	Dividend	Divisor	Quotient
Word by byte:	0123	01	(1)23
Doubleword by word:	0001 4026	0001	(1)4026

In both cases, the quotient exceeds its available space. You may be wise to include a test prior to a DIV or IDIV operation. In the first example, DIVBYTE is a one-byte divisor and the dividend is already in the AX:

```
CMP  AH,DIVBYTE        ;Compare AH to divisor
JNB  overflow-rtne     ;Exit if not smaller
DIV  DIVBYTE           ;Divide word by byte
```

In the second example, DIVWORD is a one-word divisor and the dividend is in the DX:AX.

```
CMP  DX,DIVWORD        ;Compare DX to divisor
JNB  overflow-rtne     ;Exit if not smaller
DIV  DIVWORD           ;Divide doubleword by word
```

For IDIV, the logic should account for the fact that either dividend or divisor could be negative. Since the absolute value of the divisor must be smaller, you could use the NEG instruction to set negative values temporarily to positive.

Division by Subtraction

If a quotient is too large for the divisor, you could perform successive subtraction. That is, subtract the divisor from the dividend, increment a quotient value by 1, and continue subtracting until the dividend is less than the divisor. In the following example, the dividend is in the AX, the divisor is in the BX, and the quotient is developed in the CX:

```
          SUB  CX,CX        ;Clear quotient
C20:      CMP  AX,BX        ;If dividend<divisor,
          JB   C30          ;  exit
          SUB  AX,BX        ;Subtract divisor from dividend
          INC  CX           ;Add 1 to quotient
          JMP  C20          ;Repeat
C30:      RET               ;Quotient in CX, remainder in AX
```

At the end of the routine, the CX contains the quotient and the AX contains the remainder. The example is intentionally primitive to demonstrate the technique. If the quotient is in the DX:AX, include these two operations:

1. At C20, compare AX to BX only if DX is zero.
2. After the SUB instruction, insert SBB DX,00.

Note that a very large quotient and a small divisor may cause thousands of loops.

REVERSING THE SIGN

The NEG (negate) instruction reverses the sign of a binary value, from positive to negative, and vice versa. In effect, NEG reverses the bits, just like NOT, and then adds 1 for proper two's-complement notation. Here are some examples using NEG:

```
NEG  AX        ;16 bits
NEG  BL        ;8 bits
NEG  BINAMT    ;Byte or word in memory
NEG  ECX       ;32 bits
```

For pre-80386 processors, reversing the sign of a 32-bit (or larger) value involves more steps. Assume that the DX:AX pair contain a 32-bit binary number. Because NEG cannot act on the DX:AX pair concurrently, its use causes incorrect results. The following instructions use NOT:

```
NOT  DX        ;Flip bits
NOT  AX        ;Flip bits
ADD  AX,1      ;Add 1 to AX
ADC  DX,0      ;Add carry to DX
```

One minor problem remains: It is all very well to perform arithmetic on binary data that the program itself defines. However, data that enters a program from a disk file may already be in binary format, but data entered from a terminal is in ASCII format. Although ASCII data is fine for displaying and printing, it requires special adjusting for arithmetic. But that's a topic for the next chapter.

NUMERIC DATA PROCESSORS

This section provides a general introduction to the Numeric Data Processor; a full discussion is outside the scope of this book. The system board contains a socket for an Intel Numeric Data Processor, known as a coprocessor. The 8087 coprocessor operates in conjunction with an 8088/86, the 80287 with an 80286, and the 80387 with an 80386. The coprocessor for the 80486 is built into the processor.

The coprocessor has its own instruction set and floating-point hardware for performing such operations as exponentiation and logarithmic and trigonometric functions. The eight 80-bit floating-point registers can represent numeric values up to 10 to the 400th power. The coprocessor's mathematical processing is rated at about 100 times faster than a regular processor.

The 8087 consists of eight 80-bit registers, R1–R8, in the following format:

S	exponent	significand
79	78 64	63 0

Each register has an associated 2-bit tag that indicates its status:

00	Contains a valid number
01	Contains a zero value
10	Contains an invalid amount
11	Is empty

The coprocessor recognizes seven types of numeric data:

1. Word Integer: 16 bits of binary data.

S	number
15	14 0

2. Short Integer: 32 bits of binary data.

S	number
31	30 0

3. Long Integer: 64 bits of binary data.

S	number
63	62 0

4. Short Real: 32 bits of floating-point data.

S	exponent	significand
31	30 23	22 0

5. Long Real: 64 bits of floating-point data.

S	exponent	significand
63	62 52	51 0

6. Temporary Real: 80 bits of floating-point data.

S	exponent	significand
79	78 64	63 0

7. Packed Decimal: 18 significant decimal digits.

S	zeros	significand
79	78 72	71 0

Types 1, 2, and 3 are common binary two's-complement formats. Types 4, 5, and 6 represent floating-point numbers. Type 7 contains 18 4-bit decimal digits. You can load any of these formats from memory into a coprocessor register and can store the register contents into memory. However, for its calculations the coprocessor converts all formats in its registers into temporary real. Data is stored in memory in reverse byte sequence.

The processor requests a specific operation and delivers numeric data to the coprocessor, which performs the operation and returns the result. For assembling, use the .8087, .80287, or .80387 directive.

KEY POINTS

- Watch out especially when using one-byte accumulators. The maximum signed values are $+127$ and -128.
- For multiword addition, use ADC to account for any carry from a previous ADD. If the operation is performed in a loop, use CLC to initialize the carry flag to zero.
- Use MUL or DIV for unsigned data and use IMUL or IDIV for signed data.
- For division, be especially careful of overflows. If a zero divisor is a possibility, be sure to test for the condition. Also, the divisor must be greater than the contents of the AH (if a byte) or the DX (if a word).
- For multiplying or dividing by powers of 2, use shifting for efficiency. For right shifts, use SHR for unsigned fields and SAR for signed fields. For left shifts, SHL and SAL act identically.

- Be alert for assembler defaults. For example, if FACTOR is a DB, MUL FACTOR assumes the multiplicand is AL, and DIV FACTOR assumes the dividend is AX. If FACTOR is a DW, MUL FACTOR assumes the multiplicand is AX, and DIV FACTOR assumes the dividend is DX:AX. If FACTOR is a DQ, MUL FACTOR assumes the multiplicand is EAX, and DIV FACTOR assumes the dividend is EDX:EAX.

QUESTIONS

12-1. (a) What is the maximum value in a byte for signed data and unsigned data?

     (b) What is the maximum value in a word for signed data and unsigned data?

12-2. Distinguish between a carry and an overflow.

     Questions 12-3 through 12-7 refer to this data, with words defined in reverse sequence:

```
DATAX     DW 0148H
          DW 2316H
DATAY     DW 0237H
          DW 4052H
DATAZ     DW 0
          DW 0
          DW 0
```

12-3. Code the instructions to add the following: (a) the word DATAX to the word DATAY; (b) the doubleword beginning at DATAX to the doubleword at DATAY.

12-4. Explain the effect of the following instructions:

```
STC
MOV     BX,DATAX
ADC     BX,DATAY
```

12-5. Code the instructions to multiply (MUL) the following: (a) the contents of the word DATAX by the word DATAY; (b) the doubleword beginning at DATAX by the word DATAY. Store the product in DATAZ.

12-6. Other than zero, what divisors cause an overflow error?

12-7. Code the instructions to divide (DIV) the following: (a) the contents of the word DATAX by 23; (b) the doubleword beginning at DATAX by the word DATAY.

12-8. Revise Figure 12-2 so that the routine adds three pairs of words instead of two. Name the additional words on the right WORD3A and WORD3B.

12-9. Refer to the section "Shifting the DX:AX Registers." The second part contains a more efficient method of shifting left four bits. Revise the example for a right shift of four bits.

13

ARITHMETIC II
Processing ASCII
and BCD Data

OBJECTIVE

To examine ASCII and BCD data formats, to perform arithmetic in these formats, and to cover conversions between these formats and binary.

INTRODUCTION

A computer performs arithmetic more efficiently in binary format. As seen in Chapter 12, this format causes no major problems as long as the program itself defines the data. For many purposes, new data enters a program from a keyboard as ASCII characters, in base-10 format. Similarly, the display of answers on a screen is in ASCII. For example, the number 23 in binary is 00010111, or hex 17; in ASCII, each character requires a full byte, and the ASCII number 25 internally is hex 3235.

This chapter covers techniques for converting ASCII data into binary to perform arithmetic, and converting the binary results back into ASCII for viewing. The program at the end of this chapter combines much of the material from Chapters 1 through 12.

If you have programmed in a high-level language such as C or Pascal, you are used to the compiler accounting for decimal positions. However, a computer does not recognize a decimal point in an arithmetic field. In fact, since a binary value has no provision for inserting a decimal (or binal) point, you as programmer have to account for its position.

ASCII FORMAT

Since data that you enter from a keyboard is in ASCII format, the representation in memory of an entered alphabetic value such as SAM is hex 53414D, and the representation of a numeric value such as 1234 is hex 31323334. For most purposes, an alphabetic entry such as a person's name or an item description remains unchanged in a program. But performing arithmetic on a numeric value hex such as 31323334 involves special treatment.

The following instructions perform arithmetic directly on ASCII numbers:

AAA	ASCII Adjust for Addition
AAD	ASCII Adjust for Division
AAM	ASCII Adjust for Multiplication
AAS	ASCII Adjust for Subtraction

These instructions are coded without operands and automatically adjust the AX register. The adjustment occurs because an ASCII value represents a so-called unpacked base-10 number, whereas a processor performs base-2 arithmetic.

ASCII Addition

Consider the effect of adding the ASCII numbers 8 (hex 38) and 4 (hex 34):

```
hex  38
    +34
hex  6C
```

The sum hex 6C is not a correct ASCII or binary value. However, ignore the leftmost 6 and add 6 to the rightmost hex C: hex C plus 6 = hex 12—the correct answer in terms of decimal numbers. Why add 6?—because that's the difference between hexadecimal (16) and decimal (10). That's a little oversimplified, but it does indicate the way in which AAA performs an adjustment.

As an example, assume that the AX contains hex 0038 and the BX contains hex 0034. The 38 and 34 represent two ASCII bytes that are to be added. Addition and adjustment are as follows:

```
ADD  AL,BL    ;Add hex 34 to 38
AAA           ;Adjust for ASCII add
```

The AAA operation checks the rightmost hex digit (4 bits) of the AL register. If the digit is between A and F or the auxiliary carry flag is 1, the operation adds 6 to the AL register, adds 1 to the AH register, and sets the carry and auxiliary carry flags to 1. In all cases, AAA clears to zero the leftmost hex digit of the AL. The result in the AX is:

```
                        After the ADD:    006C
                        After the AAA:    0102
```

To restore the ASCII representation, simply insert 3s in the leftmost hex digits, as follows:

```
        OR  AX,3030H    ;Result now 3132
```

All that is very well for adding one-byte numbers. Addition of multibyte ASCII numbers requires a loop that processes from right to left (low order to high order) and accounts for carries. The example in Figure 13-1 adds two three-byte ASCII numbers, ASC1 and ASC2, into a four-byte sum, ASCSUM. Note the following points:

- A CLC instruction initializes the carry flag to zero.
- The routine at A20 uses ADC for addition because any add may cause a carry that should be added to the next (left) byte.

```
TITLE     ASCADD (COM)  Adding ASCII numbers
          .MODEL  SMALL
          .CODE
          ORG     100H
BEGIN:    JMP     SHORT MAIN
;  ---------------------------------------
ASC1      DB      '578'               ;Data items
ASC2      DB      '694'
ASCSUM    DB      '0000'
;  ---------------------------------------
MAIN      PROC    NEAR
          CLC                         ;Clear carry flag
          LEA     SI,ASC1+2           ;Initialize ASCII numbers
          LEA     DI,ASC2+2
          LEA     BX,ASCSUM+3
          MOV     CX,03               ;Initialize 3 loops
A20:
          MOV     AH,00               ;Clear AH
          MOV     AL,[SI]             ;Load ASCII byte
          ADC     AL,[DI]             ;Add (with carry)
          AAA                         ;Adjust for ASCII
          MOV     [BX],AL             ;Store sum
          DEC     SI
          DEC     DI
          DEC     BX
          LOOP    A20                 ;Loop 3 times
          MOV     [BX],AH             ;At end, store carry

          LEA     BX,ASCSUM+3         ;Convert ASCSUM
          MOV     CX,04               ;   to ASCII
A30:
          OR      BYTE PTR[BX],30H
          DEC     BX
          LOOP    A30                 ;Loop 4 times
          MOV     AH,4CH
          INT     21H                 ;Exit
MAIN      ENDP
          END     BEGIN
```

Figure 13-1 ASCII Addition

- A MOV instruction clears the AH on each loop because each AAA may add 1 to the AH. ADC, however, accounts for any carry. Note that the use of XOR or SUB to clear the AH would change the carry flag.

- When looping is complete, the routine moves the AH (containing either a final 00 or 01) to the leftmost byte of ASCSUM.

- At the end, ASCSUM contains 01020702. To insert ASCII 3 in each byte, the program loops through ASCSUM in memory and ORs each byte with hex 30.

The routine did not use OR after AAA to insert leftmost 3s because OR sets the carry flag and changes the effect for the ADC instructions. A solution to save the flag settings is to push (PUSHF) the flags register, execute the OR, and then pop (POPF) the flags to restore them:

```
ADC    AL,[DI]      ;Add with carry
AAA                 ;Adjust for ASCII
PUSHF               ;Save flags
OR     AL,30H       ;Insert ASCII 3
POPF                ;Restore flags
MOV    [BX],AL      ;Store sum
```

The instructions LAHF (Load AH with Flags) and SAHF (Store AH in Flag Register) could replace PUSHF and POPF, respectively. LAHF loads the AH with the SF, ZF, AF, PF, and CF flags; SAHF stores the AH contents back into the specific flags. This example, however, already uses the AH for arithmetic overflows.

ASCII Subtraction

The AAS (ASCII Adjust for Subtraction) instruction works like AAA. AAS checks the rightmost hex digit (4 bits) of the AL. If the digit is between A and F or the auxiliary carry is 1, the operation subtracts 6 from the AL, subtracts 1 from the AH, and sets the auxiliary (AF) and carry (CF) flags. For all cases, AAS clears to zero the leftmost hex digit of the AL.

The next two examples assume that ASC1 contains hex 38 and ASC2 contains hex 34. In the first example, AAS does not need to make an adjustment because the rightmost hex digit is less than hex A:

```
                   AX    AF
MOV    AL,ASC1    ;0038
SUB    AL,ASC2    ;0004  0
AAS               ;0004  0
```

In the second example, since the rightmost digit is hex C, AAS subtracts 6 from the AL, 1 from the AH, and sets the AF and CF flags. The answer, which should be −4, is hex FF06, its 10s complement. And what can you do with that value?—a very good question.

```
                                    AX    AF
              MOV   AL,ASC2    ;0034
              SUB   AL,ASC1    ;00FC    1
              AAS              ;FF06    1
```

ASCII Multiplication

The AAM (ASCII Adjust for Multiplication) instruction corrects the result of multiplying ASCII data in the AX register. However, leftmost hex digits must first be cleared of 3s, and accordingly, the data (no longer true ASCII format) is known as unpacked decimal. For example, the ASCII number 31323334 becomes 01020304 as unpacked decimal. Also, because the adjustment is only one byte at a time, you can multiply only one-byte fields and have to code the operation as a loop.

AAM divides the AL by 10 (hex 0A) and stores the quotient in the AH and the remainder in the AL. For example, suppose that the AL contains hex 35 and the CL contains hex 39. The following multiplies the contents of the AL by the CL and converts the result to ASCII format:

```
     Instruction       Comment                             AX
     AND   CL,0FH       ;Convert CL to 09
     AND   AL,0FH       ;Convert AL to 05                   0005
     MUL   CL           ;Multiply AL by CL                  002D
     AAM                ;Convert to unpacked decimal        0405
     OR    AX,3030H     ;Convert to ASCII                   3435
```

The MUL operation generates 45 (hex 002D) in the AX. AAM divides this value by 10, generating a quotient of 04 in the AH and a remainder of 05 in the AL. The OR instruction then converts the unpacked decimal value to ASCII format.

Figure 13-2 depicts multiplying a four-byte multiplicand by a one-byte multiplier. Since AAM can accommodate only one-byte operations, the routine steps through the multiplicand one byte at a time, from right to left. At the end, the unpacked decimal product is 0108090105, which a loop routine converts to true ASCII format.

If a multiplier is greater than one byte, you have to provide for yet another loop that steps through the multiplier. It may be simpler to convert the ASCII data to binary format, covered in a later section.

ASCII Division

The AAD (ASCII Adjust for Division) instruction provides a correction of an ASCII dividend prior to dividing. However, just as with AAM, you first clear the leftmost 3s from the ASCII bytes to create unpacked decimal format. AAD allows for a two-byte dividend in the AX. Assume that the AX contains the ASCII value 3238 and the divisor, 37, is in the CL. The following performs the adjustment and the division:

```
TITLE     ASCMUL (COM)  Multiplying ASCII numbers
          .MODEL   SMALL
          .CODE
          ORG      100H
BEGIN:    JMP      MAIN
;------------------------------------------------
MULTCND DB         '3783'              ;Data items
MULTPLR DB         '5'
PRODUCT DB         5 DUP(0)
;------------------------------------------------
MAIN      PROC     NEAR
          MOV      CX,04               ;Initialize 4 loops
          LEA      SI,MULTCND+3
          LEA      DI,PRODUCT+4
          AND      MULTPLR,0FH         ;Clear ASCII 3
A20:
          MOV      AL,[SI]             ;Load ASCII char (or LODSB)
          AND      AL,0FH              ;Clear ASCII 3
          MUL      MULTPLR             ;Multiply
          AAM                          ;Adjust for ASCII
          ADD      AL,[DI]             ;Add to
          AAA                          ;  stored
          MOV      [DI],AL             ;  product
          DEC      DI
          MOV      [DI],AH             ;Store product carry
          DEC      SI
          LOOP     A20                 ;Loop 4 times

          LEA      BX,PRODUCT+4        ;Convert PRODUCT
          MOV      CX,05               ;  to ASCII
A30:
          OR       BYTE PTR[BX],30H
          DEC      BX
          LOOP     A30                 ;Loop 4 times
          MOV      AH,4CH
          INT      21H                 ;Exit
MAIN      ENDP
          END      BEGIN
```

Figure 13-2   ASCII Multiplication

Instruction	Comment	AX
AND CL,0FH	;Convert to unpacked	
AND AX,0F0FH	;Convert to unpacked	0208
AAD	;Convert to binary	001C
DIV CL	;Divide by 7	0004

AAD multiplies the AH by 10 (hex 0A), adds the product 20 (hex 14) to the AL, and clears the AH. The result, 001C, is the hex representation of decimal 28. The divisor can be only a single byte containing 01 to 09.

Figure 13-3 allows for dividing a one-byte divisor into a four-byte dividend. The routine steps through the dividend from left to right. The remainders stay in the AH register so that AAD will adjust it in the AL. At the end, the quotient in unpacked decimal format is 00090204 and the remainder in the AH is 02. Another loop (not coded) could convert the quotient to ASCII format.

If the divisor is greater than one byte, you have to provide for yet another loop to step through the divisor. Better yet, see the later section "Conversion of ASCII to Binary Format."

```
TITLE    ASCDIV (COM)  Dividing ASCII numbers
         .MODEL  SMALL
         .CODE
         ORG     100H
BEGIN:   JMP     SHORT MAIN
;-------------------------------------------------
DIVDND   DB      '3698'            ;Data items
DIVSOR   DB      '4'
QUOTNT   DB      4 DUP(0)
;-------------------------------------------------
MAIN     PROC    NEAR
         MOV     CX,04             ;Initialize 4 loops
         SUB     AH,AH             ;Clear left byte of dividend
         AND     DIVSOR,0FH        ;Clear divisor of ASCII 3
         LEA     SI,DIVDND
         LEA     DI,QUOTNT
A20:
         MOV     AL,[SI]           ;Load ASCII byte (or LODSB)
         AND     AL,0FH            ;Clear ASCII 3
         AAD                       ;Adjust for divide
         DIV     DIVSOR            ;Divide
         MOV     [DI],AL           ;Store quotient
         INC     SI
         INC     DI
         LOOP    A20               ;Loop 4 times
         MOV     AH,4CH
         INT     21H               ;Exit
MAIN     ENDP
         END     BEGIN
```

Figure 13-3   ASCII Division

BINARY-CODED DECIMAL FORMAT

In the preceding example of ASCII division, the quotient was 00090204. If you were to compress this value keeping only the right digit of each byte, the value would be 0924. This latter value is known as *binary-coded-decimal* (BCD) format (also known as *packed*) and contains only the decimal digits 0 through 9. The BCD length is one-half the ASCII length. Note, however, that the decimal number 0924 is in base 10; converted to base 16 (hexadecimal) it would appear as hex 039C.

You can perform addition and subtraction on BCD data. For this purpose, there are two adjustment instructions:

```
DAA  Decimal Adjustment for Addition
DAS  Decimal Adjustment for Subtraction
```

Once again, you have to process the fields one byte at a time. The example program in Figure 13-4 illustrates BCD addition. The procedure B10CONV converts the ASCII values ASC1 and ASC2 to BCD1 and BCD2, respectively. Processing, which is from right to left, could just as easily be left to right. Also, processing words is easier than bytes because you need two ASCII bytes to generate one BCD byte. The use of words requires an even number of bytes in the ASCII field.

The procedure C10ADD performs a loop three times to add the BCD numbers to BCDSUM. The final total is 00127263.

```
TITLE     BCDADD (COM)  Convert ASCII to BCD and add
          .MODEL  SMALL
          .CODE
          ORG     100H
BEGIN:    JMP     SHORT MAIN
;------------------------------------------------
ASC1      DB      '057836'          ;Data items
ASC2      DB      '069427'
BCD1      DB      '000'
BCD2      DB      '000'
BCDSUM    DB      4 DUP(0)
;------------------------------------------------
MAIN      PROC    NEAR
          LEA     SI,ASC1+4         ;Initialize for ASC1
          LEA     DI,BCD1+2
          CALL    B10CONV           ;Call convert routine
          LEA     SI,ASC2+4         ;Initialize for ASC2
          LEA     DI,BCD2+2
          CALL    B10CONV           ;Call convert routine
          CALL    C10ADD            ;Call add routine
          MOV     AH,4CH
          INT     21H               ;Exit
MAIN      ENDP
;                 Convert ASCII to BCD:
;                 --------------------
B10CONV   PROC
          MOV     CL,04             ;Shift factor
          MOV     DX,03             ;No. of words to convert
B20:
          MOV     AX,[SI]           ;Get ASCII pair (or LODSW)
          XCHG    AH,AL
          SHL     AL,CL             ;Shift off
          SHL     AX,CL             ;  ASCII 3s
          MOV     [DI],AH           ;Store BCD digits
          DEC     SI
          DEC     SI
          DEC     DI
          DEC     DX
          JNZ     B20
          RET
B10CONV   ENDP
;                 Add BCD numbers:
;                 ---------------
C10ADD    PROC
          XOR     AH,AH             ;Clear AH
          LEA     SI,BCD1+2         ;Initialize
          LEA     DI,BCD2+2         ;  BCD
          LEA     BX,BCDSUM+3       ;  addresses
          MOV     CX,03             ;3-byte fields
          CLC
C20:
          MOV     AL,[SI]           ;Get BCD1 (or LODSB)
          ADC     AL,[DI]           ;Add BCD2
          DAA                       ;Decimal adjust
          MOV     [BX],AL           ;Store in BCDSUM
          DEC     SI
          DEC     DI
          DEC     BX
          LOOP    C20               ;Loop 3 times
          RET
C10ADD    ENDP
          END     BEGIN
```

Figure 13-4   BCD Conversion and Arithmetic

CONVERSION OF ASCII TO BINARY FORMAT

Performing arithmetic in ASCII or BCD formats is suitable only for short fields. For most arithmetic purposes, it is more practical to convert the number into binary format. In fact, it is easier to convert from ASCII directly to binary rather than convert from ASCII to BCD to binary.

The conversion method is based on the fact that an ASCII number is in base 10 and the computer performs arithmetic in base 2. Here is the procedure:

1. Start with the rightmost byte of the ASCII number and process from right to left.
2. Strip the 3 from the left hex digit of each ASCII byte.
3. Multiply the ASCII digits progressively by 1, then 10, then 100 (hex 1, A, 64), and so forth, and sum the products.

This example converts the ASCII number 1234 to binary:

Step	*Decimal*	*Hexadecimal*
4 × 1 =	4	4
3 × 10 =	30	1E
2 × 100 =	200	C8
1 × 1000 =	1000	3E8
Total:		04D2

Try checking that hex 04D2 really equals decimal 1234. In Figure 13-5, the program converts ASCII number 1234 to binary. The length of the ASCII number, 4, is stored in ASCLEN. Instructions initialize the address of the ASCII field, ASCVAL-1, in the SI register and the length in the BX. The instruction at B20 that moves the ASCII byte to the AL is

```
        MOV    AL,[SI + BX]
```

The operation uses the address of ASCVAL-1 plus the contents of the BX (4), or ASCVAL+3 (initially, the rightmost byte of ASCVAL). Each iteration of the loop decrements BX by 1 and references the next byte to the left. For this addressing you can use BX but not CX, and consequently, you cannot use the LOOP instruction. Also, each iteration multiplies MULT10 by 10, giving a multiplier of 1, 10, 100, and so forth. At the end, BINVAL contains the correct binary value D204 (in reverse byte sequence).

The routine is coded for clarity; for faster processing, the multiplier could be stored in the SI or DI register.

```
TITLE     ASCBIN (COM)  Convert ASCII to binary format
          .MODEL   SMALL
          .CODE
          ORG      100H
BEGIN:    JMP      SHORT MAIN
; --------------------------------------------------
ASCVAL    DB       '1234'              ;Data items
BINVAL    DW       0
ASCLEN    DW       4
MULT10    DW       1
; --------------------------------------------------
MAIN      PROC     NEAR                ;Main procedure
          MOV      CX,10               ;Mult factor
          LEA      SI,ASCVAL-1         ;Address of ASCVAL
          MOV      BX,ASCLEN           ;Length of ASCVAL
B20:
          MOV      AL,[SI+BX]          ;Select ASCII character
          AND      AX,000FH            ;Remove 3-zone
          MUL      MULT10              ;Multiply by 10 factor
          ADD      BINVAL,AX           ;Add to binary
          MOV      AX,MULT10           ;Calculate next
          MUL      CX                  ;  10 factor
          MOV      MULT10,AX
          DEC      BX                  ;Last ASCII character?
          JNZ      B20                 ;  no - continue
          MOV      AH,4CH
          INT      21H                 ;Exit
MAIN      ENDP
          END      BEGIN
```

Figure 13-5   Conversion of ASCII to Binary Format

CONVERSION OF BINARY TO ASCII FORMAT

To print or display an arithmetic result, you have to convert it into ASCII format. The operation involves reversing the previous step: Instead of multiplying, simply divide the binary number by 10 (hex 0A) successively until the result is less than 10. The remainders, which can be only 0 through 9, generate the ASCII number. As an example, let's convert hex 4D2 back into decimal format:

	Quotient	Remainder
A⌐4D2	7B	4
A⌐7B	C	3
A⌐ C	1	2

Since the quotient (1) is now less than the divisor (hex A), the operation is complete. The remainders along with the last quotient form the ASCII result, from right to left, as 1234. All that remains is to store these digits in memory with ASCII 3s, as 31323334.

In Figure 13-6, the program converts a binary number to ASCII format. The routine divides the binary amount successively by 10 until the remaining quotient is less than 10, and stores the generated hex digits in ASCII format. You may find it useful if not downright entertaining to reproduce this program and trace its execution step by step.

```
TITLE    BINASC (COM)  Convert binary format to ASCII
         .MODEL   SMALL
         .CODE
         ORG      100H
BEGIN:   JMP      SHORT MAIN
; ---------------------------------------------------
ASCVAL   DB       4 DUP(' ')          ;Data items
BINVAL   DW       04D2H
; ---------------------------------------------------
MAIN     PROC     NEAR                ;Main procedure
         MOV      CX,0010             ;Divide factor
         LEA      SI,ASCVAL+3         ;Address of ASCVAL
         MOV      AX,BINVAL           ;Get binary field
C20:
         CMP      AX,0010             ;Value < 10?
         JB       C30                 ;  yes - exit
         XOR      DX,DX               ;Clear upper quotient
         DIV      CX                  ;Divide by 10
         OR       DL,30H
         MOV      [SI],DL             ;Store ASCII character
         DEC      SI
         JMP      C20
C30:
         OR       AL,30H              ;Store last quotient
         MOV      [SI],AL             ;  as ASCII character
         MOV      AH,4CH
         INT      21H                 ;Exit
MAIN     ENDP
         END      BEGIN
```

Figure 13-6 Conversion of Binary to ASCII Format

SHIFTING AND ROUNDING

Consider rounding a product to two decimal places. If the product is 12.345, add 5 to the unwanted decimal position and shift right one digit:

```
Product:              12.345
Add 5:             +       5
Rounded product:      12.350 = 12.35
```

If the product is 12.3455, add 50 and shift two digits, and if the product is 12.34555, add 500 and shift three digits:

```
   12.3455                 12.34555
+       50              +       500
   12.3505 = 12.35         12.35055 = 12.35
```

Further, a number with six decimal places requires adding 5000 and shifting four digits, and so forth. Now, since a computer normally processes binary data, 12.345 appears as hex 3039. Adding 5 to 3039 gives 303E, or 12350 in decimal format. So far, so good. But shifting one binary digit results in hex 181F, or 6175—indeed, the shift simply halves the value. We require a shift that is equivalent to shifting right one decimal digit. You can accomplish this shift by dividing by 10, or hex A:

Hex 303E divided by hex A = 4D3, or decimal 1235

Conversion of hex 4D3 to an ASCII number gives 1235. Now just insert a decimal point in the correct position, 12.35, and you can display a rounded and shifted value.

In this fashion you can round and shift any binary number. For three decimal places, add 5 and divide by 10; for four decimal places, add 50 and divide by 100. Perhaps you have noticed a pattern: The rounding factor (5, 50, 500, etc.) is always one-half of the value of the shift factor (10, 100, 1000, etc.).

Of course, a "decimal point" in a binary number is implied and is not normally present.

CONVERTING HOURS AND RATE FOR CALCULATING WAGE

The program in Figure 13-7 allows users to enter hours worked and rate of pay for employees and displays the calculated wage. For brevity, the program omits some error checking. The procedures are as follows:

B10INPT	Accepts hours and rate of pay from the terminal. These values may contain a decimal point.
D10HOUR	Initializes conversion of ASCII hours to binary.
E10RATE	Initializes conversion of ASCII rate to binary.
F10MULT	Performs the multiplication, rounding, and shifting. A wage with zero, one, or two decimal places does not require rounding or shifting. A limitation of this procedure is that it allows up to only six decimal places in wage, although that is certainly more than would normally be required.
G10WAGE	Inserts the decimal point, determines the rightmost position to begin storing ASCII characters, and converts the binary wage to ASCII.
K10DISP	Clears leading zeros to blank and displays the wage.
L10PAUS	Allows the user to view the calculated wage until pressing a key. Pressing Esc tells the program to discontinue processing.
M10ASBI	Converts ASCII to binary (a common routine for hours and for rate) and determines the number of decimal places in the entered value.
Q10SCR	Scrolls the whole screen and sets it to black on cyan.
Q15WIN	Scrolls a window in the middle of the screen where hours, rate, and wage are displayed as brown on blue.

Limitations.   A limitation in this program is that it allows only a total of six decimal places. Another limitation is the magnitude of the wage itself and the fact that shifting involves dividing by a multiple of 10 and converting to ASCII involves dividing by 10. If hours and rate contain a total that exceeds six decimal places or if the wage exceeds about 655,350, the program clears the wage to zero. In practice, a

```
                  page 60,132
        TITLE     SCREMP (EXE)  Enter hours and rate, display wage
                  .MODEL SMALL
                  .STACK 64
        ; --------------------------------------------------------
                  .DATA
        LEFCOL    EQU    28                   ;Equates for screen
        RITCOL    EQU    52
        TOPROW    EQU    10
        BOTROW    EQU    14

        HRSPAR    LABEL  BYTE                 ;Hours parameter list:
        MAXHLEN   DB     6                    ;----- --------- ----
        ACTHLEN   DB     ?
        HRSFLD    DB     6 DUP(?)

        RATEPAR   LABEL  BYTE                 ;Rate parameter list:
        MAXRLEN   DB     6                    ;---- --------- ----
        ACTRLEN   DB     ?
        RATEFLD   DB     6 DUP(?)

        MESSG1    DB     'Hours worked? ','$'
        MESSG2    DB     'Rate of pay? ','$'
        MESSG3    DB     'Wage =   '
        ASCWAGE   DB     10 DUP(30H), 13, 10,'$'
        MESSG4    DB     'Press any key to continue or Esc to quit','$'

        ADJUST    DW     ?
        BINVAL    DW     00
        BINHRS    DW     00
        BINRATE   DW     00
        COL       DB     00
        DECIND    DB     00
        MULT10    DW     01
        NODEC     DW     00
        ROW       DB     00
        SHIFT     DW     ?
        TENWD     DW     10
        ; --------------------------------------------------------
                  .CODE
        BEGIN     PROC   FAR
                  MOV    AX,@data             ;Initialize DS
                  MOV    DS,AX                ;  and ES registers
                  MOV    ES,AX
                  CALL   Q10SCR               ;Clear screen
        A20LOOP:
                  CALL   Q15WIN               ;Clear window
                  CALL   Q20CURS              ;Set cursor
                  CALL   B10INPT              ;Accept hours & rate
                  CALL   D10HOUR              ;Convert hours to binary
                  CALL   E10RATE              ;Convert rate to binary
                  CALL   F10MULT              ;Calculate wage, round
                  CALL   G10WAGE              ;Convert wage to ASCII
                  CALL   K10DISP              ;Display wage

                  CALL   L10PAUS              ;Pause for user
                  CMP    AL,1BH               ;Esc pressed?
                  JNE    A20LOOP              ;  no -- continue
        ;                                     ;  yes -- end of input
                  CALL   Q10SCR               ;Clear screen
                  MOV    AH,4CH
                  INT    21H                  ;Exit program
        BEGIN     ENDP
        ;                Input hours & rate:
        ;                ------------------
        B10INPT   PROC   NEAR
                  MOV    ROW,TOPROW+1         ;Set cursor
                  MOV    COL,LEFCOL+3
                  CALL   Q20CURS
                  INC    ROW
```

Figure 13-7 Displaying Employee Wages

```
            MOV     AH,09
            LEA     DX,MESSG1           ;Prompt for hours
            INT     21H
            MOV     AH,0AH
            LEA     DX,HRSPAR           ;Accept hours
            INT     21H
            MOV     COL,LEFCOL+3        ;Set column
            CALL    Q20CURS
            INC     ROW
            MOV     AH,09
            LEA     DX,MESSG2           ;Prompt for rate
            INT     21H
            MOV     AH,0AH
            LEA     DX,RATEPAR          ;Accept rate
            INT     21H
            RET
B10INPT ENDP
;                   Process hours:
;                   -------------
D10HOUR PROC    NEAR
            MOV     NODEC,00
            MOV     CL,ACTHLEN
            SUB     CH,CH
            LEA     SI,HRSFLD-1         ;Set right position
            ADD     SI,CX               ;  of hours
            CALL    M10ASBI             ;Convert to binary
            MOV     AX,BINVAL
            MOV     BINHRS,AX
            RET
D10HOUR ENDP
;                   Process rate:
;                   ------------
E10RATE PROC    NEAR
            MOV     CL,ACTRLEN
            SUB     CH,CH
            LEA     SI,RATEFLD-1        ;Set right position
            ADD     SI,CX               ;  of rate
            CALL    M10ASBI             ;Convert to binary
            MOV     AX,BINVAL
            MOV     BINRATE,AX
            RET
E10RATE ENDP
;                   Multiply, round, and shift:
;                   --------------------------
F10MULT PROC    NEAR
            MOV     CX,05
            LEA     DI,ASCWAGE          ;Set ASCII wage
            MOV     AX,3030H            ;  to 30s
            CLD
            REP STOSW

            MOV     SHIFT,10
            MOV     ADJUST,00
            MOV     CX,NODEC
            CMP     CL,06               ;If more than 6
            JA      F40                 ;  decimals, error
            DEC     CX
            DEC     CX
            JLE     F30                 ;Bypass if 0, 1, 2 decs
            MOV     NODEC,02
            MOV     AX,01
F20:
            MUL     TENWD               ;Calculate shift factor
            LOOP    F20
            MOV     SHIFT,AX
            SHR     AX,1                ;Calculate round value
            MOV     ADJUST,AX
F30:
            MOV     AX,BINHRS
```

Figure 13-7 Cont.

```
              MUL      BINRATE            ;Calculate wage
              ADD      AX,ADJUST          ;Round wage
              ADC      DX,00
              CMP      DX,SHIFT           ;Product too large
              JB       F50                ;  for DIV?
     F40:
              SUB      AX,AX
              JMP      F70
     F50:
              CMP      ADJUST,00          ;Shift required?
              JZ       F80                ;  no -- bypass
              DIV      SHIFT              ;Shift wage
     F70:     SUB      DX,DX              ;Clear remainder
     F80:     RET
     F10MULT ENDP
     ;                 Convert to ASCII:
     ;                 ----------------
     G10WAGE PROC      NEAR
              LEA      SI,ASCWAGE+7       ;Set decimal point
              MOV      BYTE PTR[SI],'.'
              ADD      SI,NODEC           ;Set right start pos'n
     G30:
              CMP      BYTE PTR[SI],'.'
              JNE      G40                ;Bypass if at dec pos'n
              DEC      SI
     G40:
              CMP      DX,00              ;If DX:AX < 10,
              JNZ      G50
              CMP      AX,0010            ;  operation finished
              JB       G60
     G50:
              DIV      TENWD              ;Remainder is ASCII digit
              OR       DL,30H
              MOV      [SI],DL            ;Store ASCII character
              DEC      SI
              SUB      DX,DX              ;Clear remainder
              JMP      G30
     G60:
              OR       AL,30H             ;Store last ASCII
              MOV      [SI],AL            ;  character
              RET
     G10WAGE ENDP
     ;                 Display wage:
     ;                 ------------
     K10DISP PROC      NEAR
              MOV      COL,LEFCOL+3       ;Set column
              CALL     Q20CURS
              MOV      CX,09
              LEA      SI,ASCWAGE
     K20:                                 ;Clear leading zeros
              CMP      BYTE PTR[SI],30H
              JNE      K30                ;  to blanks
              MOV      BYTE PTR[SI],20H
              INC      SI
              LOOP     K20
     K30:
              LEA      DX,MESSG3          ;Display wage
              MOV      AH,09
              INT      21H
              RET
     K10DISP ENDP
     ;                 Pause for user:
     ;                 --------------
     L10PAUS PROC      NEAR
              MOV      COL,20             ;Set cursor
              MOV      ROW,22
              CALL     Q20CURS
              MOV      AH,09
              LEA      DX,MESSG4          ;Display pause
```

Figure 13-7 Cont.

```
                INT     21H
                MOV     AH,00           ;Accept reply
                INT     16H
                RET
L10PAUS  ENDP
;                       Convert ASCII to binary:
;                       -----------------------
M10ASBI  PROC   NEAR
                MOV     MULT10,0001
                MOV     BINVAL,00
                MOV     DECIND,00
                SUB     BX,BX
M20:
                MOV     AL,[SI]         ;Get ASCII character
                CMP     AL,'.'          ;Bypass if dec point
                JNE     M40
                MOV     DECIND,01
                JMP     M90
M40:
                AND     AX,000FH
                MUL     MULT10          ;Multiply by factor
                ADD     BINVAL,AX       ;Add to binary
                MOV     AX,MULT10       ;Calculate next
                MUL     TENWD           ;  factor x 10
                MOV     MULT10,AX
                CMP     DECIND,00       ;Reached decimal point?
                JNZ     M90
                INC     BX              ;  yes - add to count
M90:
                DEC     SI
                LOOP    M20
                CMP     DECIND,00       ;End of loop
                JZ      M100            ;Any decimal point?
                ADD     NODEC,BX        ;  yes - add to total
M100:    RET
M10ASBI  ENDP
;                       Scroll whole screen:
;                       --------------------
Q10SCR   PROC   NEAR
                MOV     AX,0600H
                MOV     BH,30H          ;Color (07 for BW)
                SUB     CX,CX
                MOV     DX,184FH
                INT     10H
                RET
Q10SCR   ENDP
;                       Scroll display window:
;                       ---------------------
Q15WIN   PROC   NEAR
                MOV     AX,0605H        ;Five rows
                MOV     BH,16H          ;Color (07 for BW)
                MOV     CH,TOPROW
                MOV     CL,LEFCOL
                MOV     DH,BOTROW
                MOV     DL,RITCOL
                INT     10H
                RET
Q15WIN   ENDP
;                       Set cursor:
;                       ----------
Q20CURS  PROC   NEAR
                MOV     AH,02
                SUB     BH,BH
                MOV     DH,ROW          ;Set row
                MOV     DL,COL          ;Set column
                INT     10H
                RET
Q20CURS  ENDP
                END     BEGIN
```

Figure 13-7   Cont.

program would print a warning message or would contain subroutines to overcome these limitations.

Error checking.   A program designed for users other than the programmer should not only produce warning messages, but should also validate hours and rate. The only valid characters are numbers 0 through 9 and one decimal point. For any other character, the program should display a message and return to the input prompt. A useful instruction for validating is XLAT, which Chapter 14 covers.

Test your program thoroughly for all possible conditions: zero value, extreme high and low values, and negative values.

Negative values.   Some applications involve negative amounts, especially for reversing and correcting entries. You could allow a minus sign following a value, such as 12.34−, or preceding the value, such as −12.34. The program could check for a minus sign during conversion to binary. You may want to leave the binary number as positive and simply set an indicator to record the fact that the amount is negative. When the arithmetic is complete, the program, if required, can insert a minus sign in the ASCII field.

If you want the binary number to be negative, convert the ASCII input to binary as usual. See the section "Reversing the Sign" in Chapter 12 for changing the sign of a binary field. And watch out for using IMUL and IDIV to handle signed data. For rounding a negative amount, subtract instead of add 5.

KEY POINTS

- An ASCII field requires one byte for each character. For a numeric field, the rightmost half-byte contains the digit and the leftmost half-byte contains 3.
- Clearing the leftmost ASCII 3s to 0s converts the field to unpacked decimal data.
- Compressing ASCII characters to two digits per byte converts the field to packed or binary-coded-decimal (BCD) data.
- After an ASCII add, use AAA to adjust the answer; after an ASCII subtract, use AAS to adjust the answer.
- Before an ASCII multiplication, convert the multiplicand and multiplier to unpacked decimal by clearing the leftmost hex 3s to 0. After the multiplication, use AAM to adjust the product.
- Before an ASCII divide, convert the dividend and divisor to unpacked decimal by clearing the leftmost hex 3s, and use AAD to adjust the dividend.
- For most arithmetic purposes, convert ASCII numbers to binary. When converting from ASCII to binary format, check that the ASCII characters are valid: 30 though 39, decimal point, and possibly a minus sign.

QUESTIONS

13-1. Suppose that the AX contains ASCII 9 (hex 0039) and the BX contains ASCII 7 (hex 0037). Explain the exact results of the following unrelated operations:

(a) `ADD  AX,33H`   (b) `ADD  AX,BX`
    `AAA`   `AAA`

(c) `SUB  AX,BX`   (d) `SUB  AX,0DH`
    `AAS`   `AAS`

13-2. An unpacked decimal field named UNPAK contains hex 01040705. Code a loop that causes its contents to be proper ASCII 31343735H.

13-3. A field named ASCA contains the ASCII decimal value 173 and another field named ASCB contains ASCII 5. Code the instructions to multiply the ASCII numbers and to store the product in ASCPRO.

13-4. Use the same fields as Question 13-3 to divide ASCA by ASCB and store the quotient in ASCQUO.

13-5. Provide the manual calculations for the following:

(a) Convert ASCII decimal value 46328 to binary and show in hex.

(b) Convert the hex value back to ASCII.

13-6. Code and run a program that determines a computer's memory size (see INT 12H in Chapter 2), converts the size to ASCII format, and displays it on the screen as follows:

```
Memory size is nnn bytes
```

14

TABLE PROCESSING

OBJECTIVE

To cover the requirements for defining tables, performing table searches, and sorting table entries.

INTRODUCTION

Many program applications require tables containing such data as names, descriptions, quantities, and prices. The definition and use of tables involves only one new assembly language instruction, XLAT. Otherwise, it is simply a matter of applying what you have already learned.

This chapter begins by defining some conventional tables. Techniques for table searching are subject to the way in which tables are defined, and many methods of defining and searching other than those given here are possible. Other commonly used features covered are the use of sorting, which rearranges the sequence of data in a table and the use of linked lists, which use pointers to locate items in a table.

DEFINING TABLES

To facilitate table searching, many tables are defined methodically, with each entry defined in the same format (character or numeric), the same length, and in either ascending or descending order.

A table that you have been using throughout this book is the definition of the stack, which in the following is a table of 64 uninitialized words:

```
STACK  DW  64 DUP(?)
```

The following two tables, MONTAB and EMPTAB, initialize character and numeric values, respectively. MONTAB defines an alphabetic abbreviation of the months, and EMPTAB defines a table of employee numbers:

```
MONTAB  DB  'Jan', 'Feb', 'Mar', ..., 'Dec'
EMPTAB  DB  205, 208, 209, 212, 215, 224, ...
```

A table may also contain a mixture of numeric and character values, provided that the numeric values are consistent and the character values are consistent. In the following table of stock items, each numeric entry (stock number) is two digits (one byte) and each character entry (stock description) is nine bytes. The four dots following the description "Paper" are to show that spaces should be present and are not to be keyed into a program.

```
STOKTBL  DB  12,'Computers',14,'Paper....',17,'Diskettes', ...
```

For clarity, you may code table entries vertically:

```
STOKTBL  DB  12,  'Computers'
         DB  14,  'Paper....'
         DB  17,  'Diskettes'
         ...
```

The next example defines 50 entries each initialized to 20 blanks:

```
STORETAB DB  50 DUP(20 DUP(' '))
```

A program could use this table to store up to 50 values that it has generated internally, or it could use it to store the contents of up to 50 entries that it reads from a disk file.

Now let's examine different ways to use tables in programs.

DIRECT TABLE ADDRESSING

Suppose that a terminal user enters a numeric month such as 03 and a program is to convert it to alphabetic, as March. The routine to perform this conversion involves defining a table of alphabetic months, all of equal length. The length of entries should be 9, that of the longest name, September:

```
MONTBL  DB    'January..'
        DB    'February.'
        DB    'March....'
        ...
        DB    'December.'
```

The entry 'January' is at MONTBL+00, 'February' is at MONTBL+09, and 'March' is at MONTBL+18, and so forth. To locate month 03, the program has to perform the following steps:

1. Convert the entered month from ASCII 33 to binary 03.
2. Deduct 1 from the month: $03 - 1 = 02$.
3. Multiply the month by 9 (the length of each entry): $02 \times 9 = 18$.
4. Add this product to the address of MONTBL; the result is the address of the required description: MONTBL+18.

The technique is *direct table addressing*. Figure 14-1 provides an example of a direct access of a table of months' names, although for brevity the descriptions are three rather than nine characters long. The entered month is defined as MONIN; assume that a routine has requested a user to enter an ASCII month number into this location. Since the algorithm directly calculates the required table address, the program does not have to search through the table.

The algorithm in C10CONV uses 12 (December) for input and converts the month like this:

```
Load ASCII month in AX:                   3132
Use 3030 to XOR:                          3030
Unpacked month:                           0102
If leftmost byte nonzero, clear           0002
  and add hex 0A (decimal 10)             000C  (decimal 12)
```

The procedure in D10LOC determines the actual table location:

```
Deduct 1 from AX                          000B  (decimal 11)
Multiply by 3 (length of entries)         0021  (decimal 33)
Add address of table:                     Table+21
```

The procedure deducts 1 because the first entry is at table+0. One way to improve this program is to accept months from the keyboard and to verify that the value is between 01 and 12, inclusive.

Although direct table addressing is very efficient, it works only when entries are both *sequential* and *consecutive*. Thus you could design such a table if entries are in order of 1, 2, 3, . . . , or 106, 107, 108, . . . , or even 5, 10, 15, . . . , although you don't usually have such a neat arrangement of table values. In the next section we examine tables with values that are sequential but not consecutive.

```
                page  60,132
       TITLE    DIRECT (COM)   Direct table addressing
                .MODEL SMALL
                .CODE
                ORG     100H
       BEGIN:   JMP     SHORT MAIN
       ; -------------------------------------------------------
       THREE    DB      3
       MONIN    DB      '11'
       ALFMON   DB      '???','$'
       MONTAB   DB      'Jan','Feb','Mar','Apr','May','Jun'
                DB      'Jul','Aug','Sep','Oct','Nov','Dec'
       ; -------------------------------------------------------
       MAIN     PROC    NEAR                 ;Main procedure
                CALL    C10CONV              ;Convert to binary
                CALL    D10LOC               ;Locate month
                CALL    F10DISP              ;Display alpha month
                MOV     AH,4CH
                INT     21H                  ;Exit
       MAIN     ENDP
       ;                Convert ASCII to binary:
       ;                ------------------------
       C10CONV  PROC
                MOV     AH,MONIN             ;Set up month
                MOV     AL,MONIN+1
                XOR     AX,3030H             ;Clear ASCII 3s
                CMP     AH,00                ;Month 01-09?
                JZ      C20                  ;  Yes - bypass
                SUB     AH,AH                ;  No  - clear AH,
                ADD     AL,10                ;  correct for binary
       C20:     RET
       C10CONV  ENDP
       ;                Locate month in table:
       ;                ----------------------
       D10LOC   PROC
                LEA     SI,MONTAB
                DEC     AL                   ;Correct for table
                MUL     THREE                ;Multiply AL by 3
                ADD     SI,AX
                MOV     CX,03                ;Initialize 3-char move
                CLD
                LEA     DI,ALFMON
                REP MOVSB                    ;Move 3 characters
                RET
       D10LOC   ENDP
       ;                Display alpha month:
       ;                --------------------
       F10DISP  PROC
                MOV     AH,09                ;Request display
                LEA     DX,ALFMON
                INT     21H
                RET
       F10DISP  ENDP
                END     BEGIN
```

Figure 14-1 Direct Table Accessing

TABLE SEARCHING

Some tables consist of numbers with no apparent pattern. A typical example is a
table of stock items with consecutive numbers such as 134, 138, 141, 239, and
245. Another type of table contains ranges of values such as an income tax table.
The following sections examine these types—tables with unique entries and with
ranges—and the requirements for table searching.

Tables with Unique Entries

The stock item numbers for most firms are often not in consecutive order. Numbers tend to be grouped by category, with a leading number to indicate furniture or appliance, or to indicate department number. Also, over time, numbers are deleted and others are added. As a result, the table requires definition of stock numbers and their related descriptions (and unit prices, if required). Stock numbers and descriptions could be defined in separate tables, such as

```
STOKNOS    DB   '05','10','12',...
STOKDCR    DB   'Excavators','Lifters...','Presses...',...
```

or more clearly in the same table, with one line for each number and description:

```
          STOKTAB    DB   '05','Excavators'
                     DB   '10','Lifters...'
                     DB   '12','Presses...'
                     ...
```

The program in Figure 14-2 defines this table with six pairs of stock numbers and descriptions. The search loop at A20 begins comparing the first byte of the input stock number, STOKNIN, to the first byte of stock number in the table. If the comparison is equal, the routine compares the second bytes. If these are equal, the stock number is found and the program at A50 copies the description from the table into DESCRN.

If the comparison of first or second bytes is low, the stock number is known to be not in the table and the program displays an error message (not coded).

If the comparison of first or second bytes is high, the program increments the SI, which contains the table address, in order to compare to the next table stock number. The search loop performs a maximum of six compares. If the loop exceeds six, the stock number is known to be not in the table.

Let's verify this logic by comparing stock numbers 01, 06, and 10 to the table:

- Stock number 01 to table 05. The first byte is equal but the second is low, so the item is not in the table.
- Stock number 06 to table 05. The first byte is equal but the second is high, so compare to the next table entry: Stock number 06 to table 10. The first byte is low, so the item is not in the table.
- Stock number 10 to table 05. The first byte is high, so compare to the next table entry: stock number 10 to table 10. The first byte is equal and the second is equal, so the item is found.

In a program like this, the table could also define unit prices. The program could locate the item in the table, calculate selling price (quantity times unit price), and display the description and selling price.

```
                page    60,132
        TITLE   TABSRCH (COM)  Table search Using CMP
                .MODEL  SMALL
                .CODE
                ORG     100H
        BEGIN:  JMP     SHORT MAIN
        ; -----------------------------------------------------
        STOKNIN DB      '12'                    ;Input stock no.
        STOKTAB DB      '05','Excavators'       ;Start of table
                DB      '10','Lifters    '
                DB      '12','Presses    '
                DB      '15','Valves     '
                DB      '23','Processors'
                DB      '27','Pumps      '      ;End of table
        DESCRN  DB      10 DUP(?)               ;Save area
        ; -----------------------------------------------------

        MAIN    PROC    NEAR
                MOV     CX,06                   ;Initialize compares
                LEA     SI,STOKTAB
        A20:
                MOV     AL,STOKNIN
                CMP     AL,[SI]                 ;Stock#(1) : table
                JNE     A30                     ;Not equal - exit
                MOV     AL,STOKNIN+1            ;Equal:
                CMP     AL,[SI+1]               ;  stock#(2) : table
                JE      A50                     ;  equal -- found
        A30:
                JB      A40                     ;Low -- not in table
                ADD     SI,12                   ;High -- get next entry
                LOOP    A20
        A40:                                    ;Not in table
        ;       ...                             ;Display error message
                JMP     A90
        A50:
                MOV     CX,05                   ;Length of description
                LEA     DI,DESCRN               ;Address of description
                INC     SI
                INC     SI                      ;Extract description
                REP MOVSW                       ;  from table
        ;       ...
        A90:    MOV     AH,4CH
                INT     21H                     ;Exit
        MAIN    ENDP

                END     BEGIN
```

Figure 14-2 Table Search Using CMP

In Figure 14-2, item number is two characters and description is ten. Programming detail would vary for different number of entries and different lengths of entries. For example, to compare three-byte fields, you could use REPE CMPSB, although the instruction also involves use of the CX register.

Tables with Ranges

Income tax provides a typical example of a table with ranges of values. Consider the following imaginary table of taxable income, tax rates, and correction factors:

Taxable Income	Rate	Correction Factor
0-1000.00	.10	0.00
1000.01-2500.00	.15	050.00

Taxable Income	Rate	Correction Factor
2501.01–4250.00	.18	125.00
4250.01–6000.00	.20	260.00
6000.01 and over	.23	390.00

In the tax table, rates increase as taxable income increases. Entries for taxable income contain the high income for each step:

```
TAXTAB   DD  100000, 10, 00000
         DD  250000, 15, 05000
         DD  425000, 18, 12500
         DD  600000, 20, 26000
         DD  999999, 23, 39000
```

To perform a search of the table, the program compares the taxpayer's taxable income to the table's taxable income:

Low or equal: Use the associated rate and correction factor.

High: Increment for the next entry in the table.

The tax deduction is calculated as (taxable income × table rate) − correction factor.

Table Searching Using String Compares

REPE CMPS is useful for comparing item numbers that are two or more bytes long. The program in Figure 14-3 defines STOKTAB, but this time revised as a three-byte stock number. Since STOKNIN is the first field in the data area (following the two-byte JMP) and STOKTAB is next, they appear in the data segment as follows:

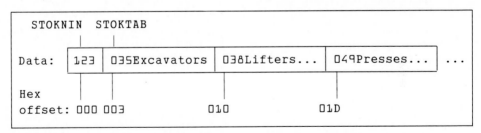

The last entry in the table contains '999' to force termination of the search, since REPE makes the CX unavailable for the LOOP instruction. The search routine compares STOKNIN to the contents of each table entry as follows:

STOKNIN	Table Entry	Result of Comparing
123	035	High: check next entry
123	038	High: check next entry

```
                              page    60,132
                   TITLE      STRSRCH (EXE)  Table search using CMPSB
                              .MODEL   SMALL
                              .STACK   64
                   ; ---------------------------------------------------
                              .DATA
0000  31 32 33     STOKNIN DB         '123'
0003  30 33 35 45 78 63  STOKTAB DB   '035','Excavators'    ;Start table
      61 76 61 74 6F 72
      73
0010  30 33 38 4C 69 66       DB      '038','Lifters    '
      74 65 72 73 20 20
      20
001D  30 34 39 50 72 65       DB      '049','Presses    '
      73 73 65 73 20 20
      20
002A  31 30 32 56 61 6C       DB      '102','Valves     '
      76 65 73 20 20 20
      20
0037  31 32 33 50 72 6F       DB      '123','Processors'
      63 65 73 73 6F 72
      73
0044  31 32 37 50 75 6D       DB      '127','Pumps      '
      70 73 20 20 20 20
      20
0051  39 39 39               DB      '999', 10 DUP(' ')   ;End table
      000A[20]
005E  000A[??]     DESCRN  DB         10 DUP(?)              ;Save area
                   ; ---------------------------------------------------
                              .CODE
0000                BEGIN   PROC    FAR
0000  B8 ---- R             MOV     AX,@data     ;Initialize segment
0003  8E D8                 MOV     DS,AX        ;  registers
0005  8E C0                 MOV     ES,AX
0007  FC                    CLD
0008  8D 3E 0003 R          LEA     DI,STOKTAB   ;Initialize table addr
000C                A20:
000C  B9 0003              MOV     CX,03        ;Compare 3 bytes
000F  8D 36 0000 R         LEA     SI,STOKNIN   ;Init'ze stock# addr
0013  F3/ A6               REPE CMPSB           ;Stock# : table
0015  74 09                JE      A30          ;  Equal - exit
0017  72 15                JB      A40          ;  Low - not in table
0019  03 F9                ADD     DI,CX        ;Add CX to offset
001B  83 C7 0A             ADD     DI,10        ;Next table item
001E  EB EC                JMP     A20
0020                A30:
0020  B9 0005              MOV     CX,05        ;Set to move 5 words
0023  8B F7                MOV     SI,DI
0025  8D 3E 005E R         LEA     DI,DESCRN    ;Init addr of descr'n
0029  F3/ A5               REP MOVSW            ;Move descr'n
                   ;        ...                 ;  from table
002B  EB 01 90             JMP     A90
002E                A40:
                   ;                   <Display error message>
002E                A90:
002E  B4 4C                MOV     AH,4CH
0030  CD 21                INT     21H          ;Exit
0032  CB                   RET
0033                BEGIN   ENDP
                              END     BEGIN
```

Figure 14-3   Table Search Using CMPSB

STOKNIN	Table Entry	Result of Comparing
123	049	High: check next entry
123	102	High: check next entry
123	123	Equal: entry found

The program initializes the DI to the offset address of STOKTAB (003), the CX to 03, and the SI to the offset of STOKNIN (000). The CMPSB operation compares byte for byte as long as the bytes are equal, and automatically increments the DI and SI registers. A comparison to the first table entry (123:035) causes termination after one byte; the DI contains 004, the SI contains 001, and the CX contains 02. For the next comparison, the DI should contain 010 and the SI should contain 000. Correcting the SI simply involves reloading the address of STOKNIN. For the address of the table entry that should be in the DI, however, the increment depends on whether the comparison ends after one, two, or three bytes. The CX contains the number of the remaining uncompared bytes, in this case, 02. Adding the CX value plus the length of the stock description gives the offset of the next table item, as follows:

```
Address in DI after CMPSB:         Hex 004
Add CX:                              + 02
Add length of description:          + 0A
Next table offset address:         Hex 010
```

Since the CX contains the number of the remaining uncompared bytes (if any), the arithmetic works for all cases, and terminates after one, two, or three comparisons. On an equal comparison, the CX contains 00 and the DI is already incremented to the address of the required description. A REP MOVSW operation then copies the description into DESCRN.

Tables with Variable-Length Entries

It is possible to define a table with variable-length entries. A special "delimiter" character such as hex 00 could follow each entry, and hex FF could distinguish the end of the table. However, be sure that no byte within an entry contains the bit configuration of a delimiter. For example, an arithmetic binary amount can contain any possible bit configuration. Use the SCAS instruction for the search.

THE XLAT (TRANSLATE) INSTRUCTION

The XLAT instruction translates the contents of a byte into another predefined value. You could use XLAT to validate the contents of data items or, if you transfer data between a PC and an IBM mainframe computer, to translate data between ASCII and EBCDIC formats.

The following example converts ASCII numbers 0–9 into EBCDIC. Since the representation in ASCII is 30–39 and in EBCDIC is F0–F9, you could use an OR operation to make the change. However, let's also convert all other characters to blank, EBCDIC hex 40. For XLAT, you define a translate table that accounts for all 256 possible characters, with EBCDIC codes inserted in the ASCII positions:

```
XLTBL    DB   48 DUP(40H)                         ;EBCDIC blanks
         DB   0F0H,0F1H,0F2H,0F3H, ...,0F9H       ;EBCDIC 0-9
         DB   198 DUP(40H)                        ;EBCDIC blanks
```

XLAT expects the address of the table in the BX register and the byte to be translated (let's name it ASCNO) in the AL register. The following performs the initialization and translation:

```
LEA  BX,XLTBL    ;Load address of table
MOV  AL,ASCNO    ;Load character to translate
XLAT             ;Translate to EBCDIC
```

XLAT uses the AL value as an offset address, in effect, the address in the BX plus the offset in the AL. If ASCNO contains 00, for example, the table address would be XLTBL+0, and XLAT would replace the 00 in the AL with hex 40 from the table. If ASCNO contains hex 32 (decimal 50), the table address is XLTBL+50. This position contains hex F1 (EBCDIC 1), which XLAT inserts in the AL register.

The program in Figure 14-4 expands this example to convert ASCII minus sign (2D) and decimal point (2E) to EBCDIC (60 and 4B, respectively) and to loop through a six-byte field. Initially, ASCNO contains −31.5 followed by a blank, or hex 2D33312E3520. At the end of the loop, EBCNO should contain hex 60F3F14BF540.

```
         page    60,132
TITLE    XLATE   (COM)  Translate ASCII to EDCDIC
         .MODEL  SMALL
         .CODE
         ORG     100H
BEGIN:   JMP     MAIN
;------------------------------------------------------------
ASCNO    DB      '-31.5 '      ;ASCII item to convert
EBCNO    DB      6 DUP(' ')    ;Converted EBCDIC item
XLTAB    DB      45 DUP(40H)   ;Translate table
         DB      60H, 4BH
         DB      40H
         DB      0F0H,0F1H,0F2H,0F3H,0F4H,0F5H,0F6H,0F7H,0F8H,0F9H
         DB      198 DUP(40H)
;------------------------------------------------------------
MAIN     PROC    NEAR          ;Main procedure
         LEA     SI,ASCNO      ;Address of ASCNO
         LEA     DI,EBCNO      ;Address of EBCNO
         MOV     CX,06         ;Length
         LEA     BX,XLTAB      ;Address of table
A20:
         MOV     AL,[SI]       ;Get ASCII character
         XLAT                  ;Translate
         MOV     [DI],AL       ;Store in EBCNO
         INC     SI
         INC     DI
         LOOP    A20           ;Repeat 6 times
;        ...
         MOV     AH,4CH
         INT     21H           ;Exit
MAIN     ENDP
         END     BEGIN
```

Figure 14-4 Conversion of ASCII to EBCDIC

DISPLAYING HEX AND ASCII CHARACTERS

The program in Figure 14-5 displays every hex value 00–FF as well as most of the related ASCII symbols. For example, the program displays the ASCII symbol S and its hex representation 53. The full display appears on the screen as a 16 by 16 matrix:

```
00  01  02  03  04  05  06  07  08  09  0A  0B  0C   0D  0E  0F
 .   .   .   .   .   .   .   .   .   .   .   .   .    .   .   .
 .   .   .   .   .   .   .   .   .   .   .   .   .    .   .   .
 .   .   .   .   .   .   .   .   .   .   .   .   .    .   .   .
F0  F1  F2  F3  F4  F5  F6  F7  F8  F9  FA  FB  FC   FD  FE  FF
```

As we saw in Figure 8-1, displaying ASCII symbols is no problem. However, displaying the hex representation of an ASCII value is more involved. For example, to display as ASCII, you have to convert hex 00 to hex 3030, hex 01 to hex 3031, and so forth.

The program initializes HEXCTR to 00 and subsequently increments it. The procedure C10HEX splits HEXCTR into its two hex digits. For example, assume that HEXCTR contains hex 4F. The routine extracts the hex 4 and uses its value and a table for a translate operation. The value returned to the AL is hex 34. The routine then extracts the hex F and translates it to hex 46. The result, hex 3446, displays as 4F.

The procedure D10DISP converts non-ASCII characters to blanks. Since DOS INT 21H service call 40H for displaying treats 1AH as an end-of-file character, the program also changes it to blank. A program using DOS service 09H would have to change the '$' terminator to a blank. When a row is full with 16 characters, the procedure displays it.

There are many other ways of converting hex digits to ASCII characters; for example, you could experiment with shifting and comparing.

SORTING TABLE ENTRIES

Often an application requires sorting data in a table into ascending or descending sequence. For example, a user may want a list of stock descriptions in ascending sequence, or a list of each sales agent's total sales in descending sequence. Typically, the data in the table is not defined as in previous examples, but is loaded from a terminal or disk. Let's make a clear distinction: This chapter covers sorting of table entries; an application that involves sorting of disk records can be much more complex.

There are a number of table sort routines varying from not efficient but clear to efficient but obscure. The sort routine in this section is fairly efficient and could serve for most table sorting. Now you may not do a lot of table sorting, and even the least efficient assembly routine may seem to execute at the speed of light. Also, the objective of this book is to explain assembly language, not sort, techniques.

```
                      page 60,132
TITLE         ASCHEX (COM)  Converting ASCII characters to hex
              .MODEL    SMALL
              .CODE
              ORG       100H
BEGIN:        JMP       SHORT MAIN
; -----------------------------------------------------------
DISPROW       DB        16 DUP(5 DUP(' ')), 13
HEXCTR        DB        00
XLATAB        DB        30H,31H,32H,33H,34H,35H,36H,37H,38H,39H
              DB        41H,42H,43H,44H,45H,46H
; -----------------------------------------------------------
MAIN          PROC      NEAR                ;Main procedure
              CALL      Q10CLR              ;Clear screen
              LEA       SI,DISPROW
A20LOOP:
              CALL      C10HEX              ;Translate
              CALL      D10DISP             ;  and display
              CMP       HEXCTR,0FFH         ;Last hex value (FF)?
              JE        A50                 ;  yes - terminate
              INC       HEXCTR              ;  no  - incr next hex
              JMP       A20LOOP
A50:          MOV       AH,4CH
              INT       21H                 ;Exit
MAIN          ENDP

C10HEX        PROC      NEAR                ;Convert to hex
              MOV       AH,00
              MOV       AL,HEXCTR           ;Get hex pair
              MOV       CL,04               ;Set shift value
              SHR       AX,CL               ;Shift off right hex digit
              LEA       BX,XLATAB           ;Set table address
              XLAT                          ;Translate hex
              MOV       [SI],AL             ;Store left character

              MOV       AL,HEXCTR
              AND       AL,0FH              ;Clear left hex digit
              XLAT                          ;Translate hex
              MOV       [SI]+1,AL           ;Store right character
              RET
C10HEX        ENDP

D10DISP       PROC      NEAR                ;Display
              MOV       AL,HEXCTR           ;Get character
              MOV       [SI]+3,AL
              CMP       AL,1AH              ;EOF character?
              JE        D20                 ;  yes - bypass
              CMP       AL,07H              ;Lower than 7?
              JB        D30                 ;  yes - ok
              CMP       AL,10H              ;Higher/equal 16?
              JAE       D30                 ;  yes - ok
D20:                                        ;Else force blank
              MOV       BYTE PTR [SI]+3,20H
D30:
              ADD       SI,05               ;Next location in row
              LEA       DI,DISPROW+80
              CMP       DI,SI               ;Filled up row?
              JNE       D40                 ;  no - bypass

              MOV       AH,40H              ;Yes - request display
              MOV       BX,01               ;  file handle
              MOV       CX,81               ;  entire row
              LEA       DX,DISPROW
              INT       21H
              LEA       SI,DISPROW          ;Reset display row
D40:          RET
D10DISP       ENDP
```

Figure 14-5 Displaying ASCII and Hex

```
Q10CLR      PROC    NEAR                ;Clear screen
            MOV     AX,0600H
            MOV     BH,61H              ;Color (07 for BW)
            MOV     CX,0000
            MOV     DX,184FH
            INT     10H
            RET
Q10CLR      ENDP
            END     BEGIN
```

Figure 14-5 (cont.)

A general approach is to compare a table entry to the entry immediately following. If the comparison is high, exchange the entries. Continue in this fashion comparing entry 1 to entry 2, entry 2 to entry 3, to the end of the table, exchanging where necessary. If you made any exchanges, repeat the entire process from the start of the table, comparing entry 1 to entry 2. If you didn't make any exchanges, the table is in sequence and you can terminate the sort.

In the following pseudocode, SWAP is an item that indicates whether an exchange was made (YES) or not made (NO).

```
G10:    Initialize address of last entry in table
G20:    Set SWAP to NO
        Initialize address of start of table
G30:    Table entry > next entry?
            Yes:  Exchange entries
                  Set SWAP to YES
        Increment for next entry in table
        At end of table?
            No:   Jump to G30
            Yes:  Does SWAP = YES?
                  Yes:  Jump to G20 (repeat sort)
                  No:   End of sort
```

The program in Figure 14-6 allows a user to enter up to 30 names from a keyboard. When all the names are entered, the program sorts the names into ascending sequence and displays the sorted names on the screen. Note that the table entries are all fixed-length 30 bytes; a routine for sorting variable-length data would be more complicated.

LINKED LISTS

A linked list contains data in what are called cells, like entries in a table but in no specified sequence. Each cell contains a pointer to the next cell in the list. (A cell may also contain a pointer to the preceding cell so that searching may proceed in either direction.) The method facilitates additions and deletions to a list without the need for expanding and contracting it.

```
            page 60,132
TITLE    NMSORT (EXE)  Sort names entered from terminal
         .MODEL  SMALL
         .STACK  64
; --------------------------------------------------------
         .DATA
NAMEPAR LABEL    BYTE                  ;Name parameter list:
MAXNLEN DB       21                    ;  maximum length
NAMELEN DB       ?                     ;  no. of chars entered
NAMEFLD DB       21 DUP(' ')           ;  name

CRLF    DB       13, 10, '$'
ENDADDR DW       ?
MESSG1  DB       'Name? ', '$'
NAMECTR DB       00
NAMETAB DB       30 DUP(20 DUP(' ')) ;Name table
NAMESAV DB       20 DUP(?), 13, 10, '$'
SWAPPED DB       00
; --------------------------------------------------------
         .CODE
BEGIN   PROC     FAR
        MOV      AX,@data             ;Initialize DS
        MOV      DS,AX                ;  and ES registers
        MOV      ES,AX
        CLD
        LEA      DI,NAMETAB
        CALL     Q10CLR               ;Clear screen
        CALL     Q20CURS              ;Set cursor
A20LOOP:
        CALL     B10READ              ;Accept name
        CMP      NAMELEN,00           ;Any more names?
        JZ       A30                  ;  no - go to sort
        CMP      NAMECTR,30           ;30 names entered?
        JE       A30                  ;  yes - go to sort
        CALL     D10STOR              ;Store entered name in table
        JMP      A20LOOP
A30:                                  ;End of input
        CALL     Q10CLR               ;Clear screen
        CALL     Q20CURS              ;  and set cursor
        CMP      NAMECTR,01           ;One or no name entered?
        JBE      A40                  ;  yes - exit
        CALL     G10SORT              ;Sort stored names
        CALL     K10DISP              ;Display sorted names
A40:    MOV      AH,4CH               ;Exit program
        INT      21H
BEGIN   ENDP

;                 Accept name as input:
;                 --------------------
B10READ PROC
        MOV      AH,09
        LEA      DX,MESSG1            ;Display prompt
        INT      21H
        MOV      AH,0AH
        LEA      DX,NAMEPAR           ;Accept name
        INT      21H
        MOV      AH,09
        LEA      DX,CRLF              ;Return/line feed
        INT      21H

        MOV      BH,00                ;Clear characters after name
        MOV      BL,NAMELEN           ;Get count of chars
        MOV      CX,21
        SUB      CX,BX                ;Calc remaining length
B20:
        MOV      NAMEFLD[BX],20H      ;Set name to blank
        INC      BX
        LOOP     B20
        RET
```

Figure 14-6   Sorting a Table of Names

```
B10READ ENDP
;                       Store name in table:
;                       --------------------
D10STOR PROC
        INC     NAMECTR             ;Add to number of names
        CLD
        LEA     SI,NAMEFLD
        MOV     CX,10
        REP MOVSW                   ;Move name to table
        RET
D10STOR ENDP
;                       Sort names in table:
;                       --------------------
G10SORT PROC
        SUB     DI,40               ;Set up stop address
        MOV     ENDADDR,DI
G20:
        MOV     SWAPPED,00          ;Set up start
        LEA     SI,NAMETAB          ; of table
G30:
        MOV     CX,20               ;Length of compare
        MOV     DI,SI
        ADD     DI,20               ;Next name for compare
        MOV     AX,DI
        MOV     BX,SI
        REPE CMPSB                  ;Compare name to next
        JBE     G40                 ;  no exchange
        CALL    H10XCHG             ;  exchange
G40:
        MOV     SI,AX
        CMP     SI,ENDADDR          ;End of table?
        JBE     G30                 ;  no - continue
        CMP     SWAPPED,00          ;Any swaps?
        JNZ     G20                 ;  yes - continue
        RET                         ;  no - end of sort
G10SORT ENDP

;                       Exchange table entries:
;                       ---------------------
H10XCHG PROC
        MOV     CX,10
        LEA     DI,NAMESAV
        MOV     SI,BX
        REP MOVSW                   ;Move lower item to save

        MOV     CX,10
        MOV     DI,BX
        REP MOVSW                   ;Move higher item to lower

        MOV     CX,10
        LEA     SI,NAMESAV
        REP MOVSW                   ;Move save to higher item
        MOV     SWAPPED,01          ;Signal that exchange made
        RET
H10XCHG ENDP
;                       Display sorted names:
;                       --------------------
K10DISP PROC
        LEA     SI,NAMETAB
K20:
        LEA     DI,NAMESAV          ;Init'ze start of table
        MOV     CX,10
        REP MOVSW
        MOV     AH,09
        LEA     DX,NAMESAV
        INT     21H                 ;Display
        DEC     NAMECTR             ;Is this last one?
        JNZ     K20                 ;  no - loop
        RET                         ;  yes - exit
```

Figure 14-6   (cont.)

```
K10DISP ENDP
;                        Clear screen:
;                        ------------
Q10CLR  PROC
        MOV     AX,0600H
        MOV     BH,61H                  ;Color (07 for BW)
        SUB     CX,CX
        MOV     DX,184FH
        INT     10H
        RET
Q10CLR  ENDP
;                        Set cursor:
;                        ----------
Q20CURS PROC
        MOV     AH,02
        SUB     BH,BH
        SUB     DX,DX                   ;Set cursor to 00,00
        INT     10H
        RET
Q20CURS ENDP

        END     BEGIN
```

Figure 14-6   (cont.)

For our purposes, the linked list contains cells with part number (four-byte ASCII value), unit price (binary word), and a pointer (binary word) to the next cell in the list. Thus each entry is eight bytes in length. The pointer is an offset from the start of the list. The linked list begins at offset 0000, the second item in the series is at 0024, the third is at 0032, and so forth:

Offset	Part no.	Price	Next address
0000	0103	12.50	0024
0008	1720	08.95	0016
0016	1827	03.75	0000
0024	0120	13.80	0032
0032	0205	25.00	0008

The item at offset 0016 contains zero as the next address, either to indicate the end of the list or to make it circular.

The program in Figure 14-7 uses the contents of the defined linked list, LINKLST, to locate a specified part number, in this case, 1720. The search begins with the first table item. The logic for using CMPSB is similar to that in Figure 14-3. The program compares part number (1720) to table item:

- Equal: the search is finished.
- Low: the item is not in the table.
- High: the program gets the offset from the table for the next item to be compared. If the offset is zero, the search ends without finding an equal; otherwise, the comparison is repeated.

```
             page    60,132
   TITLE     LINKLST (EXE)  Use of a Linked List
   ;-----------------------------------------------------
             .MODEL    SMALL
             .STACK    64              ;Define stack
             .DATA
   PARTNO    DB      '1720'            ;Part number
   LINKLST   DB      '0103'            ;Linked list table
             DW      1250, 24
             DB      '1720'
             DW      0895, 16
             DB      '1827'
             DW      0375, 00
             DB      '0120'
             DW      1380, 32
             DB      '0205'
             DW      2500, 08

             .CODE                     ;Define code segment
   BEGIN     PROC    FAR
             MOV     AX,@data          ;Set address of DATASG
             MOV     DS,AX             ;    in DS
             MOV     ES,AX             ;    and ES register
             CLD
             LEA     DI,LINKLST        ;Initialize table address
   A20:
             MOV     CX,04             ;Set to compare 4 bytes
             LEA     SI,PARTNO         ;Init'ze part# address
             REPE CMPSB                ;Part# : table
             JE      A30               ;   Equal - exit
             JB      A40               ;   Low  - not in table
             ADD     DI,CX             ;Add CX value to offset
             ADD     DI,02             ;Get offset of next item
             MOV     DX,[DI]
             LEA     DI,LINKLST
             ADD     DI,DX
             CMP     DX,00             ;Last table entry?
             JNE     A20
             JMP     A40
   A30:
   ;                 <Item Found>
             JMP     A90
   A40:
   ;                 <Display error message>

   A90:
             MOV     AX,4C00H          ;Exit
             INT     21H
   BEGIN     ENDP                      ;End of procedure
             END     BEGIN             ;End of program
```

Figure 14-7   Linked List

A more complete program could allow a user to enter any part number and could display the price as an ASCII value.

TYPE, LENGTH, AND SIZE OPERATORS

The assembler supplies a number of special operators that you may find useful. For example, the length of a table may change from time to time and you may have to modify the program for the new definition and for routines that check for the table end. But the use of the TYPE, LENGTH, and SIZE operators can enable you to reduce the number of instructions that have to be changed.

Consider this definition of a table of ten words:

```
TABLEX DW 10 DUP(?)    ;Table with 10 words
```

The program can use the TYPE operator to determine the definition (DW in this case), the LENGTH operator to determine the DUP factor (10), and the SIZE operator to determine the number of bytes (10 × 2, or 20). The following examples illustrate the three operators:

```
MOV  AX,TYPE TABLEX      ;AX = 0002 (2 bytes)
MOV  BX,LENGTH TABLEX    ;BX = 000A (10)
MOV  CX,SIZE TABLEX      ;CX = 0014 (20)
```

You may use the values that LENGTH and SIZE return to terminate a table search or a sort. For example, if the SI register contains the incremented address of a table search, test it using

```
CMP  SI,SIZE TABLEX
```

Chapter 24 describes TYPE, LENGTH, and SIZE in detail.

KEY POINTS

- For most purposes, define tables with related entries that are the same length and data format.
- Design tables based on their data format. For example, entries may be character or numeric and one, two, or more bytes each. It may be more practical to define two tables: one, for example, for three-byte item numbers and another for one-word unit prices. The search could increment the address of the item number table by 3 and the address of the price table by 2. Or, keep a count of the number of loops; on finding an equal item multiply the count by 2 (SHL one bit), and use this value as an offset to the address of the price table. (Actually, initialize the count to −1.)
- Remember that the maximum numeric value for a DB is 256 and that numeric DW and DD reverse the bytes. Also, CMP and CMPSW assume that words contain bytes in reverse sequence.
- If a table is subject to frequent changes or if several programs reference it, store it on disk. An updating program can handle changes to the table. Any program can load the table from disk and the programs need not be changed.

QUESTIONS

14-1. Define a table that contains the names of the days of the week, beginning with Sunday.

14-2. Given that Sunday equals 1, code the instructions that directly access the name from the table defined in Question 14-1. Use any suitable names.

14-3. Define three separate related tables that contain the following data: **(a)** item numbers 06, 10, 14, 21, 24; **(b)** item descriptions Videotape, Receivers, Modems, Keyboards, Diskettes; **(c)** item prices 93.95, 82.25, 90.67, 85.80, 13.85

14-4. Code a program that allows a user to enter item number (ITEMIN) and quantity (QTYIN) from the keyboard. Using the tables defined in Question 14-3, include a table search routine using ITEMIN to locate an item number in the table. Extract description and price from the tables. Calculate value (quantity × price), and display description and value on the screen.

14-5. Using the description table defined in Question 14-3, code the following: **(a)** a routine that moves the contents of the table to another (empty) table; **(b)** a routine that sorts the contents of this new table into ascending sequence by description.

14-6. A program is required to provide simple encryption of data. Define an 80-byte data area named CRYPTEXT containing any ASCII data. Arrange a translate table to convert the data somewhat randomly, for example, A to X, B to E, C to R, and so forth. Provide for all possible byte values. Arrange a second translate table that reverses (decrypts) the data. The program should perform the following steps:
- Display the original contents of CRYPTEXT on a line;
- Encrypt CRYPTEXT and display it on another line;
- Decrypt CRYPTEXT and display it on yet another line.

The third line should display the same data as the first line.

15

DISK STORAGE ORGANIZATION

OBJECTIVE

To examine the basic formats for hard disk and diskette storage, the directory, and the file allocation table.

INTRODUCTION

A programmer can survive with surprisingly little knowledge of disk organization. However, at some point, a serious programmer has to be familiar with the technical details of disk organization, particularly for developing utility programs that examine the contents of diskettes and hard disks. Where a reference to either disk or diskette is used, we use the general term *disk* in this book.

In this chapter first we explain the use of files and records, then cover the concepts of tracks, sectors, and cylinders, and provide capacity values for commonly used devices.

Also covered is the important data recorded on a disk, including the boot record (which helps the system load the DOS programs from disk into memory), the directory (which contains the name and status of each file on the disk), and the file allocation table (FAT) (which allocates disk space for files).

FILES AND RECORDS

Data on disk is stored in the form of a *file* just as you have stored your programs. Although there is no restriction on the kind of data that you may keep in a file, a typical user file would consist of *records* for customers, inventory supplies, or name and address lists. Each record contains information about a particular customer or inventory item. Within a file, all records are usually the same length and format. A record contains one or more *fields*. A customer file, for example, could consist of records that contain such fields as customer number, customer name, and balance owing. The records could be in ascending sequence by customer number, as follows:

| #1 | name | amt | | #2 | name | amt | | #3 | name | amt | . . . | #n | name | amt |

Processing for hard disk is similar to that for diskette, except that you have to supply a path name to access files in subdirectories.

DISK ORGANIZATION

For processing records, it is useful to be familiar with disk organization. Each side of a diskette and a hard disk contains a number of concentric *tracks,* numbered beginning with 00. Each track is formatted into *sectors* of 512 bytes each. A diskette has two sides, whereas a hard disk contains a number of two-sided disks.

Each time you read from or write to a diskette, the drive motor starts the diskette moving. After the data is transferred, the diskette stops moving. A hard disk is continually spinning, and when you read or write, the disk drive controller may have to move the read–write head to the required track. It then waits for the appropriate sector to reach the read–write head. Figure 15-1 illustrates these features.

A *cylinder* is a vertical set of all tracks with the same number on each side. Thus cylinder 0 is the set of tracks 0 on each side, cylinder 1 is the set of tracks 1 on each side, and so forth. For a diskette, then, cylinder 0 consists of track 0 on side 1 and track 0 on side 2, cylinder 1 consists of track 1 on side 1 and track 1 on side 2, and so forth. When writing a file, the system fills all the tracks on a cylinder, and then advances the read–write heads to the next cylinder.

DISK CAPACITY

Here are common diskette storage capacities:

Version	Tracks/Side (Cylinders)	Sectors /Track	Bytes /Sector	Total Two Sides
$5\frac{1}{4}$ in. 360KB	40	9	512	368,640
$5\frac{1}{4}$ in. 1.2MB	80	15	512	1,228,800
$3\frac{1}{2}$ in. 720KB	80	9	512	737,280
$3\frac{1}{2}$ in. 1.44MB	80	18	512	1,474,560

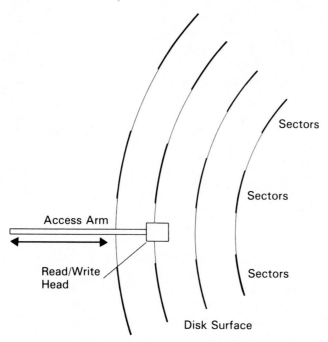

Sectors

Sectors

Access Arm

Read/Write
Head

Sectors

Disk Surface

Figure 15-1   Disk Surface and
Read/Write Head

Here are common hard disk storage capacities:

Model	Tracks/Side (Cylinders)	Sectors /Track	Bytes /Sector	Sides	Total Capacity
10 megabytes	306	17	512	4	10,653,696
20 megabytes	615	17	512	4	21,411,840
30 megabytes	615	17	512	6	32,117,760
60 megabytes	940	17	512	8	65,454,080

A reference to disk sides (heads), tracks, and sectors is by number. Side and track numbers begin with 0, whereas sector numbers begin with 1.

To account for the information stored on disk, DOS reserves certain sectors for its own purposes. The organization of diskette and hard disk varies according to their capacity. A formatted two-sided diskette with nine sectors per track contains the following:

Side 0, track 0, sector 1	Boot record
Side 0, track 0, sectors 2–3	File allocation table (FAT)
Side 0, track 0, sectors 4–7	Directory
Side 1, track 0, sectors 1–3	Directory
Side 1, track 0, sectors 4 and on	Data files

BOOT RECORD

The boot record contains instructions to help the system load the DOS programs from disk into memory. If you use FORMAT /S to format a disk, DOS copies the system modules IBMBIO.COM and IBMDOS.COM onto the first sectors of the data file area. The boot record contains the instructions that load the system programs IBMBIO.COM, IBMDOS.COM, and COMMAND.COM into memory. The boot record contains the following information:

00H	Short or far jump to the bootstrap routine at 1EH or 3EH in the boot record.
03H	Manufacturer name and DOS version number.
0BH	BIOS parameter block containing such information as bytes per sector, sectors per cluster, reserved sectors, sectors per track, and number of read–write heads.
1EH	Bootstrap loader routine for DOS versions through 3.3.
3EH	Under DOS 4.0 and on, the boot record is 200H bytes in size and the bootstrap loader routine begins at 3EH.

Records for data files begin on side 1, track 0, sector 3 through sector 9. The system stores records next on side 0, track 1, then side 1, track 1, then side 0, track 2, and so forth. This feature of filling data on opposite tracks (in the same cylinder) before proceeding to the next cylinder reduces disk head motion and is the method used on both diskettes and hard disks.

CLUSTERS

A cluster is a group of sectors that DOS treats as a unit of storage space. A cluster size is always a power of 2, such as one, two, four, or eight sectors. A file begins on a cluster boundary and requires a minimum of one cluster. Thus a 100-byte file stored on disk with eight sectors per cluster uses $8 \times 512 = 4096$ bytes of storage.

On a disk device that uses one sector per cluster, the two are the same. A disk that uses two sectors per cluster would look like this:

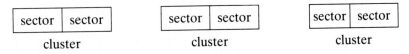

A cluster may also overlap from one track to another. A disk that uses four sectors per cluster would look like this:

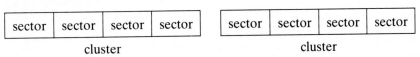

DOS stores an entry in its disk file allocation table (FAT) for each cluster for a file. Consequently, the use of clusters with multiple sectors reduces the number of entries in the FAT and enables DOS to address a larger disk storage space.

DIRECTORY

All files begin on a cluster boundary, even if they contain less than 512 bytes (or multiples of 512). DOS creates a directory entry for each file in cylinder 0 of the disk. Each entry describes the name, date, size, and location of a file on the disk. Directory entries have the following format:

Byte	Purpose
0–7	Filename as defined in the program that created the file. The first byte can also indicate file status:
	00H File has never been used
	05H First character of filename is actually E5H
	2EH Entry is for a subdirectory
	E5H File has been deleted
8–10	Filename extension.
11	File attribute defining the type of file. A file may contain more than one attribute, such as 07H for a system file that is read-only and hidden.
	00H Normal file
	01H File that can only be read
	02H Hidden file, not displayed by a directory search
	04H DOS system file, not displayed by a directory search
	08H Volume label, in the first 11 bytes
	10H Subdirectory
	20H Archive file, indicates if rewritten since last update.
12–21	Reserved for DOS.
22–23	Time of day when the file was created or last updated, stored as 16 bits in binary format as |hhhhhmmmmmmsssss|.
24–25	Date when the file was created or last updated, stored as 16 bits in binary format as |yyyyyyym|mmmddddd|. Year begins at 1980 and can be 0–119, month can be 01–12, and day can be 01–31.
26–27	Starting cluster of the file. The number is relative to the last two sectors of the directory. The first data file (with no DOS COM modules) begins at relative cluster 002. The actual side, track, and cluster depend on disk capacity.
28–31	File size in bytes. When you create a file, DOS calculates and stores its size in this field.

For fields in the directory that exceed one byte, the bytes are stored in reverse sequence.

FILE ALLOCATION TABLE

The purpose of the file allocation table (FAT) is to allocate disk space for files. If you create a new file or revise an existing file, DOS revises the FAT entries according to the location of the file on disk. The boot record is at sector 1 and the FAT begins at sector 2. The FAT contains an entry for each cluster on the disk and varies in length depending on the disk storage device. On the type of diskette where a cluster contains two sectors, the same number of FAT entries can reference twice the data.

The first byte of the FAT indicates the type of device:

FF	$5\frac{1}{4}$ in. two-sided, 8 sectors/track (320KB)
FE	$5\frac{1}{4}$ in. one-sided, 8 sectors/track (160KB)
FD	$5\frac{1}{4}$ in. two-sided, 9 sectors/track (360KB)
FC	$5\frac{1}{4}$ in. one-sided, 9 sectors/track (180KB)
F9	$5\frac{1}{4}$ in. two-sided, 15 sectors/track (1.2MB)
F9	$3\frac{1}{2}$ in. two-sided, 9 sectors/track (720KB)
F0	$3\frac{1}{2}$ in. two-sided, 9 sectors/track (1.44MB)
F8	Hard disk

The second and third bytes of the FAT contain FFFF (at the time of this writing). The following lists the organization for several types of devices, showing the starting and ending sector numbers. The column headed "Cluster" means the number of sectors per cluster:

Device	Boot	FAT	Directory	Cluster
$5\frac{1}{4}$ in. 360KB	1	2–5	6–12	2
$5\frac{1}{4}$ in. 1.2MB	1	2–15	16–29	1
$3\frac{1}{2}$ in. 720KB	1	2–7	8–14	2
$3\frac{1}{2}$ in. 1.44MB	1	2–19	20–33	1
10M hard disk	1	2–17	18–49	8
20M hard disk	1	2–83	84–115	4

For diskettes and 10M hard disks, FAT entries begin with the fourth byte and are each 12 bits in length. For hard disks greater than 10M, FAT entries begin with the fourth byte and are each 12 bits in length. The first two FAT entries, known as relative clusters 000 and 001, respectively, reference the last two clusters of the directory to indicate its size and format. The first data file begins at relative sector 002. Each FAT entry for diskettes consists of three hex digits (12 bits) to indicate the use of a particular cluster in the following format:

000	Referenced cluster is currently unused.
nnn	Relative cluster number of the next cluster for a file.
FF0–FF7	Reserved cluster or, for FF7, unusable (bad track).
FF8–FFF	Last cluster of a file.

The directory contains the starting cluster number for each file, and FAT contains a three- or four-digit hex entry that indicates the location of each additional cluster, if any. At the least for a file, FAT contains hex FFF to indicate no more records past the first cluster.

Example FAT Entries

As an example, consider a diskette containing only one file named PAYROLL.FIL stored on relative clusters 2, 3, and 4. The directory entry for this file contains the filename PAYROLL, extension FIL, hex 00 to indicate a normal file, the creation date, 002 for the first relative cluster of the file, and an entry for file size in bytes. DOS accesses the diskette and searches the directory for filename PAYROLL and extension FIL. DOS then extracts from the directory the location of the first relative cluster (2) of the file and delivers its contents to a buffer area in main memory.

The FAT could appear as follows, except that pairs of bytes would be reversed:

FAT entry:	FDF	FFF	003	004	FFF	000	000	. . .	000
Relative cluster:	0	1	2	3	4	5	6	. . .	end

In the first two FAT entries, FD indicates a two-sided nine-sector diskette, followed by FFFFH. To enter the file into memory, the system takes the following steps:

- For the second cluster, DOS accesses the FAT entry that represents relative cluster 2. From the diagram, this entry contains 003, meaning that the file continues on relative cluster 3. DOS delivers the contents of this cluster to the buffer in main memory.
- For the third cluster, DOS accesses the FAT entry that represents relative cluster 3. This entry contains 004, meaning that the file continues on relative cluster 4. DOS delivers the contents of this cluster to the buffer in main memory.
- The FAT entry for relative cluster 4 contains hex FFF to indicate no more data for this file.

DOS always stores clusters for a file in ascending sequence, although a file may be fragmented so that it resides, for example, in clusters 8, 9, 10, 14, 17, and 18.

Handling 12-Bit FAT Entries

As a simple example, a diskette directory indicates a file stored beginning at relative cluster 15. To process the first FAT entry:

- Multiply 15 by 1.5 to get 22.5.
- Access offset bytes 22 and 23 in FAT. Assume that they contain Fx FF.
- Reverse the bytes: FF Fx.
- Because the location, 15, was an odd number, use the first three digits, FFF, which tell you that there are no more clusters for this file.

Now consider a file that uses four clusters, beginning at location 15. FAT entries for bytes 22 and on, this time shown in proper reversed byte sequence, contain the following:

```
6x 01 17 80 01 FF xF
```

To find the first FAT entry, multiply 15 by 1.5 to get 22.5, and access bytes 22 and 23, as before. This time, the bytes contain 6x 01, which reverse as 01 6x. Since 15 was an odd number, use the first three digits, 016. The second cluster for the file, therefore, begins at 016.

To find the third cluster, multiply 16 by 1.5 to get 24. Access bytes 24 and 25 of FAT. These contain 17 80, which reverse as 80 17. Since 16 was an even number, use the last three digits, 017. The third cluster for the file, therefore, begins at cluster 017.

To find the fourth cluster, multiply 17 by 1.5 to get 25.5. Access bytes 25 and 26 of FAT. These contain 80 01, which reverse as 01 80. Since 17 was an even number, use the first three digits, 018. The fourth cluster for the file, therefore, begins at cluster 018.

You can use the same procedure to locate the contents of the next FAT entry in offset locations 27 and 28, FF xF, which reverse as xF FF. Since 18 was an even number, use the last three digits, FFF, which mean that this is the last entry.

Handling 16-Bit FAT Entries

As mentioned, FAT entries for hard disk with more than 10M storage are 16 bits. The directory entry provides the starting cluster for the file. Each entry indicates the next relative cluster number, and FFF8–FFFFH indicate end-of-file.

From the foregoing, you can see that all files begin on a cluster boundary. Also, what may not be so immediately clear is that a file need not be contained on adjacent clusters, but could be scattered on a disk in various sectors.

If your program has to determine the type of installed disk, it could check the FAT directly, or preferably could use DOS INT 21H service 1BH or 1CH.

DISK PROCESSING

A number of special interrupt services support disk input/output. A program that writes a file first "creates" it so that DOS can generate an entry in the directory. When all records have been written, the program "closes" the file so that DOS can complete the directory. A program that reads a file first "opens" it to ensure that the file exists. Because of the directory's design, you may process records in a disk file either sequentially or randomly.

The highest level of processing is via DOS interrupt 21H, which supports disk accessing by means of a directory and "blocking" and "unblocking" of records. The two approaches are file control blocks (FCBs), covered in Chapter 16, and file handles, covered in Chapter 17. The next lower level, also via DOS, is by means of interrupts 25H and 26H but involves absolute addressing of disk sectors. The DOS methods perform some preliminary processing before linking to BIOS. The lowest level of disk processing is via BIOS interrupt 13H, which involves direct addressing of track and sector numbers, and is covered in Chapter 18.

KEY POINTS

- Each side of a diskette and a hard disk contains a number of concentric tracks, numbered from 00. Each track is formatted into sectors of 512 bytes.
- A cylinder is the set of all tracks with the same number on each side.
- A cluster is a group of sectors that DOS treats as a unit of storage space. A cluster size is always a power of 2, such as 1, 2, 4, or 8 sectors. A file begins on a cluster boundary and requires a minimum of one cluster.
- Regardless of size, all files begin on a cluster boundary.
- The directory contains an entry for each file on a disk and indicates the filename, extension, file attribute, time, date, starting sector, and file size.
- The file allocation table (FAT) contains one entry for each cluster for each file.

QUESTIONS

15-1. What is the length in bytes of a standard sector?

15-2. What is a cylinder?

15-3. Show how to calculate the capacity of a diskette based on the number of cylinders, sectors per track, and bytes per sector for **(a)** $5\frac{1}{4}$ in., 360KB and **(b)** $3\frac{1}{2}$ in., 1.44MB.

15-4. **(a)** Where is the boot record located?
   (b) What is its purpose?

15-5. **(a)** What is a cluster?
   (b) What is its purpose?
   (c) A file is 48 bytes long. What is the disk space used for cluster sizes 1, 2, 4, and 8?

15-6. What is the indication in the directory for a deleted file?

15-7. What is the indication in the directory for **(a)** a normal file and **(b)** a hidden file?

15-8. What is the additional effect on a diskette or hard disk when you use FORMAT /S to format?

15-9. Consider a file with a size of 2890 (decimal) bytes:
   (a) Where does the system store the size?
   (b) What is the size in hexadecimal format? Show the value as the system stores it.

15-10. Where and how does the FAT indicate that the device for the FAT table is on **(a)** hard disk, **(b)** $5\frac{1}{4}$ in., 360KB, **(c)** $3\frac{1}{2}$ in., 1.44MB?

16

DISK PROCESSING I
File Control Blocks

OBJECTIVE

To examine the basic programming requirements of the original DOS functions using file control blocks to process disk files.

INTRODUCTION

In this chapter we first cover the original DOS services for disk processing and then examine the requirements for creating and processing disk files defined as sequential and as random. All of these operations were introduced by the first versions of DOS and are available under all versions.

Disk processing in this chapter involves definition of a file control block (FCB) that defines the file and a disk transfer area (DTA) that defines records. You provide its address to DOS for all disk input/output operations. No new assembly language instructions are required. Chapter 17 covers the more recent and preferred use of file handles, which support subdirectories. As a reminder, the term *cluster* denotes a group of one or more sectors of data, depending on the device.

FILE CONTROL BLOCK

For original disk I/O under DOS, you define an FCB in the data area. Since the FCB does not support path names, its use is primarily for processing files in the current directory. The FCB contains descriptive information about the file and its records, described in the following. You initialize bytes 00–15 and 32–36; DOS sets bytes 16–31.

0	*Disk drive.* For most FCB operations, 00 is the default drive, 01 is drive A, 02 is drive B, and so forth.
1–8	*Filename.* The name of the file, left-adjusted with trailing blanks, if any. The entry may be a reserved filename such as LPT1 for line printer, without a colon.
9–11	*Filename extension.* A subdivision of filename for further identification of the file, such as DOC or ASM. If less than three characters, left-adjust it. When you create a file, DOS stores its filename and extension in the directory.
12–13	*Current block number.* A block consists of 128 records. Read and write operations use the current block number and current record number (byte 32) to locate a particular record. The number is relative to the beginning of the file, where the first block is 0, the second is 1, and so forth. An open operation sets this entry to zero. DOS handles this field automatically, although you may change it for random processing.
14–15	*Logical record size.* An open operation initializes the record size to 128 (hex 80). After the open and before any read or write, you may change this entry to your own required record size.
16–19	*File size.* When a program creates a file, DOS calculates and stores its size (number of records times record size) in the directory. An open operation subsequently extracts the file size from the directory and stores it in this field. Your program may read this field but should not change it.
20–21	*Date.* DOS records the date in the directory when the file was created or last updated. An open operation extracts the date from the directory and stores it in this field.
22–31	*Reserved by DOS.*
32	*Current record number.* This entry contains the current record number (0–127) within the current block (see bytes 12–13). The system uses the current block/record to locate records in the disk file. Although the open operation sets initial record number to 0, you may set this field to begin sequential processing at any number between 0 and 127.
33–36	*Relative record number.* For random read/write, this entry must contain a relative record number. For example, to read record 25 (hex 19) randomly, set this entry to hex 19000000. To access a record randomly, the system automatically converts the relative record number to current block/record. Because there is a limit to the maximum file size (1,073,741,824 bytes), a file with a short

record size can contain more records and may have a higher maximum relative record number. If record size is greater than 64, byte 36 always contains 00.

Remember that numeric values are stored in reversed byte sequence.

Preceding the FCB is an optional seven-byte extension, which you may use for processing files with special attributes. To use the extension, code the first byte with hex FF, the second with the file attribute, and the remaining five bytes with hex zeros. Chapter 15 describes file attributes.

USING AN FCB TO CREATE A DISK FILE

For each disk file referenced, a program using original DOS disk services defines a file control block. Disk operations require the address of the FCB in the DX register and use this address to access fields within the FCB by means of DS:DX registers. Operations include creating the file, setting the disk transfer area (DTA), writing records, and closing the file.

Creating a File

On initialization, a program uses service 16H for DOS interrupt 21H to *create* a new file, as follows:

```
MOV AH,16H       ;Create
LEA DX,FCBname   ; disk file
INT 21H          ;Call DOS
```

DOS searches the directory for a filename that matches the entry in the FCB. If found, DOS reuses the space in the directory, and if not found, DOS searches for a vacant entry. The operation then initializes the file size to 0 and opens the file. The open step checks for available disk space and sets a return code in the AL register:

00   Space is available.
FF   No space is available.

Open also initializes the FCB current block number to 0 and sets a default value in the FCB record size of 128 (hex 80) bytes. Before writing a record, you may override this default with your own record size.

The Disk Transfer Area

The disk transfer area (DTA) is the start of the definition of your output record. Since the FCB contains the record size, the DTA does not require a delimiter to indicate the end of the record. Prior to a write operation, use service 1AH to supply

DOS with the address of the DTA. Only one DTA may be active at any time. The following initializes the address of the DTA:

```
MOV  AH,1AH        ;Set address
LEA  DX,DTAname    ; of DTA
INT  21H           ;Call DOS
```

If a program processes only one disk file, it needs to initialize the DTA only once for the entire execution. If a program processes more than one file, it must initialize the appropriate DTA immediately before each read or write.

Writing a Record Sequentially

To *write* a disk record sequentially, use service 15H:

```
MOV  AH,15H        ;Write record
LEA  DX,FCBname    ; sequentially
INT  21H           ;Call DOS
```

The write operation uses the information in the FCB and the address of the current DTA. If the record is the size of a sector, the operation writes the record. Otherwise, the operation fills records into a buffer area that is the length of a sector and writes the buffer when full. For example, if each record is 128 bytes long, the operation fills the buffer with four records ($4 \times 128 = 512$) and then writes the buffer into an entire disk sector.

On a successful write, DOS increments the FCB file size field (by adding the record size to it) and increments the current record number by 1. When the current record number exceeds 127, the operation sets it to 0 and increments the FCB current block number. (You could also change the current block and record number.) The write operation sets a return code in the AL register:

00 Write was successful.

01 Disk is full.

02 DTA is too small for the record.

Closing the File

When you have finished writing records, you may write an end-of-file marker (hex 1A), although it's not usually necessary, and then use service 10H to close the file:

```
MOV  AH,10H        ;Close the
LEA  DX,FCBname    ; file
INT  21H           ;Call DOS
```

The close operation writes on disk any partial data still in the DOS disk buffer and updates the directory with date and file size. The following codes are returned to the AL register:

00   Close was successful.

FF   File was not in the correct position in the directory, perhaps caused by a user changing a diskette.

Program: Using an FCB to Create a Disk File

The program in Figure 16-1 creates a disk file of names that a user enters from a keyboard. The FCB, named FCBREC in the example, contains these entries:

FCBDRIV	Disk drive 4 (or D)
FCBNAME	Name of the file, NAMEFILE
FCBEXT	File extension, DAT
FCBBLK	Current block number, initialized to 0
FCBRCSZ	Record size undefined because the open operation sets this entry to 128
FCBFLSZ	File size, as maintained by DOS
FCBSQRC	Current record number initialized to 0

The program is organized with these procedures:

BEGIN	Initializes segment registers, calls C10OPEN to create the file and to set the DTA address for DOS. and calls D10PROC to accept input. If no more input, calls G10CLSE and terminates
C10OPEN	Creates an entry for the file in the directory, sets the size of the record to 32 (hex 20), and initializes the address of the DTA
D10PROC	Prompts and accepts input of names from the terminal and calls F10WRIT to write the entered name on disk
E10DISP	Handles scrolling and setting of the cursor
F10WRIT	Writes names onto the disk file
G10CLSE	Writes an end-of-file marker and closes the file
X10ERR	Displays an error message in the event of an invalid create or write operation

Each write operation automatically adds 1 to FCBSQRC (the current record number) and hex 20 (the record size) to FCBFLSZ (the file size). Since each record is 32 bytes long, the operation fills the buffer with 16 records and then writes the

```
                page 60,132
    TITLE   FCBCREAT (EXE)  Use FCB to create file of names
                .MODEL  SMALL
                .STACK  64
;   ------------------------------------------------------
                .DATA
    RECLEN  EQU     32
    NAMEPAR LABEL   BYTE                    ;Name parameter list:
    MAXNLEN DB      RECLEN                  ;  maximum length of name
    NAMELEN DB      ?                       ;  no. of chars entered
    NAMEDTA DB      RECLEN DUP(' ')         ;  disk transfer area (DTA)

    FCBREC  LABEL   BYTE                    ;FCB for disk file:
    FCBDRIV DB      04                      ;  drive D
    FCBNAME DB      'NAMEFILE'              ;  file name
    FCBEXT  DB      'DAT'                   ;  extension
    FCBBLK  DW      0000                    ;  current block#
    FCBRCSZ DW      ?                       ;  logical record size
    FCBFLSZ DD      ?                       ;  DOS file size
            DW      ?                       ;  DOS date
            DT      ?                       ;  DOS reserved
    FCBSQRC DB      00                      ;  current record #
            DD      ?                       ;  relative record #

    CRLF    DB      13, 10, '$'
    ERRCDE  DB      00                      ;Error indicator
    PROMPT  DB      'Name? ','$'
    ROW     DB      01
    OPNMSG  DB      '*** Open error ***',  '$'
    WRTMSG  DB      '*** Write error ***', '$'
;   ------------------------------------------------------
                .CODE
    BEGIN   PROC    FAR
            MOV     AX,@data                ;Initialize data
            MOV     DS,AX                   ;  segment
            MOV     ES,AX
            MOV     AX,0600H
            CALL    Q10SCR                  ;Clear screen
            CALL    Q20CURS                 ;Set cursor
            CALL    C10OPEN                 ;Open file, set DTA
            CMP     ERRCDE,00               ;Available space?
            JZ      A20LOOP                 ;  yes - continue
            JMP     A90                     ;  no - return to DOS
    A20LOOP:
            CALL    D10PROC
            CMP     NAMELEN,00              ;End of input?
            JNE     A20LOOP                 ;  no  - continue
            CALL    G10CLSE                 ;  yes - close,
    A90:    MOV     AH,4CH                  ;  exit
            INT     21H
    BEGIN   ENDP

;               Open disk file:
;               --------------
    C10OPEN PROC    NEAR
            MOV     AH,16H                  ;Request create file
            LEA     DX,FCBREC
            INT     21H
            CMP     AL,00                   ;Available space?
            JNZ     C20                     ;  no - error

            MOV     FCBRCSZ,RECLEN          ;Record size (EQU)
            MOV     AH,1AH                  ;Request
            LEA     DX,NAMEDTA              ;  set address of DTA
            INT     21H
            RET
    C20:
            LEA     DX,OPNMSG               ;Error message
            CALL    X10ERR
            RET
```

Figure 16-1   Using an FCB to Create a File

```
C10OPEN ENDP
;                   Accept input:
;                   ------------
D10PROC PROC    NEAR
        MOV     AH,09               ;Request display
        LEA     DX,PROMPT           ;Display prompt
        INT     21H

        MOV     AH,0AH              ;Request input
        LEA     DX,NAMEPAR          ;Accept name
        INT     21H
        CALL    E10DISP             ;Handle scrolling

        CMP     NAMELEN,00          ;Was a name entered?
        JNE     D20                 ;  yes - process
        RET                         ;  no  - exit
D20:
        MOV     BH,00               ;Replace return char
        MOV     BL,NAMELEN
        MOV     NAMEDTA[BX],' '     ;Store blank
        CALL    F10WRIT             ;Call write routine

        CLD
        MOV     AX,2020H            ;Clear
        MOV     CX,RECLEN / 2       ;  name
        LEA     DI,NAMEDTA          ;  field
        REP STOSW
        RET
D10PROC ENDP
;                   Scroll & set cursor:
;                   -------------------
E10DISP PROC    NEAR
        MOV     AH,09               ;Request display
        LEA     DX,CRLF             ;Carriage ret/line feed
        INT     21H                 ;Call DOS
        CMP     ROW,18              ;Bottom of screen?
        JAE     E20                 ;  yes - bypass
        INC     ROW                 ;  no  - add to row
        RET
E20:
        MOV     AX,0601H            ;Scroll one row
        CALL    Q10SCR
        CALL    Q20CURS             ;Reset cursor
        RET
E10DISP ENDP
;                   Write disk record:
;                   -----------------
F10WRIT PROC    NEAR
        MOV     AH,15H              ;Request write
        LEA     DX,FCBREC
        INT     21H
        CMP     AL,00               ;Valid write?
        JZ      F20                 ;  yes
        LEA     DX,WRTMSG           ;  no --
        CALL    X10ERR              ;    call error routine
        MOV     NAMELEN,00
F20:    RET
F10WRIT ENDP
;                   Close disk file:
;                   ---------------
G10CLSE PROC    NEAR
        MOV     NAMEDTA,1AH         ;Set EOF mark
        CALL    F10WRIT
        MOV     AH,10H              ;Request close
        LEA     DX,FCBREC
        INT     21H
        RET
G10CLSE ENDP
;                   Scroll screen:
;                   -------------
```

Figure 16.1　(cont.)

```
Q10SCR    PROC    NEAR                    ;AX set on entry
          MOV     BH,1EH                  ;Set yellow on blue
          MOV     CX,0000
          MOV     DX,184FH
          INT     10H                     ;Scroll
          RET
Q10SCR    ENDP
;                 Set cursor:
;                 ----------
Q20CURS   PROC    NEAR
          MOV     AH,02
          MOV     BH,00
          MOV     DL,00
          MOV     DH,ROW                  ;Set cursor
          INT     10H
          RET
Q20CURS   ENDP
;                 Disk error routine:
;                 ------------------
X10ERR    PROC    NEAR
          MOV     AH,09                   ;DX contains
          INT     21H                     ;  address of message

          MOV     ERRCDE,01               ;Set error code
          RET
X10ERR    ENDP

          END     BEGIN
```

Figure 16.1 (cont.)

entire buffer onto a disk sector. The following shows the DTA and the buffer at this point:

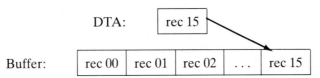

If a user enters 25 names, the record count increments from 01 to 25 (hex 19). The file size is, therefore,

$$25 \times 32 \text{ bytes} = 800 \text{ bytes, or hex } 320$$

The close operation writes the remaining nine records in the buffer onto a second sector and updates the directory for date and file size. The size is stored with reversed bytes, as 20030000. The following shows the last buffer:

Buffer: | rec 16 | rec 17 | . . . | rec 24 | hex 1A | . . . | . . . | . . . |

For simplicity, the program creates records that contain only one field. Most records, however, contain various alphabetic and binary fields and require defining the fields in the DTA. But if records contain binary numbers, do not use an EOF marker because a binary number could validly contain 1AH.

To make the program more flexible, consider allowing a user to specify which drive contains the file. At the start, the program could display a message for the user to enter the disk drive number and could then change the first byte of the FCB.

SEQUENTIAL READING OF A DISK FILE

A program that reads a disk file defines a file control block exactly how the file was created. Operations include opening the file, setting the disk transfer area (DTA), reading records, and closing the file.

Opening a File

At its start, the program uses service 0FH to open the file:

```
MOV  AH,0FH        ;Open
LEA  DX,FCBname    ; the file
INT  21H           ;Call DOS
```

The open operation checks that the directory contains an entry with the filename and extension defined in the FCB. If the entry is not in the directory, the operation returns code hex FF in the AL. If the entry is present, the operation returns code 00 in the AL and sets the following in the FCB: actual file size, date, current block number (0), and record size (hex 80). After the open, you may override this default with your own record size.

The Disk Transfer Area

The DTA defines an area for the input record, according to the format that was used to create the file. Use service 1AH (not to be confused with EOF marker 1A) to set the address of the DTA, just as for creating a disk file:

```
MOV  AH,1AH        ;Set address
LEA  DX,DTAname    ; of DTA
INT  21H           ;Call DOS
```

Reading a Record Sequentially

To read a disk record sequentially, use service call 14H:

```
MOV  AH,14H        ;Read record
LEA  DX,FCBname    ; sequentially
INT  21H           ;Call DOS
```

If successful, the read operation uses the information in the FCB to deliver the disk record beginning at the address of the DTA. The operation sets a return code in the AL register:

00   Successful read.

01   End-of-file, no data was read.

02   DTA is too small for the record.

03   End-of-file, has read a partial record filled out with zeros.

The first read operation, which references current record number 00, reads an entire sector into the DOS buffer. The operation determines the record size from the FCB and delivers to the DTA the first record from the buffer and increments the current record number in the FCB from 00 to 01. In this example, records are 32 bytes long and sectors contain 16 records:

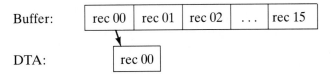

The second read executed does not have to access disk. Since the required record is already in the buffer, the operation simply transfers current record 01 from the buffer to the DTA and increments the current record number to 02. Each read operation continues in this manner until all 16 records in the buffer have been processed.

An attempt to read current record 16 causes the operation to physically read the entire next sector into the buffer. Subsequent reads then transfer each record successively from the buffer to the DTA. An attempt to read past the last record causes the operation to signal an end-of-file condition that sets the AL to hex 01, for which you should test.

Closing an Input File

Because the directory would be unchanged, it is usually not necessary to close an input file, but the practice is recommended. A program that successively opens and reads a number of files should close them because DOS limits the number of files that can be open at one time.

Program: Using an FCB to Read a Disk File

The program in Figure 16-2 reads the file that the previous program created and displays the input names on the screen. Both programs contain an identical FCB; although the names of the entries need not be the same, the operands for filename

```
TITLE     FCBREAD (EXE)  Read records created by CREATDSK
          .MODEL SMALL
          .STACK 64
;  --------------------------------------------------------
          .DATA
FCBREC   LABEL   BYTE                 ;FCB for disk file:
FCBDRIV  DB      04                   ;   drive D
FCBNAME  DB      'NAMEFILE'           ;   file name
FCBEXT   DB      'DAT'                ;   extension
FCBBLK   DW      0000                 ;   current block#
FCBRCSZ  DW      0000                 ;   logical record size
         DD      ?                    ;   DOS file size
         DW      ?                    ;   DOS date
         DT      ?                    ;   DOS reserved
FCBSQRC  DB      00                   ;   current record #
         DD      ?                    ;   relative record #

RECLEN   EQU     32                   ;Record length
NAMEFLD  DB      RECLEN DUP(' '), 13, 10, '$'

ENDCDE   DB      00
OPENMSG  DB      '*** Open error ***', '$'
READMSG  DB      '*** Read error ***', '$'
ROW      DB      00
;--------------------------------------------------------------
          .CODE
BEGIN    PROC    FAR
         MOV     AX,@data             ;Initialize data
         MOV     DS,AX                ;  segment
         MOV     ES,AX
         MOV     AX,0600H
         CALL    Q10SCR               ;Clear screen
         CALL    Q20CURS              ;Set cursor
         CALL    E10OPEN              ;Open file, set DTA
         CMP     ENDCDE,00            ;Valid open?
         JNZ     A90                  ;  no - terminate
A20LOOP:
         CALL    F10READ              ;Read disk record
         CMP     ENDCDE,00            ;Normal read?
         JNZ     A90                  ;  no  - exit
         CALL    G10DISP              ;Display name
         JMP     A20LOOP              ;Continue
A90:     MOV     AH,4CH               ;Terminate
         INT     21H
BEGIN    ENDP


;                 Open disk file:
;                 --------------
E10OPEN  PROC    NEAR
         MOV     AH,0FH               ;Request open
         LEA     DX,FCBREC
         INT     21H
         CMP     AL,00                ;File found?
         JNZ     E20                  ;  no - error

         MOV     FCBRCSZ,RECLEN       ;Set record length (EQU)
         MOV     AH,1AH
         LEA     DX,NAMEFLD           ;Set address of DTA
         INT     21H
         RET
E20:
         MOV     ENDCDE,01            ;Error message
         LEA     DX,OPENMSG
         CALL    X10ERR
         RET
E10OPEN  ENDP
;                 Read disk record:
;                 ----------------
```

Figure 16-2   Using an FCB to Read a File

```
F10READ  PROC    NEAR
         MOV     AH,14H                ;Request read
         LEA     DX,FCBREC
         INT     21H
         CMP     NAMEFLD,1AH           ;EOF marker?
         JNE     F20                   ;  no
         MOV     ENDCDE,01             ;  yes
         JMP     F90
F20:
         CMP     AL,00                 ;Normal read?
         JZ      F90                   ;  yes - exit
         MOV     ENDCDE,01             ;No:
         CMP     AL,01                 ;End-of-file?
         JZ      F90                   ;  yes - exit
         LEA     DX,READMSG            ;  no  - must be
         CALL    X10ERR                ;   invalid read
F90:
         RET
F10READ  ENDP
;                Display record:
;                ---------------
G10DISP  PROC    NEAR
         MOV     AH,09                 ;Request display
         LEA     DX,NAMEFLD
         INT     21H
         CMP     ROW,20                ;Bottom of screen?
         JAE     G30                   ;  no  - bypass
         INC     ROW                   ;  yes - incr row
         JMP     G90
G30:
         MOV     AX,0601H
         CALL    Q10SCR                ;  scroll
         CALL    Q20CURS               ;  set cursor
G90:     RET
G10DISP  ENDP

;                Scroll screen:
;                ------------
Q10SCR   PROC    NEAR                  ;AX set on entry
         MOV     BH,1EH                ;Set color
         MOV     CX,0000
         MOV     DX,184FH              ;Request scroll
         INT     10H
         RET
Q10SCR   ENDP
;                Set cursor:
;                ----------
Q20CURS  PROC    NEAR
         MOV     AH,02
         MOV     BH,00
         MOV     DH,ROW                ;Row
         MOV     DL,00                 ;Column 0
         INT     10H
         RET
Q20CURS  ENDP
;                Disk error routine:
;                ------------------
X10ERR   PROC    NEAR
         MOV     AH,09                 ;DX contains address
         INT     21H                   ;  of message
         RET
X10ERR   ENDP

         END     BEGIN
```

Figure 16.2   (cont.)

and extension must be identical. Records are 32 bytes long and a sector contains 16 records.

The program is organized as follows:

BEGIN   Initializes segment registers, calls E10OPEN to open the file and set the DTA, and calls F10READ to read a disk record. If end-of-file, the program terminates; if not end, the program calls G10DISP.

E10OPEN   Opens the file, sets the record size to the correct length of 32 (hex 20), and initializes the address of the DTA.

F10READ   Reads disk records sequentially. The read operation automatically increments the FCB current record number.

G10DISP   Displays the input record.

X10ERR   Displays an error message for an invalid open or read operation.

RANDOM PROCESSING

The discussion up to now on processing disk files sequentially is adequate for creating a file, for printing its contents, and for making changes to small files. To update a file with new data, a program restricted to sequential processing may have to read each record, change the specified ones, and write the records into another file. (It could use the same DTA but would require a different FCB.)

Some applications involve accessing a particular record on a file, such as information for a few employees or stock part numbers. For example, to access the 300th record in a file, sequential processing could involve reading through the preceding 299 records before delivering the 300th (although the system could begin at a specific current block/record number).

Although a file was created sequentially, you may access records sequentially or randomly. The requirements for random processing using an FCB simply involve inserting the required record number in the FCB relative record field and issuing a random read or write command.

Random processing uses the relative record number (bytes 33–36) in the FCB. The value is a doubleword, stored in reverse byte sequence. To locate a random record, the system automatically converts relative record number to current block (bytes 12–13) and current record (byte 32).

Random Reading

The open operation and setting of the DTA is the same for both random and sequential processing. Consider a program that is to directly access relative record number 05. Insert the number 05 into the FCB field for relative record number and request service 21H for random reading:

```
MOV  AH,21H        ;Request
LEA  DX,FCBname    ;  random read
INT  21H           ;Call DOS
```

The read operation returns a code in the AL register:

00   Successful read
01   End-of-file, no more data available
02   DTA too small for the record
03   Has read a partial record filled with zeros

A successful operation converts relative record number to current block/record. It uses this value to locate the required disk record and delivers it to the DTA.

The only valid response for a record that is supposed to exist is 00. You can cause invalid responses by such means as setting an invalid relative record number and failing to initialize a correct address in the DTA or FCB. Since these errors are easy to make, it is wise to test the AL for a nonzero return code.

When a program first requests a random record, the operation uses the directory to locate the sector where the record resides, reads the entire sector from disk into the buffer, and delivers the required record to the DTA. In this example, records are 128 bytes long and four to a sector. A request for random record number 23 causes the following four records to be read into the DTA:

record #20	record #21	record #22	record #23

When the program requests the next random record, say number 23, the operation first checks the buffer. Since the record is already there, it is transferred directly to the DTA. If the program requests a record number that is not in the buffer, the operation uses the directory to locate the record, reads the entire sector into the buffer, and delivers the record to the DTA. Accordingly, it is usually more efficient to request random record numbers that are close together.

Random Writing

The create operation and setting of the DTA is the same for both random and sequential processing. For processing an inventory file, a program could randomly read an item, change the quantity on hand, and write the record back into the same disk location. With the relative record number initialized in the FCB, a random write uses service 22H, as follows:

```
MOV  AH,22H        ;Request random
LEA  DX,FCBname    ;  write
INT  21H           ;Call DOS
```

The write operation returns a code in the AL:

00	Successful write
01	Disk full
02	DTA too small for the record

You could get a nonzero return code for a random create operation. But if you have read a record randomly and are now rewriting an updated record in the same disk location, you would expect the return code to be only 00 (unless a user changes diskettes).

The random relative record number in the FCB is a doubleword, stored in reversed byte sequence. For a small file, you may have to initialize only the leftmost byte or two. But for large files, setting a record number for three or four bytes requires some care.

Program: Reading a Disk File Randomly

The program in Figure 16-3 reads the same file created in Figure 16-1. By keying in a relative record number that is within the bounds of the file, a user can request any record to display on the screen. If the file contains 25 records, valid record numbers are 00 through 24. A number entered from the keyboard is in ASCII format, and in this case should be only one or two digits.

The program is organized as follows:

C10OPEN	Opens the file, sets the record size to 32, and sets the address of the DTA.
D10RECN	Accepts a record number from the keyboard and converts it to binary format in the FCB relative record field. An improvement would be to check that the number is valid, between 00 and 24.
F10READ	Uses the relative record number in the FCB to deliver a record to the DTA.
G10DISP	Displays the record.

The procedure D10RECN accepts a record number from the keyboard and checks its length in the parameter list. There are three possible lengths:

00	End of processing requested
01	One-digit request, stored in the AL
02	Two-digit request, stored in the AX

The procedure has to convert the ASCII number to binary. Since the value is in the AX, the AAD instruction works nicely for this purpose. The system recog-

```
                  page 60,132
        TITLE     RANREAD (EXE)  Randomly read records
                  .MODEL   SMALL
                  .STACK   64
;       -------------------------------------------------------
                  .DATA
RECLEN  EQU       32                  ;Record length
FCBREC  LABEL     BYTE                ;FCB for disk file:
FCBDRIV DB        04                  ;   drive D
FCBNAME DB        'NAMEFILE'          ;   file name
FCBEXT  DB        'DAT'               ;   extension
FCBBLK  DW        0000                ;   current block#
FCBRCSZ DW        0000                ;   logical record size
        DD        ?                   ;   DOS file size
        DW        ?                   ;   DOS date
        DT        ?                   ;   DOS reserved
        DB        00                  ;   current record#
FCBRNRC DD        00000000            ;   relative record#

RECDPAR LABEL     BYTE                ;Input parameter list:
MAXLEN  DB        3                   ;   maximum length
ACTLEN  DB        ?                   ;   actual length
RECDNO  DB        3 DUP(' ')          ;   record number

COL     DB        00
NAMEFLD DB        RECLEN DUP(' '),13,10,'$' ;DTA
OPENMSG DB        '*** Open error ***',13,10,'$'
PROMPT  DB        'Record number? $'
READMSG DB        '*** Read error ***',13,10,'$'
ROW     DB        00
ENDCDE  DB        00
;       -------------------------------------------------------
                  .CODE
BEGIN   PROC      NEAR
        MOV       AX,@data            ;Initialize data
        MOV       DS,AX               ;  segment
        MOV       ES,AX
        CALL      Q10CLR              ;Clear screen
        CALL      Q20CURS             ;Set cursor
        CALL      C10OPEN             ;Open file, set DTA
        CMP       ENDCDE,00           ;Valid open?
        JZ        A20LOOP             ;  yes - continue
        JMP       A40                 ;  no  - terminate
A20LOOP:
        CALL      D10RECN             ;Request record #
        CMP       ACTLEN,00           ;Any more requests?
        JE        A40                 ;  no  - exit
        CALL      F10READ             ;Random read
        CMP       ENDCDE,00           ;Normal read?
        JNZ       A30                 ;  no  - bypass
        CALL      G10DISP             ;Call display routine
A30:
        JMP       A20LOOP
A40:    MOV       AH,4CH
        INT       21H                 ;Terminate
BEGIN   ENDP

;                 Open disk file:
;                 --------------
C10OPEN PROC      NEAR
        MOV       AH,0FH              ;Request open file
        LEA       DX,FCBREC
        INT       21H
        CMP       AL,00               ;Valid open?
        JNZ       C20                 ;  no - error
        MOV       FCBRCSZ,RECLEN      ;Record size (EQU)
        MOV       AH,1AH
        LEA       DX,NAMEFLD          ;Set address of DTA
        INT       21H
        RET
```

Figure 16-3   Using an FCB for Random Reading

```
C20:
        LEA     DX,OPENMSG
        CALL    X10ERR              ;Error routine
        RET
C10OPEN ENDP
;               Get record number:
;               ------------------
D10RECN PROC    NEAR
        MOV     AH,09H              ;Request display
        LEA     DX,PROMPT
        INT     21H

        MOV     AH,0AH              ;Request input
        LEA     DX,RECDPAR
        INT     21H
        CMP     ACTLEN,01           ;Check length 0, 1, 2
        JB      D40                 ;Length 0, terminate
        JA      D20
        SUB     AH,AH               ;Length 1
        MOV     AL,RECDNO
        JMP     D30
D20:
        MOV     AH,RECDNO           ;Length 2
        MOV     AL,RECDNO+1
D30:
        AND     AX,0F0FH            ;Clear ASCII 3s
        AAD                         ;Convert to binary
        DEC     AX                  ;Correct (1st record is 0)
        MOV     WORD PTR FCBRNRC,AX
D40:
        MOV     COL,20
        CALL    Q20CURS             ;Set cursor
        RET
D10RECN ENDP
;               Read disk record:
;               ----------------
F10READ PROC    NEAR
        MOV     ENDCDE,00           ;Clear indicator

        MOV     AH,21H              ;Random read
        LEA     DX,FCBREC
        INT     21H
        CMP     AL,00               ;Normal read?
        JZ      F20                 ; yes - exit
        LEA     DX,READMSG          ; no - invalid,
        CALL    X10ERR              ; call error routine
F20:
        RET
F10READ ENDP

;               Display name:
;               ------------
G10DISP PROC    NEAR
        MOV     AH,09               ;Request display
        LEA     DX,NAMEFLD
        INT     21H
        INC     ROW
        MOV     COL,00
        RET
G10DISP ENDP
;               Clear screen:
;               ------------
Q10CLR  PROC    NEAR
        MOV     AX,0600H            ;Request scroll
        MOV     BH,1EH              ;Color (07 for BW)
        MOV     CX,0000
        MOV     DX,184FH
        INT     10H
        RET
```

Figure 16.3   (cont.)

```
Q10CLR   ENDP
;                    Set cursor:
;                    ----------
Q20CURS  PROC   NEAR
         MOV    AH,02                ;Request set
         MOV    BH,00                ;  cursor
         MOV    DH,ROW
         MOV    DL,COL
         INT    10H
         RET
Q20CURS  ENDP
;                    Disk error message:
;                    ------------------
X10ERR   PROC   NEAR
         MOV    AH,09                ;DX contains address
         INT    21H                  ;  of message
         INC    ROW
         MOV    ENDCDE,01
         RET
X10ERR   ENDP

         END    BEGIN
```

Figure 16.3   (cont.)

nizes the first record as number 0. The program deducts 1 from the actual number so that a user request, for example, for record 1 becomes record 0. The contents of the AX, now in binary, are moved to the leftmost two bytes of the FCB relative record field. For example, if the entered number is ASCII 12, the AX would contain 3132. AND converts this to 0102 and AAD further converts it to 000C. The result in the FCB random record field is 0C000000.

RANDOM BLOCK PROCESSING

If a program has sufficient space, one random block operation can write an entire file from the DTA onto disk and can read the entire file from disk into the DTA. This feature is especially useful for storing tables on disk, which other programs can read into memory for processing.

You may begin with any valid relative record number and any number of records, although the block must be within the file's range of records. You still first open the file and initialize the DTA.

Writing a Random Block

For random block write, initialize the required number of records in the CX register, set the starting relative record number in the FCB, and use service 28H:

```
MOV  AH,28H         ;Request random block write
MOV  CX,records     ;Set number of records
LEA  DX,FCBname     ;Address of FCB
INT  21H            ;Call DOS
```

The operation converts the FCB relative record number to current block/record. It uses this value to determine the starting disk location and sets a return code in the AL register:

00   Successful write of all records

01   No records written because of insufficient disk space

02   DTA too small for the record

The operation sets the FCB relative record field and the current block/record fields to the next record number. That is, if it wrote records 00–24, the next record is 25 (hex 19).

Reading a Random Block

For random block read, initialize the required number of records in the CX and use service 27H:

```
MOV  AH,27H       ;Request random block read
MOV  CX,records   ;Initialize number of records
LEA  DX,FCBname   ;Address of FCB
INT  21H          ;Call DOS
```

The read operation returns a code in the AL register:

00   Successful read of all records

01   Has read to end of file and last record is complete

02   DTA too small for the record and read not completed

03   End-of-file, has read a partial record

The operation stores in the CX the actual number of records read and sets the FCB relative record field and current block/record fields for the next record.

You may want to read an entire file but are uncertain of the number of records. Since the open operation initializes the FCB file size field, simply divide this value by the record length. For example, if the file size is hex 320 (800) and record length is hex 20 (32), the number of records would be hex 19 (25).

Example of Reading a Random Block

The program in Figure 16-1 created a file of names, with each record 32 bytes long. A program that performs a block read of this file would initialize the starting relative record number to 00 and the CX to 25 records. Here's the FCB and the DTA:

```
FCBREC   LABEL  BYTE              ;FCB for disk file:
FCBDRIV  DB     04                ;  drive D
```

```
FCBNAME  DB      'NAMEFILE'           ;  file name
FCBEXT   DB      'DAT'                ;  extension
FCBBLK   DW      0000                 ;  current block number
FCBRCSZ  DW      0000                 ;  logical record size
FCBFLZ   DD      ?                    ;  DOS file size
         DW      ?                    ;  DOS date
         DT      ?                    ;  DOS reserved
         DB      00                   ;  current record number
FCBRNRC  DD      00000000             ;  relative record number
DSKRECS  DB      1024 DUP(?),'$'      ;DTA for block of records
```

The program opens the file, sets the FCB record size to 32, and sets the address of the DTA:

```
MOV  AH,0FH           ;Request open
LEA  DX,FCBREC        ;Address of FCB
INT  21H
CMP  AL,00            ;Valid open?
JNZ  ⟨error-rtne⟩     ;  no-error
MOV  FCBRCSZ,0020H    ;Record size
MOV  AH,1AH
LEA  DX,DSKREC        ;Set address of DTA
INT  21H
```

For the block read, the program initializes the number of records to 25:

```
MOV  AH,27H           ;Random block read
MOV  CX,NORECS        ;Number of records
LEA  DX,FCBREC        ;Address of FCB
INT  21H
MOV  ENDCODE,AL       ;Save return code
```

The read operation converts the FCB relative record number 00 to current block 00 and current record hex 00. At the end of the operation, the FCB current record number contains hex 19 and the relative record number contains hex 19000000.

Other variations on this program could involve initializing at a record other than 00 and reading fewer than 25 records.

ABSOLUTE DISK I/O

You can use DOS INT 25H and 26H for absolute reads and writes to process a disk directly. In this case, you do not define FCBs and you lose the advantages of directory handling and blocking/deblocking of records that DOS INT 21H provides.

Since these operations treat all records as the size of a sector, they directly access a whole sector or block of sectors. Disk addressing is in terms of logical record number (absolute sector). To determine a logical record number on two-sided diskettes with nine sectors per track, count each sector from track 0, sector 1, as follows:

Track	Sector	Logical Record Number
0	1	0
0	2	1
1	1	9
1	9	17
2	9	26

A convenient formula for nine-sectored diskettes is

$$\text{Logical record number} = (\text{track} \times 9) + (\text{sector} - 1)$$

Thus the logical record number for track 2, sector 9, is

$$(2 \times 9) + (9 - 1) = 18 + 8 = 26$$

Here is the required coding for disk partitions less than 32 MBs:

```
MOV    AL,drive#       ;0 for A, 1 for B, etc.
MOV    BX,addr         ;Transfer address
MOV    CX,sectors      ;Number of sectors to read/write
MOV    DX,sector#      ;Beginning logical sector number
INT    25H or 26H      ;DOS absolute read or write
POPF                   ;Pop flags
JC     [error]
```

Absolute disk read/write operations destroy all registers except the segment registers and use the carry flag to indicate a successful (0) or unsuccessful (1) operation. An unsuccessful operation returns a nonzero code to the AL:

AL	Reason
10000000	Attachment failed to respond
01000000	Seek operation failed
00001000	Bad CRC on diskette read
00000100	Requested sector not found
00000011	Attempt to write on write-protected diskette
00000010	Other error

The INT operation pushes the flags onto the stack. On return, since the original flags are still on the stack, pop them after checking the carry flag.

Under DOS 4.0 and on, you can use these interrupts to access disk partitions that exceed 32 megabytes. The AL and CX are still used the same way. The DX is not used and the BX points to a 10-byte parameter block:

Bytes	*Description*
00H–03H	32-bit sector number
04H–05H	Number of sectors to read/write
06H–07H	Offset of buffer
08H–09H	Segment of buffer

MISCELLANEOUS DISK PROCESSING FEATURES

Among the DOS INT 21H FCB services are several useful disk operations.

INT 21H Service 0DH: Reset Disk

Normally, closing a file properly writes all remaining records and updates the directory. Under special circumstances, such as between program steps or a disaster, a program may need to reset a disk. DOS service 0DH flushes all file buffers. The operation does not automatically close the files.

```
MOV  AH,0DH   ;Request reset disk
INT  21H      ;Call DOS
```

INT 21H Service 0EH: Select Default Disk Drive

The main purpose of DOS service 0EH is to select a drive as the current default. Set the drive number in the DL, where 0 = A, 1 = B, and so forth:

```
MOV  AH,0EH   ;Request set default
MOV  DL,02    ;  drive C
INT  21H      ;Call DOS
```

The operation returns the number of drives (all types, including RAM disks) in the AL. Because DOS requires at least two logical drives A and B, it returns the value 02 for a one-drive system. (Use INT 11H for determining the actual number of drives.)

INT 21H Services 11H and 12H: Search for Directory Entries

A utility program may have to search a directory in order to access a file name, for example, to delete or rename. Accessing the first or only directory entry requires the address of an unopened FCB in the DX and service call 11H. You may also specify the address of an extended FCB.

```
MOV  AH,11H          ;Request first directory entry
LEA  DX,FCBname      ;Unopened FCB
INT  21H             ;Call DOS
```

The reference to FCBname could be offset location 5CH, the default DTA in the program segment prefix immediately preceding the program in memory (see Chapter 22).

If the operation finds no match, it returns hex FF to the AL. If it finds a match, the operation returns 00 to the AL and sets the contents of the DTA with drive number (1 = A, 2 = B, etc.), followed by file name and extension. For an extended FCB, the first byte of the DTA is hex FF, followed by five bytes of zeros and the attribute byte. The attribute determines the search pattern:

00H	Find only normal files
02H	Find hidden files and normal files
04H	Find system files and normal files
08H	Find only the volume label

If a match to a multiple request, such as *.ASM, is found, use service 12H for locating subsequent entries in the directory:

```
MOV  AH,12H          ;Request next directory entry
LEA  DX,FCBname      ;Unopened FCB
INT  21H             ;Call DOS
```

The operation returns the same values as service 11H. (Figure 16-4 in a later section illustrates these two services.) Extended services 4EH and 4FH provide access to subdirectory paths.

INT 21H Service 13H: Delete a File

DOS service 13H deletes files from within a program. Load the address of the unopened FCB in the DX register. The filename may contain wildcard characters (* and ?). Drive numbers are 0 = default, 1 = A, 2 = B, and so forth.

```
MOV  AH,13H          ;Request delete file
LEA  DX,FCBname      ;Unopened FCB
INT  21H             ;Call DOS
```

If the operation finds the requested entry (and it is not read only), it sets a delete byte in the first position of the file name in the directory and returns 00 to the AL; otherwise, it returns hex FF. Service 41H allows you to delete a file in other subdirectories.

INT 21H Service 17H: Rename File

DOS service 17H renames files from within a program. Set the old file name (change from) in the FCB in the usual location and set the new file name (change to) at FCB offset 16 (hex 12).

```
MOV  AH,17H       ;Request rename file
LEA  DX,FCBname   ;Address of FCB
INT  21H          ;Call DOS
```

Wildcard characters ? and * in the new name cause the operation to duplicate corresponding positions from the old name. A successful operation returns 00 to the AL, and an unsuccessful operation (no match or new file name already exists) returns FF. Service 56H allows you to rename a file in other subdirectories.

INT 21H Service 19H: Get Default Drive

DOS service 19H determines the default disk drive:

```
MOV  AH,19H   ;Get default drive
INT  21H      ;Call DOS
```

The operation returns a hex number in the AL, where $0 = A$, $1 = B$, and so forth. You could move this number directly into the FCB for accessing a file from the default drive, although some operations assume that $1 = A$ and $2 = B$.

INT 21H Service 1BH: Get FAT Information for Default Drive

This service returns information about the file allocation table for the default drive.

```
MOV  AH,1B   ;Request FAT information
INT  21H     ;Call DOS
```

The operation returns the following information:

AL	Number of sectors per cluster
BX	Pointer (actually DS:BX) to the first (identification) byte of the FAT
CX	Size of the physical sector, usually 512
DX	Number of clusters on the disk

The product of the AL, CX, and DX gives the capacity of the disk. Since the operation changes the DS, you should PUSH it before the interrupt and POP it after.

INT 21H Service 1CH: Get FAT Information for Specific Drive

This service returns information about the file allocation table for a specific drive. Insert the required drive number in the DL, where 0 = default, 1 = A, and so forth. The operation is otherwise identical to service 1BH.

```
MOV  AH,1CH      ;Request FAT information
MOV  DL,drive    ;Device number
INT  21H         ;Call DOS
```

INT 21H Service 23H: Get File Size

This service delivers the size of a file in terms of the number of records. Before executing this operation, set the record size in the FCB, load the address of the FCB in the DX, and leave the FCB unopened.

```
MOV  AH,23H      ;Request file size
LEA  DX,FCBname  ;Address of FCB
INT  21H         ;Call DOS
```

A successful operation returns the file size in the FCB and 00 in the AL. (If you set the record size to 1, the file size indicates the number of bytes in the file.) An unsuccessful operation returns hex FF in the AL.

INT 21H Service 24H: Set Random Record Field

You can use this service to switch from sequential to random processing. The FCB should contain the correct current block and record numbers. Load the address of the FCB in the DX.

```
MOV  AH,24H      ;Request random record
LEA  DX,FCBname  ;Address of FCB
INT  21H         ;Call DOS
```

The operation sets the random record field in the FCB based on the contents of the current block and record. No error codes are returned.

INT 21H Service 29H: Parse Filename

This service converts a command line containing a filespec of the form d:filename.ext into FCB format. You could use this service to accept a filespec from a user to copy and delete files.

You load the SI register (associated with the DS) with the address of the filespec to be parsed, the DI (associated with the ES) with the address of an area where the operation is to generate the FCB format, and the AL with a bit value that controls the parsing method:

```
MOV  AH,29H          ;Request parse filename
MOV  AL,code         ;Parsing method
LEA  DI,FCBname      ;Address of FCB (ES:DI)
LEA  SI,filespec     ;Address of filespec (DS:SI)
INT  21H             ;Call DOS
```

The codes for the parsing method are:

Bit	Value	Action
0	0	Filespec begins in the first byte location.
0	1	Scan past separators (such as blanks) to find the filespec.
1	0	Set drive ID byte in the generated FCB: missing drive = 00, A = 01, B = 02, and so forth.
1	1	Change drive ID byte in the generated FCB only if the parsed filespec specifies a drive. In this way, the FCB can have its own default drive.
2	0	Change filename in the FCB as required.
2	1	Change filename in the FCB only if the filespec contains a valid filename.
3	0	Change filename extension as required.
3	1	Change extension only if filespec contains a valid extension.

Bits 4 through 7 must be zero.

For valid data, the operation creates a standard FCB format for filename and extension, with an eight-character filename extended with blanks if necessary, a three-character extension extended with blanks if necessary, and no period between them. The operation recognizes standard punctuation and converts wildcards * and ? into a string of one or more characters. For example, PROG12.* becomes PROG12bb???. The AL returns the following codes:

00H	No wildcards encountered
01H	Wildcards converted
FFH	Invalid drive specified

After the operation, the DS:SI contains the address of the first byte after the parsed filespec, and the ES:DI contains the address of the first byte of the FCB. For a failed operation. the byte at DI + 1 is blank, although this service attempts to convert almost anything you throw at it.

For this service to work with file handles, you have to further edit the FCB to delete blanks and enter the period between filename and extension.

INT 21H Service 2EH: Set/Reset Disk Write Verification

This service enables some verification of disk write operations, that is, "proper recording" of the written data. The operation sets a switch that tells the system to verify the disk controller's cyclical redundancy check (CRC), a sophisticated form of parity checking. Setting 00 in the AL sets verify off and 01 sets verify on. The switch stays set until another operation changes it. DOS versions prior to 3.0 should also clear the DL to 0.

```
MOV  AH,2EH    ;Request verify (or MOV AX,2E01H)
MOV  AL,01     ;Set on
INT  21H       ;Call DOS
```

The operation does not return any value, since it simply sets a switch. The system subsequently responds to invalid write operations. Since a disk drive rarely records data incorrectly and the verification causes some delay, the operation is most useful where recorded data is especially critical. A related service, 54H, delivers the current setting of the verify switch.

SELECTIVELY DELETING FILES

The COM program named SDEL in Figure 16-4 illustrates DOS service calls 11H, 12H, and 13H to delete selected files. To request deletes, a user enters such commands as

```
SDEL *.*      (examine all file names)
SDEL *.BAK    (examine all BAK file names)
SDEL TEST.*   (examine all files named TEST)
```

The program, via COMMAND.COM, locates each name in the directory that matches the request. On finding a match, COMMAND.COM delivers the full program name to the program segment prefix (PSP) at hex 81 (the default DTA). The program displays the name and a prompt. You reply Y (if yes) to delete, N (if no) to keep, or press Enter to terminate.

Be sure to create this as a COM program, because an EXE program requires different addressing for the use of locations hex 5C and 81 in the PSP. As a precaution, use copied temporary files for testing.

```
          TITLE    SDEL (COM)  Delete selected files
          ;        Assumes default drive; enter as *.*, *.BAK, etc.
          CODESG   SEGMENT PARA 'Code'
                   .MODEL   SMALL
                   .CODE
                   ORG      100H
          BEGIN:   JMP      MAIN
          ; -------------------------------------------------------------
          TAB      EQU      09
          LF       EQU      10
          CR       EQU      13
          CRLF     DB       CR, LF, '$'
          DELMSG   DB       TAB, 'Erase ','$'
          ENDMSG   DB       CR, LF, 'No more directory entries', CR, LF, '$'
          ERRMSG   DB       'Write-protected disk','$'
          PROMPT   DB       'Y = Erase, N = Keep, Ent = Exit', CR, LF, '$'
          ; -------------------------------------------------------------
          MAIN     PROC     NEAR              ;Main procedure
                   MOV      AH,11H            ;Locate 1st entry
                   CALL     D10DISK
                   CMP      AL,0FFH           ;If no entries,
                   JE       A90               ; exit
                   LEA      DX,PROMPT         ;Initial prompt
                   CALL     B10DISP
          A20:
                   LEA      DX,DELMSG         ;Display delete message
                   CALL     B10DISP
                   MOV      CX,11             ;11 characters
                   MOV      SI,81H            ;Start of filename
          A30:
                   MOV      DL,[SI]           ;Get char for display
                   CALL     C10CHAR
                   INC      SI                ;Next character
                   LOOP     A30
                   MOV      DL,'?'
                   CALL     C10CHAR

                   MOV      AH,01             ;Accept 1-character
                   INT      21H               ; reply
                   CMP      AL,0DH            ;Enter character?
                   JE       A90               ; yes - exit
                   OR       AL,00100000B      ;Force lowercase
                   CMP      AL,'y'            ;Delete requested?
                   JNE      A50               ; no  - bypass
                   MOV      AH,13H            ; yes - delete entry
                   MOV      DX,80H
                   INT      21H
                   CMP      AL,0              ;Was delete valid?
                   JZ       A50               ; yes - bypass
                   LEA      DX,ERRMSG         ; no -- warn
                   CALL     B10DISP
                   JMP      A90
          A50:
                   LEA      DX,CRLF           ;Return/line feed
                   CALL     B10DISP
                   MOV      AH,12H
                   CALL     D10DISK           ;Get next directory entry
                   CMP      AL,0FFH           ;Any more?
                   JNE      A20               ; yes - loop
          A90:
                   MOV      AH,4CH            ;Exit to DOS
                   INT      21H
          MAIN     ENDP
```

Figure 16-4   Selectively Deleting Files

```
;                         Display line:
;                         ------------
B10DISP  PROC    NEAR                  ;DX set on entry
         MOV     AH,09
         INT     21H
         RET
B10DISP  ENDP
;                         Display character:
;                         -----------------
C10CHAR  PROC    NEAR                  ;DL set on entry
         MOV     AH,02
         INT     21H
         RET
C10CHAR  ENDP
;                         Read directory entry:
;                         --------------------
D10DISK  PROC    NEAR
         MOV     DX,5CH                ;Set FCB
         INT     21H
         CMP     AL,0FFH               ;More entries?
         JNE     D90
         PUSH    AX                    ;Save AL
         LEA     DX,ENDMSG
         CALL    B10DISP
         POP     AX                    ;Restore AL
D90:     RET
D10DISK  ENDP

         END     BEGIN
```

Figure 16.4   (cont.)

KEY POINTS

- A program using original DOS INT 21H service calls for disk I/O defines a file control block (FCB) for each file that it accesses.
- A block consists of 128 records. In the FCB, the current block number combined with the current record number indicates the disk record that is to be processed.
- The entries in the FCB for current block, record size, file size, and relative record number are stored in reversed byte sequence.
- All programs that reference a file define a similar FCB.
- The disk transfer area (DTA) is the location of the record that is to be written or read. You have to initialize each DTA in a program prior to a write or read operation.
- An open operation sets FCB entries for filename, extension, record size (hex 80), file size, and date. A program should change record size to the correct value.
- A program using FCB service 15H to write a file must close it at the end in order to write the records (if any) in the buffer and to complete the directory entries.
- On reads and writes under FCB services, the system automatically updates the current record number in the FCB.

- FCB service 14H read operation first checks the buffer for the required record and, if not present, performs a disk access.
- Random processing requires a record number in the relative record number entry in the FCB. Prior to performing a read or write, the system converts the number to current block/record.
- The eight bytes (doubleword) of the relative record number are stored in reversed sequence.
- If a required random record is already in the buffer, the system transfers it directly to the DTA. Otherwise, the operation accesses disk and reads into the buffer the entire sector containing the record.
- Where there is sufficient space, a random block read or write is more efficient. This feature is especially useful for loading tables.
- DOS INT 25H and 26H provide absolute disk read and write operations, but do not supply automatic directory handling, end-of-file operations, and record blocking and deblocking.

QUESTIONS

16-1. Provide the FCB services for the following operations: **(a)** create; **(b)** set DTA; **(c)** sequential write; **(d)** open; **(e)** sequential read.

16-2. A program uses the record size to which the open operation defaults.
  (a) How many records would a sector contain?
  (b) How many records would a diskette contain, assuming three tracks with nine sectors per track.
  (c) If the file in part (b) is being read sequentially, how many physical disk accesses will occur?

16-3. Write a program that allows a user to enter part numbers (3 characters), part descriptions (12 characters), and unit prices (xxx.xx) on a terminal. The program is to use FCBs to create a disk file containing these values. Remember to convert the price from ASCII to a binary word. Here is sample input data:

```
Part#  Description   Price
|023|  Assemblers    |003.15|
|024|  Linkages      |004.30|
|027|  Compilers     |005.25|
|049|  Compressors   |009.20|
|114|  Extractors    |112.50|
|117|  Haulers       |006.30|
|122|  Lifters       |105.20|
|124|  Processors    |213.35|
|127|  Labelers      |009.60|
|232|  Bailers       |056.35|
|999|                |000.00|
```

16-4. Write a program that displays the contents of the file created in Question 16-3. It will have to convert the binary value to ASCII.

16-5. Determine the current block/record for the following random record numbers: **(a)** 45; **(b)** 73; **(c)** 150; **(d)** 260.

16-6. How does random record number (decimal) 2652 appear in the FCB relative record field?

16-7. Provide the FCB service calls for the following operations: **(a)** random write; **(b)** random read; **(c)** random block write; **(d)** random block read.

16-8. Write the instructions to determine the number of records in a file. Assume that the open operation has already occurred. The name of the file size is FCBFLSZ and record size is FCBRCSZ.

16-9. Use the file created in Question 16-4 for the following requirements: **(a)** the program reads the records into a table in memory; **(b)** a user can enter part number and quantity from the keyboard; **(c)** the program searches the table for part number; **(d)** if part number is found, it uses the table price to calculate value (quantity × price); **(e)** it displays description and calculated value.

16-10. Write a small program from within DEBUG that simply executes service 29H, parse filename. Provide for the filespec at 81H and the FCB at 5CH; both are in the PSP immediately before the program. Enter various filespecs, such as B:PROGA.DOC, PROGB, PROGC.*, and C:*.ASM. Check the results at offset 5CH after each execution.

17

DISK PROCESSING II
File Handles and Extended
DOS Functions

OBJECTIVE

To cover the use of file handles and the extended DOS services for handling disk files.

INTRODUCTION

Chapter 16 covered the original FCB services for file processing, which are still available on all DOS versions. This chapter covers a number of extended services introduced by DOS 2.0 and 3.0 that do not work on earlier versions. Make sure that you have the correct DOS version before attempting to execute the operations covered in this chapter.

Many of these extended services are simpler than their counterparts in the original DOS services and are generally recommended. Some operations involve the use of an ASCIIZ string to initially identify a drive, path, and filename; a file handle for subsequent accessing of the file; and special error return codes.

THE ASCIIZ STRING

When using many of the extended services for disk processing, you first tell DOS the address of an ASCIIZ string containing the location of the file, as disk drive, directory path, and filename (all optional and within apostrophes), followed by a byte of hex zeros, thus the name ASCIIZ string. The maximum length is 128 bytes.

This example defines a drive and a filename:

```
PATHNM1 DB  'B:\TEST.ASM',0
```

This example defines a drive, a subdirectory, and a filename:

```
PATHNM2 DB  'C:\UTILITY\NU.EXE',0
```

The back slash, which may also be a forward slash, acts as a path separator. A byte of zeros terminates the string. For interrupts that require an ASCIIZ string, load its address in the DX register, for example as LEA DX,PATHNM1.

FILE HANDLES AND ERROR RETURN CODES

The extended services access files by means of a handle, a one-word number that the open and create services deliver in the AX. As discussed in Chapter 8, certain standard devices need not be opened, and you may use them directly: 00 = input, 01 = output, 02 = error output, 03 = auxiliary device, and 04 = printer.

For disk accessing, first create (for output) or open (for input) a file using an ASCIIZ string and DOS service 3CH or 3DH. A successful operation clears the carry flag to 0 and delivers the handle in the AX. Save the handle in a DW data item and use it for all subsequent disk accesses of the file. In effect, DOS creates its own FCB for the file. An unsuccessful operation sets the carry flag to 1 and returns an error code in the AX, depending on the operation. Figure 17-1 shows error codes for 01–36; other codes are concerned with networking.

If these errors aren't enough, you can also use INT 59H for additional information about an error, as covered later.

CREATING A DISK FILE

The following sections cover the requirements for creating, writing, and closing disk files for extended DOS.

INT 21H Service 3CH: Create File

For creating a new file or overwriting an old file, first use service 3CH. Load the address of the ASCIIZ string in the DX and the required attribute in the CX. Chapter 15 covers the attribute byte. Here's an example that creates a normal file, code 0:

```
PATHNM1 DB   'D:\PROG05.ASM',0
HANDLE1 DW   ?
```

01	Invalid function number	20	Unknown unit
02	File not found	21	Drive not ready
03	Path not found	22	Unknown command
04	Too many files open	23	CRC data error
05	Access denied	24	Bad request structure length
06	Invalid handle	25	Seek error
07	Memory control block destroyed	26	Unknown media type
08	Insufficient memory	27	Sector not found
09	Invalid memory block address	28	Printer out of paper
10	Invalid environment	29	Write fault
11	Invalid format	30	Read fault
12	Invalid access code	31	General failure
13	Invalid data	32	Sharing violation
15	Invalid drive specified	33	Lock violation
16	Attempt to remove directory	34	Invalid disk change
17	Not same device	35	FCB unavailable
18	No more files	36	Sharing buffer overflow
19	Write-protected disk		

Figure 17-1 Major Error Return Codes

```
    . . .
MOV  AH,3CH      ;Request create
MOV  CX,00       ; normal file
LEA  DX,PATHNM1  ;ASCIIZ string
INT  21H         ;Call DOS
JC   error       ;Exit if error
MOV  HANDLE1,AX  ;Save handle in DW
```

A valid open operation creates a directory entry with the given attribute, clears the carry flag, and sets the handle for the file in the AX. Use the handle for all subsequent operations. The named file is opened and is now available for writing. If a file by the given name already exists, the operation sets up zero length for overwriting.

For error conditions, the operation sets the carry flag and returns a code in the AX: 03, 04, or 05 (see Figure 17-1). Code 05 means that either the directory is full or the referenced filename has the read-only attribute. Be sure to check the carry flag first. For example, creating a file probably delivers handle 05 to the AX, which could easily be confused with error code 05, access denied. Related services are 5AH and 5BH, covered later.

INT 21H Service 40H: Write File

For writing records, use DOS service 40H. Load the file handle in the BX, the number of bytes to write in the CX, and the address of the output area in the DX. The following writes a 256-byte record from OUTREC:

```
HANDLE1  DW   ?
OUTREC   DB   256 DUP(' ') ;Output area
         ...
         MOV  AH,40H        ;Request write
         MOV  BX,HANDLE1     ;Handle
         MOV  CX,256         ;Record length
         LEA  DX,OUTREC      ;Address of output area
         INT  21H            ;Call DOS
         JC   error2         ;Test for error
         CMP  AX,256         ;All bytes written?
         JNE  error3
```

A valid operation writes the record from the output area, clears the carry flag, and sets the AX to the number of bytes actually written. A full disk may cause the number written to differ from the number requested, although DOS does not report this as an error. An invalid operation sets the carry flag and returns to the AX error code 05 (access denied) or 06 (invalid handle).

INT 21H Service 3EH: Close File

When you have finished writing a file, load the file handle in the BX and use DOS service 3EH to close it. The operation writes any remaining records still in the memory buffer and updates the directory and FAT.

```
         MOV  AH,3EH         ;Request close
         MOV  BX,HANDLE1     ;File handle
         INT  21H            ;Call DOS
```

The only possible error returned in the AX is 06 (invalid handle).

Program: Using a Handle to Create a File

The program in Figure 17-2 creates a file from names that a user enters from a keyboard. Major procedures are the following:

C10CREA   Uses service 3CH to create the file and saves the handle in a data item named HANDLE.

D10PROC   Accepts input from the keyboard and clears positions from the end of the name to the end of the input area to blank.

```
                 page 60,132
      TITLE      HANCREAT (EXE)   Create disk file of names
                 .MODEL   SMALL
                 .STACK   64
;     ------------------------------------------------
                 .DATA
      NAMEPAR LABEL    BYTE               ;Parameter list:
      MAXLEN  DB       30                 ;Maximum length
      NAMELEN DB       ?                  ;Actual length
      NAMEREC DB       30 DUP(' '), 0DH, 0AH    ;Entered name,
                                          ;  CR/LF for writing
      ERRCDE  DB       00                 ;Error indicator
      HANDLE  DW       ?                  ;File handle
      PATHNAM DB       'D:\NAMEFILE.DAT', 0
      PROMPT  DB       'Name? '
      ROW     DB       01
      OPNMSG  DB       '*** Open error  ***', 0DH, 0AH
      WRTMSG  DB       '*** Write error ***', 0DH, 0AH
;     ------------------------------------------------
                 .CODE
      BEGIN   PROC     FAR
              MOV      AX,@data           ;Initialize data
              MOV      DS,AX              ;  segment
              MOV      ES,AX
              MOV      AX,0600H
              CALL     Q10SCR             ;Clear screen
              CALL     Q20CURS            ;Set cursor
              CALL     C10CREA            ;Create file, set DTA
              CMP      ERRCDE,00          ;Create error?
              JZ       A20LOOP            ;  yes - continue
              JMP      A90                ;  no  - exit
      A20LOOP:
              CALL     D10PROC
              CMP      NAMELEN,00         ;End of input?
              JNE      A20LOOP            ;  no  - continue
              CALL     G10CLSE            ;  yes - close,
      A90:    MOV      AH,4CH             ;  return to DOS
              INT      21H
      BEGIN   ENDP

      ;                Create disk file:
      ;                ----------------
      C10CREA PROC     NEAR
              MOV      AH,3CH             ;Request create
              MOV      CX,00              ;Normal
              LEA      DX,PATHNAM
              INT      21H
              JC       C20                ;Error?
              MOV      HANDLE,AX          ;  no - save handle
              RET
      C20:                               ;  yes --
              LEA      DX,OPNMSG          ;  error message
              CALL     X10ERR
              RET
      C10CREA ENDP
      ;                Accept input:
      ;                ------------
      D10PROC PROC     NEAR
              MOV      AH,40H             ;Request display
              MOV      BX,01              ;Handle
              MOV      CX,06              ;Length of prompt
              LEA      DX,PROMPT          ;Display prompt
              INT      21H

              MOV      AH,0AH             ;Request input
              LEA      DX,NAMEPAR         ;Accept name
              INT      21H
              CMP      NAMELEN,00         ;Is there a name?
              JNE      D20                ;  yes --
              RET                         ;  no  - exit
```

Figure 17-2   Using a Handle to Create a File

```
D20:
            MOV     AL,20H               ;Blank for storing
            SUB     CH,CH
            MOV     CL,NAMELEN           ;Length
            LEA     DI,NAMEREC
            ADD     DI,CX                ;Address + length
            NEG     CX                   ;Calculate remaining
            ADD     CX,30                ;  length
            REP STOSB                    ;Set to blank
D90:
            CALL    F10WRIT              ;Write disk record
            CALL    E10SCRL              ;Check for scroll
            RET
D10PROC ENDP
;                   Check for scroll:
;                   ----------------
E10SCRL PROC    NEAR
            CMP     ROW,18               ;Bottom of screen?
            JAE     E10                  ;  yes - bypass
            INC     ROW                  ;  no  - add to row
            JMP     E90
E10:
            MOV     AX,0601H             ;Scroll one row
            CALL    Q10SCR
E90:        CALL    Q20CURS              ;Reset cursor
            RET
E10SCRL ENDP

;                   Write disk record:
;                   ------------------
F10WRIT PROC        NEAR
            MOV     AH,40H               ;Request write
            MOV     BX,HANDLE
            MOV     CX,32                ;30 for name + 2 for CR/LF
            LEA     DX,NAMEREC
            INT     21H
            JNC     F20                  ;Valid write?
            LEA     DX,WRTMSG            ;  no --
            CALL    X10ERR               ;  call error routine
            MOV     NAMELEN,00
F20:
            RET
F10WRIT ENDP
;                   Close disk file:
;                   ---------------
G10CLSE PROC    NEAR
            MOV     NAMEREC,1AH          ;Set EOF mark
            CALL    F10WRIT
            MOV     AH,3EH               ;Request close
            MOV     BX,HANDLE
            INT     21H
            RET
G10CLSE ENDP
;                   Scroll screen:
;                   -------------
Q10SCR  PROC    NEAR                     ;AX set on entry
            MOV     BH,1EH               ;Set yellow on blue
            MOV     CX,0000
            MOV     DX,184FH
            INT     10H                  ;Scroll
            RET
Q10SCR  ENDP
;                   Set cursor:
;                   ----------
Q20CURS PROC    NEAR
            MOV     AH,02
            MOV     BH,00
            MOV     DH,ROW               ;Set cursor
            MOV     DL,00
```

Figure 17.2   (cont.)

```
                    INT      10H
                    RET
          Q20CURS   ENDP
          ;                  Display disk error message:
          ;                  --------------------------
          X10ERR    PROC     NEAR                 ;DX contains
                    MOV      AH,40H               ;  address of message
                    MOV      BX,01
                    MOV      CX,21                ;Length
                    INT      21H
                    MOV      ERRCDE,01            ;Set error code
                    RET
          X10ERR    ENDP

                    END      BEGIN
```

Figure 17-2   (cont.)

F10WRIT   Uses service 40H to write records.

G10CLSE   At the end of processing, uses service 3EH to close the file in order to create a proper directory entry.

The input area is 30 bytes, followed by two bytes for Enter (0DH) and Line Feed (0AH), for 32 bytes in all. The program writes the 32 bytes as a fixed-length record. You could omit the Enter/Line Feed characters, but include them if you want to sort the file. The DOS SORT program requires these characters to indicate end of a record. For this example, the SORT command could be

```
      SORT D:(NAMEFILE.DAT )NAMEFILE.SRT
```

which sorts the records from NAMEFILE.DAT into ascending sequence in NAMEFILE.SRT. The program in Figure 17-3 later reads and displays the contents of NAMEFILE.SRT. Note two points. (1) The Enter/Line Feed characters are included after each record only to facilitate the sort, and could otherwise be omitted. (2) The records could be variable length, only up to the end of the names; this would involve some extra programming, as you'll see later in Figure 17-4.

READING A DISK FILE

The following sections cover the requirements for opening and reading disk files for extended DOS services.

INT 21H Service 3DH: Open File

If your program is to read a file, first use service 3DH to open it. This operation checks that the name is valid and the file is available. Load the address of the required ASCIIZ string in the DX and set an access code in the AL:

Bits	Request
0-2	000 = read only
	001 = write only
	010 = read/write
3	Reserved
4-6	Sharing mode (DOS 3.0 and on)
7	Inheritance flag (DOS 3.0 and on)

Watch out: For writing a file, use create service 3CH, not open service. The following example opens a file for reading:

```
MOV  AH,3DH        ;Request open
MOV  AL,00         ;Read only
LEA  DX,PATHNM1    ;ASCIIZ string
INT  21H           ;Call DOS
JC   error4        ;Exit if error
MOV  HANDLE2,AX    ;Save handle in DW
```

If a file by the given name exists, the operation sets the record length to 1, assumes the file's present attribute, sets the file pointer to 0 (the start of the file), clears the carry flag, and sets a handle for the file in the AX. Use the handle for all subsequent operations.

If the file does not exist, the operation sets the carry flag and returns an error code in the AX: 02, 03, 04, 05, or 12 (see Figure 17-1). Be sure to check the carry flag first. For example, creating a file probably delivers handle 05 to the AX, which could easily be confused with error code 05, access denied.

INT 21H Service 3FH: Read File

For reading records, use DOS service 3FH. Load the file handle in the BX, the number of bytes to read in the CX, and the address of the input area in the DX. The following reads a 512-byte record:

```
HANDLE2  DW   ?
INPREC   DB   512 DUP(' ')
         ...
         MOV  AH,3FH        ;Request read
         MOV  BX,HANDLE2    ;Handle
         MOV  CX,512        ;Record length
         LEA  DX,INPREC     ;Address of input area
         INT  21H           ;Call DOS
         JC   error5        ;Test for error
         CMP  AX,00         ;Zero bytes read?
         JE   endfile
```

A valid operation reads the record into memory, clears the carry flag, and sets the AX to the number of bytes actually read. Zero in the AX means an attempt to read from end of file. An invalid read sets the carry flag and returns to the AX error code 05 (access denied) or 06 (invalid handle).

Since DOS limits the number of files open at one time, a program that successively reads a number of files should close them.

Program: Using a Handle to Read a File

The program in Figure 17-3 reads the file created in Figure 17-2 and sorted by the DOS SORT command. It uses service 3DH to open the file and saves the handle in a data item named HANDLE, which service 3FH subsequently uses to read the file.

Since Enter and Line Feed already follow each record, this program does not have to advance the cursor when displaying records.

```
            page 60,132
     TITLE  HANREAD (EXE)  Use handle to read disk records
            .MODEL  SMALL
            .STACK  64
;  ------------------------------------------------------------
            .DATA
ENDCDE  DB      00                      ;End process indicator
HANDLE  DW      ?
IOAREA  DB      32 DUP(' ')
OPENMSG DB      '*** Open error ***', 0DH, 0AH
PATHNAM DB      'D:\NAMEFILE.SRT',0
READMSG DB      '*** Read error ***', 0DH, 0AH
ROW     DB      00
;------------------------------------------------------------
            .CODE
BEGIN   PROC    FAR
        MOV     AX,@data                ;Initialize data
        MOV     DS,AX                   ;  segment
        MOV     ES,AX
        MOV     AX,0600H
        CALL    Q10SCR                  ;Clear screen
        CALL    Q20CURS                 ;Set cursor
        CALL    E10OPEN                 ;Open file, set DTA
        CMP     ENDCDE,00               ;Valid open?
        JNZ     A90                     ;  no - terminate
A20LOOP:
        CALL    F10READ                 ;Read disk record
        CMP     ENDCDE,00               ;Normal read?
        JNZ     A90                     ;  no  - exit
        CALL    G10DISP                 ;  yes - display name,
        JMP     A20LOOP                 ;  continue
A90:                                    ;Terminate,
        MOV     AH,4CH                  ;  return to DOS
        INT     21H
BEGIN   ENDP
;               Open file:
;               ---------
E10OPEN PROC    NEAR
        MOV     AH,3DH                  ;Request open
        MOV     AL,00                   ;Normal file
        LEA     DX,PATHNAM
        INT     21H
        JC      E20                     ;Error?
        MOV     HANDLE,AX               ;  no - save handle
        RET
```

Figure 17-3   Using A Handle to Read a File

```
       E20:
                   MOV      ENDCDE,01          ;  yes --
                   LEA      DX,OPENMSG         ;  display
                   CALL     X10ERR             ;  error message
                   RET
       E10OPEN ENDP

       ;                     Read disk record:
       ;                     -----------------
       F10READ PROC          NEAR
                   MOV      AH,3FH             ;Request read
                   MOV      BX,HANDLE
                   MOV      CX,32              ;30 for name, 2 for CR/LF
                   LEA      DX,IOAREA
                   INT      21H
                   JC       F20               ;Error on read?
                   CMP      AX,00             ;End of file?
                   JE       F30
                   CMP      IOAREA,1AH        ;EOF marker?
                   JE       F30               ;  yes - exit
                   RET
       F20:                                   ;  no --
                   LEA      DX,READMSG         ;  invalid read
                   CALL     X10ERR
       F30:
                   MOV      ENDCDE,01          ;Force end
       F90:        RET
       F10READ ENDP
       ;                     Display name:
       ;                     ------------
       G10DISP PROC          NEAR
                   MOV      AH,40H             ;Request display
                   MOV      BX,01              ;Set handle
                   MOV      CX,32              ;  and length
                   LEA      DX,IOAREA
                   INT      21H
                   CMP      ROW,20             ;Bottom of screen?
                   JAE      G80               ;  yes - bypass
                   INC      ROW               ;  no - increment row
                   JMP      G90
       G80:
                   MOV      AX,0601H
                   CALL     Q10SCR             ;Scroll
                   CALL     Q20CURS            ;Set cursor
       G90:        RET
       G10DISP ENDP
       ;                     Scroll screen:
       ;                     -------------
       Q10SCR  PROC          NEAR               ;AX set on entry
                   MOV      BH,1EH             ;Set color
                   MOV      CX,0000
                   MOV      DX,184FH           ;Request scroll
                   INT      10H
                   RET
       Q10SCR  ENDP
       ;                     Set cursor:
       ;                     ----------
       Q20CURS PROC          NEAR
                   MOV      AH,02              ;Request set
                   MOV      BH,00              ;  cursor
                   MOV      DH,ROW             ;  row
                   MOV      DL,00              ;  column
                   INT      10H
                   RET
       Q20CURS ENDP
       ;                     Display disk error message:
       ;                     --------------------------
       X10ERR  PROC          NEAR
                   MOV      AH,40H             ;DX contains address
                   MOV      BX,01              ;Handle
                   MOV      CX,20              ;Length
                   INT      21H               ;  of message
                   RET
       X10ERR  ENDP

                   END      BEGIN
```

Figure 17.3 (cont.)

ASCII FILES

The preceding examples created files and read them, but you may also want to process ASCII files that DOS or an editor has created. All you need to know are the organization of the directory and FAT and the way in which the system stores data in a sector. DOS stores your data in an ASM file, for example, exactly the way that you key it, including the characters for Tab (09H), Enter (0DH), and Line Feed (0AH). To conserve disk space, DOS does not store blanks that appear on the screen immediately preceding a Tab character nor blanks on a line to the right of an Enter character. The following illustrates an assembly instruction as it appears on the screen:

⟨Tab⟩MOV⟨Tab⟩AH,09⟨Enter⟩

The hex representation for this ASCII data would be

094D4F560941482C30390D0A

where 09 is Tab, 0D is Enter, and 0A is Line Feed. When TYPE or an editor read the file, the Tab, Enter, and Line Feed characters automatically adjust the data on a screen.

Let's now examine the program in Figure 17-4 that reads and displays the file, HANREAD.ASM (the example from Figure 17-3), one sector at a time. If you have already keyed and tested HANREAD, you can easily copy it to a new name.

The program performs much the same functions as DOS TYPE, where each line displays up to the Enter/Line Feed characters. Scrolling is a problem. If you perform no special tests for bottom of screen, the operation automatically displays new lines over old, and if the old line is longer, old characters still appear to the right. For proper scrolling, you have to count rows and test for the bottom of the screen. Since lines in an ASCII file are variable length, you have to scan for the end of each line before displaying it.

The program reads a full sector of data into SECTOR. The procedure G10XFER transfers one byte at a time from SECTOR to DISAREA, where the characters are to be displayed. When a Line Feed is encountered, the routine displays the contents of DISAREA up to and including the Line Feed. [The display screen accepts Tab characters (09H) and automatically sets the cursor on the next location evenly divisible by 8.]

The program has to check for end of sector (read another sector) and end of display area. For conventional ASCII files such as ASM files, each line is relatively short and is sure to terminate with Enter/Line Feed. Non-ASCII files such as EXE and OBJ do not have "lines," and our program has to check for end of DISAREA to avoid crashing. The program is intended to display only ASCII files, but the test is insurance against unexpected files.

These are the steps in G10XFER:

1. Initialize the address of SECTOR.
2. Initialize the address of DISAREA.

```
               page 60,132
  TITLE     ASCREAD (EXE)  Read an ASCII file
               .MODEL  SMALL
               .STACK  64
  ; -----------------------------------------------------------
               .DATA
  DISAREA DB       120 DUP(' ')       ;Display area
  ENDCDE  DW       00                 ;End process indicator
  HANDLE  DW       0                  ;File handle
  OPENMSG DB       '*** Open error ***'
  PATHNAM DB       'D:\HANREAD.ASM', 0
  ROW     DB       00
  SECTOR  DB       512 DUP(' ')       ;Input area
  ; -----------------------------------------------------------
               .CODE
  BEGIN   PROC    FAR                 ;Main procedure
               MOV     AX,@data        ;Initialize data
               MOV     DS,AX           ;  segment
               MOV     ES,AX
               MOV     AX,0600H
               CALL    Q10SCR          ;Clear screen
               CALL    Q20CURS         ;Set cursor
               CALL    E10OPEN         ;Open file
               CMP     ENDCDE,00       ;Valid open?
               JNE     A90             ;  no -- exit
  A20LOOP:                             ;  yes - continue
               CALL    R10READ         ;Read 1st disk sector
               CMP     ENDCDE,00       ;End-file, no data?
               JE      A90             ;  yes - exit
               CALL    G10XFER         ;Display/read
  A90:
               MOV AH,3EH              ;Request close file
               MOV BX,HANDLE
               INT 21H
               MOV     AH,4CH          ;Terminate
               INT     21H
  BEGIN   ENDP
  ;               Open disk file:
  ;               --------------
  E10OPEN PROC    NEAR
               MOV     AH,3DH          ;Request open
               MOV     AL,00           ;Read only
               LEA     DX,PATHNAM
               INT     21H
               JNC     E20             ;Test carry flag,
               CALL    X10ERR          ;  error if set
               RET
  E20:
               MOV     HANDLE,AX       ;Save handle
               RET
  E10OPEN ENDP


  ;               Transfer data to display line:
  ;               ------------------------------
  G10XFER PROC    NEAR
               CLD                     ;Set left-to-right
               LEA     SI,SECTOR
  G20:
               LEA     DI,DISAREA
  G30:
               LEA     DX,SECTOR+512
               CMP     SI,DX           ;End of sector?
               JNE     G40             ;  no - bypass
               CALL    R10READ         ;  yes - read next
               CMP     ENDCDE,00       ;End of file?
               JE      G80             ;  yes - exit
               LEA     SI,SECTOR
```

Figure 17-4   Reading an ASCII File

```
G40:
        LEA     DX,DISAREA+80
        CMP     DI,DX                ;End of DISAREA?
        JB      G50                  ;  no - bypass
        MOV     [DI],0D0AH           ;  yes - set CR/LF,
        CALL    H10DISP              ;   and display
        LEA     DI,DISAREA
G50:
        LODSB                        ;[SI] to AL, INC SI
        STOSB                        ;AL to [DI], INC DI
        CMP     AL,1AH               ;End-of-file?
        JE      G80                  ;  yes - exit
        CMP     AL,0AH               ;Line feed?
        JNE     G30                  ;  no  - loop
        CALL    H10DISP              ;  yes - display
        JMP     G20
G80:
        CALL    H10DISP              ;Display last line
G90:    RET
G10XFER ENDP
;               Display line:
;               ------------
H10DISP PROC    NEAR
        MOV     AH,40H               ;Request display
        MOV     BX,01                ;Handle
        LEA     CX,DISAREA           ;Calculate
        NEG     CX                   ;  length of
        ADD     CX,DI                ;  line
        LEA     DX,DISAREA
        INT     21H
        CMP     ROW,22               ;Bottom of screen?
        JAE     H20                  ;  no - exit
        INC     ROW
        JMP     H90
H20:
        MOV     AX,0601H             ;Scroll
        CALL    Q10SCR
        CALL    Q20CURS
H90:    RET
H10DISP ENDP
;               Scroll screen:
;               -------------
Q10SCR  PROC    NEAR                 ;AX set on entry
        MOV     BH,1EH               ;Set color
        MOV     CX,0000              ;Scroll
        MOV     DX,184FH
        INT     10H
        RET
Q10SCR  ENDP
;               Set cursor:
;               ----------
Q20CURS PROC    NEAR
        MOV     AH,02                ;Request set
        MOV     BH,00                ;  cursor
        MOV     DH,ROW
        MOV     DL,00
        INT     10H
        RET
Q20CURS ENDP
;               Read disk sector:
;               ----------------
R10READ PROC    NEAR
        MOV     AH,3FH               ;Request read
        MOV     BX,HANDLE            ;Device
        MOV     CX,512               ;Length
        LEA     DX,SECTOR            ;Buffer
        INT     21H
        MOV     ENDCDE,AX
        RET
```

Figure 17.4   (cont.)

```
R10READ  ENDP
;                       Display disk error message:
;                       ---------------------------
X10ERR   PROC   NEAR
         MOV    AH,40H                ;Request display
         MOV    BX,01                 ;Handle
         MOV    CX,18                 ;Length
         LEA    DX,OPENMSG
         INT    21H
         MOV    ENDCDE,01             ;Error indicator
         RET
X10ERR   ENDP

         END    BEGIN
```

Figure 17.4   (cont.)

3. If at end of SECTOR, read the next sector. If at end-of-file, exit; otherwise, initialize the address of SECTOR.

4. If at end of DISAREA, force Enter/Line Feed, display the line, and initialize DISAREA.

5. Get a character from SECTOR and store it in DISAREA.

6. If the character is end-of-file (1AH), exit.

7. If the character is Line Feed (0AH), display the line and go to step 2, otherwise, go to step 3.

Try running this program under DEBUG with an appropriate drive number and ASCII file. After each disk input, display the contents of the input area and see how DOS has formatted your records. To enhance this program, prompt a user to enter the filename and extension.

OTHER EXTENDED DOS SERVICES

DOS provides many additional services; the major ones are included next.

INT 21H Service 36H: Get Free Disk Space

This service delivers information about the space on a disk device. Load the drive number (0 = default, 1 = A, 2 = B, etc.) in the DL and request service 36H:

```
MOV  AH,36H    ;Request default
MOV  DL,0      ; drive
INT  21H       ;Call DOS
```

For an invalid device number, the operation sets hex FFFF in the AX; otherwise, it returns:

AX   Number of sectors per cluster
BX   Number of available clusters

CX	Number of bytes per sector
DX	Total number of clusters on device

The product of AX, CX, and DX gives the disk capacity. DOS versions prior to 2.0 could use service 1BH (get FAT information) for similar data.

INT 21H Service 39H: Create Subdirectory

This service creates a subdirectory, just like the DOS command MKDIR. You load the DX with the address of an ASCIIZ string containing the drive and directory pathname.

```
MOV  AH,39H        ;Request create subdirectory
LEA  DX,ASCstring  ;Address of ASCIIZ string
INT  21H
```

An error sets the carry flag and returns code 03 or 05 in the AX.

INT 21H Service 3AH: Remove Subdirectory

This service deletes a subdirectory, just like the DOS command RMDIR. You load the DX with the address of an ASCIIZ string containing the drive and directory pathname. You cannot delete the current directory or a subdirectory containing files.

```
MOV  AH,3AH        ;Request delete subdirectory
LEA  DX,ASCstring  ;Address of ASCIIZ string
INT  21H
```

An error sets the carry flag and returns code 03, 05, or 15 in the AX.

INT 21H Service 3BH: Change Current Directory

This service changes the current directory to one that you specify, just like the DOS command CHDIR. You load the DX with the address of an ASCIIZ string containing the new drive and directory pathname.

```
MOV  AH,3BH        ;Request change directory
LEA  DX,ASCstring  ;Address of ASCIIZ string
INT  21H
```

An error sets the carry flag and returns code 03 (path not found) in the AX.

INT 21H Service 41H: Delete File

Use service 41H to delete a file (but not "read-only") from within a program. Load the address in the DX of an ASCIIZ string containing device path and filename, with no wildcard references.

```
MOV  AH,41H       ;Request delete
LEA  DX,PATHNAM   ; ASCIIZ string
INT  21H          ;Call DOS
```

An invalid operation sets the carry flag and returns in the AX code 02 (file not found), 03 (path not found), or 05 (access denied).

INT 21H Service 42H: Move File Pointer

DOS maintains a file pointer that open initializes to 0 and subsequent sequential reads and writes increment for each record processed. You can use service 42H (move file pointer) for setting the file pointer anywhere within a file, and then use other services for random retrieval or updating.

Set the file handle in the BX and the required offset as bytes in the CX:DX. For a move up to 65,535, set 0 in the CX and the number in the DX. Also, set a method code in the AL that tells the operation the point from which to take the offset:

00	Take the offset from the start of the file.
01	Take the offset from the current location of the file pointer, which could be anywhere within the file, including the start.
02	Take the offset from the end-of-file. You can determine the file size (and its consequent end-of-file) by setting the CX:DX to zero and using method code 02. Another use for this method code is for adding records to the end-of-file.

The following example moves the pointer 1024 bytes from the start of a file:

```
MOV  AH,42H       ;Request move pointer
MOV  AL,00        ; to start of file
LEA  BX,HANDLE1   ;Set handle
MOV  CX,00
MOV  DX,1024      ;1024-byte offset
INT  21H          ;Call DOS
JC   error
```

A valid operation clears the carry flag and delivers the new pointer location in the DX:AX. You may then perform a read or write interrupt for random processing.

An invalid operation sets the carry flag and returns in the AX code 01 (invalid method code) or 06 (invalid handle).

INT 21H Service 43H: Get/Set File Attribute

You may use service 43H to check or change a file attribute in the directory. Bit 0 is read-only, 1 is hidden, 2 is system, and 5 is archive. Load the address of an ASCIIZ string in the DX. To check the attribute, set 00 in the AL. To change attribute, set 01 in the AL and the new attribute in the CX. The following sets normal attribute:

```
MOV  AH,43H          ;Request
MOV  AL,01           ;  set normal
MOV  CX,00           ;  attribute
LEA  DX,PATHNM2      ;ASCIIZ string
INT  21H             ;Call DOS
```

A check of attribute returns the current attribute to the CX; a change of attribute sets the directory entry to the attribute in the CX. An invalid operation sets the carry flag and returns to the AX code 01, 02, 03, or 05.

INT 21H Service 44H: I/O Control for Devices

This elaborate service, IOCTL, communicates information between a program and an open device. The operation also includes keyboard input and display output. You load a function value in the AL to request one of a number of actions. An invalid operation, such as invalid file handle, sets the carry flag and returns a standard error code to the AX.

AL function 00H: get device information.   Load the file handle in the BX. The operation returns the following in the DX, according to bit:

0	Standard console input (if bit 7 = 1)
1	Standard console output (if bit 7 = 1)
2	Null device (if bit 7 = 1)
3	Clock device (if bit 7 = 1)
4	Reserved
5	0 = process in ASCII mode (1AH is EOF)
	1 = process in binary mode
6	For input, 0 = EOF, 1 = not EOF
7	0 = disk drive, 1 = other device
14	0 = device cannot process strings by functions 2, 3, 4, and 5
	1 = device can process strings by functions 2 and 3

Bits 0 through 3 apply only to nondisk devices (bit 7 = 1). For disk devices (bit 7 = 0), the bits indicate drive number, where 0 = A, 1 = B, and so forth.

AL function 01H: set device information.   Load the file handle in the BX and the bit setup in the DL for bits 0–7, as shown for function 00H. The operation sets device information accordingly.

AL function 02H: read from device.   The operation reads control strings from a character device. Load the file handle in the BX, the number of bytes to read in the CX, and the address of the data area in the DX. A successful operation returns to the AX the number of bytes transferred.

AL function 03H: write to device.   The operation writes control strings to a character device. The setup is otherwise the same as for function 02H.

AL function 04H: read from drive.   The operation reads control strings from a drive. Load the drive (0 = default, 1 = A, etc.) in the BL, the number of bytes to read in the CX, and the address of the data area in the DX. A successful operation returns to the AX the number of bytes transferred.

AL function 05H: write to drive.   The operation writes control strings to a drive. The setup is otherwise the same as for function 04H.

AL function 06H: get input status.   This service checks whether a file handle is ready for input. Load the handle in the BX. The operation returns a code in the AL:

A device: 00H = not ready, FFH = ready
A file: 00H = EOF reached, FFH = EOF not reached

AL function 07H: get output status.   This service checks whether a file handle is ready for output. The setup is otherwise the same as for function 06H.

AL function 08H: determine if device removable (DOS 3.0 and on).   This service determines whether the device contains removable media, such as diskette. Load the BL with the drive number (0 = default, 1 = A, etc.). The operation returns a code in the AX: 00H = removable, 01H = fixed, and 0FH = invalid drive number in BL.

AL function 09H: determine if device local or remote (DOS 3.0 and on).   The setup is similar to that for function 08H. The operation returns a value in bit 12 of the DX: 0 = local and 1 = remote.

AL function 0AH: determine if handle local or remote (DOS 3.0 and on).
The setup is similar to that for function 09H. The operation returns a value in bit 15
of the DX: 0 = local and 1 = remote.

Other functions concerned with disk drives and file sharing are outside the
scope of this book.

INT 21H Service 45H: Duplicate a File Handle

You can use this service to give a file more than one handle, although you may find
few occasions ever to do so.

```
MOV  AH,45H       ;Request duplicate handle
MOV  BX,handle    ;Present handle to be duplicated
INT  21H
```

The operation returns a new handle (the next one available) in the AX or, if an
error, sets the carry flag and returns an error code (04 or 06). The use of old and new
handles is identical. See also service 46H.

INT 21H Service 46H: Force Duplicate of File Handle

This service is similar to service 45H except that this one can assign a specific file
handle. You could use this service to redirect output, for example. For this service,
you load the BX with the original handle and the CX with the second handle. Some
combinations may not work; for example, handle 00 is keyboard input and 04 is
printer output, and 03 (auxiliary) cannot be redirected.

INT 21H Service 47H: Get Current Directory

DOS service 47H determines the current directory for any drive. Define a space
large enough to contain the longest possible pathname (up to 64 bytes), and load its
name in the SI. Identify the drive in the DL by 0 = default, 1 = A, 2 = B, and so
forth.

```
MOV  AH,47H       ;Request get directory
MOV  DL,drive     ;Drive
LEA  SI,buffer    ;64-bye buffer space
INT  21H
```

A valid operation delivers the current directory (but not the drive) to the named
address, such as

```
ASSEMBLE\EXAMPLES0
```

A byte of hex zeros identifies the end of the pathname. If the requested directory is the root, the value returned is only a byte of hex 00. In this way, you can get the current pathname in order to access any file in a subdirectory. An invalid drive number sets the carry flag and returns code 15 in the AX. See the example in Figure 17-5.

INT 21H Services 4EH and 4FH: Find Matching File

These operations are similar to original services 11H and 12H. Use service 4EH to begin a search in a directory and 4FH to continue it. For beginning the search, load the address of an ASCIIZ string containing pathname in the DX; the string may contain wildcard characters ? and *. Set the file attribute in the CX—any combination of normal (bit 0), hidden (bit 1), system (bit 2), or directory (bit 3).

```
        MOV   AH,4EH          ;Request first match
        MOV   CX,00H          ;Normal attribute

        TITLE   GETPATH (COM)  Get current directory
                .MODEL   SMALL
                .CODE
                ORG      100H
        BEGIN:  JMP      SHORT MAIN
        ; ----------------------------------------------
        PATHNAM DB       65 DUP(' ')      ;Current pathname
        ; ----------------------------------------------
        MAIN    PROC     NEAR
                MOV      AH,19H            ;Get default drive
                INT      21H
                ADD      AL,41H            ;Change hex no. to letter
                MOV      DL,AL             ;  0=A, 1=B, etc.
                CALL     B10DISP           ;Display drive number,
                MOV      DL,':'
                CALL     B10DISP           ;  colon,
                MOV      DL,'\'
                CALL     B10DISP           ;  backslash

                MOV      AH,47H
                MOV      DL,00             ;Get pathname
                LEA      SI,PATHNAM
                INT      21H
        A10LOOP:
                CMP      BYTE PTR [SI],0   ;End of pathname?
                JE       A20              ;  yes - exit
                MOV      AL,[SI]          ;Display pathname
                MOV      DL,AL            ;  one byte at
                CALL     B10DISP          ;  a time
                INC      SI
                JMP      A10LOOP          ;Repeat
        A20:    MOV      AH,4CH           ;Exit to DOS
                INT      21H
        MAIN    ENDP

        B10DISP PROC     NEAR             ;DL set on entry
                MOV      AH,02            ;Request display
                INT      21H
                RET
        B10DISP ENDP

                END      BEGIN
```

Figure 17-5   Get Current Directory

```
          LEA DX,PATHNM1    ;ASCIIZ string
          INT 21H           ;Call DOS
```

An operation that locates a match fills the current DTA in the FCB at 80H with the following:

00–20	Reserved by DOS for subsequent search
21–21	File attribute
22–23	File time
24–25	File date
26–29	File size: low word then high word
30–42	Name and extension as an ASCIIZ string followed by hex 00

The operation does not change the carry flag. Error return codes in the AX are 02 (file not found), 03 (path not found), and 18 (no more files).

A unique use for service 4EH is to determine whether a reference is to a *filename* or to a *subdirectory*. For example, if the returned attribute is 10H, the reference is to a subdirectory. The operation also returns the file size. Thus you may use service 4EH to determine the size of a file and service 36H to check the space available for writing it.

If you used service 4EH to begin a search on wildcards, use service 4FH to find subsequent entries. Between use of these operations, leave the current DTA intact.

```
          MOV AH,4FH    ;Request next match
          INT 21H       ;Call DOS
```

The only return code in the AX is 18 (no more files). The operation does not change the carry flag.

INT 21H Service 54H: Get Verify State

You can use this service to determine the status of the disk write verify flag. (See service 2EH in Chapter 16 for setting the switch.) The operation returns to the AL 00H for verify off and 01H for verify on.

INT 21H Service 56H: Rename a File

This service can rename a file from within a program. Load the DX with the address of an ASCIIZ string containing the old drive, path, and name of the file to be renamed. Load the DI (actually ES:DI) with the address of a new ASCIIZ string containing the drive, path, and name, with no wildcards. Drive numbers, if used, must be the same in both strings. Since paths need not be the same, the operation can both rename a file and move it to another directory.

```
MOV  AH,56H          ;Request rename file
LEA  DX,oldstring    ;DS:DX
LEA  DI,newstring    ;ES:DI
INT  21H             ;Call DOS
```

An error sets the carry flag and returns in the AX codes 02 (file not found), 03 (path not found), 05 (access denied), and 17 (not same device).

INT 21H Service 57H: Get/Set a File's Date and Time

This service enables a program to get or set the date and time for an open file. The formats for time and date are the same as those in the directory:

Bits for Time		Bits for Date	
0BH–0FH	Hours	09H–0FH	Year (relative to 1980)
05H–0AH	Minutes	05H–08H	Month
00H–04H	Seconds	00H–04H	Day of month

(Seconds are in the form of number of 2-second increments, 0–29.) Load the request (0 = get, 1 = set) in the AL and the file handle in the BX. For a set request, load time in the CX and date in the DX.

```
MOV  AH,57H          ;Request date/time
MOV  AL,01           ;Set
MOV  BX,handle       ;File handle
MOV  CX,time         ;New time
MOV  DX,date         ;New date
INT  21H
```

A valid get operation returns the time in the CX and the date in the DX; a valid set operation changes the date/time entries for the file. An invalid operation sets the carry flag and returns in the AX code 01 (invalid function) or 06 (invalid handle).

INT 21H Service 59H: Get Extended Error (DOS 3.0 and on)

This service provides additional information about errors after execution of INT 21H services that set the carry flag, FCB services that return hex FF, and INT 24H error handlers. You set the BX with the DOS version: 0000H for versions 3.0 through 3.3. The operation returns the error class in the BH, a suggested action in the BL, locus in the CH, and—watch for this—destroys the CL, DI, DS (!), DX, ES, and SI registers. PUSH any required registers prior to this interrupt and POP them afterward.

Error class.   This code, returned in the BH, provides the following:

01   Out of resource, such as space or channel.
02   Temporary situation (not an error), such as locked file that should go
      away.
03   Lack of proper authorization.
04   System software error, not this program.
05   Hardware failure.
06   Serious DOS error, not this program.
07   Error in this program, such as inconsistent request.
08   Requested item not found.
09   Improper file or disk format.
10   File or item is locked.
11   Disk error, such as CRC error or wrong disk.
12   Item already exists.
13   Unknown error class.

Action.   This code, returned in the BL, provides information on the action
to take:

01   Retry a few times; may have to ask user to terminate.
02   Pause first and retry a few times.
03   Ask user to reenter proper request.
04   Close files and terminate the program.
05   Terminate the program immediately, do not close files.
06   Ignore the error.
07   Request user to perform an action (such as change diskette) and retry
      the operation.

Locus.   This code, returned in the CH, provides additional information on
locating an error:

01   Unknown situation, can't help
02   Disk storage problem
03   Network problem
04   Serial device problem
05   Memory problem

INT 21H Service 5AH: Create a Unique File (DOS 3.0 and on)

This service would be useful where a program creates temporary files, especially in networks where the names of other files may be unknown and the program is to avoid accidentally overwriting them. The operation creates a file with a unique name within the path.

Load the CX with the required file attribute and the DX with the address of an ASCIIZ path—drive (if necessary) and subdirectory (if any), followed by 12 bytes for the new filename:

```
d:\subdirectory\[12 bytes]
```

A successful operation delivers the file handle to the AX and appends the new filename to the ASCIIZ string. An invalid operation sets the carry flag and returns an error code in the AX.

INT 21H Service 5BH: Create a New File (DOS 3.0 and on)

This service creates a file only if the named file does not already exist, and is otherwise identical to service 3CH. A valid operation clears the carry flag and returns the file handle in the AX. An invalid operation (including an identical filename) sets the carry flag and returns a code in the AX. You could use this service where you don't want to overwrite a file.

KEY POINTS

- Many of the extended DOS services reference an ASCIIZ string that consists of a directory path followed by a byte of hex zeros.
- The create and open services return a file handle that you use for subsequent file accessing.
- On errors, many of the services set the carry flag and return an error code in the AX.
- The create service is used when writing a file and the open service when reading a file.
- A file that has been written should be closed so that the operation may update the directory.

QUESTIONS

17-1. What are the error return codes for **(a)** file not found and **(b)** invalid handle?

17-2. Define an ASCIIZ string named PATH1 for a file named CUST.LST on drive C.

17-3. For the file in Question 17-2, provide the instructions to **(a)** define an item named

CUSTHAN for the file handle, **(b)** create the file, **(c)** write a record from CUSTOUT (128 bytes), and **(d)** close the file. Test for errors.

17-4. For the file in Question 17-3, code the instructions to **(a)** open the file and **(b)** read records into CUSTIN. Test for errors.

17-5. Under what circumstances should you close a file that is used only for input?

17-6. Revise the program in Figure 17-4 so that a user at a keyboard can enter a filename for displaying. Provide for any number of requests and for pressing only the Enter key to cause termination.

17-7. Write a program that allows a user to enter part numbers (3 characters), part descriptions (12 characters), and unit prices (xxx.xx) on a terminal. The program is to use file handles to create a disk file containing these values. Remember to convert the price from ASCII to binary. Following is sample input data:

Part	Description	Price
|023|	Assemblers	|00315|
|024|	Linkages	|00430|
|027|	Compilers	|00525|
|049|	Compressors	|00920|
|114|	Extractors	|11250|
|117|	Haulers	|00630|
|122|	Lifters	|10520|
|124|	Processors	|21335|
|127|	Labelers	|00960|
|232|	Bailers	|05635|
|999|		|00000|

17-8. Write a program that displays the contents of the file created in Question 17-7. It will have to convert the binary value to ASCII.

17-9. Use the file created in Question 17-7 for the following requirements: **(a)** the program reads the records into a table in memory; **(b)** a user can enter part number and quantity from the keyboard; **(c)** the program searches the table for part number; **(d)** if part number is found, it uses the table price to calculate value (quantity × price); **(e)** it displays description and calculated value.

17-10. Figure 16-4 showed how to use FCB services for selectively deleting files. Revise the program for file handles.

18

DISK PROCESSING III:
BIOS Disk Operations

OBJECTIVE

To examine basic programming requirements for using the BIOS functions to read, write, format, and verify disks.

INTRODUCTION

You can code directly at the BIOS level for disk processing, although BIOS supplies no automatic use of the directory or blocking and deblocking of records. BIOS disk operation INT 13H treats "records" as the size of a sector, and disk addressing is in terms of actual track and sector number. Operations involve resetting the drive, reading, writing, verifying, and formatting.

Most of these operations are for experienced software developers who are aware of the potential danger in their misuse. Also, BIOS versions vary according to the processor used, such as 8086, 80286, 80386, and 80486 and even by models, such as XT-286, PC Convertible, and AT prior to 11/15/85.

STATUS BYTE

Most of the INT 13H services return a status code to the AH register. Service 01 requests it specifically, whereas other operations that fail set the carry flag and return a status code to identify the cause. Here are the major codes:

AH	Reason
00000000	No error
00000001	Bad command passed to controller
00000010	Address mark on disk not found
00000011	Writing on protected disk attempted
00000100	Required sector not found
00000101	Reset operation failed
00000111	Drive parameters wrong
00001000	DMA (direct memory access) overrun
00001001	DMA across a 64K boundary attempted
00010000	Bad CRC on a read encountered
00100000	Controller failed
01000000	Seek operation failed
10000000	Device failed to respond
10111011	Undefined error

If an interrupt operation returns an error, a program's usual action is to reset the disk (service 00) and to retry the operation three times. If there is still an error, display a message and give the user a chance to change the diskette, if that's a solution.

BASIC BIOS DISK OPERATIONS

This section covers the BIOS INT 13H disk services. The operation requires a service code in the AH register.

INT 13H Service 00: Reset Disk System

Use this operation after another disk operation returns a serious error. The operation performs a hard reset to the diskette or hard drive controller. That is, the next time the drive is accessed, it first resets to cylinder 0. If a hard disk is installed, set the DL to a value of 80H or more for a hard drive and the usual code (0 = A, 1 = B, etc.) for a diskette. An error sets the carry flag and returns a status code in the AH. Service 0DH is a related operation.

INT 13H Service 01: Read Disk Status

This operation returns to the AH the status from the last disk operation. (See status byte in the preceding section.) If a hard drive is installed, set the DL to a value of

80H or more for hard disk and the usual code (0 = drive A, etc.) for diskette. An error sets the carry flag and returns a status code in the AH.

INT 13H Service 02: Read Sectors

The operation reads a specified number of sectors on the same track into memory. Initialize the following registers:

AL	Number of sectors, up to the maximum for a track
AH	Track number
CL	Starting sector number
DH	Head (side) number (0 or 1 for diskette)
DL	Drive number for hard drive (80H or more) or diskette (0 = A)
ES:BX	Address of the I/O buffer in the data area, which should be large enough for all the sectors to be read. (BX in this case is subject to ES, thus the form ES:BX.)

The following example reads one sector into an area named INSECT, which should be large enough to contain all the data:

```
MOV  AH,02       ;Request read
MOV  AL,01       ;One sector
LEA  BX,INSECT   ;Input buffer at ES:BX
MOV  CH,05       ;Track 05
MOV  CL,03       ;Sector 03
MOV  DH,00       ;Head 00
MOV  DL,01       ;Drive 01 (B)
INT  13H         ;Call BIOS
```

On return, the AL contains the number of sectors that the operation actually reads. The DS, BX, CX, and DX registers are preserved. An error sets the carry flag and returns a status code in the AH.

For most situations, a program would specify only one sector or all sectors for a track. It would initialize the CH and CL and increment them to read sectors sequentially. Once the sector number exceeds the maximum for a track, you have to reset it to 01 and either increment the track number or change from side 0 to side 1 of the disk.

INT 13H Service 03: Write Sectors

This operation, the opposite of service 02, writes a specified area from memory (usually, 512 bytes or a multiple of 512) onto designated formatted sectors. Load registers and handle processing just as for service 02. On return, the AL contains the number of sectors that the operation actually wrote. The DS, BX, CX, and DX registers are preserved. An error sets the carry flag and returns a status code in the AH.

INT 13H Service 04: Verify Sectors

This operation simply checks that the specified sectors can be read, and performs a cyclical redundancy check. When an operation writes a sector, the disk controller calculates and writes a CRC checksum based on the bits that are set. This service reads the sector, recalculates the checksum, and compares it to the stored value. You could use this service after a write (service 03) to ensure more reliable output at a cost of more I/O time. Load the registers just as for service 02, but since the operation does not perform true verification, there is no need to set an address in the ES:BX. On return, the AL contains the number of sectors actually verified. The DS, BX, CX, and DX registers are preserved. An error sets the carry flag and returns a status code in the AH.

USING BIOS TO READ SECTORS

Now let's examine the program in Figure 18-1, which uses BIOS interrupt 13H to read sectors from disk. The program is based on the example in Figure 16-3 with the following changes:

1. There is now no FCB definition or open routine.
2. The program has to calculate each disk address. After each read, it increments the sector number. In C10ADDR, when the sector reaches 10, the routine resets the sector to 01. If the side is 1, the program increments track number; side number is then changed, if 0 to 1 and if 1 to 0. This works only for disks that contain nine sectors per track.
3. CURADR contains the beginning track/sector (which the program incre- ments) and ENDADR contains the ending track/sector. One way to enhance the program is to prompt a user for starting and ending track/sector.

Suggestion: Run this program under DEBUG. Trace through the instructions that initialize the segment registers. Adjust the start and end sectors to the location of the FAT (its location varies by operating system version). Use G (go) to execute, and examine the FAT and directory entries in the input area.

As an alternative to DEBUG, your program could convert the ASCII charac- ters in the input area to their hex equivalents and display the hex values just as DEBUG does (see the program in Figure 14-5). In this way, you could examine the contents of any sector, even "hidden" ones and could allow a user to enter changes and write the changed sector back onto disk.

Note that when DOS creates a file, it may insert records in available sectors, which may not be contiguous on disk. Thus you can't expect BIOS INT 13H to read a file sequentially.

```
TITLE     BIOREAD (EXE)   Read disk sectors via BIOS
          .MODEL   SMALL
          .STACK   64
; -----------------------------------------------------------
          .DATA
CURADR   DW      0304H           ;Beginning track/sector
ENDADR   DW      0501H           ;Ending track/sector
ENDCDE   DB      00              ;End process indicator
READMSG  DB      '*** Read error ***$'
RECDIN   DB      512 DUP(' ')    ;Input area
SIDE     DB      00
; -----------------------------------------------------------
          .CODE
BEGIN    PROC    FAR
         MOV     AX,@data
         MOV     DS,AX
         MOV     ES,AX
         MOV     AX,0600H        ;Request scroll
A20LOOP:
         CALL    Q10SCR          ;Clear screen
         CALL    Q20CURS         ;Set cursor
         CALL    C10ADDR         ;Calculate disk address
         MOV     CX,CURADR
         MOV     DX,ENDADR
         CMP     CX,DX           ;At ending sector?
         JE      A90             ;  yes - exit
         CALL    F10READ         ;Read disk record
         CMP     ENDCDE,00       ;Normal read?
         JNZ     A90             ;  no  - exit
         CALL    G10DISP         ;Display sector
         JMP     A20LOOP         ;Repeat
A90:     MOV     AH,4CH
         INT     21H             ;Terminate
BEGIN    ENDP
;                Calculate next disk address:
;                ----------------------------
C10ADDR  PROC    NEAR
         MOV     CX,CURADR
         CMP     CL,10           ;Past last sector?
         JNE     C90             ;  no - exit
         CMP     SIDE,00         ;Bypass if side 0
         JE      C20
         INC     CH              ;Increment track
C20:
         XOR     SIDE,01         ;Change side
         MOV     CL,01           ;Set sector to 1
         MOV     CURADR,CX
C90:     RET
C10ADDR  ENDP
;                Read disk sector:
;                ----------------
F10READ  PROC    NEAR
         MOV     AH,02           ;Request read
         MOV     AL,01           ;Number of sectors
         LEA     BX,RECDIN       ;Address of buffer
         MOV     CX,CURADR       ;Track/sector
         MOV     DH,SIDE         ;Side
         MOV     DL,01           ;Drive B
         INT     13H             ;Request input
         CMP     AH,00           ;Normal read?
         JZ      F90             ;  yes - exit
         MOV     ENDCDE,01       ;  no:
         CALL    X10ERR          ;    invalid read
F90:
         INC     CURADR          ;Increment sector
         RET
F10READ  ENDP
```

Figure 18-1   Using BIOS to Read Disk Sectors

```
;                      Display sector:
;                      --------------
G10DISP  PROC    NEAR
         MOV     AH,40H           ;Request display
         MOV     BX,01            ;Handle
         MOV     CX,512           ;Length
         LEA     DX,RECDIN
         INT     21H
         RET
G10DISP  ENDP
;                      Clear screen:
;                      ------------
Q10SCR   PROC    NEAR
         MOV     AX,0600H         ;Full screen
         MOV     BH,1EH           ;Set color
         MOV     CX,0000          ;Request scroll
         MOV     DX,184FH
         INT     10H
         RET
Q10SCR   ENDP
;                      Set cursor:
;                      ----------
Q20CURS  PROC    NEAR
         MOV     AH,02            ;Request set
         MOV     BH,00            ;  cursor
         MOV     DX,0000
         INT     10H
         RET
Q20CURS  ENDP
;                      Display disk error message:
;                      --------------------------
X10ERR   PROC    NEAR
         MOV     AH,40H           ;Request display
         MOV     BX,01            ;Handle
         MOV     CX,18            ;Length of message
         LEA     DX,READMSG
         INT     21H
         RET
X10ERR   ENDP
         END     BEGIN
```

Figure 18-1 Cont.

OTHER BIOS DISK OPERATIONS

Other BIOS disk operations may involve an 80286 or 80386 system. Many were introduced with the AT and PS/2 systems and many are concerned only with hard disks.

INT 13H Service 05: Format Tracks

This operation formats tracks according to one of four different sizes. (The standard size is 512.) Read–write operations require format information to locate a requested sector. This section describes the procedure for formatting diskettes. For this service, load the number of sectors to format in the AL, track number in the CH, head number in the DH, and drive number in the DL. Also, load the ES:BX registers with an address that points to a group of address fields for a track. For each sector on a track there must be one four-byte entry of the form T/H/S/B, where

---

T = track number

H = head (surface) number

S = sector number

B = bytes per sector (00 = 128, 01 = 256, 02 = 512, 03 = 1024)

For example, if you format track 03, head 00, and 512 bytes per sector, the first entry for the track is hex 03000102, followed by one entry for each remaining sector. An error sets the carry flag and returns a status code in the AH.

You may define sectors in normal sequence as 1, 2, . . . , 9 or you may interleave them. For an interleave factor of 2, sectors are in this logical sequence: 1, 3, 5, 7, 9, 2, 4, 6, 8. Interleaving is common on hard disks and often provides better disk performance.

Use service 17H first to set the diskette type. PS/2 and AT computers also require service 18H prior to execution of this service. Related services are 06 and 07.

INT 13H Service 06: Format and Set Flags

This service formats specified hard disk tracks and sets flags for bad sectors.

INT 13H Service 07: Format at Specified Track

This service formats hard disks beginning at a specified track and is the normal operation for formatting a whole disk.

INT 13H Service 08: Get Drive Parameters

This useful service returns information about a hard disk. Load the drive number (80H–87H) in the DL. A successful operation returns:

CH	High cylinder/track number
CL	High sector number and high-order two bits of cylinder number
DH	High head number
DL	Number of drives attached to the controller

An error sets the carry flag and returns a status code in the AH. You can also use this service for diskettes; the operation returns an address in the ES:DI that points to an 11-byte parameter table.

INT 13H Service 09: Initialize Drive

BIOS performs this service when you boot up your computer, according to a hard disk table in BIOS. The DL contains the drive number (80H–87H). INT 41H and INT 46H are related operations.

INT 13H Service 0AH: Read Extended Sector Buffer

The sector buffer on hard disks includes the 512 bytes of data plus four bytes for an error correction code (ECC), used for error checking and correcting of the data. Writers of disk utility programs are likely to use this service, which can read the whole sector buffer.

Load the number of sectors (up to the maximum for the drive) in the AL, the address of the buffer in the ES:BX, cylinder (track) number in the CH, sector number in the CL, head number in the DH, and drive in the DL (80H–87H). An error sets the carry flag and returns a status code in the AH.

INT 13H Service 0BH: Write Extended Sector Buffer

This service is similar to service 0AH except that this one writes the sector buffer onto disk.

INT 13H Service 0CH: Seek Cylinder

This service positions the read/write head on a hard disk at a specified cylinder (track). Load the cylinder number in the CH, sector number and high-order two bits of cylinder number in the CL, head number in the DH, and drive (80H–87H) in the DL. An error sets the carry flag and returns a status code in the AH.

INT 13H Service 0DH: Alternate Disk Reset

This service is similar to service 00, although this one is restricted to hard disks. Load the drive (80H–87H) in the DL. An error sets the carry flag and returns a status code in the AH.

INT 13H Service 0EH: Read Sector Buffer

This service is similar to service 0AH, although this one reads a sector and not the ECC bytes.

INT 13H Service 0FH: Write Sector Buffer

This service is similar to service 0BH, although this one writes a sector and not the ECC bytes.

INT 13H Services 10H: Test for Drive Ready, 11H: Recalibrate Hard Drive, 12H: ROM Diagnostics, 13H: Drive Diagnostics, and 14H: Controller Diagnostics

These services perform internal diagnostics and report specified information for BIOS and for advanced utility programs. An error sets the carry flag and returns a status code in the AH.

INT 13H Service 15H: Get Disk Type

This service returns information about a disk drive. Load the drive (0 = A, etc. for diskette or 80H–87H for hard disk) in the DL. The operation returns a code in the AH:

00   No disk present
01   Diskette drive that does not sense a change of diskette
02   Diskette drive that senses a change of diskette
03   Hard disk drive

For return code 03, the CX:DX pair contains the total number of disk sectors on the drive. An error sets the carry flag and returns a status code in the AH.

INT 13H Service 16H: Change of Diskette Status

This service checks for changes of diskettes for the PS/2 and AT, which can sense a change. For no change of disk, the operation clears the carry flag and returns 00 to the AH. For a change of disk, the operation sets the carry flag, returns 06 to the AH, and the drive number that had a change to the DL. An error also sets the carry flag and returns a code in the AH—an unexpected source of confusion.

INT 13H Service 17H: Set Diskette Type

This service sets up the combination of drive and diskette for a PS/2 or AT (after 6/10/85). Use this service along with service 05 for disk formatting. Load the drive number (0 = A, etc.) in the DL and the disk type in the AL. Disk types are

01   360K diskette in 360K drive
02   360K diskette in 1.2M drive
03   1.2M diskette in 1.2M drive
04   720K diskette in 720K drive

The operation clears (valid) or sets (invalid) the carry flag and returns a status in the AH register.

INT 13H Service 18H: Set Media Type for Format

For PS/2 and AT (after 11/15/85) computers, use this service before calling service 05. Load the number of tracks in the CH (low-order 8 bits), and the CL with the number of tracks (high 2 bits in bits 7–6) and sectors per track (bits 5–0). The AH and carry flag indicate the status of the operation. A valid operation returns in the ES:DI a pointer to an 11-byte parameter table.

INT 13H Service 19H: Park Disk Heads

For this service, PS/2 computers require the drive number in the DL. For all models, the operation clears (valid) or sets (invalid) the carry flag and returns a status code in the AH register.

KEY POINTS

- BIOS INT 13H provides direct access to track and sector.
- BIOS INT 13H does not supply automatic directory handling, end-of-file operations, and blocking and deblocking of records.
- The verify sector operation performs an elementary check of data written at some cost of processing time.
- A program should check for the status byte after each BIOS disk operation.

QUESTIONS

18-1. What are the two major disadvantages of using BIOS INT 13H? That is, why is the use of DOS interrupts usually preferred?

18-2. Under what circumstances would a programmer use BIOS INT 13H?

18-3. Most INT 13H operations return a status code.
  (a) Where is the code returned?
  (b) What does code 00H mean?
  (c) What does code 03H mean?

18-4. What is the standard procedure for an error returned by INT 13H?

18-5. Code the instructions to reset the diskette controller.

18-6. Code the instructions to read the diskette status.

18-7. Code the instructions for BIOS INT 13H to read one sector using memory address INDSK, drive A, head 0, track 6, and sector 3.

18-8. Code the instructions for BIOS INT 13H to write three sectors using memory address OUTDSK, drive B, head 0, track 8, and sector 1.

18-9. After the write in Question 18-8, how would you check for an attempt to write on a protected disk?

18-10. Based on Question 18-8, code the instructions to verify the write operation.

19

PRINTING

OBJECTIVE

To describe the requirements for printing using DOS and BIOS interrupts.

INTRODUCTION

Compared to screen and disk handling, printing appears to be a simple process. There are only a few operations involved, all done either through DOS INT 21H or through BIOS INT 17H. The commands to the printer include form feed, line feed, and carriage return.

One classification of printers is according to printer interface. Parallel printers accept eight bits at a time from the processor, whereas serial printers accept data from the processor one bit at a time.

Printers also may accept even, odd, or no parity bit. A printer must understand a signal from the processor, for example, to eject to a new page, to feed one line down a page, or to tab across a page. The processor also must understand a signal from a printer that indicates it is busy or out of paper. Unfortunately, many types of printers respond differently to signals from a processor, and one of the more difficult tasks for software specialists is to interface their programs to printers.

COMMON PRINTER CONTROL CHARACTERS

The standard characters that control printing include the following:

Decimal	Hex	Function
08	08	Backspace
09	09	Horizontal tab
10	0A	Line feed (advance one line)
11	0B	Vertical tab
12	0C	Form feed (advance to next page)
13	0D	Carriage return (return to left margin)

Horizontal tab.   Horizontal tab (hex 09) works only on printers that have the feature and the printer tabs are set up. Otherwise, the printer may ignore the command. You can print blank spaces to get around an inability to tab.

Line feed.   Line feed (hex 0A) advances a single line and two successive line feeds cause a double space. Virtually all printers recognize this command.

Form feed.   Initializing the paper when you power up a printer determines the starting position for the top of a page. The default length for a page is 11 inches. Neither the processor nor the printer automatically checks for the bottom of a page. If your program continues printing down a page, it eventually prints over the page perforation and onto the top of the next page. To control paging, count the lines as they print, and on reaching the maximum for a page (such as 55 lines), execute a form feed (hex 0C), then reset the line count to 0 or 1. Virtually all printers recognize this command.

At the end of printing, deliver a command such as line feed or form feed to force printing the last line still in the printer's buffer. Issuing form feed at the end of execution also facilitates tearing off the last page.

Carriage return.   Carriage return (hex 0D) resets the printer to its leftmost margin and is normally accompanied by a line feed command. Virtually all printers recognize this command. This character is Enter or Return on the keyboard.

USING EXTENDED DOS TO PRINT

DOS 2.0 introduced file handles, which we have used in the chapters on screen handling and disk processing. To print, use DOS INT 21H service 40H. Load file handle 04 the BX, the number of characters to print in the CX, and the address of the text in the DX.

The following example prints 25 characters from a data item named HEADG beginning at the leftmost margin. Carriage return (0DH) and line feed (0AH) in HEADG reset the carriage and advance one line.

```
HEADG DB    'Industrial Bicycle Mfrs', 0DH, 0AH
      . . .
      MOV AH,40H       ;Request output
      MOV BX,04        ;Handle for printer
      MOV CX,25        ;25 characters
      LEA DX,HEADG     ;Print area
      INT 21H          ;Call DOS
```

A successful operation prints the text, clears the carry flag, and returns the number of characters printed in the AX. An unsuccessful operation sets the carry flag and returns error code 05 (access denied) or 06 (invalid handle) in the AX. (An end-of-file marker (Ctrl-Z or hex A) in the data also causes the operation to terminate.)

PRINTING WITH PAGE OVERFLOW AND HEADINGS

The program in Figure 19-1 is similar to the one in Figure 8-2 that accepts names from the keyboard and displays them down the screen. This program, however, directs the names to the printer. Each printed page contains a heading followed by a double space and the entered names in the following format:

```
List of Employee Names    Page 01
Clancy Alderson
Janet Brown
David Christie
. . .
```

The program counts each line printed and, on reaching the "bottom" of a page, ejects the forms to the top of the next page. Major procedures are the following:

D10INPT	Prompts for and accepts a name from the keyboard.
E10PRNT	If at the end of a page, calls M10PAGE; prints the name (its length is based on the actual length in the input parameter list).
M10PAGE	Advances to a new page; prints the heading; resets line count and adds to page count.
P10OUT	Common routine, handles actual request to print.

At the beginning of execution, it is necessary to print a heading, but not to eject to a new page. To this end, M10PAGE bypasses the form feed if PAGECTR contains 01, its initial value. PAGECTR is defined as

```
PAGECTR DB 'O1'
```

```
TITLE    PRTNAME (EXE)  Accept entered names and print
         .MODEL   SMALL
         .STACK   64
; ----------------------------------------------------
         .DATA
NAMEPAR  LABEL   BYTE                 ;Parameter list:
MAXNLEN  DB      20                   ;  maximum length of name
NAMELEN  DB      ?                    ;  actual length entered
NAMEFLD  DB      20 DUP(' ')          ;  name entered
                                      ;Heading line:
HEADG    DB      'List of Employee Names    Page  '
PAGECTR  DB      '01', 0AH, 0AH

FFEED    DB      0CH                  ;Form feed
LFEED    DB      0AH                  ;Line feed
LINECTR  DB      01
PROMPT   DB      'Name? '
; ----------------------------------------------------
         .CODE
BEGIN    PROC    FAR
         MOV     AX,@data             ;Initialize data
         MOV     DS,AX                ;  segment
         MOV     ES,AX
         CALL    Q10CLR               ;Clear screen
         CALL    M10PAGE              ;Page heading
A20LOOP:
         MOV     DX,0000              ;Set cursor to 00,00
         CALL    Q20CURS
         CALL    D10INPT              ;Provide input of name
         CALL    Q10CLR
         CMP     NAMELEN,00           ;No name entered?
         JE      A30                  ;  no name, exit
         CALL    E10PRNT              ;  name, prepare printing
         JMP     A20LOOP
A30:
         MOV     CX,01                ;End --
         LEA     DX,FFEED             ;  one character
         CALL    P10OUT               ;  for form feed,
         MOV     AH,4CH               ;  return to DOS
         INT     21H
BEGIN    ENDP
;                Accept input of name:
;                ---------------------
D10INPT  PROC    NEAR
         MOV     AH,40H               ;Request
         MOV     BX,01                ;  display
         MOV     CX,05                ;  5 characters
         LEA     DX,PROMPT
         INT     21H                  ;Call DOS
         MOV     AH,0AH               ;Request input
         LEA     DX,NAMEPAR
         INT     21H                  ;Call DOS
         RET
D10INPT  ENDP
;                Prepare for printing:
;                ---------------------
E10PRNT  PROC    NEAR
         CMP     LINECTR,60           ;End of page?
         JB      E20                  ;  no - bypass
         CALL    M10PAGE              ;  yes - print heading

E20:
         MOV     CH,00
         MOV     CL,NAMELEN           ;Set no. of characters
         LEA     DX,NAMEFLD           ;Set address of name
         CALL    P10OUT               ;Print name
         MOV     CX,01                ;One
         LEA     DX,LFEED             ;  line feed
         CALL    P10OUT
```

Figure 19-1 Printing with Page Overflow and Headings

```
            INC     LINECTR                 ;Add to line count
            RET
E10PRNT ENDP
;                   Page heading routine:
;                   --------------------
M10PAGE PROC    NEAR
            CMP     WORD PTR PAGECTR,3130H  ;First page?
            JE      M30                     ; yes - bypass
            MOV     CX,01                   ;
            LEA     DX,FFEED                ; no --
            CALL    P10OUT                  ; form feed,
            MOV     LINECTR,03              ; reset line count
M30:
            MOV     CX,36                   ;Length of heading
            LEA     DX,HEADG                ;Address of heading
M40:
            CALL    P10OUT
            INC     PAGECTR+1               ;Add to page count
            CMP     PAGECTR+1,3AH           ;Page no. = hex 3A?
            JNE     M50                     ; no  - bypass
            MOV     PAGECTR+1,30H           ; yes - set to ASCII
            INC     PAGECTR                 ;
M50:        RET
M10PAGE ENDP
;                   Print routine:
;                   -------------
P10OUT  PROC    NEAR                        ;CX and DX set on entry
            MOV     AH,40H                  ;Request print
            MOV     BX,04                   ;Handle
            INT     21H                     ;Call DOS
            RET
P10OUT  ENDP
;                   Clear screen:
;                   ------------
Q10CLR  PROC    NEAR
            MOV     AX,0600H                ;Request scroll
            MOV     BH,60H                  ;Color (07 for BW)
            MOV     CX,0000                 ;From 00,00
            MOV     DX,184FH                ;  to 24,79
            INT     10H                     ;Call BIOS
            RET
Q10CLR  ENDP
;                   Set cursor row/col:
;                   ------------------
Q20CURS PROC    NEAR                        ;DX set on entry
            MOV     AH,02                   ;Request set cursor
            MOV     BH,00                   ;Page number 0
            INT     10H                     ;Call BIOS
            RET
Q20CURS ENDP
            END     BEGIN
```

Figure 19-1 Cont.

which generates an ASCII number, hex 3031. The routine in M10PAGE increments PAGECTR by 1 so that it becomes progressively 3032, 3033, and so forth. The value is valid up to 3039 and then becomes 303A, which would print as 0:. If the rightmost byte of PAGECTR contains hex 3A, the routine changes it to hex 30 and adds 1 to the leftmost byte. Hex 303A becomes 3130, or 10.

Placing a test for end of page before (rather than after) printing a name ensures that the last page has at least one name under the title.

PRINTING ASCII FILES AND HANDLING TABS

A common procedure, performed for example by the video adapter, is to expand a Tab character (09) with blanks to the next location evenly divisible by 8. Thus tab stops could be at locations 8, 16, 24, and so forth, so that all locations between 0 and 7 tab to 8, those between 8 and 15 tab to 16, and so forth. Some printers, however, ignore tab characters. DOS PRINT, for example, which prints ASCII files (such as assembly language source programs), has to check each character that it sends to the printer. If a tab, the program expands blanks to the next 8-byte location.

The program in Figure 19-2 requests a user to enter the name of a file and prints its contents. The program is similar to the one in Figure 17-3 that displays files, but this one has to expand tab stops for the printer. You'll find the logic in G10XFER, following label G60. Following are three examples of tab stops for positions 1, 9, and 21:

Present print location:	1	9	21
Binary value:	00000001	00001001	00010101
Clear rightmost 3 bits:	00000000	00001000	00010000
Add 8:	00001000	00010000	00011000
New tabbed location:	8	16	24

The program is organized as follows:

C10PRMP	Requests the user to enter a file name. Pressing only the Enter key causes the program to assume the user is finished.
E10OPEN	Opens the requested disk file.
G10XFER	Checks for end of sector, end of file, end of display area, line feed, and tab. Basically, sends regular characters to the display area.
P10PRNT	Prints the display line and clears it.
R10READ	Reads a sector from the file.

Carriage return, line feed, and form feed should work on all printers. You could modify this program to count the lines printed and force a form feed when near the bottom of a page, at line 62 or so. Some users prefer to use an editor program to embed form feed characters directly in their ASCII files, at the exact location where they want a page break, such as at the end of a program procedure. The usual method is to hold down the Alt key and press numbers on the numeric keypad: 012 for form feed.

You could revise this program for original DOS service 05 to send each character directly to the printer, thereby eliminating the definition and use of a display area.

```
TITLE    PRINASC (EXE)  Read and print disk records
         .MODEL  SMALL
         .STACK  64
;  --------------------------------------------------
         .DATA
PATHPAR LABEL  BYTE                   ;Parameter list for
MAXLEN  DB     32                     ;  input of
NAMELEN DB     ?                      ;  filename
FILENAM DB     32 DUP(' ')

COUNT   DW     00
DISAREA DB     120 DUP(' ')           ;Display area
ENDCDE  DW     00                     ;End process indicator
FFEED   DB     0CH
HANDLE  DW     0
OPENMSG DB     '*** Open error ***'
PROMPT  DB     'Name of file? '
SECTOR  DB     512 DUP(' ')           ;Input area for file
;  --------------------------------------------------
         .CODE
BEGIN   PROC   FAR                    ;Main procedure
        MOV    AX,@data               ;Initialize data
        MOV    DS,AX                  ;  segment
        MOV    ES,AX
        CALL   Q10SCR                 ;Clear screen
        CALL   Q20CURS                ;Set cursor
A10LOOP:
        MOV    ENDCDE,00              ;Initialize
        CALL   C10PRMP                ;Request filename
        CMP    NAMELEN,00             ;Any request?
        JE     A90                    ;  No -- exit
        CALL   E10OPEN                ;Open file, set DTA
        CMP    ENDCDE,00              ;Valid open?
        JNE    A80                    ;  no -- request again
        CALL   R10READ                ;Read 1st disk sector
        CMP    ENDCDE,00              ;End-file, no data?
        JE     A80                    ;  yes -- request next
        CALL   G10XFER                ;Print/read
A80:
        JMP    A10LOOP                ;Repeat
A90:    MOV    AH,4CH                 ;Terminate
        INT    21H
BEGIN   ENDP
;                    Request file name:
;                    ------------------
C10PRMP PROC   NEAR
        MOV    AH,40H                 ;Prompt for filename
        MOV    BX,01
        MOV    CX,13
        LEA    DX,PROMPT
        INT    21H
        MOV    AH,0AH                 ;Accept filename
        LEA    DX,PATHPAR
        INT    21H
        MOV    BL,NAMELEN             ;Insert
        MOV    BH,00                  ;  zero at end
        MOV    FILENAM[BX],0          ;  filename
C90:    RET
C10PRMP ENDP


;                    Open disk file:
;                    --------------
E10OPEN PROC   NEAR
        MOV    AH,3DH                 ;Request open
        MOV    AL,00                  ;Read only
        LEA    DX,FILENAM
        INT    21H
        JNC    E20                    ;Test carry flag,
        CALL   X10ERR                 ;  error if set
        RET
```

Figure 19-2   Printing an ASCII File

```
E20:
        MOV     HANDLE,AX           ;Save handle
        MOV     AX,2020H
        MOV     CX,256              ;Clear sector
        LEA     DI,SECTOR           ;  area to blank
        REP STOSW
        RET
E10OPEN ENDP
;               Transfer data to print line:
;               ----------------------------
G10XFER PROC    NEAR
        CLD                         ;Set left-to-right
        LEA     SI,SECTOR           ;Initialize
G20:
        LEA     DI,DISAREA
        MOV     COUNT,00
G30:
        LEA     DX,SECTOR+512
        CMP     SI,DX               ;End of sector?
        JNE     G40                 ;  no -- bypass
        CALL    R10READ             ;  yes -- read next
        CMP     ENDCDE,00           ;End of file?
        JE      G80                 ;  yes -- exit
        LEA     SI,SECTOR
G40:
        MOV     BX,COUNT
        CMP     BX,80               ;At end of display area?
        JB      G50                 ;  no -- bypass
        MOV     [DI+BX],0D0AH       ;  yes - set CR/LF
        CALL    P10PRNT
        LEA     DI,DISAREA          ;Reinitialize
        MOV     COUNT,00
G50:
        LODSB                       ;[SI] to AL, INC SI
        MOV     BX,COUNT
        MOV     [DI+BX],AL          ;Character to print line
        INC     BX
        CMP     AL,1AH              ;End-of-file?
        JE      G80                 ;  yes -- exit
        CMP     AL,0AH              ;Line feed?
        JNE     G60
        CALL    P10PRNT             ;Call print
        JMP     G20
G60:
        CMP     AL,09H              ;Tab character?
        JNE     G70
        DEC     BX                  ;  yes -- reset BX
        MOV     BYTE PTR [DI+BX],20H ;Clear tab to blank
        AND     BX,0FFF8H           ;Clear rightmost 3 bits
        ADD     BX,08               ;  & add 8 -> tab stop
G70:
        MOV     COUNT,BX
        JMP     G30
G80:    MOV     BX,COUNT            ;End of file
        MOV     BYTE PTR [DI+BX],0CH ;Form feed
        CALL    P10PRNT             ;Print last line
G90:    RET
G10XFER ENDP
;               Print line:
;               ----------
P10PRNT PROC    NEAR
        MOV     AH,40H              ;Request print
        MOV     BX,04
        MOV     CX,COUNT            ;Length
        INC     CX
        LEA     DX,DISAREA
        INT     21H
        MOV     AX,2020H            ;Clear display line
        MOV     CX,60
        LEA     DI,DISAREA
```

Figure 19-2 Cont.

```
                REP STOSW
                RET
P10PRNT ENDP
;                       Read disk sector:
;                       ----------------
R10READ PROC    NEAR
        MOV     AH,3FH                 ;Request read
        MOV     BX,HANDLE              ;Device
        MOV     CX,512                 ;Length
        LEA     DX,SECTOR              ;Buffer
        INT     21H
        MOV     ENDCDE,AX
        RET
R10READ ENDP
;                       Scroll screen:
;                       -------------
Q10SCR  PROC    NEAR
        MOV     AX,0600H
        MOV     BH,1EH                 ;Set color
        MOV     CX,0000                ;Scroll
        MOV     DX,184FH
        INT     10H
        RET
Q10SCR  ENDP
;                       Set cursor:
;                       ----------
Q20CURS PROC    NEAR
        MOV     AH,02                  ;Request set
        MOV     BH,00                  ;  cursor
        MOV     DX,00
        INT     10H
        RET
Q20CURS ENDP
;                       Display disk error message:
;                       --------------------------
X10ERR  PROC    NEAR
        MOV     AH,40H                 ;Request display
        MOV     BX,01                  ;Handle
        MOV     CX,18                  ;Length
        LEA     DX,OPENMSG             ;Error message
        INT     21H
        MOV     ENDCDE,01              ;Error indicator
        RET
X10ERR  ENDP
        END     BEGIN
```

Figure 19-2   Cont.

USING ORIGINAL DOS TO PRINT

Original DOS service 05 provides print facilities. Load service 05 in the AH register, the character that you want to print in the DL, and issue INT 21H, as follows:

```
        MOV AH,05       ;Request print service
        MOV DL,char     ;Character to print
        INT 21H         ;Call DOS
```

These instructions are adequate for sending print control characters. However,
printing typically involves a full or partial line of text and requires stepping through
a line formatted in the data area.

The following illustrates printing a full line. It first initializes the address of

HEADG in the SI register and sets the CX to the length of HEADG. The loop at P20 extracts each character successively from HEADG and sends it to the printer. Since the first character in HEADG is a form feed and the last two characters are line feed, the heading prints at the top of a new page and is followed by a double space.

```
HEADG  DB     0CH,'Industrial Bicycle Mfrs',0DH,0AH,0AH
       . . .
       MOV    CX,27       ;Initialize length and
       LEA    SI,HEADG    ; address of heading
P20:
       MOV    AH,05       ;Request to print
       MOV    DL,[SI]     ;Character from heading
       INT    21H         ;Call DOS
       INC    SI          ;Next character in heading
       LOOP   P20         ;Loop 27 times
```

If the printer power is not on, DOS returns a message "out of paper" repetitively. If you turn on the power, the program begins printing correctly. You can also press Ctrl/Break to cancel execution.

SPECIAL PRINTER COMMANDS

We have already examined the use of a number of basic printer commands, such as form feed and carriage return. Other commands suitable for many common printers include:

Decimal	Hex	Action
15	0F	Turn on condensed mode
14	0E	Turn on expanded mode
18	12	Turn off condensed mode
20	14	Turn off expanded mode

Some commands require a preceding Esc (escape) character (hex 1B). Some of these commands, depending on the printer, include:

1B 30	Set line spacing to eight lines per inch
1B 32	Set line spacing to six lines per inch
1B 45	Set on emphasized printing mode
1B 46	Set off emphasized printing mode

You can send command codes to a printer in two different ways:

1. Define commands in the data area. The following sets condensed mode, eight
    lines per inch, prints a title, and causes carriage return and line feed oper-
    ations:

    ```
    HEADG    DB    OFH, 1BH, 30H, 'Title... ', ODH, OAH
    ```

2. Use immediate instructions:

    ```
    MOV  AH,05     ;Request print
    MOV  DL,OFH    ;Send condensed mode character
    INT  21H
    ```

All following characters print in condensed mode until the program sends a
command that resets the mode.

These commands don't necessarily work for all printer models. Check your
printer manual for its specific commands.

USING BIOS INT 17H TO PRINT

Valid printers for BIOS interrupt 17H are 0 (the default), 1, and 2 for LPT1, LPT2,
and LPT3, respectively. The operation provides three different services specified in
the AH register.

INT 17H Service 00: Print a Character

This operation causes printing of one character and allows for printer numbers 0, 1,
or 2. Load the character in the AL and the printer number in the DX:

```
MOV  AH,00     ;Request print
MOV  AL,char   ;Character to be printed
MOV  DX,00     ;Select printer number 0
INT  17H       ;Call BIOS
```

If the operation cannot print the character, it returns 01 to the AH register. You
would normally use service 02 first to check the printer status.

INT 17H Service 01: Initialize the Printer Port

This service resets the printer and initializes it for data.

```
MOV  AH,01     ;Request initialize port
MOV  DX,00     ;Select printer port number 0
INT  17H       ;Call BIOS
```

Since the operation sends a form feed character, use it to set the printer to the top-of-page position, although most printers do this automatically when turned on. The operation returns a status code in the AH with one or more bits set to 1:

Bit	Cause
0	Time out
3	Input/output error
4	Selected
5	Out of paper
6	Acknowledged from printer
7	Not busy

If the printer is already switched on, the operation returns hex 90 (binary 10010000)—the printer is not "busy" and is "selected," a valid condition. Printer "errors" are bit 5 (out of paper) and bit 3 (output error). If the printer is not switched on, the operation returns hex B0, or binary 10110000, indicating "out of paper."

INT 17H Service 02: Get Printer Port Status

The purpose of this service is to determine the status of the printer. The operation returns the same printer port status as service 01.

```
MOV   AH,02          ;Request read port
MOV   DX,00          ;Select printer port number 0
INT   17H            ;Call BIOS
TEST  AH,00101001B   ;Ready?
JNZ   errormsg       ;No—display message
```

When the program runs, if the printer is not initially turned on, BIOS is unable to return a message automatically—your program is supposed to test and act upon the printer status. If your program does not check the status, your only indication is the cursor blinking. If you turn on the printer at this point, some of the output data is lost. Consequently, before BIOS print operations, check the port status; if there is an error, display a message. (The DOS operation performs this checking automatically, although its message "out of paper" applies to various conditions.) When the printer is switched on, the message no longer displays and printing begins normally with no loss of data.

At any time, a printer may run out of forms or may be inadvertently switched off. If you are writing a program for others to use, include a status test before every attempt to print.

KEY POINTS

- Before attempting to print, turn on the power and have the printer loaded with an adequate supply of paper.
- After printing is completed, use line feed or form feed to clear the printer buffer.
- DOS provides a message if there is a printer error, but BIOS returns only a status code. When using BIOS INT 17H, check the printer status before printing.

QUESTIONS

19-1. Provide the printer control characters for **(a)** horizontal tab, **(b)** form feed, **(c)** backspace, and **(d)** carriage return.

19-2. Code a program using DOS service 40H for the following requirements: **(a)** eject the forms to the next page; **(b)** print your name; **(c)** perform carriage return and line feed and print your address; **(d)** perform carriage return and line feed and print your city/state; **(e)** eject the forms.

19-3. Revise Question 19-2 for using DOS service 05.

19-4. Code a heading line that sets condensed mode, defines a title (any name), provides for carriage return and form feed operations, and turns off condensed mode.

19-5. BIOS interrupt 17H for printing returns an error code.
   (a) Where is the code returned?
   (b) What does code 08H mean?
   (c) What does code 90H mean?

19-6. Revise Question 19-2 for using BIOS INT 17H. Include a test for printer status.

19-7. Revise Question 19-2 so that the program performs parts (b), (c), and (d) five times.

19-8. Revise Figure 19-1 to run under DOS service 05.

19-9. Revise Figure 19-2 so that it also displays printed lines.

20

MACRO WRITING

OBJECTIVE

To explain the definition and use of macro instructions.

INTRODUCTION

For each symbolic instruction, the assembler generates one machine language instruction. But for each coded statement in a high-level language such as Pascal or C, the compiler generates one or more (often many) machine language instructions. In this regard, you can think of a high-level language as consisting of *macro* statements.

The assembler has facilities that programmers use to define macros. You define a specific name for the macro along with the assembly language instructions that the macro is to generate. Then, whenever you need to execute the instructions, simply code the name of the macro, and the assembler generates your defined instructions.

Macros are useful for the following purposes:

- To simplify and to reduce the amount of coding
- To streamline an assembly language program to make it more readable
- To reduce errors caused by repetitive coding

Examples of possible macros are input/output operations that load registers and perform interrupts, conversion of ASCII and binary data, multiple-word arithmetic operations, string handling routines, and divide by subtraction.

A SIMPLE MACRO DEFINITION

A macro definition appears before any defined segment. Let's examine a simple *macro definition* named INITZ, which initializes the segment registers for an EXE program:

```
INITZ   MACRO                   ;Define macro
        MOV     AX,@data    ; } Body of
        MOV     DS,AX       ; } macro
        MOV     ES,AX       ; } definition
        ENDM                    ;End of macro
```

The name of the macro is INITZ, although any other unique valid name is acceptable. The MACRO directive tells the assembler that the following instructions up to ENDM are to be part of a macro definition. The ENDM directive terminates the macro definition. The instructions between MACRO and ENDM comprise the body of the macro definition.

The names referenced in the macro definition, @data, AX, DS, and ES, must be defined elsewhere in the program or otherwise be known to the assembler. You subsequently use the macro instruction INITZ in the code segment where you want to initialize the registers. When the assembler encounters the macro instruction INITZ, it scans a table of symbolic instructions, and failing to find an entry, checks for macro instructions. Since the program contains a definition of the macro INITZ, the assembler substitutes the body of the definition, generating the instructions— the *macro expansion*. A program would use this macro instruction only once, although other macros are designed to be used any number of times, and each time the assembler generates the same macro expansion.

Figure 20-1 provides a listing of the assembled program. The macro expansion shows the number 1 to the left of each instruction to indicate that a macro instruction generated it. A macro expansion indicates only generated object code, so that directives like ASSUME or PAGE would not appear.

In a later section we explain how to catalog macros in a library and how to include them automatically in any program.

USING PARAMETERS IN MACROS

To make a macro flexible, you can define names in a macro as *dummy arguments*. The following macro definition named PROMPT provides for the use of DOS service 09H to display any message. When using the macro instruction, the pro-

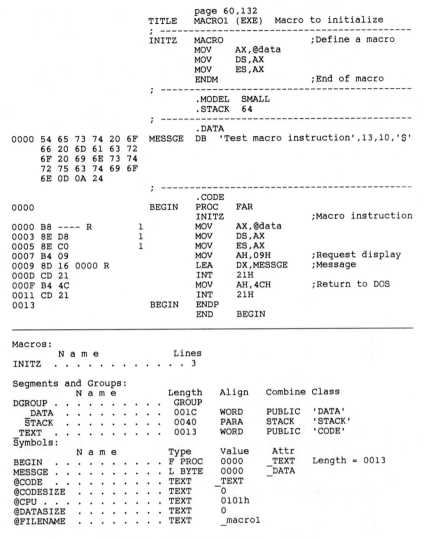

```
                              page 60,132
                     TITLE    MACRO1 (EXE)  Macro to initialize
                     ; -----------------------------------------------
                     INITZ    MACRO                    ;Define a macro
                              MOV      AX,@data
                              MOV      DS,AX
                              MOV      ES,AX
                              ENDM                     ;End of macro
                     ; -----------------------------------------------
                              .MODEL   SMALL
                              .STACK   64
                     ; -----------------------------------------------
                              .DATA
0000 54 65 73 74 20 6F MESSGE DB       'Test macro instruction',13,10,'$'
     66 20 6D 61 63 72
     6F 20 69 6E 73 74
     72 75 63 74 69 6F
     6E 0D 0A 24
                     ; -----------------------------------------------
                              .CODE
0000                 BEGIN    PROC     FAR
                              INITZ                    ;Macro instruction
0000 B8 ---- R     1          MOV      AX,@data
0003 8E D8         1          MOV      DS,AX
0005 8E C0         1          MOV      ES,AX
0007 B4 09                    MOV      AH,09H          ;Request display
0009 8D 16 0000 R             LEA      DX,MESSGE       ;Message
000D CD 21                    INT      21H
000F B4 4C                    MOV      AH,4CH          ;Return to DOS
0011 CD 21                    INT      21H
0013                 BEGIN    ENDP
                              END      BEGIN
```

```
Macros:
        N a m e                 Lines
INITZ . . . . . . . . . . . . 3

Segments and Groups:
            N a m e           Length   Align   Combine Class
DGROUP . . . . . . . . . . .  GROUP
    DATA . . . . . . . . . .  001C     WORD    PUBLIC  'DATA'
    STACK  . . . . . . . . .  0040     PARA    STACK   'STACK'
    TEXT . . . . . . . . . .  0013     WORD    PUBLIC  'CODE'
Symbols:
            N a m e           Type     Value   Attr
BEGIN  . . . . . . . . . . .  F PROC   0000     _TEXT   Length = 0013
MESSGE . . . . . . . . . . .  L BYTE   0000     _DATA
@CODE  . . . . . . . . . . .  TEXT     _TEXT
@CODESIZE  . . . . . . . . .  TEXT     0
@CPU . . . . . . . . . . . .  TEXT     0101h
@DATASIZE  . . . . . . . . .  TEXT     0
@FILENAME  . . . . . . . . .  TEXT     _macro1
```

Figure 20-1   Simple Assembled Macro-Instruction

grammer has to supply the name of the message, which references a data area terminated by a dollar sign.

```
PROMPT    MACRO    MESSGE        ;Dummy argument
          MOV      AH,09H
          LEA      DX,MESSGE
          INT      21H
          ENDM                   ;End of macro
```

A dummy argument in a macro definition tells the assembler to match its name with any occurrence of the same name in the macro body. The dummy argument MESSGE also occurs in the LEA instruction. A dummy argument may have any valid name.

When using the macro instruction PROMPT, supply as a parameter the actual name of the message to be displayed, for example as

```
PROMPT  MESSAGE2
```

In this case, MESSAGE2 would be properly defined in the data segment. The parameter in the macro instruction matches the dummy argument in the original macro definition:

Macro definition: PROMPT   MACRO   MESSGE   (argument)

Macro instruction: PROMPT   MESSAGE2 (parameter)

The assembler has already matched the argument in the original macro definition with the LEA statement in the body. It now substitutes the parameters of the macro instruction with the dummy argument in the macro definition: MESSGE matches MESSG2 in the macro definition. The assembler substitutes MESSG2 for the occurrence of MESSGE in the LEA instruction, and would substitute it for any other occurrence.

The macro definition and macro expansion are shown in full in Figure 20-2. The program also defines the macro INITZ at the start and uses it in the code segment.

A dummy argument may have any legal name, including a register name such as CX. You may define a macro with any number of dummy arguments, separated by commas, up to column 120 of a line. It substitutes parameters of the macro instruction with dummy arguments in the macro definition, entry for entry, from left to right.

COMMENTS

Comments may appear in a macro definition to clarify its purpose. A COMMENT directive or a semicolon indicates a comment line, as in the following example:

```
PROMPT  MACRO   MESSGE
;               This macro permits display of messages
        MOV     AH,09H
        LEA     DX,MESSGE
        INT     21H
        ENDM
```

```
                              TITLE    MACRO2 (EXE)  Use of parameters
                              ; -------------------------------------------
                              INITZ    MACRO                     ;Define macro
                                       MOV      AX,@data
                                       MOV      DS,AX
                                       MOV      ES,AX
                                       ENDM                      ;End of macro
                              PROMPT   MACRO    MESSGE           ;Define macro
                                       MOV      AH,09
                                       LEA      DX,MESSGE
                                       INT      21H
                                       ENDM                      ;End of macro
                              ; -------------------------------------------
                                       .MODEL   SMALL
                                       .STACK   64
                              ; -------------------------------------------
                                       .DATA
  0000 43 75 73 74 6F 6D     MESSG1   DB       'Customer name?', '$'
       65 72 20 6E 61 6D
       65 3F 24
  000F 43 75 73 74 6F 6D     MESSG2   DB       'Customer address?', '$'
       65 72 20 61 64 64
       72 65 73 73 3F 24
                              ; -------------------------------------------
                                       .CODE
  0000                        BEGIN    PROC     FAR
                                       INITZ
  0000  B8 ---- R          1          MOV      AX,@data
  0003  8E D8              1          MOV      DS,AX
  0005  8E C0              1          MOV      ES,AX
                                       PROMPT MESSG2
  0007  B4 09              1          MOV      AH,09
  0009  8D 16 000F R       1          LEA      DX,MESSG2
  000D  CD 21              1          INT      21H
  000F  B4 4C                         MOV      AH,4CH            ;Return to DOS
  0011  CD 21                         INT      21H
  0013                        BEGIN    ENDP
                                       END      BEGIN
```

Figure 20-2   Use of Macro Parameters

Because the default is to list only instructions that generate object code, the assembler does not automatically display a comment when this macro definition is expanded. If you want a comment to appear within an expansion, use the listing directive .LALL ("list all," including the leading period) prior to requesting the macro instruction:

```
.LALL
PROMPT MESSAGE1
```

A macro definition could contain a number of comments, some of which you may want to list and some to suppress. Still use .LALL, but code double semicolons (;;) before comments that are always to be suppressed. (The assembler default is .XALL, which causes a listing only of instructions that generate object code.) You may not want any of the source code of a macro expansion to list, especially if the macro instruction is used several times in a program. Code the listing directive .SALL ("suppress all"), which reduces the size of the printed program, although it has no effect on the size of the object module.

A listing directive holds effect throughout a program until another listing directive is encountered. You can place them in a program to cause some macros to display comments, some to display the macro expansion, and some to suppress these.

The program in Figure 20-3 illustrates the preceding features. The program defines the two macros, INITZ and PROMPT, described earlier. The code segment contains the listing directive .SALL to suppress the expansion of INITZ and the first expansion of PROMPT. For the second use of PROMPT, the listing directive .LALL causes the assembler to print the comment and the expansion of the macro. However, in the macro definition for PROMPT, the comment containing a double semicolon (;;) still does not print in this macro expansion.

```
                          TITLE     MACRO3 (EXE)  Use of .LALL & .SALL
                          ; ------------------------------------------------
                          INITZ     MACRO
                                    MOV       AX,@data
                                    MOV       DS,AX
                                    MOV       ES,AX
                                    ENDM
                          ; ------------------------------------------------
                          PROMPT    MACRO     MESSGE
                          ;         This macro displays any message
                          ;;        Generates code that calls DOS service
                                    MOV       AH,09          ;Request display
                                    LEA       DX,MESSGE
                                    INT       21H
                                    ENDM
                          ; ------------------------------------------------
                                    .MODEL    SMALL
                                    .STACK    64
                          ; ------------------------------------------------
                                    .DATA
0000 43 75 73 74 6F 6D    MESSG1    DB        'Customer name?', 13, 10, '$'
     65 72 20 6E 61 6D
     65 3F 0D 0A 24
0011 43 75 73 74 6F 6D    MESSG2    DB        'Customer address?', 13, 10, '$'
     65 72 20 61 64 64
     72 65 73 73 3F 0D
     0A 24

                          ; ------------------------------------------------
                                    .CODE
0000                      BEGIN     PROC      FAR
                                    .SALL
                                    INITZ
                                    PROMPT MESSG1
                                    .LALL
                                    PROMPT MESSG2
                        1 ;         This macro displays any message
000F B4 09              1           MOV       AH,09          ;Request display
0011 8D 16 0011 R       1           LEA       DX,MESSG2
0015 CD 21              1           INT       21H
0017 B4 4C                          MOV       AH,4CH         ;Return to DOS
0019 CD 21                          INT       21H
001B                      BEGIN     ENDP
                                    END       BEGIN
```

Figure 20-3   Listing and Suppression of Macro Expansions

USING A MACRO WITHIN A MACRO DEFINITION

A macro definition may contain a reference to another defined macro. Consider a simple macro named DOS21 that loads a service in the AH register and calls DOS INT 21H:

```
DOS21   MACRO     DOSFUNC
        MOV       AH,DOSFUNC
        INT       21H
        ENDM
```

To use the DOS21 macro for accepting input from the keyboard, code

```
        LEA       DX,NAMEPAR
        DOS21     0AH
```

Suppose you have another macro named DISP that uses service 02 in the AH register to display a character:

```
DISP  MACRO     CHAR
      MOV       AH,02
      MOV       DL,CHAR
      INT       21H
      ENDM
```

To display an asterisk, for example, code the macro as DISP '*'. You could change DISP to take advantage of the DOS21H macro, as

```
DISP  MACRO     CHAR
      MOV       DL,CHAR
      DOS21     02
      ENDM
```

Now if you code the DISP macro as DISP '*', the assembler generates

```
        MOV     DL,'*'
        MOV     AH,02
        INT     21H
```

THE LOCAL DIRECTIVE

Some macros require definition of a data item or an instruction label. If you use the macro more than once in the same program, the assembler defines the data item or label for each occurrence, and generates an error message because of duplicate names. Use the LOCAL directive to ensure that each generated name is unique, and code it immediately after the MACRO statement, even before comments. Its general format is

LOCAL	dummy-1, dummy-2, ...	;One or more dummy arguments

Figure 20-4 illustrates the use of LOCAL. The purpose of the program is to perform division by successive subtraction. The routine subtracts the divisor from

```
                              TITLE    MACRO4 (EXE)  Use of LOCAL
                              ; --------------------------------------------------
                              INITZ    MACRO
                                       MOV      AX,@data
                                       MOV      DS,AX
                                       MOV      ES,AX
                                       ENDM
                              DIVIDE   MACRO    DIVIDEND,DIVISOR,QUOTIENT
                                       LOCAL    COMP
                                       LOCAL    OUT
                              ;        AX = div'd, BX = divisor, CX = quotient
                                       MOV      AX,DIVIDEND  ;Set dividend
                                       MOV      BX,DIVISOR   ;Set divisor
                                       SUB      CX,CX        ;Clear quotient
                              COMP:
                                       CMP      AX,BX        ;Div'd < div'r?
                                       JB       OUT          ;  yes - exit
                                       SUB      AX,BX        ;Div'd - divisor
                                       INC      CX           ;Add to quotient
                                       JMP      COMP
                              OUT:
                                       MOV      QUOTIENT,CX  ;Store quotient
                                       ENDM
                              ; --------------------------------------------------
                                       .MODEL   SMALL
                                       .STACK   64
                              ; --------------------------------------------------
                                       .DATA
0000 0096                     DIVDND   DW       150          ;Dividend
0002 001B                     DIVSOR   DW       27           ;Divisor
0004 0000                     QUOTNT   DW       ?            ;Quotient
                              ; --------------------------------------------------
                                       .CODE
0000                          BEGIN    PROC     FAR
                                       .LALL
                                       INITZ
0000 B8 ---- R        1                MOV      AX,@data
0003 8E D8            1                MOV      DS,AX
0005 8E C0            1                MOV      ES,AX
                              DIVIDE DIVDND,DIVSOR,QUOTNT
                      1;               AX = div'd, BX = divisor, CX = quotient
0007 A1 0000 R        1                MOV      AX,DIVDND    ;Set dividend
000A 8B 1E 0002 R     1                MOV      BX,DIVSOR    ;Set divisor
000E 2B C9            1                SUB      CX,CX        ;Clear quotient
0010                  1??0000:
0010 3B C3            1                CMP      AX,BX        ;Div'd < div'r?
0012 72 05            1                JB       ??0001       ;  yes - exit
0014 2B C3            1                SUB      AX,BX        ;Div'd - divisor
0016 41               1                INC      CX           ;Add to quotient
0017 EB F7            1                JMP      ??0000
0019                  1??0001:
0019 89 0E 0004 R     1                MOV      QUOTNT,CX    ;Store quotient
001D B4 4C                             MOV      AH,4CH
001F CD 21                             INT      21H          ;Exit to DOS
0021                          BEGIN    ENDP
                                       END      BEGIN
```

Figure 20-4 Use of LOCAL

the dividend and adds 1 to the quotient until the dividend is less than the divisor. The procedure requires two labels: COMP for the loop address, and OUT for exiting on completion. Both COMP and OUT are defined as LOCAL and may have any legal names.

In the macro expansion, the generated symbolic label for COMP is ??0000 and for OUT is ??0001. If the DIVIDE macro instruction were used again in the same program, the symbolic labels for the next macro expansion would become ??0002 and ??0003, respectively. In this way, the feature ensures that generated labels are unique.

INCLUDES FROM A MACRO LIBRARY

Defining a macro such as INITZ or INITZ and using it just once in a program is not very productive. A better approach is to catalog your macros in a disk library under a descriptive name, such as MACRO.LIB:

```
INIT     MACRO    CSNAME,DSNAME,SSNAME
         . . .
         ENDM
PROMPT   MACRO    MESSGE
         . . .
         ENDM
```

To use any of the cataloged macros, instead of a MACRO definition at the start of the program, use an INCLUDE directive like this:

```
INCLUDE C:MACRO.LIB
. . .
INIT CSEG,DATA,STACK
```

The assembler accesses the file named MACRO.LIB (in this case) on drive C, and includes both macro definitions INIT and PROMPT into the program. In this example, only INIT is actually required. As coded, the assembled listing will contain a copy of the macro definition indicated by the letter C in column 30 of the LST file. Following the macro instruction is the expansion of the macro along with its generated object code indicated by + in column 31.

Since a MASM assembly is a two-pass operation, you can use the following statements to cause INCLUDE to occur only on pass 1 (instead of both passes):

```
IF1
        INCLUDE C:MACRO.LIB
ENDIF
```

IF1 and ENDIF are conditional directives. IF1 tells the assembler to access the named library only on pass 1 of the assembly. ENDIF terminates the IF logic. A copy of the macro definition no longer appears on the listing—a saving of both time and space.

The program in Figure 20-5 contains the previously described IF1, INCLUDE, and ENDIF statements, although the assembler lists only the ENDIF in the LST file. The two macro instructions used in the code segment, INIT and PROMPT, are both cataloged in MACRO.LIB. They were simply stored together as a disk file under that name by means of an editor program.

The placement of INCLUDE is not critical, but must appear before a macro instruction that references the library entry.

The PURGE Directive

An INCLUDE statement causes the assembler to include all the macro definitions that are in the specified library. For example, a library contains the macros INIT, PROMPT, and DIVIDE, but a program requires only INIT. The PURGE directive enables you to "delete" unwanted macros PROMPT and DIVIDE from the current assembly:

```
IF1
        INCLUDE C:\MACRO.LIB      ;Include full library
ENDIF
PURGE  PROMPT,DIVIDE             ;Delete unneeded macros
. . .
INIT   CSEG,DATA,STACK           ;Use remaining macro
```

A PURGE operation facilitates only an assembly and has no effect on macros stored in the library.

```
                          TITLE   MACRO5 (EXE)  Test of INCLUDE
                          ; ------------------------------------------
                                  .MODEL SMALL
                                  .STACK 64
                          ; ------------------------------------------
                                  .DATA
0000 54 65 73 74 20 6F    MESSGE  DB       'Test of macro','$'
     66 20 6D 61 63 72
     6F 24
                          ; ------------------------------------------
                                  .CODE
0000                      BEGIN   PROC    FAR
                                  INITZ
0000 B8 ---- R         1          MOV     AX,@data
0003 8E D8             1          MOV     DS,AX
0005 8E C0             1          MOV     ES,AX
                                  PROMPT  MESSGE
0007 B4 09             1          MOV     AH,09          ;Request display
0009 8D 16 0000 R      1          LEA     DX,MESSGE
000D CD 21             1          INT     21H
000F B4 4C                        MOV     AH,4CH
0011 CD 21                        INT     21H            ;Exit to DOS
0013                      BEGIN   ENDP
                                  END     BEGIN
```

Figure 20-5   Use of Library INCLUDE

CONCATENATION

The ampersand (&) character tells the assembler to join (concatenate) text or symbols. The following MOVE macro provides for MOVSB, MOVSW, or MOVSD:

```
MOVE    MACRO   TAG
        REP MOVS&TAG
        ENDM
```

A user could code the macro instruction as MOVE B, MOVE W, or MOVE D. The assembler concatenates the parameter with the MOVS instruction, as REP MOVSB, REP MOVSW, or REP MOVSD. This example is somewhat trivial and is for illustrative purposes.

REPETITION DIRECTIVES

The repetition directives REPT, IRP, and IRPC cause the assembler to repeat a block of statements, terminated by ENDM. These directives do not have to be contained in a MACRO definition, but if they are, one ENDM is required to terminate the repetition and a second ENDM to terminate the MACRO definition.

REPT: Repeat

The REPT operation causes repetition of a block of statements up to ENDM according to the number of times in the expression entry:

```
REPT expression
```

The following initializes the value N to 0, and then repeats generation of DB N five times:

```
N =         0
REPT 5
N =         N + 1
DB          N
ENDM
```

The result is five generated DB statements, DB 1 through DB 5. A use for REPT could be to define a table or part of a table. The next example generates five MOVSB instructions and is equivalent to REP MOVSB where the CX contains 05:

```
REPT    5
MOVSB
ENDM
```

IRP: Indefinite Repeat

The IRP operation causes a repeat of a block of instructions up to the ENDM. Here is the general format:

```
IRP  dummy,⟨arguments⟩
```

The arguments, contained in angle brackets, are any number of legal symbols, string, numeric, or arithmetic constants. The assembler generates a block of code for each argument. In the following example, the assembler generates DB 3, DB 9, DB 17, DB 25, and DB 28:

```
IRP  N,⟨3,9,17,25,28⟩
DB   N
```

IRPC: Indefinite Repeat Character

The IRPC operation causes a repeat of the block of statements up to the ENDM. Here is the general format:

```
IRPC  dummy,string
```

The assembler generates a block of code for each character in the "string." In the following example, the assembler generates DW 3 through DW 8:

```
IRPC  N,345678
DW    N
ENDM
```

CONDITIONAL DIRECTIVES

Assembly language supports a number of conditional directives. We used IF1 earlier to include a library entry only during pass 1 of an assembly. Conditional directives are most useful within a macro definition but are not limited to that purpose. Every IF directive must have a matching ENDIF to terminate a tested condition. One optional ELSE may provide an alternative action:

```
IFxx    (condition) ⎫
...                 ⎪
ELSE    (optional)  ⎬ conditional
...                 ⎪ block
ENDIF   (end of IF) ⎭
```

Omission of ENDIF causes an error message: "Undeterminated conditional." If a condition being examined is true, the assembler executes the conditional block up to the ELSE, or if no ELSE up to the ENDIF. If the condition is false, the assembler executes the conditional block following the ELSE, or if no ELSE it does not generate any of the conditional block.

The following explains the various conditional directives:

IF expression	If the assembler evaluates the expression to nonzero, it assembles the statements within the conditional block.
IFE expression	If the assembler evaluates the expression to zero, it assembles the statements within the conditional block.
IF1 (no expression)	If the assembler is processing pass 1, it acts on the statements in the conditional block.
IF2 (no expression)	If the assembler is processing pass 2, it acts on the statements in the conditional block.
IFDEF symbol	If the symbol is defined in the program or is declared as EXTRN, the assembler processes the statements in the conditional block.
IFNDEF symbol	If the symbol is not defined or is not declared as EXTRN, the assembler processes the statements in the conditional block.
IFB ⟨argument⟩	If the argument is blank, the assembler processes the statements in the conditional block. The argument requires angle brackets.
IFNB ⟨argument⟩	If the argument is not blank, the assembler processes the statements in the conditional block. The argument requires angle brackets.
IFIDN ⟨arg-1⟩,⟨arg-2⟩	If the argument-1 string is identical to the argument-2 string, the assembler processes the statements in the conditional block. The arguments require angle brackets.
IFDIF ⟨arg-1⟩,⟨arg-2⟩	If the argument-1 string is different from the argument-2 string, the assembler processes the statements in the conditional block. The arguments require angle brackets.

IF and IFE can use the relational operators EQ, NE, LT, LE, GT, and GE, for example as

```
IF expression1 EQ expression2
```

Here's a simple example of IFNB (if not blank). All INT 21H requests require a service in the AH register, whereas some requests also require a value in the DX. The following macro, DOS21, uses IFNB to test for a nonblank argument for the DX:

```
DOS21  MACRO    DOSFUNC,DXADDRES
       MOV      AH,DOSFUNC
       IFNB     ⟨DXADDRES⟩
       MOV      DX,OFFSET DXADDRES
       ENDIF
       INT      21H
       ENDM
```

Using DOS21 for simple keyboard input requires service 01 in the AH:

```
DOS21    01
```

The assembler generates MOV AH,01 and INT 21H. Input of a character string requires service 0AH in the AH and the input address in the DX:

```
DOS21    0AH,IPFIELD
```

The assembler generates both MOV instructions and INT 21H.

The EXITM Directive

A macro definition may contain a conditional directive that tests for a serious condition. If the condition is true, the assembler is to exit from any further macro expansion. The EXITM directive serves this purpose:

```
IFxx [condition]
...  (invalid condition)
EXITM
...
ENDIF
```

If the assembler encounters EXITM in its expansion, it discontinues the macro expansion and resumes processing after the ENDM. You can also use EXITM to terminate REPT, IRP, and IRPC even if they are contained within a macro definition.

Macro Using IF and IFNDEF Conditions

The skeleton program in Figure 20-6 contains a macro definition named DIVIDE that generates a routine to perform division by successive subtraction. A user has to

```
                   TITLE    MACRO6 (EXE)  Test of IF and IFNDEF
                   ; -------------------------------------------------
                   INITZ    MACRO                       ;Define a macro
                            MOV      AX,@data
                            MOV      DS,AX
                            MOV      ES,AX
                            ENDM                        ;End of macro
                   DIVIDE   MACRO    DIVIDEND,DIVISOR,QUOTIENT
                            LOCAL    COMP
                            LOCAL    OUT
                            CNTR     = 0
                   ;        AX = div'nd, BX = div'r, CX = quot't
                            IFNDEF DIVIDEND
                   ;                 Dividend not defined
                            CNTR     = CNTR +1
                            ENDIF
                            IFNDEF DIVISOR
                   ;                 Divisor not defined
                            CNTR     = CNTR +1
                            ENDIF
                            IFNDEF QUOTIENT
                   ;                 Quotient not defined
                            CNTR     = CNTR + 1
                            ENDIF
                            IF       CNTR
                   ;                 Macro expansion terminated
                            EXITM
                            ENDIF
                            MOV      AX,DIVIDEND         ;Set dividend
                            MOV      BX,DIVISOR          ;Set divisor
                            SUB      CX,CX              ;Clear quotient
                   COMP:
                            CMP      AX,BX              ;Div'd < div'r?
                            JB       OUT                ;  yes - exit
                            SUB      AX,BX              ;Div'd - div'r
                            INC      CX                 ;Add to quotient
                            JMP      COMP
                   OUT:
                            MOV      QUOTIENT,CX        ;Store quotient
                            ENDM
                   ; -------------------------------------------------
                            .MODEL   SMALL
                            .STACK   64
                            .DATA
0000 0096          DIVDND   DW       150                ;Dividend
0002 001B          DIVSOR   DW       27                 ;Divisor
0004 0000          QUOTNT   DW       ?                  ;Quotient
                   ; -------------------------------------------------
                            .CODE
0000               BEGIN    PROC     FAR
                            .LALL
                            INITZ
0000 B8 ---- R    1         MOV      AX,@data
0003 8E D8        1         MOV      DS,AX
0005 8E C0        1         MOV      ES,AX
                            DIVIDE DIVDND,DIVSOR,QUOTNT
= 0000            1         CNTR     = 0
                  1 ;       AX = div'nd, BX = div'r, CX = quot't
0007 A1 0000 R    1         MOV      AX,DIVDND          ;Set dividend
000A 8B 1E 0002 R 1         MOV      BX,DIVSOR          ;Set divisor
000E 2B C9        1         SUB      CX,CX              ;Clear quotient
0010              1 ??0000:
0010 3B C3        1         CMP      AX,BX              ;Div'd < div'r?
0012 72 05        1         JB       ??0001             ;  yes - exit
0014 2B C3        1         SUB      AX,BX              ;Div'd - div'r
0016 41           1         INC      CX                 ;Add to quotient
0017 EB F7        1         JMP      ??0000
0019              1 ??0001:
```

Figure 20-6 Use of IF and IFNDEF

```
0019 89 0E 0004 R 1              MOV    QUOTNT,CX          ;Store quotient
                                 DIVIDE DIDND,DIVSOR,QUOT
  = 0000             1           CNTR   = 0
                     1 ;         AX = div'nd, BX = div'r, CX = quot't
                     1           IFNDEF DIDND
                     1 ;                Dividend not defined
  = 0001             1           CNTR   = CNTR +1
                     1           ENDIF
                     1           IFNDEF QUOT
                     1 ;                Quotient not defined
  = 0002             1           CNTR   = CNTR + 1
                     1           ENDIF
                     1           IF     CNTR
                     1 ;                Macro expansion terminated
                     1           EXITM
001D  B4 4C                      MOV    AH,4CH
001F  CD 21                      INT    21H                ;Exit to DOS
0021               BEGIN         ENDP
                                 END    BEGIN
```

Figure 20-6   Cont.

code the macro instruction with parameters for dividend, divisor, and quotient, in that order. The macro uses IFNDEF to check whether the program actually contains their definitions. For any entry not defined, the macro increments a field named CNTR. Technically, CNTR could have any legal name and is for temporary use in a macro definition. After checking the three parameters, the macro checks CNTR for nonzero:

```
     IF   CNTR
;        Macro expansion terminated
     EXITM
     ENDIF
```

If CNTR has been set to a nonzero value, the assembler generates the comment and exits (EXITM) from any further macro expansion. Note that an initial instruction clears CNTR to 0, and also that the IFNDEF blocks need only to set CNTR to 1 rather than increment it.

    If the assembler passes all the tests safely, it generates the macro expansion. In the code segment, the second DIVIDE macro instruction contains an invalid dividend and quotient and generates only comments. One way to improve the macro would be to test whether the divisor is nonzero and whether the dividend and divisor have the same sign; for this purpose, use assembly language code rather than conditional directives.

Macro Using IFIDN Condition

The skeleton program in Figure 20-7 contains a macro definition named MOVIF that generates MOVSB or MOVSW depending on a supplied parameter. A user has to code the macro instruction with a parameter B (byte) or W (word) to indicate whether MOVS is to be MOVSB or MOVSW.

```
                       TITLE   MACRO7 (EXE)  Tests of IFIDN
                       ; --------------------------------------------
                       INITZ   MACRO                   ;Define a macro
                               MOV     AX,@data
                               MOV     DS,AX
                               MOV     ES,AX
                               ENDM                    ;End of macro
                       MOVIF   MACRO   TAG             ;Define a macro
                               IFIDN   <&TAG>,<B>
                               REP MOVSB
                               EXITM
                               ENDIF
                               IFIDN   <&TAG>,<W>
                               REP MOVSW
                               ELSE
                       ;       No B or W tag -- default to B
                               REP MOVSB
                               ENDIF
                               ENDM                    ;End of macro
                       ; --------------------------------------------
                               .MODEL SMALL
                               .STACK 64
                               .CODE
     0000              BEGIN   PROC    FAR
                               .LALL
                               INITZ
     0000 B8 ---- R    1       MOV     AX,@data
     0003 8E D8        1       MOV     DS,AX
     0005 8E C0        1       MOV     ES,AX
                               MOVIF   B
                       1       IFIDN   <B>,<B>
     0007 F3/ A4       1       REP MOVSB
                       1       EXITM
                               MOVIF   W
                       1       IFIDN   <W>,<W>
     0009 F3/ A5       1       REP MOVSW
                       1       ENDIF
                               MOVIF
                       1       ELSE
                       1 ;     No B or W tag -- default to B
     000B F3/ A4       1       REP MOVSB
                       1       ENDIF
     000D B4 4C                MOV     AH,4CH
     000F CD 21                INT     21H             ;Exit to DOS
     0011              BEGIN   ENDP
                               END     BEGIN
```

Figure 20-7   Use of IFIDN

The first two statements of the macro definition are

```
     MOVIF  MACRO  TAG
            IFIDN  <&TAG>,<B>
```

The IFIDN conditional directive compares the supplied parameter (supposedly B or W) to the string B. If the two are identical, the assembler generates REP MOVSB. The normal use of the ampersand (&) operator is for concatenation. However, the operand ⟨TAG⟩ without an ampersand does not work.

If a user does not supply B or W, the assembler generates a comment and a default to MOVSB.

The examples in the code segment test MOVIF three times: for B, for W, and for invalid. Don't attempt to execute this program as it stands, since the CX and DX registers need to contain proper values. Admittedly, this macro is not very useful; its purpose is to illustrate the use of conditional directives in a simple manner. By this point, however, you should be able to code some large useful macros.

KEY POINTS

- The use of macros in assembly language can result in more readable and more productive code.
- A macro definition requires a MACRO directive, a block of one or more statements known as the body that the macro definition is to generate, and an ENDM directive to terminate the definition.
- A macro instruction is the use of the macro in a program. The code that a macro instruction generates is the macro expansion.
- The .SALL, .LALL, and .XALL directives control the listing of comments and the object code generated in a macro expansion.
- The LOCAL directive facilitates using names within a macro definition, and must appear immediately after the macro statement.
- The use of dummy arguments in a macro definition allows a user to code parameters for more flexibility.
- A macro library makes macros available to other programs.
- Conditional directives enable you to validate macro parameters.

QUESTIONS

20-1. Under what circumstances would the use of macros be recommended?

20-2. Code the first and last lines for a simple macro named SETUP.

20-3. Distinguish between the body of a macro definition and the macro expansion.

20-4. What is a dummy argument?

20-5. Code the required instructions:
   (a) Suppress all instructions that a macro generates.
   (b) List only instructions that generate object code.

20-6. Code two macro definitions that perform multiplication: (a) MULTBY is to generate code that multiplies byte times byte; (b) MULTWD is to generate code that multiplies word times word.
   Include the multiplicands and multipliers as dummy arguments in the macro definition. Test execution of the macros with a small program that also defines the required data fields.

20-7. Store the macros defined in Question 20-6 in a macro library. Revise the program to INCLUDE the library entries during pass 1 of the assembly.

20-8. Write a macro named BIPRINT that uses BIOS INT 17H to print. The macro should include a test for status and should provide for any defined print line with any length.

20-9. Revise the macro in Figure 20-6 to bypass the division if the divisor is zero.

21

LINKING TO SUBPROGRAMS

OBJECTIVE

To cover the programming techniques involved in linking and executing separately assembled programs.

INTRODUCTION

Up to this point, program examples have consisted of one assembled module. It is possible, however, to execute a program that consists of a main program and one or more separately assembled subprograms. The following are reasons for organizing a program into subprograms:

- It may be desirable to link between languages, for example to combine the computing power of a high-level language with the processing efficiency of assembler.
- A program written as one module could be too large for the assembler to process.
- Parts of a program may be written by different teams who assemble their modules separately.
- Because of the large size of an executable module, it may be necessary to overlay parts of it during execution.

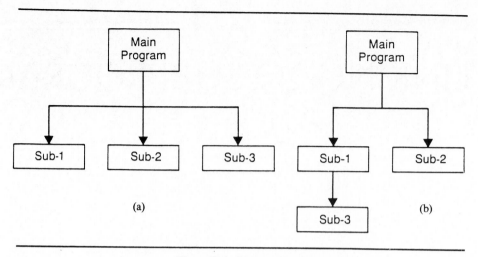

Figure 21-1   Program Hierarchy

Each program is assembled separately and generates its own unique object (OBJ) module. The linker then links the object modules into one combined executable (EXE) module. Typically, the main program is the one that begins execution, and it calls one or more subprograms. Subprograms in turn may call other subprograms.

Figure 21-1 shows two examples of a hierarchy of a main program and three subprograms. In Figure 21-1(a), the main program calls subprograms 1, 2, and 3. In Figure 21-1(b), the main program calls subprograms 1 and 2, and only subprogram 1 calls subprogram 3.

There are numerous variations of subprogram organization, but the organization has to make sense to the assembler, to the linker, and to execution. You also have to watch out for situations in which, for example, subprogram 1 calls subprogram 2, which calls subprogram 3, which in turn calls subprogram 1. This process, known as recursion, can be made to work, but if not handled carefully, can cause interesting execution bugs.

SEGMENTS

This section covers a number of the options used for segments. The general format for the full SEGMENT directive is

seg-name	SEGMENT	[align][combine]['class']

Align Type

The align operator tells the assembler to align the named segment beginning on a particular storage boundary:

BYTE   Byte boundary, for a segment of a subprogram that is to be combined with that of another program

WORD   Even boundary, for a segment of a subprogram that is to be combined with that of another program

DWORD   Doubleword boundary, normally for the 80386/486

PARA   Paragraph boundary (divisible by hex 10), the default and most commonly used for both main and subprograms

PAGE   Page boundary (divisible by hex 100)

Combine Type

The combine operator tells the assembler and linker whether to combine segments or keep them separate. Combine types that are relevant to this chapter are NONE, PUBLIC, and COMMON.

NONE   The segment is to be logically separate from other segments, although they may end up to be physically adjacent. This type is the default for full segment directives.

PUBLIC   The linker is to combine into one segment those segments that are defined as PUBLIC and have the same segment name and class. This type is the default for simplified segment directives.

COMMON   If COMMON segments have the same name and class, the linker gives them the same base address. For execution, the second segment overlays the first one. The largest segment determines the length of the common area.

Class Option

You can assign the same class name to related segments so that the assembler and linker group them together. That is, they are to appear as segments one after the other, but not combined into one segment unless the PUBLIC combine option is also coded. The class entry may contain any legal name, contained in single quotes, although the name 'code' is recommended for the code segment.

The following two statements generate identical results, namely an independent code segment aligned on a paragraph boundary:

```
CODESEG   SEGMENT    PARA NONE 'Code'
CODESEG   SEGMENT    'Code'
```

Note: We explained full segment directives in Chapter 4, but have used the simplified segment directives in following chapters. Since full segment directives can provide tighter control over assembling and linking subprograms, most examples in this chapter use them.

INTRASEGMENT CALLS

CALL instructions used to this point have been intrasegment calls—that is, within the same code segment. An intrasegment CALL is near if the called procedure is defined as or defaults to NEAR. The CALL operation pushes the IP register onto the stack and replaces the IP with the offset of the destination address.

Consider an intrasegment CALL that consists of object code E8 2000, where E8 is the operation code and 2000 is the offset of the called procedure. The operation pushes the IP onto the stack and stores the 2000 as offset 0020 in the IP. The processor then combines the current address in the CS with the offset in the IP for the next instruction to execute. On exit from the called procedure, a RET instruction pops the stored IP off the stack into the IP and returns to the instruction following the CALL.

```
            CALL nearproc     ;Near call: push IP,
            . . .             ;  link to nearproc
nearproc    PROC NEAR
            . . .
            RET               ;Near return: pop IP, return
nearproc    ENDP
```

An intrasegment call may be near (as described) or far if the call is to a far procedure within the same segment.

INTERSEGMENT CALLS

A CALL is far if the called procedure is defined as FAR or EXTRN. The CALL operation first pushes the contents of the CS register onto the stack and inserts an intersegment address into the CS. It then pushes the IP onto the stack and inserts an offset address in the IP. In this way, both the address in the code segment and the offset are saved for the return from the called subprogram. A call to another segment is always an intersegment far call.

```
              CALL farproc    ;Far call: push CS,
              . . .           ;  IP, link to farproc
farproc    PROC FAR

              . . .
              RET             ;Far return: pop IP, CS
farproc    ENDP             ;  return
```

Consider an intersegment CALL that consists of object code 9A 0002 AF04. Hex 9A is the operation code for an intersegment CALL. The operation stores the 0002 as 0200 in the IP and stores the AF04 as 04AF in the CS. These combine to establish the address of the first instruction in the called subprogram to execute:

```
Code segment            04AF0
Offset in IP          +  0200
Effective address       04CF0
```

On exit from the called procedure, an intersegment (far) RET pops both the original IP and CS addresses back into their respective registers. The CS:IP pair now points to the address of the instruction following the original CALL, where execution resumes.

EXTRN AND PUBLIC ATTRIBUTES

Consider a main program (MAINPROG) that calls a subprogram (SUBPROG). An intersegment CALL is required as shown in Figure 21-2.

The CALL in MAINPROG has to know that SUBPROG exists outside this segment (or else the assembler generates an error message that SUBPROG is an undefined symbol). The directive EXTRN SUBPROG:FAR performs this function—it notifies the assembler that any reference to SUBPROG is to a FAR label that is defined externally, in another assembly. Because the assembler has no

```
              EXTRN      SUBPROG:FAR
MAINPROG:     . . .
                       CALL SUBPROG

              PUBLIC     SUBPROG
SUBPROG:      . . .
              . . .
              RET
```

Figure 21-2 Intersegment CALL

way of knowing whether this is true, it generates "empty" object code operands in the CALL, which the linker is to fill:

```
9A 0000 ---- E   CALL subprogram
```

SUBPROG contains a PUBLIC directive that tells the assembler and linker that another module has to know the address of SUBPROG. In a later step, when both MAINPROG and SUBPROG are successfully assembled into object modules, they may be linked as follows:

LINK Prompt	*Reply*
`Object Modules[.OBJ]:`	`B:MAINPROG+B:SUBPROG`
`Run File[filespec.EXE]:`	`B:COMBPROG` (or any legal name)
`List File[NUL.MAP]:`	`CON`
`Libraries[.LIB]:`	`[Enter]`

The linker matches EXTRNs in one object module with PUBLICs in the other and inserts any required offset addresses. It then combines the two object modules into one executable module. If unable to match references, the linker supplies error messages—watch for these before attempting execution.

The EXTRN Directive

The EXTRN directive tells the assembler that the named item—a data item, procedure, or label—is defined in another assembly. It has the following format:

```
EXTRN name:type [, ... ]
```

You can define more than one name up to the end of a line or code additional EXTRN statements. The other assembly module must define the name and identify it as PUBLIC. The type entry may be ABS (a constant), BYTE, DWORD, FAR, NEAR, WORD, or a name defined by an EQU, and must be valid in terms of the actual definition of name.

- BYTE, WORD, and DWORD identify data items that this module references but another module defines.
- NEAR and FAR identify a procedure or instruction label that this module references but another module defines.

THE PUBLIC Directive

The PUBLIC directive tells the assembler and linker that the address of a specified symbol defined in the current assembly is to be available to other modules. The general format is

```
PUBLIC symbol [, ... ]
```

You can define more than one symbol up to the end of a line or code additional PUBLIC statements. The symbol entry can be a label (including PROC labels), a variable, or a number. Invalid entries include register names and EQU symbols that define values greater than two bytes.

Let's now examine different ways of making data known between programs: using EXTRN and PUBLIC, defining common data in subprograms, and passing parameters.

USE OF EXTRN AND PUBLIC FOR A LABEL

The program in Figure 21-3 consists of a main program, CALLMUL1, and a subprogram, SUBMUL1, both using full segment directives. The main program defines segments for the stack, data, and code. The data segment defines QTY and PRICE. The code segment loads the AX with PRICE and the BX with QTY and then calls the subprogram. An EXTRN in the main program defines the entry point to the subprogram as SUBMUL1.

The subprogram contains a PUBLIC statement (after the ASSUME) that makes SUBMUL1 known to the linker as the entry point for execution. This subprogram simply multiplies the contents of the AX (price) by the BX (quantity) and develops the product in the DX:AX pair as hex 002E 4000.

Since the subprogram does not define any data, it does not need a data segment; it could, but only this subprogram would recognize such data.

As well, the subprogram does not define a stack segment because it references the same stack addresses as the main program. Consequently, the stack defined in the main program is available to the subprogram. The linker requires definition of at least one stack for an EXE program, and the definition in the main program serves this purpose.

Now let's examine the symbol tables following each assembly. Note that the symbol table for the main program shows SUBMUL1 as Far and External. The symbol table for the subprogram shows SUBMUL1 as F (for Far) and Global. The term global implies that the name is known "globally" outside this subprogram.

The link map at the end of the listing shows the organization of the program in memory. Note that there are two code segments, one for each assembly, but at different starting addresses, since their combine types are NONE. These appear in the sequence that you enter when linking, with the main program normally first. In this case, the code segment for the main program starts at offset hex 00090, and the code segment for the subprogram at hex 000B0.

A trace of program execution disclosed that the CS register contained 141E[0] and CALL SUBMUL1 generated

```
9A 000 2014 (your segment value may differ)
```

```
                     TITLE    CALLMUL1 (EXE)  Call subprogram
                             EXTRN   SUBMUL1:FAR
                   ; ----------------------------------------------
0000                         STACKSG SEGMENT PARA STACK 'Stack'
0000  0040[????]             DW      64 DUP(?)
0080                         STACKSG ENDS
                   ; ----------------------------------------------
0000                         DATASG  SEGMENT PARA 'Data'
0000  0140                   QTY     DW      0140H
0002  2500                   PRICE   DW      2500H
0004                         DATASG  ENDS
                   ; ----------------------------------------------
0000                         CODESG  SEGMENT PARA 'Code'
0000                         BEGIN   PROC    FAR
                                     ASSUME CS:CODESG,DS:DATASG,SS:STACKSG
0000  B8 ---- R                      MOV     AX,DATASG
0003  8E D8                          MOV     DS,AX
0005  A1 0002 R                      MOV     AX,PRICE       ;Set up price
0008  8B 1E 0000 R                   MOV     BX,QTY         ;  and quantity
000C  9A 0000 ---- E                 CALL    SUBMUL1        ;Call subprogram
0011  B4 4C                          MOV     AH,4CH         ;Return
0013  CD 21                          INT     21H
0015                         BEGIN   ENDP
0015                         CODESG  ENDS
                                     END     BEGIN

Segments and Groups:
          N a m e        Length  Align   Combine Class
CODESG . . . . . . . . . 0015    PARA    NONE    'CODE'
DATASG . . . . . . . . . 0004    PARA    NONE    'DATA'
STACKSG  . . . . . . . . 0080    PARA    STACK   'STACK'
Symbols:
          N a m e        Type    Value   Attr
BEGIN  . . . . . . . . . F PROC  0000    CODESG  Length = 0015
PRICE  . . . . . . . . . L WORD  0002    DATASG
QTY  . . . . . . . . . . L WORD  0000    DATASG
SUBMUL1  . . . . . . . . L FAR   0000            External
```

```
                     TITLE    SUBMUL1 Called subprogram
                   ; --------------------------------
0000                         CODESG  SEGMENT PARA 'Code'
0000                         SUBMUL1 PROC    FAR
                                     ASSUME CS:CODESG
                                     PUBLIC SUBMUL1
0000  F7 E3                          MUL     BX             ;AX = price, BX = qty
0002  CB                             RET                    ;DX:AX = product
0003                         SUBMUL1 ENDP
0003                         CODESG  ENDS
                                     END     SUBMUL1

Segments and Groups:
       ·  N a m e        Length  Align   Combine Class
CODESG . . . . . . . . . 0003    PARA    NONE    'CODE'
Symbols:
          N a m e        Type    Value   Attr
SUBMUL1  . . . . . . . . F PROC  0000    CODESG  Global  Length=0003
```

```
     Link Map
     Object Modules: CALLMUL1+SUBMUL1

     Start  Stop   Length Name           Class
     00000H 0007FH 00080H STACKSG        STACK
     00080H 00083H 00004H DATASG         DATA
     00090H 000A4H 00015H CODESG         CODE    <-- Note: 2 code
     000B0H 000B2H 00003H CODESG         CODE    <--   segments

     Program entry point at 0009:0000
```

Figure 21-3   Use of EXTRN and PUBLIC

The machine code for an intersegment CALL is hex 9A. The operation pushes the IP register onto the stack and loads 0000 in the IP. It then pushes the CS containing 141E[0] onto the stack and loads 1420[0] in the CS. (We'll show the register contents in normal, not reversed, byte order.) The next instruction to execute is CS:IP, or 1420[0] plus 0020. What is at 14200? Well, the main program began with the CS register containing 141E[0]. According to the map, the main code segment offset begins at offset 00090 and the subprogram offset begins at offset 000B0, 20H bytes apart. Adding the main program's CS value plus 20H supplies the effective address of the subprogram's code segment:

```
CS address              141E0
IP offset              +00020
Effective address       14200
```

The linker determines this address just as we have and substitutes it in the CALL operand. SUBMUL1 multiplies the two values, with the product in the DX:AX, and makes a far return to CALLMUL1.

USE OF PUBLIC IN THE CODE SEGMENT

Our next example in Figure 21-4 provides a variation on Figure 21-3. There is one change in the main program, CALLMUL2, and one change in the subprogram, SUBPROG2, both involving the use of PUBLIC in the SEGMENT directive for both code segments:

```
CODESG  SEGMENT  PARA PUBLIC 'Code'
```

There are interesting results in the link map and the CALL object code. In the symbol table following each assembly, the combine-type for CODESG is PUBLIC, whereas in Figure 21-3 it is NONE. More interesting is the link map at the end that now shows only one code segment. The fact that both segments have the same name (DATASG), class ('Code'), and PUBLIC attribute caused the linker to combine the two logical code segments into one physical code segment. Further, a trace of machine execution showed that the CALL instruction in the program is a far call, even though the call is in the same segment:

```
9A 2000 1E14 (your segment value may differ)
```

This instruction stores hex 2000 in the IP as 0020 and hex 1E14 in the CS register as 141E[0]. Because the subprogram shares a common code segment with the main program, the CS register is set to the same starting address, 141E. But the CS:IP now provide:

```
                          TITLE    CALLMUL2 (EXE)  Call subprogram
                                   EXTRN    SUBMUL2:FAR
                          ; ------------------------------------------
0000                      STACKSG  SEGMENT PARA STACK 'Stack'
0000 0040[????]                    DW      64 DUP(?)
0080                      STACKSG  ENDS
                          ; ------------------------------------------
0000                      DATASG   SEGMENT PARA 'Data'
0000 0140                 QTY      DW      0140H
0002 2500                 PRICE    DW      2500H
0004                      DATASG   ENDS
                          ; ------------------------------------------
0000                      CODESG   SEGMENT PARA PUBLIC 'Code'
0000                      BEGIN    PROC    FAR
                                   ASSUME  CS:CODESG,DS:DATASG,SS:STACKSG
0000 B8 ---- R                     MOV     AX,DATASG
0003 8E D8                         MOV     DS,AX
0005 A1 0002 R                     MOV     AX,PRICE      ;Set up price
0008 8B 1E 0000 R                  MOV     BX,QTY        ; & quantity
000C 9A 0000 ---- E                CALL    SUBMUL2       ;Call subprogram
0011 B4 4C                         MOV     AH,4CH        ;Return
0013 CD 21                         INT     21H
0015                      BEGIN    ENDP
0015                      CODESG   ENDS
                                   END     BEGIN

Segments and Groups:
          N a m e              Length Align   Combine Class
CODESG . . . . . . . . . . . . 0015   PARA    PUBLIC  'CODE'
DATASG . . . . . . . . . . . . 0004   PARA    NONE    'DATA'
STACKSG  . . . . . . . . . . . 0080   PARA    STACK   'STACK'
Symbols:
          N a m e              Type   Value   Attr
BEGIN  . . . . . . . . . . . . F PROC 0000    CODESG  Length = 0015
PRICE  . . . . . . . . . . . . L WORD 0002    DATASG
QTY  . . . . . . . . . . . . . L WORD 0000    DATASG
SUBMUL2  . . . . . . . . . . . L FAR          0000    External
```

```
                          TITLE    SUBMUL2 Called subprogram
                          ; --------------------------------
0000                      CODESG   SEGMENT PARA PUBLIC 'Code'
0000                      SUBMUL2  PROC    FAR
                                   ASSUME  CS:CODESG
                                   PUBLIC  SUBMUL2
0000 F7 E3                         MUL     BX         ;AX = price, BX = qty
0002 CB                            RET                ;DX:AX = product
0003                      SUBMUL2  ENDP
0003                      CODESG   ENDS
                                   END     SUBMUL2

Segments and Groups:
          N a m e              Length Align   Combine Class
CODESG . . . . . . . . . . . . 0003   PARA    PUBLIC  'CODE'
Symbols:
          N a m e              Type   Value   Attr
SUBMUL2  . . . . . . . . . . . F PROC 0000    CODESG  Global Length=0003
```

```
    Link Map
    Object Modules: CALLMUL2+SUBMUL2

    Start   Stop    Length  Name          Class
    00000H  0007FH  00080H  STACKSG       STACK
    00080H  00083H  00004H  DATASG        DATA
    00090H  000B2H  00023H  CODESG        CODE  <-- 1 code segment

    Program entry point at 0009:0000
```

Figure 21-4   Code Segment Defined as PUBLIC

```
CS address              141E0
IP offset             + 0020
Effective address       14200
```

The code segment of the subprogram therefore presumably begins at hex 14200. Is this correct? The link map doesn't make this point clear, but you can infer the address from the listing of the main program, which ends at offset 0015. Since the code segment for the subprogram is defined as PARA, it begins on a paragraph boundary (evenly divisible by hex 10, so that the rightmost digit is 0):

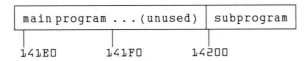

The linker sets the subprogram at the first paragraph boundary immediately following the main program, at offset 00020. Therefore, the code segment of the subprogram begins at 141E0 plus 0020, or 14200.

Since the PUBLIC type combines segments into one segment, you could also use it for a COM program. Now let's see how the linker handles data defined in a main program and referenced in a subprogram.

SIMPLIFIED SEGMENT DIRECTIVES

Figure 21-5 shows the previous program example defined with simplified segment directives. Figure 21-4 defines the code segments as PUBLIC and Figure 21-5 defaults to PUBLIC, so that both examples generate one code segment. However, the use of simplified segment directives causes some significant differences. First, the segments in the link map are in the sequence code, data, and stack (although this has no effect on program execution). Second, the subprogram's code segment (_TEXT) aligns on a word boundary. A trace of machine execution showed the following object code for the CALL:

```
9A 1600 1514 (your segment value may differ)
```

Because the subprogram shares a common code segment with the main program, the CS register is set to the same starting address, 1415.

```
CS address              14150
IP offset             + 0016
Effective address       14166
```

The code segment of the subprogram begins at hex 14166. You can infer the address from the listing of the main program, which ends at offset 0015. Since the map

```
                            TITLE     CALLML2A (EXE)  Call subprogram
                            .MODEL    SMALL
                            .STACK    64
                            EXTRN     SUBML2A:FAR
                   ; --------------------------------------------
                            .DATA
0000 0140          QTY      DW        0140H
0002 2500          PRICE    DW        2500H
                   ; --------------------------------------------
                            .CODE
0000               BEGIN    PROC      FAR
0000 B8 ---- R              MOV       AX,@data
0003 8E D8                  MOV       DS,AX
0005 A1 0002 R              MOV       AX,PRICE      ;Set up price
0008 8B 1E 0000 R           MOV       BX,QTY        ;  and quantity
000C 9A 0000 ---- E         CALL      SUBML2A       ;Call subprogram
0011 B4 4C                  MOV       AH,4CH        ;Return
0013 CD 21                  INT       21H
0015               BEGIN    ENDP
                            END       BEGIN
```

```
Segments and Groups:
            N a m e                Length Align  Combine Class
DGROUP . . . . . . . . . . . . GROUP
  _DATA  . . . . . . . . . . 0004   WORD   PUBLIC  'DATA'
  STACK  . . . . . . . . . . 0040   PARA   STACK   'STACK'
_TEXT  . . . . . . . . . . . 0015   WORD   PUBLIC  'CODE'
Symbols:
            N a m e            Type    Value   Attr
BEGIN . . . . . . . . . .F PROC 0000   _TEXT   Length = 0015
PRICE . . . . . . . . . .L WORD 0002   _DATA
QTY . . . . . . . . . . .L WORD 0000   _DATA
SUBML2A . . . . . . . . .L FAR  0000           External
```

```
                            TITLE     SUBML2A Called subprogram
                            .MODEL SMALL
                            .CODE
0000               SUBML2A  PROC      FAR
                            PUBLIC SUBML2A
0000 F7 E3                  MUL       BX            ;AX = price, BX = qty
0002 CB                     RET                     ;DX:AX = product
0003               SUBML2A  ENDP
                            END       SUBML2A
```

```
Segments and Groups:
            N a m e                Length Align  Combine Class
DGROUP . . . . . . . . . . . . GROUP
  _DATA  . . . . . . . . . . 0000   WORD   PUBLIC  'DATA'
_TEXT  . . . . . . . . . . . 0003   WORD   PUBLIC  'CODE'
Symbols:
            N a m e            Type    Value   Attr
SUBML2A . . . . . . . . .F PROC 0000   _TEXT Global Length=0003
```

```
    Link Map
    Object Modules: CALLML2A+SUBML2A

    Start  Stop   Length Name          Class
    00000H 00018H 00019H _TEXT         CODE
    0001AH 0001DH 00004H _DATA         DATA
    00020H 0005FH 00040H STACK         STACK

    Program entry point at 0000:0000
```

Figure 21-5 Use of Simplified Segment Directives

shows the main code segment beginning at 00000H, the next word boundary is at 00016H. Thus the code segment for this program is 19H bytes long, whereas for the previous program it is 23H bytes long (because its subprogram aligned on a paragraph boundary).

COMMON DATA IN SUBPROGRAMS

A common requirement is to process data in one assembly module that is defined in another assembly module. Let's modify the preceding examples so that although the main program still defines QTY and PRICE, the subprogram now inserts their values into the BX and AX. Figure 21-6 gives the revised coding. The new changes are the following:

- The main program CALLMUL3 defines QTY and PRICE as PUBLIC. The data segment is also defined with the PUBLIC attribute. Note in the symbol table the Global attribute for QTY and PRICE.
- The subprogram SUBMUL3 defines QTY and PRICE as EXTRN, and both as WORD. This definition informs the assembler as to the length of the two fields. The assembler can generate the correct operation code for the MOV instructions, but the linker will have to complete the operands. (Note in the symbol table that PRICE and QTY are External.)

The assembler lists the MOV instructions in the subprogram as

```
A1  0000 E      MOV  AX,PRICE
8B  1E 0000 E   MOV  BX,QTY
```

Object code A1 means move a word from memory to the AX, whereas 8B means move a word from memory to the BX. (AX operations often require fewer bytes.) Tracing execution reveals that the linker has completed the object code operands as follows:

```
A1  0200
8B  1E 0000
```

The object code is now identical to that generated for the previous examples where the MOV instructions are in the calling program. This is a logical result because the operands in all three programs reference the same DS register and the same offset addresses.

The main program and the subprogram may define any other data items, but only those defined as PUBLIC and EXTRN are known in common.

```
                    TITLE   CALLMUL3 (EXE)  Call subprogram
                    EXTRN   SUBMUL3:FAR
                    PUBLIC  QTY,PRICE
                  ; --------------------------------------------
0000                STACKSG SEGMENT PARA STACK 'Stack'
0000 0040[????]             DW      64 DUP(?)
0080                STACKSG ENDS
                  ; --------------------------------------------
0000                DATASG  SEGMENT PARA PUBLIC 'Data'
0000 0140           QTY     DW      0140H
0002 2500           PRICE   DW      2500H
0004                DATASG  ENDS
                  ; --------------------------------------------
0000                CODESG  SEGMENT PARA PUBLIC 'Code'
0000                BEGIN   PROC    FAR
                            ASSUME  CS:CODESG,DS:DATASG,SS:STACKSG
0000 B8 ---- R              MOV     AX,DATASG
0003 8E D8                  MOV     DS,AX
0005 9A 0000 ---- E         CALL    SUBMUL3        ;Call subprogram
000A B4 4C                  MOV     AH,4CH         ;Return
000C CD 21                  INT     21H
000E                BEGIN   ENDP
000E                CODESG  ENDS
                            END     BEGIN

Segments and Groups:
          N a m e             Length Align  Combine Class
CODESG . . . . . . . . . . .  000E   PARA   PUBLIC  'CODE'
DATASG . . . . . . . . .      0004   PARA   PUBLIC  'DATA'
STACKSG  . . . . . . . .      0080   PARA   STACK   'STACK'
Symbols:
          N a m e             Type   Value  Attr
BEGIN . . . . . . . . . .     .F PROC 0000   CODESG  Length = 000E
PRICE . . . . . . . . .       .L WORD 0002   DATASG  Global
QTY . . . . . . . . . .       .L WORD 0000   DATASG  Global
SUBMUL3 . . . . . . . . .     .L FAR  0000           External
```

```
                    TITLE   SUBMUL3 Called subprogram
                    EXTRN   QTY:WORD,PRICE:WORD
                  ; ----------------------------------
0000                CODESG  SEGMENT PARA PUBLIC 'CODE'
0000                SUBMUL3 PROC    FAR
                            ASSUME  CS:CODESG
                            PUBLIC  SUBMUL3
0000 A1 0000 E              MOV     AX,PRICE
0003 8B 1E 0000 E           MOV     BX,QTY
0007 F7 E3                  MUL     BX             ;DX:AX = product
0009 CB                     RET
000A                SUBMUL3 ENDP
000A                CODESG  ENDS
                            END     SUBMUL3

Segments and Groups:
          N a m e             Length Align  Combine Class
CODESG . . . . . . . . . .    000A   PARA   PUBLIC  'CODE'
Symbols:
          N a m e             Type   Value  Attr
PRICE . . . . . . . . .       .V WORD 0000   External
QTY . . . . . . . . . .       .V WORD 0000   External
SUBMUL3 . . . . . . . .       .F PROC 0000   CODESG Global Length=000A
```

```
    Link Map
    Object Modules: CALLMUL3+SUBMUL3

    Start  Stop   Length Name           Class
    00000H 0007FH 00080H STACKSG        STACK
    00080H 00083H 00004H DATASG         DATA
    00090H 000A9H 0001AH CODESG         CODE

    Program entry point at 0009:0000
```

Figure 21-6 Common Data in Subprograms

DEFINING DATA IN BOTH PROGRAMS

In the preceding example, CALLMUL3 defined QTY and PRICE, whereas SUBMUL3 did not define any data. The reason SUBMUL3 can reference CALLMUL3's data is because it does not change the address in the DS register, which still points to CALLMUL3's data segment. But programs are not always so simple, and subprograms often have to define their own data as well as reference data in the calling program.

Let's perform a variation on the previous program. The next example in Figure 21-7 defines QTY in CALLMUL4 but defines PRICE in SUBMUL4. From CALLMUL4's point of view, PRICE does not exist, although SUBMUL4 has to know the location of both items. SUBMUL4's code segment has to get QTY first while the DS register still contains the address of CALLMUL4's data segment. SUBMUL4 then pushes the DS on the stack and loads the address of its own data segment. SUBMUL4 can now get PRICE and perform the multiplication.

Before returning to CALLMUL4, SUBMUL4 has to pop the DS off the stack so that CALLMUL4 can access its own data segment. (It's not technically necessary in this case because CALLMUL4 happens to return to DOS immediately, but we'll do it as a standard practice.)

As a final note, you could make both data segments PUBLIC, with the same name and class. In this case, the linker combines them and SUBMUL4 doesn't have to push and pop the DS because the programs use the same data segment and DS address. We'll leave this variation as an exercise for you to revise and trace under DEBUG. SUBMUL4's code segment could look like this:

```
EXTRN    QTY:WORD
ASSUME   CS:CODESG,DS:DATASG
PUBLIC   SUBMUL4
MOV      AX,PRICE    ;PRICE in own data segment
MOV      BX,QTY      ;QTY in CALLMUL4
MUL      BX
RET
```

PASSING PARAMETERS

Another way of making data know to a called subprogram is by passing parameters, in which a program passes data physically via the stack. In this case, ensure that each PUSH references a word (or doubleword on advance systems), in either memory or a register.

In Figure 21-8, the calling program CALLMUL5 pushes both PRICE and QTY prior to calling the subprogram SUBMUL5. Initially, the SP contained the size of the stack, 80H. Each word pushed onto the stack decrements the SP by 2.

```
                      TITLE     CALLMUL4 (EXE) Call subprogram
                      EXTRN     SUBMUL4:FAR
                      PUBLIC    QTY
                  ; -------------------------------------------
0000              STACKSG SEGMENT PARA STACK 'Stack'
0000  0040[????]          DW      64 DUP(?)
0080              STACKSG ENDS
                  ; -------------------------------------------
0000              DATASG  SEGMENT PARA 'Data'
0000 0140         QTY     DW      0140H
0002              DATASG  ENDS
                  ; -------------------------------------------
0000              CODESG  SEGMENT PARA 'Code'
0000              BEGIN   PROC    FAR
                          ASSUME  CS:CODESG,DS:DATASG,SS:STACKSG
0000 B8 ---- R            MOV     AX,DATASG
0003 8E D8                MOV     DS,AX
0005 9A 0000 ---- E       CALL    SUBMUL4          ;Call subprogram
000A B4 4C                MOV     AH,4CH           ;Exit
000C CD 21                INT     21H
000E              BEGIN   ENDP
000E              CODESG  ENDS
                          END     BEGIN

Segments and Groups:
        N a m e               Length Align  Combine Class
CODESG . . . . . . . . . . . 000E  PARA    NONE    'CODE'
DATASG . . . . . . . . . . . 0002  PARA    NONE    'DATA'
STACKSG . . . . . . . . . . 0080  PARA    STACK   'STACK'
Symbols:
        N a m e               Type   Value  Attr
BEGIN . . . . . . . . . .F PROC 0000   CODESG  Length = 000E
QTY . . . . . . . . . . .L WORD 0000   DATASG  Global
SUBMUL4 . . . . . . . . .L FAR  0000           External
```

```
                      TITLE     SUBMUL4 Called subprogram
                      EXTRN     QTY:WORD
                  ; -------------------------------------------
0000              DATASG  SEGMENT PARA 'Data'
0000 2500         PRICE   DW      2500H
0002              DATASG  ENDS
                  ; -------------------------------------------
0000              CODESG  SEGMENT PARA 'CODE'
0000              SUBMUL4 PROC    FAR
                          ASSUME  CS:CODESG
                          PUBLIC  SUBMUL4
0000 8B 1E 0000 E         MOV     BX,QTY          ;Get QTY from CALLMUL
0004 1E                   PUSH    DS              ;Save CALLMUL's DS
                          ASSUME  DS:DATASG
0005 B8 ---- R            MOV     AX,DATASG       ;Set up own DS
0008 8E D8                MOV     DS,AX
000A A1 0000 R            MOV     AX,PRICE        ;Price from own data segment
000D F7 E3                MUL     BX              ;DX:AX = product
000F 1F                   POP     DS              ;Restore CALLMUL's DS
0010 CB                   RET
0011              SUBMUL4 ENDP
0011              CODESG  ENDS
                          END     SUBMUL4

Segments and Groups:
        N a m e               Length Align  Combine Class
CODESG . . . . . . . . .     0011  PARA    NONE    'CODE'
DATASG . . . . . . . . .     0002  PARA    NONE    'DATA'
Symbols:
        N a m e               Type   Value  Attr
PRICE . . . . . . . . . . L WORD 0000   DATASG
QTY . . . . . . . . . . . V WORD 0000           External
SUBMUL4 . . . . . . . . . F PROC 0000   CODESG Global Length=0011
```

Figure 21-7   Defining Data in Both Programs

```
Link Map
Object Modules: CALLMUL3+SUBMUL3

Start  Stop   Length Name                Class
00000H 0007FH 00080H STACKSG             STACK
00080H 00081H 00002H DATASG              DATA
00090H 00091H 00002H DATASG              DATA
000A0H 000ADH 0000EH CODESG              CODE
000B0H 000C0H 00011H CODESG              CODE

Program entry point at 000A:0000
```

Figure 21-7 Cont.

After the CALL, the stack appears as follows:

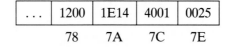

. . .	1200	1E14	4001	0025
	78	7A	7C	7E

1. A PUSH loaded PRICE (2500) onto the stack at 7E.
2. A PUSH loaded QTY (0140) onto the stack at 7C.
3. CALL pushed the contents of the CS (141E for this execution) onto the stack at 7A. Since the subprogram is PUBLIC, the linker combines the two code segments and the CS address is the same for both.
4. CALL also pushed the contents of the IP register, 0012, onto the stack at 78.

The called program requires use of the BP to access the parameters in the stack. Its first action is to save the contents of the BP for the calling program by pushing it onto the stack. In this case, the BP happens to contain zero, and PUSH stores it in the stack at offset 76:

0000	1200	1E14	4001	0025
76	78	7A	7C	7E

The program then inserts the contents of the SP (0076) into the BP because the BP (but not the SP) is usable as an index register. Since the BP now also contains 0076, price is in the stack at BP + 8 (offset 7E) and quantity is at BP + 6 (offset 7C). The routine transfers these values from the stack to the AX and BX, respectively, and performs the multiplication.

Before returning to the calling program, the routine pops the BP (returning the zero address to the BP), which increments the SP by 2, from 76 to 78.

The last instruction, RET, is a far return to the calling program that performs the following:

• Pops the word now at the top of the stack (1200) to the IP and increments the SP by 2, from 78 to 7A.

```
                              TITLE    CALLMUL5 (EXE)  Passing parameters
                              EXTRN    SUBMUL5:FAR
                         ; ------------------------------------------------
0000                     STACKSG SEGMENT PARA STACK 'Stack'
0000 0040[????]                  DW      64 DUP(?)
0080                     STACKSG ENDS
                         ; ------------------------------------------------
0000                     DATASG  SEGMENT PARA 'Data'
0000 0140                QTY     DW      0140H
0002 2500                PRICE   DW      2500H
0004                     DATASG  ENDS
                         ; ------------------------------------------------
0000                     CODESG  SEGMENT PARA PUBLIC 'Code'
0000                     BEGIN   PROC    FAR
                                 ASSUME  CS:CODESG,DS:DATASG,SS:STACKSG
0000 B8 ---- R                   MOV     AX,DATASG
0003 8E D8                       MOV     DS,AX
0005 FF 36 0002 R                PUSH    PRICE
0009 FF 36 0000 R                PUSH    QTY
000D 9A 0000 ---- E              CALL    SUBMUL5         ;Call subprogram
0012 B4 4C                       MOV     AH,4CH          ;Return
0014 CD 21                       INT     21H
0016                     BEGIN   ENDP
0016                     CODESG  ENDS
                                 END     BEGIN

Segments and Groups:
              N a m e              Length Align  Combine Class
CODESG . . . . . . . . . . . 0016   PARA   PUBLIC  'CODE'
DATASG . . . . . . . . . . . 0004   PARA   NONE    'DATA'
STACKSG . . . . . . . . . .  0080   PARA   STACK   'STACK'
Symbols:
              N a m e              Type  Value   Attr
BEGIN . . . . . . . . . .    F PROC 0000   CODESG  Length = 0016
PRICE . . . . . . . . . .    L WORD 0002   DATASG
QTY . . . . . . . . . . .    L WORD 0000   DATASG
SUBMUL5 . . . . . . . .      L FAR  0000           External
```

```
                              TITLE    SUBMUL5 Called subprogram
0000                     CODESG  SEGMENT PARA PUBLIC 'Code'
0000                     SUBMUL5 PROC    FAR
                                 ASSUME  CS:CODESG
                                 PUBLIC  SUBMUL5
0000 55                          PUSH    BP
0001 8B EC                       MOV     BP,SP
0003 8B 46 08                    MOV     AX,[BP+8]       ;Get price
0006 8B 5E 06                    MOV     BX,[BP+6]       ;Get quantity
0009 F7 E3                       MUL     BX              ;DX:AX = product
000B 5D                          POP     BP
000C CA 0004                     RET     4
000F                     SUBMUL5 ENDP
000F                     CODESG  ENDS
                                 END

Segments and Groups:
              N a m e              Length Align  Combine Class
CODESG . . . . . . . . . . . 000F   PARA   PUBLIC  'CODE'
Symbols:
              N a m e              Type  Value   Attr
SUBMUL5 . . . . . . . .      F PROC 0000   CODESG  Global Length=000F
```

```
    Link Map
    Object Modules: CALLMUL5+SUBMUL5

    Start  Stop   Length Name            Class
    00000H 0007FH 00080H STACKSG         STACK
    00080H 00083H 00004H DATASG          DATA
    00090H 000BEH 0002FH CODESG          CODE

    Program entry point at 0009:0000
```

Figure 21-8 Passing Parameters

- Pops the word now at the top (141E) onto the CS and increments the SP by 2, from 7A to 7C.
- Because of the two passed parameters at 7C and 7E, the RET instruction is coded as

```
RET 4
```

The 4, known as a *pop value,* contains the number of bytes in the passed parameters (two one-word parameters in this case). The RET operation also adds the pop value to the SP, correcting it to 80. In effect, because the parameters in the stack are no longer required, the operation discards them and returns correctly to the calling program. Note that the POP and RET operations increment the SP but don't actually erase the contents of the stack.

If you follow the general rules discussed in this chapter, you should be able to link a program consisting of more than two assembly modules and to make data known in all the modules. But watch out for the size of the stack—for large programs, defining 64 words could be a wise precaution.

In Chapter 22 we cover some important concepts on memory management and executing overlay programs. In Chapter 24 we provide additional features of segments, including defining more than one code or data segment in the same assembly module and the use of GROUP to combine these into a common segment.

LINKING PASCAL AND ASSEMBLY LANGUAGE PROGRAMS

In this section we explain how to link IBM and MicroSoft Pascal to assembly language programs. The simple Pascal program in Figure 21-9 links to an assembly subprogram. The Pascal program is compiled to produce an OBJ module and the assembly program is assembled to produce an OBJ module. The linker then combines these two OBJ modules into one EXE executable module.

The Pascal program defines two items named temp_row and temp_col and accepts entries for row and column from the keyboard into these variables. It then sends the addresses of temp_row and temp_col as parameters to the assembly subprogram to set the cursor to this location. The Pascal program defines the name of the assembly subprogram in a procedure as move_cursor and defines the two parameters as extern. The statement in the Pascal program that "calls" the name of the assembly subprogram and passes the parameters is

```
move_curs( temp_row, temp_col);
```

Values pushed onto the stack are the calling program's stack pointer, return segment pointer, return offset, and the addresses of the two passed parameters. The following shows the offsets for each entry in the stack:

```
program pascall ( input, output );

    procedure move_curs( const row: integer;
                         const col: integer ); extern;
    var
        temp_row:        integer;
        temp_col:        integer;


    begin
        write( 'Enter cursor row: ' );
        readln( temp_row );

        write( 'Enter cursor column: ' );
        readln( temp_col );

        move_curs( temp_row, temp_col );
        write( 'New cursor location' );
    end.
```

```
TITLE   MOVCUR  Assembler subprogram called by Pascal
        PUBLIC MOVE_CURS
;------------------------------------------------------------
;    MOVE_CURS: Set cursor on screen at passed location
;    Passed:    const row       Row and column where
;               const col       cursor is to be set
;    Returned:  nothing
;------------------------------------------------------------
CODESEG        SEGMENT PARA PUBLIC 'CODE'

MOVE_CURS    PROC FAR
             ASSUME CS:CODESEG
             PUSH    BP              ;Caller's BP register
             MOV     BP,SP           ;Point to parameters passed

             MOV     SI,[BP+8]       ;SI points to row
             MOV     DH,[SI]         ;Move row to DH

             MOV     SI,[BP+6]       ;SI points to column
             MOV     DL,[SI]         ;Move column to DL

             MOV     AH,02           ;Move cursor
             MOV     BH,0            ;Page #0
             INT     10H

             POP     BP              ;Return to caller
             RET     4
MOVE_CURS    ENDP
CODESEG ENDS
             END
```

Figure 21-9   Linking Pascal to Assembler

00	Caller's stack pointer
02	Caller's return segment pointer
04	Caller's return offset
06	Address of second parameter
08	Address of first parameter

The assembly subprogram is going to use the BP register. Consequently, you have to push it onto the stack to save its address for the return to the Pascal calling program. Note that the steps in the called subprogram are similar to the example in Figure 21-7.

The SP register normally addresses entries in the stack. But since you cannot use the SP to act as an index register, the step after pushing the BP is to move the address in the SP to the BP. This step enables you to use the BP as an index register to access entries in the stack.

The next step is to access the addresses of the two parameters in the stack. The first passed parameter, the row, is at offset 08 in the stack and can be accessed by BP + 08. The second passed parameter, the column, is at offset 06 and can be accessed by BP + 06.

The two addresses in the stack have to be transferred to one of the available index registers: BX, DI, or SI. This example uses [BP + 08] to move the address of the row to the SI and then uses [SI] to move the contents of the passed parameter to the DH register.

The column is transferred to the DL register in a similar way. Then the subprogram uses the row and column in the DX register to call BIOS to set the cursor. On exit, the subprogram pops the BP. The RET instruction requires an operand value that is two times the number of parameters—in this case, 2×2, or 4. Values are automatically popped off the stack and control transfers back to the calling program.

If you change a segment register, be sure to PUSH it on entry and POP it on exit. You can also use the stack to pass values from a subprogram to a calling program. Although this subprogram doesn't return values, Pascal would expect a subprogram to return a single word in the AX and a pair of words in the DX:AX.

Following the two programs is the map that the linker generated. The first entry is for the Pascal program named PASCALL; the second entry is for the assembly subprogram named CODESEG (the name of the code segment). A number of Pascal subroutines follow. This rather trivial program has resulted in hex 5720 bytes of memory—over 20K. A compiler language typically generates considerable overhead regardless of the size of the source program.

LINKING C AND ASSEMBLY LANGUAGE PROGRAMS

The problem with describing linkage of C to assembly language programs is that versions of C have different conventions, and for precise requirements, refer to your C manual. Some points of interest:

- Most versions of C pass parameters onto the stack in a sequence that is reverse to that of other languages. Consider the following C statement:

```
Adds (m, n);
```

The statement pushes n and m on the stack in that order and calls Adds. On return from the called module, the C module (not the assembly module) adds 4 to the SP to discard the passed parameters. The typical procedure for accessing the two passed parameters is as follows:

```
PUSH  BP
MOV   BP,SP
MOV   DH,[BP + 4]
MOV   DL,[BP + 6]
 . . .
POP   BP
RET
```

- For C versions that are sensitive to uppercase and lowercase, the name of the assembly module should be the same case as the C program's reference.
- Some C versions require that an assembly program that changes the DI and SI registers should push them on entry and pop them on exit.
- The assembly program should return values, if required, as one word in the AX or two words in the DX:AX pair.
- For some C versions, an assembly program that sets the DF flag should clear it (CLD) before returning.

Linking Turbo C with Turbo Assembler

Turbo C provides two ways of interfacing with Turbo Assembler: by inline code and by separate assembly modules.

Inline assembly code.   For compiling the C module, you request TCC.EXE (the command version of Turbo C). You simply insert assembly statements, preceded by the keyword asm, in the source code, such as

```
asm INC WORD PTR FLDX
```

Separate assembly modules.   For this conventional method, you code the C and assembly programs separately. Use TCC to compile the C module, TASM to assemble the assembly module, and TLINK to link them.

Use of names.   The Turbo Assembler modules must use a naming convention for segments and variables that is compatible with Turbo C. All assembler references to functions and variables in the C module must begin with an underscore character. Further, since C is case-sensitive, the assembly module should use the same case (upper or lower) for variable names common to the C module.

Registers.   The assembly module may freely use the AX, BX, CX, DX, ES, and flags registers. It may also use the BP, SP, CS, DS, SS, DI, and SI registers provided that it saves and restores them.

Passing parameters.   Turbo C pushes passed parameters onto the stack, from right to left if there are more than one.

KEY POINTS

- In a main program that calls a subprogram, define the entry point as EXTRN; in the subprogram define the entry point as PUBLIC.
- Handle recursion carefully—that is, subprogram 1 calls subprogram 2, which in turn calls subprogram 1.
- If two code segments are to be linked into one segment, define them with the same name, same class, and the PUBLIC combine type.
- To simplify programming, begin execution with the main program.
- It is also generally easier (but not necessary) to define common data in the main program. The main program defines the common data as PUBLIC and the subprogram (or subprograms) defines the common data as EXTRN.

QUESTIONS

21-1. Provide four reasons for organizing a program into subprograms.

The next three questions refer to the general format for the SEGMENT directive:

```
seg-name SEGMENT [align] [combine] ['class']
```

21-2. **(a)** For the SEGMENT directive's align option, what is the default?
(b) What is the effect of the BYTE option? (That is, what action does the assembler take?)

21-3. **(a)** For the SEGMENT directive's combine option, what is the default?
(b) When would you use the PUBLIC option?
(c) When would you use the COMMON option?

21-4. **(a)** What should the code segment's class option be for the SEGMENT directive?
(b) Two segments have the same class but not the PUBLIC combine option. What is the effect?
(c) Two segments have the same class and both have the PUBLIC combine option. What is the effect?

21-5. Distinguish between an intrasegment call and an intersegment call.

21-6. A program named MAINPRO is to call a subprogram named SUBPRO.
(a) What statement in MAINPRO tells the assembler that the name SUBPRO is defined outside its own assembly?
(b) What statement in SUBPRO is required to make its name known to MAINPRO?

21-7. Assume that MAINPRO in Question 21-6 has defined variables named QTY as DB, VALUE as DW, and PRICE as DW. SUBPRO is to divide VALUE by QTY and is to store the quotient in PRICE.
(a) How does MAINPRO tell the assembler that the three variables are to be known outside this assembly?
(b) How does SUBPRO tell the assembler that the three variables are defined in another assembly?

21-8. Combine Questions 21-6 and 21-7 into a working program and test it.

21-9. Revise Question 21-8 so that MAINPRO passes all three variables as parameters. Note, however, that SUBPRO is to return the calculated price intact in its parameter.

21-10. Here's an exercise that should keep you occupied. Expand Question 21-9 so that MAINPRO permits a user to enter quantity and value on the keyboard; SUBCONV converts the ASCII amounts to binary; SUBCALC calculates the price; and SUBDISP converts the binary price to ASCII and displays the result.

22

DOS MEMORY MANAGEMENT

OBJECTIVE

To describe DOS initialization, the program segment prefix, the environment, memory control, the program loader, and resident programs.

INTRODUCTION

In this chapter we describe DOS organization in detail, including DOS initialization, the program segment prefix, the environment, memory control, the steps that the system takes in loading an executable module into memory for execution, and resident programs.

The four major DOS programs provide a particular service:

1. The *boot record* is on track 0, sector 1, of the DOS diskette and on any disk that you use FORMAT /S to format. When you initiate the system (assuming that DOS is in drive A or C), the system automatically loads the boot record from disk into memory. This program then loads IBMBIO.COM from disk into memory.

2. *IBMBIO.COM* is a low-level interface to the BIOS routines in ROM. (Under MS-DOS, this file is known as IO.SYS.) On initiation, IBMBIO.COM determines device and equipment status and sets interrupt table addresses for interrupts up to 20H. IBMBIO.COM also handles input/output between

memory and external devices such as video monitor and disk. It then loads IBMDOS.COM and COMMAND.COM.

3. *IBMDOS.COM* is a high-level interface to programs that loads into memory after IBMBIO.COM and sets interrupt table addresses for interrupts 20H through 3FH. (Under MS-DOS, this file is known as MSDOS.SYS.) IBMDOS.COM manages the directory and files on disk, handles blocking and deblocking of disk records, handles INT 21H functions, and performs a number of other service functions.

4. *COMMAND.COM* handles the various commands such as DIR and CHKDSK and runs requested COM, EXE, and BAT programs. It consists of three parts: a small resident portion, an initialization portion, and a transient portion. COMMAND.COM, covered in detail in the next section, is responsible for loading executable programs from disk into memory.

Figure 22-1 shows a map of memory after DOS has loaded. Details may vary by computer model.

Beginning Address	Contents
00000	Interrupt address table (details in Chapter 23)
00400	BIOS data area (details in Chapter 23)
00500	DOS communication area
xxxx0	IBMBIO.COM
xxxx0	IBMDOS.COM:
xxxx0	Resident portion of COMMAND.COM
	DOS buffers and control areas
	Installable device drivers
	Resident programs (if any)
	User programs
	. . .
xxxx0	Transient portion of COMMAND.COM, stored at top of RAM
A0000	Used by EGA and VGA adapters
B0000	Used for monochrome displays
B8000	Used by color adapters
C0000	ROM expansion area: hard disk adapters, EGA ROM
D0000	ROM expansion area: EMS window
E0000	ROM expansion area: PS/2 BIOS ROM
F0000	System ROM area

Figure 22-1   Map of Memory

DOS COMMUNICATION AREA

DOS has its own communication area beginning at memory address 0500H. Programmers appear to have little need for this area. Following are the fields that are documented:

050:00H	A one-byte print screen status flag, where
	00H = Not active or a successful PrtSc operation
	01H = PrtSc in progress
	FFH = PrtSc encountered an error
050:01H	Used by BASIC
050:04H	Status byte for single-drive mode
050:10–21H	Used by BASIC
050:22–2FH	Used by DOS for diskette initialization
050:30–33H	Used by MODE command

COMMAND.COM

The system loads the three portions of COMMAND.COM into memory either permanently during a session or temporarily as required. The following describes the three parts of COMMAND.COM.

The *resident portion* immediately loads IBMDOS.COM (and its data areas) where it resides during processing. The resident portion handles all errors for disk I/O and the following interrupts:

INT 22H	Terminate address
INT 23H	Ctrl/Break handler
INT 24H	Error detection on disk read/write or a bad memory image of the file allocation table (FAT)
INT 27H	Terminate but stay resident

The *initialization portion* immediately follows the resident portion and contains the setup for AUTOEXEC files. When the system starts up, this portion initially takes control, prompts for the date, and determines the segment address where the system is to load programs for execution.

None of these initialization routines is required again during a session. Consequently, your first request to load a program from disk causes DOS to overlay it in this section of memory.

The *transient portion* of COMMAND.COM is loaded into the highest area of memory. "Transient" implies that DOS may overlay this area with other requested programs, if necessary. The transient portion displays the familiar screen prompt, and accepts and executes requests. It contains a relocation loader facility that loads COM and EXE files from disk into memory for execution. When you request execution of a program, the transient portion constructs a program segment in the lowest available memory location. It creates the PSP at 00H and loads your requested executable program at offset 100H, sets exit addresses, and gives control to your loaded program. Here is the sequence:

```
IBMBIO.COM
IBMDOS.COM
COMMAND.COM (resident)
Program segment:
     program segment prefix
     executable program
. . .
COMMAND.COM (transient, may be overlaid)
```

Normal termination of a program causes a return to the resident portion of COMMAND.COM. If the transient portion was overlaid, the resident portion reloads it into memory.

PROGRAM SEGMENT PREFIX

DOS loads COM and EXE programs for execution into a program segment and creates a program segment prefix (PSP) at offset 0 and the program at 100H of the segment. The PSP contains the following fields according to relative hex position:

00–01	An INT 20H instruction (hex CD20)
02–03	The segment address of the last paragraph of memory allocated to the program, as xxxx0 For example, 640K is indicated as hex 00A0, meaning A0000[0].
04–09	Reserved
0A–0D	Terminate address (segment address for INT 22H)
0E–11	Ctrl/Break exit address (segment address for INT 23H)
12–15	Critical error exit address (segment address for INT 24H)
16–17	Reserved
18–2B	Default file handle table
2C–2D	Segment address of program's environment
2E–31	Reserved
32–33	Length of the file handle table
34–37	Far pointer to handle table
38–4F	Reserved

50–51	Call to DOS function (an INT 21H and RETF)
52–5B	Reserved
5C–6B	Parameter area 1, formatted as standard unopened file control block (FCB #1)
6C–7F	Parameter area 2, formatted as standard unopened file control block (FCB #2); overlaid if FCB at 5CH is opened
80–FF	Buffer for default disk transfer area (DTA)

PSP 18–2BH: Default File Handle Table

Each byte in the file handle table refers to an entry in a DOS table that defines the related device or driver. Initially, the table contains 0101010002FF...FF, where the first 01 refers to the keyboard, the second 01 to the screen, and so forth:

Table	Device	Handle	Device
01	Console	0	Keyboard (standard input)
01	Console	1	Screen (standard input)
01	Console	2	Screen (standard error)
00	COM1 (serial port)	3	Auxiliary
02	Printer	4	Standard printer
FF	Unassigned	5	Unassigned

The table of 20 handles explains why DOS allows a maximum of 20 files open at one time. Normally, the PSP word at 32H contains the length of the table (14H, or 20) and 34H contains its segment address in the form IP:CS, where the IP is 18H (the offset in the PSP) and the CS is the segment address of the PSP.

Programs that need more than 20 open files have to release memory (INT 21H service 4AH) and use service 67H (set handle count) with the new handle limit (up to 65,535) in the BX. The amount of memory required is one byte per handle, rounded up to the next byte paragraph plus 16 bytes. The operation creates the new handle table outside the PSP and updates locations 32H and 34H in the PSP.

PSP 2C–2D: Segment Address of Environment

Every program loaded for execution has a related environment that DOS stores in memory beginning on a paragraph boundary before the program segment. The default size is 160 bytes, with a maximum of 32K since DOS 3.2. The environment contains such DOS commands as COMSPEC, PATH, PROMPT, and SET that are applicable to the program.

PSP 5C–6B: Standard Unopened FCB-1

DOS formats this area with a dummy or real file control block (FCB), based on the characters (if any) that you enter following a request for a program name for execution, such as MASM B:PROGRAM1.ASM.

PSP 6C–7F: Standard Unopened FCB-2

DOS also formats this area with a dummy or real file control block (FCB), based on the characters (if any) that you enter when you request a program name for execution.

PSP 80–FF: Default DTA Buffer

The portion of the PSP beginning at 80H is called a default buffer for the disk transfer area. For an FCB file, if the record length is 128 bytes, technically you could use this area as its DTA, although few would do this. More important, DOS initializes this area with the text (if any) that a user keys in following the requested program name. The first byte contains the number of keys (if any) pressed immediately following the entered program name, followed by any actual characters entered. Following is any garbage already in memory from a previous program.

The following four examples should clarify the contents and purpose of the FCBs and the default buffer.

Example 1: Command with No Operand

Suppose that you cause a program named CALCIT.EXE to execute by entering CALCIT [Enter]. When DOS constructs the PSP for this program, it sets up FCB-1, FCB-2, and the default DTA as

```
5CH FCB-1:    00 20 20 20 20 20 20 20 20 20 20 20 . . .
6CH FCB-2:    00 20 20 20 20 20 20 20 20 20 20 20 . . .
80H DTA:      00 0D . . .
```

FCB-1 and FCB-2 are both dummy FCBs. The first byte, 00H, refers to the default drive number. The following bytes for filename and extension are blank, since no text following the keyed program name was entered. The first byte of the DTA contains the number of bytes keyed in after the name CALCIT, not including the Enter character. Since no keys other than Enter were pressed, the number is zero. The second byte contains the Enter character, 0DH, that was pressed.

Example 2: Command with Text Operand

Suppose that you want to execute a program named COLOR and pass a parameter "BY" that tells the program to set color blue (B) on yellow (Y) background. You type the program name followed by the parameter, as COLOR BY. DOS sets the following in the PSP:

```
5CH FCB-1:    00 42 59 20 20 20 20 20 20 20 20 20 . . .
6CH FCB-2:    00 20 20 20 20 20 20 20 20 20 20 20 . . .
80H DTA:      03 20 42 59 0D . . .
```

DOS has attempted to set up a FCB for FCB-1 with 00H as the default drive and 4259H (BY) as the filename. Note that DOS doesn't know whether the filename is valid. The bytes in the DTA at 80H mean length of 3, a space, "BY," and the Enter character, respectively. Other than the length, this field contains exactly what was typed.

Example 3: Command with a Filename Operand

Programs like DEL allow users to enter a file name after the program name. If you key in, for example, DEL B:CALCIT.OBJ [Enter], the PSP contains the following:

```
5CH FCB-1:    02 43 41 4C 43 49 54 20 20 4F 42 4A . . .
               C  A  L  C  I  T        O  B  J
6CH FCB-2:    00 20 20 20 20 20 20 20 20 20 20 20 . . .
80H DTA:      0D 20 42 3A 43 41 4C 43 49 54 2E 4F 42 4A 0D . . .
                 B  :  C  A  L  C  I  T  .  O  B  J
```

The first character of FCB-1 indicates drive number (02 = B in this case), followed by the name of the file, CALCIT, that the program is to reference. Following are two blanks that complete the eight-character filename and then the extension, OBJ. The bytes in the DTA contain a length of 13 (0DH) followed by exactly what was typed.

Example 4: Command with Two Filename Operands

Consider entering a command followed by two parameters, such as

```
COPY A:FILEA.ASM B:FILEB.ASM
```

DOS sets the FCBs in the PSP with the following:

```
5CH FCB-1:    01 46 49 4C 45 41 20 20 20 41 53 4D . . .
               F  I  L  E  A           A  S  M
6CH FCB-2:    02 46 49 4C 45 42 20 20 20 41 53 4D . . .
               F  I  L  E  B           A  S  M
```

The first byte for FCB-1, 01, refers to drive A, and the first byte for FCB-2, 02, refers to drive B. For the DTA, the bytes would contain the number of characters entered (10H), a space (20H), A:FILEA B:FILEB, and the Enter character (0DH).

Accessing the PSP

Since the PSP immediately precedes your program, you can access its areas in order to process specified files or to take special action. To locate the DTA, a COM program can simply set 80H in the SI register and access the bytes:

```
MOV  SI,80H            ;Address of DTA
CMP  BYTE PTR[SI],0    ;Check buffer
JE   EXIT              ;zero--no data
```

An EXE program can't always assume that its code segment immediately follows the PSP. However, on initialization, the DS and ES contain the address of the PSP, so you could save the ES after initializing the DS:

```
MOV  AX,DSEG       ;Initialize DS
MOV  DS,AX
MOV  SAVEPSP,ES    ;Save address of PSP
```

Later, you could use the saved address for accessing the PSP buffer:

```
MOV  SI,SAVEPSP
CMP  BYTE PTR[SI+80H],0    ;Check PSP buffer
JE   EXIT                  ;zero--no data
```

DOS version 3.0 introduced INT 62H, which delivers the address of the current PSP in the BX register, and which you may use to access data in the PSP. The following example saves the address of the PSP in the ES register:

```
MOV  AH,62H    ;Request address of PSP
INT  21H
MOV  ES,BX     ;Save address in ES
```

Extended Example Using the PSP

The example COM program in this section sets the attribute of a file to normal (00H). A user would key in the program name followed by the name of the file, such as NORMATR D:filename.ext. The program checks for the Enter character and replaces it with a byte of hex zeros, for an ASCIIZ string. A user could also type in the drive number and directory path.

```
TITLE    NORMATR    'Set file attribute to normal'
CODESG   SEGMENT    PARA
         ASSUME     CS:CODESG
         ORG        100H
BEGIN:   MOV        AL,0DH              ;Search character (Enter)
```

```
               MOV      CX,21                ;Number of bytes
               MOV      DI,82H               ;Start address in PSP
               REPNZ SCASB                   ;Scan for Enter
               JNZ      ***                  ;Not found--error
               DEC      DI                   ;Found:
               MOV      BYTE PTR [DI],0       ;Replace with 00H
               MOV      AH,43H                ;DOS service call
               MOV      AL,01                 ;  to set attribute
               MOV      CX,00                 ;  to normal
               MOV      DX,82H                ;  ASCIIZ string in PSP
               INT      21H
               JC       ***                  ;Write error
               RET
CODESG         ENDS
               END      BEGIN
```

DOS MEMORY CONTROL

DOS allows any number of programs to be loaded and to stay resident. Examples include VDISK, MOUSE, SIDEKICK, and PROKEY. DOS sets up one or two *memory control blocks* (MCBs) for each loaded program. Preceding each memory control block is a memory control record beginning on a paragraph boundary:

00–00	Code, where 'M' means more blocks to follow and 'Z' means zero blocks to follow (the last block). (This is a useful interpretation, but not necessarily the original intention.)
01–02	Segment address of the owner's PSP. 0800 means that it belongs to IBMDOS.COM and 0000 means that it is released and available.
03–04	Length of memory control block in paragraphs.
05–07	Reserved.
08–0F	ASCII program name (for DOS 4.0 and on).

A forward linked list (of sorts) connects memory control blocks. The first memory control block, set up and owned by IBMDOS.COM, contains DOS file buffers, FCBs used by file handle functions, and device drivers loaded by DEVICE commands in CONFIG.SYS.

The second memory control block is the resident portion of COMMAND.COM with its own PSP. As of DOS 4.0, a few special programs such as FASTOPEN and SHARE may be loaded before COMMAND.COM.

The third memory control block is the master environment containing the COMSPEC command, PROMPT commands, PATH commands, and any strings set by SET.

Succeeding blocks include any TSR programs and the currently executing program. These programs each have two blocks: a copy of the environment and the program segment with the PSP and the executable module.

The first MCB, which belongs to IBMDOS.COM, can be located by means of an undocumented feature, INT 21H service 52H. The operation returns the segment address of IBMDOS.COM in the ES and an offset in the BX. ES:[BX-4] points to a doubleword in IP:CS format that contains the address of this MCB.

To find subsequent MCBs in the chain:

1. Use the address of the memory control record.
2. Add 1 to its segment address to get the start of its MCB.
3. Add the length from 03–04 of the memory control record.

You now have the segment address of the next memory control record.

To determine the paragraphs of memory available to DOS for the last program, find the memory control record with Z in byte 0 and perform the preceding calculations. The last block has available to it all remaining higher memory.

Partial Example

This session used DOS version 4.01 and loaded COMMAND.COM, VDISK, and DEBUG. DEBUG displayed the required memory contents. Watch out for reversed byte sequence.

1. Service 52H returned 02CC[0] in the ES and 0026 in the BX. Since we want the four bytes to the left at 0022, use D 02CC:22 to display the contents:

                     00 00 56 0B

    in IP:CS format. The address of the first MCB is therefore at 0B56[0].
2. Use D B56:0 to display the first MCB:

                     4D 08 00 AE 05 . . .

    The 4D (M) means more MCBs follow, 0800 (0008H) means that this MCB belongs to IBMDOS.COM, and AE05 (05AEH) is the length of the MCB.
3. Locate the second MCB (COMMAND.COM):

Location of first MCB	B56[0]
Add 1 paragraph	+ 1[0]
Add length of the MCB	+ 5AE[0]
Location of next MCB	1105[0]

    Use D 1105:0 to display the second MCB:

                     4D 06 11 64 01 . . .

You could also examine the contents of COMMAND.COM at this point.

4. Locate the third memory control block, the master environment:

Location of previous MCB	1105[0]
Add 1 paragraph	+ 1[0]
Add length of the MCB	+ 164[0]
Location of next MCB	126A[0]

Use D 126A:0 to display the third MCB:

4D . . . .

You could also examine the contents of the master environment at this point. You can also locate the remaining MCBs in a similar fashion. Note that succeeding programs have one MCB for their environment and one for their program segment. The last memory control record has 5AH ('Z') in its first byte. If you display from within DEBUG, this is its own MCB.

Memory Allocation Strategy

On loading a program, DOS uses one of three strategies:

1. *First fit: (default).* DOS searches from the lowest address in memory for the first block that is large enough, usually the last or only one.
2. *Best fit: (DOS 3.0 and on).* DOS searches for the smallest available block in memory that is large enough.
3. *Last fit: (DOS 3.0 and on).* DOS searches from the highest memory address for the first block that is large enough.

Best-fit and last-fit strategies are appropriate to multitasking systems, which could have fragmented memory because of programs running concurrently. When a program is terminated, its memory is released to the system.

INT 21H service 58H (get/set memory allocation strategy) allows queries and changes to this strategy. For getting the strategy, the AL contains 00 on entry and the BL returns 00 for first fit, 01 for best fit, and 02 for last fit. For setting a strategy, on entry the AL contains 01 and the BL contains 00 for first fit, 01 for best fit, and 02 for last fit. An error sets the carry flag and returns 01 (invalid function) in the AX.

PROGRAM LOADER

On loading both COM and EXE programs, DOS performs the following:

1. Sets up memory control blocks for the program's environment and for the program segment
2. Creates a program segment prefix at location 00H of the program segment and loads the program at 100H

Other than these steps, however, the load and execute steps differ for COM and EXE programs. A major difference is that the linker inserts a special header record in an EXE file when storing it on disk.

Loading and Executing a COM Program

Since the organization of a COM file is relatively simple, DOS needs to know only that the file extension is COM. As described earlier, a program segment prefix precedes COM and EXE programs loaded in memory. The first two bytes of the PSP contain the INT 20H instruction (return to DOS). On loading a COM program, DOS

- Sets the four segment registers with the address of the first byte of the PSP.
- Sets the stack pointer to the end of the 64K segment, offset FFFEH (or to the end of memory if the segment is not large enough) and pushes a zero word on the stack.
- Sets the instruction pointer to 100H (the size of the PSP) and allows control to proceed to the address generated by CS:IP, the first location immediately following the PSP. This is the first byte of your program, and should contain an executable instruction. Figure 22-2 illustrates this initialization.

You can use RET to exit from the program. RET pops the zero (that the loader pushed initially onto the stack) into the IP. CS:IP now generate an address that is the location of the first byte of the PSP, containing INT 20H. When that instruction executes, control returns to the resident portion of COMMAND.COM. (If a program uses INT 21H service 4CH instead of RET to terminate, control passes directly to COMMAND.COM.)

Loading and Executing an EXE Program

The linker stores on disk an EXE module that consists of two parts: (1) a header record containing control and relocation information and (2) the actual load module.

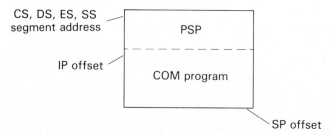

Figure 22-2   Initialization of a COM Program

The header is a minimum of 512 bytes in size and may be longer if there are many relocatable items. The header contains information about the size of the executable module, where it is to be loaded in memory, the address of the stack, and relocation offsets to be inserted into incomplete machine addresses, according to relative hex position:

00–01	Hex 4D5A ('MZ'). Identifies the file as an EXE file.
02–03	Number of bytes in the last block of the EXE file.
04–05	Size of the file including the header, in 512-byte block increments.
06–07	Number of relocation table items (see 1CH).
08–09	Size of the header in 16-byte (paragraph) increments, to help DOS locate the start of the executable module following this header. The minimum number is 20H (32), where $32 \times 16 = 512$ bytes.
0A–0B	Minimum count of paragraphs that must reside above the end of the program when loaded.
0C–0D	High/low loader switch. You decide when linking whether the program is to load for execution at a low (the usual) or a high memory address. Hex 0000 indicates high and FFFF indicates low. Otherwise, this location contains the maximum count of paragraphs that must reside above the end of the loaded program.
0E–0F	Offset location in the executable module of the stack segment.
10–11	Offset that the loader is to insert in the SP register when transferring control to the executable module. The value is the defined size of the stack.
12–13	Checksum value—the sum of all the words in the file (ignoring overflows) used as a validation check for lost data.
14–15	Offset (usually but not necessarily 00H) that the loader is to insert in the IP register when transferring control to the executable module.
16–17	Offset in the executable module of the code segment, which the loader inserts in the CS register. If the code segment is first, the offset would be zero.
18–19	Offset of the first relocation item in this file, recognized by "— R" in the LST listing.
1A–1B	Overlay number: zero (the usual) means that the header references the resident portion of the EXE file.
1C–end	Relocation table containing a variable number of relocation items, as identified at offset 06.

Position 06 of the header indicates the number of items in the executable module that are to be relocated. Each relocation item, beginning at header 1C, consists of a two-byte offset value and a two-byte segment value.

The system constructs memory control blocks for the environment and the program segment. Following are the steps that DOS performs when loading and initializing an EXE program:

- Reads the formatted part of the header into memory.
- Calculates the size of the executable module (total file size in position 04H minus header size at position 08H) and reads the module into memory at the start segment.
- Reads the relocation table items into a work area and adds the value of each table item to the start segment value.
- Sets the DS and ES registers to the segment address of the PSP.
- Sets the SS register to the address of the PSP plus 100H (the size of the PSP) plus the SS offset value (at 0EH). It also sets the SP register to the value at 10H, the size of the stack.
- Sets the CS to the address of the PSP plus 100H (the size of the PSP) plus the CS offset value in the header (at 16H) to the CS. It also sets the IP with the offset at 14H. The CS:IP pair provide the starting address of the code segment and, in effect, program execution. Figure 22-3 illustrates this initialization.

DOS is finished with the EXE header and discards it. The CS and SS registers are set correctly, but your program has to set the DS (and ES) for its own data segment:

```
MOV  AX,datasegname   ;Set DS and ES registers
MOV  DS,AX            ; to address
MOV  ES,AX            ; of data segment
```

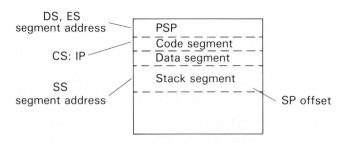

Figure 22-3   Initialization of an EXE Program

Example of Loading an EXE Program

Consider the following MAP that the linker generated for an EXE program:

```
Start      Stop      Length   Name     Class
00000H     0003AH    003BH    CSEG     Code
00040H     0005AH    001BH    DSEG     Data
00060H     0007FH    0020H    STACK    Stack
Program entry point at 0000:0000
```

The map provides the relative (not actual) location of each of the three segments. The H following each value indicates hexadecimal format. Note that some linkers arrange these segments in alphabetic sequence by name.

According to the map, the code segment (CSEG), is to start at 00000H—its relative location is the beginning of the executable module, and its length is 003BH bytes. The data segment, DSEG, begins at 00040H and has a length of 001BH. This is the first address following CSEG that aligns on a paragraph boundary (evenly divisible by 10H). The stack segment, STACK, begins at 00060H, the first address following DSEG that aligns on a paragraph boundary.

DEBUG is no help in examining a header record because when loading a program for execution, DOS replaces the header with a PSP. However, there are various utility programs on the market (or you can write your own) that allow you to view the hex contents of any disk sector. The header for this example program contains the following relevant information, according to hex location. The contents of fields are in hex and in reverse byte sequence:

00   Hex 4D5A

02   Number of bytes in last block: 5B00

04   Size of file including header in 512-byte blocks: 0200 (Hex $0002 \times 512 = 1024$)

06   Number of relocation table items following formatted portion of header: 0100, that is, 0001

08   Size of header in 16-byte increments: 2000. (0020H = 32, and $32 \times 16 = 512$)

0C   Load in low memory: FFFFH

0E   Offset location of stack segment: 6000, or 0060H

10   Address to insert in SP: 2000, or 0020H

14   Offset for IP: 0000

16   Offset for CS: 0000

18   Offset for first relocation item: 1E00, or 001EH

When DEBUG loaded the program, the registers contained the following:

```
SP = 0020   DS = 138F   ES = 138F
SS = 13A5   CS = 139F   IP = 0000
```

For EXE modules, the loader sets the DS and ES to the address of the PSP and sets the CS, IP, SS, and SP to values from the header record.

CS Register

According to the DS register when the program loaded, the address of the PSP is at 138F[0]H. Since the PSP is 100H bytes long, the executable module follows immediately at 138F0 + 100 = 139F[0]H, which the loader inserts in the CS register. The CS register indicates the starting address of the code portion (CSEG) of the program. You can use the DEBUG dump command, D CS:0000, to view the machine code in memory. The code is identical to the hex portion of the assembler LST printout, other than operands that LST tags as R.

SS Register

The loader used the value 60H in the header (at 0EH) to set the SS register.

Start address of PSP (see DS)	138F0
Length of PSP	+ 100
Offset of stack (see the map)	+ 60
Address of stack	13A50

SP Register

The loader used 20H from the header (at 10H) to initialize the stack pointer to the length of the stack. In this example, the stack was defined as 16 DUP(?), that is, 16 two-byte fields = 32, or 20H. The SP points to the current top of the stack.

DS Register

The loader uses the DS register to establish the starting point for the PSP. Because the header does not contain a starting address for the DS, your program has to initialize it:

```
0004 B8 ---- R    MOV AX,DSEG
0007 8E D8        MOV DS,AX
```

The assembler has left unfilled the machine address of DSEG, which becomes an entry in the relocation table in the header, discussed earlier. DEBUG shows the completed instruction as

```
                                B8 A313
```

A313 loads into the DS as 13A3. We now have at the start of execution

Register	Address	Map Offset
CS	139F[0]H	00H
DS	13A3[0]H	40H
SS	13A5[0]H	60H

As an exercise, trace any of your linked programs through DEBUG and note the changed values in the registers:

Instruction	Registers Changed
MOV AX,DSEG	IP and AX
MOV DS,AX	IP and DS
MOV ES,AX	IP and ES

The DS now contains the correct address of the data segment. You can use D DS:00 to view the contents of DSEG and use D SS:00 to view the contents of the stack.

ALLOCATING AND FREEING MEMORY

DOS services allow you to allocate an area of memory, to release an area, and to modify the size of an area. The most likely uses for these services are for programs that load other programs for execution and for resident programs. Under DOS, which is designed as a single-user environment, a program that needs to load another program for execution has to release some of its memory space.

Service 48H: Allocate Memory

To allocate memory space for a program, you request in the BX the number of paragraphs for the program. The operation begins at the first memory control block and steps through each block until it locates a space large enough for the request, usually at the high end of memory.

A successful operation clears the carry flag and returns in the AX the segment address of the allocated memory block. An unsuccessful operation sets the carry flag and returns in the AX an error code (07 = memory control block destroyed and 08 = insufficient memory) and in the BX the size in paragraphs of the largest block available. A memory control block destroyed means that the operation found a block in which the first byte was not 'M' or 'Z'.

Service 49H: Free Allocated Memory

This service frees allocated memory, commonly used to release a resident program. You first load in the ES the segment address of the block to be returned. A successful operation clears the carry flag and stores 00H in the second and third bytes of the memory control block, meaning that it is no longer in use. An unsuccessful operation sets the carry flag and returns in the AX an error code (07 = memory control block destroyed and 09 = invalid memory block address).

Service 4AH: Modify Allocated Memory Block

This service can increase or decrease the size of a memory control block. You initialize the BX with the number of paragraphs to retain for the program and the ES with the address of the program segment prefix. A program can calculate its own size by subtracting the end of the last segment from the address of the PSP. You'll have to ensure that you use the last segment if your linker rearranges segments in alphabetic sequence.

A successful operation clears the carry flag. An unsuccessful operation sets the carry flag and returns in the AX an error code (07 = memory control block destroyed, 08 = insufficient memory, and 09 = invalid memory block address) and (if an attempt to increase) returns in the BX the maximum possible size. The wrong address in the ES will cause error 07.

LOAD OR EXECUTE A PROGRAM FUNCTION

Let's now examine how to load and execute a program from within another program. INT 21H service 4BH enables one program to load another program into memory for optional execution. Load the address of a parameter block in the BX (actually ES:BX) and the address of the path name for the called program in the DX. The path name is an ASCIIZ string in uppercase letters. Set the AL with function code 00 for load and execute or 03 for load only.

AL = 00 Load and Execute

The operation establishes a program segment prefix for the new program and sets the control-break and terminate addresses to the instruction following this function. Since all registers, including the stack, are changed, this operation is not for novices. The parameter block addressed by the ES:BX has the following format:

Offset	Purpose
00	Word segment address of environment string to be passed at PSP + 2CH. A zero address means that the loaded program is to inherit the environment of its parent.
02	Doubleword pointer to command line for placing at PSP + 80H.
06	Doubleword pointer to default FCB-1 for passing at PSP + 5CH.
10	Doubleword pointer to default FCB-2 for passing at PSP + 6CH.

The doubleword pointers have the form offset:segment-address.

AL = 03 Load Overlay

The operation loads a program or block of code, *but does not establish a PSP or begin its execution.* Thus the code requested could be a program overlay. The parameter block addressed by the ES:BX has the following format:

Offset	Purpose
00	Word segment address where file is to be loaded
02	Word relocation factor to apply to the image

An error sets the carry flag and returns in the AX error codes 01, 02, 05, 08, 10, or 11, described in Figure 17-1.

The EXE program in Figure 22-4 requests DOS to perform the DIR command for drive D. The program first uses service 4AH to reduce its memory requirements to its actual size—the difference between its last (dummy) segment ZNDSEG and the start of its PSP. Note that at this point the ES still contains the address of the PSP as loaded on entry. (The ASSUME statements preceding and following MOV BX,SEG ZNDSEG appear to be required for MASM 5.1 but not for some other assemblers.) The module is 80 bytes in size, so that the PSP (10H paragraphs) and the program (8 paragraphs) total 18H paragraphs.

Service 4BH with function 00 in the AL handles the loading and execution of COMMAND.COM. The program displays the directory entries for drive D.

PROGRAM OVERLAYS

Figure 22-4 illustrated a program that uses DOS service 4BH to load and execute another program. The program in Figure 22-5 uses the same service, but this time just to load a program into memory. The process consists of three programs: CALLOVER, SUBPRG1, and SUBPRG2.

```
         TITLE    EXDOS (EXE) DOS service 4BH to execute DIR
         ; ----------------------------------------------------------
         SSEG     SEGMENT PARA STACK 'Stack'
                  DW      32(?)
         SSEG     ENDS
         ; ----------------------------------------------------------
         DSEG     SEGMENT PARA 'Data'
         PARAREA  LABEL   BYTE                 ;Parameter block for load/exec:
                  DW      0                    ;  address of envir. string
                  DW      OFFSET DIRCOM        ;  pointer to command line
                  DW      DSEG
                  DW      OFFSET FCB1          ;  pointer to default FCB1
                  DW      DSEG
                  DW      OFFSET FCB2          ;  pointer to default FCB2
                  DW      DSEG
         DIRCOM   DB      17,'/C DIR D:',13,0
         FCB1     DB      16 DUP(0)
         FCB2     DB      16 DUP(0)
         PROGNAM  DB      'D:COMMAND.COM',0
         DSEG     ENDS
         ; ----------------------------------------------------------
         CSEG     SEGMENT PARA 'Code'
                  ASSUME  CS:CSEG,DS:DSEG,SS:SSEG,ES:DSEG
         BEGIN    PROC    FAR
                  MOV     AH,4AH               ;Reduce allocated memory space
                  ASSUME  CS:ZNDSEG
                  MOV     BX,SEG ZNDSEG        ;Ending segment
                  ASSUME  CS:CSEG
                  MOV     CX,ES                ;  minus start of
                  SUB     BX,CX                ;  program segment
                  INT     21H
                  JC      E10ERR               ;Not enough space?
                  MOV     AX,DSEG
                  MOV     DS,AX                ;Set DS and ES
                  MOV     ES,AX
                  MOV     AH,4BH               ;Request load
                  MOV     AL,00                ;  and execute
                  LEA     BX,PARAREA           ;  COMMAND.COM
                  LEA     DX,PROGNAM
                  INT     21H                  ;Call DOS
                  JC      E20ERR               ;Execute error?
                  MOV     AL,00                ;OK -- no error code
                  JMP     X10XIT
         E10ERR:
                  MOV     AL,01                ;Error code 1
                  JMP     X10XIT
         E20ERR:
                  MOV     AL,02                ;Error code 2
                  JMP     X10XIT
         X10XIT:
                  MOV     AH,4CH               ;Request terminate
                  INT     21H                  ;Return to DOS
         BEGIN    ENDP
         CSEG     ENDS

         ZNDSEG   SEGMENT                      ;Dummy segment
         ZNDSEG   ENDS
                  END     BEGIN
```

Figure 22-4   Execution of DIR from within a Program

CALLOVER is the main program with these segments:

```
STACKSG SEGMENT PARA STACK 'Stack1'
DATASG  SEGMENT PARA 'Data1'
CODESG  SEGMENT PARA 'Code1'
ZENDSG  SEGMENT                                ;Dummy (empty) segment
```

```
TITLE    CALLOVER (EXE)  Call subprogram and overlay
         EXTRN   SUBPRG1:FAR
; --------------------------------------------------
STACKSG SEGMENT PARA STACK 'Stack1'
         DW      64 DUP(?)
STACKSG ENDS
; --------------------------------------------------
DATASG  SEGMENT PARA 'Data1'
PARABLK LABEL   WORD             ;Parameter block
         DW      0               ;
         DW      0               ;
FILENAM DB      'D:\SUBPRG2.EXE',0
ERRMSG1 DB      'Modify mem error'
ERRMSG2 DB      'Allocate error  '
ERRMSG3 DB      'Seg call error  '
DATASG  ENDS
; --------------------------------------------------
CODESG  SEGMENT PARA 'Code1'
BEGIN   PROC    FAR
         ASSUME  CS:CODESG,DS:DATASG,SS:STACKSG
         MOV     AX,DATASG
         MOV     DS,AX
         CALL    Q10SCR           ;Scroll screen
         CALL    SUBPRG1          ;Call subprogram 1

         MOV     AH,4AH           ;Shrink memory
         ASSUME  CS:ZENDSG
         MOV     BX,SEG ZENDSG    ;Address of end program
         ASSUME  CS:CODESG
         MOV     CX,ES            ;Address of PSP
         SUB     BX,CX            ;Size of this program
         INT     21H
         JC      A30ERR           ;If error, exit

         MOV     AX,DS            ;Initialize ES for
         MOV     ES,AX            ;  this service
         MOV     AH,48H           ;Allocate memory for overlay
         MOV     BX,40            ;40 paragraphs
         INT     21H
         JC      A40ERR           ;If error, exit
         MOV     PARABLK,AX       ;Save segment address

         MOV     AH,4BH           ;Load overlay program
         MOV     AL,03            ;  with no execute
         LEA     BX,PARABLK
         LEA     DX,FILENAM
         INT     21H
         JC      A50ERR           ;If error, exit

         MOV     AX,PARABLK       ;Exchange two words
         MOV     PARABLK+2,AX     ;  of PARABLK
         MOV     PARABLK,20H      ;Set CS offset to 20H
         LEA     BX,PARABLK
         CALL    DWORD PTR [BX]   ;Call subprogram 2
         JMP     A90
A30ERR:
         CALL    Q20SET           ;Set cursor
         LEA     DX,ERRMSG1
         CALL    Q30DISP          ;Display message
         JMP     A90
A40ERR:
         CALL    Q20SET           ;Set cursor
         LEA     DX,ERRMSG2
         CALL    Q30DISP          ;Display message
         JMP     A90
A50ERR:
         CALL    Q20SET           ;Set cursor
         LEA     DX,ERRMSG3
         CALL    Q30DISP          ;Display message
         JMP     A90
```

Figure 22-5   Call Subprogram and Overlay

```
A90:
        MOV     AH,4CH              ;Exit
        INT     21H
BEGIN   ENDP
;               Video screen services:
;               ----------------------
Q10SCR  PROC    NEAR
        MOV     AX,0600
        MOV     BH,1EH              ;Set color
        MOV     CX,0000             ;Scroll
        MOV     DX,184FH
        INT     10H
        RET
Q10SCR  ENDP

Q20SET  PROC
        MOV     AH,02               ;Request set
        MOV     BH,00               ;  cursor
        MOV     DH,12
        MOV     DL,00
        INT     10H
        RET
Q20SET  ENDP

Q30DISP PROC                        ;DX set on entry
        MOV     AH,40H              ;Request display
        MOV     BX,01               ;Handle
        MOV     CX,16               ;Length
        INT     21H
        RET
Q30DISP ENDP
CODESG  ENDS

ZENDSG  SEGMENT                     ;Dummy (empty) segment
ZENDSG  ENDS
        END     BEGIN
```

```
TITLE   SUBPRG1 Called subprogram
; ------------------------------------------
DATASG  SEGMENT PARA 'Data2'
SUBMSG  DB      'Subprogram 1 reporting'
DATASG  ENDS
CODESG  SEGMENT PARA 'Code2'
SUBPRG1 PROC    FAR
        ASSUME  CS:CODESG,DS:DATASG
        PUBLIC  SUBPRG1
        PUSH    DS                  ;Save caller's DS
        MOV     AX,DATASG           ;Initialize DS
        MOV     DS,AX
        MOV     AH,02               ;Request set
        MOV     BH,00               ;  cursor
        MOV     DH,05
        MOV     DL,00
        INT     10H
        MOV     AH,40H              ;Request display
        MOV     BX,01               ;Handle
        MOV     CX,22               ;Length
        LEA     DX,SUBMSG
        INT     21H
        POP     DS                  ;Restore DS for caller
        RET
SUBPRG1 ENDP
CODESG  ENDS
        END
```

Figure 22-5   Cont.

```
TITLE    SUBPRG2 Called overlay subprogram
; ---------------------------------------
DATASG   SEGMENT PARA 'Data'
SUBMSG   DB      'Subprogram 2 reporting'
DATASG   ENDS

CODESG   SEGMENT PARA 'Code'
SUBPRG2  PROC    FAR
         ASSUME  CS:CODESG,DS:DATASG
         PUSH    DS              ;Save caller's DS
         MOV     AX,CS           ;Set address of first
         MOV     DS,AX           ;  segment in DS
         MOV     AH,02           ;Request set
         MOV     BH,00           ;  cursor
         MOV     DH,10
         MOV     DL,00
         INT     10H
         MOV     AH,40H          ;Request display
         MOV     BX,01           ;Handle
         MOV     CX,22           ;Length
         LEA     DX,SUBMSG
         INT     21H
         POP     DS              ;Restore caller's DS
         RET
SUBPRG2  ENDP
CODESG   ENDS
         END
```

Figure 22-5   Cont.

SUBPRG1 is linked with and called by CALLOVER. Its segments are

```
DATASG  SEGMENT PARA 'Data2'
CODESG  SEGMENT PARA 'Code2'
```

CALLOVER's segments are linked first—that's why their class names differ: 'Data1', 'Data2', 'Code1', 'Code2', and so forth. Here's the link map for CALLOVER+SUBPRG1:

```
Start    Stop     Length   Name      Class
00000H   0007FH   00080H   STACKSG   Stack1
00080H   000C2H   00043H   DATASG    Data1
000D0H   0016DH   0009EH   CODESG    Code1
00170H   00170H   00000H   ZENDSG
00170H   0018FH   00016H   DATASG    Data2
00190H   001AFH   00020H   CODESG    Code2
```

SUBPRG2 is also called by CALLOVER but is linked separately. Its segments are:

```
DATASG  SEGMENT  PARA 'Data'
CODESG  SEGMENT  PARA 'Code'
```

SUBPRG2's link map looked like this:

```
Start   Stop    Length  Name    Class
00000H  00015H  00016H  DATASG  Data
00020H  0003EH  0001FH  CODESG  Code
```

When CALLOVER+SUBPRG1 are loaded into memory for execution, CALLOVER calls and executes SUBPRG1 in normal fashion. The near CALL initializes the IP correctly, but since SUBPRG1 has its own data segment, it has to push CALLOVER's DS and establish its own address. SUBPRG1 sets the cursor, displays a message, pops the DS, and returns to CALLOVER.

To overlay SUBPRG2 on SUBPRG1, CALLOVER has to shrink its memory space, since DOS has given it all available memory. CALLOVER's highest segment is ZENDSG, which is empty. CALLOVER subtracts the address of its PSP (still in the ES) from the address of ZENDSG. The difference is 270H (27H paragraphs), calculated as the size of the PSP (100H) plus the offset of ZENDSG (170H), which is delivered to DOS by service 4AH.

DOS service 48H then allocates memory to allow space for SUBPRG2 to be loaded (overlaid) on top of SUBPRG1, arbitrarily set to 40H paragraphs. The operation returns the loading address in the AX register, which CALLOVER stores in PARABLK. This is the first word of a parameter block to be used by service 4BH.

Service 4BH with function 03 in the AL loads SUBPRG2 into memory. The service references CS and PARABLK: The first word contains the segment address where the overlay is to load and the second word is an offset, in this case, zero. A diagram may help make these steps clearer:

	After Initial Load		*After Service 4AH Shrinks Memory*		*After Service 48H Allocates Memory*
000	PSP	000	PSP	000	PSP
	- - - - - -		- - - - - -		- - - - - -
100	CALLOVER	100	CALLOVER	100	CALLOVER
	- - - - - -				- - - - - -
270	SUBPRG1			270	SUBPRG2

The far CALL to SUBPRG2 requires a reference defined as IP:CS, but PARABLK is in the form CS:IP. The CS value is moved to the second word and 20H is stored in the first word for the IP, since the link map showed that value as the offset of SUBPRG2's code segment. The next instructions load the address of PARABLK in the BX and call SUBPRG2:

```
LEA   BX,PARABLK
CALL  DWORD PTR [BX]
```

Note that CALLOVER doesn't reference SUBPRG2 by name in its code segment and so doesn't require an EXTRN statement. Since SUBPRG2 has its own data segment, it first pushes the DS onto the stack and initializes its own address. But SUBPRG2 wasn't linked with CALLOVER. As a result, the instruction MOV AX,DATASG would set the AX only with the offset address of DATASG, 0[0]H, and not its segment address. We do know that CALL set the CS with the address of the first segment, which (according to the map) happens to be the address of the data segment. Moving the CS to the DS gives the correct address in the DS. Note that if SUBPRG2's code and data segments were in a different sequence, the coding would have to be somewhat different.

SUBPRG2 sets the cursor, displays a message, pops the DS, and returns to CALLOVER. DEBUG was indispensable in developing this program.

RESIDENT PROGRAMS

A number of popular commercial programs, such as Prokey, Superkey, Homebase, and Sidekick, are designed to reside in memory while other programs run, and you can activate their services through special keystrokes. You load resident programs after DOS loads and before activating other normal processing programs. They are almost always COM programs and are also known as "terminate but stay resident" (TSR) programs.

The easy part of writing a resident program is getting it to reside. Instead of normal termination, you exit by means of INT 21H service 31H (previously, INT 27H). The operation requires the size of the program in the DX register:

```
MOV  AH,4CH       ;Request TSR
MOV  DX,prog-size ;Size of program
INT  21H
```

When you execute the initialization routine, DOS reserves the memory block where the program resides and loads subsequent programs higher in memory.

The not-so-easy part of writing a resident program involves activating it after it is resident, since it is not internal to DOS as are DIR, COPY, and CLS. A common approach is to modify the interrupt services table so that the resident program interrupts all keystrokes, acts on a special keystroke or combination, and passes on all other keystrokes. The effect is that a resident program typically, but not necessarily, consists of the following:

1. A section that redefines locations in the interrupt services table.
2. A procedure that executes only the first time the program runs and that performs the following:
   • Replaces the address in the interrupt services table with its own address.
   • Establishes the size of the portion that is to remain resident.

• Uses an interrupt that tells DOS to terminate this program and to attach the specified portion in memory.

3. A procedure that remains resident and that is activated, for example, by special keyboard input or in some cases by the timer clock.

In effect, the initialization procedure sets up all the conditions to make the resident program work, and then allows itself to be erased. The organization of memory now appears as follows:

Interrupt services table	
IBMBIO.COM & IBMDOS.COM	
COMMAND.COM	
Resident portion of program	(stays in memory)
Initialization portion of program	(overlaid by next program)
Rest of available memory	

The program in Figure 22-6 illustrates a resident program that beeps when you use the numeric keypad when NumLock is on. This program has to intercept INT 09H, keyboard input, to check for the key pressed. The program uses two INT 21H service calls for manipulating the interrupt services table, since there is no assurance that more advanced computers will have the interrupt table located in the same memory locations.

Service 35H: Get Interrupt Address

You load the AL with the required interrupt number:

```
MOV  AH,35H    ;Request interrupt address
MOV  AL,int#   ;Interrupt number
INT  21H
```

The operation returns the address of the interrupt in ES:BX as code segment:offset. For conventional memory, a request for the address of INT 09H returns 00H in the ES and 24H (36) in the BX.

Service 25H: Set Interrupt Address

You load the required interrupt number in the AL and the new address in the DX:

```
MOV  AH,25H      ;Request interrupt address
MOV  AL,int#     ;Interrupt number
LEA  DX,newaddr  ;New address for interrupt
INT  21H
```

```
                page 60,132
TITLE           TESTNUM (COM)  Beep if use numeric keypad when NumLock on
BIODATA  SEGMENT AT 40H              ;BIOS data area
         ORG     17H
KBSTAT   DB      ?                    ;Keyboard status byte
BIODATA  ENDS
;        --------------------------------------------------
CODESG   SEGMENT PARA
         ASSUME  CS:CODESG,DS:BIODATA
         ORG     100H
BEGIN:
         JMP     INITZE               ;Jump to initialization
SAVINT9  DD      ?
TESTNUM:
         PUSH    AX                   ;Save registers
         PUSH    CX
         PUSH    DS

         MOV     AX,BIODATA           ;Segment address of
         MOV     DS,AX                ;  BIOS data area
         MOV     AL,KBSTAT            ;Get keyboard flag
         TEST    AL,00100000B         ;NumLock state?
         JZ      EXIT                 ;No -- exit

         IN      AL,60H               ;Get keystroke from port
         CMP     AL,71                ;Scan code < 71?
         JL      EXIT                 ;  yes -- exit
         CMP     AL,83                ;Scan code > 83?
         JG      EXIT                 ;  yes -- exit
                                      ;Must be from numeric keypad
         MOV     AL,10110110B         ;Set frequency
         OUT     43H,AL
         MOV     AX,1000
         OUT     42H,AL
         MOV     AL,AH
         OUT     42H,AL
         IN      AL,61H               ;Turn on speaker
         MOV     AH,AL
         OR      AL,03
         OUT     61H,AL
         MOV     CX,5000              ;Set duration
PAUSE:
         LOOP    PAUSE
         MOV     AL,AH                ;Turn off speaker
         OUT     61H,AL
EXIT:
         POP     DS                   ;Restore registers
         POP     CX
         POP     AX
         JMP     CS:SAVINT9           ;Resume INT 09

;        Initialization routine
;        ----------------------
INITZE:
         CLI                          ;Prevent further interrupts
         MOV     AL,09                ;Get address of INT 09
         MOV     AH,35H               ;  in ES:BX
         INT     21H
         MOV     WORD PTR SAVINT9,BX  ;  and save it
         MOV     WORD PTR SAVINT9+2,ES

         MOV     AL,09                ;Set new address for INT 09
         MOV     DX,OFFSET TESTNUM ;  in TESTNUM
         MOV     AH,25H
         INT     21H

         MOV     DX,OFFSET INITZE ;Set size of resident portion
         MOV     AH,31H               ;Request stay resident
         STI                          ;Restore interrupts
         INT     21H
CODESG   ENDS
         END     BEGIN
```

Figure 22-6   Resident Program

The operation replaces the present address of the interrupt with your new address.

The following points about the resident program are of interest:

BIODATA defines the BIOS data segment beginning at 40[0], in particular the keyboard flags byte, called here KBSTAT, that reflects the status of the keyboard. Bit 5 on (1) means that NumLock is on.

CODESG begins the code segment of the COM program. The first executable instruction, JMP INITZE, transfers past the resident portion to the INITZE procedure near the end. This routine first uses CLI to prevent any further interrupts at this time. It uses DOS service 35H to locate the address of INT 09 in the interrupt services table. The operation returns the address in the ES:BX, which this routine stores in INT9SAV. Service 25H then sets the program's own address for INT 09 in the interrupt table, TESTNUM, the entry point to the resident program. In effect, the program saves INT 09's address and replaces it with its own address. The last step establishes the size of the resident portion (all the code up to INITZE) in the DX and uses DOS service 31H (terminate but stay resident) to exit. The code from INITZE to the end gets overlaid by the next program that is loaded for execution.

TESTNUM is the name of the resident procedure that is activated when a user presses a key. The system transfers to the address of INT 09 in the interrupt service table, which has been changed to the address of TESTNUM. Since the interrupt may happen, for example, while the user is in DOS or an editor or word processing program, this program has to save the registers that it uses. The program accesses the keyboard flag to determine whether NumLock is on and the numeric keypad was pressed (a keyboard scan code between 71 and 83 inclusive). If so, the program beeps the speaker. The use of the speaker is explained in Chapter 23 under "Generating Sound." Final instructions involve restoring the pushed registers—in reverse sequence—and jumping to INT9SAV, which contains the original INT 09 address. Since we've patched into it, we now release control back to the interrupt.

The next example should help make the procedure clear. First is a conventional operation without a TSR intercepting the interrupt:

1. A user presses a key and the keyboard sends interrupt 09 to BIOS.
2. BIOS uses the address of INT 09 in the interrupt services table to locate its BIOS routine.
3. Control then transfers to the BIOS routine.
4. The routine gets the character and (if it's a standard character) delivers it to the keyboard buffer.

Next is the procedure for the resident program:

1. A user presses a key and the keyboard sends interrupt 09 to BIOS.
2. BIOS uses the address of INT 09 in the interrupt services table to locate its BIOS routine.
3. But the table now contains the address of TESTNUM, the resident program, where control transfers.

4. TESTNUM checks for NumLock on and checks the character for a numeric keypad number.
5. TESTNUM exits by jumping to the original saved INT 09 address, which transfers control to the BIOS routine.
6. The BIOS routine gets the character and (if it's a standard character) delivers it to the keyboard buffer.

Since this program is intended to be illustrative, you can modify or expand it for your own purposes. A few commercial programs that also replace the table address of interrupt 09 don't allow concurrent use of a resident program like this one.

Service 34H: Get Address of DOS Busy Flag

This is an undocumented interrupt used internally by DOS. Some TSRs also use it when requesting a DOS interrupt to check whether one is already currently active. Since DOS is not reentrant, the TSR has to wait until DOS is no longer busy. The service returns the address of the DOS busy flag, INDOS, in the ES:BX. The flag contains the number of DOS functions currently active—0 for none. You may enter DOS only if INDOS is 0.

KEY POINTS

- The boot record is on track 0, sector 1, of any disk that you use FORMAT /S to format. When you initiate the system, the system automatically loads the boot record from disk into memory. This program then loads IBMBIO.COM from disk into memory.
- IBMBIO.COM (or IO.SYS.) is a low-level interface to the BIOS routines in ROM. On initiation, IBMBIO.COM determines device and equipment status and sets interrupt table addresses for interrupts up to 20H. IBMBIO.COM also handles input/output between memory and external devices and loads IBMDOS.COM and COMMAND.COM.
- IBMDOS.COM (or MSDOS.SYS.) is a high-level interface to programs that loads into memory after IBMBIO.COM. Operations include setting interrupt table addresses for interrupts 20H through 3FH, managing the directory and files on disk, handling blocking and deblocking of disk records, and handling INT 21H functions.
- COMMAND.COM handles the various commands such as DIR and CHKDSK and runs requested COM, EXE, and BAT programs. It consists of three parts: a small resident portion, an initialization portion, and a transient portion. COMMAND.COM is responsible for loading executable programs from disk into memory.

- DOS loads COM and EXE programs for execution into a program segment and creates a program segment prefix (PSP) at offset 0 and the program at 100H of the segment. Useful fields within the PSP include parameter area 1 at 5CH, parameter area 2 at 6CH, and default disk transfer area at 80H.

- DOS sets up one or two memory control blocks (MCBs) for each loaded program. Preceding each MCB is a memory control record beginning on a paragraph boundary.

- On loading both COM and EXE programs, DOS sets up memory control blocks for the program's environment and for the program segment, creates a PSP at location 00H of the program segment, and loads the program at 100H.

- On loading a COM program, DOS sets the segment registers with the address of the PSP, sets the stack pointer to the end of the 64K segment, pushes a zero word on the stack, and sets the instruction pointer to 100H (the size of the PSP). Control then proceeds to the address generated by CS:IP, the first location immediately following the PSP.

- The linker stores on disk an EXE module that consists of a header record containing control and relocation information and the actual load module.

- When loading and initializing an EXE program, DOS reads the header record into memory, calculates the size of the executable module, and reads the module into memory at the start segment. It reads the relocation table items into a work area and adds the value of each table item to the start segment value. It sets the DS and ES to the segment address of the PSP, sets the SS to the address of the PSP plus 100H plus the SS offset value, sets the SP to the size of the stack, and sets the CS to the address of the PSP plus 100H plus the CS offset value in the header to the CS. It also sets the IP with the offset at 14H. The CS:IP pair provide the starting address of the code segment and, in effect, program execution.

- DOS INT 21H service 49H, which frees allocated memory, is commonly used to release a resident program.

- DOS INT 21H service 4AH can increase or decrease the size of a memory control block.

- You load resident programs after DOS loads and before activating other normal processing programs. Instead of normal termination, you exit by means of INT 21H service 31H, which requires the size of the program in the DX register.

QUESTIONS

22-1. **(a)** Where is the boot record located?
  (b) What is its purpose?

22-2. What is the purpose of IBMBIO.COM (IO.SYS.)?

22-3. What is the purpose of IBMDOS.COM (MSDOS.SYS.)?

22-4. Where generally are the following portions of COMMAND.COM located in memory, and what is their purpose?
(a) Resident; (b) initialization; (c) transient.

22-5. (a) Where is the program segment prefix located? (b) What is its size?

22-6. A user types in the instruction FUDGE C:ALF.DOC to request execution of a FUDGE program. Show the hex contents in the program's PSP at
(a) 5CH, parameter area 1 (FCB 1) and (b) 80H, the default DTA.

22-7. Your program has to determine what PATH commands are set for its environment. Explain where your program may find its own environment. (*Note:* The program's environment, not the DOS master environment.)

22-8. A COM program is loaded for execution with its PSP beginning at location hex 2BA1[0]. What address does DOS store in each of the following registers. (Don't bother with reversed byte notation.)
(a) CS; (b) DS; (c) ES; (d) SS.

22-9. A link map for an EXE program showed the following:

```
Start   Stop    Length  Name    Class
00000H  0002FH  00030H  STACK   STACK
00030H  0005BH  0002CH  CODESG  CODE
00060H  0007CH  0001DH  DATASG  DATA
```

DOS loads the program with the PSP beginning at location hex 1A25[0]. Show the contents of each of the registers at the time of loading. Show calculations where appropriate. (Ignore reversed byte notation.) (a) CS; (b) DS; (c) ES; (d) SS; (e) SP.

22-10. A memory control record begins at location EB6[0] and contains the following: 4D C00E 0A00 . . . .
(a) What does the 4D (M) mean to DOS?
(b) How would the contents differ if this were the last memory control block?
(c) What is the memory location of the next memory control record? Show calculations.

22-11. (a) Resident programs commonly intercept keyboard input. Where and what exactly is this intercepted address?
(b) In what two significant ways does coding termination of a resident program differ from coding termination of a normal program?

23

BIOS AND DOS DATA AREAS AND INTERRUPTS

OBJECTIVE

To describe the BIOS and DOS interrupt services.

INTRODUCTION

In this chapter we describe the various types of interrupts, the interrupt procedure, the boot procedure, details of the BIOS and DOS interrupt services, ports, and generation of sound through the PC's speaker.

INTERRUPTS

An interrupt is an operation that interrupts execution of a program so that the system can take special action. The interrupt routine executes and normally returns to the interrupted procedure, which resumes its execution.

BIOS (basic input/output system) and DOS establish an interrupt service table in memory locations 0–3FFH. The table provides for 255 (hex FF) interrupts, each with a related four-byte address in the form IP:CS.

BIOS handles interrupts 00H–1FH and DOS handles interrupts 20H–3FH. We have already used a number of interrupts for video display, disk input/output, and printing.

External and Internal Interrupts

An *external* interrupt is caused by a device that is external to the processor. The two lines that can signal external interrupts are the nonmaskable interrupt (NMI) line and the interrupt request (INTR) line. The NMI line reports memory and I/O parity errors. The processor always acts on this interrupt, even if you use CLI to clear the interrupt flag in an attempt to disable external interrupts. The INTR line reports requests from external devices, namely interrupts 05H through 0FH, for the timer, keyboard, serial ports, fixed disk, diskette drives, and parallel ports.

An *internal* interrupt occurs as a result of execution of an INT instruction, execution of a divide operation that causes an overflow, execution in single-step mode, or request for an external interrupt, such as disk I/O. Programs commonly use internal interrupts to access BIOS and DOS procedures. They are nonmaskable.

THE BOOT PROCESS

On the PC, ROM resides beginning at location FFFF0H. Turning on the power causes a "cold boot." The processor enters a reset state, sets all memory locations to 0, performs a parity check of memory, and sets the CS register to FFFF[0]H and the IP register to zero. The first instruction to execute therefore is at FFFF:0, or FFFF0, the entry point to BIOS. BIOS also stores the value 1234H at 40[0]:72H to tell a subsequent Ctrl/Alt/Del (warm reboot) not to perform the preceding power-on self-test.

BIOS checks the various ports to identify and initialize devices that are attached, including INT 11H (equipment determination) and INT 12H (memory size determination). BIOS then establishes, beginning at location 0 of memory, the interrupt service table that contains addresses of interrupt routines.

BIOS next determines whether a disk containing DOS is present and, if so, it executes INT 19H to access the first disk sector containing the bootstrap loader. This program loads DOS files IBMBIO.COM, IBMDOS.COM, and COMMAND.COM from disk into memory. At this point, memory appears as

> Interrupt services table
> BIOS data area
> IBMBIO.COM and IBMDOS.COM (or IO.SYS and MSDOS.SYS)
> Resident portion of COMMAND.COM
> Available for any program's use
> Transient portion of COMMAND.COM at end of RAM
> ROM BIOS

BIOS DATA AREA

BIOS maintains its own data area in lower memory beginning at segment address 40[0]H. A useful exercise is to use DEBUG to examine these fields. Here they are listed by offset.

Serial Port Data Area

00H–07H   Four words, addresses of up to four serial ports

Parallel Port Data Area

08H–0FH   Four words, addresses of up to four parallel ports

System Equipment Data Area

10H–11H   Equipment status, a primitive indication of installed devices, which you can access with INT 11H:

Bit	Device
15,14	Number of printers attached
11–9	Number of RS232 serial adapters
7,6	Number of diskette devices: $00 = 1, 01 = 2, 10 = 3$, and $11 = 4$
5,4	Initial video mode: 00 = unused $01 = 40 \times 25$ color $10 = 80 \times 25$ color $11 = 80 \times 25$ monochrome
2	Pointing device (PS/2)
1	1 = math coprocessor is present
0	1 = diskette drive is present

Miscellaneous Data Area

12H–12H   Manufacturer's test flags.

Memory Size Data Area

13H–14H   Amount of memory on system board in K bytes
15H–16H   Amount of expansion memory in K bytes

Keyboard Data Area 1

17H–17H   First byte of current shift status:

Bit	Action	Bit	Action
7	Insert toggled	3	Alt pressed
6	CapsLock toggled	2	Ctrl pressed
5	NumLock toggled	1	Left shift pressed
4	Scroll Lock toggled	0	Right shift pressed

18H–18H   Second byte of current shift status:

Bit	Action	Bit	Action
7	Insert pressed	3	Ctrl/NumLock pressed
6	CapsLock pressed	2	SysReq pressed
5	NumLock pressed	1	Left Alt pressed
4	Scroll Lock pressed	0	Left Ctrl pressed

19H–19H   Alternate keyboard entry for ASCII characters
1AH–1BH   Pointer to keyboard buffer head
1CH–1DH   Pointer to keyboard buffer tail
1EH–3DH   Keyboard buffer

Diskette Drive Data Area

3EH–3EH   Disk seek status. Bit number 0 refers to drive A, 1 to B, 2 to
               C, and 3 to D. A bit value of 0 means that the next seek is to
               reposition to cylinder 0 to recalibrate the drive.

3FH–3FH   Disk motor status. If bit 7 = 1, a write operation is in progress.
               Bit number 0 refers to drive A, 1 to B, 2 to C, and 3 to D; a bit
               value of 0 means that the motor is on.

40H–40H   Motor count for time-out until motor turn-off.

41H–41H   Disk status, indicating an error on the last diskette drive oper-
               ation:

00H	No error	09H	Attempt to DMA across
01H	Invalid drive parameter		64K boundary
02H	Address mark not found	0CH	Media type not found
03H	Write-protect error	10H	CRC error on read
04H	Sector not found	20H	Controller error

06H	Diskette change line active	40H	Seek failed
08H	DMA overrun	80H	Drive not ready
42H–48H	Diskette drive controller status.		

Video Control Data Area 1

49H–49H　　　Current video mode, indicated by a 1-bit:

Bit	Mode	Bit	Mode
7	Monochrome	3	80×25 color
6	640×200 monochrome	2	80×25 monochrome
5	320×200 monochrome	1	40×25 color
4	320×200 color	0	40×25 monochrome

4AH–4BH	Number of columns on screen
4CH–4DH	Size of video page buffer
4EH–4FH	Starting offset of video buffer
50H–5FH	Eight words for current starting location for each of eight pages, numbered 0–7
60H–61H	Starting and ending line of cursor
62H–62H	Currently active display page
63H–64H	Port address of active display, where monochrome is 3B4H and color is 3D4H
65H–65H	Current setting of the video mode register
66H–66H	Current color palette

System Data Area

67H–68H	Data edge time count
69H–6AH	Cyclical redundancy check (CRC) register
6BH–6BH	Last input value
6CH–6DH	Lower half of timer
6EH–6FH	Higher half of timer
70H–70H	Timer overflow (1 if gone past midnight)
71H–71H	Ctrl/Break sets bit 7 to 1
72H–73H	Memory reset flag: if contents are 1234H, Ctrl/Alt/Del causes a warm (rather than cold) reboot

Hard Disk Data Area

74H–74H	Hard disk status (details in Chapter 18)
75H–75H	Number of hard disks attached

Time-Out Data Area

78H–7BH	Time-out for parallel ports
7CH–7FH	Time-out for serial ports

Keyboard Data Area 2

80H–81H	Offset address for start of keyboard buffer
82H–83H	Offset address for end of keyboard buffer

Video Control Data Area 2

84H–8AH	Number of rows on screen (minus 1), character height, and status

Diskette/Hard Disk Data Area

8BH–95H	Controller and error status

Keyboard Data Area 3

96H–96H	Keyboard mode state and type flags

Bit	Action	Bit	Action
7	Read ID in progress	3	Right Alt pressed
6	Last character first ID	2	Right Ctrl pressed
5	Force NumLock if read ID and KBX	1	Last code was E0 hidden code
4	101/102 keyboard installed	0	Last code was E1 hidden code

97H–97H	Keyboard LED Flags

Real-Time Clock Data Area

98H–A7H	Status of wait flags

Save Pointer Data Area

A8H–ABH   Pointers to various BIOS tables

Miscellaneous Data Area 2

ACH–FFH   Reserved area
50:00H   Print screen status byte (INT 05H)

An area of interest for the PC, XT, and AT computers is at F0H, a 16-byte interapplication communication area (IAC), where a program can write information for another program to read.

INTERRUPT SERVICES

The operand of an interrupt instruction such as INT 12H identifies the type of request. For each type, the system maintains an address in the interrupt services table beginning in location 0000 (although advanced models may use different locations). Since there are 256 entries each four bytes long, the table occupies the first 1024 bytes of memory, from 00H through 3FFH. Thus bytes 0–3 contain the address for interrupt 0, bytes 4–7 for interrupt 1, and so forth.

Each address consists of a one-word offset and a one-word code segment address (IP:CS) that relate to a BIOS or DOS routine that handles a specific interrupt type. The interrupt inserts the code segment address and offset into the CS and IP registers, respectively.

An interrupt pushes on the stack the contents of the flags register, the CS, and the IP. For example, the table address of interrupt 12H (which returns the memory size in the AX register) is 0048H (12H × 4 = 48H). The operation extracts the four-byte address from location 0048H and stores two bytes in the IP and two in the CS. The address that results from the CS:IP registers is the start of a routine in the BIOS area, which now executes. The interrupt returns via an IRET (Interrupt Return) instruction, which pops the IP, CS, and flags from the stack and returns to the instruction following the interrupt.

BIOS INTERRUPTS

This section covers the BIOS interrupts 00–1FH.

INT 00H: divide by zero.   An attempt to divide by zero, which invokes the interrupt, displays a message, and usually hangs the system. Program developers are familiar with this error because destroying a segment register may accidentally cause this interrupt.

INT 01H: single step.   Used by DEBUG and other debuggers to cause single-stepping through execution.

INT 02H: nonmaskable interrupt.   Used by serious hardware conditions such as parity errors that are always enabled. Thus a program issuing a CLI instruction does not affect them.

INT 03H: break point.   Used by debugging programs to stop execution. DEBUG's Go or Proceed commands set this interrupt at the appropriate stop location in the program. DEBUG undoes single-step mode and allows the program to execute normally up to INT 03H, where DEBUG resets single-step mode.

INT 04H: overflow.   May be caused by an arithmetic operation, although usually no action takes place.

INT 05H: print screen.   Causes the contents of the screen to print. Issuing INT 05H activates it internally, and pressing the Ctrl/PrtSc keys activates it externally. The operation enables interrupts and saves the cursor position. No registers are affected. Address 50:00 in the BIOS data area contains the status of the operation.

INT 08H: timer.   A hardware interrupt that updates the system time and (if necessary) date. A programmable timer chip generates an interrupt every 54.9254 milliseconds, about 18.2 times a second.

INT 09H: keyboard interrupt.   Caused by pressing or releasing a key on the keyboard, described in detail in Chapter 10.

INT 0DH: video control.   Generated during CRT vertical retraces, for video control.

INT 0EH: diskette control.   Signals diskette attention, such as completion of an operation.

INT 0FH: printer control.   Used for control of a printer.

INT 10H: video display.   Accepts a number of service calls in the AH for screen mode, setting the cursor, scrolling, and displaying, described in detail in Chapter 9.

INT 11H: equipment determination.   Determines the optional devices on the system and returns a value to the AX. At power-up time, the system executes this operation and stores the AX in location 40:10H. See the earlier section "BIOS Data Area" for details.

INT 12H: memory size determination.   Returns in the AX the size of memory on the system board in terms of contiguous 1K bytes such that 640K memory is 0280H, as determined during power-on.

INT 13H: disk input/output.   Accepts a number of services in the AH for disk status, read sectors, write sectors, verify, format, and get diagnostics, covered in Chapter 16.

INT 14H: communications input/output.   Provides byte stream I/O to the RS232 communication port. The DX should contain the number of the RS232 adapter (0–3 for COM1, 2, 3, and 4). A number of services is established through the AH register.

Service 00: Initialize Communications Port.   Set the following parameters in the AL according to bit number:

Baud Rate	Parity	Stopbit	Word Length
7 – 5	4 – 3	2	1 – 0
000 = 110	00 = none	0 = 1	10 = 7 bits
001 = 150	01 = odd	1 = 2	11 = 8 bits
010 = 300	10 = none		
011 = 600	11 = even		
100 = 1200			
101 = 2400			
110 = 4800			
111 = 9600			

The operation returns the status of the communications port in the AX (see service 03 for details). Here's an example that sets COM1 to 1200 baud, no parity, 1 stop bit, and 8-bit data length:

```
MOV  AH,00            ;Request initialize port
MOV  AL,10000011B     ;Parameters
MOV  DX,00            ;COM1 serial port
INT  14H              ;Call BIOS
```

Service 01: Transmit Character.   Load the AL with the character that the routine is to transmit and the DX with the port number. On return, the operation sets the port status in the AH (see service 03). If the operation is unable to transmit the byte, it also sets bit 7 of the AH, although the normal purpose of this bit is to report a time-out error. Execute service 00 before using this service.

Service 02: Receive Character.   Load the port number in the DX. The operation accepts a character from the communications line into the AL. It also sets the AH with the port status (see service 03) for error bits 7, 4, 3, 2, and 1. Thus a nonzero value in the AX indicates an input error. Execute service 00 before using this service.

Service 03: Return Status of Communications Port.   Load the port number in the DX. The operation returns the line status in the AH and modem status in the AL:

AH (Line Status)	AL (Modem Status)
7 Time out	7 Received line signal detect
6 Trans shift register empty	6 Ring indicator
5 Trans hold register empty	5 Data set ready
4 Break detect	4 Clear to send
3 Framing error	3 Delta receive line signal detect
2 Parity error	2 Trailing edge ring detector
1 Overrun error	1 Delta data set ready
0 Data ready	0 Delta clear to send

Other services for PS/2s are 04 (extended initialize) and 05 (extended communications port control). Programmers, however, typically bypass BIOS altogether to handle communications.

INT 15H: system services.   This rather exotic operation provides a large number of services such as processing cassette tape (early PCs), power-on self-testing, reading system status, joystick support, determining extended memory size, and switching the processor to protected mode. For example, on 80286/386 computers, with service code 88H in the AH, the operation returns in the AX the number of K bytes of extended memory (0580H means 1408 bytes). Since the operation exits without resetting interrupts, use it like this:

```
MOV  AH,88H    ;Request extended memory
INT  15H       ;from BIOS
STI            ;Restore interrupts
```

INT 16H: keyboard input.   Accepts a number of service calls in the AH for basic keyboard input, covered in Chapter 9.

INT 17H: printer output.   Provides a number of services for printing, discussed Chapter 19.

INT 18H: ROM BASIC entry.   Called by BIOS if the system starts up with no disk containing the DOS system programs.

INT 19H: bootstrap loader.   If a disk(ette) device is available with the DOS system programs, reads track 0, sector 1, into the boot location in memory at 7C00H and transfers control to this location. If there is no disk drive, transfers to the ROM BASIC entry point via INT 18H. It is possible to use this as a software interrupt; it does not clear the screen or initialize data in ROM BIOS.

INT 1AH: read and set time.   Reads or sets the time of day according to a code in the AH:

> *00 Read clock.* Returns the high portion of the count in the CX and the low portion in the DX. If the time has passed 24 hours since the last read, the operation sets the AL to nonzero.
>
> *01 Set clock.* Load the high portion of the count in the CX and the low portion in the DX.

To determine how long a routine executes, you could set the clock to zero, then read it at the end of processing. Services 02–07 handle time and date for AT and PS/2 computers for real-time clock services.

INT 1BH: get control on keyboard break.   When Ctrl/Break keys are pressed, causes ROM BIOS to transfer control to this address, where a flag is set.

INT 1CH: get control of timer interrupt.   Called by INT 08H.

INT 1DH: pointer to video initialization table.   The interrupt address of the video controller's parameter table containing such items as number of screen columns.

INT 1EH: pointer to diskette parameter table.   The interrupt address of the diskette base table.

INT 1FH: pointer to graphics table.   In high resolution graphics mode, enables access to characters 128–255 in a 1K table containing eight bytes per character. (Graphics mode normally offers direct access only to ASCII characters 0–127.)

DOS INTERRUPTS

The two DOS modules, IBMBIO.COM and IBMDOS.COM, facilitate using BIOS. Since these modules provide much of the additional required testing, the DOS operations are generally easier to use than their BIOS counterparts and are generally more machine independent.

IBMBIO.COM provides a low-level interface to BIOS. This is an I/O handler program that facilitates reading data from external devices into memory and writing data from memory onto external devices.

IBMDOS.COM contains a file manager and a number of service functions such as blocking and deblocking disk records. When a user program requests INT 21H, the operation delivers to IBMDOS.COM information via the contents of registers. To complete the request, IBMDOS.COM may translate the information into one or more calls to IBMBIO.COM, which in turn calls BIOS. The following shows the relationship:

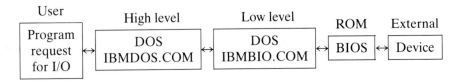

Interrupts 20H through 3FH are reserved for DOS operations, some of which reference the PSP directly according to these PSP offsets:

0AH   Terminate address (see INT 22H)
0EH   Ctrl/Break address (see INT 23H)
12H   Critical error address (see INT 24H)

Following are the DOS interrupts:

INT 20H: terminate program.   Terminates execution, restores addresses for Ctrl/Break and critical errors, flushes register buffers, and returns control to DOS. It would normally be placed in the main procedure and the CS should contain the address of the PSP on exit. The preferred termination is INT 21H service 4BH.

INT 21H: DOS service request.   The main DOS operation, which requires a service code in the AH and which is described later.

INT 22H: terminate address.   Copies the address of this interrupt in the program's PSP when DOS loads a program for execution. On program termination, DOS transfers control to the address of this interrupt location. You do not need to issue this interrupt.

INT 23H: ctrl/break address.   Designed to transfer control to a DOS routine when you press Ctrl/Break or Ctrl/C. The routine terminates program execution (or a batch file). A program could also change this address to its own routine to perform special action without program termination. You do not need to issue this interrupt.

INT 24H: critical error handler vector.   Along with the preceding two interrupts, is concerned with the addresses that DOS initializes in the PSP. When DOS recognizes a critical error (often a disk or printer operation), it uses this interrupt to transfer control. Further discussion soon gets unduly complicated and is outside the scope of this book.

INT 25H: absolute disk read.   Reads one or more disk sectors, covered in Chapter 16.

INT 26H: absolute disk write.   Writes one or more disk sectors, covered in Chapter 16.

INT 27H: terminate but stay resident.   Causes a COM program to remain in memory, covered in Chapter 22.

INT 2FH: multiplex interrupt.   Involves communications between programs, principally regarding print spoolers.

INT 33H: mouse interface.   Provides for mouse input.

DOS INT 21H SERVICES

Following are the original DOS services. You load the service in the AH register and request INT 21H.

00	Terminate program. Basically the same as INT 20H and considered obsolete.
01	Keyboard input with echo (see Chapter 10).
02	Display output (see Chapter 8).
03	Communications input. Reads a character from the serial port into the AL. Since this is a primitive service, BIOS INT 14H is preferred.
04	Communications output. Insert in the DL the character to transmit. BIOS INT 14H is preferred.
05	Printer output (see Chapter 19).
06	Direct keyboard and display (see Chapter 10).
07	Direct keyboard input without echo (see Chapter 10).
08	Keyboard input without echo (see Chapter 10).
09	Display string (see Chapter 8).
0A	Buffered keyboard input (see Chapter 10).
0B	Check keyboard status (see Chapter 10).
0C	Clear keyboard buffer and invoke input (see Chapter 10).

0D	Reset disk (see Chapter 16).
0E	Select current disk drive (see Chapter 16).
0F	Open FCB file (see Chapter 16).
10	Close FCB file (see Chapter 16).
11	Search for first matching disk entry (see Chapter 16).
12	Search for next matching disk entry (see Chapter 16).
13	Delete FCB file (see Chapter 16).
14	Read FCB sequential record (see Chapter 16).
15	Write FCB sequential record (see Chapter 16).
16	Create FCB file (see Chapter 16).
17	Rename FCB file (see Chapter 16).
19	Determine default disk drive (see Chapter 16).
1A	Set disk transfer area (see Chapter 16).
1B	Get FAT information for current drive (see Chapter 16).
1C	Get FAT information for specific drive (see Chapter 16).
21	Read FCB random record (see Chapter 16).
22	Write FCB random record (see Chapter 16).
23	Get FCB file size (see Chapter 16).
24	Set random FCB record field (see Chapter 16).
25	Set interrupt table address (see Chapter 22).
26	Create new program segment prefix. Use is not recommended.
27	Read random disk block (see Chapter 16).
28	Write random disk block (see Chapter 16).
29	Parse filename (see Chapter 16).
2A	Get system date. Returns in binary day of week (Sunday = 0) in AL, year (1980–2099) in CX, month in DH, day in DL.
2B	Set system date. Set year (1980–2099) in CX, month in DH, and day of month in DL. On return, AL is 00H for valid or FFH for invalid.
2C	Get system time. Returns hours in CH, minutes in CL, seconds in DH, hundredths seconds in DL.
2D	Set system time. Set hour (0–23) in CH, minutes in CL, seconds in DH, and hundredths seconds in DL. On return, AL is 00H for valid or FFH for invalid.
2E	Set/reset disk verification (see Chapter 16).

DOS 2.0 introduced the following extended services:

2F	Get address of current disk transfer area (see Chapter 16 and see service 1AH for setting the address.)

30   Get version number of DOS. Returns minor number in AH and major number in AL and clears BX and CX.

31   Terminate but stay resident (see Chapter 22).

32   Get disk parameters (undocumented). Load the drive number in the DX (where 0 = default, 1 = a, etc.). The operation returns an address in the DS:BX that points to a data area containing low-level information about the data structure of the drive. In the following table, DOS 3.3 means all versions up to and including it and DOS 4.0 means all versions since:

Offset			
DOS 3.3	*DOS 4.0*	*Length*	*Contents*
00H	00H	Byte	Drive number
01H	01H	Byte	Logical unit
02H	02H	Word	Bytes per sector
04H	04H	Byte	Sectors per cluster minus 1
05H	05H	Byte	Shift count of sectors per cluster
06H	06H	Word	Number of reserved boot sectors
08H	08H	Byte	Copies of FAT
09H	09H	Word	Maximum root directory entries
0BH	0BH	Word	First data sector
0DH	0DH	Word	Highest cluster number plus 1
0FH	0FH	Byte/word	Sectors per FAT
10H	11H	Word	First directory sector
12H	13H	Dword	Address of device driver
16H	17H	Byte	Media descriptor byte
17H	18H	Byte	Access flag (0 if disk was accessed)
18H	19H	Dword	Pointer to next parameter block
1CH	1DH	Dword	Reserved

33   Get or check Ctrl/Break state. For get, load 00 in AL; for set, load 01 in AL and 00 in DL for off or 01 for on. Setting off means that DOS checks for Ctrl/Break pressed only in limited situations, such as video output.

34   Get DOS busy flag address (see Chapter 22).

35   Get interrupt table address (see Chapter 22).

36   Get free disk space (see Chapter 17).

38   Get/set country-dependent information.

39   Create subdirectory (MKDIR) (see Chapter 17).

3A   Remove subdirectory (RMDIR) (see Chapter 17).

3B   Change current directory (CHDIR) (see Chapter 17).

3C   Create file (see Chapter 17).

3D   Open file (see Chapter 17).

3E	Close file (see Chapter 17).
3F	Read from file (see Chapters 8, 17, and 19).
40	Write to file (see Chapters 8, 17, and 19).
41	Delete file from directory (see Chapter 17).
42	Move file pointer (see Chapter 17).
43	Check or change file attribute (see Chapter 17).
44	Provide I/O control for devices (see Chapter 17).
45	Duplicate a file handle (see Chapter 17).
46	Force duplicate of handle (see Chapter 17).
47	Get current directory (see Chapter 17).
48	Allocate memory block (see Chapter 22).
49	Free allocated memory block (see Chapter 22).
4A	Modify allocated memory block (see Chapter 22).
4B	Load/execute a program (see Chapter 22).
4C	Terminate program (see Chapter 3).
4D	Retrieve return code of a subprocess (see Chapter 3).
4E	Find first matching directory entry (see Chapter 17).
4F	Find next matching directory entry (see Chapter 17).
52	Get address of IBMDOS.COM (undocumented) (see Chapter 22).
54	Get verify state (see Chapter 17).
56	Rename a file (see Chapter 17).
57	Get/set file date and time (see Chapter 17).
58	Get/set memory allocation strategy (see Chapter 22).

DOS 3.0 introduced the following extended services:

59	Get extended error code (see Chapter 17).
5A	Create a unique file (see Chapter 17).
5B	Create a new file (see Chapter 17).
5C	Lock/unlock file access. For networking and multitasking environments.
62	Get address of PSP (see Chapter 22).

DOS 3.1 introduced the following extended services, in AH/AL:

4409	Check if device is local or remote (see Chapter 17).
440A	Check if handle is local or remote (see Chapter 17).
5E00	Get machine name. For use under a local area network.
5E02	Set printer setup. For use under a local area network.

5E03	Get printer setup. For use under a local area network.
5F02	Get redirection list entry. For use under a local area network.
5F03	Redirect device. For use under a local area network.
5F04	Cancel redirection. For use under a local area network.

DOS 3.2 introduced the following extended services, in AX:

440D	Provide generic IOCTL.
440E	Get drive assignment.
440F	Set next logical drive letter.

DOS 3.3 introduced the following extended services:

440C	Code page switching.
65	Get extended country information.
66	Get/set global code page.
67	Set handle count (see Chapter 22).
68	Commit file.

DOS 4.0 introduced the following extended service:

33	Get/set system values. Load function 05 in the AL. The operation returns the boot drive ID in the DL (1 = A). (Formerly Ctrl/Break check.)
6C	Extended open file. Combines services 3CH (create file), 3DH (open file), and 5BH (create unique file).

SETTING THE CTRL/BREAK ADDRESS

When a user presses the Ctrl/Break or Ctrl/C keys, the normal procedure is for the program to terminate and return to DOS. You may want your program to provide its own routine to handle this situation. The following example uses INT 21H service call 25H to set the address for Ctrl/Break in the interrupt table (INT 23H) for its own routine, C10BRK. The routine could reinitialize the program or do whatever is necessary.

```
        MOV    AH,25H        ;Request set table address
        MOV    AL,23H        ;  for interrupt 23H
        LEA    DX,C10BRK     ;New address
        INT    21H           ;Call DOS
        . . .
C10BRK:                      ;Ctrl/Break routine
        . . .
        IRET                 ;Interrupt return
```

PORTS

A port is a device that connects a processor to the external world. Through a port a processor receives a signal from an input device and sends a signal to an output device. Ports are identified by their address, in the range of 0H–3FFH, or 1024 in all. Note that these are not conventional memory addresses. It is possible to use the IN and OUT instructions to handle I/O directly at the port level:

IN transfers data from an input port to the AL if byte and AX if word. The general format is

```
IN  accum-reg,port
```

OUT transfers data to an output port from the AL if a byte and from the AX if a word. The general format is

```
OUT  port,accum-reg
```

You can specify a port address statically or dynamically:

Statically.   Use an operand from 0 through 255 directly as

```
Input    IN  AL,port#   ;Input one byte
Output   OUT port#,AX   ;Output one word
```

Dynamically.   Use the contents of the DX register, 0 through 65,535, indirectly. This method is suitable for incrementing the DX in order to process consecutive port addresses. Here is an example that uses port 60H:

```
MOV DX,60H   ;Port 60H (keyboard)
IN  AL,DX    ;Get byte
```

Following is a list of some port addresses:

020H–023H	Interrupt mask registers
040H–043H	Timer/counter
060H	Input from the keyboard
061H	Speaker (bits 0 and 1)
200H–20FH	Game controller
278H–27FH	Parallel printer adapter LPT3
2F8H–2FFH	Serial port COM2
378H–37FH	Parallel printer adapter LPT2
3B0H–3BBH	Monochrome display adapter
3BCH–3BFH	Parallel printer adapter LPT1
3C0H–3CFH	Enhanced graphics adapter

3D0H–3DFH	Color graphics adapter	
3F0H–3F7H	Disk controller	
3F8H–3FFH	Serial port COM1	

The recommended practice is to use DOS and BIOS interrupts. You may safely bypass BIOS when you access ports 21, 40–42, 60, 61, and 201. For example, on boot-up a ROM BIOS routine scans for the serial and parallel port adapters. If found, it places the serial port addresses in the BIOS data area beginning at memory location 40:00H and the parallel addresses beginning at location 40:08H. Each has space for four one-word entries. The BIOS table for a system with two serial ports and two parallel ports could look like this:

```
40:00    F803    COM1
40:02    F802    COM2
40:04    0000    unused
40:06    0000    unused
40:08    7803    LPT1
40:0A    7802    LPT2
40:0C    0000    unused
40:0E    0000    unused
```

If you use BIOS INT 17H to print a character, you insert the printer number in the DX register:

```
MOV  AH,00     ;Request print
MOV  AL,char   ;Character to print
MOV  DX,0      ;Printer 0 = LPT1
INT  17H       ;Call BIOS
```

Many programs allow for printing only via the first parallel port. If you have two printers attached, as LPT1 and LPT2, you could use the program in Figure 23-1 to reverse (toggle) their addresses in the BIOS table.

GENERATING SOUND

The PC generates sound by means of a built-in permanent magnet speaker. You can select one of two ways to drive the speaker or combine both ways: (1) Use bit 1 of port 61H to activate the Intel 8255A-5 Programmable Peripheral Interface (PPI) chip or (2) use the gating of the Intel 8353-5 Programmable Interval Timer (PIT). The clock generates a 1.19318-MHz signal. The PPI controls gate 2 at bit 0 of port 61H.

The program in Figure 23-2 generates a series of notes in ascending frequency.

```
TITLE     LPTPORT (COM)  Switch printer ports betw LPT1 & 2
BIOSDAT SEGMENT AT 40H            ;BIOS data area
        ORG     8H               ;Printer port addresses
PARLPRT DW      4 DUP(?)         ;4 words
BIOSDAT ENDS

CODESG  SEGMENT PARA 'code'
        ASSUME  DS:BIOSDAT,CS:CODESG
        ORG     100H
BEGIN:
        MOV     AX,BIOSDAT
        MOV     DS,AX

        MOV     AX,PARLPRT(0)    ;LPT1 address to AX
        MOV     BX,PARLPRT(2)    ;LPT2 address to BX
        MOV     PARLPRT(0),BX    ;Exchange addresses
        MOV     PARLPRT(2),AX    ;Exchange addresses
        RET
CODESG  ENDS
        END     BEGIN
```

Figure 23-1   Switch Printer Ports

DURTION provides the length of each note and TONE determines its frequency. The program initially accesses port 61H and saves the value that the operation delivers. A CLI instruction clears the interrupt flag to enable a constant tone. The interval timer generates a clock tick of 18.2 ticks per second that (unless you code CLI) interrupts execution of your program and causes the tone to wobble.

The contents of TONE determines its frequency; high values cause low frequencies and low values cause high frequencies. After the routine B10SPKR plays each note, it increases the frequency of TONE by means of a right shift of one bit (effectively halving its value). Since decreasing TONE in this example also reduces how long it plays, the routine also increases DURTION by means of a left shift of one bit (effectively doubling its value).

The program terminates when TONE is reduced to 0. The initial values in DURTION and TONE don't have any technical significance. You can experiment with other values and try execution without the CLI. You could also revise the program to generate notes that decrease in frequency; initialize TONE to 01 and DURTION to a high value. On each loop, increase the value in TONE, decrease the value in DURTION, and terminate when DURTION equals 0.

You could use any variation of the logic to play a sequence of notes, in order, for example, to draw a user's attention.

KEY POINTS

- ROM resides beginning at location FFFF0H. Turning on the power causes a "cold boot." The processor enters a reset state, sets all memory locations to 0, performs a parity check of memory, and sets the CS register to FFFF[0]H and the IP register to zero. The first instruction to execute therefore is at FFFF:0, or FFFF0, the entry point to BIOS.

```
TITLE     SOUND    (COM)  Produce sound from speaker
SOUNSG  SEGMENT PARA 'Code'
        ASSUME  CS:SOUNSG,DS:SOUNSG,SS:SOUNSG
        ORG     100H
BEGIN:  JMP     SHORT MAIN
; --------------------------------------------------
DURTION DW      1000                ;Length of tone
TONE    DW      256H                ;Frequency
; --------------------------------------------------
MAIN    PROC    NEAR
        IN      AL,61H              ;Get port data
        PUSH    AX                  ;  & save
        CLI                         ;Clear interrupts
        CALL    B10SPKR             ;Produce sound
        POP     AX                  ;Reset
        OUT     61H,AL              ;  port value
        STI                         ;Reset interrupts
        RET
MAIN    ENDP

B10SPKR PROC    NEAR
B20:    MOV     DX,DURTION          ;Set duration of sound
B30:
        AND     AL,11111100B        ;Clear bits 0 & 1
        OUT     61H,AL              ;Transmit to speaker
        MOV     CX,TONE             ;Set length
B40:
        LOOP    B40                 ;Time delay
        OR      AL,00000010B        ;Set bit 1 on
        OUT     61H,AL              ;Transmit to speaker
        MOV     CX,TONE             ;Set length
B50:
        LOOP    B50                 ;Time delay
        DEC     DX                  ;Reduce duration
        JNZ     B30                 ;Continue?
        SHL     DURTION,1           ;  no - increase length
        SHR     TONE,1              ;Reduce frequency
        JNZ     B20                 ;Now zero?
        RET                         ;  yes - exit
B10SPKR ENDP

SOUNSG  ENDS
        END     BEGIN
```

Figure 23-2   Generating Sound

- On boot-up, BIOS checks the various ports to identify and initialize devices that are attached. BIOS then establishes beginning at location 0 of memory an interrupt service table that contains addresses for interrupts that occur. Two operations that BIOS performs are equipment and memory size determination. If a disk containing DOS is present, BIOS accesses the first disk sector containing the bootstrap loader. This program loads DOS files IBMBIO.COM, IBMDOS.COM, and COMMAND.COM from disk into memory.
- BIOS maintains its own data area in lower memory beginning at segment address 40[0]H. Relevant data areas include serial port, parallel port, system equipment, keyboard, diskette drive, video control, hard disk, and real-time clock.
- The operand of an interrupt instruction such as INT 12H identifies the type of request. For each of the 256 possible types, the system maintains a four-byte

address in the interrupt services table at locations 0000H through 3FFH. Thus bytes 0–3 contain the address for interrupt 0, bytes 4–7 for interrupt 1, and so forth.

- BIOS interrupts range from 00H through 1FH and include divide by zero, print screen, timer, video control, diskette control, video display I/O, equipment and memory size determination, disk I/O, communications I/O, keyboard input, printer output, and bootstrap loader.

- Interrupts 20H through 3FH are reserved for DOS operations. The most important DOS interrupt is 21H, which handles such operations as keyboard input, display output, printer output, reset disk, open/close file, delete file, read/write sequential record, read/write random record, terminate but stay resident, create subdirectory, and terminate program.

- Through a port a processor receives a signal from an input device and sends a signal to an output device. Ports are identified by their address, in the range 0H–3FFH, or 1024 in all.

QUESTIONS

23-1. Distinguish between an external and an internal interrupt.

23-2. Distinguish between an NMI line and an INTR line.

23-3. (a) What is the memory location of the entry point to BIOS?
(b) On power-up, how does the system direct itself to this address?

23-4. On bootup, BIOS performs interrupts 11H, 12H, and 19H. What is their purpose?

23-5. What is the beginning location of the BIOS data area?

23-6. (a) What are the installed devices if the equipment status byte contains 01000010 01100011?
(b) What interrupt accesses this byte?

23-7. Identify the following BIOS interrupts: (a) divide by zero; (b) print screen; (c) keyboard interrupt; (d) video display; (e) disk I/O; (f) keyboard input; (g) printer output.

23-8. Identify the following DOS 21H services: (a) 05H; (b) 0AH; (c) 0FH; (d) 16H; (e) 35H; (f) 3CH; (g) 3DH; (h) 3FH; (i) 40H.

23-9. Refer to Figure 23-1 and code the instructions to reverse the addresses for COM1 and COM2.

24

OPERATORS AND DIRECTIVES

OBJECTIVE

To describe in detail the assembly language operators and directives.

INTRODUCTION

The various assembly language features at first tend to be somewhat overwhelming. But once you have become familiar with the simpler and more common features described in earlier chapters, you should find the descriptions in this chapter more easily understood and a handy reference. This chapter describes the various type specifiers, operators, and directives. The assembler manual contains a few other marginally useful features.

TYPE SPECIFIERS

Type specifiers can provide the size of a data variable or the distance of an instruction label. Type specifiers that give the *size* of a data variable are BYTE, WORD, DWORD, FWORD, QWORD, and TBYTE. Those that give the *distance* of an instruction label are NEAR, FAR, and PROC. A near address is simply the offset and is assumed to be in the current segment; a far address consists of a segment address and an offset and can be used to access another segment.

The PTR and THIS operators and the COM, EXTRN, LABEL, and PROC directives use type specifiers.

OPERATORS

An operator provides a facility for changing or analyzing operands during an assembly. Operators are divided into various categories.

Calculation operators: arithmetic, index, logical, shift, and structure field name

Macro operators: various types, covered in Chapter 20

Record operators: MASK and WIDTH, covered later in this chapter under the RECORD directive

Relational operators: one type

Segment operators: OFFSET, SEG, and segment override

Type (or attribute) operators: HIGH, LENGTH, LOW, PTR, SHORT, SIZE, THIS, and TYPE

Since a knowledge of these categories is not necessary, we'll cover the operators in alphabetic sequence.

Arithmetic Operators

These operators include the familiar arithmetic signs and perform arithmetic during an assembly. In most cases, you could perform the calculation yourself, although the advantage of using these operators is that every time you change the program and reassemble, the assembler automatically recalculates their values.

Sign	Type	Used as	Effect
+	Addition	FLD1+25	Adds 25 to address of FLD1
+	Positive	+FLD1	Treats FLD1 as positive
−	Subtraction	FLD2−FLD1	Calculates difference between two offset addresses
−	Negation	−FLD1	Reverses sign
*	Multiplication	value*3	Multiplies value by 3
/	Division	value/3	Divides value by 3
MOD	Remainder	value1 MOD value2	Delivers remainder for value1/value2

Except for addition (+) and subtraction (−), all operators must be integer constants. The following examples of integer expressions are related:

```
value1 = 13*4        ;42
value1 = value1/6    ;42/6 = 7
value1 = -value1 - 3 ;(-7) - (3) = -10
```

HIGH Operator

This operator returns the high (leftmost) byte of an expression. See also LOW operator. Here is an example:

```
EQUVAL    EQU  1234H
          . . .
          MOV  CL,HIGH EQUVAL    ;Load 12H in CL
```

INDEX Operators

For a direct memory reference, one operand of an instruction specifies the name of a defined variable, as shown by COUNTER in the instruction ADD CX,COUNTER. During execution, the processor locates the specified variable in memory by combining the offset value of the variable with the address in the data segment.

For indexed memory, an operand references a base or index register, constants, offset variables, and variables. The index operator, which uses square brackets, acts like a plus (+) sign. A typical use of indexing is to reference data items in tables. You can use the following operations to reference indexed memory:

- [constant] containing an immediate number or name in square brackets. For example, load the fifth entry of TABLEA into the CL:

```
MOV  CL,TABLEA[4]    ;Get the fifth entry from TABLEA
```

Note that TABLEA[0] is the first entry.

- Base register BX as [BX] in association with the DS segment register, and base register BP as [BP] in association with the SS segment register. For example, use the offset address in the BX (combined with the segment address in the DS register) and move the referenced item to the DX:

```
MOV  DX,[BX]    ;Base register DS:BX
```

- Index register DI as [DI] and index register SI as [SI], both in association with the DS segment register. For example, combine the address in the DS with the offset address in the SI, and move the referenced item to the AX:

```
            MOV  AX,[SI]    ;Index register DS:SI
```

- Combined index registers. For example, move the contents of the AX to the address determined by combining the DS address, the BX offset, the SI offset, plus the constant 4:

```
      MOV  [BX + SI + 4],AX    ;Base + index + constant
```

You can combine these operands in any sequence, but don't combine two base registers [BX + BP] or two index registers [DI + SI]. Only the index registers must be in square brackets. The preceding example could also be coded [BX + SI] + 4.

LENGTH Operator

The LENGTH operator returns the number of entries defined by a DUP operation. The following MOV instruction returns the length 10 to the DX:

```
      TABLEA  DW   10 DUP(?)
              . . .
              MOV  DX,LENGTH TABLEA
```

If the operand does not contain a DUP entry, the operator returns the value 01. See also the SIZE and TYPE operators.

Logical Operators

These operators perform logical operations on the bits in an expression.

Operator	Used as	Effect
AND	expression1 AND expression2	Ands the bits
OR	expression1 OR expression2	Ors the bits
XOR	expression1 XOR expression2	Exclusive Ors the bits
NOT	NOT expression1	Complements the bits

Here are two examples:

```
   MOV AL,00111100B AND 01010101B ;Load 00010100B
   MOV BL,NOT 01010101B           ;Load 10101010B
```

LOW Operator

This operator returns the low (rightmost) byte of an expression (see also HIGH operator). Here is an example:

```
EQUVAL    EQU  1234H
          . . .
          MOV  CL,LOW EQUVAL   ;Load 34H in CL
```

OFFSET Operator

The OFFSET operator returns the offset address of a variable or label (that is, the relative address within the data segment or code segment). The general format is

```
OFFSET variable or label
```

The following MOV returns the offset address of TABLEA:

```
MOV DX,OFFSET TABLEA
```

Note that LEA doesn't require OFFSET to return the same value:

```
LEA DX,TABLEA
```

MASK Operator

See RECORD Directive in the section "Directives."

PTR Operator

The PTR operator can be used on data variables and instruction labels. It uses the type specifiers BYTE, WORD, FWORD, DWORD, QWORD, or TBYTE to override the defined type (DB, DW, DF, DD, DF, or DT) for variables. It uses the type specifiers NEAR, FAR, or PROC to override implied distance of labels. Its general format is

```
type PTR expression
```

The type is the new attribute such as BYTE. The expression refers to a variable or constant. Following are examples of the PTR operator. Watch out for FLDW, where the bytes are in reverse sequence.

```
FLDB DB   22H
     DB   35H
FLDW DW   2672H                 ;Stored as 7226
     . . .
     MOV  AH,BYTE PTR FLDW      ;Move first byte (72)
     ADD  BL,BYTE PTR FLDW+1    ;Add second byte (26)
     MOV  BYTE PTR FLDW,05      ;Move 05 to first byte
```

```
MOV  AX,WORD PTR FLDB      ;Move two bytes (2235) to AX
CALL FAR PTR[BX]           ;Call far procedure
```

A feature that performs a similar function to PTR is the LABEL directive, described later.

SEG Operator

The SEG operator returns the address of the segment in which a specified variable or label is placed. Programs that combine separately assembled segments would most likely use this operator. The general format is

```
SEG  variable or label
```

The following MOV instructions return the address of the segment in which the referenced names are defined:

```
MOV  DX,SEG FLDW   ;Address of data segment
MOV  DX,SEG A20    ;Address of code segment
```

Segment Override Operator

This operator, coded as a colon (:), calculates the address of a label or variable relative to a particular segment. The general format is

```
segment:expression
```

The segment can be any of the segment registers, or a segment or group name. The expression can be a constant, an expression, or a SEG expression. These examples override the DS segment register:

```
MOV  BH,ES:10H    ;Load from ES plus offset 10H
MOV  CX,SS:[BX]   ;Load from SS plus offset in BX
```

SHL and SHR Operators

The operators SHL and SHR shift an expression during an assembly. The general formats are

```
expression SHL  count
expression SHR  count
```

In the following example, the operation shifts the bit constant three bits to the right:

```
MOV  BL,01011101B SHR 3  ;Load 00001011B
```

SHORT Operator

The purpose of the SHORT operator is to modify the NEAR attribute of a JMP destination that is within +127 and −128 bytes.

```
JMP SHORT label
```

The assembler reduces the machine code operand from two bytes to one. This feature is useful for near jumps that branch forward, since otherwise the assembler initially doesn't know the distance of the jump address and assumes a far jump.

SIZE Operator

The SIZE operator returns the product of LENGTH times TYPE and is useful only if the referenced variable contains the DUP entry. The general format is

```
SIZE variable
```

See TYPE Operator for an example.

THIS Operator

The THIS operator creates an operand with segment and offset values that are equal to that of the current location counter. The general format is

```
THIS type
```

The type specifiers can be BYTE, WORD, DWORD, FWORD, QWORD, or TBYTE for variables and NEAR, FAR, or PROC for labels. You typically use THIS with the EQU or equal-sign (=) directives. The following example defines FLDA:

```
FLDA EQU  THIS BYTE
```

The segment is the same as if you used the LABEL directive:

```
FLDA LABEL   BYTE
```

TYPE Operator

The TYPE operator returns the number of bytes according to the definition of the referenced variable. However, the operation always returns 1 for a string variable and 0 for a constant.

Definition	Number of Bytes for Numeric Variable
DB	1
DW	2
DD	4
DF	6
DQ	8
DT	10
STRUC	Number of bytes defined by STRUC
NEAR label	Hex FFFF
FAR label	Hex FFFE

The general format of TYPE is

```
TYPE variable or label
```

The following examples illustrate TYPE, LENGTH, and SIZE operators:

```
FLDB    DB   ?
TABLEA  DW   20 DUP(?)          ;Define 20 words
        . . .
        MOV  AX,TYPE FLDB       ;AX = 0001H
        MOV  AX,TYPE TABLEA     ;AX = 0002H
        MOV  CX,LENGTH TABLEA   ;CX = 000AH (10)
        MOV  DX,SIZE TABLEA     ;DX = 0014H (20)
```

Since TABLEA is defined as DW, TYPE returns 0002, LENGTH returns 000AH based on the DUP entry, and SIZE returns type times length, or 14H (20).

WIDTH Operator

See RECORD Directive in the following section.

DIRECTIVES

In this section we describe most of the assembly language directives. Chapter 5 covers in detail the directives for defining data (DB, DW, etc.) and Chapter 20 covers the directives for macro instructions; they aren't repeated here. Directives are divided into various categories.

Code labels: ALIGN, ENDP, EVEN, LABEL, and PROC
Conditional assembly: IF, ELSE, and others, covered in Chapter 20

Conditional errors: .ERR, .ERR1, and others

Data allocation: ALIGN, EQU, EVEN, LABEL, and ORG. DB, DW, DD, DF, DQ, and DT covered in Chapter 5

Listing control: .CREF, .LIST, PAGE, SUBTTL, TITLE, .XCREF, and .XLIST, covered in this chapter. .LALL, .LFCOND, .SALL, .SFCOND, .TFCOND, and .XALL, covered in Chapter 20

Macros: ENDM, EXITM, LOCAL, MACRO, and PURGE, covered in Chapter 20

Miscellaneous: COMMENT, INCLUDE, INCLUDELIB, NAME, &OUT, and .RADIX

Processor: .8086, .286, .286P, .386, .386P, .8087, .287, and .387

Repeat blocks: IRP, IRPC, and REPT, covered in Chapter 20

Segment: .ALPHA, ASSUME, DOSSEG, END, ENDS, GROUP, SEGMENT, and .SEQ

Scope: COMM, EXTRN, and PUBLIC

Simplified segment: .CODE, .CONST, .DATA, .DATA?, DOSSEG, .FARDATA, .FARDATA?, .MODEL, and .STACK

Since a knowledge of these categories is not necessary, we'll cover the directives (other than macro-related ones) in alphabetic sequence.

ALIGN Directive

MASM 5.0 introduced the ALIGN directive to force the assembler to align the next segment according to a given operand. The general format is

```
ALIGN number
```

The number must be a power of 2, such as 2, 4, 8, or 16. For the statement ALIGN 4, the assembler advances its location counter to the next address that is evenly divisible by 4. If the location counter is already at the required address, it is not advanced. The assembler fills unused bytes with 0s for data and NOPs for instructions. Note that ALIGN 2 has the same effect as EVEN.

Alignment is no advantage on the 8088 processor, which accesses only one byte at a time, but can speed up the 8086 and 80186-80486 processors.

.ALPHA Directive

This directive, placed at or near the start of a program, tells the assembler to arrange segments in alphabetic sequence. It overrides the assembler option /S (see also the .SEQ directive).

ASSUME Directive

ASSUME tells the assembler to associate segment names with the CS, DS, ES, and SS segment registers. The general format is

```
ASSUME  seg-reg:seg-name [, ... ]
```

Valid seg-reg entries are CS, DS, ES, and SS, and FS and GS on the 80386/486. Valid seg-names are those of segment registers, NOTHING, GROUPs, and a SEG expression. One ASSUME statement may assign up to four segment registers, in any sequence.

In the following ASSUME statement, CODESG, DATASG, and STACK are the names the program has used to define the segments:

```
ASSUME  CS:CODESG,DS:DATASG,SS:STACK,ES:DATASG
```

Omission of a segment reference is the same as coding NOTHING. Use of the keyword NOTHING also cancels any previous ASSUME for a specified segment register:

```
ASSUME  ES:NOTHING
```

Suppose that you do not assign the DS register or use NOTHING to cancel it. In order to reference a data item in the data segment, an instruction operand may use the segment override operator (:) to reference the DS register:

```
MOV  AX,DS:[BX]    ;Use indexed address
MOV  AX,DS:FLDW    ;Move contents of FLDW
```

Of course, the DS register must contain a valid address. The simplified segment directives automatically generate an ASSUME.

.CODE Directive

This is a simplified segment directive introduced by MASM 5.0 and TASM 1.0 to define the code segment. The general format is

```
.CODE [name]
```

All executable code must be placed in this segment. The MEDIUM and LARGE memory models permit multiple code segments, which you distinguish by means of the name operand. See also the .MODEL directive.

COMM Directive

Defining a variable as COMM gives it both the PUBLIC and EXTRN attributes. In this way, you would not have to define the variable as PUBLIC in one module and EXTRN in another. The general format is

```
COMM [NEAR/FAR] label:size[:count]
```

- COMM is coded within a data segment.
- NEAR or FAR can be coded or allowed to default, although the default varies by memory model.
- Label is the name of the variable. Note that the variable cannot have an initial value.
- Size can be any of the type specifiers BYTE, WORD, DWORD, QWORD, or TBYTE.
- Count indicates the number of elements for the variable. The default is 1.

This example defines FLDCOM with the COMM attribute:

```
COMM NEAR FLDCOM:WORD
```

COMMENT Directive

This directive is useful for multiple lines of comments. The general format is

```
COMMENT delimiter [comments]
        [comments]
delimiter [comments]
```

The delimiter is the first nonblank character, such as * or + , following COMMENT. The comments terminate on the line on which the second delimiter appears. This example uses an asterisk as a delimiter:

```
COMMENT  *  This routine scans
            the input stream
            for invalid
         *  characters.
```

.CONST Directive

This is a simplified segment directive introduced by MASM 5.0 to define a data (or constant-data) segment with the 'const' class (see also the .MODEL directive).

.CREF Directive

This directive (the default) tells the assembler to generate a cross-reference table. It would be used following a .XCREF directive that caused suppression of the table.

.DATA and .DATA? Directives

These are a simplified segment directives introduced by MASM 5.0 to define data segments. .DATA defines an initialized near data segment and .DATA? defines an uninitialized near data segment, usually used when linking to a high-level language. For a stand-alone assembly program, you may also define uninitialized near data in a .DATA segment (see also the .FARDATA and .MODEL directives).

DOSSEG Directive

You may use a number of ways to control the sequence in which the assembler arranges segments. (Some IBM versions arrange them alphabetically.) You may code the .SEQ or .ALPHA directives at the start of a program, or you can enter the /S or /A assembler options at assembly time. The DOSSEG directive tells the assembler to ignore all other requests and to adopt the DOS segment sequence, basically code, data, and stack. Code this directive at or near the start of the program.

END Directive

The END directive is placed at the end of a source program. The general format is

```
END [start-address]
```

The optional start-address indicates the location in the code segment (usually, the first instruction) where execution is to begin. The system loader uses this address to initialize the CS register. If your program consists of only one module, define a start-address. If it consists of a number of modules, only one has a start-address.

ENDP Directive

This directive indicates the end of a procedure. The general format is

```
label ENDP
```

The label is the same as the one that defines the procedure.

ENDS Directive

This directive indicates the end of a segment or structure. The general format is

```
label ENDS
```

The label is the same as the one that defines the segment or structure.

EQU Directive

The EQU directive is used to redefine a data name or variable with another data name, variable, or immediate value. The directive should be defined in a program before it is referenced. The formats for numeric and string equates differ:

Numeric equate	name EQU expression
String equate	name EQU ⟨string⟩

The assembler replaces each occurrence of the name with the operand. Since an equate is used for simple replacement, it uses no additional storage in the object program.

Examples of numeric equates:

```
COUNTER DW     0
SUM     EQU    COUNTER   ;Another name for COUNTER
TEN     EQU    10        ;Numeric value
        . . .
        INC    SUM       ;Increment COUNTER
        ADD    SUM,TEN   ;Add 10 to COUNTER
```

Examples of string equates:

```
PRODMSG EQU    ('Enter product number:')
BYPTR   EQU    (BYTE PTR)
        . . .
MESSGE1 DB     PRODMSG            ;Replace with string
        . . .
        MOV    SAVE,BYPTR [BX]    ;Replace with string
```

The angle brackets were introduced by MASM 5.0 so that you may clearly indicate a string operand.

.ERR Directives

These conditional error directives can be used for debugging and testing for errors during an assembly.

Directive	*Error Forced*
.ERR	When encountered
.ERR1	During pass 1 of an assembly
.ERR2	During pass 2 of an assembly
.ERRE	By true (0) expression
.ERRNZ	By false (not 0) expression
.ERRDEF	By defined symbol
.ERRNDEF	By not defined symbol
.ERRB	By blank string
.ERRNB	By not blank string
.ERRIDN[I]	By identical strings
.ERRDIF[I]	By different strings

You could use these in macros and in conditional assembly statements. In the following conditional assembly statements, the assembler displays a message if the condition is not true:

```
IF      condition
        . . .
ELSE    .ERR
        %OUT[message]
ENDIF
```

EVEN Directive

EVEN tells the assembler to advance its location counter if necessary so that the next defined data item or instruction is aligned on an even storage boundary. This feature makes processing more efficient on processors that access 16 or 32 bits at a time (see also the ALIGN directive).

In the following example, BYTELOCN is a one-byte field on an even boundary. The assembler's location counter is now at 0017. EVEN causes the assembler to advance the location counter one byte to 0018:

```
0016    BYTELOCN DB   ?
0017             EVEN       (advances location counter)
[0017            NOP]
0018    WORDLOCN DW   ?
```

EXTRN Directive

The EXTRN directive informs the assembler and linker of data variables and labels that this assembly references but that another module (linked to this one) defines. The general format is

```
EXTRN   name:type[, . . . ]
```

The name entry is an item defined in another assembly and declared in it as PUBLIC. The type specifier can refer to

- Data items: ABS (a constant), BYTE, WORD, DWORD, FWORD, QWORD, TBYTE. Code the EXTRN in the segment where the item occurs.
- Distance: NEAR or FAR. Code NEAR in the segment where the item occurs and code FAR anywhere.

In the next example, the calling program defines CONVAL as PUBLIC and as a DW. The called subprogram identifies CONVAL (in another segment) as EXTRN and FAR.

Calling program:

```
DSEG1     SEGMENT
          PUBLIC      CONVAL
          . . .
CONVAL    DW          ?
          . . .
DSEG1     ENDS
```

Called subprogram:

```
          EXTRN       CONVAL:FAR
DSEG2     SEGMENT
          . . .
          MOV         AX,CONVAL
          . . .
DSEG2     ENDS
```

In Chapter 21 we give examples of EXTRN.

.FARDATA and .FARDATA? Directives

These are simplified segment directives introduced by MASM 5.0 to define data segments. .FARDATA defines an initialized far data segment and .FARDATA? defines an uninitialized far data segment. For a stand-alone assembly program, you may also define uninitialized far data in a .FARDATA segment (see also the .DATA and .MODEL directives).

GROUP Directive

A program may contain several segments of the same type (code, data, stack). The purpose of the GROUP directive is to collect them under one name so that they reside within one segment, usually a data segment. The general format is

```
name GROUP seg-name [, ... ]
```

The following GROUP combines SEG1 and SEG2 in the same assembly module:

```
GROUPX      GROUP       SEG1, SEG2
SEG1        SEGMENT     PARA 'Data'
            ASSUME      DS:GROUPX
             . . .
SEG1        ENDS
;
SEG2        SEGMENT     PARA 'Data'
            ASSUME      DS:GROUPX
             . . .
SEG2        ENDS
```

The effect of using GROUP is similar to giving the segments the same name and the PUBLIC attribute.

INCLUDE Directive

You may have sections of assembly code or macro instructions that various programs use. You can store these in separate disk files available for use by any program. Consider a routine that converts ASCII code to binary is stored on drive C in a file named CONVERT.LIB. To access the file, insert an INCLUDE statement such as

```
INCLUDE C:CONVERT.LIB
```

at the location in the source program where you would normally code the ASCII conversion routine. The assembler locates the file on disk and includes the statements in with your own program. (If the assembler cannot find the file, it issues an error message and ignores the INCLUDE.)

For each line included, the assembler prints a C in column 30 of the LST file and begins the source code in column 33.

In Chapter 20 we give a practical example of INCLUDE and explain how to include only for pass 1 of an assembly.

LABEL Directive

The LABEL directive enables you to redefine the attribute of a data variable or instruction label. The general format is

```
name LABEL type-specifier
```

For labels, you can use LABEL to redefine executable code as NEAR, FAR, or PROC, such as for a secondary entry point to a procedure. For variables, you can use the type specifiers BYTE, WORD, DWORD, FWORD, QWORD, TBYTE, or structure name to redefine data items and the names of structures. LABEL enables you, for example, to define a field as both DB and DW. The following illustrates the use of BYTE and WORD types:

```
REDEFB  LABEL  BYTE
FIELDW  DW     2532H
REDEFW  LABEL  WORD
FIELDB  DB     25H
        DB     32H
        . . .
        MOV    AL,REDEFB    ;Move 1st byte
        MOV    BX,REDEFW    ;Move 2 bytes
```

The first MOV instruction moves only the first byte of FIELDW. The second MOV moves the two bytes beginning at FIELDB. The PTR operator performs a similar function.

.LIST Directive

The .LIST directive (the default) causes the assembler to list the source program. You may use the .XLIST directive anywhere in an assembly source program to discontinue listing it. A typical situation is where statements are common to other programs and you don't need another listing. .LIST resumes the listing. Code these with no operand.

.MODEL Directive

This directive, introduced by MASM 5.0, is one of the simplified segment directives. It creates default segments and the required ASSUME and GROUP statements. The general format is

```
.MODEL  memory-model
```

The memory models are

SMALL	All data in one segment and all code in one segment.
MEDIUM	All data in one segment but code in more than one segment.
COMPACT	Data in more than one segment but code in one segment.
LARGE	Both data and code in more than one segment but no array may exceed 64K.
HUGE	Both data and code in more than one segment and arrays may exceed 64K.

The .STACK directive defines the stack, .CODE defines the code segment, and any or all of .DATA, .DATA?, .FARDATA, and .FARDATA? may define data segments. Here is an example:

```
.MODEL  SMALL
.STACK  120
.DATA
        [data items]
.CODE
        [instructions]
END
```

ORG Directive

The assembler uses a location counter to account for its relative position in a data or code segment. Consider a data segment with the following definitions:

Offset	Name	Operation	Operand	Location Counter
00	FLDA	DW	2542H	02
02	FLDB	DB	36H	03
03	FLDC	DW	212EH	05
05	FLDD	DD	00000705H	09

Initially, the location counter is set to 00. Since FLDA is two bytes, the location counter is incremented to 02 for the location of the next item. Since FLDB is one byte, the location counter is incremented to 03, and so forth. You can use the ORG directive to change the contents of the location counter and accordingly the location of the next defined items. The general format is

```
        ORG  expression
```

The expression may be an absolute number, not a symbolic name, and must form a two-byte absolute number. Consider the following data items to be defined immediately after FLDD in the previous definition:

Offset	Name	Operation	Operand	Location Counter
		ORG	0	00
00	FLDX	DB	?	01
01	FLDY	DW	?	02
03	FLDZ	DB	?	04
		ORG	$ + 5	09

The first ORG resets the location counter to 00. The variables that follow, FLDX, FLDY, and FLDZ, define the same memory locations as FLDA, FLDB, and FLDC, respectively:

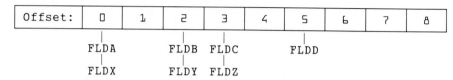

An operand containing a dollar symbol ($) as in the second ORG previously given refers to the current value in the location counter. The operand $ + 5 therefore sets the location counter to 04 + 5, or 09, which is the same setting after the definition of FLDD.

A reference to FLDC is to a one-word field at offset 03, and a reference to FLDZ is to a one-byte field at offset 03:

```
MOV  AX,FLDC    ;One word
MOV  AL,FLDZ    ;One byte
```

You can use this ORG feature to redefine memory locations. But be sure that ORG resets the location counter to the correct value and that you account for all redefined memory locations. Also, the redefined variables should not contain defined constants—these would overlay constants on top of the original constants. ORG cannot appear within a STRUC definition.

%OUT Directive

This directive tells the assembler to direct a message to the standard output device (usually the printer). The general format is

```
%OUT  message
```

The .ERR directives section gives an example.

PAGE Directive

The PAGE directive at the start of a source program specifies the maximum number of lines to list on a page and the maximum number of characters on a line. Its general format is

```
PAGE [[length],width]
```

The following example sets 60 lines per page and 132 characters per line:

```
PAGE  60,132
```

Lines per page may range from 10 to 255, and characters per line may range from 60 to 132. Omission of a PAGE statement causes the assembler to assume PAGE 50,80. You may also force a page to eject at a specific line, such as at the end of a segment. At the required line, code PAGE with no operand.

PROC Directive

A procedure is a block of code that begins with the PROC directive and terminates with ENDP. A typical use is for a subroutine within the code segment. Although technically you can enter a procedure in-line or by a JMP instruction, the normal practice is to use CALL to enter and RET to exit. The CALL operand may be a NEAR or FAR type specifier, and RET assumes the same type.

A procedure that is in the same segment as the calling procedure is a NEAR procedure and is accessed by an offset:

```
proc-name PROC [NEAR]
```

An omitted operand defaults to NEAR. If a called procedure is external to the calling segment, it must be declared as PUBLIC and you should use CALL to enter it.

For an EXE program, the main PROC that is the entry point for execution must be FAR. Also, a called procedure under a different ASSUME CS value must have the FAR attribute:

```
            PUBLIC   proc-name
proc-name   PROC     FAR
```

A far label may be in another segment, which CALL accesses by a segment address and offset.

Processor Directives

These directives define the processors that the assembler is to recognize. The normal placement for these directives is at the start of a source program, although you could code them inside a program where you want a processor enabled or disabled. A reference to the 8086 includes the 8088.

Directive	Enables Instructions for Processors
.8086	8086 and 8087 coprocessor
.186	8086, 8087, and 80186 additional instructions
.286	8086, 80287 coprocessor, and 80286 additional instructions
.286P	All of .286 plus the 80286 privileged instructions
.386	8086, 80387 coprocessor, and 80386 additional instructions

Directive	*Enables Instructions for Processors*
.386P	All of .386 plus the 80386 privileged instructions
.8087	8087 coprocessor (and prevents assembly of instructions unique to the 80287 and 80387)
.287	80287 coprocessor
.387	80387 coprocessor

PUBLIC Directive

The purpose of the PUBLIC directive is to inform the assembler and linker that the identified symbols in an assembly are to be referenced by other modules linked with this one. The general format is

```
PUBLIC symbol[, ...]
```

The symbol can be a label, a number (up to two bytes), or a variable. See EXTRN earlier and Chapter 20 for examples.

RECORD Directive

The RECORD directive enables you to define patterns of bits. One purpose is to define switch indicators either as one bit or as multibit. The general format is

```
record-name RECORD field-name:width[=exp] [, ... ]
```

Record name and field names may be any unique valid identifiers. Following each field name is a colon (:) and a "width"—the number of bits. The range of the width entry is 1 to 16 bits:

Number of Defined Bits	*Default Size*
1–8	8
9–16	16

Any length up to 8 becomes 8 bits, and 9 to 16 becomes 16, right-adjusted if necessary. The following example defines RECORD:

```
BITREC  RECORD  BIT1:3,BIT2:7,BIT3:6
```

BIT1 defines the first 3 bits of BITREC, BIT2 defines the next 7, and BIT3 defines the last 6. The total is 16 bits, or one word. You can initialize values in RECORD as follows:

```
BITREC2 RECORD  BIT1:3=101B,BIT2:7=0110110B,BIT3:6=011010B
```

Suppose that a definition of RECORD is at the front of the data segment. Within the data segment there should be another statement that allocates storage for the record. Define a unique valid name, the record name, and an operand consisting of angle brackets (the "less than," "greater than" symbols):

```
DEFBITS BITREC ()
```

The allocation above generates object code AD9AH (stored as 9AAD) in the data segment. The angle brackets may also contain entries that redefine BITREC.

The program in Figure 24-1 defines BITREC as RECORD, but without initial values in the record fields. In this case, an allocation statement in the data segment initializes each field as shown within angle brackets.

Record-specific operators are WIDTH, shift count, and MASK. The use of these operators permits you to change a RECORD definition without having to change the instructions that reference it.

WIDTH operator.   The WIDTH operator returns a width as the number of bits in a RECORD or in a RECORD field. For example, in Figure 24-1 following A10 are two examples of WIDTH. The first MOV returns the width of the entire RECORD BITREC (16 bits); the second MOV returns the width of the record field BIT2 (7 bits). In both cases, the assembler has generated an immediate operand for width.

Shift count.   A direct reference to a RECORD field such as

```
MOV CL,BIT2
```

does not refer to the contents of BIT2 (indeed, that would be rather difficult). Instead, the assembler generates an immediate operand that contains a "shift count" to help you isolate the field. The immediate value represents the number of bits that you would have to shift BIT2 to right-adjust it. In Figure 24-1, the three examples following B10 return the shift count for BIT1, BIT2, and BIT3.

MASK operator.   The MASK operator returns a "mask" of 1-bits representing the specified field, and in effect defines the bit positions that the field occupies. For example, the MASK for each of the fields defined in BITREC is:

Field	Binary	Hex
BIT1	1110000000000000	E000
BIT2	0001111111000000	1FC0
BIT3	0000000000111111	003F

In Figure 24-1, the three instructions following C10 return the MASK values for BIT1, BIT2, and BIT3. The instructions following D10 and E10 isolate BIT2

```
                    TITLE   TRECORD (COM)  Test of RECORD Directive
0000                CODESG  SEGMENT PARA 'Code'
                    ASSUME  CS:CODESG,DS:CODESG,SS:CODESG
0100                ORG     100H
0100 EB 02    BEGIN:  JMP     SHORT MAIN
              ; --------------------------------------------------------
              BITREC  RECORD  BIT1:3,BIT2:7,BIT3:6   ;Define record
0102 AD9A     DEFBITS BITREC  <101B,0110110B,011010B> ;Init. record
              ; --------------------------------------------------------
0104          MAIN    PROC    NEAR
0104          A10:                                    ;Width:
0104 B7 10            MOV     BH,WIDTH BITREC         ;  of record (16)
0106 B0 07            MOV     AL,WIDTH BIT2           ;  of field  (07)
0108          B10:                                    ;Shift count:
0108 B1 0D            MOV     CL,BIT1                 ;  hex 0D
010A B1 06            MOV     CL,BIT2                 ;      06
010C B1 00            MOV     CL,BIT3                 ;      00
010E          C10:                                    ;Mask:
010E B8 E000          MOV     AX,MASK BIT1            ;  hex E000
0111 BB 1FC0          MOV     BX,MASK BIT2            ;      1FC0
0114 B9 003F          MOV     CX,MASK BIT3            ;      003F
0117          D10:                                    ;Isolate BIT2:
0117 A1 0102 R        MOV     AX,DEFBITS              ;  get record
011A 25 1FC0          AND     AX,MASK BIT2            ;  clear BIT1 & 3
011D B1 06            MOV     CL,BIT2                 ;  get shift 06
011F D3 E8            SHR     AX,CL                   ;  shift right
0121          E10:                                    ;Isolate BIT1:
0121 A1 0102 R        MOV     AX,DEFBITS              ;  get record
0124 B1 0D            MOV     CL,BIT1                 ;  get shift 13
0126 D3 E8            SHR     AX,CL                   ;  shift right
0128 B4 4C            MOV     AH,4CH                  ;Exit
012A CD 21            INT     21H
012C          MAIN    ENDP
012C          CODESG  ENDS
                      END     BEGIN
```

Structures and Records:

N a m e	Width	# fields		
	Shift	Width	Mask	Initial
BITREC	0010	0003		
BIT1	000D	0003	E000	0000
BIT2	0006	0007	1FC0	0000
BIT3	0000	0006	003F	0000

Segments and Groups:

N a m e	Length	Align	Combine	Class
CODESG	012C	PARA	NONE	'CODE'

Symbols:

N a m e	Type	Value	Attr	
A10	L NEAR	0104	CODESG	
B10	L NEAR	0108	CODESG	
BEGIN	L NEAR	0100	CODESG	
BIT1	000D			
BIT2	0006			
BIT3	0000			
C10	L NEAR	010E	CODESG	
D10	L NEAR	0117	CODESG	
DEFBITS	L WORD	0102	CODESG	
E10	L NEAR	0121	CODESG	
MAIN	N PROC	0104	CODESG	Length=0028

Figure 24-1 Use of RECORD Directive

and BIT1 from BITREC, respectively. D10 gets the record into the AX register and uses a MASK of BIT2 to AND it:

```
Record:          101 0110110 011010
AND MASK BIT2:   000 1111111 000000
Result:          000 0110110 000000
```

The effect is to clear all bits except those of BIT2. The next two instructions cause the AX to shift 6 bits so that BIT2 is right-adjusted:

```
                    0000000000110110  (0036H)
```

The example following E10 gets the record into the AX, and because BIT1 is the leftmost field, the routine simply uses its shift factor to shift right 13 bits:

```
                    0000000000000101  (0005H)
```

SEGMENT Directive

An assembly module consists of one or more segments, part of a segment, or even parts of several segments. The general format for a segment is

```
seg-name SEGMENT [align] [combine] ['class']
...
seg-nameENDS
```

All operands are optional. The following describes the entries for align, combine, and class:

Align.   The align operand indicates the starting boundary for a segment:

BYTE	Next address
WORD	Next even address (divisible by 2)
DWORD	Next doubleword address (divisible by 4)
PARA	Next paragraph (divisible by 10H)
PAGE	Next page address (divisible by 100H)

PARA is commonly used for all types of segments. BYTE and WORD can be used for segments that are to be combined within another segment, usually a data segment. DWORD is normally used with the 80386 processor.

Combine.   The combine operands NONE, PUBLIC, STACK, and COMMON indicate the way the linker is to handle a segment:

NONE (default). The segment is to be logically separate from other segments, although it may end up to be physically adjacent. The segment is presumed to have its own base address.

PUBLIC. LINK loads PUBLIC segments of the same name and class adjacent to one another segment. One base address is presumed for all such PUBLIC segments.

STACK. LINK treats STACK the same as PUBLIC. There must be at least one STACK defined in a linked EXE program. If there is more than one, the stack pointer (SP) is set to the start of the first stack.

COMMON. If COMMON segments have the same name and class, the linker gives them the same base address. For execution, the second segment overlays the first one. The largest segment determines the length of the common area.

AT paragraph address. The paragraph must be defined previously. The entry facilitates defining labels and variables at fixed offsets within fixed areas of memory, such as the interrupt table in low memory or the BIOS data area at 40[0]H. For example, the code in ROM defines the location of the video display buffer as:

```
VIDEO-RAM  SEGMENT  AT  0B800H
```

The assembler creates a dummy segment that provides in effect an image of memory locations.

'class'.   The class entry can help the linker associate segments with different names, identify segments, and control their order. Class may contain any legal name, contained in single quotes. The linker uses it to relate segments that have the same name and class. Typical examples are 'Data' and 'Code'. If you define a class as 'Code', the linker expects it to contain instruction code. Also, the CODEVIEW debugger expects this class for the code segment.

The linker combines the following two segments with the same name (CSEG) and class ('Code') into one physical segment under the same segment register:

```
          _____
Assembly    CSEG    SEGMENT PARA PUBLIC 'Code'
module 1            ASSUME  CS:CSEG
                      . . .
            CSEG    ENDS
          _____
Assembly    CSEG    SEGMENT PARA PUBLIC 'Code'
module 2            ASSUME  CS:CSEG
                      . . .
            CSEG    ENDS
```

Since you may want to control the ordering of segments within a program, it is useful to understand how the linker handles it. The original order of the segment names provides the basic sequence, which you may override by means of the PUBLIC attribute and class names. Here's an example that links two object modules. Both modules contain a segment named DSEG1 with the PUBLIC attribute and identical class names:

Before linking the OBJ modules:

```
module 1   SSEG   SEGMENT   PARA STACK
module 1   DSEG1  SEGMENT   PARA PUBLIC 'Data'
module 1   DSEG2  SEGMENT   PARA
module 1   CSEG   SEGMENT   PARA 'Code'
module 2   DSEG1  SEGMENT   PARA PUBLIC 'Data'
module 2   DSEG2  SEGMENT   PARA
module 2   CSEG   SEGMENT   PARA 'Code'
```

After linking into one EXE module:

```
module 1     CSEG   SEGMENT   PARA 'Code'
module 2     CSEG   SEGMENT   PARA 'Code'
module 1+2   DSEG1  SEGMENT   PARA PUBLIC 'Data'
module 1     DSEG2  SEGMENT   PARA
module 2     DSEG2  SEGMENT   PARA
module 1     SSEG   SEGMENT   PARA STACK
```

You may nest segments provided that a nested segment is completely contained within the other. In the following example, SEG2 is completely contained within SEG1:

```
┌───SEG1    SEGMENT
│          . . .        SEG1 begins
│  ┌─SEG2    SEGMENT
│  │       . . .        SEG2 area
│  └─SEG2    ENDS
│          . . .        SEG1 resumes
└───SEG1    ENDS
```

The .ALPHA, .SEQ, DOSSEG directives and the assembler options /A and /S can also control segment order. For combining segments into groups, see the GROUP directive.

.SEQ Directive

This directive (the default), placed at or near the start of a program, tells the assembler to leave segments in their original sequence. It overrides the assembler option /A (see also the .ALPHA directive).

.STACK Directive

This is a simplified segment directive introduced by MASM 5.0 to define the stack. The general format is

```
.STACK [size]
```

The default stack size is 1024 bytes, which you may override (see also the .MODEL directive).

STRUC Directive

The STRUC directive facilitates defining related fields within a structure. Its general format is

```
struc-name    STRUC
              . . .
              [defined fields]
              . . .
struc-name    ENDS
```

A structure begins with its name and the directive STRUC and terminates with the structure name and the directive ENDS. The assembler stores the contained defined fields one after the other from the start of the structure. Valid entries are DB, DW, DD, DQ, and DT definitions with optional field names.

In Figure 24-2, STRUC defines a parameter list named PARLIST for input of a name from the keyboard. A subsequent statement allocates storage for the structure:

```
PARAMS PARLIST ()
```

The allocate statement makes the structure addressable within the program. The angle brackets (less than, greater than symbols) in the operand are empty in this example, but you may use them to redefine (override) data within a structure.

Instructions may reference a structure name directly. To reference fields within a structure, instructions must qualify them by using the allocate name of the structure (PARAMS in the example) followed by a period that connects it with the field name, as

```
MOV  AL,PARAMS.ACTLEN
```

You can use the allocate statement to redefine the contents of fields within a structure.

```
                           page 60,132
                   TITLE   DSTRUC  (COM)  Defining a structure
0000               CODESG  SEGMENT PARA 'Code'
                           ASSUME  CS:CODESG,DS:CODESG,SS:CODESG
0100                       ORG     100H
0100 EB 29         BEGIN:  JMP     SHORT MAIN
                   ; ---------------------------------------------
                   PARLIST STRUC                   ;Parameter list
0000 19            MAXLEN  DB      25              ;
0001 00            ACTLEN  DB      ?               ;
0002 0019[20]      NAMEIN  DB      25 DUP(' ')     ;
001B               PARLIST ENDS                    ;

0102  19           PARAMS  PARLIST <>              ;Allocate structure
0103  00
0104  0019[20]

011D 57 68 61 74 20 69  PROMPT  DB      'What is name?', '$'
     73 20 6E 61 6D 65
     3F 24
                   ; ---------------------------------------------
012B               MAIN    PROC    NEAR
012B B4 09                 MOV     AH,09           ;Display prompt
012D 8D 16 011D R          LEA     DX,PROMPT
0131 CD 21                 INT     21H
0133 B4 0A                 MOV     AH,0AH          ;Accept input
0135 8D 16 0102 R          LEA     DX,PARAMS
0139 CD 21                 INT     21H
013B A0 0103 R             MOV     AL,PARAMS.ACTLEN ;Length of
                   ;       ...                     ; input
013E B4 4C                 MOV     AH,4CH          ;Exit
0140 CD 21                 INT     21H
0142               MAIN    ENDP
0142               CODESG  ENDS
                           END     BEGIN
```

```
Structures and Records:
          N a m e          Width    # fields
                           Shift   Width   Mask    Initial
PARLIST . . . . . . . . . .001B    0003
 MAXLEN . . . . . . . . . .0000
 ACTLEN . . . . . . . . . .0001
 NAMEIN . . . . . . . . . .0002

Segments and Groups:
          N a m e          Length  Align  Combine Class
CODESG . . . . . . . . . . 0142    PARA   NONE    'CODE'
Symbols:
          N a m e          Type    Value   Attr
BEGIN . . . . . . . . . . L NEAR   0100    CODESG
MAIN . . . . . . . . . . . N PROC  012B    CODESG   Length = 0017
PARAMS . . . . . . . . . . L 0102          CODESG
PROMPT . . . . . . . . . . L BYTE  011D    CODESG
BIT2 . . . . . . . . . . . 0006
BIT3 . . . . . . . . . . . 0000
C10 . . . . . . . . . . . L NEAR   010E    CODESG
D10 . . . . . . . . . . . L NEAR   0117    CODESG
DEFBITS . . . . . . . . . L WORD   0102    CODESG
E10 . . . . . . . . . . . L NEAR   0121    CODESG
MAIN . . . . . . . . . . . N PROC  0104    CODESG Length=0028
```

Figure 24-2   Example of a Structure

SUBTTL Directive

The SUBTTL directive causes a subtitle up to 60 characters to print on line 3 of each page of a source listing. You may code SUBTTL any number of times. The general format is

```
SUBTTL text
```

TITLE Directive

The TITLE directive causes a title up to 60 characters to print on line 2 of each page of a source listing. You may code TITLE once, at the start. The general format is

```
TITLE text
```

.XCREF Directive

This directive tells the assembler to suppress the cross-reference table. The general format is

```
.XCREF [name [,name] ...]
```

Omitting the operand causes suppression of all entries in the table. You can also suppress the cross-reference of specified items. Here are examples of .XCREF and .CREF:

```
.XCREF                  ;Suppress cross-reference
...
.CREF                   ;Restore cross-reference
...
.XREF FIELDA,FIELDB     ;Suppress cross-reference of FIELDA and
                         FIELDB.
```

.XLIST Directive

You may use the .XLIST directive anywhere in a source program to discontinue printing an assembled program. A typical situation would be where the statements are common to other programs and you don't need another listing. The .LIST directive (the default) resumes the listing. Code these with no operand.

25

INSTRUCTION REFERENCE

OBJECTIVE

To explain machine code and to provide a description of the instruction set.

INTRODUCTION

In this chapter we explain machine code and provide a list of symbolic instructions with an explanation of their purpose.

Many instructions have a specific purpose so that a one-byte instruction code is adequate. The following are examples:

```
Object      Symbolic
 code      instruction              Comment
  40        INC AX        ;Increment AX
  50        PUSH AX       ;Push AX
  C3        RET (short)   ;Short return from procedure
  CB        RET (far)     ;Far return from procedure
  FD        STD           ;Set direction flag
```

None of these instructions makes a direct reference to memory. Instructions that specify an immediate operand, an 8-bit register, two registers, or a reference to memory require more complex machine code.

REGISTER NOTATION

Instructions that reference a register may contain three bits that indicate the particular register and a "w" bit that indicates whether the "width" is byte or word. Also, only certain instructions may access segment registers. Figure 25-1 shows the complete register notations.

Here's the symbolic and machine code for a MOV instruction with a one-byte immediate operand:

```
MOV  AH,00    10110 100 00000000
               |   |||
               w  reg = AH
```

In this case, the first byte of machine code indicates a width of one byte (w = 0) and refers to the AH register (100). Here's a MOV instruction that contains a one-word immediate operand:

```
MOV  AX,00    10111 000 00000000 00000000
               |   |||
               w  reg = AX
```

The first byte of machine code indicates a width of one word (w = 1) and refers to the AX register (000). For other instructions, w and reg may occupy different positions.

ADDRESSING MODE BYTE

The mode byte, where it exists, occupies the second byte of machine code and consists of the following three elements:

mod   A 2-bit mode, where 11 refers to a register and 00, 01, and 10 refer to a memory location

```
General, Base, and Index Registers:
   Bits        w = 0         w = 1
   000          AL            AX
   001          CL            CX
   010          DL            DX
   011          BL            BX
   100          AH            SP
   101          CH            BP
   110          DH            SI
   111          BH            DI

Bits for segment register:
        00          ES
        01          CS
        10          SS
        11          DS
```

Figure 25-1 Register Notation

reg   A 3-bit reference to a register

r/m   A 3-bit reference to a register or memory, where r indicates which register and m indicates a memory address

Also, the first byte of machine code may contain a "d" bit that indicates the direction of flow. For d = 1, the register is the source and for d = 2, the register is the destination. Here's an example of adding the AX to the BX:

```
ADD BX,AX    00000011   11 011 000
                        dw mod reg r/m
```

In this example, d = 1 means that mod (11) and reg (011) describe operand 1 and r/m (000) describes operand 2. Since w = 1, the width is a word. Therefore, the instruction is to add the AX (000) to the BX (011).

The second byte of the object instruction indicates most modes of addressing memory. In the next section we examine the addressing mode in more detail.

Mod Bits

The two mod bits distinguish between addressing of registers and memory. The following explains their purpose:

00   r/m bits give the exact addressing option; there is no offset byte.

01   r/m bits give the exact addressing option; there is one offset byte.

10   r/m bits give the exact addressing option; there are two offset bytes.

11   r/m specifies a register. The "w" bit (in the operation code byte) determines whether a reference is to an 8- or 16-bit register.

Reg Bits

The three reg bits, in association with the w bit, determine the actual 8- or 16-bit register.

R/M Bits

The three r/m (register/memory) bits, in association with mod, determine the addressing mode, as shown in Figure 25-2.

r/m	mod=00	mod=01	mod=10	mod=11 w=0	mod=11 w=1
000	BX+SI	BX+SI+disp	BX+SI+disp	AL	AX
001	BX+DI	BX+DI+disp	BX+DI+disp	CL	CX
010	BP+SI	BP+SI+disp	BP+SI+disp	DL	DX
011	BP+DI	BP+DI+disp	BP+DI+disp	BL	BX
100	SI	SI+disp	SI+disp	AH	SP
101	DI	DI+disp	DI+disp	CH	BP
110	Direct	BP+disp	BP+disp	DH	SI
111	BX	BX+disp	BX+disp	BH	DI

Figure 25-2 The r/m Bits

TWO-BYTE INSTRUCTIONS

The first example of a two-byte instruction adds the AX to the BX:

```
ADD BX,AX    0000 0011   11 011 000
                         dw mod reg   r/m
```

d   1: reg plus w describe operand 1 (BX), and mod plus r/m plus w describe operand 2 (AX).

w   1: The width is word.

mod   11: Operand 2 is a register.

reg   011: Operand 1 is the BX register.

r/m   000: Operand 2 is the AX register.

The second example multiplies the AL by the BL:

```
MUL BL 11110110   11 100  011
                  w mod reg   r/m
```

The processor assumes that the multiplicand is in the AL if byte, the AX if word, and the EAX if doubleword. The width (w = 0) is byte, mod references a register, and the register is the BL (011). Reg = 100 is not meaningful here.

THREE-BYTE INSTRUCTIONS

The following MOV generates three bytes of machine code:

```
MOV mem-word,AX    10100001 dddddddd dddddddd
```

A move from the accumulator (AX or AL) needs to know only whether the operation is byte or word. In this example, w = 1 means word, and the 16-bit AX is understood. The use of AL in operand-2 would cause the w bit to be 0. Byte 2 and byte 3 contain the offset to the memory location. The use of the accumulator register is often more efficient than the use of other registers.

FOUR-BYTE INSTRUCTIONS

The first example of a four-byte instruction multiplies the AL by a memory location.

```
MUL mem-byte    11110110   00 100 110 x--x x--x
                           w mod reg   r/m
```

For this instruction, reg is always 100. Mod = 00 indicates a memory reference, and r/m = 110 means a direct reference to memory. The machine instruction also contains two following bytes that provide the offset to this memory location.

The second example illustrates the LEA instruction, which specifies a word address:

```
LEA DX,mem   10001101 00 010 110   x--x x--x
             LEA    mod reg  r/m
```

Reg = 010 designates the DX register. Mod = 00 and r/m = 110 indicate a direct reference to a memory address. Two following bytes provide the offset to this location.

INSTRUCTION SET

This section covers the instruction set in alphabetic sequence. Similar instructions are grouped together for brevity. In addition to the preceding discussion of mode byte and width bit, the following abbreviations are relevant:

addr	Address of a memory location
addr-high	Rightmost byte of an address
addr-low	Leftmost byte of an address
data	Immediate operand (8-bit if $w = 0$, 16-bit if $w = 1$)
data-high	Rightmost byte of an immediate operand
data-low	Leftmost byte of an immediate operand
disp	Displacement (offset value)
reg	Reference to a register

The 80186-486 processors support a number of specialized instructions not covered here: ARPL, BOUND, CLTS, ENTER, LAR, LEAVE, LGDT, LIDT, LLDT, LMSW, LSL, LTR, SGDT, SIDT, SLDT, SMSW, STR, VERR, and VERW. Instructions unique to the 80486 are BSWAP, XADD, CMPXCHG, INVD, WBINVD, and INVLPG, also not covered here.

AAA: ASCII Adjust for Addition

Operation. Corrects the sum of two ASCII bytes in the AL. If the rightmost four bits of the AL have a value greater than 9 or if the AF flag is set to 1, AAA adds 1 to the AH and sets the AF and CF flags. Otherwise, the AF and CF are cleared. AAA always clears the leftmost four bits of the AL.

Flags. Affects AF and CF (OF, PF, SF, and ZF are undefined).

Source Code.   AAA (no operand)

Object Code.   00110111

AAD: ASCII Adjust for Division

Operation.   Corrects for division of ASCII values. Use AAD before dividing into an unpacked decimal value in the AX (strip out ASCII 3s). AAD corrects the dividend to a binary value in the AL for a subsequent binary divide. It multiplies the AH by 10, adds the product to the AL, and clears the AH.

Flags.   Affects PF, SF, and ZF (AF, CF, and OF are undefined).

Source Code.   AAD (no operand)

Object Code. |11010101|00001010|

AAM: ASCII Adjust for Multiplication

Operation.   Corrects the product generated by multiplying two unpacked decimal values. AAM divides the AL by 10 and stores the quotient in the AH and the remainder in the AL.

Flags.   Affects PF, SF, and ZF (AF, CF, and OF are undefined).

Source Code.   AAM (no operand)

Object Code. |11010100|00001010|

AAS: ASCII Adjust for Subtraction

Operation.   Corrects subtraction of two ASCII bytes in the AL. If the rightmost four bits have a value greater than 9 or if the CF flag is 1, AAS subtracts 6 from the AL, subtracts 1 from the AH, and sets the AF and CF flags. Otherwise, the AF and CF are cleared. AAS always clears the leftmost four bits of the AL.

Flags.   Affects AF and CF (OF, PF, SF, and ZF are undefined).

Source Code.   AAS (no operand)

Object Code.   00111111

ADC: Add with Carry

Operation.   Typically used in multiword binary addition to carry an overflowed 1-bit into the next stage of arithmetic. If the CF flag is set, ADC first adds 1 to operand 1. ADC then adds operand 2 to operand 1, just as ADD does.

Flags.   Affects AF, CF, OF, PF, SF, and ZF.

Source Code.   ADC {register/memory},{register/memory/immediate}

Object Code.   (three formats)

```
Reg/mem with reg:          |000100dw|modregr/m|
Immed to accum'r:          |0001010w|data |data if w=1|
Immed to reg/mem: |100000sw|mod010r/m|---data----|data if sw=01|
```

ADD: Add Binary Numbers

Operation.   Adds binary values from memory, register, or immediate to a register, or adds values in a register or immediate to memory. Values may be byte, word, or doubleword (80386/486).

Flags.   Affects AF, CF, OF, PF, SF, and ZF.

Source Code.   ADD {register/memory},{register/memory/immediate}

Object Code.   (three formats)

```
Reg/mem with reg:  |000000dw|modregr/m|
Immed to accum'r:  |0000010w|--data--|data if w=1|
Immed to reg/mem:  |100000sw|mod000r/m|---data---|data if sw=01|
```

AND: Logical AND

Operation.   Performs a logical AND operation on bits of two operands. Both operands are bytes, words, or doublewords (80386/486), which AND matches bit for bit. If both matched bits are 1, the operand 1 bit is set; otherwise, it is cleared (see also OR, XOR, and TEST).

Flags.   Affects CF (0), OF (0), PF, SF, and ZF (AF is undefined).

Source Code.   AND {register/memory},{register/memory/immediate}

Object Code.   (three formats)

```
Reg/mem with reg:  |001000dw|modregr/m|
Immed to accum'r:  |0010010w|---data----|data if w=1|
Immed to reg/mem:  |1010000w|mod 100 r/m|---data----|data if w=1|
```

BSF and BSR: Bit Scan (80386/486)

Operation.   Scans a bit string for the first 1-bit. BSF scans from right to left, and BSR scans from left to right. The operand 2 register (16 or 32 bits) contains the string to be scanned. The operation returns the position of the bit (if any) in the operand 1 register.

Flags.   Affects ZF.

Source Code.   BSF/BSR register,{register/memory}

Object Code.   BSF:|00001111|10111100|modregr/m|
                  BSR:|00001111|10111101|modregr/m|

BT/BTC/BTR/BTS: Bit Test (80386/486)

Operation.   Copies a specified bit into the CF flag. Operand 1 contains the bit string being tested and operand 2 indicates its position. BTC complements the bit by reversing its value in operand 1. BTR resets the bit by clearing it to 0. BTS sets the bit to 1.

Flags.   Affects CF.

Source Code.   BT/BTC/BTR/BTS {register/memory},{register/immediate}

Object Code

```
Immed to reg:   00001111 10111010 mod***r/m
Reg/mem to reg: 00001111 10***010 modregr/m
    (*** means BT=100, BTC=111, BTR=110, BTS=101)
```

CALL: Call a Procedure

Operation.   Calls a near or far procedure. The assembler generates a near CALL if the called procedure is NEAR or a far CALL if the called procedure is FAR. For near, CALL decrements the SP by 2 and pushes the IP (the address of the next instruction) onto the stack. It then loads the IP with the destination offset address. For far, CALL decrements the SP, pushes the CS onto the stack, and loads an intersegment pointer onto the stack. It then pushes and loads the IP. A subsequent near or far RET undoes these steps on return.

Flags.   None.

Source Code.   CALL {register/memory}

Object Code.   (four formats)

```
Direct within segment:   |11101000|disp-low|disp-high|
Indirect within segment: |11111111|mod010r/m|
Indirect intersegment:   |11111111|mod011r/m|
Direct intersegment:
             |10011010|offset-low|offset-high|seg-low|seg-high|
```

CBW: Convert Byte to Word

Operation.   Extends a one-byte signed value in the AL to a word by duplicating the sign (bit 7) of the AL through the bits in the AH (see also CWD, CWDE, and CDQ).

Flags.   None.

Source Code.   CBW (no operand)

Object Code.   10011000

CDQ: Convert Doubleword to Quadword (80386/486)

Operation.   Extends a 32-bit signed value in the EAX to a 64-bit value in the EDX:EAX pair (see also CBW, CWD, and CWDE).

Flags.   None.

Source Code.   CDQ (no operand)

Object Code.   10011001

CLC: Clear Carry Flag

Operation.   Clears the CF flag so that, for example, an ADC does not add a 1-bit (see also STC).

Flags.   CF (becomes 0).

Source Code.   CLC (no operand)

Object Code.   11111000

CLD: Clear Direction Flag

Operation.   Clears the DF flag, to cause string operations such as MOVS to process from left to right (see also STD).

Flags.   DF (becomes 0).

Source Code.   CLD (no operand)

Object Code.   11111100

CLI: Clear Interrupt Flag

Operation.   Clears the IF flag, to disable maskable external interrupts (see also STI).

Flags.   IF (becomes 0).

Source Code.   CLI (no operand)

Object Code.   11111010

CMC: Complement Carry Flag

Operation.   Complements the CF flag: reverses the CF bit value—0 becomes 1 and 1 becomes 0.

Flags.   CF (reversed).

Source Code.   CMC (no operand)

Object Code.   11110101

CMP: Compare

Operation.   Compares the contents of two data fields. CMP internally subtracts operand 2 from operand 1 but does not change the values. Both operands are byte, word, or doubleword (80386/486). CMP may compare register, memory, or immediate to a register or compare register or immediate to memory (see also CMPS).

Flags.   Affects AF, CF, OF, PF, SF, and ZF.

Source Code.   CMP {register/memory},{register/memory/immediate}

Object Code.   (three formats)

```
Reg/mem with reg:   |001110dw|modregr/m|
Immed to accum'r:   |0011110w|---data--|data if w=1|
Immed to reg/mem:   |100000sw|mod111r/m|---data----|data if sw=0|
```

CMPS/CMPSB/CMPSW/CMPSD: Compare String

Operation.   Compares strings of any length in memory. A REPn prefix normally precedes these instructions, along with a maximum value in the CX. CMPSB compares bytes, CMPSW compares words, and CMPSD (80386/486) compares doublewords. The DS:SI registers address operand 1 and the ES:DI registers address operand 2. If the DF flag is 0, the operation compares left to right and increments the SI and DI. If the DF is 1, it compares from right to left and decrements the SI and DI. REPn decrements the CX by 1 for each repetition. The operation terminates when the compared value is found (REPNE) or not found (REPE) or the CX is decremented to 0; the DI and SI are advanced past the byte that caused termination.

Flags.   Affects AF, CF, OF, PF, SF, and ZF.

Source Code.   [REPnn] CMPSB/CMPSW/CMPSD (no operand)

Object Code.   `1010011w`

CWD: Convert Word to Doubleword

Operation.   Extends a one-word signed value in the AX to a doubleword by duplicating the sign (bit 15) of the AX through the DX, typically to generate a 32-bit dividend (see also CBW, CWDE, and CDQ).

Flags.   None.

Source Code.   CWD (no operand)

Object Code.   `10011001`

CWDE: Convert Word to Doubleword Extended (80386/486)

Operation. Extends a one-word signed value in the AX to a doubleword in the EAX by duplicating the sign (bit 15) of the AX, typically to generate a 32-bit dividend (see also CBW, CWD, and CDQ).

Flags. None.

Source Code. CWDE (no operand)

Object Code. 10011000

DAA: Decimal Adjust for Addition

Operation. Corrects the result of adding two BCD (packed decimal) items in the AL. If the rightmost four bits have a value greater than 9 or the AF flag is 1, DAA adds 6 to the AL and sets the AF. If the AL contains a value greater than 9FH or the CF flag is 1, DAA adds 60H to the AL and sets the CF. Otherwise, the AF and CF are cleared (see also DAS).

Flags. Affects AF, CF, PF, SF, and ZF (OF undefined).

Source Code. DAA (no operand)

Object Code. 00100111

DAS: Decimal Adjust for Subtraction

Operation. Corrects the result of subtracting two BCD (packed decimal) fields in the AL. If the rightmost four bits have a value greater than 9 or the AF flag is 1, DAS subtracts 60H from the AL and sets the CF flag. Otherwise, the AF and CF are cleared (see also DAA).

Flags. Affects AF, CF, PF, SF, and ZF (OF undefined).

Source Code. DAS (no operand)

Object Code. 00101111 (no operand)

DEC: Decrement by 1

Operation. Decrements 1 from a byte, word, or doubleword (80386/486) in a register or memory (see also INC).

Flags. Affects AF, OF, PF, SF, and ZF.

Source Code. DEC {register/memory}

Object Code. (two formats)

```
Register:    |01001reg|
Reg/memory:  |1111111w|mod001r/m|
```

DIV: Unsigned Division

Operation.   Divides an unsigned dividend by an unsigned divisor. DIV treats a leftmost 1-bit as a data bit, not a minus sign. Here are the three types of division:

Dividend (Operand 1)	Divisor (Operand 2)	Quotient	Remainder	Example
16-bit AX	8-bit reg/memory	AL	AH	DIV BH
32-bit DX:AX	16-bit reg/memory	AX	DX	DIV CX
64-bit EDX:EAX	32-bit reg/memory	EAX	EDX	DIV ECX

Division by zero causes a zero-divide interrupt (see also IDIV).

Flags.   Affects AF, CF, OF, PF, SF, and ZF (all undefined).

Source Code.   DIV {register/memory}

Object Code. |1111011w|mod110r/m|

ESC: Escape

Operation.   Facilitates use of coprocessors such as the 80287 to perform special operations. ESC provides the coprocessor with an instruction and operand for execution.

Flags.   None.

Source Code.   ESC immediate,{register/memory}

Object Code. |11011xxx|modxxxr/m| (x-bits are not important)

HLT: Enter Halt State

Operation.   Causes the processor to enter a halt state while waiting for an interrupt. HLT terminates with the CS and IP registers pointing to the instruction following the HLT. When an interrupt occurs, the processor pushes the CS and IP on the stack and executes the interrupt routine. On return, an IRET instruction pops the stack and processing resumes following the original HLT.

Flags.   None.

Source Code.   HLT (no operand)

Object Code.   11110100

IDIV: Signed (Integer) Division

Operation.   Divides a signed dividend by a signed divisor. IDIV treats a leftmost 1-bit as a negative sign. Here are the three types of division:

Dividend (Operand 1)	Divisor (Operand 2)	Quotient	Remainder	Example
16-bit AX	8-bit reg/memory	AL	AH	IDIV BH
32-bit DX:AX	16-bit reg/memory	AX	DX	IDIV CX
64-bit EDX:EAX	32-bit reg/memory	EAX	EDX	IDIV ECX

Division by zero causes a zero-divide interrupt. See CBW and CWD to extend the length of a signed dividend (see also DIV).

Flags.   Affects AF, CF, OF, PF, SF, and ZF.

Source Code.   IDIV {register/memory}

Object Code. |1111011w|mod111r/m|

IMUL: Signed (Integer) Multiplication

Operation.   Multiplies a signed multiplicand by a signed multiplier. IMUL treats a leftmost 1-bit as a negative sign. Here are the operations for all processors:

Multiplicand (Operand 1)	Multiplier (Operand 2)	Product	Example
8-bit AL	8-bit register/memory	AX	IMUL BL
16-bit AX	16-bit register/memory	DX:AX	IMUL BX
32-bit EAX	32-bit register/memory	EDX:EAX	IMUL ECX

Three other IMUL formats are available for processors other than the 8088/86 (see also MUL).

Flags.   Affects CF and OF (AF, PF, SF, and ZF are undefined).

Source Code.

IMUL {register/memory} (all processors)
IMUL register,immediate (80186-486)
IMUL register,register,immediate (80186-486)
IMUL register,{register/memory} (80386-486)

Object Code. |1111011w|mod101r/m| (first format)

IN: Input Byte or Word

Operation.   Transfers from an input port a byte to the AL or a word to the AX. Code the port as a fixed numeric operand (as IN AX,port#) or as a variable in the

DX (as IN AX,DX). Use the DX if the port number is greater than 256. The 80186-486 also support an INS (Input String) instruction (see also OUT).

Flags.   None.

Source Code.   IN {AL/AX},{portno/DX}

Object Code.   (two formats)

      Variable port: |1110110w|
      Fixed port: |1110010w|--port--|

INC: Increment by 1

Operation.   Increments by 1 a byte, word, or doubleword (80386/486) in a register or memory, coded, for example, as INC CX (see also DEC).

Flags.   Affects AF, OF, PF, SF, and ZF.

Source Code.   INC {register/memory}

Object Code.   (two formats)

      Register: |01000reg|
      Reg/memory: |1111111w|mod000r/m|

INT: Interrupt

Operation.   Interrupts processing and transfers control to one of the 256 interrupt (vector) addresses. INT performs the following: (1) Decrements the SP by 2, pushes the flags onto the stack, and resets the IF and TF flags; (2) decrements the SP by 2, pushes the CS onto the stack, and places the high-order word of the interrupt address in the CS; and (3) decrements the CS by 2, pushes the IP onto the stack, and fills the IP with the low-order word of the interrupt address. For the 80386/486, INT pushes a 16-bit IP for 16-bit segments and a 32-bit IP for 32-bit segments. IRET returns from the interrupt routine.

Flags.   Affects IF and TF.

Source Code.   INT number

Object Code. |1100110v|-- type--| (if v = 0 type is 3)

INTO: Interrupt on Overflow

Operation.   Causes an interrupt (usually harmless) if an overflow has occurred (the OF is set to 1) and performs an INT 04. The interrupt address is at location 10H of the interrupt service table (see also INT).

Flags.   None.

Source Code.   INTO (no operand)

Object Code.   `11001110`

IRET: Interrupt Return

Operation.   Provides a far return from an interrupt routine. IRET performs the following: (1) pops the word at the top of the stack into the IP, increments the SP by 2, and pops the top of the stack into the CS; and (2) increments the SP by 2 and pops the top of the stack into the flags register. This procedure undoes the steps that the interrupt originally took and performs a return. For the 80386/486, use IRETD (doubleword) to pop a 32-bit IP (see also RET).

Flags.   Affects all.

Source Code.   IRET

Object Code.   `11001111` (no operand)

JA/JNBE: Jump Above or Jump If Not Below/Equal

Operation.   Used after a test of unsigned data. If the CF flag is 0 (no carry) and the ZF flag is 0 (nonzero), the instruction adds the operand offset to the IP and performs a jump. The jump must be short (-128 to 127 bytes) except for the 80386/486, which may be near.

Flags.   None.

Source Code.   JA/JNBE label

Object Code.   `|01110111|--disp--|`

JAE/JNB: Jump If Above/Equal or Jump If Not Below

Operation.   Used after a test of unsigned data. If the CF flag is 0 (no carry), the instruction adds the operand offset to the IP and performs a jump. The jump must be short (-128 to 127 bytes) except for the 80386/486, which may be near.

Flags.   None.

Source Code.   JAE/JNB label

Object Code.   `|01110011|--disp--|`

JB/JNAE: Jump If Below or Jump If Not Above/Equal

Operation.   Used after a test of unsigned data. If the CF flag is 1 (carry), the instruction adds the operand offset to the IP and performs a jump. The jump must be short (-128 to 127 bytes) except for the 80386/486, which may be near.

Flags.   None.

Source Code.   JB/JNAE label

Object Code. |01110010|--disp--|

JBE/JNA: Jump If Below/Equal or Jump If Not Above

Operation.   Used after a test of unsigned data. If the CF flag is 1 (carry) or the AF flag is 1, the instruction adds the operand offset to the IP and performs a jump. The jump must be short (−128 to 127 bytes) except for the 80386/486, which may be near.

Flags.   None.

Source Code.   JBE/JNA label

Object Code. |01110110|--disp--|

JC: Jump If Carry

Operation.   See JB/JNAE (identical operations).

JCXZ/JECXZ: Jump If CX Is Zero or Jump If JECXZ Is Zero

Operation.   Jumps to a specified address if the CX or the ECX (80386/486) contains zero. The operation could be useful at the start of a loop, although limited to a short jump.

Flags.   None.

Source Code.   JCXZ/JECXZ label

Object Code for JCXZ. |11100011|--disp--|

JE/JZ: Jump If Equal or Jump If Zero

Operation.   Used after a test of signed or unsigned data. If the ZF flag is 1 (zero condition), the instruction adds the operand offset to the IP and performs a jump. The jump must be short (−128 to 127 bytes) except for the 80386/486, which may be near.

Flags.   None.

Source Code.   JE/JZ label

Object Code. |01110100|--disp--|

JG/JNLE: Jump If Greater or Jump If Not Less/Equal

Operation.   Used after a test of signed data. If the ZF flag is 0 (nonzero) and the SF flag equals the OF (both 0 or both 1), the instruction adds the operand offset to the IP and performs a jump. The jump must be short (−128 to 127 bytes) except for the 80386/486, which may be near.

Flags.   None.

Source Code.   JG/JNLE label

Object Code. |01111111|--disp--|

JGE/JNL: Jump If Greater/Equal or Jump If Not Less

Operation.   Used after a test of signed data. If the SF flag equals the OF (both 0 or both 1), the instruction adds the operand offset to the IP and performs a jump. The jump must be short (−128 to 127 bytes) except for the 80386/486, which may be near.

Flags.   None.

Source Code.   JGE/JNL label

Object Code. |01111101|--disp--|

JL/JNGE: Jump If Less or Jump If Greater/Equal

Operation.   Used after a test of signed data. If the SF flag is not equal to the OF, the instruction adds the operand offset to the IP and performs a jump. The jump must be short (−128 to 127 bytes) except for the 80386/486, which may be near.

Flags.   None.

Source Code.   JL/JNGE label

Object Code. |01111100|--disp--|

JLE/JNG: Jump If Less/Equal or Jump If Not Greater

Operation.   Used after a test of signed data. If the ZF flag is 1 (zero condition) or if the SF flag is not equal to the OF, the instruction adds the operand offset to the IP and performs a jump. The jump must be short (−128 to 127 bytes) except for the 80386/486, which may be near.

Flags.   None.

Source Code.   JLE/JNG label

Object Code. |01111110|--disp--|

JMP: Unconditional Jump

Operation.   Jumps to a designated address under any condition. A JMP address may be short (−128 to +127 bytes), near (within 32K), or far (another segment). A short JMP replaces the IP with a destination offset address. A far jump (such as JMP FAR PTR label) replaces the CS:IP with a new segment address.

Flags.   None.

Source Code.   JMP {register/memory}

Object Code.   (five formats)

Direct within seg short: `|11101011|--disp---|`
Direct within segment: `|11101001|disp-low|disp-high|`
Indirect within segment: `|11111111|mod100r/m|`
Indirect intersegment: `|11111111|mod101r/m|`
Direct intersegment:
                            `|11101010|offset-low|offset-high|seg-low|seg-high|`

JNC: Jump If No Carry

Operation.   See JAE/JNB (identical operations).

JNE/JNZ: Jump If Not Equal or Jump If Not Zero

Operation.   Used after a test of signed data. If the ZF flag is 0 (nonzero), the instruction adds the operand offset to the IP and performs a jump. The jump must be short (−128 to 127 bytes) except for the 80386/486, which may be near.

Flags.   None.

Source Code.   JNE/JNZ label

Object Code.   `|01110101|--disp--|`

JNO: Jump If No Overflow

Operation.   Jumps if an operation caused no overflow. If the OF flag is 0, the instruction adds the operand offset to the IP and performs a jump. The jump must be short (−128 to 127 bytes) except for the 80386/486, which may be near (see also JO).

Flags.   None.

Source Code.   JNO label

Object Code.   `|01110001|--disp--|`

JNP/JPO: Jump If No Parity or Jump If Parity Odd

Operation.   Jumps if an operation caused no (or odd) parity—an operation has set an odd number of bits on in the low-order 8 bits. If the PF flag is 0 (odd parity), the instruction adds the operand offset to the IP and performs a jump. The jump must be short (−128 to 127 bytes) except for the 80386/486, which may be near (see also JP/JPE).

Flags.   None.

Source Code.   JNP/JPO label

Object Code. |01111011|--disp--|

JNS: Jump If No Sign

Operation.   Jumps if an operation set the sign to positive. If the SF flag is 0 (positive), JNS adds the operand offset to the IP and performs a jump. The jump must be short (-128 to 127 bytes) except for the 80386/486, which may be near (see also JS).

Flags.   None.

Source Code.   JNS label

Object Code. |01111001|--disp--|

JO: Jump If Overflow

Operation.   Jumps if an operation caused an overflow. If the OF flag is 1 (overflow), JO adds the operand offset to the IP and performs a jump. The jump must be short (-128 to 127 bytes) except for the 80386/486, which may be near (see also JNO).

Flags.   None.

Source Code.   JO label

Object Code. |01110000|--disp--|

JP/JPE: Jump If Parity or Jump If Parity Even

Operation.   Jumps if an operation caused even parity—an operation has set an even number of bits on in the low-order 8 bits. If the PF flag is 1 (even parity), the instruction adds the operand offset to the IP and performs a jump. The jump must be short (-128 to 127 bytes) except for the 80386/486, which may be near (see also JNP/JPO).

Flags.   None.

Source Code.   JP/JPE label

Object Code. |01111010|--disp--|

JS: Jump If Sign

Operation.   Jumps if an operation set the sign to negative. If the SF flag is 1 (negative), JS adds the operand offset to the IP and performs the jump. The jump must be short (-128 to 127 bytes) except for the 80386/486, which may be near (see also JNS).

Flags.   None.

Source Code.   JS label

Object Code. |01111000|--disp--|

LAHF: Load AH from Flags

Operation.   Loads the rightmost 8 bits of the flags register into the AH (see also SAHF).

Flags.   None.

Source Code.   LAHF (no operand)

Object Code.   10011111

LDS/LES/LFS/LGS/LSS: Load Segment Register

Operation.   Initializes a far address and offset of a data item so that succeeding instructions can access it. Operand 1 references any of the general, index, or pointer registers. Operand 2 references four bytes in memory containing an offset and a segment address. The operation loads the segment address in the segment register and the offset address in the operand 1 register.

Flags.   None.

Source Code.   LDS/LES/LFS/LGS/LSS register,memory

Object Code.

```
LDS:    |11000101|mod reg r/m|
LES:    |11000100|mod reg r/m|
LFS:    |00001111|10110100|mod reg r/m| (80386/486)
LGS:    |00001111|10110101|mod reg r/m| (80386/486)
LSS:    |00001111|10110010|mod reg r/m| (80386/486)
```

LEA: Load Effective Address

Operation.   Loads a near (offset) address into a register.

Flags.   None.

Source Code.   LEA register,memory

Object Code.   10001101

LES/LFS/LGS: Load Extra Segment Register

Operation.   See LDS.

LOCK: Lock Bus

Operation.   Prevent 80287 or other (co)processors from changing a data item at the same time. LOCK is a one-byte prefix that you may code immediately before any instruction. The operation sends a signal to the other processor to prevent it from using the data until the next instruction is completed.

Flags.   None.

Source Code.   LOCK instruction

Object Code.   11110000

LODS/LODSB/LODSW: Load Byte or Word String

Operation.   Loads the accumulator register with a value from memory. Although LODS is a string operation, it does not require a REP prefix. The DS:SI registers address a byte (if LODSB), word (if LODSW), or doubleword (if LODSD) and load it from memory into the AL, AX, or EAX. If the DF flag is 0, the operation adds 1 (if byte), 2 (if word), or 4 (if doubleword) to the SI; otherwise, it subtracts 1, 2, or 4.

Flags.   None.

Source Code.   LODS/LODSB/LODSW (no operand)

Object Code.   1010110w

LOOP: Loop until Complete

Operation.   Controls executing a routine a specified number of times. The CX should contain a count before starting the loop. LOOP appears at the end of the loop and decrements the CX by 1. If the CX is nonzero, the instruction transfers to the operand address at the start of the loop (adds the offset in the IP); otherwise it drops through to the next instruction. The offset must be a short jump.

Flags.   None.

Source Code.   LOOP label

Object Code. |11100010|--disp--|

LOOPE/LOOPZ: Loop While Equal or Loop While Zero

Operation.   Controls repetitive execution of a routine. LOOPE/LOOPZ are similar to LOOP except that they terminate if the CX is 0 or if the ZF flag is 0 (nonzero condition) (see also LOOPNE/LOOPNZ).

Flags.   None.

Source Code.   LOOPE/LOOPZ label

Object Code. |11100001|--disp--|

LOOPNE/LOOPNZ: Loop While Not Equal or Loop While Not Zero

Operation.   Controls repetitive execution of a routine. LOOPNE/LOOPNZ are similar to LOOP except that they terminate if the CX is 0 or if the ZF flag is 1 (zero condition) (see also LOOPE/LOOPZ).

Flags.   None.

Source Code.   LOOPNE/LOOPNZ label

Object Code.   `11100000|--disp--|`

LSS: Load Stack Segment Register

Operation.   See LDS.

MOV: Move Data

Operation.   Transfers data between two registers or between a register and memory, and transfers immediate data to a register or memory. The referenced data defines the number of bytes (one, two, or four) moved; the operands must agree in size. MOV cannot transfer between two memory locations (use MOVS), immediate data to a segment register, or a segment register to a segment register. (see also MOVSX/MOVZX).

Flags.   None.

Source Code.   MOV {register/memory},{register/memory/immediate}

Object Code.   (seven formats)

Reg/mem to/from reg:	`|100010dw|modregr/m|`
Immed to reg/mem:	`|1100011w|mod000r/m|---data---|data if w=1|`
Immed to register:	`|1011wreg|---data---|data if w=1|`
Mem to accumulator:	`|1010000w| addr-low| addr-high |`
Accumulator to mem:	`|1010001w| addr-low| addr-high |`
Reg/mem to seg reg:	`|10001110|mod0sgr/m|(sg=seg reg)`
Seg reg to reg/mem:	`|10001100|mod0sgr/m|(sg=seg reg)`

MOVS/MOVSB/MOVSW/MOVSD: Move String

Operation.   Moves data between memory locations. Normally used with the REP prefix and a length in the CX, MOVSB moves bytes, MOVSW moves words, and MOVSD (80386/486) moves doublewords. ES:DI address operand 1 and DS:SI address operand 2. If the DF flag is 0, the operation moves data from left to right and increments the DI and SI by 1, 2, or 4. If the DF is 1, the operation moves data from right to left and decrements the DI and SI. REP decrements the CX by 1 for each repetition. The operation terminates when the CX is decremented to 0; the DI and SI are advanced past the last byte moved.

Flags.   None.

Source Code.   [REP] MOVSB/MOVSW/MOVSD (no operand)

Object Code.   `1010010w`

MOVSX/MOVZX: Move and Fill (80386/486)

Operation.   Copies an 8- or 16-bit source operand into a 16- or 32-bit destination operand. MOVSX fills the sign bit into leftmost bits and MOVZX fills zero bits.

Flags.   None.

Source Code.   MOVSX/MOVZX {register/memory},{register/memory/ immediate}

MUL: Unsigned Multiplication

Operation.   Multiplies an unsigned multiplicand by an unsigned multiplier. MUL treats a leftmost 1-bit as a data bit, not a negative sign. Here are the three operations:

Multiplicand (Operand 1)	Multiplier (Operand 2)	Product	Example
`8-bit AL`	`8-bit register/memory`	`AX`	`MUL BL`
`16-bit AX`	`16-bit register/memory`	`DX:AX`	`MUL BX`
`32-bit EAX`	`32-bit register/memory`	`EDX:EAX`	`MUL ECX`

(see also IMUL).

Flags.   Affects CF and OF (AF, PF, SF, and ZF are undefined).

Source Code.   MUL {register/memory}

Object Code.   `|1111011w|mod100r/m|`

NEG: Negate

Operation.   Reverses a binary value from positive to negative and from negative to positive. NEG provides two's complement of the specified operand: subtracts the operand from zero and adds 1. Operands may be a byte, word, or doubleword (80386/486) in a register or memory (see also NOT).

Flags.   Affects AF, CF, OF, PF, SF, and ZF.

Source Code.   NEG {register/memory}

Object Code.   `|1111011w|mod011r/m|`

NOP: No Operation

Operation.   Used to delete or insert machine code or to delay execution for purposes of timing. NOP simply performs a null operation: XCHG AX,AX.

Flags.   None.

Source Code.   NOP (no operand)

Object Code.   10010000

NOT: Logical NOT

Operation.   Changes 0-bits to 1-bits, and vice versa. The operand is a byte, word, or doubleword (80386/486) in a register or memory (see also NEG).

Flags.   None.

Source Code.   NOT {register/memory}

Object Code. |1111011w|mod 010 r/m|

OR: Logical OR

Operation.   Performs a logical OR operation on bits of two operands. Both operands are bytes, words, or doublewords (80386/486), which OR matches bit for bit. If either matched bit is 1, the operand 1 bit becomes 1, and is otherwise unchanged. (see also AND and XOR).

Flags.   Affects CF (0), OF (0), PF, SF, and ZF (AF is undefined).

Source Code.   OR {register/memory},{register/memory/immediate}

Object Code.   (three formats)

Reg/mem with reg:	|000010dw|modregr/m|
Immed to accum'r:	|0000110w|---data--|data if w=1|
Immed to reg/mem:	|1000000w|mod001r/m|---data----|data if w=1|

OUT: Output Byte or Word

Operation.   Transfers to an output port a byte from the AL or a word from the AX. The port is a fixed numeric operand (as OUT port#,AX) or a variable in the DX (as OUT DX,AX). Use the DX if the port number is greater than 256. The 80186-486 also support an OUTS (Out String) instruction (see also IN).

Flags.   None.

Source Code.   OUT {portno/DX},{AL/AX}

Object Code.

| Variable port: |1110111w|
| Fixed port: |1110011w|--port--|

POP: Pop Word off Stack

Operation.   Pops a word or doubleword (80386/486) previously pushed on the stack to a specified destination—general register, segment register, or memory. The SP points to the current (double)word at the top of the stack; POP transfers it to the specified destination and increments the SP by 2 or 4 (see also PUSH).

Flags.   None.

Source Code.   POP {register/memory}

Object Code.   (three formats)

| Register: |01011reg|
| Segment reg: |000sg111|(sg implies segment reg)
| Reg/memory: |10001111|mod 000 r/m|

POPA: Pop All General Registers (80186-486)

Operation.   Pops the top eight words from the stack into the DI, SI, BP, SP, BX, DX, CX, AX in that order and increments the SP by 16. Normally, a PUSHA has pushed the registers. For the 80386/486, POPAD handles doublewords and increments the SP by 32. The SP value is discarded rather than loaded.

Flags.   Affects none.

Source Code.   POPA/POPAD (no operand)

Object Code.   01100001

POPF: Pop Flags off Stack

Operation.   Pops the top word from the stack to the flags register and increments the SP by 2. Normally, a PUSHF has pushed the flags. For the 80386/486, POPFD handles doublewords and increments the SP by 4.

Flags.   Affects all.

Source Code.   POPF/POPFD (no operand)

Object Code.   10011101

PUSH: Push onto Stack

Operation.   Pushes a word or doubleword (80386/486) on the stack for later use. The SP register points to the current (double)word at the top of the stack. PUSH decrements the SP by 2 or 4 and transfers a (double)word from the specified operand to the new top of the stack. The source may be a general register, segment register, or memory (see also POP and PUSHF).

Flags. None.

Source Code.

> PUSH {register/memory} (all processors)
> PUSH immediate   (80186-486)

Object Code.   (three formats)

> Register: |01010reg|
> Segment reg: |000sg110|(sg implies segment reg)
> Reg/memory: |11111111|mod110r/m|

PUSHA: Push All General Registers (80186-486)

Operation.   Pushes the AX, CX, DX, BX, SP, BP, SI, DI, in that order, on the stack and decrements the SP by 16. For the 80386/486, PUSHAD handles doublewords and decrements the SP by 32. Normally, a POPA later pops the registers.

Flags. Affects none.

Source Code.   PUSHA/PUSHAD (no operand)

Object Code.   01100000

PUSHF: Push Flags onto Stack

Operation.   Pushes the contents of the flags register on the stack for later use. PUSHF decrements the SP by 2 and transfers the flags to the new top of the stack. For the 80386/486, PUSHFD handles doublewords and decrements the SP by 4 (see also POPF and PUSH).

Flags. Affects none.

Source Code.   PUSHF (no operand)

Object Code.   10011100

RCL/RCR: Rotate Left through Carry and Rotate Right through Carry

Operation.   Rotates bits through the CF flag. The operation rotates bits left or right in a byte, word, or doubleword (80386/486) in a register or memory. The operand can be an immediate constant or a reference to the CL. On the 8088/86, then constant may be only 1; a larger rotate must be in the CL. On the 80186-486, the constant may be up to 31. For RCL, the leftmost bit enters the CF and the CF bit enters bit 0 of the destination; all other bits rotate left. For RCR, bit 0 enters the CF and the CF bit enters the leftmost bit of the destination; all other bits rotate right (see also ROL and ROR).

Flags.   Affects CF and OF.

Source Code.   RCL/RCR {register/memory},{CL/immediate}

Object Code.

```
    RCL:     |110100cw|mod010r/m|(if c=0 shift is 1;
    RCR:     |110100cw|mod011r/m| if c=1 shift is in CL)
```

REP/REPE/REPZ/REPNE/REPNZ: Repeat String

Operation.   Repeats a string operation a specified number of times. These are optional repeat prefixes coded before string instructions CMPS, MOVS, SCAS, and STOS. Load the CX with a count prior to execution. The operation decrements the CX by 1 for each execution of the string instruction. For REP, the operation repeats until CX is 0. For REPE/REPZ (repeat while equal/zero), the operation repeats until CX is 0 or until ZF is 0 (unequal/nonzero condition). For REPNE/REPNZ (repeat while not equal/zero), the operation repeats until CX is 0 or until ZF is 1 (equal/zero condition).

Flags.   See the associated string instruction.

Source Code.   REP/REPE/REPZ/REPNE/REPNZ string-instruction

Object Code.

```
    REP/REPNE:     11110010
    REPE:          11110011
```

RET: Return from a Procedure

Operation.   Returns from a procedure previously entered by a near or far CALL. The assembler generates a near RET if it is within a procedure labeled NEAR, and a far RET if it is within a procedure labeled FAR. For near, RET moves the word at the top of the stack to the IP and increments the SP by 2. For far, RET moves the words at the top of the stack to the IP and CS and increments the SP by 4. Any numeric operand (a pop value as RET 4) is added to the SP.

Flags.   None.

Source Code.   RET [pop-value]

Object Code.   (four formats)

Within a segment: |11000011|
Within a segment with pop-value: |11000010|data-low|data-high|
Intersegment: |11001011|
Intersegment with pop-value: |11001010|data-low|data-high|

RETF and RETN: Return from a Far or Near Procedure

Operation.   Returns from a procedure previously entered by a near or far CALL. These instructions were introduced by MASM 5.0. You can code a near or far return explicitly and can code the procedure without PROC or ENDP directives. Use CALL NEAR/FAR PTR label to call the procedure (see RET for details).

Flags.   None.

Source Code.   RETF/RETN [pop-value]

Object Code.   See RET.

ROL/ROR: Rotate Left and Rotate Right

Operation.   Rotates bits left or right in a byte, word, or doubleword (80386/486) in a register or memory. The operand can be an immediate constant or a reference to the CL. On the 8088/86, the constant may be only 1; a larger rotate must be in the CL. On the 80186-486, the constant may be up to 31. For ROL, the leftmost bit enters bit 0 of the destination; all other bits rotate left. For ROR, bit 0 enters the leftmost bit of the destination; all other bits rotate right (see also RCL and RCR).

Flags.   Affects CF and OF.

Source Code.   ROL/ROR {register/memory},{CL/immediate}

Object Code.

ROL: |110100cw|mod000r/m| (if c=0 count=1;
ROR: |110100cw|mod001r/m| if c=1 count is in CL)

SAHF: Store AH Contents in Flags

Operation.   Stores bits from the AH in the rightmost bits of the flags register (see also LAHF).

Flags.   Affects AF, CF, PF, SF, and ZF.

Source Code.   SAHF (no operand)

Object Code.   10011110

SAL/SAR: Shift Algebraic Left or Shift Algebraic Right

Operation.   Shifts bits left or right in a byte, word, or doubleword in a register or memory. The operand can be an immediate constant or a reference to the CL. On the 8088/86, the constant may be only 1; a larger shift must be in the CL. On the 80186-486, the constant may be up to 31.

SAL shifts bits left a specified number and fills 0 bits in vacated positions to the right. SAL acts exactly like SHL. SAR is an arithmetic shift that considers the sign of the referenced field. SAR shifts bits to the right a specified number and fills the sign bit (0 or 1) to the left. All bits shifted off are lost.

Flags.   Affects CF, OF, PF, SF, and ZF (AF is undefined).

Source Code.   SAL/SAR {register/memory},{CL/immediate}

Object Code.

```
SAL:    |110100cw|mod100r/m| (If c=0 count=1;
SAR:    |110100cw|mod111r/m|  if c=1 count in CL)
```

SBB: Subtract with Borrow

Operation.   Typically used in multiword binary subtraction to carry an overflowed 1 bit into the next stage of arithmetic. If the CF flag is set, SBB first subtracts 1 from operand 1. SBB always subtracts operand 2 from operand 1, just like SUB (see also ADC).

Flags.   Affects AF, CF, OF, PF, SF, and ZF.

Source Code.   SBB {register/memory},{register/memory/immediate}

Object Code.   (three formats)

```
Reg/mem with reg:       |000110dw|modregr/m|
Immed from accum'r:     |0001110w|---data--|data if w = 1|
Immed from reg/mem:
                        |100000sw|mod011r/m|---data----|data if sw = 01|
```

SCAS/SCASB/SCASW/SCASD: Scan String

Operation.   Scans a string in memory for a specified value. For SCASB load the value in the AL, for SCASW load the value in the AX, and for SCASD load the value in the EAX. ES:DI reference the string in memory that is to be scanned. The operations are normally used with a REPE/REPNE prefix along with a count in the CX. If the DF flag is 0, the operation scans memory from left to right and increments the DI. If the DF is 1, the operation scans memory from right to left and decrements the DI. REPn decrements the CX for each repetition. The operation terminates on an equal (REPNE) or an unequal (REPE) or when the CX is decremented to 0.

Flags.   Affects AF, CF, OF, PF, SF, and ZF.

Source Code.   [REPnn] SCASB/SCASW/SCASD (no operand)

Object Code.   `1010111w`

SETnn: Set Bytes Conditionally (80386/486)

Operation.   Sets a specified byte based on a condition. This is a group of 30 instructions including SETE, SETNE, SETC, and SETNS that parallel conditional jumps. If a tested condition is true, the operation sets the 8-bit operand to 1, otherwise to 0. An example:

```
CMP AX,BX    ;Compare contents of AX to BX
SETE CL      ;If equal, set CL to 1, else to 0
```

Flags.   None.

Source Code.   SETnn {register/memory}

Object Code.   `00001111|1001cond|mod000r/m` (cond varies according to condition tested)

SHL/SHR: Shift Logical Left or Shift Logical Right

Operation.   Shifts bits left or right in a byte, word, or doubleword in a register or memory. The operand can be an immediate constant or a reference to the CL. On the 8088/86, the constant may be only 1; a larger shift must be in the CL. On the 80186-486, the constant may be up to 31. SHL and SHR are logical shifts that treat the sign bit as a data bit.

SHL shift bits left a specified number and fills 0 bits in vacated positions to the right. SHL acts exactly like SAL. SHR shifts bits to the right a specified number and fills 0 bits to the left. All bits shifted off are lost.

Flags.   Affects CF, OF, PF, SF, and ZF (AF is undefined).

Source Code.   SHL/SHR {register/memory},{CL/immediate}

Object Code.

SHL: `|110100cw|mod100r/m|` (If c = 0 count = 1;

SHR: `|110100cw|mod101r/m|` if c = 1 count in CL)

SHLD/SHRD: Shift Double Precision (80386/486)

Operation.   Shifts multiple bits into an operand. The instructions require three operands. Operand 1 is a 16- or 32-bit register or memory location containing the value to be shifted. Operand 2 is a register (same size as operand 1) containing the bits to be shifted into operand 1. Operand 3 is the CL or an immediate constant containing the shift value.

Flags.   CF, PF, SF, and ZF (AF and OF are undefined).

Source Code.   SHLD/SHRD {register/memory},register,{CL/immediate}

Object Code.   Omitted.

STC: Set Carry Flag

Operation.   Sets the CF flag to 1 (see also CLC).

Flags.   CF (becomes 1).

Source Code.   STC (no operand)

Object Code.   11111001

STD: Set Direction Flag

Operation.   Sets the DF flag to 1 to cause string operations such as MOVS to process from right to left (see also CLD).

Flags.   DF (becomes 1).

Source Code.   STD (no operand)

Object Code.   11111101

STI: Set Interrupt Flag

Operation.   Sets the IF flag to 1 to enable maskable external interrupts after execution of the next instruction (see also CLI).

Flags.   IF (becomes 1).

Source Code.   STI (no operand)

Object Code.   11111011

STOS/STOSB/STOSW/STOSD: Store String

Operation.   Stores the contents of the accumulator in memory. When used with a REP prefix along with a count in the CX, the operation duplicates a string value a specified number of times, suitable for such actions as clearing an area of memory. For STOSB load the value in the AL, for STOSW load the value in the AX, and for STOSD load the value in the EAX. ES:DI reference a location in memory where the value is to be stored. If the DF flag is 0, the operation stores in memory from left to right and increments the DI. If the DF is 1, the operation stores from right to left and decrements the DI. REP decrements the CX for each repetition and terminates when it becomes 0.

Flags.   None.

Source Code.   [REP] STOSB/STOSW/STOSD (no operand)

Object Code.   `1010101w`

SUB: Subtract Binary Values

Operation.   Subtracts binary values in a register, memory, or immediate from a register or subtracts values in a register or immediate from memory. Values may be byte, word, or doubleword (80386/486) (see also SBB).

Flags.   Affects AF, CF, OF, PF, SF, and ZF.

Source Code.   SUB {register/memory},{register/memory/immediate}

Object Code.   (three formats)

> Reg/mem with reg: `|001010dw|modregr/m|`
> Immed from accum'r   `|0010110w|---data--|data if w=1|`
> Immed from reg/mem:
> `|100000sw|mod101r/m|---data----|data if sw=01|`

TEST: Test Bits

Operation.   Tests a field for a specific bit configuration. TEST acts like AND but does not change the destination operand. Both operands are bytes, words, or doublewords (80386/486) in a register or memory; operand 2 may be immediate. TEST uses AND logic to set flags, which you may test with JE or JNE.

Flags.   Affects CF, OF, PF, SF, and ZF (AF is undefined).

Source Code.   TEST {register/memory},{register/memory/immediate}

Object Code.   (three formats)

> Reg/mem and reg: `|1000010w|modregr/m|`
> Immed to accum'r: `|1010100w|---data--|data if w=1|`
> Immed to reg/mem: `|1111011w|mod000r/m|---data----|data if w=1|`

WAIT: Put Processor in Wait State

Operation.   Allows the processor to remain in a wait state until an external interrupt occurs in order to synchronize it with an external device or coprocessor. The processor waits until the device finishes executing and resumes processing on receiving a signal in the TEST pin.

Flags.   None.

Source Code.   WAIT (no operand)

Object Code.   `10011011`

XCHG: Exchange

Operation.   Exchanges data between two registers (as XCHG AH,BL) or between a register and memory (as XCHG CX,word).

Flags.   None.

Source Code.   XCHG {register/memory},{register/memory}

Object Code.   (two formats)

> Reg with accumulator: |10010reg|
> Reg/mem with reg: |1000011w|mod reg r/m|

XLAT: Translate

Operation.   Translates bytes into a different format, such as ASCII to EBCDIC. You define a table and load its address in the BX. Load the AL with a value that is to be translated. XLAT uses the AL value as an offset into the table, selects the byte from the table, and stores it in the AL.

Flags.   none.

Source Code.   XLAT [AL] (AL operand is optional)

Object Code.   11010111

XOR: Exclusive OR

Operation.   Performs a logical exclusive OR on bits of two operands. Both operands are bytes, words, or doublewords (80386/486), which XOR matches bit for bit. If matched bits are the same, XOR sets the operand 1 bit to 0, and if different to 1 (see also AND and OR).

Flags.   Affects CF (0), OF (0), PF, SF, and ZF (AF is undefined).

Source Code.   XOR {register/memory},{register/memory/immediate}

Object Code.   (three formats)

> Reg/mem with reg: |001100dw|mod reg r/m|
> Immed to reg/mem: |1000000w|mod 110 r/m|---data----|data if w=1|
> Immed to accum'r: |0011010w|---data----|data if w=1|

= Appendix A =

ASCII CHARACTER CODES

Table A-1 lists the representation for the entire 256 ASCII character codes (hex 00 through FF) along with their hexadecimal representation. Note that hex 20 is the standard space or blank. Characters from hex 00 through hex 1F, which have not been printed, include controls for printers and data transmission and are:

Hex	Character	Hex	Character	Hex	Character
00	(Null)	01	Happy face	02	Happy face
03	Heart	04	Diamond	05	Club
06	Spade	07	(Beep)	08	(Back space)
09	(Tab)	0A	(Line feed)	0B	(Vertical tab)
0C	(Form Feed)	0D	(Return)	0E	(Shift out)
0F	(Shift in)	10	(Data line esc)	11	(Dev ctl 1)
12	(Dev ctl 2)	13	(Dev ctl 3)	14	(Dev ctl 4)
15	(Neg acknowledge)	16	(Synch idle)	17	(End tran block)
18	(Cancel)	19	(End of medium)	1A	(Substitute)
1B	(Escape)	1C	(File separator)	1D	(Group separator)
1E	(Record separator)	1F	(Unit separator)		

```
00     01     02     03 ♥ 04 ♦ 05 ♣ 06 ♠ 07     08     09     0A     0B     0C     0D     0E     0F
10     11     12     13     14     15     16     17     18     19     1A     1B     1C     1D     1E     1F
20     21 !  22 "  23 #  24 $  25 %  26 &  27 '  28 (  29 )  2A *  2B +  2C ,  2D -  2E .  2F /
30 0  31 1  32 2  33 3  34 4  35 5  36 6  37 7  38 8  39 9  3A :  3B ;  3C <  3D =  3E >  3F ?
40 @  41 A  42 B  43 C  44 D  45 E  46 F  47 G  48 H  49 I  4A J  4B K  4C L  4D M  4E N  4F O
50 P  51 Q  52 R  53 S  54 T  55 U  56 V  57 W  58 X  59 Y  5A Z  5B [  5C \  5D ]  5E ^  5F _
60 `  61 a  62 b  63 c  64 d  65 e  66 f  67 g  68 h  69 i  6A j  6B k  6C l  6D m  6E n  6F o
70 p  71 q  72 r  73 s  74 t  75 u  76 v  77 w  78 x  79 y  7A z  7B {  7C |  7D }  7E ~  7F
80 ç  81 ü  82 é  83 â  84 ä  85 à  86 å  87 ç  88 ê  89 ë  8A è  8B ï  8C î  8D ì  8E Ä  8F Å
90 É  91 æ  92 Æ  93 ô  94 ö  95 ò  96 û  97 ù  98 ÿ  99 Ö  9A Ü  9B ¢  9C £  9D ¥  9E ₧  9F ƒ
A0 á  A1 í  A2 ó  A3 ú  A4 ñ  A5 Ñ  A6 ª  A7 º  A8 ¿  A9 ⌐  AA ¬  AB ½  AC ¼  AD ¡  AE «  AF »
B0 ░  B1 ▒  B2 ▓  B3 │  B4 ┤  B5 ╡  B6 ╢  B7 ╖  B8 ╕  B9 ╣  BA ║  BB ╗  BC ╝  BD ╜  BE ╛  BF ┐
C0 └  C1 ┴  C2 ┬  C3 ├  C4 ─  C5 ┼  C6 ╞  C7 ╟  C8 ╚  C9 ╔  CA ╩  CB ╦  CC ╠  CD ═  CE ╬  CF ╧
D0 ╨  D1 ╤  D2 ╥  D3 ╙  D4 ╘  D5 ╒  D6 ╓  D7 ╫  D8 ╪  D9 ┘  DA ┌  DB █  DC ▄  DD ▌  DE ▐  DF ▀
E0 α  E1 ß  E2 Γ  E3 π  E4 Σ  E5 σ  E6 µ  E7 τ  E8 Φ  E9 θ  EA Ω  EB δ  EC ∞  ED φ  EE ε  EF ∩
F0 ≡  F1 ±  F2 ≥  F3 ≤  F4 ⌠  F5 ⌡  F6 ÷  F7 ≈  F8 °  F9 ∙  FA ·  FB √  FC ⁿ  FD ²  FE ■  FF
```

Table A-1   ASCII Character Set

Appendix B
HEXADECIMAL/DECIMAL CONVERSION

In this appendix we provide the steps in converting between hexadecimal and decimal formats. In the first section we show how to convert hex A7B8 to decimal 42,936 and the second section, how to convert 42,936 back to hex A7B8.

CONVERTING HEXADECIMAL TO DECIMAL

To convert hex number A7B8 to a decimal number, start with the leftmost hex digit (A), continuously multiply each hex digit by 16, and accumulate the results. Since multiplication is in decimal, convert hex digits A through F to decimal 10 through 15.

First digit: A (10)	10
Multiply by 16	$\times\ \underline{16}$
	160
Add next digit, 7	$+\ \underline{\quad 7}$
	167
Multiply by 16	$\times\ \underline{\ 16}$
	2672
Add next digit, B (11)	$+\ \underline{\quad 11}$
	2683
Multiply by 16	$\times\ \underline{\quad 16}$
	42,928
Add next digit, 8	$+\ \underline{\qquad 8}$
Decimal value	42,936

You can also use a conversion table. For hex A7B8, think of the rightmost digit (8) as position 1, the next digit to the left (B) as position 2, the next digit (7) as position 3, and the leftmost digit (A) as position 4. Refer to Table B-1 and locate the value for each hex digit:

```
For position 1 (8), column 1  =        8
For position 2 (B), column 2  =      176
For position 3 (7), column 3  =    1,792
For position 4 (A), column 4  =   40,960
Decimal value                     42,936
```

CONVERTING DECIMAL TO HEXADECIMAL

To convert decimal number 42,936 to hexadecimal, first divide the original number 42,936 by 16; the remainder becomes the rightmost hex digit, 6. Next divide the new quotient 2683 by 16; the remainder, 11 or B, becomes the next hex digit to the left. Develop the hex number from the remainders of each step of the division. Continue in this manner until the quotient is zero.

Operation	Quotient	Remainder	Hex	
42,936 / 16	2683	8	8	(rightmost)
2,683 / 16	167	11	B	
167 / 16	10	7	7	
10 / 16	0	10	A	(leftmost)

You can also use Table B-1 to convert decimal to hexadecimal. For decimal number 42,936, locate the number that is equal to or next smaller. Note the equivalent hex number and its position in the table. Subtract the decimal value of that hex digit from 42,936, and locate the difference in the table. The procedure works as follows:

	Decimal	Hex
Starting decimal value	42,936	
Subtract next smaller number	−40,960	A000
Difference	1,976	
Subtract next smaller number	−1,792	700
Difference	184	
Subtract next smaller number	−176	B0
Difference	8	8
Final hex number		A7B8

Table B-1 Hexadecimal/Decimal Conversion

Hex	8 (Dec)	7 (Dec)	6 (Dec)	5 (Dec)	4 (Dec)	3 (Dec)	2 (Dec)	1 (Dec)
0	0	0	0	0	0	0	0	0
1	268,435,456	16,777,216	1,048,576	65,536	4,096	256	16	1
2	536,870,912	33,554,432	2,097,152	131,072	8,192	512	32	2
3	805,306,368	50,331,648	3,145,728	196,608	12,288	768	48	3
4	1,073,741,824	67,108,864	4,194,304	262,144	16,384	1,024	64	4
5	1,342,177,280	83,886,080	5,242,880	327,680	20,480	1,280	80	5
6	1,610,612,736	100,663,296	6,291,456	393,216	24,576	1,536	96	6
7	1,879,048,192	117,440,512	7,340,032	458,752	28,672	1,792	112	7
8	2,147,483,648	134,217,728	8,388,608	524,288	32,768	2,048	128	8
9	2,415,919,104	150,994,944	9,437,184	589,824	36,864	2,304	144	9
A	2,684,354,560	167,772,160	10,485,760	655,360	40,960	2,560	160	10
B	2,952,790,016	184,549,376	11,534,336	720,896	45,056	2,816	176	11
C	3,221,225,472	201,326,592	12,582,912	786,432	49,152	3,072	192	12
D	3,489,660,928	218,103,808	13,631,488	851,968	53,248	3,328	208	13
E	3,758,096,384	234,881,024	14,680,064	917,504	57,344	3,584	224	14
F	4,026,531,840	251,658,240	15,728,640	983,040	61,440	3,840	240	15

— Appendix C —

RESERVED WORDS

If used to define a data item, many of the following reserved words may confuse the assembler or may cause an assembler error, in some cases serious.

Register Names

AH	CH	DL	EDI	GS
AL	CL	DS	EDX	IP
AX	CS	DX	EIP	SI
BH	CX	EAX	ES	SP
BL	DH	EBP	ES	SS
BP	DI	EBX	ESI	
BX	DI	ECX	FS	

Symbolic Instructions

AAA	ARPL	CDQ	CMPSn	ESC
AAD	BOUND	CLC	CWDn	HLT
AAM	BSF	CLD	DAA	IDIV
AAS	BSR	CLI	DAS	IMUL
ADC	BTn	CLTS	DEC	IN
ADD	CALL	CMC	DIV	INC
AND	CBW	CMP	ENTER	INSw

INT	JNLE	LOCK	POPAD	SCASn
INTO	JNO	LODSn	POPF	SETnn
IRET	JNP	LOOP	POPFD	SGDT
JA	JNS	LOOPE	PUSH	SHL
JAE	JNZ	LOOPNE	PUSHAD	SHLD
JB	JO	LOOPNZ	PUSHF	SHR
JBE	JP	LOOPZ	PUSHFD	SHRD
JCXZ	JPE	LSL	RCL	SIDT
JE	JPO	LSS	RCR	SLDT
JECXZ	JS	LSS	REN	SMSW
JG	JZ	LTR	REP	STC
JGE	LAHF	MOV	REPE	STD
JL	LAR	MOVSn	REPNE	STI
JLE	LDS	MOVSX	REPNZ	STOSn
JMP	LEA	MOVZX	REPZ	STR
JNA	LEAVE	MUL	RET	SUB
JNAE	LES	NEG	RETF	TEST
JNB	LFS	NOP	ROL	VERR
JNBE	LGDT	NOT	ROR	VERRW
JNE	LGS	OR	SAHF	WAIT
JNG	LIDT	OUTn	SAL	XCHG
JNGE	LLDT	POP	SAR	XLAT
JNL	LMSW	POPA	SBB	XOR

Directives

ALIGN	ENDIF	IFIDN	PUBLIC
.ALPHA	ENDM	IFNB	PURGE
ASSUME	ENDP	IFNDEF	.RADIX
.CODE	ENDS	INCLUDE	RECORD
COMM	EQU	INCLUDELIB	REPT
COMMENT	.ERRnn	IRP	.SALL
.CONST	EVEN	IRPC	SEGMENT
.CREF	EXITM	LABEL	.SEQ
.DATA	EXTRN	.LALL	.SFCOND
.DATA?	.FARDATA	.LFCOND	.STACK
DB	.FARDATA?	.LIST	STRUC
DD	GROUP	LOCAL	SUBTTL
DF	IF	MACRO	.TFCOND
DOSSEG	IF1	.MODEL	TITLE
DQ	IF2	NAME	.XALL
DT	IFB	ORG	.XCREF
DW	IFDEF	OUT	.XLIST
ELSE	IFDIF	PAGE	
END	IFE	PROC	

Operators

AND	HIGH	NEAR	SHR
BYTE	LE	NOT	SIZE
COMMENT	LENGTH	NOTHING	STACK
CON	LINE	OFFSET	THIS
DUP	LOW	OR	TYPE
EQ	LT	PTR	WIDTH
FAR	MASK	SEG	WORD
GE	MOD	SHL	XOR
GT	NE	SHORT	

═ Appendix D ═
ASSEMBLER AND LINK OPTIONS

The IBM assembler program is MASM.EXE, MicroSoft versions are MASM.EXE and QuickAssembler, Borland's is TASM.EXE, and SLR System's is OPTASM, all of which are similar. Examples in this appendix use disk drives A: and B:users of hard disk or RAM disk can substitute the appropriate drive.

ASSEMBLING A PROGRAM

To assemble a source program, insert the assembler diskette in drive A and your program diskette in drive B. You use a command line to request an assembly, although MASM also provides for prompts.

Assembling with a Command Line

The general format for using a command line to assemble is

```
MASM/TASM [options] source[,object][,listing][,crossref]
```

- Options are explained later.
- Source identifies the source program. The assembler assumes the extension .ASM, so you need not enter it. You can also enter disk drive.
- Object provides for a generated OBJ file. The filename and drive may be the same as or different from the source.
- Listing provides for a generated LST file that contains the source and object code. The filename and drive may be the same as or different from the source.
- Crossref provides for a generated file containing symbols for a cross-reference listing. The extension is .CRF for MASM and .XRF for TASM. The filename and drive may be the same or different.

This example spells out all the files:

```
MASM B:name.ASM,B:name.OBJ,B:name.LST,B:name.CRF
```

The following shortcut command allows for defaults for object, listing, and cross-reference files, all with the same name:

```
MASM B:filename,B:,B:,B:
```

This example requests a cross-reference but no listing file:

```
MASM B:filename,B:,,B:
```

Assembling without a Command Line

You can enter just the name of the your program with no command line. TASM simply displays the general format for the command and an explanation of options, whereas MASM displays these prompts one at a time:

```
Source filename [.ASM]:
Object filename [filename.OBJ]:
Source listing [NUL.LST]:
Cross-reference [NUL.CRF]:
```

For the first prompt, type drive (if it's not the default) and filename. Accept the extension ASM, which the assembler assumes. The second prompt identifies the name of the OBJ file, with the same filename, which you may change. If necessary, enter a drive number. The third prompt assumes that you do not want a listing of the assembled program. The fourth prompt assumes that you do not want a cross-reference listing. Enter B: to get one on drive B.

Assembler Options

Assembler options for MASM, TASM, and OPTASM include the following:

/A	Arrange source segments in alphabetic sequence.
/C	Create a cross-reference file.
/D	MASM: Produce listing files on both pass 1 and 2 to locate phase errors. For TASM, /Dsymbol means define a symbol.
/E	Accept 80×87 coprocessor instructions and generate linkage to BASIC, C, or FORTRAN for emulated floating-point instructions.
/H	Display assembler options with a brief explanation. Enter /H with no file names or other options.
/L	Create a normal listing file.
/ML	Make all names case sensitive.
/MU	Convert all names to uppercase.
/MX	Make public and external names case sensitive.
/N	Suppress generation of the symbol table.
/R	Real 8087 support.
/S	Leave source segments in original sequence.
/T	(Terse) Display diagnostics at end of assembly only if an error is encountered.
/V	(Verbose) Display at end of assembly the number of lines and symbols processed (not OPTASM).
/Wn	Set level of warning messages: $0 =$ display only severe errors; $1 =$ display severe errors and serious warnings (the default); $2 =$ display severe errors, serious warnings, and advisory warnings.
/Z	Display source lines on the screen for errors.
/ZD	Include line-number information in the object file for CodeView, TurboDebugger, or SYMDEB.
/ZI	Include line-number and symbolic information in the object file for CodeView, TurboDebugger, or SYMDEB.

You may request options in either prompt or command-line mode. For prompts, you could code MASM/A/V [Enter], for example, then enter the usual filename. Or, you may enter options in any prompt line, for example as

```
Source filename [.ASM]: /A/V filename or filename /A/V [Enter]
```

The /A/V options tell the assembler to write segments in alphabetic sequence and to display additional diagnostics at the end of the assembly.

Additional Turbo Assembler Features

Turbo Assembler lets you assemble multiple files in one command line, each with its own options. You can also use DOS wildcards (* and ?). To assemble all source programs in the current directory, enter TASM *. To assemble all source programs named PROG1.ASM, PROG2.ASM, and so on, enter TASM PROG?. You can enter groups (or sets) of filenames, with each group separated by a semicolon. The following command assembles PROGA and PROGB with the /C option and PROGC with the /A option:

```
TASM /C PROGA PROGB; /A PROGC
```

Tables

Following an assembler LST listing are tables that describe structures and records, segments and groups, and symbols.

Segment and group table.   This table has the following heading:

```
Name Length Align Combine Class
```

The name column gives the names of all segments and groups in alphabetic sequence. The length column gives the size in hex of each segment. The align column gives the alignment type, such as BYTE, WORD, or PARA. Combine lists the defined combine type, such as STACK for a stack, NONE where no type is coded, PUBLIC for external definitions, or a hex address for AT types. The class column lists the segment class names, as coded in the SEGMENT statement.

Symbol table.   A symbol table has the following heading:

```
Name Type Value Attribute
```

The name column lists the names of all defined items in alphabetic sequence. The type column gives the type:

L NEAR or L FAR: A near or far label
N PROC or F PROC: A near or far procedure
BYTE, WORD, DWORD, FWORD, QWORD, TBYTE: A data item
ALIAS: An alias for another symbol
NUMBER: An absolute label
OPCODE: An equate for an instruction operand
TEXT: An equate for text

The value column gives the hex offset from the beginning of a segment for names, labels, and procedures. The attribute column lists a symbol's attributes, including its segment and length.

Appendix D

CROSS-REFERENCE FILE

A CRF or XRF file is used to produce a cross-reference listing of a program's labels, symbols, and variables, However, you have to use CREF for IBM and MicroSoft or TCREF for Borland to convert it to a sorted cross-reference file. You can key in CREF or TCREF with or without a command line.

Using a Command Line

The general format for using a command line is

```
CREF/TCREF xreffile,reffile
```

The command line contains references to the original cross-reference file (CRF or XRF) and to a generated REF file. The following example causes CREF to write a cross-reference file named ASMPROG.REF on drive D:

```
CREF/TCREF D:ASMPROG,D:
```

Omitting the Command Line

You can enter just the name of a program with no command line. TCREF simply displays the general format for the command and an explanation of options, whereas CREF displays these prompts:

```
Cref filename [.CRF]:
List filename [cross-ref.REF]:
```

For the first prompt, enter the name of the file, without a CRF extension. For the second prompt, you can enter the drive number only and accept the default file name.

LINKING A PROGRAM

To convert an OBJ module to an EXE module, insert the DOS diskette in drive A and your program diskette in drive B. The IBM and Microsoft linker is LINK and the Borland's is TLINK. For LINK and TLINK, you use a command line to request linking; LINK also provides for prompts.

Linking with a Command Line

The general format for using a command line to link is

```
LINK/TLINK [options] objfile,exefile[,mapfile][,libraryfile]
```

- Options are described later.
- Objfile identifies the object file generated by the assembler. The linker assumes the extension .OBJ, so you need not enter it. You can also enter the disk drive number.
- Exefile provides for generating an EXE file. The filename and drive may be the same as or different from the source.
- Mapfile provides for generating a file with an extension .MAP that indicates the relative location and the size of each segment and any errors that LINK has found. A typical error is failure to define a stack segment. Entering CON tells the linker to display the map on the screen (instead of writing it on disk) so that you can view it immediately for errors.
- Libraryfile provides for the libraries option.

To link more than one object file into an executable module, combine them in one line like this:

```
LINK B:PROGA + B:PROGB + B:PROGC
```

Linking with No Command Line

You can enter just the name of the linker with no command line. TLINK simply displays the general format for the command and an explanation of options, whereas LINK displays these prompts:

```
Object Modules [.OBJ]:
Run File [filename.EXE]:
List File [NUL.MAP]:
Libraries [.LIB]:
```

Type the drive (if it's not the default) and filename. Accept the extension OBJ, which the linker assumes. The second prompt assumes the same filename, which you may change. If necessary, enter the drive number. The third prompt assumes no listing of the link map. The last prompt refers to the DOS library option.

For the last three prompts, just press Enter to accept the default. This example tells the linker to produce EXE and CON files:

```
Object Modules [.OBJ]: B:ASMPROG [Enter]
Run File [ASMPROG.EXE]: B: [Enter]
List File [NUL.MAP]: CON [Enter]
Libraries [.LIB]: [Enter]
```

Debugging Options

If you intend to use CodeView, TurboDebugger, or SYMDEB, use the assembler's /ZI option for assembling. For linking, use DOS LINK's /CO option in either command-line or prompt mode, or Turbo TLINK's /V option:

```
LINK /CO filename...
TLINK /V filename...
```

Converting Turbo Object Files to COM Programs

Borland's TLINK also allows you to convert an object program directly to COM format, provided that the source program was originally coded according to COM requirements. Use the /T option:

```
TLINK /T objfile,comfile,CON
```

EXE2BIN OPTIONS

The DOS EXE2BIN program converts EXE modules generating by MASM into COM modules, provided that the source program was originally coded according to COM requirements. Insert the DOS diskette in drive A and the diskette containing the EXE file in drive B. Enter the following command:

```
EXE2BIN B:filename B:filename.COM
```

The first operand is the name of the EXE file, which you enter without an extension. The second operand is the name of the COM file; you may change the name, but be sure to code a COM extension. Delete the OBJ and EXE files.

— Appendix E —
THE DOS DEBUG PROGRAM

The DEBUG program on the DOS disk is useful for writing very small programs, for debugging assembly language programs, and for examining the contents of a file or memory. You may enter one of two commands to start DEBUG.

1. To create a file or examine memory, enter DEBUG with no filespec: DEBUG.
2. To modify or debug a program (COM or EXE) or to modify a file, enter DEBUG with a filespec, such as DEBUG D:PROGC.COM. DOS loads DEBUG into memory, and DEBUG displays a hyphen (-) as a prompt. The memory area for your program is known as a program segment. The CS, DS, ES, and SS registers are initialized with the address of the program segment prefix (PSP), and your work area begins at PSP + 100H.

A reference to a memory address may be in terms of a segment and offset, such as DS:120 or an offset only, such as 120. You may also make direct references to memory addresses, such as 40:417, where 40[0]H is the segment and 417H is the offset. DEBUG assumes that all entered numbers are hexadecimal, so you do not enter the trailing H. The F1 and F3 keys work for DEBUG just as they do for DOS; that is, F1 duplicates the previous command one key at a time, and F3 duplicates the entire previous command. Also, DEBUG does not distinguish between uppercase and lowercase letters.

Following is a description of each DEBUG command, in alphabetic sequence. Press Enter after each DEBUG statement.

A (Assemble).   Translate assembly source statements into machine code. The operation is especially useful for writing small assembly programs and for testing small segments of code, such as interrupts. The default address is CS:0100H and the general format is

```
A [address]
```

The following example creates an assembly program consisting of four instructions. You code the assembly statements; DEBUG generates on the left the code segment (shown here as xxxx:) and an offset:

```
             A(or A 100) [Enter]
xxxx:0100    MOV DX,1A [Enter]
xxxx:0103    MOV CX,4C [Enter]
xxxx:0106    ADD CX,DX [Enter]
xxxx:0109    RET [Enter]
             [Enter]
```

Since DEBUG sets the IP to 100H because of the size of the PSP, you may code A or A 100. The last Enter key (that's two in a row) tells DEBUG to end the program. You can now use the trace (T) command to execute it and the unassemble (U) command to see the machine code.

You can change any of these instructions. For example, to change the ADD at 106H to SUB:

```
             A 106 [Enter]
xxxx:0106    SUB CX,DX [Enter]
             [Enter]
```

When you reexecute the program, the IP is still incremented. Use the register (R) command to reset it to 100H.

C (Compare).   Compare the contents of two blocks of memory. The default register is the DS and the general format is

```
C [range] [address]
```

You may code the command one of two ways: (1) a starting address (compare from), a length, and a starting address (compare to), or (2) a starting address and an ending address (compare from) and a starting address (compare to). These examples compare bytes beginning at DS:050 to bytes beginning at DS:300:

```
C 050 L30 300   Compare using a length of 30H
C 050 080 300   Compare using a range
```

The operation displays the addresses and contents of unequal bytes.

D (Dump or display).   Display the contents of a portion of memory in hex and ASCII. The default register is the DS and the general format is

```
D [address] or D [range]
```

You may specify a starting address or a starting address with a range. Omission of a range or length causes a default to hex 80.

```
D 200       Display 80H bytes beginning at DS:200H
D           Display 80H bytes beginning from last display
D CS:150    Display 80 bytes beginning at CS:150H
D DS:20 L5  Display 5 bytes beginning at DS:20H
D 300 32C   Display the bytes from 300H through 32CH
```

E (Enter).   Enter data or machine instructions. The default register is the DS and the general format is

```
E address [list]
```

The operation allows two options: to replace bytes with those in a list or to provide sequential editing of bytes. Examples of the first option follow:

```
E 105 13 3A 21      Enter three bytes beginning at DS:105H
E CS:211 21 2A      Enter two bytes beginning at CS:211H
E 110 "anything"    Enter character string beginning at
                    DS:110H
```

For the second option, enter the address that you want displayed:

```
E 12C   Show contents of DS:12CH
```

The operation waits for your input. Enter one or more bytes of hex values, separated by a space, beginning at DS:12CH.

F (Fill).   Fill a range of memory locations with values in a list. The default register is the DS. The general format is

```
F range list
```

These examples fill beginning at DS:214H with bytes containing repetitions of "SAM":

```
F 214 L21 "SAM"    Use a length of 21H
F 214 234 "SAM"    Use a range, 214H through 234H
```

G (Go).   Execute a machine language program that you are debugging through to a specified breakpoint. Be sure to examine the machine code listing for valid IP addresses, because an invalid address may cause unpredictable results. Also, set breakpoints only in your own program, not in DOS or BIOS. The operation executes through interrupts and pauses if necessary to wait for keyboard input. The default register is the CS. The general format is

```
G [=address] address [address...]
```

The entry =address provides an optional starting address. The other entries provide up to ten breakpoint addresses. This example tells DEBUG to execute up to 11A:

```
G 11A
```

H (Hexadecimal).   Show the sum of and difference between two hex values. Code this as H value value. The maximum length is four hex digits. For example, H 14F 22 displays the result 171 12D.

I (Input).   Input and display one byte from a port. Code this as I portaddress.

L (Load).   Load a file or disk sectors into memory. The default register is CS:100 and the general format is

```
L [address [drive sector sector]]
```

To load a file, note that it should be already named (see N):

```
N filespec    Name the file
L             Load it at CS:100H
```

The following example loads beginning at CS:100 from drive 0 (A), starting at sector 20H for 15H sectors:

```
L 100 0 20 15
```

M (Move).   Move (or copy) the contents of memory locations. The default register is the DS and the general format is

```
M range address
```

These examples copy the bytes beginning at DS:050H through 150H into the address beginning at DS:400H:

```
M DS:50 L100 DS:400   Use a length
M DS:50 150 DS:400    Use a range
```

N (Name).   Name a program or a file that you intend to read from or write onto disk. Code the command as N filespec, such as

```
                    N D:SAM.COM
```

The operation sets the name at CS:80 in the PSP. For this example, the first byte at CS:80 contains the length (0AH), followed by the space and the filespec. You may then use L (Load) or W (Write) to read or write the file.

O (Output).   Send a byte to port. Code this as O portaddress byte.

P (Proceed).   Execute a subroutine call (CALL), a loop (LOOP), an interrupt (INT), or a repeat string instruction (REP) through to the next instruction. The general format is

```
                 P [=address] [value]
```

where =address is an optional starting address and value is an optional number of instructions to proceed. For example, if your trace of execution is at an INT 21H instruction, just enter P to execute through it.

Q (Quit).   Exit DEBUG. The operation does not save files; use W for that purpose.

R (Register).   Display the contents of registers and the next instruction. The general format is

```
                 R [registername]
```

The following examples illustrate its use:

```
R       Display all registers
R DX    Display the DX. DEBUG gives you an option:
        1. Press Enter—no change to the contents
        2. Enter 1-4 hex characters to change the contents
R F     Display the flags register
R IP    Display the IP
11A     DEBUG displays its contents, for example, 11AH
100     You enter 100H to change its contents
```

S (Search).   Search memory for characters in a list. The default register is the DS and the general format is

```
S range list
```

If found, the operation delivers the addresses; otherwise it does not respond. This example searches beginning at DS:300 for 2000H bytes for the word "HELP":

```
S 300 L 2000 "HELP"
```

This example searches from CS:100 through CS:400 for a byte containing 51H:

```
S CS:100 400 51
```

T (Trace).   Execute a program in single-step mode. Note that you should not trace through DOS interrupts (use P or G instead). The default register is the CS:IP and the general format is

```
T [=address] [value]
```

The optional entry =address tells DEBUG where to begin the trace and the optional value gives the number of instructions to trace. Omission of the operands causes DEBUG to execute the next instruction and to display the registers. Here are two examples:

```
T         Execute one instruction
T 10      Execute 16 (10H) instructions
```

U (Unassemble).   Unassemble machine instructions. The default register is the CS:IP and the general format is

```
U [address] or U [range]
```

The area specified should contain valid machine code. The operation displays symbolic instructions. Here are three examples:

```
U 0100      Unassemble 32 bytes beginning at CS:100
U           Unassemble 32 bytes since last U, if any
U 100 140   Unassemble from 100H through 140H
```

W (Write).   Write a file from DEBUG. The file should first be named if it wasn't already loaded. The default register is the CS and the general format is

```
W [address [drive start-sector number-of-sectors]]
```

Write program files only with a COM extension, since W does not support the EXE format. (To modify an EXE program, change the extension temporarily.) This example uses W with no operands and has to set the size of the file in the CX register:

```
N filespec    Name the file
R CX          Request CX register
length        Insert file size
W             Write the file
```

You may also write the file directly to disk sectors, although this practice requires considerable care.

— Appendix F —

KEYBOARD SCAN CODES

Following are the scan codes for the first (or only) 83 keys on the keyboard. These are all available through services 00, 01, 02, 10H, 11H, and 12H of INT 16H.

Hex	Key	Hex	Key	Hex	Key
01	Esc	1D	Ctrl	39	Spacebar
02	! and 1	1E	A and a	3A	CapsLock
03	@ and 2	1F	S and s	3B	F1
04	# and 3	20	D and d	3C	F2
05	$ and 4	21	F and f	3D	F3
06	% and 5	22	G and g	3E	F4
07	^ and 6	23	H and h	3F	F5
08	= and 7	24	J and j	40	F6
09	* and 8	25	K and k	41	F7
0A	(and 9	26	L and l	42	F8
0B	) and 0	27	: and ;	43	F9
0C	_ and -	28	'' and '	44	F10
0D	+ and =	29	~ and '	45	NumLock
0E	Backspace	2A	LeftShift	46	ScrollLock
0F	Tab	2B	¦ and \	47	7 and Home
10	Q and q	2C	Z and z	48	8 and Up Arrow
11	W and w	2D	X and x	49	9 and PgUp
12	E and e	2E	C and c	4A	- (grey)
13	R and r	2F	V and v	4B	4 and Left Arrow
14	T and t	30	B and b	4C	5 (keypad)
15	Y and y	31	N and n	4D	6 and Right Arrow
16	U and u	32	M and m	4E	+ (grey)
17	I and i	33	< and ,	4F	1 and End
18	O and o	34	> and .	50	2 and Down Arrow
19	P and p	35	? and /	51	3 and PgDn
1A	{ and [	36	RightShift	52	0 and Ins
1B	} and]	37	PrtSc and *	53	. and Del
1C	Enter	38	Alt		

Scan codes for combination keys:

54-5D	Shift F1 through Shift F10
5E-67	Ctrl F1 through Ctrl F10
68-71	Alt F1 through Alt F10
72	Ctrl PrtSc
73	Ctrl Left Arrow
74	Ctrl Right Arrow
75	Ctrl End
76	Ctrl PgDn
77	Ctrl Home
78-81	Alt 1 through Alt 10

The additional scan codes for the enhanced keyboard begin at 85H. These are available only through services 10H, 11H, and 12H of INT 16H.

Hex	Key	Hex	Key	Hex	Key
85	F11	90	Ctrl +	9B	Alt Left Arrow
86	F12	91	Ctrl Down Arrow	9D	Alt Right Arrow
87	Shift F11	92	Ctrl Insert	9F	Alt End
88	Shift F12	93	Ctrl Delete	A0	Alt Down Arrow
89	Ctrl F11	94	Ctrl Tab	A1	Alt PgDn
8A	Ctrl F12	95	Ctrl /	A2	Alt Insert
8B	Alt F11	96	Ctrl *	A3	Alt Delete
8C	Alt F12	97	Alt Home	A4	Alt /
8D	Ctrl Up Arrow	98	Alt Up Arrow	A5	Alt Tab
8E	Ctrl –	99	Alt PgUp	A6	Alt Enter
8F	Ctrl 5				

ANSWERS TO SELECTED QUESTIONS

Chapter 1

1-1. **(a)** 0101;   **(c)** 10101.

1-2. **(a)** 00100010;   **(c)** 00100000.

1-3. **(a)** 11101101;   **(c)** 11000111.

1-4. **(a)** 00111000;   **(c)** 00000010.

1-5. **(a)** 51;   **(c)** 5D.

1-6. **(a)** 23C8;   **(c)** 8000.

1-7. **(a)** 13;   **(c)** 59;   **(e)** FFF.

1-8. **(a)** 01010000;   **(c)** 00100011.

1-10. ROM (read-only memory) is permanent and performs startup procedures and handles input/output. RAM (random-access memory) is temporary and is the area where programs and data reside when executing.

1-12. **(a)** A section of a program, up to 64K in size, containing code, data, or the stack.

1-13. Stack, data, and code.

1-14. **(a)** AX, BX, CX, DX, DI, SI;   **(c)** AX and DX;   **(e)** flags.

Chapter 2

2-1. **(a)** 5A302.

2-3. **(a)** B82946.

2-4. E CS:101 54.

2-5. **(a)**
```
MOV   AX,3004
ADD   AX,3000
RET
```
(c) R and IP to set the IP to 0.

2-6. The product is hex 0612.

2-8. Use the N command to name the program (as COM), set the length in the CX, and use the W command to write it.

2-11. **(a)** DOS defines the stack for a COM program.

Chapter 3

3-1. **(a)** TITLE.

3-2. **(a), (b),** and **(c)** are valid; **(d)** is invalid because it starts with a number; **(e)** is valid only if it refers to the AX register.

3-5. **(a)** Causes alignment of a segment on a boundary, such as a paragraph.

3-6. **(a)** Provides a section of related code, such as a subroutine.

3-7. **(a)** END; **(c)** ENDS.

3-8. A number of executable instructions cause control to return to the operating system; END is a directive that tells the assembler that there are no more instructions to assemble.

3-11. ASSUME CS:CDSEG,DS:DATSEG,SS:STKSEG.

Chapter 4

4-2. B:TEMPY, B:, B:, and B:.

4-3. **(a)** DEBUG B:TEMPY.EXE; **(b)** B:TEMPY.

4-4. **(a)** Assembly language source program; **(c)** assembled listing file with source and object code; **(e)** assembled object file.

4-5.
```
MOV   AX,DATSEG
MOV   DS,AX
```
4-6.
```
MOV   AL,30H
SHL   AL,1
MOV   BL,18H
MUL   BL
```
4-8. The data segment should appear as follows:
```
FLDA   DB   28H
FLDB   DB   14H
FLDC   DW   ?
```

Chapter 5

5-1. **(a)** 2;   **(c)** 10;   **(e)** 8.

5-2. TITLE1   DB   'RGB Electronics'

5-3. **(a)** FLDA DD 73H

   (c) FLDC DW ?

   (e) FLDE DW 16, 19, 20, 27, 30

5-4. **(a)** ASCII 3236;   **(b)** hex 1A.

5-5. **(a)** 26;   **(c)** 3A732500.

5-6. **(a)** MOV AX, 320

   (c) ADD BX, 40H

   (e) SHL FLDB, 1 (or SAL)

Chapter 6

6-1. 64K.

6-4. It uses the high area of the COM program or, if insufficient space, uses the end of memory.

6-5. **(a)** EXE2BIN SAMPLE SAMPLE.COM.

Chapter 7

7-1. **(a)** +127 and −128;   **(b)** The operand is a one-byte value allowing for hex 00 through 7F (0 through +128) and hex 80 through FF (−128 through −1).

7-2. **(a)** 62B;   **(c)** 5EA

7-3. Following is one of many possible solutions:

```
            MOV     AX, 00
            MOV     BX, 01
            MOV     CX, 12
            MOV     DX, 00
    B20:
            ADD     AX, BX    ; Number is in AX
            MOV     BX, DX
            MOV     DX, AX
            LOOP    B20
```

7-4. **(a)** CMP DX, CX   **(c)** JCXZ address   **(e)** CMP BX, AX
   JA address or   CMP CX, 0   JLE or JNG
            JZ address

7-5. **(a)** OF (1);   **(c)** ZF (1);   **(e)** DF (1).

7-7. The first (main) PROC must be FAR because the operating system links to its address for execution. A NEAR attribute means that the address is within this particular program (that is, within the assembly).

7-9. Three (one for each CALL).

7-10. **(a)** 1001 1010;   **(c)** 1111 1011;   **(e)** 0000 0000.

7-12. **(a)** 5CDCH;   **(c)** CDC8H;   **(e)** 3737H;   **(g)** 72B9H.

Chapter 8

8-1. Row = 18H and column = 4FH.

8-3.
```
MOV   AX,060BH   ;Request
MOV   BH,07      ; clear
MOV   CX,0C00H   ; screen
MOV   DX,164FH
INT   10H
```

8-4. **(a)** Original DOS service call:
```
MSSGE   DB        'What is the date (mm/dd/yy)?',07H,'$'
        MOV       AH,09       ;Request display
        LEA       DX,MSSGE    ; of date
        INT       21H
```

8-5. **(a)** Original DOS service call:
```
DATEPAR LABEL BYTE
MAXLEN  DB     9                 ;Space for slashes and enter
ACTLEN  DB     ?
DATEFLD DB     9 DUP(' ')
        . . .
        MOV    AH,0AH            ;Request input
        LEA    DX,DATEPAR   ; of date
        INT    21H
```

8-6. **(a)** 00.

Chapter 9

9-1. **(a)** 0000 0001;   **(c)** 0111 1000.

9-2. **(a)** 1011 0101;   **(c)** 1000 1100.

9-3. **(a)**
```
MOV   AH,00       ;Request set mode
MOV   AL,02       ; 80-column monochrome
INT   10H
```
(c)
```
MOV   AH,060AH    ;Request scroll 10 lines
MOV   BH,07       ;Normal video
MOV   CX,0000     ;Entire screen
MOV   DX,184FH
INT   10H
```

9-4. Eight colors for background and 16 for foreground.

9-5.
```
MOV   AH,09         ;Display
MOV   AL,04         ;Diamond
MOV   BH,00         ;Page number 0
MOV   BL,01011010B  ;Light green on magenta
MOV   CX,05         ;Five times
INT   10H
```

9-9. Low resolution: four bits per pixel gives 16 colors.
Medium resolution: two bits per pixel gives 4 colors.
High resolution: one bit per pixel gives two "colors" (BW).

9-11. First set graphics mode, then use INT 10H (AH = 0BH) to set background color.

9-12. First set graphics mode.
```
MOV   AH,0DH   ;Read dot
MOV   CX,13    ;Column
MOV   DX,12    ;Row
INT   10H
```

Chapter 10

10-1. **(a)** Location 40:17H (417H).
10-2. **(a)** Keyboard input with echo. Requires two interrupts if an extended function.
10-4. **(a)** 48; **(c)** 47.
10-6. Use INT 16H for input and test for the scan code.
10-8. On any press or release of a key.
10-10. **(a)** Location 40:1EH (41EH).

Chapter 11

11-4. **(a)**
```
              JCXZ   label2
      label1: MOV    AX,[SI]
              MOV    [DI],AX
              INC    DI
              INC    DI
              INC    SI
              INC    SI
              LOOP   label1
      label2: ...
```
11-5. Set the DF for right-to-left move. For MOVSB, initialize at NAME1 + 9 and NAME2 + 9. For MOVSW, initialize at NAME1 + 8 and NAME2 + 8.
11-6. **(a)**
```
    CLD                     ;Left to right
    LEA    SI,CONAME        ;Initialize
    LEA    DI,PRLINE        ; to move
    MOV    CX,20            ; 20 bytes
    REP MOVSB               ;Move
```
  (c)
```
    CLD
    LEA    SI,CONAME+2      ;Start at 3rd byte
    LODSW                   ;Load 2 bytes
```
  (e)
```
    CLD                     ;Left to right
    MOV    CX,20            ;20 bytes
    LEA    SI,CONAME        ;Initialize
    LEA    DI,PRLINE        ; address
    REPE CMPSB              ;Compare
```
11-7. Here is one solution:
```
H10SCAS  PROC        NEAR
         CLD                      ;Left to right
                     MOV  CX,10 ;10 bytes
         LEA         DI,NAME1     ;Initialize address
         MOV         AL,'e'       ; and scan character
```

```
         H20:
                    REPNE  SCASB                              ;Scan
                    JNE           H30                         ;Found?
                    CMP           BYTE PTR[DI],'r'            ;Yes-next byte
                    JNE           H20                         ; equals 'r'?
                    MOV           AH,03
         H30:       RET
         H10SCAS    ENDP
11-8.    PATTERN    DB     03H,04H,05H,0B4H
         DISPLAY    DB     80 DUP(' '),'$'
                    CLD                      ;Left to right
                    LEA    SI,PATTERN        ;Initialize
                    LEA    DI,DISPLAY        ; address
                    MOV    CX,20             ;20 bytes
                    REP MOVSW                ;Move pattern
```
Then use INT 21H to display the variable DISPLAY.

Chapter 12

12-1. **(a)** 127 and 255.

12-3. **(a)**
```
    MOV  AX,DATAY
    ADD  AX,DATAX
    MOV  DATAY,AX
```
(b) See Figure 12-2 for multiword addition.

12-4. STC sets the carry flag. The sum is hex 0148 plus hex 0237 plus 1.

12-5. **(a)**
```
    MOV  AX,DATAX
    MUL  DATAY
```
(b) See Figure 12-4 for multiplying doubleword by word.

12-7. **(a)**
```
    MOV  AX,DATAX
    MOV  BL,25
    DIV  BL
```

Chapter 13

13-1. **(a)** ADD generates hex 6C, and AAA generates hex 0102.
(c) SUB generates hex 02, and AAS has no effect.

13-2.
```
            LEA    SI,UNPAK       ;Initialize address
            MOV    CX,04          ; and 4 loops
    B20:
            OR     [SI],30H       ;Insert ASCII 3
            INC    SI             ;Increment for next byte
            LOOP   B20            ;Loop 4 times
```

13-3. Use Figure 13-2 as a guide, but initialize CX to 03.

13-4. Use Figure 13-3 as a guide, but initialize CX to 03.

13-5. **(a)** Convert ASCII to binary:

	Decimal		*Hex*
$8 \times 1 =$	8		8
$2 \times 10 =$	20		14
$3 \times 100 =$	300		12C
$6 \times 1000 =$	6000		1770
$4 \times 10000 =$	40000		9C40
			B4F8

Chapter 14

```
14-1.   WKDAYS   DB      'Sunday...'
                 DB      'Monday...'
                 DB      'Tuesday...'
                 ...
14-2.   DAYNO    DB              ?
        DAYNAM   DB              9 DUP(?)
        NINE     DB              9
                 ...
                 LEA     SI,WKDAYS    ;Address of table
                 SUB     AH,AH        ;Clear AH
                 MOV     AL,DAYNO     ;Day of week
                 DEC     AL           ;Decrement day,
                 MUL     NINE         ;  gives location in table
                 ADD     SI,AX        ;Add to address of table
                 MOV     CX,09        ;Nine characters
                 LEA     DI,DAYNAM    ;Address of destination
                 REP MOVSB            ;Move 9 chars from table
14-3.   (a) ITEMNO   DB      '06','10','14','21','24'
        (c) ITPRICE  DW      9395,8225,9067,8580,1385
```

14-4. A possible organization is into the following procedures:

Subroutine	*Purpose*
B10READ	Display prompt, accept item number.
C10SRCH	Search table, display message if invalid item.
D10MOVE	Extract description and price from table.
E10CONV	Convert quantity from ASCII to binary.
F10CALC	Calculate value (quantity × price).
G10CONV	Convert value from binary to ASCII.
K10DISP	Display description and value on screen.

14-5. The following routine copies the table. Refer to Figure 14-6 for sorting table entries.

```
        SORTAB   DB              5 DUP(9 DUP(?))
                 ...
                 LEA     SI,ITDESC    ;Initialize
                 LEA     DI,SORTAB    ;  table address and
```

```
MOV            CX,45          ; number of characters
CLD                           ;Left to right
REP MOVSB                     ;Move
```

14-6. The intention is to use XLAT for translation.

Chapter 15

15-1. 512.

15-3. **(a)** 40 cylinders × 9 sectors × 2 sides × 512 bytes = 368,640.

15-4. **(a)** side 0, track 0, sector 1.

15-5. **(a)** A group of sectors (1, 2, 4, or 8) that DOS treats as a unit of storage space on a disk.

15-6. In the directory, the first byte of file name is set to E5H.

15-9. **(a)** Positions 28–31 of the directory;   **(b)** hex 0B4A, stored as 4A0B.

15-10. **(a)** The first byte of the FAT contains F8H.

Chapter 16

16-1. All the service calls involve INT 21H: **(a)** 16H;   **(c)** 15H;   **(e)** 14H.

16-2. **(a)** 4;   **(b)** 108 (9 sectors × 3 tracks × 4 records/track);   **(c)** one access per sector, or 27 in all.

16-3. Use Figure 16-1 as a guide for creating a disk file, and Figure 13-5 for conversion from ASCII to binary.

16-4. Use Figure 16-2 as a guide for reading the disk file, and Figure 13-6 for conversion from binary to ASCII.

16-5. **(a)** Block 0, record 44;   **(c)** block 1, record 21.

16-6. Decimal 2652 is hex 0A5C, stored as 5C0A0000.

16-7. The service calls involve INT 21H: **(a)** 22H;   **(c)** 28H.

16-8. FCBFLSZ contains the size of the file in bytes (number of records times length of records), and FCBRCSZ contains the length of records. Divide FCBFLSZ (four bytes in the DX:AX) by FCBRCSZ (two bytes).

16-9. The section "Random Block Processing" provides an example of reading a block.

16-10. Chapter 13 shows how to convert ASCII numbers to binary.

Chapter 17

17-1. **(a)** 02.

17-3. **(b)**
```
        MOV    AH,3CH         ;Request create
        MOV    CX,00          ;Normal file
        LEA    DX,PATH1       ;ASCIIZ string
        INT    21H            ;Call DOS
        JC     error          ;Exit if error
        MOV    CUSTHAN,AX     ;Save handle
```

17-4. **(a)**
```
        MOV    AH,3DH         ;Request open
        MOV    AL,00          ;Read only
        LEA    DX,PATH1       ;ASCIIZ string
```

```
INT   21H           ;Call DOS
JC    error         ;Exit if error
MOV   CUSTHAN,AX    ;Save handle
```

17-5.   Where a program opens many files.

17-7.   The program uses file handles and is otherwise the same as Question 16-3, which uses FCBs.

17-8.   The program uses file handles and is otherwise the same as Question 16-4, which uses FCBs.

Chapter 18

18-2.   Most likely developers of disk utility programs.

18-3.   **(a)** In the AH.

18-5.   Use INT 13H and AH = 00.

18-6.   Use INT 13H and AH = 01.

18-8.
```
MOV   AH,03         ;Request write
MOV   AL,03         ;3 sectors
LEA   BX,OUTDSK     ;Output area
MOV   CH,08         ;Track 08
MOV   CL,01         ;Sector 01
MOV   DH,00         ;Head 0
MOV   DL,01         ;Drive B
INT   13H
```

18-9.   The status byte in the AH contains 00000011.

Chapter 19

19-1.   **(a)** 09.

19-3.   **(a)**
```
MOV   AH,05         ;Request print
MOV   DL,0CH        ;Form feed
INT   21H
```

   (b)
```
      LEA   SI,NAMEFLD    ;Initialize name
      MOV   CX,length     ; and length
B20:
      MOV   AH,05         ;Request print
      MOV   DL,[SI]       ;Character from name
      INT   21H           ;Call DOS
      INC   SI            ;Next character in name
      LOOP  B20           ;Loop length times
```

   (c)   You could code a line feed (0AH) in front of address. The solution is similar to part (b).

   (e)   Issue another form feed (0CH).

19-4.   HEADNG DB 13, 10, 15, 'Title', 12

19-5.   **(a)** In the AH.

19-7.   You won't be able to use CX for looping five times because the loop that prints the name uses the CX. You could use the BX as follows:

```
          MOV   BX,05
    C20:

          . . .
          DEC   BX
          JNZ   C20
```

Chapter 20

20-1. The introduction to this chapter gives three reasons.

20-2. The statements include MACRO and ENDM.

20-5. (a) SALL.

20-6. (a)
```
    MULTBY  MACRO   MULTPR,MULTCD
            MOV     AL,MULTCD
            MUL     MULTPR
            ENDM
```

20-7. To include the macro in pass 1, code the following:

```
    IF1
            INCLUDE library-name
    ENDIF
```

20-8. The macro definition could begin with:

```
    BIPRINT MACRO PRTLINE,PRLEN
```
PRTLINE and PRLEN are dummy arguments for the address and length of the line to be printed. Refer to Chapter 19 for using BIOS INT 17H to print.

20-9. Note that you cannot use a conditional IF to test for a zero divisor. A conditional IF works only during assembly, whereas the test must occur during program execution. Code assembly instructions such as these:

```
    CMP  DIVISOR,00    ;Zero divisor?
    JNZ  (bypass)      ;No-bypass
    CALL (error message routine)
```

Chapter 21

21-1. The introduction to this chapter gives reasons.

21-2. (a) PARA.

21-3. (a) NONE.

21-4. (a) 'code'.

21-6. (a) EXTRN SUBPRO:FAR

21-7. (a) PUBLIC QTY,VALUE,PRICE

21-8. Use Figure 21-6 as a guide.

21-9. Use Figure 21-8 as a guide for passing parameters. However, this question involves pushing three variables onto the stack. The called program therefore has to access [BP + 10] for the third entry (PRICE) in the stack. You can define your own standard for returning PRICE through the stack. Watch also for the pop value in the RET operand.

21-10. This program involves material in Chapters 8 (screen I/0), 13 (conversion between ASCII and binary), 12 (binary multiplication), and 21 (linkage to subprograms). Be especially careful of the stack.

Chapter 22

22-1. (a) In sector 1, track 0.

22-2. A low-level interface to the BIOS routines in ROM.

22-4. (a) Following IBMDOS.COM.

22-5. (a) The first 256 bytes of a program when loaded in memory for execution.

22-6. 5CH:03 41 4C 46 20 20 20 20 20 44 4F 43
80H:0A 20 43 3A 41 4C 46 2E 44 4F 43 0D

22-8. (a) 2BA1.

22-9. (a) 1A25[0] + 100H (PSP) + 30H = 1A38[0].

22-10. (a) It means start of an MCB (not the last one).

22-11. (a) INT 09H, in the interrupt services table at 24H.

Chapter 23

23-1. These types are discussed in the section on interrupts at the start of this chapter.

23-2. These lines are discussed in the section on interrupts at the start of this chapter.

23-3. (a) FFFF[0]H.

23-5. At 40[0]H.

23-6. (a) See BIOS data area at offset 10H–11H.

23-7. (a) INT 00H.

23-8. (a) Print screen.

23-9. Note that the figure reverses the parallel ports, LPT1 and LPT2.

INDEX